Aalto and America

November 2012

Aalto and America

EDITED BY STANFORD ANDERSON, GAIL FENSKE, AND DAVID FIXLER

for Cheryl and Dave,
who have an eye for
good design and who
appreciate nature —

Gail

Yale University Press
NEW HAVEN AND LONDON

Production of this book has been supported by the Graham Foundation for
Advanced Studies in the Fine Arts

Designed by Hecht Design, Arlington MA, USA
Printed in Singapore

Library of Congress Cataloging-in-Publication Data

Aalto and America / edited by Stanford Anderson, Gail Fenske, and David Fixler.
     p. cm.
Includes bibliographical references and index.
ISBN 978-0-300-17600-1 (alk. paper)

1. Aalto, Alvar, 1898-1976--Criticism and interpretation. 2. Architecture--United
States--History--20th century. I. Aalto, Alvar, 1898-1976. II. Anderson, Stanford.
III. Fenske, Gail. IV. Fixler, David.

NA1455.F53A23 2011
720.92--dc22   2011004832

A catalogue record for this book is available from The British Library

Contents

Acknowledgements

As co-editors of Aalto and America, our connection to the subject of this book extends far beyond the beginnings of the project ten years ago. Stanford Anderson has held a longstanding interest in the strain of modern architecture for which Aalto stands as the preeminent representative; Gail Fenske has published on the modern architect William Wurster, Dean at MIT during Aalto's primary years of activity in America, the late 1940s; and a half-century later, David Fixler directed the restoration of Aalto's Baker House Dormitory.

The editors shared a vision for Aalto and America, but the project could not have been realized without the significant contributions of a number of institutions and individuals besides our own. Most important, we appreciate and respect the project's authors for their formidable intellectual contribution. In working with each of them, we gained new insights on Aalto and his work. All of the authors graciously accommodated our editorial suggestions, which allowed the development of essays that collectively reflect the many facets of Aalto's encounter with America.

Without the assistance of the librarians, archivists, and their staffs who excavated the documents and materials essential to our research, the project simply would not have been possible. At the Alvar Aalto Museum in Jyväskylä and Helsinki, Finland, we are thankful for the assistance of the Aalto Academy Director Esa Laaksonen and his secretary, Merja Vainio, Curator Katariina Pakoma, Curator Arne Heporauta, Curator Mia Hipeli, and Hanni Sippo. At the Archive of the Museum of Finnish Architecture, Helsinki, the Head of Research, Timo Tuomi, and staff graciously accommodated our requests. We also thank the Director of the Aalto Foundation, Markku Lahti, and architect Tapani Mustonen. The MIT Museum's Architecture & Design Collection were indispensible to our research; we are especially grateful to the former Curator of Architecture & Design, Kimberly Alexander. We also appreciate the assistance of the staff at MIT's Institute Archives & Special Collections, the University of California, Berkeley's Environmental Design Archives, and at the Boston Public Library, Fine Arts Department.

Colleagues and staff at our respective institutions provided indispensible logistical and administrative support. We are especially indebted to Anne Simunovic, Assistant to the Head, Department of Architecture, MIT; Anne Deveau, Principal Administrative Assistant, Program in History, Theory & Criticism, Department of Architecture, MIT; Baker Housemasters Professor Will Watson and Myra Harrison, and Victoria Sirianni and Susan Personette from MIT Facilities. We would also like to thank Rebecca Chamberlain, Jack Valleli, Kathaleen Brearly, and Nicola Pezolet. In the School of Architecture, Art & Historic Preservation at Roger Williams University, we appreciate the assistance of Architecture Librarian, John Schlinke. At the architectural firm Perry Dean Rogers and Partners, architects for the Baker House renovation project, we thank Steven Foote, Martha Pilgreen and in particular the late Charles F. Rogers II, principal in charge; and at EYP Architecture and Engineering, Inc., Boston, Tom Birdsey, Leila Kamal, and Cahal Stephens.

Each of us benefitted immensely from inspiring conversations with friends and colleagues at various stages of the project's development. We would especially like to note the late Lawrence Anderson, Richard Chafee, Mark Jarzombek, Markus Mäkelä, John Rhodes, Marc Treib, Andrew Saint, the late Paul Byard, Harry Charrington, John Ellis, David Foxe, Ana Gabby, the late Olav Hammarström, Klaus Herdeg, Hélène Lipstadt, Frank Matero, Henry Moss, the late Veli Paatela, Paul David Pearson, Nicholas Ray, Peter Reed, and the late Göran Schildt. In Jyväskylä and Helsinki, Esa Laaksonen and Pekka Korvenmaa graciously offered their expertise and insights on local architecture. Closer to home, the thoughtful viewpoint of Larry Speck sharpened our perspective on Baker House.

At Yale University Press, we are extraordinarily grateful for the support of our editors, Michelle Komie in New Haven and Sally Salvesen in London, and of the Press's director, John Donatich. We are deeply indebted to the press's three anonymous reviewers, whose thoughtful comments strongly informed the shaping of the manuscript. More recently, Sophie Sheldrake and Catherine Bowe have overseen all aspects of the book's production. We are also grateful to our manuscript editor, Molly Balikov, designers Alice Hecht and Anne Dauchy of Hecht Design, cartographer Dennis McClendon, and indexer Margie Towery. For photography, we appreciate the collaboration of Erica Stoller at ESTO and Richard Strode of Strode Photographic, Portland, Oregon.

For funding and leave time, we are grateful to the Graham Foundation and especially to its former Director, Richard Solomon; to Adele Santos, Dean of the MIT School of Architecture and Planning; to Roger Williams University's Foundation to Promote Scholarship and Teaching; and to EYP in Boston.

We are fortunate that those closest to us shared our interest in the project, inspiring its progress as it advanced through innumerable revisions to take shape as this book: Nancy Royal, Don Cecich, Phyllis Halpern, Matthew and Andrew Fixler, and the late Michael Fixler.

But most of all, as co-editors we have each other to acknowledge. Of course, we each had our respective roles in the project and we know what those are. We had countless meetings, long conversations, and did not always agree. Still, we are pleased to recognize that Aalto and America is the product of a remarkable collaboration.

Stanford Anderson

Gail Fenske

David Fixler

Boston, Massachusetts, 2011

Contributors

Stanford Anderson, architect and Professor of History and Architecture at the Massachusetts Institute of Technology in Cambridge, Massachusetts, has taught at MIT since 1963 (Head of Department 1991–2005). In 2004, he was named AIA/ACSA Topaz Laureate, the highest North American award in architectural education. His research and writing focuses on architectural theory, modern architecture, American urbanism, and epistemology and historiography. Among his publications are *Peter Behrens: A New Architecture for the Twentieth Century* and *Eladio Dieste and Innovation in Structural Art.*

Paul Bentel is a partner in the studio of Bentel & Bentel, Architects/Planners AIA, and Adjunct Associate Professor of Architecture and History at Columbia University. He is a Fellow of the American Institute of Architects. Prior to receiving his graduate degree in architecture, he was a sculptor in Pietrasanta, Italy. He holds a PhD in the History, Theory, and Criticism of Architecture from MIT.

Gail Fenske is Professor of Architecture in the School of Architecture, Art & Historic Preservation at Roger Williams University. She has held visiting professorships at Wellesley College and MIT. She is the author of *The Skyscraper and the City: The Woolworth Building and the Making of Modern New York* as well as several essays in scholarly books on modern architecture and urbanism, among them an essay on William W. Wurster and the California Bay Region Style in Martha Pollak, editor, *The Education of the Architect.* She received a PhD in the History, Theory, and Criticism of Architecture from MIT.

David Fixler is an architect with EYP specializing in the rehabilitation of modern architecture. A graduate of Columbia University, his projects include the renovation of Aalto's Baker House at MIT, the United Nations Headquarters in New York, and work on Louis Kahn's Richards Labs at the University of Pennsylvania. Fixler's writings on architectural history, preservation and design have been published internationally. He has taught and lectured widely, organized conferences on a broad range of topics, and is an officer in several international scholarly and professional organizations, including serving as co-founder and President of DOCOMOMO-US/ New England.

Sarah Williams Goldhagen is the architecture critic of *The New Republic* and a scholar and theorist of modern and contemporary architecture. The author of *Louis Kahn's Situated Modernism* and editor, with Rejean Legault, of *Anxious Modernisms: Experimentation in Postwar Architectural Culture,* Goldhagen has published widely, in both scholarly and popular journals, on a broad array of topics. She is currently writing a book on how people experience the contemporary built environment.

Kari Jormakka studied architecture at Otaniemi Technical University and Tampere University of Technology. He also studied philosophy at Helsinki University, receiving a Master's in 1985, a PhD in 1991, and a Habilitation in 1993. He has taught at Tampere University, the Ohio State University, University of Illinois, Bauhaus University in Weimar, Harvard Graduate School of Design, and Vienna University of Technology, where he has been Ordinarius Professor since 1998. Author of many books and numerous papers on architectural history and theory, his publications include as co-author "The Use and Abuse of Paper: Essays on Alvar Aalto" and *Constructing Architecture: Notes on Theory and Criticism in Architecture and the Arts.*

Pekka Korvenmaa is Professor of Design and Culture and Vice Dean at the Aalto University School of Art and Design Helsinki. He has published on Finnish architectural and design history in Finland and internationally since the early 1980s with an emphasis on the post-WWII era and the relationship between design, technology, and production. Among his works are "Aalto and Finnish Industry," in Peter Reed, editor, *Between Humanism and Materialism* and as editor, *Sunila, 1936–1954*, volume seven in the series *Alvar Aalto*. He has recently published *Finnish Design: A Concise History*.

Dörte Kuhlmann has taught at the Institute of Architectural Sciences, Vienna University of Technology since 1998, where she is professor of architectural theory, gender studies, and design, and head of the faculty council. She is the author of several books on contemporary architecture and gender studies including *Mensch und Natur: Alvar Aalto in Deutschland*, and has curated two exhibitions on Finnish architecture: "Wood with a Difference" and "Wooden Boxes." She has also taught and lectured at the Institute for European Studies Vienna, Bauhaus University Weimar, UBT Pristina Kosovo, SCI-Arc Los Angeles, and University of Illinois Chicago.

Sarah Menin is an independent scholar and academic, having been Reader in Architectural History and Theory at Newcastle University, where she is now a Visiting Fellow. Her research examines the role of the psyche in the architectural sphere. She has published widely in academic journals. Her books include *Nature and Space: Aalto and Le Corbusier* (with Flora Samuel), *Constructing Place: Mind and Matter,* and *An Architecture of Invitation: Colin St John Wilson* (with Stephen Kite). She continues to practice architecture.

Ákos Moravánszky is Professor of the Theory of Architecture at the Institut gta of ETH Zurich. He studied architecture at the Technical University in Budapest and received his doctorgrade from the Technical University in Vienna in 1980. He has been a Research Fellow at the Zentralinstitut für Kunstgeschichte in Munich, a Research Associate at the Getty Center for History of Art and the Humanities, and for five years taught as a Visiting Professor at MIT. His research interests include the history of East and Middle European architecture in the 19th–20th centuries and the history of architectural theory. He is author of *Competing Visions: Aesthetic Invention and Social Imagination in Central European Architecture, 1867–1918*.

Juhani Pallasmaa, Architect SAFA, Hon. FAIA, Int. FRIBA, has practiced architecture since the early 60s and established Pallasmaa Architects in 1983. He is also active in urban planning and exhibition, product, and graphic design. He has taught and lectured on five continents and has served as Dean at the Helsinki University of Technology and Director of the Museum of Finnish Architecture. He has published numerous books and essays on the philosophies of architecture and art. Among his books are *The Embodied Image: Imagination and Imagery in Architecture, Conversaciones con Alvar Aalto, The Thinking Hand: Embodied and Existential Wisdom in Architecture,* and *Encounters: Architectural Essays*.

Eeva-Liisa Pelkonen is Associate Professor at Yale School of Architecture, where she directs the Master of Environmental Design Program. Her research focuses on the language of modern architecture viewed from various national and historical perspectives. She recently published *Alvar Aalto: Architecture, Modernity, and Geopolitics*. She is also author of *Achtung Architektur! Image and Phantasm in Contemporary Austrian Architecture,* co-editor with Donald Albrecht of *Eero Saarinen: Shaping the Future,* and author of *Kevin Roche: Architecture as Environment*. She holds an M. Arch from Tampere Technical University, Master of Environmental Design from Yale, and PhD from Columbia University. In 2010, the President of Finland recognized her with the award of a knighthood in the order of the White Rose.

Matthew A. Postal is an architectural historian specializing in 20th-century architecture, urbanism and interiors. Since 1998, he has conducted research on New York architecture for the Landmarks Preservation Commission of New York. He is also Adjunct Professor at the New York School of Interior Design and Lewis & Clark College. He is the co-author of the *Guide to New York City Landmarks* and *10 Architectural Walks in Manhattan*. He holds a PhD in art history from the Graduate Center of the City University of New York.

Lawrence W. Speck is an architect and educator. His architectural projects have been profiled in major architectural journals in the United States, England, Germany, Italy, China, Brazil, Japan, Turkey and Australia. He has written three books, among them *Technology, Sustainability, and Cultural Identity* with Reed Kroloff, several chapters in books, and has published numerous articles in professional journals. A faculty member at University of Texas at Austin since 1975, he served as Dean of the School of Architecture from 1992 to 2001. In 2011, he was named AIA/ACSA Topaz Laureate, the highest award given to an architectural educator in North America.

Michael Spens is Professor of Architecture, Dundee University. Since 1995, he has served as the Director of the International Committee for the restoration of Viipuri Library, now the Vyborg City Library in Russia. With his book, *Vipurii Library, 1927–1935*, which he wrote in consultation with the Russian site architect, Sergei Kravchenko, Spens brought the plight of the library to public attention. In 1996, he formed a British committee in support of the library's restoration, which in 2002 became a fund-raising trust. While facilitating the restoration, a collaboration of Finnish and Russian architects, he conducted research on Aalto's Mount Angel Library near Portland, Oregon. He was recognized by the President of Finland with a knighthood awarded in 2001.

Michael Trencher is Professor, School of Architecture, Pratt Institute, Brooklyn, New York. Over his 40 year career he has taught a wide variety of subjects including specialized electives on Aalto and traveling seminars in Finland. He is the author of *The Alvar Aalto Guide*. His photographs formed the basis for the Universe/Rizzoli edition, *Alvar Aalto Masterworks*, for which he also wrote the introduction. Trencher has also edited and condensed an English language edition of Schildt's three major biographic texts for proposed publication by Rizzoli/Otava.

Professor Sir Colin St. John Wilson RA (1922–2007) was a teacher and finally Professor and Head of School at the Cambridge School of Architecture. "Sandy" Wilson joined the London County Council Architects' Department after wartime service in the Royal Navy and consequently became involved in the design polemics and the construction of post war Britain. His built work consisted mostly of university and public buildings, the largest of which was the British Library, on which he was engaged almost continuously from 1962 until 1996. His carefully conceived lectures for students formed the starting point for many of his articles and books.

Chronology

Cranbrook
late fall

New York
Oct 13–mid-Dec

1938

Yosemite and
Gold Rush towns
late May

San Francisco
May 25

Los Angeles
mid-May

Arizona and
New Mexico
early Jun

Chicago
mid-May

Yale
New Haven
Apr 14–May 9

New York
early Mar

1939

MIT
Cambridge
Oct 8–17

Cape
Cod
May

New York
Mar 19

Fallingwater
Bear Run
Aug 3–22

1940

1898   Born on February 3 in Kuortane, Finland.

1923   Establishes his architectural practice in Jyväskylä, Finland.

1924   Marries Aino Marsio, an architect employed in his office.

1933   Establishes his architectural office in Helsinki, Finland.

1937   American architect William W. Wurster and landscape architect Thomas Church and his wife Elizabeth visit Aalto at his home in Munkkiniemi, a neighborhood of Helsinki. Lawrence B. Anderson, Assistant Professor of Architecture at MIT, visits Aalto in Helsinki.

1938   *Alvar Aalto: Architecture and Furniture* opens on March 15 at the Museum of Modern Art in New York. The exhibition catalog is the first book on Aalto.

FIRST VISIT Aalto departs from *Gothenburg*, Sweden aboard the Gripsholm for the United States on October 13. He arrives on October 23 and stays for two months. His primary sphere of activity is New York City and the Museum of Modern Art. He meets with Alfred H. Barr, Jr., director; John McAndrew, curator of architecture and industrial art; James Johnson Sweeney, future curator of painting and sculpture; Edgar Kaufmann, Jr., future curator of design; and Nelson Rockefeller, future president of the Museum. He lectures at the Museum of Modern Art, Yale University, and New York University. In late fall, he visits the Finnish émigré architect, Eliel Saarinen at the Cranbrook Academy of Art in Bloomfield Hills, Michigan.

1939   **SECOND VISIT** Departs with Aino on March 4, sailing via Sweden on the *Queen Mary* and arriving in New York City. He supervises construction of the Finland Pavilion for the New York World's Fair. It opens on May 1.

Delivers a series of seven lectures at Yale University between April 14 and May 9, the last of which describes his recent Villa Mairea, "A House for a Rich Art Collector."

In early May, the Aaltos travel to Chicago (with Harry and Marie Gullichsen) to see Moholy-Nagy's "New Bauhaus." In mid-May they meet the architect Richard Neutra in Los Angeles, and go on to San Francisco to visit William W. Wurster, arriving on May 25. On June 1, Aalto holds a meeting on his "Institute for Architectural Research" in Wurster's office in San Francisco. He meets Lewis Mumford. They also travel to Yosemite National Park and to the "Gold Rush" towns of the Sierra Nevada, including Sutter's Creek.

Aino and Alvar Aalto's furniture and decorative arts are exhibited at the Golden Gate International Exhibition.

In New York by June 13, they return to Finland, arriving for midsummer (June 21).

Winter War between Finland and the Soviet Union, November 1939 – March 1940.

1940   **THIRD VISIT** Leaves for Sweden on March 4, with Aino and their two children. They sail on the *Drottningholm*, arriving in New York City on March 19. Aalto meets Buckminster Fuller.

On April 25 and 26, he gives two lectures at MIT. Other university lectures include: Yale, Princeton, Pratt Institute, Dartmouth College, and the Cranbrook Academy of Art.

In the spring, the Aaltos visit Edgar Kaufmann, Jr., at Fallingwater, Bear Run, Pennsylvania. They visit Cape Cod in May.

In June, Aalto corresponds with William Burchard regarding an appointment at MIT and on July 22 is appointed Research Professor there.

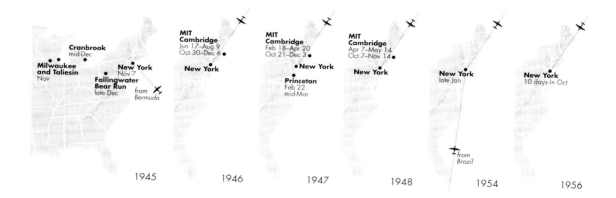

In July, the Aaltos visit William Lescaze in New Jersey and Walter Gropius in Lincoln, Massachusetts.

They stay with Edgar Kaufmann, Jr., at Fallingwater between August 3 and August 22.

In his "Working Program for Architectural Research at MIT" of September 3, Aalto persuades the School of Architecture and the Bemis Foundation to establish an architectural laboratory for examining the production of flexible building units.

Aalto begins his appointment as Research Professor on October 8, but stays for little over a week. Finland's War Office orders his return on October 17.

1941   The Continuation War (1941–44). Finland regains from Russia its pre-1940 territories, including East Karelia, and then loses them again.

1943   The Finland–America Association, of which Aalto is an active member, is founded on July 1.

1944   The exhibition "Built in USA, 1932–44," curated by Elizabeth Bauer Mock, opens at the Museum of Modern Art in New York. It notes Aalto's works as exemplary of the new "humanizing" philosophy of modern design.

1944   Aalto, serving as Chairman (1943–58) of SAFA (Association of Finnish Architects), brings the exhibition *America Builds*, organized by the Museum of Modern Art, from Stockholm to Helsinki. In conjunction with the exhibition he writes the essay, "The Intellectual Background of American Architecture."

1945   Lapland War. German troops retreat from Finland, leaving Rovaniemi destroyed. World War II ends in September.

FOURTH VISIT   Travels by air for the first time, arriving in New York (via Bermuda) on November 7. He teaches as a design critic at MIT in November and December. A luncheon is held in his honor at the Manhattan Club, New York, on November 23, 1945.

In late November, Aalto travels to Milwaukee, Wisconsin, to hear a lecture by Frank Lloyd Wright, followed by a two-day stay at Taliesen in Spring Green, Wisconsin. In mid-December, he goes to Cranbrook via New York to spend the Christmas holiday with the Saarinens.

He returns to Finland on February 2, 1946.

1946   **FIFTH VISIT** Aalto is appointed Visiting Professor at MIT. He arrives on June 17, and stays until August 9. He presents his ideas for a new "senior house" to the MIT Corporation. In the fall, Aalto is selected by the MIT Corporation to design the Senior Dormitory.

SIXTH VISIT   He returns to teach at MIT between October 30 and December 6.

1947   **SEVENTH VISIT**   Arrives in New York on February 18. In addition to teaching at MIT, Aalto works on the design for the Senior Dormitory. On February 28 he receives an honorary degree from Princeton University. He returns to Finland on April 20.

EIGHTH VISIT   Teaches at MIT between October 21 and December 3. He receives the commission for the Woodberry Poetry Room at Harvard University's Lamont Library.

1961

Miami
May 9

1963

1964

1967

1948 In February, Philip Johnson and Alfred Barr, Jr. hold the symposium, "What is Happening to Modern Architecture" at the Museum of Modern Art in New York. Henry-Russell Hitchcock and Lewis Mumford debate the "new humanism."

NINTH VISIT At MIT between April 7 and May 14.

TENTH VISIT In the fall, he arrives on October 7 and stays until November 14. He supervises construction of the Senior Dormitory.

1949 Aino Aalto dies.

The Senior Dormitory (Baker House) is dedicated in June. Aalto is not present, although he had intended to return to MIT in fall 1949.

1952 Marries Elissa Mäkiniemi.

1954 **ELEVENTH VISIT** Stops in New York with Elissa for ten days on their return from Brazil. He works with Wallace Harrison on design sketches for Lincoln Center.

1955 Elected a Member of the Academy in Finland.

1957 Awarded the Gold Medal by the Royal Institute of British Architects, London.

William W. Wurster, Catherine Bauer Wurster, and their daughter travel to Finland to visit Aalto.

1961 **TWELFTH VISIT** Arrives in New York in June to meet with Edgar Kaufmann, Jr., regarding the Kaufmann Conference Rooms at the Institute for International Education, across from the United Nations Headquarters.

1963 **THIRTEENTH VISIT** Awarded the Gold Medal from the American Institute of Architects. It is presented at the Institute's annual convention in Miami, Florida. He visits the site of the Kaufmann Conference Rooms in New York. He returns to MIT's School of Architecture and Planning and sees the completed Baker House.

1964 **FOURTEENTH VISIT** Aalto and Elissa arrive in New York in August. He receives an honorary doctorate from Columbia University and attends the dedication of the Edgar J. Kaufmann Conference Rooms.

Aalto is invited to design Mount Angel Abbey Library, St. Benedict, Oregon.

1967 **FIFTEENTH VISIT** Receives the Thomas Jefferson Medal at Jefferson's Monticello, near Charlottesville, Virginia. He visits the site of Mount Angel Abbey Library for the first time.

1968 The National Institute of Arts and Letters (now the American Academy of Arts and Letters) makes Aalto a foreign honorary member. Its president, George F. Kennan, travels to Helsinki to confer the award on Aalto at the United States Embassy.

1970 Mount Angel Library is completed and dedicated in May 1970. Aalto is not present.

1976 Aalto dies on May 11 in Helsinki.

Introduction

Stanford Anderson

By any measure Alvar Aalto counts as one of the few giants among twentieth-century modernist architects and is the most significant Finnish architect of the last century. Recent literature on Aalto reflects that high standing, notably stimulated by the centennial of his birth, in 1998. Students of Aalto largely examine his career in either or both of two contexts: the distinct character of his homeland at the periphery of Europe, or his recognized standing in European architectural culture.

Even the centennial exhibition and catalogue of the Museum of Modern Art in New York gave sparse attention to Aalto's relationship with America, which is all the more surprising for the fact that New York, and indeed the Museum itself, figured large in Aalto's experience of America.[1] He visited New York City in 1938, but that experience began when Aalto won the competition to create the Finland Pavilion at the 1939 World's Fair in New York with a design that marked a shift in his career.

The arrival of Alvar Aalto and his first wife, Aino Marsio Aalto, in America was occasioned by the construction of the World's Fair pavilion, a notable event soon enmeshed in far more diverse and equally influential activities, including Aalto's appointment as a research professor at the Massachusetts Institute of Technology (MIT), a title he always valued. Several essays in this volume tell this story, which is briefly rehearsed here.

After World War II, a period without major architectural commissions, Aalto returned to a position at MIT and, most notably, the opportunity to build a dormitory for MIT, an institution now of increased scientific and cultural ambition. The result was a building innovative both within its type and in Aalto's career. Several essays in the present volume convincingly argue not only for the significance of Baker House, as the dormitory came to be known, but also for its crucial impact on the production, particularly in Finland, of what have been called the "mature years" of Aalto's career.[2]

The story of Aalto and America deserves a telling in depth, and its significance is supported by the devoted labor of sixteen scholars, critics, and architects, European (especially Finnish) and American, who joined to produce this volume.

The Book

Following this introduction, three parts provide the structure of *Aalto and America*. The debated position of Aalto as a modernist, and the challenge he represented within that framework, must be assessed if we are to understand the impact of America on Aalto's thought and work. This assessment along with insights into the historiography of Aalto studies form part 1.

As stated, Aalto's engagement with America was not a simple phenomenon. He was not a tourist or casual traveler, nor merely an astute observer (as was Le Corbusier); rather, his engagement was complex, multidimensional, and involved virtually all facets of his life and work. Given his stature, Aalto's experience of America merits a detailed examination, the subject of part 2.

Three of Aalto's works in America—the Finland Pavilion, Baker House, and the library for Mount Angel Abbey in Oregon—are outstanding in the context of his life's work. In part 3, each of these works receives unprecedented attention—the pavilion and the library in the informed and attentive studies of individual scholars, and Baker House in multiple insightful essays from complementary perspectives. The presentation of all of Aalto's work in America is fulfilled with essays on the Woodberry Poetry Room at Harvard University and the Edgar J. Kaufmann Conference Rooms in New York.

Interpreting Aalto

Always greet with skepticism broad, generalizing claims for distinctive periods, styles, or movements in architecture. There was and is more to be gained from a careful consideration of the differences among the justly renowned works of Le Corbusier, Ludwig Mies van der Rohe, and Walter Gropius than was provided by Henry-Russell Hitchcock, Jr., and Philip Johnson when they subsumed those masters under a few stylistic rubrics and the heading of "International Style" at the Museum of Modern Art in 1932.[3]

This triumvirate of modern architects continued to be joined, with different emphases, hierarchies, and penumbra, in the work of early historians of modern architecture, notably Nikolaus Pevsner and Sigfried Giedion.[4] The practice continues to this day in the too-ready American references to "International Style" and the European catch-all of "functionalism," a conceptual term reduced to one of style. Stylistic categorization under the term "functionalism" served as the "other" in polemics advancing postmodernism and continues today in the same role for the proponents of the temporal necessity for voluptuous forms facilitated by computer-aided design and fabrication.[5]

There are those architects whose work is characteristically viewed for its individuality: Frank Lloyd Wright, Hugo Häring, Rudolf Schindler, Hans Scharoun, and others, as well as those who are seen as eccentrics. Aalto's work too is often recognized for its particularity, yet historians and critics assimilated him to the canon of modern architecture.

Aalto holds an anomalous position which is reflected in the essays of this book. Several of the contributors point out that the classic generalizing text of the history of modern architecture, Giedion's *Space, Time and Architecture: The Growth of a New Tradition*, began with devoted attention to the triumvirate, but with each succeeding edition increased its favorable attention to Aalto until images of his works outnumbered those of any other architect.[6] Aalto was the emerging figure among the canonical masters of modern architecture. Indeed, Dörte Kuhlmann sees Aalto as numbering among the "five most significant masters of modernism," but also as implicitly distinguished from the triumvirate, due to his work's role as a remedy for the shortcomings of heroic functionalism as perceived by postwar criticism, which found it "inhumane, mechanical, placeless, alienating, and standardized." In contrast, Sarah Williams Goldhagen begins her essay by noting that Aalto, despite his considerable renown, receives appreciation from a limited, self-selected audience. Goldhagen is not wrong in that assessment, but then the other old masters no longer have the devoted groups of a generation ago either. One might argue that among contemporary architects, Aalto and his work receive allegiances of increasing significance; senior architects of the stature of Álvaro Siza and Rafael Moneo profess the significance of Aalto in their own development.[7] Shigeru Ban, a strong emerging figure in architecture, conceived Aalto exhibitions with sympathetic installations of his own design, first in Tokyo and recently in a prominent London exhibition and catalogue that united the names of Aalto and Ban.[8] In his contribution, Colin St. John Wilson reminds the reader of one of the roots of this continuing attention to Aalto. Wilson's essay succinctly restates his sustained position advocating the "other tradition" of modern architecture with Aalto at its center. Wilson's claim for such a tradition entails that Aalto and his work must stand, after all, in coherent relation to other architects, noting in particular Häring, Scharoun, and Gunnar Asplund.

Do we then witness a battle of styles within Aalto's work? Aalto's two acclaimed early works, the library of Viipuri and the sanatorium of Paimio, gave him a foothold in the modernist pantheon that he forsook in the apostasy of the Villa Mairea (1937–39) and, more boldly and publicly, in the 1939 Finland Pavilion in New York—thus arguably establishing himself as the kingpin of an opposed stylistic group. Sarah Menin, in her contribution to this volume, asserts something of the kind: "The fact that…Aalto threw down a gauntlet to modernists in Finland's pavilion offers a significant correlation of creativity and personal vulnerability."

Most of the contributors find that Aalto's various works, despite their formal diversity, form a coherent oeuvre, which stands apart from that of the triumvirate. Sarah Goldhagen gives attention to both the Viipuri and Paimio constructions in her fresh and concerted argument for the distinctiveness of Aalto's entire career in architecture. In a particularly thoughtful architectural analysis, Michael Spens draws a convincing line from one of Aalto's first important buildings, the library in Viipuri, to one of his last, the library of Mount Angel Abbey, in Oregon. Yet one of these libraries could not be mistaken for the other. What unites Aalto's work—and potentially the work of other architects within Wilson's "tradition"—is not form.

Sandy Wilson holds an important place in this book, both for his devotion to Aalto's work and for the significance of his claims. It sorrows us that, late in the editorial process, we lost his voice. Nonetheless, *Aalto and America* is an independent inquiry by a new generation of historians and critics that, within the book's limited frame, seeks to bring our best understanding to certain aspects of Aalto and his work. Essays and particular arguments counter as well as parallel Wilson's thought.

Having said that, and staking a claim for the independent thought of the authors, I acknowledge that many of our essays contribute to an appreciation of Aalto that Wilson would have welcomed. Many of our authors share a conviction that what distinguished Aalto was a devoted commitment to the particularities of each project. If there was a battle, it was not one of style but of process and intent. Aalto's commitments are not to be understood in shallow, mere utilitarian terms. Aalto objected to what he saw as the narrow sense of function that he perceived in the thought and work of self-defined functionalists of the interwar years—Hannes Meyer, for example. Yet his objection prepared the way for a not wholly distinct advocacy in his call for a more profound sense of function. In 1940, Aalto asserted that the problem with rationalism in architecture was that it had not gone far enough.[9]

Aalto spoke repeatedly of his acceptance of functionalism, but on the condition that it must be conceived to address human needs deeply, including psychological and sociological needs. Aalto did not write a book advocating alliance with thought stemming from the social sciences, as did Richard Neutra.[10] Aalto's work, however, is a more eloquent witness of this devotion to human need, both individually and socially. Lawrence Speck constructs his essay on Baker House to reveal even quite mundane aspects of the building as within Aalto's complex understanding of functionalism.

Sarah Goldhagen gives important new depth to this professed attention to human need. She too touches on many mundane details—familiar ones like Aalto's design of a noiseless wash basin in the patients' rooms at Paimio and not so familiar ones like the waste baskets for the library of Viipuri. These particularities are seen as committed design decisions revealing the sophisticated, if partly intuitive, process stemming from Aalto's own commitment to the individual and social needs of people. Goldhagen demonstrates how that commitment, in Aalto's early years, was informed by his attentive respect for fundamental work in psychology at the beginning of the twentieth century, with particular concern for cognition and reason grounded in physiological psychology. Those psychological theories are now superseded, yet they are simultaneously both foundational for and subsumed by contemporary advancements in psychology and physiology. Goldhagen can read the implications of these advancements back into Aalto's work perhaps because he was working, often with self-acknowledged intuition, in a different discipline. Her essay enlightens us about Aalto and offers fresh thoughts on an enhanced, non-Heideggerian phenomenological approach to the understanding of architecture.

Among the essays that give further evidence of Aalto's profound attention to human need—whether in the shape of a handrail, the qualities of light employed, or the subtleties of psychological well-being—are those of Menin on the Finland Pavilion, Speck and other authors on Baker House, Kari Jormakka on the Woodberry Poetry Room, and Spens on the Mount Angel Abbey Library. If one attends carefully to an Aalto building and its details, it is difficult not to embrace "the methodical accommodation of circumstance," a thought that I once borrowed from Aalto.[11] Stepping back from the building under study, the conviction of Aalto's attention to human need, even to its finer circumstances, is only reinforced by differences among his buildings. As Speck points out, Baker House had international critical acclaim and positive reception by MIT from the outset (and so it continues); yet Aalto did not again create a building with serpentine curves or a dramatic hanging stairway. Forms were invented for a purpose, not as something to be visited on other circumstances. Such self-visitations are rampant with noted architects today.

The essayists of *Aalto and America* make recurrent commitments to the concept of the primacy of process, and the accommodation of circumstance in Aalto's work. Kuhlmann specifically mentions such matters with regard to Aalto's concern with light. She perceives, however, a satisfying provision of diversity rather than a more profound architectural program. She then offers a firmer challenge: "Aalto's deviations from *Neue Sachlichkeit* norms are not so much sensitive responses to the functional and other specificities of each situation as they are semiotic responses to the abstract issues raised by the critics."

I admit that I first bristle at this assertion for more than one reason. In *The International Style: Architecture since 1922*, Hitchcock and Johnson deviated from *Neue Sachlichkeit* norms precisely to avoid functional specificities: for example, they chastised Gropius for a beam at the Bauhaus with gussets that diminished the purity of its form.[12] Yes, Aalto deviated from the norms of *Neue Sachlichkeit*—from the mechanistic norms of *Neue Sachlichkeit* toward a more profound sense of human need. The well-received work at Viipuri and Paimio was contemporary with *Neue Sachlichkeit*. If the ensuing, greater deviations of Villa Mairea and the Finland Pavilion in New York elicited criticism, negative and positive, the work still preceded the criticism. I find it hard to imagine that Aalto was blocked at the drawing board while seeking "semiotic responses to the abstract issues raised by the critics."

There is of course another, sympathetic reading of Kuhlmann's statement. What if "Aalto" is not Aalto at his drawing board, but the Aalto of critical discourse? Some readers might still sense that Kuhlmann offers a false dichotomy in the sentence as written. But one could read Kuhlmann as saying that Aalto's "sensitive responses to the functional and other specificities of each situation" (which Kuhlmann also notes) are *also* "semiotic responses to the abstract issues raised by the critics." In this reading, Kuhlmann offers a particularly fruitful approach, precisely because "Aalto," the subject of critical discourse, supported by Aalto's differentiated projects, methodically responsive to circumstance, is open to multiple readings. It is the richness of the source material Aalto offers that has allowed Aalto's work to be integrated into quite different realms of critical discourse.

Paul Bentel, in his study of Baker House, presents a still more extensive catalogue of changing critical assessments of Aalto. He would not disagree with Kuhlmann since he recognizes the remarkable plasticity of the interpretations of Aalto, but he is emphatic in not stopping with the historiographic or semiotic conclusion. For Bentel, "it is . . . troubling that historical narration diminishes the artifact by yielding to it a meaning that only partially reflects its intrinsic value as architecture." He also notes, "Despite the role of the building as a historical touchstone, our strong reactions to Baker House's sculptural forms, its robust material features, and its idiosyncratic plan suggest that it is possible for the building to outperform its historical persona." So it cuts both ways: while Baker House provokes discourse, the understanding of Baker House, and more, is formed by successive dialogues. Thus Bentel insists on returning to the concrete experience of the work by ever-changing observers.

We are returned to the necessity of asking, what are the underlying conditions of Aalto's complexity and richness? Our responses appear not only with Bentel but in other contributors' concerted analyses of Aalto's American works (especially the 1939 Finland Pavilion, Baker House, and the Mount Angel Abbey Library) and notably in the cognitive propositions of Goldhagen.

Aalto in and on America

The present work is titled *Aalto and America* because beyond the matter of fact that Aalto built in America, Aalto also had important relations and activities in this country that influenced his thinking about both America and his work. It was a mark of his stature that Aalto won the competitions to design the Finland Pavilions for both the World's Fair in Paris in 1937 and in New York in 1939. Yet it is also true that Aalto's introduction to New York was unusually fortunate, both for the crucial moment in his career and the stature of the people and institutions he engaged. The commission for the 1939 pavilion first brought Aalto to America, a subject addressed by Sarah Menin's essay on the pavilion, which informs us of the events closely related to that project.

Aalto was immediately and increasingly involved with much more than the pavilion, including his solo exhibition at the Museum of Modern Art in 1938; the marketing of his furniture; his association with wealthy and culturally well-placed New Yorkers, including the Rockefellers and key members of MoMA; and explorations of possible research institutes and publications. Almost immediately, with worsening political conditions in Europe and the Soviet–Finnish Winter War, Aalto became a political envoy and what Eeva-Liisa Pelkonen calls a "one-man propaganda unit" in America for the Finnish government. With the loss of the eastern territory of Karelia, Finland faced resettlement issues that provoked further research, design, and funding enterprises for Aalto, to a significant degree in America.

Pelkonen considers these events in Aalto's life and gives close attention to the complex political conditions of Finland in those years, a country squeezed between the Soviet Union and Nazi Germany, attacked by the Russians, used as a pawn by both powers, and eventually strategically allied with Germany. Pelkonen reveals not only Aalto's important engagements in those years but also his psychological vulnerability.

This book is not the place for a biography of Aalto.[13] However, for the decade of Aalto's most significant transactions with America, from the late 1930s to the late 1940s, the essays by Pelkonen, Juhani Pallasmaa, and Gail Fenske offer biographical insights through their careful attention to the events of those years.

Pekka Korvenmaa examines more concrete, or literally "material," matters: the commonality of wood construction in both Finland and America and Aalto's shared interest in the rationalization of basic housing as he found it in America, particularly in Albert Farwell Bemis's research at MIT.[14] Events were such that Aalto conducted his work in design, modular research, standardization, and construction of houses almost wholly in Finland, enabled through his close, even personal, ties with the Gullichsen family and the Ahlström corporation.

Fenske broadens the scope of the theme of Aalto and America, beginning with Americans—notably Philip Johnson and William Wilson Wurster, —the latter of whom visited Aalto in Finland before Aalto's travels to New York. Fenske follows Aalto beyond New York to California, where Aalto traveled to solidify his close relation with Wurster. Fenske also details Aalto's significant relations with MIT, beginning with the overture from John Burchard, director of the housing research–oriented Albert Farwell Bemis Foundation of MIT. With Aalto's appointment as a research professor, MIT intended to join in a wider program to support both house design and a plan for "An American Town in Finland," part of a Finnish resettlement program. Aalto's time at MIT was cut short by his required return to Finland, but his efforts continued in Finland. At the end of the war, his friend Wurster had fortuitously become the dean of the School of Architecture at MIT, strengthening their mutual interests. Aalto's most significant postwar engagement at MIT was the commission for the dormitory Baker House. Fenske joins Michael Trencher in explaining how Wurster and Aalto conceived of Baker House not just as a dormitory, but as part of a program to humanize this technological university—a program that was in concert with new Institute policy, extending to curricular changes and to succeeding officers of the Institute.

While Fenske provides the required depth to understand Aalto *in* America, Juhani Pallasmaa, with his profound knowledge both of Finland and Aalto, directs our attention to Aalto *on* America. In his contribution, he observes Aalto in America, as in his sympathetic attention to Eliel Saarinen and the Cranbrook Academy and his visit with Frank Lloyd Wright at Taliesin. But Pallasmaa is especially revealing of "Aalto and America" during Aalto's time in Finland before, during, and after his American years.

Pallasmaa begins with Aalto's childhood interest in America's myths of the West. Recognizing Aalto's period in which America was envisioned positively, and when professional opportunities beckoned, Pallasmaa also takes us to Aalto's later disenchantment. To account for Aalto's departure from MIT and a promising scene in America, Pallasmaa does not turn to the pressing events of 1940 and Aalto's military order to return as Menin emphasizes, but rather to Aalto's deep ties to the "Nordic landscape, culture, and values of life." He recites Giedion's claim that "Finland is with Aalto wherever he goes," and closes with his own assessment: Aalto's "artistic sensibilities grew from the Finnish landscape and cultural soil to the degree that even his architectural works abroad are reflections of the characteristics of his Nordic homeland."

But this "Finnishness" argument seems to cut both ways. Aalto could have his Finland wherever he went. Pallasmaa himself, in introducing the argument, begins by acknowledging Aalto's "cosmopolitan and internationalist character." We might do well to probe Aalto's cosmopolitanism.

Both Fenske and Pelkonen comment on the Aaltos' appreciation of California, stimulated by their positive perception of the "mixture of races and cultural impulses."[15] Pelkonen writes of Aalto's assessment of the difference between American and European culture and society, and a concern to challenge European nationalism and its root in the idea of cultural and ethnic homogeneity. Consequently, when he looked inward, Aalto found the advantages of Finland having two languages and participating in Nordic cooperation.

In her contribution, Pelkonen takes us deep into Aalto's Finland. Though Aalto's library commission in Viipuri took him to Karelia, romanticized as the primitive locus of Finnish culture, he seems not to have traveled or sketched in the Karelian countryside. When he wrote on Karelian architecture in 1941, he assessed it with universal principles, avoiding vernacularism that would be too easily, especially in that moment, associated with regressive political programs. Aalto, writing after the loss of the eastern province of Karelia, deemed the heartland of Finnishness, avoided nationalism to the point of finding it unnecessary to draw national boundaries in the matter of material culture.[16] It comes as no surprise that Kuhlmann finds that Aalto, whether at home or abroad, worked against tradition.

Non-essentialist theories of cosmopolitanism accept the complexity of a cosmopolitan ethos and traits engendered by one's place of birth and maturation. There is reason to see Aalto as such a cosmopolitan. As cited by Pallasmaa, Aalto wrote already in 1922: "And when we see how in times past one succeeded in being international, free of prejudices and at the same time true to oneself, we can with full awareness receive currents from ancient Italy, from Spain, and from modern America."[17] It appears more faithful to Aalto's thought and actions, and more compelling as an example for our hopes in globalizing times, if we can see Aalto as one who always drew from his roots but was still more a citizen of the world.[18]

Aalto's Work in America

Part 4 of this book presents close accounts of all the work built by Aalto in America. Sarah Menin's detailed study of the Finland Pavilion for the 1939 World's Fair in New York concludes: "In the pavilion, with its remarkable architectural form, Aalto was seeking to yoke Finnish culture both backward to the heart of the forest and forward to the heart of the twentieth century—to engage both its progress and its grief." It is in the nature of the work that both Aalto and Menin must engage "Finnishness," but they take us far beyond the recurrent evocations of the curvilinear shores of lakes and islands.

Following Menin's chapter are five essays that provide different takes on the most noted of Aalto's American works, Baker House dormitory at MIT. Michael Trencher's "Baker House: The Individual and Mass Housing, a Delicate Balance" is perceptive in placing Baker House in the context of both Soviet collective housing and Le Corbusier's Swiss Pavilion dormitory at the Cité Internationale Universitaire de Paris. Trencher's essay is ingenious in that he does justice to all the projects and shows that Aalto was both attentive to, and finally independent of, the precedent projects. Trencher is convincing in his finding of Aalto's independence in his balancing of the group and the individual in a humanistic and supporting manner, just that which Wurster and Aalto had envisioned for MIT.

Lawrence Speck, in his contribution, situates Aalto as central to that strain of modernist thought that values a deep, humane interpretation of functionalism, and presents Baker House as exemplary of this sustained ambition on the part of Aalto.

Ákos Moravánszky inventively plays off the distinctive coarse brickwork of Baker House to inform us of modernist ambitions to use brick as a basis of modular standardization, and then returns us to "Aalto's construction of a building material." For Moravánszky, "Baker House was an experiment with brick as the basic element of architechnological standardization. In an iconological sense, however, the emphasis was on the archaic rather than on the technological." With Aalto working for a technological university in a period of self-examination and a search for a more humane education and environment, Moravánszky observes, "Aalto spoke of the material experiments in architecture as a play rich in historical resonance. He was convinced that the architect can play and experiment with the values of a society, rather than simply 'express' them."

Aalto's choice of low-quality, coarse bricks from which the clinkers were *not* eliminated, their self-supporting but not load-bearing use, and the arrangement of standard bricks in a serpentine wall are all distinctive aspects of Baker House. Yet our authors also rightly recall that red brick is a standard of Boston and even of the prestigious Harvard University nearby, up the Charles River. Bay windows are also common in Boston; not that they are serpentine, but they too form rhythmic street facades and offer views up and down the street. As Pallasmaa describes, for Aalto architecture was "not an abstract and contextually detached professional practice, but rather…a mediation between landscape, material culture, and people." It is no paradox that such mediation might, for Aalto, be a lesson from his homeland, that Finland was with him in America, so to speak; yet at the same time he was sounding depths of New England culture, not only with bricks but also in the traits discussed by other of our contributors on Baker House.

It may be argued, as notably David Fixler does, that not only did MIT and America benefit from Aalto's experience and architectural profundity, but Aalto carried something back as well. It is in the years following Baker House that the brilliant mature work of Aalto's red (brick) period yielded such masterpieces as the Säynätsalo town hall and the National Pensions Institute and House of Culture in Helsinki. Of course they represent much more than a new commitment to red brick; they are also part of a new, varied, independent form-making that was Aalto's, but already rehearsed at MIT.

Wilson recalls Aalto professing that critical assessments in architecture should be formed from what a building is like thirty years after its making, and tests this proposition with a favorable account, by two MIT students, of Baker House after that interval.[19] After fifty years of use, assessments by both critics and students remained positive, but renovation to meet new technical standards was necessary. Fixler, the renovation architect for Baker House, writes here from the authority of his careful preliminary studies, design, and implementation of the renewal of Baker House. Fixler also puts this work in the context of the vexed issues of restoration or renovation of works of modern architecture.

Paul Bentel's study of Baker House is largely historiographic, but with the addition of an insistence on a return to careful, rewarding attention to this powerful building. It was such attention that gave Aalto, and specifically Baker House, a significance in American architectural discourse that, as Fenske points out, challenged and even overcame the primacy of Gropius and The Architects Collaborative (TAC) at Harvard.

As Aalto was designing Baker House, he received a small but distinguished commission from Harvard, the Woodberry Poetry Room to be housed in Lamont Library, then also in a design stage. The poetry reading room as a place of activity was already in existence. Kari Jormakka describes its intended role as a location for undergraduate student learning opportunities that also fulfills a larger program. Students come not only to read but to hear recordings of major poets reciting their own poetry. Many of the recordings are the result of initiatives of the Poetry Room, including sponsored visits and readings at Harvard. Jormakka's incisive analysis demonstrates Aalto's achievement in this small architectonic environment, set in the context of a work, Lamont Library, that cautiously introduced modern architecture to the famed Harvard Yard. It is a great pity that Harvard was not a faithful custodian in the recent renovation of the poetry room.

Edgar Kaufmann, Jr., devoted his life to architecture, from an early (if brief) apprenticeship with Frank Lloyd Wright to a role in the early stages of the architecture and design program at the Museum of Modern Art to a late professorship at Columbia University.[20] In his time at MoMA, he was attentive to Alvar Aalto and continued an appreciation of Aalto's work. In the early 1960s Kaufmann took the opportunity to suggest and finance a set of conference rooms for the Institute of International Education in New York, on the top floors of its office building facing the United Nations Plaza. In his essay in the present volume, Matthew Postal describes these origins and the dedication of the rooms to Edgar Kaufmann, Sr., the patron of both Wright's Fallingwater and of the Kaufmann House in Palm Springs, California, by Richard Neutra. Postal details the complexity of the remote, New York–Helsinki design and partial fabrication process, ending in a work of value but perhaps one not wholly satisfactory to either of the protagonists.

The final essay of *Aalto and America* is that of Michael Spens on the library for the Mount Angel Abbey. Spens places the library in the tradition of Benedictine monasteries stemming from Monte Cassino in Italy. With far more detail, he traces the origin of the abbey's library from Aalto's first library, that of Viipuri, through the many examples of this important building type in Aalto's oeuvre. However, Spens always returns to his close reading of the abbey library itself. He succeeds in what he claims: that this library is indeed a masterpiece, unjustly placed in relative neglect in the critical literature on Aalto and modern architecture. Concluding his argument, Spens writes: "Aalto's buildings recognize the flows, pools, and eddies of circulation around them, human and material. . . . These spaces are transmuted into the internal containers for human movement, separation, and congregation, and these qualities are channeled and duly accommodated within tactile surfaces and perceivable orientations. Thus the concept of phenology, as it is known today, has already been instinctively realized by Aalto in his work, where a particular site in his mind was always deemed to extend its sphere far beyond the immediate 'footprint' of the building plan."

Sarah Goldhagen and Michael Spens wrote unaware of each other's essay, yet their works, revealing a more considered phenomenology, in theory and in practice, complement one another. And in so doing they form excellent bookends to this collection of essays.

1 Peter Reed, ed., *Alvar Aalto: Between Humanism and Materialism* (New York: Museum of Modern Art, 1998).

2 Göran Schildt, *Alvar Aalto: The Mature Years* (New York: Rizzoli, 1991).

3 Henry-Russell Hitchcock, Jr., and Philip Johnson, *The International Style: Architecture since 1922* (New York: W. W. Norton, 1932; reprinted with new forewords, 1966 and 1995).

4 Nikolaus Pevsner, *Pioneers of Modern Design from William Morris to Walter Gropius* (New York: Museum of Modern Art, 1949); Sigfried Giedion, *Space, Time and Architecture: The Growth of a New Tradition* (Cambridge, Mass.: Harvard Univ. Press, 1941).

5 Stanford Anderson, "The Fiction of Function," *Assemblage* 2 (Feb. 1987): 18–31.

6 Sigfried Giedion, *Space, Time and Architecture: The Growth of a New Tradition*, 5th ed. (Cambridge, Mass.: Harvard Univ. Press, 1967).

7 Álvaro Siza delivered a lecture, titled simply "Aalto," on the relations of his thought and work to those of Aalto at the conference "Interpreting Aalto: Baker House and MIT," organized by Stanford Anderson and held at MIT's Kresge Auditorium on 1–2 Oct. 1999. This conference also served as the jumping-off point for the present volume. See also Siza, "Alvar Aalto," in *Álvaro Siza: Complete Works*, ed. Kenneth Frampton (London: Phaidon, 2000), 572–73. Rafael Moneo, in the small space of his Pritzker Architecture Prize biography (http://www.pritzkerprize.com/laureates/1996/bio.html, accessed 29 May 2011) draws attention to his early contact with Aalto, and Nicholas Ray finds Moneo's "thinking is probably as close to Aalto's as any of his generation." Ray, *Alvar Aalto* (New Haven, Conn.: Yale Univ. Press, 2005), 194.

8 "Alvar Aalto," Axis Gallery, Tokyo (1986); "Alvar Aalto through the Eyes of Shigeru Ban," Barbican Art Gallery, London (Spring 2007). Juhani Pallasmaa and Tomoko Sato, eds., *Alvar Aalto through the Eyes of Shigeru Ban* (London: Blackdog, 2007).

9 Alvar Aalto, "The Humanizing of Architecture: Functionalism Must Take the Human Point of View to Achieve Its Full Effectiveness," *Technology Review*, Nov. 1940, 14–16, 36; republished several times including as "The Humanizing of Architecture," in *Alvar Aalto in His Own Words*, ed. Göran Schildt (New York: Rizzoli, 1998), 102-07.

10 Richard Neutra, *Survival through Design* (1954; London: Oxford Univ. Press, 1969).

11 Stanford Anderson, "Aalto and 'Methodical Accommodation to Circumstance'" and "Aalto und 'die methodische Anpassung an Gegebenheiten,'" in *Alvar Aalto in Seven Buildings/Alvar Aalto in sieben Bauwerken*, ed. Timo Tuomi and others (Helsinki: Museum of Finnish Architecture, 1998), 142–49, 192. Also in editions with Finnish, Swedish, and Portuguese translations.

12 Hitchcock and Johnson, *International Style* (New York: Norton, 1932 and 1966), 142.

13 The standard biography of Aalto is in three independently published volumes by Göran Schildt: *Alvar Aalto: The Early Years* (New York: Rizzoli, 1984); *Alvar Aalto: The Decisive Years* (Rizzoli, 1986); and *Alvar Aalto: The Mature Years* (Rizzoli, 1991).

14 Albert Farwell Bemis led research on housing at MIT, which culminated in the publication of Bemis and John Burchard, *The Evolving House*, 3 vols. (Cambridge, Mass.: MIT Press, 1933–36).

15 Alvar Aalto, quoted in Schildt, *Alvar Aalto: The Decisive Years*, 179.

16 Alvar Aalto, "Karjalan rakennustaide," *Uusi Suomi*, 2 Nov. 1941, 12; published in translation as "Karelian Architecture" in *Alvar Aalto in His Own Words*, ed. Göran Schildt (New York: Rizzoli, 1997), 115–19.

17 Alvar Aalto, "Menneitten aikojen motiivit," *Arkkitehti* 2 (1922); published in translation as "Motifs from Past Ages," in *Alvar Aalto in His Own Words*, 32-35.

18 Kwame Anthony Appiah, *Cosmopolitanism: Ethics in a World of Strangers* (New York: W. W. Norton, 2006).

19 Deborah Poodry and Victoria Ozonoff, "Coffins, Pies and Couches: Aalto at MIT," *Spazio e Società* 18 (June 1982): 105.

20 I wish to take this opportunity to make a correction and apology. Late in the process, Edgar Kaufmann, Jr., became the advisor to my doctoral dissertation at Columbia University. I was under pressure to finish and these were precisely the most troubled days of student political activity both at MIT, where I taught, and still more at Columbia, where the campus was closed. Kaufmann was attentive to my needs, reviewing chapters immediately and staging a defense with distinguished professors at the home of one of them, George Collins. I write all this by way of explaining that I felt both appreciation and respect for Edgar Kaufmann. Eventually my dissertation was published. When I received my first copy, I opened it randomly, as it happened, to the acknowledgments and my eyes fell on my appreciation to "Edward Kaufmann." This typo was made more hurtful by the fact that there was an Edward Kaufmann in New York architectural circles at the time. Though I am sure there are more errors, this is still the only one in the book of which I am conscious. I cannot account for how this failure occurred and went unattended (and a failure MIT Press would not correct or note in the paperback edition). I am pleased to somewhat assuage my guilt with this notice. Learn more of Edgar Kaufmann in the essay by Matthew Postal in this volume.

Aalto's Modernism

The essays of part 1 propose intellectual and critical contexts in which to place the thought and work of Alvar Aalto. No essay in this collection was conceived to set a critical agenda for the other essays. Yet while Sarah Goldhagen's "Aalto's Embodied Rationalism" is her own insightful construction of the thought and work of Alvar Aalto, it also serves both to inform and to be tested by the work of the other contributors.

Goldhagen's emphasis is revealed in her title. She explores Aalto's interest at the beginnings of his career in the noted physiological psychology of early-twentieth-century Germany. Such simultaneously rational and physical programs for understanding our perceptual mechanisms and sensibilities are reflected in Aalto's repeated arguments in favor of a functionalism that is deeply informed by human needs and experience. Goldhagen sees in Aalto's thought and work a conflation of rationalism and humanism that informs a deep comprehension of the cognitive realities of human experience. She examines several of Aalto's major architectural works to reveal his partially intuitive, cognitive enterprise more fully. Goldhagen also argues that Aalto's work can be seen through a "prism of phenomenology" that is non-Heideggerian and still developing in contemporary cognitive linguistics and neuroscience.

Dörte Kuhlmann's "Floating Signifiers: Interpreting Aalto" is a semiotic analysis of the historical and critical reception of Aalto. The fruitfulness of Kuhlmann's approach stems from the distinctiveness and complexity of Aalto's thought and work that in turn inspires diverse and still changing interpretations. Following an early point when critics would incorporate Aalto in the emerging modernist canon, other possibilities have emerged according to the changing demands of architectural discourse, each open to conflicting evaluations. Among these are interpretations of his work as a deviant challenge within modernism, a more personal and expressive version of modernism, a phenomenologically informed alternative to modernism, an anticipation of postmodernism, and competing versions of Aalto in his Finnish context—positions that embed him in his Finnishness or see him as a Finn of broad cultural perceptions. Kuhlmann invokes the thought of Claude Lévi-Strauss and Jacques Lacan in finding a reciprocity between Aalto's singular achievement in architecture and the proposition that the play of signification always exceeds the constraints we imagine operate on expression.

The essay by Colin St. John Wilson will perhaps be the last authored presentation of Wilson's long-term advocacy of his theory of "Aalto and the Other Tradition." Aalto's thought is grounded, he argues, in the Aristotelian distinction between Pure Art ("that serves only itself") and Practical Art ("that serves an end other than itself"). Architecture being unequivocally a Practical Art, Wilson continues his endorsement of Aalto's work for its "life-enhancing response to a real situation." Wilson sees Aalto's deeply informed commitment to this position as one whose authority has continued to deepen and offer the promise of fruitful development.

Sandy Wilson died in 2007, before we could complete this collaboration, but his essay serves as a sign of his continuing, committed, and generous love of architecture devoted to people, individually and collectively. **S.A.**

Aalto's Embodied Rationalism

Sarah Williams Goldhagen

In the story of modernism, told and retold, interpreted and reinterpreted, Alvar Aalto is often treated as the most important, greatest early modernist who doesn't fit. The mainstream, nearly filmic narrative begins (or not) with the work of Frank Lloyd Wright, and then, in a series of cuts, presents a central cast of characters in which Le Corbusier, Ludwig Mies van der Rohe, J. J. P. Oud (sometimes), and Walter Gropius play leading roles. Afterward, and separately, comes the short on Aalto. The story of this northern outlier, lauded throughout his career and to this day by an underpopulated if devoted coterie of architects, scholars, and theorists, remains some sort of outtake played in an ancillary modernist theater.

Puzzling out Aalto's uneasy exclusion from the canonical narrative of modernism is not difficult, as many of his design methods contravene its central precepts. If modernism was concerned with standardization, Aalto often complained that the *Neue Sachlichkeit* approach to standardization bulldozed human particularities, and he advocated and practiced instead what he called the "flexible standardization" of a building's parts but never the architectural whole, which he insisted should be planned and constructed with attention to a site's topography, the needs of users, and so on. In his own work, Aalto flagrantly, almost defiantly celebrated the idiosyncrasies of handicraft. If modernists embraced at least the pretense of structural rationalism, Aalto exhibited an only occasional interest in the structure of his buildings and refused to bend over backwards to integrate structure with form. He masked hybrid structural solutions freely: load-bearing masonry here,

steel beams or poured concrete there.[1] If modernism insisted on the symbolic importance and pragmatic superiority of new materials, Aalto liberally mixed old with new—wood; reinforced, poured, and prefabricated concrete; steel; brick. If modernism whispered or shouted transparency, Aalto's buildings revel in their opacity. If modernism suffered from a deep ambivalence toward typology and historic precedent, Aalto unhesitatingly drew from Erik Gunnar Asplund's Stockholm Public Library, Le Corbusier's Villa Savoye, the Vesnin brothers' project for *Pravda*, Italian Renaissance palazzi, Finnish country churches, Karelian courtyard farmhouses, Greek amphitheaters, and more. If modernism mandated a functional approach to planning, and consequently a formal abstraction, Aalto's buildings pulsate with figuration and metaphors.[2] If modernism redefined architecture as space, Aalto continued to be fascinated by the object. If modernism aspired to universalism, Aalto—putatively, at least—practiced particularism.

At times, Aalto opportunistically encouraged this partial renegade status within the field and, to be sure, seeing his architecture thus has borne ripe fruit.[3] This canonical view of his relationship to modernism has nurtured architectural practices, critical questions, and scholarly interpretations about the chronological development of modernism and the complexity of modernist attitudes to regionalism, standardization, and functionalism, all of which have advanced contemporary architectural practice and historical understanding. Still, the basic paradox remains. Indisputably, Aalto's work is modernist. But how?

To answer this question is not the straightforward undertaking it might seem to be. Doing so requires unpacking a number of tightly boxed concepts about how we as users and makers of buildings look at and comprehend our built world. These concepts include how we understand human cognition, the philosophical concept of rationalism, and rationalism's role in the construction of modernism.

For Aalto, rationalism and humanism so intermeshed that the concepts were practically coterminous. Even if this makes for a somewhat counterintuitive notion of rationalism, Aalto's redefined rationalism better describes the cognitive realities of human experience than did the multiple rationalisms advanced by his contemporaneous modernist colleagues. Aalto's conflation of rationalism with humanism makes sense when each term is reflected through the prism of phenomenology, which has taken various forms, from early-twentieth-century scientific psychology to mid-twentieth-century phenomenological philosophy to contemporary cognitive linguistics and neuroscience. Aalto developed his singular and lasting approach to modernism partly by learning, partly by intuiting a model of human cognition and reason grounded in what today is commonly called phenomenology.[4]

Understanding Aalto's rationalism requires traveling through a dense forest on what may at times seem a crooked path. First, his commitment to rationalism must be explored. Then the intertwined philosophical and architectural traditions of rationalism must be untangled in order to properly articulate Aalto's conception of rationalism by placing it within these longstanding intellectual traditions. Only then can the alternative notion of rationalism, embodied rationalism, be explicated and shown to be the cognitive and historical framework from which Aalto developed his architecture. These explorations clear the ground for revisiting two buildings that Aalto, when he came to America, repeatedly claimed foundational to his later work and indeed central to his philosophy of architecture: the sanatorium in Paimio (1929–1932) and the municipal library in Viipuri (1927–1935; Viipuri is now in Russia and renamed Vyborg).

When Aalto's notions of rationalism and humanism, and the architecture that he built out of those ideas, are seen from these multiple, overlapping vantage points, the importance of these buildings for understanding Aalto's later work in America becomes clear. Aalto's extravasation from the central discourse of modernism also disappears, and a more theoretically adequate and historically accurate conception of modernism and Aalto's critical project within it emerges.

Triangulated Rationalism

Throughout his career, Aalto broadcast and rebroadcast his commitments to modernism and rationalism. He contended that modernists (by which he largely meant his colleagues in the Congrès Internationaux d'Architects Modernes, or CIAM) had "no reason" to dispense with the pursuit of rationalism, which itself was not wrong. But he gently suggested that how his colleagues conceptualized reason and rationalism was shallow, even wrong-headed: rationalism "has not gone deep enough."[5] By equating rationalism with the rationalization of the building process, or with structural or mathematical logic, these architects violated basic human needs. In a barely veiled reference to Le Corbusier, who declared that his model dwellings for the Weissenhofsiedlung were "as efficient as a railway car," Aalto wrote, "By the word 'economical' I do not mean the economy that prevailed in the early days in the railway cars of the Pullman Company." Pullman cars were "said to be practical and economical, but the wise traveler was quick to point out that their practicality and economy provided significant advantages only to the Pullman company, not to the passengers."[6] Similarly, according to Aalto, attempts to "rationalize" lighting (surely a reference to the lighting designs emerging from the Bauhaus workshops) "introduced little else but blindingly white porcelain spheres or opal cubes"—again, reaping profits for the manufacturer, but visiting upon the consumer little more than headaches and hotspots.[7]

Modernist architects needed to expand their understanding of rationalism, to analyze "more of the qualities" intrinsic to the architecture they designed. Comparing the array of human needs architecture accommodates to hues on a color spectrum, Aalto contended that architects must consider not only architecture's "visible" colors—program, economy, technology, hygiene, site—but also its invisible "ultraviolet band." There the "purely human questions" lurk. Buildings should serve everyday human needs. Early in his career,

Aalto effusively imagined a visitor in a new house, standing in the entrance foyer, catching glimpses of its less formal upper story "with its bedrooms, children's rooms and a line with drying articles of clothing on it, hanging there as a somewhat careless piece of evidence of the chores of everyday life."[8] Architectural environments must at once accommodate users and slow them down; they should force them to appreciate "the value of the fleeting moment."[9] Sometimes, he acknowledged, architectural methods "resemble scientific ones": an analytical, rational approach to the multiplicity of human needs, and a "process of research, such as science employs, can be adopted also in architecture." Nevertheless, "always there will be more of instinct and art" in this process—intuition, he asserted, "can sometimes be extremely rational."[10]

Whatever Aalto meant by rationalism, his use of the term certainly differed in both degree and kind from that of many of his colleagues. To elucidate these worlds of difference we need to take ten steps backwards and examine the term "rationalism" in modern architecture and modern philosophy, because it is on philosophical notions of rationalism that the early modernist approach to rationalism largely rests.

In discussions of modern architecture, "rationalism" elicits a fairly standard set of meanings.[11] Twentieth-century rationalism, often riddled with contradiction in individual practices, is the intertwined theoretical legacy of two nineteenth-century pedagogical traditions: the structural rationalism of Eugène-Emmanuel Viollet-le-Duc and his successor, Auguste Choisy, and the typological functionalism of Jean-Nicholas-Louis Durand.[12]

The best known modernists of the 1920s in the techno-rational strain, such as Le Corbusier, Gropius, and Mies van der Rohe, conjoined structural rationalism and typological functionalism to establish a set of guiding principles, which they applied in practice in such sundry combinations that rationalism became nearly topological, a single lump of theoretical clay ever-transforming into a multiplicity of forms. Mies van der Rohe, for example, became the supposedly unschooled successor to nineteenth-century structural rationalism while rejecting typological functionalism as unsuited to the psychic and locational needs of ever-transitory modern man.[13] Le Corbusier and Gropius insisted on pressing new technologies into what they claimed were architecture's logical structural, functional, and aesthetic ends. A sometime adjunct to this latter strain of rationalism mandated that architectural design should be developed according to the dictates of the anticipated construction process, preferably mass production.

The formal incarnation of techno-rationalism is most famously represented by designs such as Mies van der Rohe's project for a Concrete Office Block (1922), Le Corbusier's Maison Dom-Ino (1914–1915), and Gropius' Bauhaus at Dessau (1926). Each is shaped by a species of Euclidean geometry, which, formally, became the symbolic language of rationalist design. A cube, a cone, a sphere, a cylinder, and a pyramid appear above a bird's eye view of ancient Rome in Le Corbusier's *Vers une architecture*; in *Urbanisme*, he amusingly incarnates modernity itself in the straight line.[14] For Gropius, Durand's geometrically neutral grid figuratively supplied the graph paper on which one could design buildings with an eye toward their eventual mass production. Many famous modernist buildings discursively engage the grid in plan and elevation, even if they occasionally violate its unforgiving orthogonal dictates, sneaking non–geometrically derived curves on top or within.

For some of the techno-rationalists' contemporaries, such as Hugo Häring and Hans Scharoun, rationalism in design did not begin from a building's formal disposition but from the architect's handling of human social functions. Often called organic functionalists, these architects owed to Durand their insistence that a building's shape and plan suit its projected use. Yet they rejected typology as so saturated in historical precedent that it prohibited individuated solutions to architectural design. A new architecture need serve *modern* life. For the organic functionalists, a building's design must emerge first from the specifics of program and site.

Most architects and critics of the 1920s, and even today, considered these two best known theoretical strains of modernist practice, techno-rationalism and organic functionalism, to be diametrically opposed.[15] And not without reason. Techno-rationalists began from the object, organic functionalists from its users. Techno-rationalists employed (or purported to employ) mathematical systems of geometry or physics; organic functionalists shunned such abstractions (even as they occasionally used them) in favor of the contingencies of site and patterns of human social interaction. Techno-rationalism revered systematic, parsed-out logic; organic functionalism followed pragmatic analysis of the empirical world. Techno-rationalism, straight lines; organic functionalism, curves.

Early modernist theory's binary opposition of these approaches indicates the loose affiliation of each with an epistemological tradition that itself has been historically opposed to the other: the intellectualism of René Descartes on the one hand, and the empiricism of Edmund Burke and John Locke on the other.[16] The philosophical debate on rationalism versus empiricism is longstanding, and need not be examined in depth here. Suffice it to say that the debate revolves around the extent to which people gain knowledge by way of information acquired through the senses. Descartes's "I think, therefore I am" famously epitomizes the intellectualist position: the mind at all times knows its own ideas; thought is wholly conscious; the structure of the mind is directly accessible to itself; certain forms of knowledge are constructed without input from sensory experience.[17] The empiricist tradition rests on most of these same premises but differs in its contention that *only* from data acquired through sensory experience can human knowledge emerge.

In early-twentieth-century architectural discourse, the parallels between these two dominant strains of modernism and their philosophical analogues—intellectualism and techno-rationalism on the one hand, empiricism and organic functionalism on the other— are not exact. Still, they are suggestive. The techno-rationalists propounded formal, rule-bound, abstract systems of logic and analysis which bore the stamp of Cartesian intellectualism. The organic functionalists asserted that design should begin with the architect's study of the empirical world, with *data* gathered from the projected users' sensory experiences, patterns of social interaction, and experience of the site.

Not surprisingly, the tendency of early modernist architects and critics to oppose techno-rationalism to organic functionalism blinded them to effective continuities between the two traditions, as is true in the case of their philosophical second cousins.[18] Both techno-rationalists and organic functionalists operate from the premise that the mind can know or excavate its own ideas, that human thought is largely conscious, and that the mind's structure is accessible to itself. Both employ a logic-driven approach, differing only on *what kind* of data is offered up to human cognition. Both insist that architecture reflect and serve the conditions of modern life. Both hold that the makers and users of buildings are thinking subjects capable of cognitions dispassionately constructed from rational analysis, and that each thinking subject is categorically distinct from the object world of other people and of buildings, cities, and nature.

Techno-rationalists and organic functionalists both disliked surrealism, an artistic movement that celebrated personal self-expression and the irrational.[19] Surrealism, led by Hans Arp, André Breton, Giorgio de Chirico, Max Ernst, and others, established rapid-fire currency among avant-garde intellectuals in the same years that techno-rationalism and organic functionalism earned widespread recognition.[20] Surrealist artists, and their occasional architect-friends—Berthold Lubetkin, Friedrich Kiesler, Paul Nelson, and (sometimes) Le Corbusier come to mind— impudently assembled a here-and-there aesthetic that they believed expressed, and even provoked, primal human drives. Analysis, logic, and empirical data were shunned. Surrealism celebrated the poetic, the associative, and the uncanny.

Surrealism was the stepchild of Freud's id, that shadowy unconscious force the Viennese psycho-analyst contended is twinned to and navigated by the necessary strictures of the prudential ego. Like his philosophical confederates, Freud presumed the thinking subject and the object world split, with the id militating against grounded interpretations of empirically verifiable realities. Reason's "other," the id is the ghost ever threatening the smooth operation of the human machine, perverting one's cognitions of and interactions with the object world. The cognitive style of the id is everything that its putative opposites are not: organic, primal, ecstatic, symbolic.

Embodied Rationalism

Throughout the twentieth century and even today, this three-point philosophical model of human cognition—intellection, empiricism, and irrationalism—governs much scientific as well as humanistic thought, art and architecture included. Although popularly taken as commonsensical, in truth it is an isosceles triangle of unstable dimensions, ever-tottering, still yet to collapse.

At the foundation of this triangulated model of human cognition is the assumption that cognition and reason are the collaborative product of successively executed faculties. This model of cognition has been character-ized by George Lakoff, a cognitive linguist, and Mark Johnson, a philosopher, as "the Society of Mind."[21] In it, input is processed bottom up. Both intellection and empiricism posit that the human senses receive bits of information and then hand them up to perception, the brain's preliminary synthetic faculty. Perception registers the information and then transmits it to its "higher" (and more sophisticated) processor, imagi-nation, at which point the mind forms a preliminary interpretation of the data received. Imagination, how-ever, is inevitably colored by feeling—undisciplined, irrational, and out of control; an unruly child or a threat-eningly emotive woman. In cognitive pursuit of "true" understanding, the brain's higher-level function, reason, remains dissatisfied with interpretations that rely solely on putatively lower-level processes such as sensation, perception, imagination, and feeling. Searching for a more solid foundation on which to rest its conclusions, the brain hands its preliminary interpretation up to its preexisting data bank of received wisdom—memory. Yet memory too distorts. So this already highly pro-cessed cognition is once more handed upward, this time to the mind's most sophisticated arbiter, reason. Reason is unlike in kind to the mind's lower-caste members: it is unflinchingly guided by discipline, logic, and analysis. Bound by rules and clear-sighted, reason plays the man of cool systematization.

Recent scholarship, including work by Lakoff and Johnson, in a number of overlapping but professionally distinct disciplines such as language acquisition, cogni-tive linguistics, gesture analyses, historical linguistics, and neuroscience, falsifies both the triangulated model of human reason and unreason and the Society of Mind paradigm of cognition on which it rests. Facilitated in part by recent developments in biotechnology such as computerized data analysis, PET scans and functional Magnetic Resonance Imaging, this research, which draws from several longstanding intellectual traditions, determines that the machinations of the human mind do not concord with any part of the "common sense" three-point model of cognition, neither Cartesian intel-lectualism, nor empiricism, nor the Freudian notion of the irrational. Cartesian intellectualism does not exist. The presumption it shares with empiricism, that a

divide separates the thinking subject from her per-ceived world, is misconceived. Consequently, accepted notions of the irrational as the "other" of rationalism need also to be toppled.

A twenty-first-century view of human cognition, one that leaves the Society of Mind behind, is earning ever-wider acceptance in the sciences and social sciences. It holds that human cognition is approximately 90 percent *unconscious*, and demonstrates that human cog-nition—and therefore, human reason and knowledge—is intricately structured in determinative patterns by the reality of a person's bodily inhabitation of the world.[22] *Contra* the Society of Mind, cognition is not the progressive analytic synthesis of information received from the external world via the senses. Everyday and "higher" cognitions often emerge unconsciously and intersensorily; they are unavoidably imaginative and emotion-driven. How I interpret what I see is inter-meshed with what I have seen and what I anticipate seeing; with what I hear, have heard, and anticipate hearing; with what I touch, have touched, and antici-pate touching.

A simple, powerful falsifier of the triangulated model of human cognition lies in the global, cross-cultural universality of body-based metaphors that are used to describe everyday human experience.[23] In every known language, spoken and non-spoken, humans employ, and as far as scholars know always have employed, the same or an extremely similar set of metaphors to characterize emotional and intellectual states and to describe how they attain knowledge about the world. The coupling of human affection with physical warmth exemplifies this phenomenon.[24] This so-called primary metaphor is probably forged during infancy, in what linguists and neurologists call a "cross-domain associa-tion": newborns conflate the psychological experience of affection with the physical warmth they experi-ence in the close embrace of their caretaker's body. "Affection equals warmth" becomes "neurally instanti-ated" in the brain as a cognitive schema. From then on, "we are not free to think just anything."[25]

Some cognitive scientists point out that infants in all cultures begin to employ primary metaphors in the same developmental sequence, which strongly suggests their neurological basis. A host of other such metaphors reveals additional cognitive schemas, all hung on the scaffolding of human embodiment.

"I feel at home there" conflates the emotional state of feeling secure with the physical experience of inhabiting a spatial container—in this instance, a familiar building. Such familiar cognitive schemas belong to a vast and fluid body of primary metaphors, common in aggregate to every culture, framing intellectual and emotional cognitive states around the blunt fact of human embodiment. Users and listeners comprehend these primary metaphors—despite their sometimes patent illogic—precisely because the cognitions each describes are born of our irreducible physiological constitution as human beings.

The cognitive framing of emotional states often refers to bodily movement through space and time. In day-to-day physio-perceptual experience, moments abound in which people routinely orient themselves emotionally with respect to other people, other objects, and other containers. Cognitive orientation schemas are instantiated in such primary metaphors as "change is motion," which are exemplified in familiar phrases such as "I'm getting to a better place"; that is, a change in emotional or intellectual state is metaphorically equated to a change in physical location. Some primary metaphors are so clichéd that their tropic qualities are nearly indiscernible: when a person says "I'm getting there" or "I'm making progress," she equates psychic advancement with forward, and sometimes upward, movement toward a psychologically pre-established if literally amorphous destination. Acquiring knowledge is walking from the unseeing state of darkness into vision and light: "there's light at the end of the tunnel." In this instance as well the brain's neurological architecture likely underlies the consistency and the universality of these metaphors: neuroscientists now believe that the brain's locus of reason also manages perception and motor control.

The diachronic and synchronic persistence of such primary metaphors confirms that our minds develop in total integration with our bodily experience. An embodied theory of the mind does not belie that human consciousness is profoundly inflected by political, economic, scientific, social, and cultural phenomena. Nor does embodied rationalism fail to recognize the wide variability across cultures and over time in how people interpret the primary metaphors and cognitive schemas they employ. Yet the facts on the ground remain. The space of the world is not, and could never

be, exterior to the space of the bodily self. In terms of how we inhabit the world as thinking subjects, the self is, as Merleau-Ponty wrote, "the zero degree of spatiality." The simple antonymic relationship of "here," within or of our body, to "there," outside it, says so.[26] No throne elevates reason above sensory experience, as the Society of Mind model of cognition suggests. Rationality is "imbued with a sensibility, and vice versa."[27] Reason is unconscious and intuitive; it is simultaneously "rational" and "irrational," analytical and poetic, systematic and associative, logical and metaphoric.[28]

Embodied Rationalism and Experimental Psychology

Among twentieth-century intellectuals who accepted the existence of a rational human faculty, only phenomenologically oriented experimental psychologists, phenomenological philosophers, and those in related fields questioned the substantive premises of the three-point model of human cognition. In some cases, the insights of these thinkers foreshadowed contemporary findings on the embodied mind; conversely, recent research attests to the correctness of phenomenology's fundamental principles. Aalto's early intellectual biography and projects strongly suggest that he should be counted among the members of this group. As Eeva-Liisa Pelkonen has shown, from his student days he knew the basic precepts if not the specifics of proto-phenomenological experimental psychology. Certainly, by the late 1920s, he was extremely familiar with its central ideas.[29]

Founded in the mid-nineteenth century and centered in Germany, scientific or experimental psychology encompassed adjacent and related fields such as phonetics, linguistics, aesthetics, philosophy, and the study of culture.[30] The physicist Gustav Fechner (1801–1887) first advanced some of its principles in his *Elements of Psychophysics* in 1860. His best-known pupil, Wilhelm Wundt (1832–1920), developed his mentor's ideas into a scholarly agenda to investigate scientifically a vast constellation of human cognitive processes.[31] Founding a laboratory of experimental psychology at the University of Leipzig in 1874, Wundt's wide-ranging research included systematic, controlled experiments on human reaction times in muscular sensations and reflexes, on the experience of binocular vision, and on the visual perception of color. Through such experiments, Wundt established many of experimental psychology's paradigmatic precepts: that human perception is an act of creative synthesis; that emotion is a determining factor in any and all mental processes; and that no split divides human consciousness (the subject) from the physical world (the object). By the 1880s, Wundt was devoting much of his work to exploring the philosophical and cultural implications of his scientific findings. He founded the journal *Philosophical Studies* in 1881 and wrote what would eventually become a ten-volume study, *Cultural Psychology* (1900–1920).

From the University of Leipzig, where Wundt presided over the laboratory of experimental psychology and taught for over forty-five years, he legitimized the discipline, shaped its research agendas, and disseminated its findings. Wundt was enormously popular among students—enrollment in his lecture classes sometimes exceeded six hundred—and in his lifetime he granted more doctorates in psychology than any other scientist in Germany. He hired like-minded and widely influential scholars, including the art historian August Schmarsow (1853–1936), who was chair of the university's department of art history from 1893 to 1919. By 1914, Wundt's laboratory of experimental psychology had become the leading center and model for psychological research in the world, replicated all over Europe, as well as in the United States, India, and Japan.

Wundt's colleague Schmarsow pursued a new way to interpret artistic intention and experience by calling for what he specifically described, referencing Kant, as a phenomenologically based approach.[32] Criticizing Alois Riegl's *Spätrömische Kunstindustrie* (1901) as too narrowly focused on optical experience to the exclusion of the other senses, Schmarsow contended that if experimental psychology took a too strictly scientific approach to the study of aesthetics it would get on "the wrong track," unrealistically abstracting human consciousness "from all the contingencies of the earthly scene."[33]

Cognition, Schmarsow contended, encompassed "the whole physis of the perceiver," including an awareness of that "physis," or body. Any notion of reason must encompass the imagination and the "play of associative factors."[34] Foreshadowing Merleau-Ponty, Schmarsow posited the human body as degree zero in the human perception of space and time, writing that our cognitive understanding of verticality drew from our phenomenological experience of standing, of measure from "the reach of our arms" and a person's projected or actual position in and movement through space.

By 1900 experimental psychology developed two estuaries, equally wide: one more philosophical, represented in the work of Wundt and Schmarsow, and one more scientifically oriented, propounded most prominently by Theodor Lipps (1851–1914), whose Psychological Institute in Munich was founded in 1894 and quickly became the main institutional competitor to Wundt's laboratory in Leipzig. Lipps, best known among art historians as the founder of empathy theory, rejected what he held was the Leipzig school's overemphasis on subjectivism. Advocating a strictly scientific approach, Lipps disseminated his research on human physiological response to sensory stimuli in numerous books on the human perception of time, music, space, and visuality. Like Wundt, Lipps also wrote on aesthetics, and he founded the well-known journal *Beiträge zur Aesthetik*, which he edited for many years.

Although Schmarsow pointedly criticized Lipps's approach as overly driven by scientific method and pursuits, both the Munich and the Leipzig schools of experimental psychology insisted on the centrality of human embodiment to an understanding of cognition and reason. Thus by the early twentieth century, a number of prominent psychologists and aestheticians held that human cognition and reason is fundamentally embodied, fundamentally intersensory, and fundamentally creative; that emotion, memory, and imagination are integral to human reason; and that the commonly accepted gulf dividing subject from object does not exist. These early experimental psychologists had not identified the more or less stable set of cognitive schemas, basic-level categories, and primary metaphors that form the foundation for the operations of human cognition and reason. Still, this German scholarship in psychology, philosophy, and aesthetics established a body of knowledge and intellectual positions that today's research, with its more refined research tools and methods, confirms in its essence though vastly elaborates on in its details.

How might this knowledge of experimental psychology, or of phenomenology, or of cognitive neuroscience and linguistics, change or develop our understanding of Aalto's modernism? If we reexamine Aalto's work and intellectual development in light of this intellectual background, many of his design practices and theoretical statements that appear to violate the basic premises of canonical modernism can be recast as a transparent project to articulate a modern architecture that takes advantage of the opportunities modernity presents, ameliorates the psychic casualties it leaves in its wake, and springs from the essentially embodied nature of cognition. Aalto drew on primary metaphors and cognitive schemas even in his earliest published writings on architecture, often conceptualizing them with the somewhat blunt instruments he had at hand: the scientific language of experimental psychology.

Aalto Embodied

From 1900 to 1921—the years of Aalto's childhood, his basic education at the lyceum in Jyväskylä, and his architectural training in Helsinki—European intellectuals in the sciences, the arts, philosophy, and culture were schooled in the basic insights and findings of proto-phenomenological experimental psychology. Although the field was centered in Germany, interest in its findings extended into Germanophile countries, including Finland.[35] By 1902 Uppsala University in Sweden established a major psychology laboratory, and by 1917, when Aalto was nineteen years old, a member of the department of pedagogy at the University of Jyväskylä was advocating the founding of a laboratory of experimental psychology.[36]

Aalto read German fluently and closely followed intellectual currents in Europe. During his basic training in Jyväskylä, he learned of empathy theory and, more broadly, the basic precepts of experimental psychology.[37] As a young man and throughout his career, he sketched mainly in perspective, an embodied (if still artificially constructed) point of view, and he never drew in axonometric—the disembodied language of mathematically abstracted spatial depiction. His writings are saturated with the precepts of embodied rationalism: at the age of twenty-six he wrote that the beauty of a hilltop town in Tuscany (which he saw on his honeymoon in 1924) shone forth especially "when seen from the level of the human eye, that is, from the ground level," because only from this perspective was "a vision the senses receive whole and undisrupted, adapted to human size and limitations."[38]

Proposing a sauna for a hilltop ridge in Jyväskylä to serve as a national monument to Finnish culture, Aalto described his "Roman bath—a Finnish sauna" as a building "caress[ing] the senses" to spark deep memories and profound emotions. Swimming in the language of the sensorium, he describes his imagined sauna's smells, textures, and sights: the aroma of burning spruce and juniper twigs, the warmth of "a stove with a crackling fire of choice logs," the soft, warm light emitting from a colored lamp, the textures of "changing rooms covered with beautiful Nordic woven fabrics."[39] Such early writings and projects intimate the young Finnish architect's grasp of the intersensory and often unconscious nature of cognition and reason's deep enmeshment with emotion and bodily experience.

When earning his architectural degree at the Polytechnic Institute in Helsinki in the years 1916–1921, Aalto became close to several of his professors, including Selim Lindqvist, who paid far closer attention to architectural and intellectual trends in Europe than to the national romantic movement that predominated in Finland at the time, and who was especially interested in the *Jugendstil* movement that had been so deeply influenced by the ideas of Lipps.[40] When Aalto moved in 1927 to Turku, he had chosen a coastal city where intellectual, economic, and social exchange with Stockholm and the rest of Europe dominated local culture. After 1928 he became still more deeply involved in European architectural discourse and was further exposed to proto-phenomenological experimental psychology during trips to Germany, when he became familiar with the work of early modernist artists at the Bauhaus, including Oskar Schlemmer, Paul Klee, and, most importantly, László Moholy-Nagy, who became Aalto's lifelong friend.[41] The interest of Klee and Moholy-Nagy in experimental psychology is well documented (FIG. 1); the latter explicitly used the discipline's contemporary jargon, describing his artistic project as the "psycho-biological" experience of man, by which he meant the sentient person's intersubjective relationship with space, time, and light.[42]

From the mid-1920s onward, Aalto felt his way toward a formal idiom equal to and shaped by his understanding of the embodied nature of human cognition. Repeatedly his writings invoke the language of experimental psychology: he argued that "the rationalist working method" must encompass "psychological requirements" such as neurophysiology and the "general physiological properties" of human beings.[43] "My aim," he wrote, "was to show that real rationalism means dealing with *all* questions related to the object. . . . [The architect must] take a rational attitude also to demands that are often dismissed as vague issues of individual taste, but are shown by more detailed analysis to be derived partly from neurophysiology, and partly from psychology." Once architects adopt such an approach, he continued, explicitly connecting his sort of rationalism with the humanism he often discussed, "we will have extended the rationalist working method enough to make it easier to prevent inhuman results."[44] Rationalism "should be extended to the psychological domain," he insisted. "Only one book has not yet been published anywhere in the world, *The Physiological Home*."[45]

Repeatedly, Aalto spoke about how humans appropriate architecture, how architecture's forms entangle with a person's sensory perceptions and an intellectual cognition of everyday experience. His proposal for a blackened interior of a "rational cinema" emerged from his observation that "modern man's retina is beleaguered with images (photographs, printed matter, street advertisements, cinema) from morning till night."[46] The designer of a successful cinema, therefore, must peel this particularly new, quintessentially modern program away from the apparently similar typology of the auditorium or theater. When a person watches a film, he observed, lighting is "crucial . . . The clarity of the picture depends on absolute darkness."[47] He explained that when shown in current cinemas, films typically project a great deal of light back into the viewer's eyes, resulting in visual discomfort and greatly compromising the viewer's perception of image quality. His solution was to blacken the cinema's interior completely and to install a wash-board like arrangement of raised vertical slats, in which the sides facing the screen were painted with a matte, light-absorbing black.

Throughout his career, Aalto repeatedly invoked the word "human," asserting that architecture should "serve human life," or that it must "humanize" an overwrought world. These vague, sometimes repetitious incantations to humanism—the word "human" or its derivations appear no less than thirty-two times

FIGURE 01 *Paul Klee*, Uncomposed in Space, *watercolor, pen, chalk, and pencil on paper on cardboard (1929), (31.7 x 24.5 cm). Zentrum Paul Klee, Bern, on loan from a private collection.*

in one of his articles—can be and at times have been misleading. They allude not, as some writers have assumed or concluded, to a kinder, gentler modernism, nor to the European classical tradition, nor to a regionalist-inspired, woody familiarity of the British New Empiricism or the Bay Region style in the United States. By "humanism" Aalto meant to exhort modernists to create a rationalist architecture of the *human being*: a physiological, perceiving, thinking creature whose experiences and cognitions are by their very nature phenomenological.

FIGURE 02 *Aalto, Paimio Sanatorium, Finland, 1929–32. Main entrance.*

Astonishing Rationalism

During his first teaching stint at MIT, in 1940, Aalto published in the Institute's journal *Technology Review* an article describing for his American audience his two most celebrated Finnish projects, the sanatorium in Paimio (**FIG. 2**) and the town library in Viipuri. Years after the putative shift in his work to a "mature" regionalism, Aalto presents these early projects as central to his intellectual and architectural vision. Nowhere does he emphasize their regionalism. Instead he explains that in designing the Paimio and Viipuri buildings, he rejected extra-phenomenological compositional systems such as the grid, then so popular among techno-rationalists. Such undifferentiated, mathematically regularized notions of space were and are wholly antithetical to the premises of "the humanizing of architecture," which is the title of the article. His buildings, Aalto explains, were designed around the rhythms and patterns of daily life. Their spaces emanated from the body, degree zero of human cognitive experience. In describing these buildings Aalto reveals how he shaped them, from conception to built form, around the human mind's fundamentally intersensory, fundamentally metaphoric apprehension of the world. The principles that underlay these projects' designs, Aalto hoped, might inspire his students and colleagues to redirect modernism, which he portrays as a right-thinking movement gone astray.[48]

Discussing the Paimio Sanatorium, Aalto explains that the design emerged only after he conducted "experiments" examining his projected users' daily rituals and routines, their psychological reactions to room forms, to shades and degrees of colors, to types and intensities of light. Echoing experimental psychology's research experiments conducted at the universities in Leipzig and Munich, he recounts analyzing the impact on patients of variations in temperature, types or degrees of ventilation, and levels of noise. From the "results" of these "experiments," he concluded that the sanatorium's design needed to address an intertwined array of physiognomic, phenomenological, and cognitive phenomena particular to its afflicted users' needs. The organizing spatial principle for patients' rooms needed to differ from that of ordinary rooms. In a perhaps direct, perhaps unconscious, and perhaps completely unrelated allusion to one of Schmarsow's best-known premises—that spatial experience depends on a vertically-aligned, ambulatory, embodied subject—Aalto wrote that although most interior architectural spaces accommodate an ambulatory person whose body is oriented along a vertical axis, Paimio's patients would be lying down (**FIG. 3**). Hence a sanatorium's spatial organization needed to dissimilate the ordinary room in that it should be designed not around a vertical axis in motion but around a stationary, low-slung, horizontal one.[49]

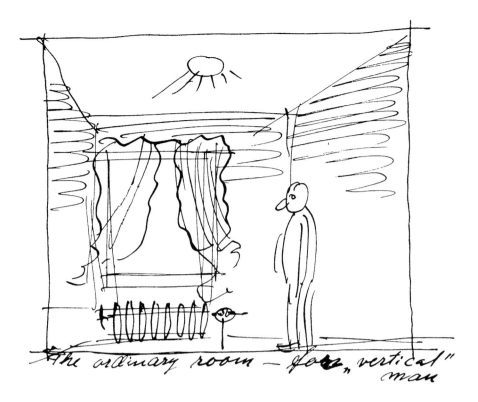

The ordinary room — for "vertical" man

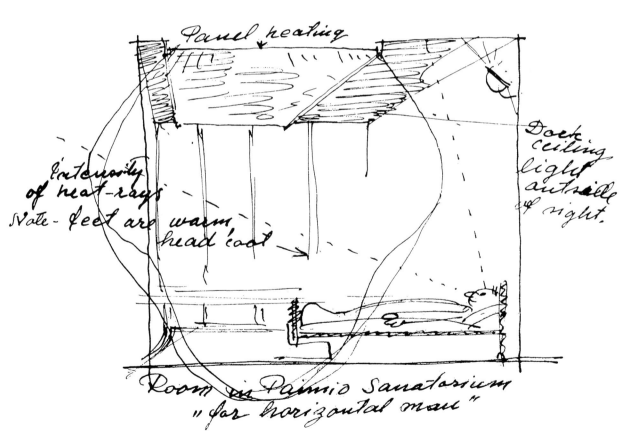

Panel heating

Intensity of heat-rays Note - feet are warm head cool

Dark ceiling light outside of sight.

Room in Paimio Sanatorium "for horizontal man"

FIGURE 03 *Aalto, Paimio Sanatorium. Sketch of typical patient resting, from "The Humanizing of Architecture," Technology Review (Nov. 1940).*

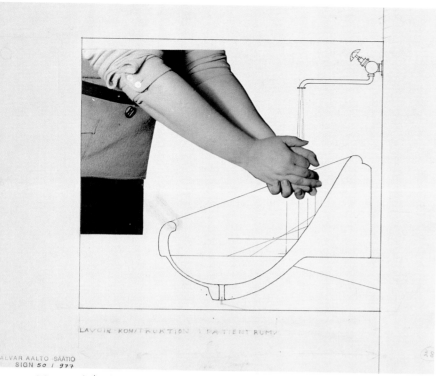

FIGURE 04 *Aalto, Paimio Sanatorium. Custom sinks in patients' rooms.*

in the hallways outside invalids' rooms so that pipes could be serviced without disturbing a patient's rest. He packed one wall in each room with sound-absorbing materials. Most famously, he specially designed "noiseless sinks," reconfiguring the conventional sink basin to reduce the auditory disruption of tap water splashing at acute angles onto an impermeable porcelain surface (**FIG. 4**). The floor plans were also designed to reinforce the patient's associations of warmth, brightness, and tranquility, with rooms arranged so that the patient could move easily from bed to wall-length desk (**FIGS. 5–6**). Once seated, she could look out large, plate glass windows into the surrounding forest, an omnipresent reminder of her needed escape from urban life. In between the double-glazed windows Aalto threaded a heating element to warm the glass, a material highly sensitive to variations in temperature. Ensconced at her desk, the patient could read, write, or just look, resting her feet on the curving footrest protruding from that typically recessed moment in a room where floor meets wall.

One consequence, he continued, would be that ceilings, which architects typically over- (or, more accurately, under-)look, took on an unusually prominent role in the design. Aalto thought through how his infirm users would respond, visually and perceptually, to different ceiling colors and illumination schemes. He oriented their bedrooms south-southeast, which, he explained, offered the most variable natural light, basking resting invalids in the morning's softer rays while shading their eyes from the sharp glare of the afternoon sun. He painted some walls to reflect light, others to absorb it, depending on how much sun each would receive in different seasons and at different times of day. In the interest of visual variety, he exaggerated tonal variation in the ceilings with a dark hued, highly saturated (and therefore perceptually variable) bluish-green. No overhead fixtures cast light into the resting patient's eyes: Aalto explains that his scheme for artificial lighting, combined with the room's dark tonal values, would greatly reduce eye-stressing glare.

Aalto recounts the multitude of ways in which his analysis of his prospective users' auditory, sensorimotor, tactile, proprioceptive, and psychological experiences guided the design of the patients' rooms. Quiet reigned. He placed access panels to plumbing fixtures

Knowledge Is Light

Describing his design for the library in Viipuri, Aalto revealed a similarly phenomenologically informed sensibility. In this case, he also discussed at length his explicitly metaphoric conception for the project.

Interpretations of the Viipuri Library typically begin with the project's stylistic evolution from the initial competition drawings of 1927 to the final design of 1933–1934. The competition-winning scheme depicts an Asplundian, lightly ornamented neoclassicism which is consistent with Aalto's design for the Muurame Church of 1927–1929, complete with an over-scaled doorway that alludes directly to the Stockholm Public Library. When he took up designing the final, executed scheme after a four-year delay, Aalto instead composed two rectangles joined on one long side, with the smaller slid off the larger's line of symmetry. A foyer, near the corner of the smaller, single-story block, contained a dog-leg staircase backed floor-to-ceiling with plate glass. All figurative ornament was gone.

Undoubtedly, the built project's style echoes the formal language he saw in the work of his European colleagues in the Congrès Internationaux d'Architects Modernes, which he joined in 1928, attending its

FIGURE 05 *Aalto, Paimio sanatorium. Patients' room, with room-length desk under plate-glass windows.*

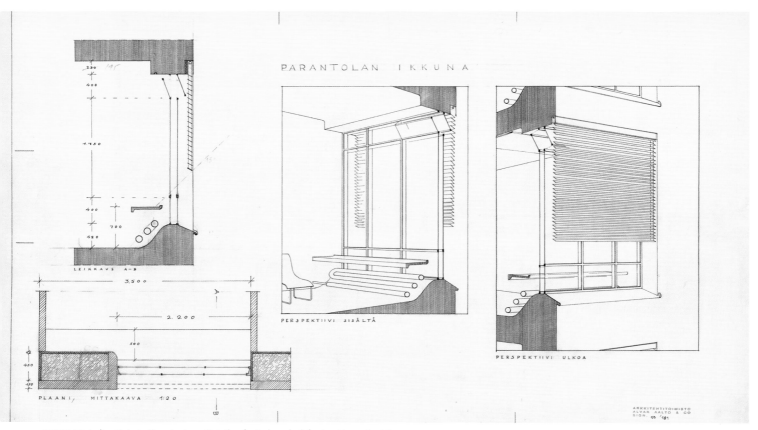

FIGURE 06 *Aalto, Paimio Sanatorium. Details of window-desk-footrest in patients' rooms.*

first conference in Frankfurt in 1929. Aalto's idiom did change from the first to the final schemes of the library, yet in "The Humanizing of Architecture" Aalto insisted that throughout the long design process the library's central concept held. "When I designed the city library at Viipuri," he wrote, "I pursued the solution with the help of primitive sketches from some kind of fantastic mountain landscapes with cliffs lit up by suns in different positions" (**FIG. 7**). Aalto never really explained the meaning of this image, which he implied had come to him spontaneously. But from this vision, he "gradually arrived at the [architectural] concept for the library building" (**FIG. 8**).[50] The compositional transformation of the library project's idiom, he insisted, owed more to the particularities of its re-siting: whereas the initial site for the project was more formal, as constructed, the building faces both a formal park and an informal woodland beyond. The configuration of this final site inspired Aalto, he wrote, to seek a less symmetrical, less historicizing composition.[51]

Taking Aalto at his word and delving not into the project's stylistic transformations but instead into the meaning of those initial, "primitive" sketches, his guiding concept for the building and its continuity throughout its conception and execution is clarified. His sketchy imaginings elicit a raft of primary metaphors steering the central compositional features of the library design. To adduce only examples discussed in the preceding section on embodied rationalism, the idea of ascending a fantastic mountainscape evokes some of the primary metaphors described by Lakoff and Johnson such as "knowledge is light," "the acquisition of knowledge is ascent up a path toward a pre-given destination," and "thinking is seeing." Climbing a mountain, surveying and contemplating the views as light and shadows change with the day's passing, anticipating the monumental isolation and psychic clarity of the summit: these metaphors constitute the Viipuri Library's central organizational tropes.

Giving architectural form to this vision of ascent inspired Aalto to employ a sectional approach. For the primary spatial sequence he exaggerated the user's procession from the distracting cacophony and visual "bombardment" of everyday life to an internalized,

FIGURE 07 *Aalto, sketch of "fantastic mountain" as inspiration for Viipuri Library reading room.*

silent world. From one secondary entrance, that closest to the street, the user enters a periodical reading room (located below the main reading room) filled with rows of shoulder-height reading stands (FIG. 9). The room metaphorically evokes the transitory hustle and bustle of modern life: one imagines a user taking a quick detour inside on his way to work to scan the day's headlines, and then running back out without ever so much as sitting down.

By contrast, from the main entrance foyer (which leads to an auditorium), a user walks on an axis toward the light-filled monumental staircase, and slowly ascends into a large, double-height, single-span, multilevel room that falls away from the access desk at its apex like cliffs from a mountain summit (FIG. 10). The reading room, Aalto wrote, needed "a conserving and externally closed character." No views open up to the distractions of the world. Aalto packed the brick walls with sound-absorbing materials and made them "exceptionally strong." Creating an otherworldly realm of silence, the reading room's visual, auditory, tactile, and spatial features focus the user on the central purpose of her destination. Here, as Aalto put it, is the place where books and people meet.[52] Vertically, bookshelves line the room; horizontally, large communal reading tables offer surfaces on which to lay out one's work. Another part of the room is filled with rows of individual carrels, each furnished with a bentwood storage unit to facilitate the reader's use of space without inhibiting her views of the roomscape, of other cliffs, of other people.

In designing the reading room, Aalto wrote, he was principally concerned with the interrelationship of the

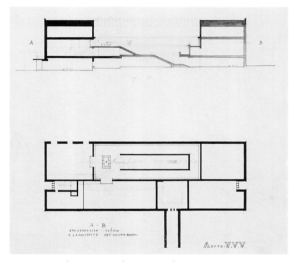

FIGURE 08 *Aalto, Viipuri Library. Initial competition entry, 1927, plan and section.*

FIGURE 09 *Aalto, Viipuri Library. Periodical reading room.*

FIGURE 10 *Aalto, Viipuri Library. Main reading room.*

reader, the book, and light. He determined that physiologically, a reader needs even, indirect light for two reasons: so that distracting shadows would not fall on one's open book, and so that bright light would not reflect from the white page back into one's eyes. The architectural solution lay in the library's fifty-seven conical concrete skylights, each nearly four feet wide and six feet deep. The shape of the cones was determined by the angle the summer sun reaches at the summer solstice in Viipuri (**FIG. 11**). Each skylight also contains retractable spotlights, which can be switched on and off to compensate for glare or shadows as the sun moves across the sky (**FIG. 12**). This system, Aalto explained, makes it possible in the Viipuri reading room, as at the top of a mountain, for light to come from "millions of directions."[53]

These skylights fulfill the physiologically and phenomenologically determined program Aalto set for himself in the library project: reader, book, light. Together with the room's multileveled, horizontally and vertically expansive form, they also comprise the room's central compositional trope: a fantastic mountain landscape lit by many suns. This reading room is replete with accommodation to the bodily basis of human cognitive experience, with its reliance on cognitive schemas and primary metaphors. To reach it, the user must literally and figuratively ascend in order to attain a goal. The reading room is shaped around the user's bodily aspect when engaged in different pursuits: a researcher standing or moving about, a reader quietly sitting in imaginative thought (**SEE FIG. 12**).

FIGURE 11 *Aalto, Viipuri Library. Sketch of reader under natural light in the main reading room.*

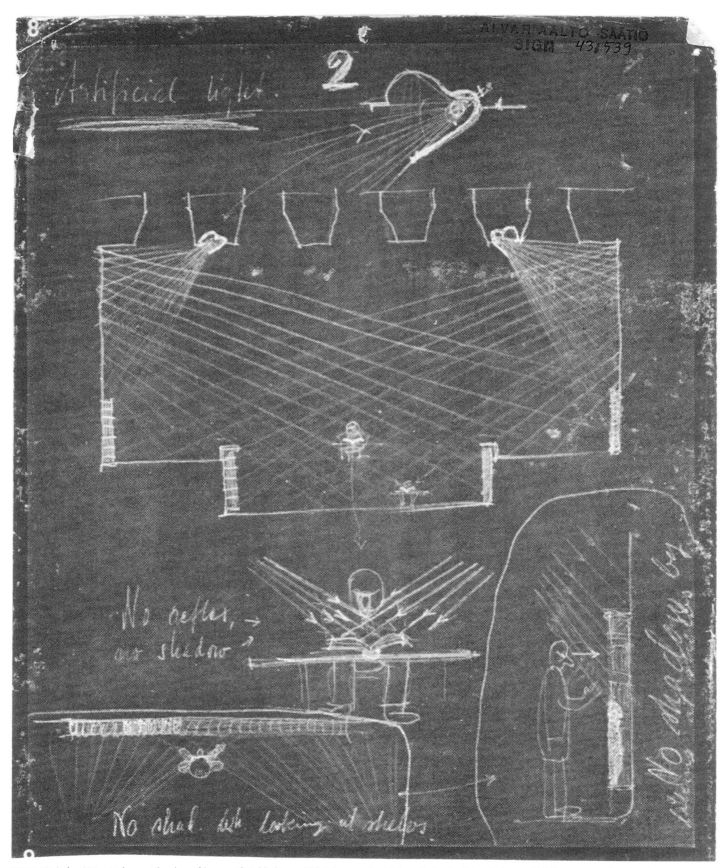

FIGURE 12 *Aalto, Viipuri Library. Sketches of how artificial light would fall from conical lightwells (top); of how light would fall onto a reader's book (center); of light falling on bookstacks as a researcher stands perusing the books (lower right and bottom).*

Aalto's kit-of-parts organization for the library plan explicitly differentiates—programmatically, architecturally, and experientially—between what he called the "social" block and the block in which the reading room is housed. In choosing such an organization Aalto drew on the cognitive schema "emotional states are physical containers" (as in the primary metaphor discussed earlier, "I feel at home there," to describe the sense of emotional well-being). The larger block, designed around the reader, silent and opaque to the external world, contains mainly the multi-leveled reading room. The smaller, narrower, single-story "social" block housing offices, the periodical and children's reading rooms, and, most famously, the wavy-ceilinged auditorium, nurture connections among people and between people and the social and natural world beyond. The principal entrance to the social block, adjacent to the woodland park, begins in a foyer bathed in the filtered light of layered transparency, a space of transition from nature and urbanity to the sheltered world of social interchange and private scholarly pursuit. Aalto, symbolically emphasizing the liminality of the foyer, trained vines to grow inside the floor-to-ceiling windows (FIG. 13).

Aalto continues this theme of filtered layers of transparency between the space of the world and the communal spaces of the social block by containing the social activities within while offering his user the chance to imaginatively project her escape to a quieter world. Such a compositional strategy is especially evident in his design of the auditorium, where he reinforces the user's peripheral awareness of the informal woodland park beyond by butting the wavy-shaped ceiling up against the rectangular plate-glass windows (FIG. 14). The windows look out into the forest canopy, as uneven and fluid as the ceiling inside. Aalto echoes this intermeshing of his projected user's fluid and multidirectional experience of the space of the world and her axial and directional experience of space of the library in the corridor walls leading to the auditorium: at one moment, an apparently load-bearing wall breaks into a trunk-like pair of columns; at another, these walls break into curves that arc this way, then that, gently shepherding visitors inside.

FIGURE 13 *Aalto, Viipuri Library. Northeast foyer with vines trained to grow up wires inside the windows.*

FIGURE 14 *Aalto, Viipuri Library. View of auditorium from exterior, with ceiling visible inside.*

Aalto explained how he had decided on the famously wavy ceiling of the long, narrow auditorium by considering the acoustical experience of both listeners and lecturers. Although he spoke of the social block as the "block for the ear," his theoretical declarations and compositional gestures indicate that he referred to the ear not just in its biological sense: "I conceive acoustic questions mainly as physiological and psychological questions," he wrote. "Purely mechanical solutions are not justifiable." He imagined a lecture hall without a lecture; rather, the room is filled with participants in a discussion, sound waves traveling frontwards and backwards. Revealing his socially democratic ideals, Aalto wrote that even in the design of a lecture hall, "general discussions should be just as important as individual performances."[54]

As in the Viipuri reading room, Aalto's physiognomically derived solution becomes the compositional datum for the auditorium space, which formally instantiates the back-and-forth movement of conversation that it technically facilitates. Finally, the dropped ceiling, which hides both the room's mechanical equipment and its structural armature, brings the room's vertical scale more into line with that of the human body.

Throughout the building, architectural details offer rich and highly variable tactile, visual, auditory, and experiential moments. Moving through the spaces of the library offers multiple opportunities for heightened sensory awareness, through stucco walls, rubber flooring, plate glass, steel, and a wide variety of woods—sycamore, oak, birch, red beech, and teak—each material placed according to its color, grain, tactile qualities, and the level of wear Aalto anticipated that it would receive.[55] The midsections of many interior columns are wrapped with wooden slats, offering extra stimulus and proprioceptive markers to passing hands. Woven wastebaskets are furnished with a rectangular shelf placed above their circular apertures, offering the user a surface so that she might shuffle through collected papers, separating wanted from unwanted (FIG. 15). Here, as in the Paimio Sanatorium, Aalto detailed and furnished the building by thinking through the users' often overlooked, sometimes invisible everyday needs.

Aalto's use of organic curves, careful attention to natural light, metaphoric references to the forms of nature (and in other instances also to local vernacular traditions), and frequent use of wood, are often gathered

into the rubric of his putative regionalism. Very often, his work exhibits an extraordinary sensitivity to the inflections, nuances, and character of a particular site or locale. Yet Aalto's regionalism, if we must employ that term, constituted part of his larger agenda: to create an architecture of embodied rationalism. The Viipuri Library and Paimio Sanatorium established the framework on which Aalto drew in his design of the Baker House dormitory and many other subsequent works. They are all "regionalist" in that sensitivity to site, season, place, and memory inevitably figures into a phenomenologically grounded modernist architecture. After all, a perceiving, thinking subject situates him or herself in a place, at a time, and on the ground.

Enlarging Rationalism

In both the Viipuri Library and the Paimio Sanatorium, Aalto offers a model of what he called for in "The Humanizing of Architecture": the "enlargement of rational method to encompass related fields."[56] Aalto's enlarged rationalism is based on the phenomenological principles of embodied cognition: to paraphrase his own words, his rationalism would "prevent inhuman" (and therefore instead effectuate "humanist") results. Aalto's embodied rationalism, developed early in his career before he arrived in the United States, continued to guide his approach to design for the rest of his career, and to create a number of iconic projects, many of which justly hold their place as some of the twentieth century's greatest buildings. Such projects include the town hall and library at Säynätsalo, the Cultural Center in Wolfsburg, the MIT dormitory in Cambridge, Massachusetts, and the House of Culture and the National Pensions Institute buildings in Helsinki. In each of these projects, Aalto developed a quiet, nuanced, phenomenologically dense architecture that remains unparalleled in the history of modernism.

Aalto identified with and embraced the conditions of modern life, and believed that Western culture was in the midst of an all-encompassing break with the past. He consumed with nearly child-like enthusiasm products that became the emblems of twentieth-century modernity, such as the automobile, the cinema, and the phonograph. As an artist he moved in the society of modernism and befriended many of its most vigorous proponents. And as an architect, he insisted on and incorporated the central tenets of the new architectural

FIGURE 15 *Aalto, Viipuri Library. Wastebasket, with moveable sorting shelf attached.*

credo that he believed would advance a new architecture. This included incorporating new technologies when appropriate to the task at hand: the elevator at the Paimio Sanatorium was one of the earliest glass elevators in Finland, and his flexible standardization of building parts for low-cost housing and his furniture designs relied heavily on the techniques of mass production that simply were not possible before the technological innovations of the twentieth century.

In other words, Aalto practiced what are indisputably the core tenets of modernism: that architectural form must be radically reevaluated in light of conditions of modernity; that a new architecture must be devised that is appropriate to the conditions of modern life; that this new architecture must express the conundrums and ameliorate the ills visited on humanity by modernity; and that it must accommodate not just the powerful but also the less powerful or even

the disempowered. This new architecture must create more than just monuments; it must create architectural spaces in the service of an ordinary life well lived.

Although Aalto arguably gave embodied rationalism its fullest and first architectural manifestation, other well-known avant-garde architects of his generation, including J. J. P. Oud, Bruno Taut, Hans Scharoun, El Lissitsky, and the Vesnin brothers, also explored embodied rationalism's compositional and intellectual principles, albeit in what may initially appear to be a dizzying, misleading multiplicity of forms. Why this phenomenologically oriented strain of embodied rationalism remains so little explored is a story for another essay. What is clear is that an unrecognized form of rationalism has coursed through the history of modernism, which the work of Alvar Aalto can help us to see, not only with our eyes, but also with our minds.[57]

1 Edward R. Ford writes that each of the Paimio Sanatorium's four wings has a different structural system, a variation that is not evident from the building's external appearance. Ford, *The Details of Modern Architecture, Volume 2: 1928 to 1988* (Cambridge, Mass.: MIT Press, 1996), 121. He adds that in the Viipuri Library, structure is "seldom exposed" (122).

2 Richard Weston has been most insistent and insightful in unfolding the symbolic dimensions of Aalto's work, for example, in Weston, "Between Nature and Culture: Reflections on the Villa Mairea," in *Alvar Aalto: Toward a Human Modernism*, ed. Winfried Nerdinger (New York: Prestel, 1999), 61–76.

3 Eeva-Liisa Pelkonen discusses Aalto's opportunism in "Empathic Affinities: Alvar Aalto and His Architectural Milieus" (PhD diss., Columbia University, 2003), which was subsequently revised and published as *Alvar Aalto: Architecture, Modernity, Geopolitics* (New Haven, Conn.: Yale Univ. Press, 2009).

4 In the architectural history and theory of twentieth-century modernism, phenomenology is very often—one might even say almost always—associated with the mystical, anti-modern phenomenology of Martin Heidegger. For examples, see many of the essays in George Dodds and Robert Tavernor, eds., *Body and Building: Essays on the Changing Relation of Body and Architecture* (Cambridge, Mass.: MIT Press, 2002); Karsten Harries, *The Ethical Function of Architecture* (Cambridge, Mass.: MIT Press, 1998); Steven Holl, Juhani Pallasmaa, and Alberto Pérez-Gómez, *Questions of Perception: Phenomenology of Architecture* (San Francisco: William Stout, 2006); Juhani Pallasmaa, *The Eyes of the Skin: Architecture and the Senses* (New York, John Wiley, 2005); Alberto Pérez-Gómez, *Architecture and the Crisis of Modern Science* (Cambridge, Mass.: MIT Press, 1983); and Christian Norberg-Schulz, *Genius Loci: Toward a Phenomenology of Architecture* (New York: Rizzoli, 1983).

Phenomenology's close association with Heideggerian philosophy—with all its mystical, anti-modern, and even quasi-fascistic implications—has, in the discourse of the history and theory of modernism in architecture, provoked ambivalence or hostility, or has simply been ignored by the two other dominant strains in the field: Marxist and post-Marxist studies influenced by the Frankfurt school, and psychoanalytically oriented studies influenced by Sigmund Freud and his followers. For examples of such ambivalence or hostility, see Jorge Otero-Pailos, *Architecture's Historical Turn: Phenomenology and the Rise of the Postmodern* (Minneapolis: Univ. of Minnesota Press, 2010); Mitchell W. Schwarzer, "The Emergence of Architectural Space: August Schmarsow's Theory of *Raumgestaltung*," *Assemblage* 15 (Aug. 1991): 48–61; Mark Jarzombek, *The Psychologizing of Modernity: Art, Architecture, and History* (New York: Cambridge Univ. Press, 2000); and Jarzombek, "Joseph August Lux: Werkbund Promoter, Historian of a Lost Modernity," *Journal of Society of Architectural Historians* 63:2 (June 2004): 202–19.

In addition to Jarzombek's *Psychologizing of Modernity*, see three other examples of more recent scholarship in the field that touch on the strain of phenomenology or embodied cognition discussed here: Sandy Isenstadt, "Richard Neutra and the Psychology of Architectural Consumption," in *Anxious Modernisms: Experimentation in Postwar Architectural Culture*, ed. Sarah Williams Goldhagen and Réjean Legault (Cambridge, Mass.: MIT Press, 2001), 97–117; Dell Upton, "Architecture in Everyday Life," *New Literary History* 33:4 (Autumn 2002): 707; and Upton, *Another City: Urban Life and Urban Spaces in the New American Republic* (New Haven, Conn.: Yale Univ. Press, 2008). On the differences between Heideggerian phenomenology and the sort of phenomenology or embodied cognition discussed here, most famously propounded by Maurice Merleau-Ponty, see Dermot Moran, *Introduction to Phenomenology* (London: Routledge, 2000), esp. 412.

5 Alvar Aalto, "The Humanizing of Architecture," (1940), in *Alvar Aalto in His Own Words*, ed. Göran Schildt (New York: Rizzoli, 1998), 102–7.

6 Alvar Aalto, "The Housing Problem" (1930), in *Alvar Aalto in His Own Words*, ed. Schildt, 80. Of the bedrooms in the double house at the Weissenhofsiedlung, Le Corbusier wrote: "By day, the sleeper becomes a parlor car," referring to the transformability of the overnight cubicles on Pullman trains. Quoted in Karen Kirsch, *The Weissenhofsiedlung: Experimental Housing Built for the Deutscher Werkbund, Stuttgart, 1927* (New York: Rizzoli, 1989), 114.

7 Alvar Aalto, "Rationalism and Man" (1935), in *Alvar Aalto in His Own Words*, ed. Schildt, 91. The subsequent two quotations by Aalto are from the same essay.

8 Alvar Aalto, "From Doorstep to Living Room" (1926), in *Alvar Aalto in His Own Words*, ed. Schildt, 55.

9 Alvar Aalto, "The Stockholm Exhibition 1930" (1930), in *Alvar Aalto in His Own Words*, ed. Schildt, 76.

10 The first three quotations are from Aalto, "Rationalism and Man," 91; the quotation on intuition is from an interview by Göran Schildt, in *Alvar Aalto in His Own Words*, ed. Schildt, 269–75.

11 For discussions of rationalism in modern architecture, see Adrian Forty, *Words and Buildings: A Vocabulary of Modern Architecture* (New York: Thames & Hudson, 2000), 174–95, 276–91; Vittorio Magnago Lampugnani, ed., *Encyclopedia of Twentieth-Century Architecture* (New York: Harry N. Abrams, 1986), 275–78; and Antoine Picon, introduction to Jean-Nicholas-Louis Durand, *Précis of the Lectures on Architecture* (Santa Monica, Calif.: Getty Publications, 2000), 1–68.

12 Reyner Banham, *Theory and Design in the First Machine Age* (New York: Praeger, 1960), 9–34; Kenneth Frampton, *Modern Architecture: A Critical History*, 3rd ed. (New York: Thames & Hudson, 1992), esp. 12–19; Robin Middleton and David Watkin, *Neoclassical and Nineteenth-Century Architecture* (New York: Rizzoli, 1987).

13 See Vittorio Magnago Lampugnani, "Berlin Modernism and the Architecture of the Metropolis," in *Mies in Berlin*, ed. Terence Riley and Barry Bergdoll (New York: Museum of Modern Art, 2002), 35–65; and, from the same source, Detlef Mertins, "Architectures of Becoming: Mies van der Rohe and the Avant Garde," 106–33.

14 Le Corbusier, *Vers une architecture* (Paris: G. Crès, 1923), translated as *Toward an Architecture* (Los Angeles: Getty Research Institute, 2007); *Urbanisme* (Paris: G. Crès, 1925), translated as *The City of Tomorrow and Its Planning* (London: John Rodker, 1929). Le Corbusier writes that "man, by reason of his very nature, practices order; that his actions and his thoughts are dictated by the straight line and the right angle, that the straight line and the right angle is instinctive in him and that his mind apprehends it as a lofty objective." Le Corbusier, *The City of To-morrow*, 17.

15 For selected examples of this diametric opposition of techno-rationalism and organic functionalism (widely ranging in date), see Adolf Behne, *The Modern Functional Building* (1926; Santa Monica, Calif.: Getty Publications, 1996); Sigfried Giedion, *Space, Time and Architecture: The Growth of a New Tradition* (Cambridge, Mass.: Harvard Univ. Press, 1941); Peter Blundell-Jones, *Hugo Häring: The Organic versus the Geometric* (Stuttgart, Germany: Axel Menges, 1999); and Colin St. John Wilson, *The Other Tradition of Modern Architecture: The Uncompleted Project* (London: Academy Editions, 1995). Such oppositions do not begin to capture the actual complexity of modernism in architecture: see Sarah Williams Goldhagen, "Something to Talk About: Modernism, Discourse, Style," *Journal of the Society of Architectural Historians* 64 (Summer 2006): 144–67.

16 Peter Markie, "Rationalism vs. Empiricism," *Stanford Encyclopedia of Philosophy*, http://plato.stanford.edu/entries/rationalism-empiricism/, accessed 29 March 2011.

17 George Lakoff and Mark Johnson, *Philosophy in the Flesh: The Embodied Mind and Its Challenge to Western Thought* (New York: Basic, 1999), 391-414.

18 Markie, "Rationalism vs. Empiricism," *idem*.

19 On the general history of surrealism, see Gérard Durozi, *History of the Surrealist Movement* (1997; Chicago: Univ. of Chicago Press, 2002).

20 On the impact of surrealism on architecture, see, for example, John Allan, *Berthold Lubetkin: Architecture and the Tradition of Progress* (London: Royal Institute of British Architects Publications, 1992); Romy Golan, *Modernity and Nostalgia: Art and Politics between the Wars* (New Haven, Conn.: Yale Univ. Press, 1995); Caroline Maniaque, *Le Corbusier et les maisons Jaoul* (Paris: Picard, 2005); Thomas Michal, ed., *Surrealism and Architecture* (London: Routledge, 2005); Don Quaintance, "Modern Art in a Modern Setting: Frederick Kiesler's Design of Art of This Century," in *Peggy Guggenheim and Frederick Kiesler: The Story of the Art of This Century*, ed. Susan Davidson and Philip Rylands (New York: Guggenheim Museum Publications, 2004), 207–73; Terence Riley and Joseph Abram, *The Filter of Reason: The World of Paul Nelson*

(New York: Rizzoli, 1990); and Anthony Vidler, *The Architectural Uncanny: Essays in the Modern Unhomely* (Cambridge, Mass.: MIT Press, 1992).

21 Lakoff and Johnson, *Philosophy in the Flesh,* 410–14.

22 See Francisco Varela, Evan T. Thompson, and Eleanor Rosch, *The Embodied Mind: Cognitive Science and the Human Experience* (Cambridge, Mass.: MIT Press, 1991); many of the essays in José Luis Bermúdez, Anthony Marcel, and Naomi Eilan, eds., *The Body and the Self* (Cambridge, Mass.: MIT Press, 1995); Anthony Damasio, *Descartes' Error: Emotion, Reason, and the Human Brain* (New York: Avon, 1994); Damasio, *The Feeling of What Happens: Body and Emotion in the Making of Consciousness* (New York: Mariner, 2000); George Lakoff and Mark Johnson, *Metaphors We Live By* (Chicago: Univ. of Chicago Press, 1980) and their *Philosophy in the Flesh;* Mark L. Johnson, "Embodied Reason," in *Perspectives on Embodiment: The Intersections of Nature and Culture,* ed. Gail Weiss and Honi Fern Haber (New York: Routledge, 1999), 81–102; and Steven Pinker, *The Language Instinct: How the Mind Creates Language* (New York: Williams Morrow, 1994).

23 Andrew N. Meltzoff and M. Keith Moore, "Infants' Understanding of People and Things: From Body Imitation to Folk Psychology," in *The Body and the Self,* ed. José Luis Bermúdez and others (Cambridge, Mass.: MIT Press), 43–69.

24 Shaun Gallagher, "Body Schema and Intentionality," in *The Body and the Self,* ed. Bermúdez, Marcel, and Eilan, 225–244; Maurice Merleau-Ponty, *The Phenomenology of Perception* (London: Routledge, 1962), 118–19; Merleau-Ponty, "The Eye and the Mind," *The Primacy of Perception* (Evanston, Ill.: Northwestern Univ. Press, 1964), 159–92. On Merleau-Ponty, see also Moran, *Introduction to Phenomenology,* 391–434; Hubert L. Dreyfus, "Merleau-Ponty and Recent Cognitive Science," 129–50; and Richard Shusterman, "The Silent, Limping Body of Philosophy," in *The Cambridge Companion to Merleau-Ponty,* ed. Taylor Carman and Mark B. N. Hansen (New York: Cambridge Univ. Press, 2005), 151–80.

25 Lakoff and Johnson, *Philosophy in the Flesh,* 5. The discussion of primary metaphors and cognitive schemas in the subsequent two paragraphs is based on pages 30–38 and 45–94 from Lakoff's and Johnson's book.

26 Merleau-Ponty writes in *Phenomenology of Perception:* "The word 'here' applied to my body does not refer to a determinate position in relation to other positions or to external co-ordinates, but the laying down of first co-ordinates" (100).

27 Moran, *Introduction to Phenomenology,* 423 (from a discussion of Merleau-Ponty).

28 Johnson, "Embodied Reason"; and Lakoff and Johnson, *Philosophy in the Flesh,* 122–37.

29 Pelkonen first brought to light Aalto's exposure to empathy theory, and later to scientific psychology, in her "Empathic Affinities," chap. 3–4, although she takes her analysis of Aalto's work and his ideas in a very different (and fruitful) direction than I do here.

30 Duane P. Schultz and Sydney Ellen Schultz, *A History of Modern Psychology,* 8th ed. (Belmont, Calif.: Wadsworth, 2004); and Harry Francis Mallgrave and Eleftherios Ikonomou, introduction to *Empathy, Form, and Space: Problems in German Aesthetics, 1873–1893* (Santa Monica, Calif.: Getty Publications, 1994), 1–85.

31 Wilhelm Wundt, *Principles of Physiological Psychology* (1874; New York: Macmillan, 1904); see also the section on Wundt in Schultz and Schultz, *History of Modern Psychology,* 87–100; and R. I. Watson, Sr., *The Great Psychologists,* 4th ed. (New York: J. B. Lippincott, 1978), chap. 12.

32 On Schmarsow, see Mallgrave and Ikonomou, introduction to *Empathy, Form, and Space,* 60–66.

33 See August Schmarsow, "The Essence of Architectural Creation" (1893), in *Empathy, Form, and Space,* ed. Mallgrave and Ikonomou, 281–97 (the phrase "earthly scene" appears on p.291). See also Michael Podro, *The Critical Historians of Art* (New Haven, Conn.: Yale Univ. Press, 1982), 143–49; and Schwarzer, "The Emergence of Architectural Space."

34 Schmarsow, "Essence of Architectural Creation," 283.

35 Ritva Wäre, *"Finnish art nouveau: the marriage of early modernism and national romanticism"* 2006 Architecture 1900 – in a new light. (Stockholm: Arkitekturmuseet), 48-61. https://tuhat.halvi.helsinki.fi/portal/en/persons/ritva-t-ware%2813ab3cf7-a0ba-498c-99dc-cd259aa0b520%29/publications.html

36 Jyväskylä Department of Psychology website, http://www.ytk/laitokset/psykologia. Experimental psychology within the academy only became institutionalized as a separate discipline in the 1940s. Schultz and Schultz, *History of Modern Psychology,* 100. For background information, see also Mark Jarzombek, *Psychologizing of Modernity.*

37 Pelkonen, "Empathic Affinities,"*Alvar Aalto: Architecture, Modernity and Geopolitics,* 26–27.

38 Alvar Aalto, "The Hilltop Town" (1924), in *Alvar Aalto in His Own Words,* ed. Schildt, 49.

39 Alvar Aalto, "Temple Baths on Jyväskylä Ridge" (1925), in *Alvar Aalto in His Own Words,* ed. Schildt, 18–19.

40 Göran Schildt, "Alvar Aalto," *The Grove Dictionary of Art Online* (New York: Grove's Dictionaries, 1999). http://www.oxfordartonline.com/subscriber/article/grove/art/T000023

41 Paul Klee's interest in phenomenology is discussed in Victoria Salley, "The Master Years," in *Paul Klee: Selected by Genius, 1917–1933,* ed. Roland Doschka (New York: Prestel, 2001), 12–14. Göran Schildt discusses Aalto's friendship with Moholy-Nagy in *Alvar Aalto: The Decisive Years* (New York: Rizzoli, 1986), 70–78.

42 See, for example, Lásló Moholy-Nagy, *Vom Material zu Architektur* (Munich: Lagen, 1929).

43 Aalto, "Rationalism and Man," 92.

44 Aalto, "Rationalism and Man," 92, emphasis added.

45 Aalto, "Housing Problem," 83.

46 Alvar Aalto, "An Independence Monument in Helsinki: The Olympic Stadium" (1927), in *Alvar Aalto in His Own Words,* ed. Schildt, 64–66.

47 Alvar Aalto, "The Rational Cinema" (1928), in *Alvar Aalto in His Own Words,* ed. Schildt, 66–71.

48 Aalto, "Humanizing of Architecture," 14–15.

49 Schmarsow, "Essence of Architectural Creation," 289; also, in same volume, Mallgrave and Ikonomou, introduction to *Empathy, Form, and Space,* 15. Note that Eeva-Liisa Pelkonen's appendix to her doctoral dissertation, which lists the contents of Aalto's library, does not include any works by Schmarsow.

50 Aalto, quoted in Michael Spens, *Viipuri Library, 1927–1935: Alvar Aalto* (London: Academy Editions, 1994), 36.

51 Alvar Aalto, "Municipal Library in Viipuri: Description of the Building's Construction," *Municipal Library, Viipuri* (Jyväskylä, Finland: Alvar Aalto Museum, 1997), unpaginated. On the design process of the library, see also Spens, *Vipurii Library.*

52 All quotations Aalto, "Municipal Library in Viipuri."

53 Aalto, "Humanizing of Architecture," 36.

54 Aalto, "Municipal Library in Viipuri."

55 Aalto, "Municipal Library in Viipuri."

56 Aalto, "Humanizing of Architecture," 15.

57 On the complexity of modernism and its many under- or unexplored strains, see Sarah Williams Goldhagen, "Coda: Reconceptualizing the Modern," in *Anxious Modernisms,* ed. Goldhagen and Legault, 301–23; and Goldhagen, "Something to Talk About."

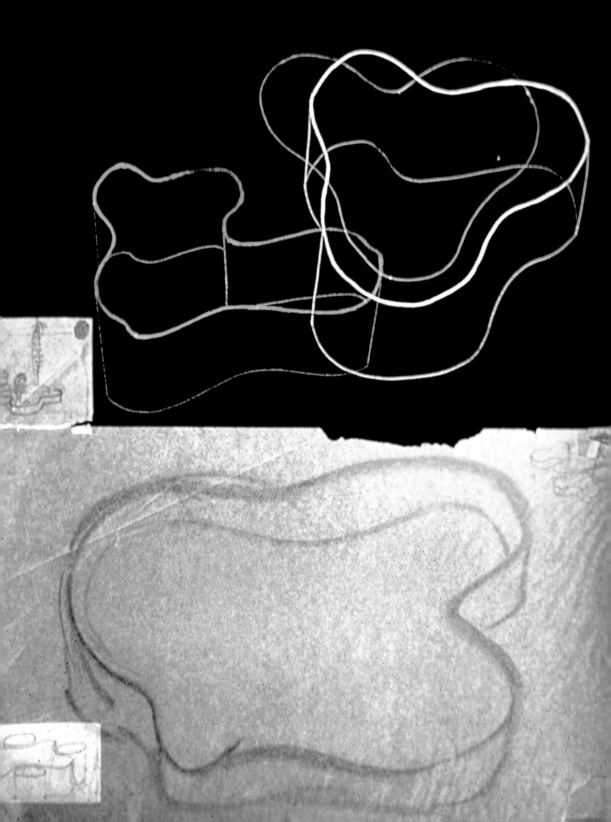

Floating Signifiers: Interpreting Aalto

Dörte Kuhlmann

In the essay "In Lieu of an Article," Alvar Aalto tells of an unnamed professor waking up from a nightmare in a cold sweat and crying out: "Who is going to save me from Vällingby?"[1] To the Finnish architect, the Stockholm suburb represented all that was wrong with modern architecture: anonymity, repetition, scalelessness. Aalto himself is often seen as representing a different kind of modernism, one that is sensitive to human and social issues and close to nature.

However, it is not easy to determine exactly what it is that makes Aalto's architecture human, natural, or organic. I will argue that such descriptions may involve the use of what in the 1960s Claude Lévi-Strauss and Jacques Lacan termed "floating signifiers." A floating signifier can be invested with all kinds of meanings since it holds open a space for that which exceeds expression.

FIGURE 01 *Le Corbusier, Unité Berlin apartment block, Hansaviertel, Berlin, 1955–57. Le Corbusier's ideas cast in concrete.*

Although there is an "inadequation" between the two halves of the equation (the signifier and the signified) there is a relation, one that results in a "*surabondance de significant*," an excess that is, according to Lévi-Strauss, "*absolument necessaire*" in symbolic thought. Moreover, floating signifiers often have strong emotive qualities, as Lévi-Strauss explained. He suggested that since their origin humans have possessed an integral stock of signifiers that they are at a loss to allocate to a signified which is given as such without being known.[2]

Polarities

Critics who identify Aalto as a specifically human or natural architect usually oppose him to international Corbusian modernism, which is asserted to be responsible for inhuman house-machines and lifeless, overscaled, and monofunctional housing developments. Yet one cannot accuse Le Corbusier of ignoring the needs of the human being or society. In his prolific writings, the champion of modernism never failed to stress the necessities of *soleil, espace, et verdure* or the importance of human scale and proportioning, and always considered the possibilities of solving social ills with architectural and urban means. To make his point, Le Corbusier went so far as to cast explanations of his ambitions on the facades of his Unité buildings (**FIG. 1**).

Despite such programmatic statements, Le Corbusier was known as the creator of "machines for living in." Although his work after the early 1930s rarely reflected this ethic, Le Corbusier was normally not regarded as an architect with a particular interest in the human being or in nature. In contrast, Aalto's Hansaviertel housing

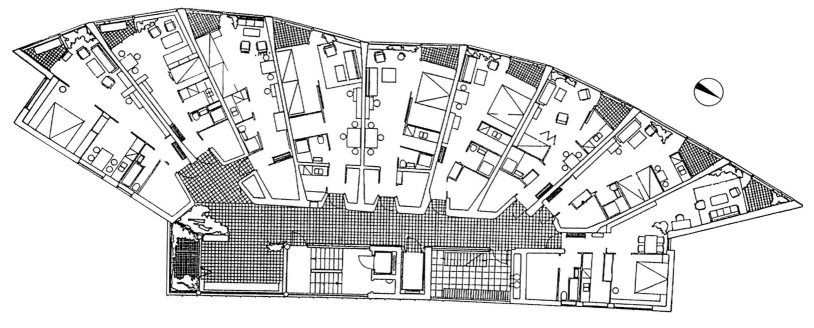

FIGURE 02 *Aalto, Neue Vahr apartment block, Bremen, Germany, 1958–62. Plan of first floor.*

block, built for the same Interbau exhibition in 1957 as Le Corbusier's Berlin Unité, was invariably described as an example of human architecture. The same can even be said of another residential building that Aalto erected in Germany, the Neue Vahr, in Bremen (1958–62). In what follows, the focus will be on these two buildings since both of them received much publicity from national as well as international critics, providing interesting sources for analyses of Aalto's position within the modernist discourse.

A typical reading of Aalto can be found in Robert Venturi's *Complexity and Contradiction*. The author contrasts Le Corbusier's Unité d'Habitation in Marseilles with Aalto's Neue Vahr, explaining that "Aalto has taken the rectangular order of Le Corbusier's basic dwelling unit, which makes up his high-rise apartment slabs, and distorted it into diagonals in order to orient the dwelling unit toward the south for light and for the view."[3] Moreover, the apartments are distorted in different ways, so that as a result there are nine different apartment types on each floor **(FIG. 2)**. This concept contrasts strikingly with Le Corbusier's repetitive use of the same apartment plan.

In this regard, the Neue Vahr can be seen as a variation of the strategy already found in Aalto's Baker House (1946–49), in Cambridge, Massachusetts. To explain the proliferation of types of rooms, many critics, such as Richard Weston and Colin St. John Wilson, refer to Aalto's sensitivity to site, climate, and material, claiming that the serpentine form of the dormitory was carefully calculated so that each room would have a desirable view of the Charles River. Likewise, in the Neue Vahr each floor consists of different apartments supposedly fine-tuned to views and sunlight. Venturi seems to assume as much when he writes: "The inherently rectangular order of structure and space of Aalto's apartment house in Bremen yields to the inner needs for light and space toward the south, like the growth of a flower toward the sun."[4] However, this explanation, even if it were correct, would have been incomprehensible to Le Corbusier who had derived his Unité concept from an analysis of light angles, solar cycles, and other data that he presents at length in his book *La ville radieuse* (1934). If indeed the direction of sunlight was the driving force in Aalto's design, should not a straight bar form, such as that of the Unité, be preferred? If, according to some criterion, a specific orientation of the apartment is better than another one, it would seem logical to provide the same ideal condition to all nine of the apartments, and not just one. If, however, any of the west orientations is fine, then it seems unlikely that the particular plan configuration would have been derived from an analysis of sunlight.

Cultural Fields

To understand why Aalto and Le Corbusier seem to be measured and interpreted according to quite different criteria, we might turn to Aalto himself. In 1963, he stated: "According to Karl Marx, there have been few wars in the world in which more than three enemies have fought one another. Architecture, however, has more than three thousand enemies simultaneously trying to conquer the field."[5] This observation anticipates Pierre Bourdieu's notion of social fields as stages in a battle for cultural capital and domination.

Bourdieu conceives of society as consisting of various fields of action such as economy, culture, and education. In all of these practices, the actors compete for capital that is either material or symbolic. Those with the greatest capital that is specific to the field are dominant. Those who seek to gain dominance try to modify the rules of the field so that their capital is increased and that of the rulers devalued. The mandarins resist any such changes in order to protect the value of their capital. In the cultural field, symbolic capital may consist largely of floating signifiers; such capital is particularly resistant to devaluation.

The cultural field is one of almost pure symbolic domination, occupied by objects, skills, and practices with little use value. Therefore, the struggle is governed by a pure logic of positionality, or of difference and distinction. The "subject" of the production of a work of art—of its value and its meaning—is not the individual artist who creates the object in its materiality, but rather the entire set of agents engaged in the field, or the *habitus* in relation to a position in the field.[6]

This view of art as a field and of an artwork as a position is exemplified in Venturi's analyses throughout *Complexity and Contradiction*, which can be viewed as attempts to constitute an expanded field of modernist architectural discourse by comparing and cross-referencing masterpieces of architecture from every period, often from the Italian Renaissance and baroque. Thus, the question of interpretation is the question of situating a particular building within a context of acknowledged masterpieces and not, for example, considering how a building satisfies verifiable functions. It is therefore important to view the Neue Vahr as a variation of the canonic solution of the Unité, thus contributing to the same discourse as Le Corbusier, but presenting a variant that can be seen as a contrasting position within the field (**FIG. 3**).

To see the difficulties raised in the critical evaluation of Aalto's work, it is best to consider a particular example, such as the Wolfsburg Cultural Center. Aalto has been applauded for his subtle use of light in the library of this building. Instead of uniform artificial lighting, Aalto designed a variety of "barrel" or "slit" skylights to illuminate each section of the library, including the children's department, the main reading hall, and the catalogue section (**FIGS. 4–6**). Each lighting configuration delivers a slightly different ambience, presumably tailored to the needs of each reading situation. Nonetheless, it is quite difficult to determine the needs that would best be met with exactly those

FIGURE 03 *Le Corbusier, Unité Berlin. View of facade.*

FIGURE 04 *Aalto, Wolfsburg Cultural Center, Wolfsburg, Germany, 1958–61. Skylights at the roof.*

FIGURE 05 *Aalto, Wolfsburg Cultural Center library. View of the interior.*

FIGURE 06 *Aalto, Wolfsburg Cultural Center library. Other skylights from interior.*

lighting conditions that Aalto´s ingenious skylights produce. Perhaps the diversity of lighting techniques is supposed to call attention to the functional uniqueness of each room; hence, variety is here more important than the exact match between function and the architectural solution.

The same could be said of the Neue Vahr apartment plans. If an entire floor were to make one apartment, the inhabitant could always occupy the room with the best sunlight at a given time of the day. As things are,

however, each apartment only receives light from one direction, which can be optimal only for a relatively brief time. Moreover, although the fan shape has the advantage of maximizing the width of the west facade, it also narrows the inner part of the plan and is thus hardly ideal in terms of space or light.

To justify the difference in apartment plans, one could, of course, appeal to Aalto's emphasis on individuality against the ideology of the *Normalmensch*, as preached by the heroic functionalists. However, unless the architect can determine the specific wishes of each future inhabitant and match each inhabitant with the appropriately tailored apartment, there is no guarantee of a functional gain from the variations. Still, the variation in the apartment plans can symbolize Aalto's respect for the individual, just as for the inhabitants, the absence of a uniform appearance may support a sense of individuality, without actually corresponding functionally to individual needs.

In this sense, Aalto's deviations from *Neue Sachlichkeit* norms are not so much sensitive responses to the functional and other specificities of each situation as they are semiotic responses to the abstract issues raised by the critics. From this point of view, we may even regard Aalto's architecture metaphorically as a floating signifier in the discourse of architectural modernism: it is about "response," "variation," and "individuality," as thematized by contemporary ideologists of the modern movement such as Sigfried Giedion, Göran Schildt, and Henry-Russell Hitchcock to name but a few.

Dialectical Oppositions and Synthetic Triads

The characterization of Aalto's singular achievement in architecture is bound up with the changing demands of the discourse. Aalto's status as one of the five most significant masters of modernism is linked to the postwar criticism of heroic functionalism for being inhumane, mechanical, placeless, alienating, and standardized. In contrast, Aalto's work has been seen as remedying these lacks in the otherwise healthy modern movement.

The majority of historians and critics emphasize three aspects in Aalto's architecture that set it apart from any other architect's work and explain his importance: his concern for the human qualities of the environment, his

Finnishness, and his love of nature. For such characterizations Bourdieu's notion of social fields provides an especially illuminating framework for analysis. The notion of Aalto's architecture as organic, for example, is meaningful in the context of the modernist discourse in that other, diametrically opposed positions are occupied by the likes of Le Corbusier, Ludwig Mies van der Rohe, and Walter Gropius. Were the field extended to include Hugo Häring, Josef Frank, or vernacular architecture, the position of Aalto would change radically. Likewise, Aalto's Finnishness becomes striking if he is set in a discourse structured around opposite poles, one being the West, as exemplified by the United States or Western Europe (France or Germany), and the other being the East, as exemplified by either Russia or Japan and China. In such an interpretive context, Sigfried Giedion, for example, saw Finland as a country in the middle, and therefore believed Aalto to be uniquely equipped to bring the opposing poles together in a new, Hegelian synthesis.

For Giedion, the polarization of the architectural field suggested the need for a synthetic "third." Perhaps influenced by German Romantic philosophy, Giedion liked to conceptualize everything in triads, denouncing the extremes and praising the reconciliation of opposites. In the 1920s and 1930s, orthodox functionalism was seen as one extreme, originally contrasted with expressionism and, after its demise, with conservative, somewhat *Heimatstil*-inspired developments. Similar bipolar structure could be discerned even within modernism itself. As the secretary of the Congrès Internationaux d'Architects Modernes (CIAM), Giedion's self-appointed task was to repair the loss of the center within the modern movement by discovering a complement to Le Corbusier, the embodiment of heroic functionalism, excessive rationalism, and inhuman machinism.

However, in the late 1920s, Le Corbusier had already shown signs of taking modernism in a different direction, perhaps in response to changes in the political atmosphere. The first sign of renouncing the rationalism of *L'Esprit nouveau* was his design of the Beistegui penthouse (1929–31) with a roof garden that collages historicist elements without any reasonable functional justification.[7] At about this time, he also began experimenting with vernacular materials and primitive building methods, as in the Maison de Mandrot (1929–32), the Maison Errazuris (1930), and the Petite

Maison de Weekend (1935). His formal language also began to change. The Mundaneum project of 1929 was unabashedly historicist, a spiraling ziggurat whose form was barely justifiable as an exhibition building. Freeform curves were only used as accents in the plans or roof gardens of the white villas, but in the 1930s they appear as major elements, such as the curved masonry wall in the Swiss Pavilion of 1930. Only two years later, the Plan Obus for Algiers featured a curved roadway on top of dwellings in different styles, including Moorish, Louis XVI, Italian Renaissance, and modern. Finally, the references to the intuitive sources of form became more frequent in Le Corbusier's writings in the 1930s, culminating in his 1950s eulogy of the "ineffable" as the ultimate essence of architecture.

In other words, Le Corbusier was among the first to deploy in his designs natural materials; free-form shapes; postmodern collages of local, vernacular, and historicist references; and nonfunctional elements—and justify it all with arguments about intuition. Indeed, Giedion did credit him for having introduced Antoni Gaudí to the modernist avant garde.[8] Still, Giedion never presented Le Corbusier as the initiator of the new, organic trend in modern architecture. Because of his definitive position as *the* leader of the architectural field, Le Corbusier's subversions of the International Style in the 1930s could be seen as signs of capitulation to the conservatives, whereas in Aalto's case, similar primitivism or curved forms as in the New York World's Fair pavilion of 1939 could be imputed to his origins in exotic and unspoiled Finland.[9] Thus, Aalto could be described as a new force offering fresh alternatives to standard rationalism.

Aalto as the Finnish Architect

For Giedion, it was important to argue that the new masters of organic modernism drew inspiration from the original home countries (preferably at the cultural fringe); otherwise, the rejection of the rationalist language of forms might have appeared capricious, a product of superficial fashions.

Since Giedion's second edition of *Space, Time, and Architecture* (1949), it has been the rule for critics to associate Aalto's works with Finland. However, Aalto's countrymen did not originally recognize his buildings as particularly Finnish. In the mid-1930s, the architect

FIGURE 07 Aalto, Villa Mairea, Noormarkku, Finland, 1937–39. View of tearoom.

FIGURE 08 *Aalto, Villa Mairea. Exterior of sauna.*

and critic Gustaf Strengell remarked that the interiors of the Viipuri Library (1933) exhibited strikingly Japanese characteristics in their use of light wood in its natural state.[10] The Villa Mairea is even more international: it collages Corbusian modernism with Japanese tea-rooms, African bound columns, cubist paintings, and continental *Heimatstil* (**FIGS. 7, 8**). Apparently, the agglomeration of foreign influences in the Villa Mairea is so overwhelming as to make it a perfect example of what Roland Barthes called an empty sign, so that it gradually became a paradigm of "Finnish" as well as "natural" architecture within the discursive field of modernism.[11]

The Savoy Vase is perhaps even a better illustration of Aalto's purported Finnishness, as it is often seen as referring to the lakes and islands of Finland. The vase was part of a series of designs for which Aalto won the 1936 competition organized by the glassworks of Karhula and Iittala. The prime aim of the competition was to acquire designs suitable for showing at the Paris World's Fair in 1937. In the original competition drawings, Aalto used a cubist device á la Fernand Léger, contrasting and overlaying organic lines with independent blocks of color. In addition to its use in cubist painting, this technique was also popular in advertising and graphic design as can be seen, for example, in Joseph Binder's poster for the Austrian Werkbund's 1935 Christmas exhibition (**FIGS. 9, 10**).[12] Certainly, Aalto was familiar with the softly curved, organic shapes that had been produced by Hans Arp since about 1930. Throughout his career Aalto himself often acknowledged the influence of contemporary art on his designs and seems to have seen in abstract art a model for his architecture: "Abstract art . . . is a medium that can transport us directly into the human current of feelings that has almost been lost by the written word."[13] Even in architecture similar shapes had been around for a while; one might argue that the Savoy Vase is in fact a miniature version of Mies van der Rohe's Glass Skyscraper (1922). The title of

FIGURE 09 *Joseph Binder, poster for the "Weihnachts-Ausstellung des neuen Werkbundes Österreichs,"
Vienna, 1935.*

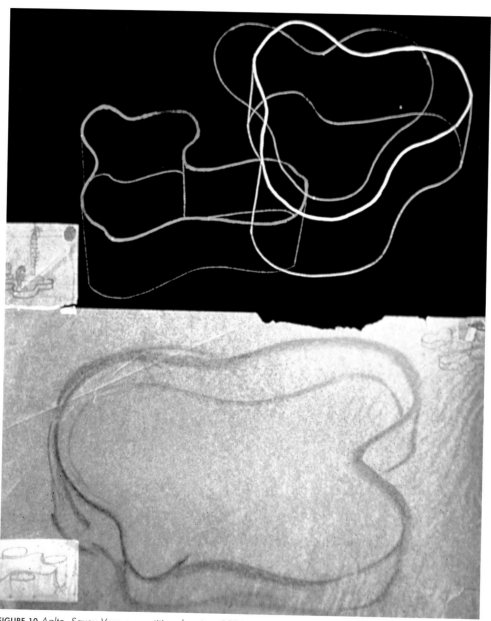

FIGURE 10 *Aalto, Savoy Vase competition drawing, 1936*

Aalto's competition entry—*Eskimoerindens skinnbuxa* (The leather pants of an Eskimo woman)—makes no reference to modern art or architecture, but neither does it suggest that Aalto was inspired by Finland or by landscape.

Despite the lack of a connection, the vase was seen as particularly Finnish in the context of the Paris World's Fair, which of course was all about national identities, invented or not.

Aalto as the Natural Architect

In addition to Finland, "nature" is almost always evoked in the descriptions of Aalto's buildings, even though "natural architecture" may be an oxymoron. The meaning of "natural architecture" in criticism is hard to grasp, and often this floating signifier is simultaneously identified as "organic architecture." The most common meanings of "natural" (or "organic") architecture can be roughly grouped in four categories. First, "natural" sometimes means that the shapes of a building resemble plants or animals. Second, architecture can be "natural" if "natural" materials are used. Third, sometimes "natural" is to be understood as "growing out of the site," "local," or even "contextual." Fourth, "natural" can mean that the building process imitates natural processes in terms of growth or function.

Compared with the designs of Imre Makovecz or Herb Greene, Aalto´s buildings are not particularly biomorphic. Nonetheless, his free-form wooden grills on the ceilings of the Neue Vahr, the ceiling decoration in the Hansaviertel, and his rounded floor plans are usually associated with nature even though the buildings are located in an urban setting (**FIG. 11**). If one compares Aalto again with Le Corbusier, who also used free forms in Ronchamp and on the roof garden of the Unité d'Habitation in Marseille, it would seem more accurate to identify these elements as references to contemporary abstract art and architecture.[14] However, Aalto's wooden grills allowed the reading that Aalto, coming from a country of unspoiled nature, had indeed a special connection to wood and hence to nature. In this sense one could argue that he used the means of abstraction for a sharper perception of the natural environment than that offered by any other architect and thus sensitized the user to nature even in urban locations.

FIGURE 11 *Aalto, Neue Vahr. Ceiling detail.*

FIGURE 12 *Aalto, Wolfsburg Cultural Center. View of the exterior.*

Materials that could be seen as proverbially natural never dominate in Aalto's buildings. Rather, they are made of brick or concrete with facades of plaster or cladding of marble or granite, often imported. In the Wolfsburg Cultural Center, Aalto created striped facades with marble from Italy, Greece, and Sweden and syenite from the Pamir Mountains. Aalto may have derived such striping from the cathedral in Siena, according to Göran Schildt (FIG. 12).[15] Because of its traditional use for public monuments and its value, marble has always occupied the position of a cultural item instead of a natural material. Aalto himself explained that Carrara marble was for him "the original stone for monumental architectural forms."[16]

However, Aalto also often employed timber details in various forms in many of his buildings and even used vernacular grass roofs in the Villa Mairea. Such apparently minor details played an important role in categorizing Aalto as a proponent of organic architecture, distancing him from orthodox rationalists. This affiliation was acknowledged by the press; for example, in 1957 the German magazine *Bauen+Wohnen* wrote: "Aalto's experiments do not violate the nature of wood; he stays close to nature but of course in a new and bold way. While Mies van der Rohe is a classicist, Aalto could almost be called a romantic who wants to make visible the forces inherent in the material."[17] It seems that Aalto used natural materials and wood for decorative or semiotic purposes, rather than in the more organic way critics often demand of a true "natural architecture."

The more abstract senses of "natural architecture" seem to apply better to Aalto's works. To return to Venturi's assessment of the Neue Vahr, it is important not to overlook his metaphor about the building opening up to light "like the growth of a flower toward the sun."[18] This can be interpreted either as a formal metaphor or as a reference to the form-giving process resembling the natural growth of a plant. The idea that the design finds its form in response to the conditions it must meet is a typical modernist one but not one particularly endorsed by Aalto. Rather, he stressed that his own design method would often take the opposite direction in that he would first come up with an idea and then integrate the required functions.[19] Another sense of a "natural" design method was evoked by Aalto, as well as by many later critics, namely that the buildings are designed without elaborate theories but

through intuition, somewhat as nature is thought to create organisms. This understanding accords with Aalto's reputation, but it has been seriously challenged by recent studies that demonstrate pervasive geometrical regularities in his designs, including the Villa Mairea (1937–39), the House of Culture (1952–58), and the Riola Church (1975–78).[20]

Yet Aalto stressed on several occasions that he drew inspiration and even design principles from nature. For example, he argued that nature provides the best model for standardization in architecture in that "in nature, standardization is almost exclusively applied to the smallest possible unit, the cell."[21] While the idea is intriguing, it is hard to define which architectural element could be thought of as a cell. Instead of thinking of a room, for example, as a standard unit to be repeated, Aalto suggested that the brick might be such a cell. However, this extreme view does not significantly further the cause of standardization.[22] Yet one should not misunderstand Aalto's reference to organic standardization as a more or less accurate adaptation of this term to the needs of a specific individual. Rather, it is a reference to the manifold solutions in nature one may find to a circumscribed problem of function.: "The blossoms of an apple tree are standardized, and yet they are all different. That is how we, too, shall learn to build."[23] In architecture, such flexible standardization might let the environment appear less monotonous to its inhabitants, "a kind of standardization that does not force life into a mold, but actually enhances its rich variety." Thus Aalto offered numerous variations with unspecified functions, which are open to interpretation by the users and critics of his buildings.

Aalto as a Regionalist or Contextualist Architect

Another reading of an organic approach concerns the adjustment of the building to its environment. The idea is that a building should naturally grow out of its site, as a plant would grow in a specific place. In this sense, Edward R. Ford characterizes Aalto as "the hero of regionalist architecture, responding to climate, site, . . . [and] material."[24] This was not always the case. Early in his career, in 1930, Aalto had proposed in an orthodox functionalist manner that "new buildings must not be

FIGURE 13 *Aalto, Neue Vahr. View of the exterior.*

adjusted to fit in the surrounding built environment but must be able to develop in a healthy way."[25] During the 1940s he changed his opinion considerably, yet many of his later buildings, both in the city and in the country, seem to lack any connection to their environment at first glance. Only on deeper investigation can subtle contextual references be discerned.

The Neue Vahr tower, described by Malcolm Quantrill as "one of the most elegant towers to emerge in post-war European architecture," is a case in point **(FIG. 13)**.[26] While Aalto's later works are characteristically additive conglomerations of elements that refer to the buildings' surroundings or to their functions, as is the case with the Wolfsburg Cultural Center or the Mount Angel Abbey Library, the Neue Vahr is a freestanding tower that seemingly ignores its context. Apparently it was Aalto's intention to set up a significant landmark in the middle of the new neighborhood. At least this was the understanding of a contemporary critic who wrote: "In this very unusual solution to a very banal problem one can see a living protest against the sterile general attitude of the rest of the Neue Vahr."[27]

While the Neue Vahr is not particularly contextualist, the architectural press lauded Aalto's Rautatalo office building in Helsinki as an exceptionally successful example of contextualism. Completed in 1955, the building stands next to a 1920s bank by Eliel Saarinen. In his presentation of the building in the *Arkkitehti* magazine, Aalto mentions that the new building related to its surroundings with the rhythm of its facade.[28] However, such a device was already in the 1950s a standard move and would hardly have justified the Rautatalo's reputation as an exceptionally successful example of contextualism. A closer look at the building reveals another, more original contextualist device: the Miesian curtain wall is flanked by two curved pilasters of brick. In their form and material, they continue the main motive of Saarinen's bank: the semicircular brick piers.[29] This very sophisticated solution allows the critics to sense the *genius loci*: the brick corner pilasters can be read as minimal markers that indicated respect for the built context without giving up the modernist agenda.

In more general terms, the combination of brick with steel and glass in Aalto's architecture in the 1950s supported his reputation as an architect interested in natural materials and perhaps even tradition, but at the same time Aalto's use of brick occasionally seems to work against the regionalist ideal. Exposed brick in the Baker House dormitory can be seen as a contextual gesture, as brick is a typical material on elite New England campuses and in Boston in particular. However, most of the masterpieces from Aalto's "brick period," such as the Säynätsalo Town Hall (1949–52), the National Pensions Institute (1953–57), and the Otaniemi Technical University (1949–68), are located in Finland, where brick is not a characteristic material. The predominant Finnish building material was wood; many National Romantic architects in Finland around 1900 tended to view brick as Russian.[30] Nonetheless, brick became very popular in Finland during the 1920s neoclassicism and later in the National Romanticism of the late 1930s to the early 1950s.

Aalto's decision to use brick may also have been partly inspired by Eliel Saarinen. After immigrating to the United States in 1922, Saarinen continued to employ exposed brick in his architecture, but his classical tendencies were infused with art deco and arts and crafts elements, most visibly in the campus of the Cranbrook Academy of Art in Michigan. Although the two Finnish architects were not very close in their native country,

FIGURE 14 *Eliel Saarinen, Cranbrook Academy of Art, Bloomfield Hills, Mich., 1925–30. Detail of brick.*

FIGURE 15 *Aalto, Baker House dormitory, Massachusetts Institute of Technology, Cambridge, Mass., 1946–49. Detail of brick.*

Aalto visited Saarinen at Cranbrook in 1939 and even spent Christmas with the Saarinens in 1946. It was around this time when Saarinen invited him to become a partner in his Cranbrook office.[31] However, Aalto decided against this offer and rejected Saarinen's over-sophisticated brickwork; nonetheless he quoted Saarinen with the deformed bricks at the Baker House dormitory (FIGS. 14, 15).

The use of irregular bricks is not the only feature that Aalto and Saarinen shared. Saarinen's First Christian Church (1942) in Columbus, Indiana, features walls and staircases with detailing similar to that of the Villa Mairea, and the parish house of the same church has a curved wooden ceiling in the basement auditorium,

which is somewhat reminiscent of the lecture room of the Viipuri Library. Saarinen and Aalto were certainly the best known Finnish architects at the time in the United States, and while they worked very much in the international context, these slight deviations from the mainstream emphasized the Finnishness of their work.

Considering the fact that Aalto himself connected brick architecture with central Europe, it is especially surprising that in the Neue Vahr he opted for international white modernism. Since the times of the Hansa League, brick has had strong regional connotations for Northern Germany. Popular in the Middle Ages and the Renaissance, it was rediscovered first by the historicists of the late nineteenth century and then in the 1920s by Dutch and German expressionists who regarded brick as a primitive, original material. Aalto's theoretical position may explain his unorthodox handling of local traditions, for he believed that a national architecture was not a matter of reproducing tradition: "We don't need what is known as traditional architecture, and work that merely applies inherited forms superficially does not deserve to be called national. Nor do we need any deliberate quest for individuality as such. Nonetheless, we must of course always demand individual thinking."[32] In keeping with this principle, in both Finland and Germany Aalto worked explicitly against tradition and put more emphasis on the symbolic self-identity of the community than on local traditions and building techniques.[33]

Aalto as the Human Architect

Despite having proposed in 1934 the building of residential towers in the park landscape of the Munkkiniemi neighborhood of Helsinki, Aalto later became known for criticizing high-rise buildings as inhuman and alienating.[34] However, he was appointed to build the twenty-two-story Neue Vahr in Bremen in June 1958 and a little later another sixteen-story residential tower in Lucerne.[35]

The reason why the Neue Vahr commission was given to Aalto has to do with a local controversy in Bremen, generated by Ernst May's master plan for the new development. As the local press called it, "Sing-Sing," "an impossible extreme," and "depressing machines for living," the client, the nonprofit housing organization GEWOBA, was determined to find a socially oriented architect and thereby set an example for future social

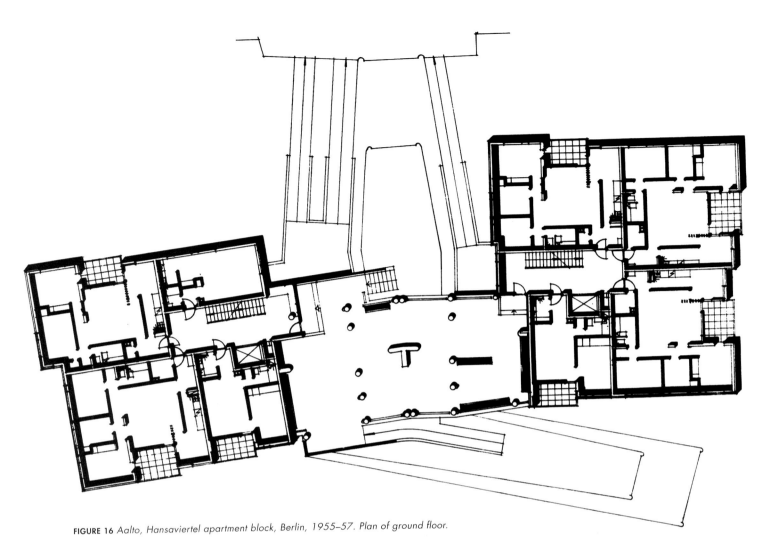

FIGURE 16 *Aalto, Hansaviertel apartment block, Berlin, 1955–57. Plan of ground floor.*

housing in Germany.[36] Thus, they picked Aalto, who had established his reputation as the human modernist at the Interbau exhibition in Berlin in 1957.

Referring to his Hansaviertel housing block, the Swiss magazine *Werk* praised his "extraordinary close, practical, psychological, and pure human relation" toward problems of dwelling and claimed that Aalto, in contrast to his colleagues, did not build "theories" but rather "designed . . . a life-sustaining environment of a purity and intimacy unequalled by any other building at the exhibition."[37] *Bauwelt* commented: "Aalto also came and built among all of those rectangular boxes a building which, despite being mass housing, accommodates issues of orientation, privacy, and the diverse wishes of the occupants under one roof. It is not without reason that precisely Aalto's building was described as the most human: scale, material and consideration of the function of dwelling led to

that judgment."[38] In Berlin, the impression of Aalto as a humanist was further supported by his building having no more than eight stories and seventy-eight apartments—in contrast to Le Corbusier's Berlin Unité, which housed seven times as many inhabitants. By comparison the Unité was seen as anonymous mass housing of the machine age while Aalto's Hansaviertel stood for social values. Le Corbusier did not hesitate to make the windowless *rue intérieure* of his building 420 feet long and only 9 feet wide, whereas in the Hansaviertel block, Aalto grouped the family around a multifunctional atrium and applied the same pattern to organize each floor around the staircase as a core, uniting the two parts of the building with a shared entrance area on the ground floor (FIG. 16). While Le Corbusier strove to satisfy the physical needs of the inhabitants, Aalto's approach in Berlin was more a symbolic presentation of humanness or community values.

FIGURE 17 *Aalto, Opera House, Essen, Germany, 1959–64. Exterior at entry.*

Conclusion

Aalto's image in criticism does not reflect his sensitivity to region, nature, or the human being in an abstract sense as much as it responds to the critical debates on the lack of "regional," "natural," and "human" qualities in international modernism. Thus, in Göran Schildt's characterization of Aalto as "the secret opponent within the modern movement," the word "within" should be stressed. Unlike renegades and mavericks, such as Josef Frank or Friedensreich Hundertwasser, Aalto did not undermine the cultural field of modernism but exercised his critique internally. Many of his 1950s buildings, for example, addressed the "placelessness" of modern architecture about which critics had complained.

During the past decades, interpretations of Aalto's work have taken different directions. He partly has been seen as a proponent of functionalism, nationalism, or organicism, or as a precursor of postmodernism and numerous other tendencies. His buildings speak a strong formal language and often evoke natural imagery, like the Opera House in Essen that has been nick-named a "tree trunk," but his shapes remain abstract enough to acquit him of any charges of copying forms or of repeating old metaphors (FIG. 17). In this regard he anticipated recent ideas about "weak form" and "weak thought" in striving for the "betweenness" which allows multiple new readings without ignoring tradition.[39] Aalto's secret may have been his skeptical position toward orthodox modernism, for he didn't believe in the possibility of finding final solutions, as his contemporaries did: "I am considering here only one aspect of this vast paper struggle: the striving for the absolute. Every epoch, whether long or short, or only part of an epoch has the tendency to believe that its time possesses a definitive character."[40]

1 Alvar Aalto, "In Lieu of an Article" (1958), in *Alvar Aalto in His Own Words,* ed. Göran Schildt (New York: Rizzoli, 1998), 263–4.

2 Claude Lévi-Strauss, *Introduction to the Work of Marcel Mauss,* trans. Felicity Baker (London: Routledge & Kegan Paul, 1987), 62. Elaborating on the idea of floating signifiers, he stated that in our attempt to understand the world, we always dispose of a surplus of meaning periodically re-allotted by the mythopoetical imagination, so that the wholeness of meaning becomes precisely the main task of art.

3 Robert Venturi, *Complexity and Contradiction* (New York: Museum of Modern Art, 1966), 56. In a personal communication, Stanford Anderson points out that the Neue Vahr apartments face southwest to northwest. Further, in Venturi's illustrated plans of Neue Vahr and a Unité by Le Corbusier, assuming the convention of north upward, Venturi deployed the Neue Vahr plan to fit his claim and the Unité plan to undermine Le Corbusier's attention to sun orientation. Running the Unité north–south, Le Corbusier gave each of his double-facing apartments east and west exposure. Also, the Unité has atypical apartments to the south.

4 Venturi, *Complexity and Contradiction,* 85. As concerns the Neue Vahr, I suggest Aalto intended the west orientation of apartments for young people who return home in the evening.

5 Quoted in Göran Schildt, *Alvar Aalto: The Mature Years* (New York: Rizzoli, 1991), 248.

6 Pierre Bourdieu, *Distinction: A Social Critique of the Judgement of Taste* (Cambridge, Mass.: Harvard Univ. Press, 1984); Pierre Bourdieu, "The Production of Belief: Contribution to an Economy of Symbolic Goods," *Media, Culture, and Society* 2 (1980), 261–93.

7 Kari Jormakka, Jacqueline Gargus, and Douglas Graf, "The Use and Abuse of Paper," *Datutop* 20 (1999): 17.

8 See Sigfried Giedion, *Space, Time and Architecture: The Growth of a New Tradition* (5th ed., Cambridge, Mass.: Harvard Univ. Press, 1980), 874. According to Mark Wigley's lecture 1996 "On Site," presented at the fourth Bienal de Arquitectura Española in Barcelona, Garcia Mercadal had invited Le Corbusier to Madrid but Josep Luis Sert diverted him to Barcelona where he had the opportunity to see Gaudí's buildings.

9 Le Corbusier's subversions of the International Style may be seen as signs of capitulation to the conservatives because the use, for example, of natural stone, primitive wooden constructions, and irregularities in the craft were familiar devices of various *Heimatstil* movements. They were, thus, already ideologically occupied in the highly polarized discourse of architecture, at least in the German context.

10 Quoted in Göran Schildt, *Alvar Aalto: The Decisive Years* (New York: Rizzoli, 1986), 114.

11 Roland Barthes, *The Eiffel Tower and Other Mythologies* (New York: Hill & Wang, 1979), 4; Juhani Pallasmaa, "Alvar Aalto: Toward a Synthetic Functionalism," in *Alvar Aalto: Between Humanism and Materialism,* ed. Peter Reed (New York: Museum of Modern Art, 1998), 32.

12 Bernhard Denscher, *Österreichische Plakatkunst, 1898–1938* (Vienna: Verlag Brandstätter, 1992), 111; see also Jormakka, Gargus, and Graf, "Use and Abuse of Paper," 72.

13 Aalto quoted in Marc Treib, "Aalto's Nature," in *Alvar Aalto,* ed. Reed, 60.

14 Marc Treib, "Aalto's Nature," in *Alvar Aalto,* ed. Reed, 60.

15 Schildt, *Alvar Aalto: Mature Years,* 193.

16 Alvar Aalto, "The Relationship between Architecture, Painting, and Sculpture" (1970), in *Alvar Aalto in His Own Words,* Schildt, 268.

17 Antonio Hernandez, "Möbel aus Holz und Stahl: Alvar Aalto und Mies van der Rohe," *Bauen und Wohnen* 8 (1957), 262.

18 Venturi, *Complexity and Contradiction,* 85.

19 Alvar Aalto, quoted in Oszkar Winkler, *Alvar Aalto* (Berlin: Henschelverlag, 1987), 32.

20 See, for example, Klaus Herdeg, *The Decorated Diagram: Harvard Architecture and the Failure of the Bauhaus Legacy* (Cambridge, Mass.: MIT Press, 1983), 32; Juhani Pallasmaa, ed., *Alvar Aalto: Villa Mairea, 1938–39* (Helsinki: Alvar Aalto Foundation/Mairea Foundation, 1998), 81; and Jormakka, Gargus, and Graf, "Use and Abuse of Paper," 48–49, 95–101, 136.

21 Alvar Aalto, "Influence of Structure and Material on Contemporary Architecture" (1938), in *Alvar Aalto in His Own Words,* Schildt, 100.

22 In 1957 Aalto wrote of an Indian architect who came to Finland and asked what module Aalto's office employed. "I did not answer him, because I did not know that. One of my chief lieutenants was sitting on my right. He answered. He said, 'One millimeter or less.'" Lee Hodgden, who worked in Aalto's office in the 1950s, claims he was the unnamed lieutenant. In an interview with Kari Jormakka in Ithaca, N.Y., on 3 Oct. 2001, Hodgden said that he had told the visitor—who actually came from Le Corbusier's office—that the module of the office was a brick. See Schildt, *Alvar Aalto in His Own Words,* 202.

23 Alvar Aalto, "Interview for Finnish Television, July 1972," in *Alvar Aalto in His Own Words,* Schildt, 271. The following quotation is from the same source.

24 Edward R. Ford, *The Details of Modern Architecture, Volume 2: 1928 to 1988* (Cambridge, Mass.: MIT Press, 1996), 119.

25 Alvar Aalto, "Bostadsbebyggelsen på gammal stadsplan," *Byggmästaren* (Stockholm), (1930), 22.

26 Malcolm Quantrill, *Alvar Aalto: A Critical Study* (New York: Schocken, 1989), 205–6.

27 "22-geschossiger Appartementturm mit Südwestwohnungen in der 'Neuen Vahr' in Bremen," *Bauen und Wohnen* 7 (1963), 458.

28 Alvar Aalto, "Rautatalo, Keskuskatu 3, Helsinki," *Arkkitehti* 9 (1955), 128–137.

29 Kari Jormakka, "Constructing Architecture," *Datutop* 15 (1991), 19.

30 Alvar Aalto, "Between Humanism and Materialism" (1955), in *Alvar Aalto in His Own Words,* Schildt, 180.

31 Schildt, *Alvar Aalto: The Early Years* (New York: Rizzoli, 1984), 163.

32 Alvar Aalto, seemingly endorsing views of André Lurçat, in "Instead of an Interview. André Lurçat in Finland" (1934), in *Alvar Aalto in His Own Words,* Schildt, 84.

33 "22-geschossiger Appartementturm," 458.

34 Peter Reed, "Alvar Aalto and the New Humanism of the Postwar Era," in *Alvar Aalto,* ed. Reed, 108–9.

35 Aalto built the Schönbühl high-rise tower in Lucerne in 1965–68.

36 Hans-Joachim Wallenhorst, *Die Chronik der GEWOBA 1924 bis 1992* (Bremen, Germany: GEWOBA, 1993), 242–43.

37 "Der Wohnbau von Alvar Aalto an der Interbau Berlin 1957," *Werk* 1 (1958), 9.

38 Günther Kühne, "Alvar Aalto baut in Deutschland," *Bauwelt* 41 (1962), 1143.

39 See Peter Eisenman, "En Terror Firma: in Trails of Grotextes," in *Peter Eisenman: Recent Projects,* ed. Arie Graafland (Nijmegen, Netherlands: SUN, 1989), 19–24; and Eisenman, "Die blaue Linie," *Aura und Exzess: Zur Überwindung der Metaphysik der Architektur* (Vienna: Passagen Verlag, 1995), 148.

40 Alvar Aalto, quoted in Karl Fleig, *Alvar Aalto* (1978; Zürich: Verlag für Architektur Artemis, 1984), 3:13.

Aalto and the Other Tradition

Colin St. John Wilson

Alvar Aalto is commonly credited with outspoken disdain for practitioners writing about architecture. This notion came to be so commonly held that Robert Venturi, in his contribution to the memorial issue on Aalto in *L'Architecture d'aujourd'hui* in 1977, declared that one of the things he most admired in Aalto was the fact that he did not write.[1] It was a perfectly excusable misrepresentation in the light of Aalto's own statements, of which the most famous is his declaration that the Creator created paper for drawing architecture on; everything else is, at least for Aalto, to misuse paper.[2] Actually Aalto wrote so many pieces and recorded so many lectures that Göran Schildt, in assembling the second, enlarged edition of Aalto's writings, declared of the 280 pages of text, "[They] represent perhaps 15% of all the material known to me."[3] Aalto's increasingly dismissive statements about critical theory were largely provoked by the critical stance of the "young Turks" whose rationalism (grounded in the theory of their teacher Aulis Blomstedt) took on the status in the early 1960s of a challenge to Aalto's dominating influence in Finland. That conflict has long since been put to rest; what endures is a large body of cogently argued theory, which is convincingly substantiated in an equally large body of built work. Together, I believe they represent a point of view whose authority has continued to deepen and which today offers more promise of fruitful development than that of his more orthodox contemporaries.

The earliest writings date from 1922, thus not part of that first flood of brilliant iconoclastic statements from Le Corbusier, Ludwig Mies van der Rohe, and (earlier still) Adolf Loos. Nevertheless they were well formed before the orthodoxies of the Congrès Internationaux d'Architects Modernes (or CIAM, whose first meeting took place in 1928) began to be formulated. Right from the start they were characterized by remarkable self-confidence and independence. Aalto believed passionately in the obligation to challenge received ideas. His favorite writers were Voltaire, Friedrich Nietzsche, and George Bernard Shaw, and a strain of anarchistic irreverence was ingrained in his character. Another of

his mentors was the great Finnish philosopher of art Yrjö Hirn, whose book *The Origins of Art* emphasizes the central role of play in the creative process.[4] Just how Aalto put this concept to work in his design practice is beautifully described in his article "The Trout and the Stream," which describes an important episode in the design process for the Viipuri Library. Immersed in the density and contradictory nature of the parameters in the building program, he broke out of designer's block by engaging in what he called "quite childlike compositions. . . . [I was] getting my range as it were with naïve drawings."[5] Out of the resulting (and now famous) "doodles" of mountains and rotating suns came the celebrated light-cones in the ceiling of the reading room **(FACING PAGE IMAGE)**.

In general terms, however, I believe that the fundamental soundness of his approach lies in the fact that it is firmly grounded in the crucial classical (Aristotelian) distinction between Pure Art ("that serves only itself") and Practical Art ("that serves an end other than itself"). Architecture is unequivocally a Practical Art, and the primary source of its inspiration lies in the fact that it is, in a phrase of Alberti, "born of necessity, nourished by convenience, dignified by use."[6] The fulfillment and embodiment of purpose in the creation of forms of life is its essence.

My first exposure to Aalto's way of thinking was at his Gold Medal Discourse at the Royal Institute of British Architects in 1957. Aalto opened with the following statement: "Our time is full of enthusiasm for . . . architecture because of the architectural revolution that has been taking place during these last decades. . . . The architectural revolution is still going on, but it is like all revolutions: it starts with enthusiasm and it stops with some sort of dictatorship."[7]

The impact of this statement was riveting. At a time when all the critics were celebrating the victory of modern architecture, and Unité d'Habitations and Seagram Buildings were sprouting like mushrooms over the face of the earth, here we were being warned by this extraordinary man that this triumph was self-deception masking "bad faith" and broken promises.

He identified two sources of bad faith in current practice. The first was formalism. As early as 1927 he wrote: "We cannot create new form where there is no new content"[8] In the promotion of stylistic criteria he detected "the smell of Hollywood"; the concept of "style" as a generating agent was fundamentally contrary to his commitment to an open-ended search for a form responsive to context, way of life, and *genius loci* of the task in question. To him, as to the European avant-garde in general, the attempt by Hitchcock and Johnson in their book *The International Style* to identify what was perceived to be a "revolution" as a mere change of taste was poisonous.[9] The second source of bad faith was the glamorizing of technology. Aalto's idea of hell for the common man was the moment when "mechanization takes command"; he saw the priority attributed to technical values as misplaced, assigning value to the issue of "how?" over the true priority of the questions "why?" and "for whom?." Aalto then challenged us to take up a fighting position against these two major forms of betrayal.

Aalto was ten years younger than the first of the modern masters, and right from the start he held himself at a critical distance from them and, above all, from the hardening orthodoxies of CIAM. Whereas for them the enemy was the dead hand of the Past, for him the enemy was the bad faith of the Present. This critical realism was perhaps the main source of his attraction to my own generation. Critical irreverence was intrinsic to his character, albeit of the constructive type that Paul Valéry defined as "creative doubt." "We should at all times be prepared to doubt and criticize" was Aalto's motto. Of "the frequently despised philosophy of doubt" he wrote that on the highest plane doubt could be transformed into its apparent opposite, love in a critical sense: "It can result in a love for 'the little man,' which works as a safeguard whenever the mechanical forms of modern life threaten to smother individuality."[10]

Aalto believed that the one true claim to originality of the modern movement lay in the undertaking to serve "everyman"—the emancipatory movement stemming from the writings of William Morris and the early socialists. Aalto's phrase for it was "the democratization of architecture." He summed up his working philosophy in the watchword of his famous telegram to John Ely

Burchard at MIT in 1947: "Architecture, the real thing, is only where man stands in [the] centre."[11] We must examine carefully what he meant by this. For lesser folk, the claim might merely be a sentimental political aspiration, but for Aalto it was the springboard for a deeply poetic interpretation of the activities and occasions and physical context of society. The range of building types that he addressed was wider than that of any other architect and the range of his invention matched the diversity of each form of life. Hugo Häring was expelled from the CIAM group for his objections to Le Corbusier's codification of forms and functions into Cartesian categories for instant implementation. He wrote, "We want to examine things and allow them to discover their own forms. . . . It goes against the grain with us . . . to force upon them laws of any kind."[12] This statement of 1925 defines very precisely what was already Aalto's "creative doubt" about CIAM. In my book *The Other Tradition of Modern Architecture*, I argue that at its very birth CIAM provoked the resistance of a number of individual architects.[13] Among these were Aalto, Häring, Erik Gunnar Asplund, and Hans Scharoun, whose subsequent body of work can be seen as a counter-thesis, or "other tradition," to that of orthodox CIAM and the "International Style."

Aalto's originality lay in the way he took this argument forward both in analysis and in design practice. Through an immensely rich response to the sensuous realm of body language, he invented a whole world of forms that could create a presence and a place that, like a human face, have a memorability we do not normally enjoy in our daily commerce with the man-made world. In his paper "Rationalism and Man" (1935), he began to discriminate the range and levels of sensibility at work:

We might say that one way to produce a more humane built environment is to extend our definition of rationalism. We must analyze more of the qualities associated with an object than we have done so far. All the demands that could be thought of with respect to the quality of an object form a kind of graded scale, perhaps a series like the spectrum. The red band of the spectrum covers social considerations, the orange one questions of construction, and so forth up to the ultraviolet band, invisible to the eye; this area perhaps conceals the demands that are closest to the human individual and thus elude definition. Be this as it may, it is in the band that contains the purely human questions that we will find most of what is new. . . .Even if a more precise analysis were to lead to the conclusion that some emotional concept is the sum of elements that are physically or otherwise measurable, we would still soon find ourselves outside the realm of physics. . . .As soon as we include psychological requirements or, rather, as soon as we are able to include them, we will have extended the rationalist working method enough to make it easier to prevent inhuman results.[14]

In his paper "The Humanizing of Architecture" (1940), he took the argument further: "It is not the rationalization itself which was wrong in the first and now past period of Modern architecture. The fault lies in the fact that the rationalization has not gone deep enough. The present phase of Modern architecture is doubtless a new one, with the special aim of solving problems in the humanitarian and psychological fields. This new period, however, is not in contradiction to the first period of technical rationalization. Rather, it is to be understood as an enlargement of rational methods to encompass related fields."[15]

As a teacher, Aalto enjoyed incomparable success in practicing what he preached, "success" in this sense measured by the extent to which his buildings have proved to their inhabitants that they have fully and joyfully served the end for which they were created. To anticipate and allow for such a process to run its course, he said that "it is not what a building looks like on its opening day, but what it is like thirty years later that matters."[16] None of his contemporaries offered such a hostage to fortune! Most of his buildings that I have seen have survived lovingly in the hands and the hearts of those who dwell in them. It is no coincidence that exactly thirty years after the opening of Baker House, two MIT students (Deborah Poodry and Victoria Ozonoff) published the results of a survey among the inhabitants of the building. The findings of that review (and its analysis of the evolution of the design) may be familiar, but I cannot resist quoting the authors' summary praise for "the effectiveness of Aalto's simultaneous concerns for the particular needs of the individual inhabitant, and for the support necessary to develop a group living experience. . . . If the design was that of a Master, the result has been active participation."[17] In *The Other Tradition of Modern Architecture* I compare the success of this building with the design methods and less happy outcome of its contemporary rival at the Harvard Graduate Center. The comparison provides an exemplary case study of the difference between Aalto's searching quest for a life-enhancing response to a real situation and the plodding orthodoxy of CIAM. There can be no more damning refutation of the charge by Hitchcock that Baker House was just a piece of expressionist eccentricity than Aalto's analytic comparison of twelve alternative solutions that has the elegance of a Cuvier classification of organisms (**FIGS. 1–4 p.196**).[18] What could be more appropriate than to dissolve that misreading and, by looking deep into both the process and the product, to draw from Aalto's work the inspiration that it has to offer for our thinking in the future.

1 Robert Venturi, "Le Palladio du Mouvement Moderne," *L'Architecture d'aujourd'hui*, 191 (1977), 119–20.

2 "God made paper for drawing architecture on. Everything else—at least to me—is a misuse of paper. *Torheit*—as Zarathustra would say." Alvar Aalto, "In Lieu of an Article" (1958), in *Alvar Aalto in His Own Words*, ed. Schildt, 264.

3 Göran Schildt, ed., *Alvar Aalto in His Own Words* (New York: Rizzoli, 1998), 9.

4 Yrjö Hirn, *The Origins of Art: A Psychological and Sociological Inquiry* (London: Macmillan, 1900).

5 Alvar Aalto, "The Trout and the Stream" (1947), in *Alvar Aalto in His Own Words*, Schildt, 107–9.

6 Leon Battista Alberti, *De re aedificatoria*, 1485, book 1, chap. 9. Here, in the translation of Joseph Rykwert, Neil Leach, and Robert Tavernor, *On the Art of Building in Ten Books* (Cambridge, Mass.: MIT Press, 1988), 24. The Leoni edition, *The Architecture of Leon Battista Alberti in Ten Books* (London, 1726) reads: "For all building in general, if you consider it well, owes its Birth to Necessity, was nursed by Convenience, and embellished by Use; Pleasure was the last Thing consulted in it, which is never truly obtained by Things that are immoderate" (13).

7 Alvar Aalto, RIBA Annual Discourse (1957) reprinted as "The Enemies of Good Architecture," in *Alvar Aalto in His Own Words*, Schildt, 202–6

8 Alvar Aalto, "The Latest Trends in Architecture," (1 Jan. 1928), in *Alvar Aalto in His Own Words*, Schildt, 58–64.

9 Henry-Russell Hitchcock, Jr., and Philip Johnson, *The International Style: Architecture since 1922* (New York: W. W. Norton, 1932). It is to Hitchcock's credit that in his preface to the 1966 re-issue of *The International Style* he wrote a gracefully chastened note: "Had we written it a few years later . . . we would have had to face . . . the rise to international prominence of Aalto," p. ix.

10 Alvar Aalto, "What is Culture?" (1958), in *Alvar Aalto in His Own Words*, Schildt, 15–17. Wilson chose not to include the final words of that sentence: "and harmonious life." ed.

11 Quoted in Deborah Poodry and Victoria Ozonoff, "Coffins, Pies and Couches: Aalto at MIT," *Spazio e Società* 18 (June 1982), 105.

12 Hugo Häring, "Wege zur Form," *Die Form*, no. 1 (Oct. 1925); reprinted in *Hugo Häring: Schriften, Entwürfe, Bauten*, ed. Heinrich Lauterbach and Jürgen Joedicke (Stuttgart, Germany: Karl Krämer, 1965), 13–14. Translation for the author by Fritz Stoll.

13 Colin St.John Wilson, *The Other Tradition of Modern Architecture* (London: Academy Editions, 1995).

14 Alvar Aalto, "Rationalism and Man" (1935), in *Alvar Aalto in His Own Words*, Schildt, 91.

15 Alvar Aalto, "The Humanizing of Architecture" (1940), in *Alvar Aalto in His Own Words*, Schildt, 102.

16 From a conversation with the author, Villa Mairea, July 1960.

17 Poodry and Ozonoff, "Coffins, Pies and Couches," 104–23. See also the analysis of their findings in Wilson, *Other Tradition of Modern Architecture*, 93–102.

18 A view expressed in conversation with the author during Hitchcock's visit to Cambridge University in the summer of 1957.

Aalto and America

The following essays assess Alvar Aalto's perceptions of America as an architect and critic. They also document and explore his activity in America as an architect, intellectual, professor, and diplomat for Finland.

In his "Aalto's Image of America," Juhani Pallasmaa provides an overview of Aalto's changing architectural philosophy (from that of a "rationalist" to one of a synthetic humanist), his changing political convictions, and his changing viewpoint as an enthusiast and eventually a critic of American politics and culture. The essays that follow document with independent chronologies the three phases of Aalto's American involvement. Eeva-Liisa Pelkonen focuses on the discovery and interpretation of Aalto's work by the Museum of Modern Art, beginning in 1937. Pekka Korvenmaa explores Aalto's research of the American housing industry and his professorship at MIT's School of Architecture around 1940. Gail Fenske examines his return to MIT in 1945 as a design critic at the invitation of his friend William W. Wurster, the California modernist; his commission for Baker House in 1946; and his eventual return to Finland.

These chronological essays take up independent themes that together illustrate the faceted nature of Aalto's encounter with America. Pelkonen's essay is a subtle reading of the interrelationship between international politics and architectural culture in the years leading up to World War II, a politically charged time during which the ideologies of nationalism, internationalism, and regionalism competed in shaping the Museum of Modern Art's interpretation of modernism and with it, of Aalto's work. The museum's exhibition "Architecture and Furniture: Aalto" opened well before his arrival in America for the first time in 1938. Aalto's discovery of American "regionalist" architecture during his second trip of 1939 supported his argument for the development of Finnish architecture along the same lines, an argument made poignant by Finland's loss of its regional heartland, Karelia, to the Soviets during the Winter War of 1939–40.

Korvenmaa takes up Aalto's research of the housing industry in the United States, working through the Finnish Information Office as a diplomat in the wake of the Winter War with the objective of advancing Finnish war-time reconstruction. At the center of Korvenmaa's analysis is the project "An American Town in Finland," for which Aalto raised U.S. and Finnish capital and he established a research laboratory at MIT. Fenske examines the relationship between Aalto and Wurster, who, during his tenure as the dean of the School of Architecture and Planning at MIT from 1944 to 1950 and as a representative of the regionalist ideology in modern architecture and criticism, focused on creating an institutional environment especially receptive to Aalto's work and ideas—in particular, to his design for Baker House. Fenske concludes part 3 with Aalto's official departure for Finland, just after Wurster's return to California; Aalto's deepening "Finnishness" paralleled Wurster's consciousness of being a "California architect."

After Aalto's MIT appointment officially ended in 1951, he would return to the United States in the early 1960s and finally in 1967 to visit the site of Mount Angel Abbey near Portland, Oregon. But as the essays in part 3 demonstrate, the late 1930s and 1940s constituted the primary years of Aalto's engagement with America's architecture, intellectual life, cities, and landscapes. In highlighting the larger contextual themes of international politics, housing research, and modernist criticism and design, the essays call attention to the many dimensions of Aalto's experience with America.   **G.F.**

Cape Cod. Hurricane

Aalto's Image of America

Juhani Pallasmaa

After the 1860s America—or Amerikka, as it has been popularly called in Finland—became the ideal land for numerous Finns. Finnish liberals began to admire American democracy, culture, and lifestyle, which were seen as the great ideal and a progressive alternative to the spiritual tiredness and moral as well as political decline of the Old World.[1] The interest in immigrating to this "Land of the Future" eventually turned into a real "America Fever" and by 1930, 320,000 immigrants from Finland were living in the United States.[2] The region of Alvar Aalto's childhood life in the vicinity of the western coastline was among the areas with the highest immigration rate.[3]

The enthusiastic Alvar Aalto, always thirsty for knowledge, must have become interested in American culture early in his youth. In two of his earliest articles, published in a popular magazine in the beginning of the 1920s, Aalto mentions Buffalo Bill, Old Shatterhand, Nick Carter, Nat Pinkerton, and Huckleberry Finn as his childhood literary heroes of Indian and detective stories.[4] Later, he would play out this interest during his travels in America (**FIG. 1**).

Aalto also mentioned the United States in 1922 in one of his earliest published and serious writings on the dialectics of local tradition and external influences: "Seeing how people were able to be international and unprejudiced in times past, and yet remain true to themselves, we may accept impulses from the old Italy, from Spain and from the new America with open eyes."[5]

Since the 1890s, the Finns have considered Eliel Saarinen a cultural hero who participated in creating the cultural image of the country, an image that eventually influenced Finland's gaining of political independence in 1917. The success of Aalto's esteemed older colleague in the famous Chicago Tribune Tower competition in 1922, one year after Aalto's graduation as an architect, and Saarinen's subsequent emigration to the United States must have been a subject of much collegiate discussion and admiration among Finnish architects in those days.[6] Aalto evidently had developed a special personal interest in Saarinen's artistic personality and career, since he acknowledged the decisive impact of an early encounter with Saarinen's work at the age of nine.[7] By the mid-1930s, Aalto had inherited Saarinen's position as the leading figure of the Finnish architectural scene. In 1931, *Suomen Kuvalehti*, the esteemed Finnish weekly news journal, ran images of Saarinen and his Chicago Tribune Tower project on the cover of issue no. 38 and a photograph of Aalto's

FIGURE 01 *Alvar Aalto on horseback near Fort Williams, Arizona, 1939.*

FIGURE 02–03 *Two covers of the leading Finnish news journal* Suomen Kuvalehti *in 1931 symbolize the shift in the leadership of Finnish architecture. Issue 38: Eliel Saarinen with the backdrop of his second-prize winning Chicago Tribune Tower entry of 1922. Issue 45: Alvar Aalto's revolutionary Paimio Sanatorium under construction.*

revolutionary Paimio Sanatorium under construction on the cover of issue no. 45, signifying the change in the leadership of Finnish architecture (FIGS. 2–4).

The fact that already in the early 1920s Aalto had lectured on the architecture of Manhattan at the Association of Finnish Architects together with the esteemed critic and writer Gustaf Strengell, his elder colleague, speaks of the seriousness of his interest in America.[8] According to the recollection of his Swedish colleague Hakon Ahlberg, Aalto sought information about the United States from him in 1930.[9] The actual motive for Aalto's interest at that time is not known, however.

FIGURE 04 *Alvar Aalto in the garden of the Saarinen House at Cranbrook Academy of Art, Bloomfield Hills, Mich., 1938.*

From Socialist Ideals
to a Philosophy of Doubt

In the late 1920s and early 1930s, Alvar Aalto adopted a liberal leftist orientation, which clearly shifted his interest toward socialist ideas. One would expect that Aalto's leftist values might have distanced him from American culture, but his socialist affinities proved to be rather short-lived. Besides, instead of being viewed as ideological and political adversaries, the United States and the Soviet Union were seen as two alternative social utopias in the early 1930s.

Aalto was closely associated with Acceptera, the radical modernist group of Swedish architects known for its leftist aspirations, and the similarly inclined Projektio film club in Helsinki, which gave him a radical leftist label in his own country.[10] He was one of the founders of the film club and served as its chairman during its short-lived existence. The club showed avant-garde films by Sergei Eisenstein, Vsevolod Pudovkin, Luis Buñuel, Josef von Sternberg and Yuli Raizman, and others. Some of the films had been banned by official censors because of their political or sexual content.

Many of Aalto's closest continental friends from the Bauhaus and Congrès Internationaux d'Architecture Moderne (CIAM) circles, such as Walter Gropius, Ernst May, Le Corbusier, André Lurcat, and Hans Schmidt, had warm and optimistic views of the social experiment of the Soviet Union, the other "land of the future." Aalto's leftist attitudes culminated in his attack against speculative private capitalism and his defense of the Soviet system of housing in 1932 in the *Granskaren* journal, published in his hometown of Turku from 1927 to 1933.[11] He also contributed an article titled "A Good Home" to a magazine edited by two extreme leftist Finns. It defended the idea of planned economy and criticizing individualism in housing: "Then [after the failure of the individualistic production of housing] we will have to adopt a planned economy in the production of its collective complements, under a management working scientifically, as if in a laboratory."[12] Aalto's frequent use of the notion "scientific" during the 1930s carries a distinct Marxist tone.

Toward the end of the decade, Aalto clarified his independent position between the rightist and leftist ideologies competing on the European political scene. After the Soviet Union attacked Finland in November 1939, Aalto wrote: "The war in Finland is not a struggle between socialist and capitalist rule, but a war in which the aggressor represents an imperialism that has completely betrayed socialism and dragged its name in the mud, besides which it has shown itself to lack all organizational capacity. . . . Thus the struggle is between a bad system masquerading behind 'the socialist view of the world' and a deep, genuine social mentality."[13] Here Aalto makes a determined distinction between an ideological dogma and humanist social aspirations.

Aalto's interaction with representatives of Swedish social democratic politics and culture as well as his expanding friendships in England and the United States helped him steer out of his contemporaries' ideological polarization. Still, a leftist undertone continued in Aalto's aspiration for a "classless society," which was, for instance, the social ideal that he shared with the Gullichsens [Harry and Maire Gullichsen], the clients of his seminal Villa Mairea (1938–39).[14]

After a short period of ideological enthusiasm, however, Aalto's social and political views were dominated by his skepticism and philosophy of doubt. In a speech delivered at the centennial celebration of his high school in Jyväskylä, more than twenty years later, Aalto spoke of the virtue of doubt: "'Going outside oneself'—seeing things outside one's own limited perspective or that of the surroundings—sows the seed of doubt. The frequently despised philosophy of doubt is an absolute prerequisite for anyone wishing to contribute to culture, assuming that this doubt is transformed into a positive force. For criticism conveys the message 'I do not follow the tide,' and on the highest plane doubt can be transformed into its apparent opposite, love in a critical sense, love that endures, because it rests on critically tested ground."[15] This philosophy of doubt enabled him to shift pragmatically from one way of thinking to another without becoming ideologically tied.

Aalto expressed his critical social and political views boldly. During the invited visit of a delegation of Finnish architects to Berlin in 1943, Aalto ridiculed the Nazi ideology in a manner that bordered on the

FIGURE 05 *The Aaltos' daughter Hanni at Wright's "Fallingwater" house, Bear Run, Penn., 1940. Photo: Aino Aalto.*

Aalto's American Friendships and Connections

Aalto's ideological independence was already in evidence as he began, early on, to use America as an ironic example of a populist culture. For instance, in the late 1920s he ridiculed the sensationalism of American cinema and "the American patent" on Statues of Liberty.[21] Yet Aalto's interest in America was certainly strengthened by personal contacts with American architects and the early recognition and publication of his work in the United States.[22]

The English-speaking world gained familiarity with Aalto through the early success of his furniture in England, as well as through his acquaintance with the British journalist P. Morton Shand, who arranged the first exhibition of Aalto's furniture at Fortnum and Mason's store in London in 1933, and with the historian and critic James M. Richards, among others. But Aalto's personal contacts in America predated those in England. In 1929, the New York architectural critic Robert W. Slott got in touch with him, requesting photographs of his newest work. Philip Johnson contacted Aalto in Stockholm in 1930 and, a year later, in Berlin while preparing the seminal book *The International Style* in collaboration with Henry-Russell Hitchcock, Jr. During the mid-1930s, Aalto befriended the sculptor Alexander Calder in Paris—another American, whose sanguine attitude to life and art as well as sense of humor appealed to him. By 1933, Aalto also had made friends with the New York architect and critic Albert Frey, who planned to publish images of the Paimio Sanatorium in the *Architectural Record*, and the New York architect William Lescaze, who had designed one of the seminal American modernist buildings, the Philadelphia Savings Fund Society Building (1929–32), in collaboration with George Howe.

In 1936, Aalto met the young New York architect Harmon H. Goldstone, whose friendship was to become of great importance, particularly when Aalto made his first visit to the United States in 1938. Further, Aalto began two deep friendships in 1937, with William W. Wurster of Berkeley, California, and Lawrence B. Anderson of the Massachusetts Institute of Technology; these would become seminal for him during his later visits and successive stays in the United States, in particular for his appointment as a research professor

politically dangerous.[16] As Göran Schildt has shown, anarchistic attitudes, in the authentic sense of the notion, were characteristic for Aalto.[17] After World War II, Aalto became disillusioned with politics and democratic processes of decision-making altogether. "Biologically democracy is a very difficult process," he said in his Royal Institute of British Architects discourse in 1957.[18] As a consequence, he never voted in Finland's national and communal elections. Furthermore, he simultaneously accepted commissions from the Finnish business and industrial worlds as well as the Communist party.[19] Aalto explained his social and political independence: "Society is divided into factions, but I build for everybody. In other words, I must see society as a unity. . . . Society has devised instruments that enable various groups, such as trade unions and political parties, to promote their interest, but as an architect I cannot commit myself at this level. My starting point is that of the humanist, if such a solemn word can be used."[20]

at MIT in 1940 and his reappointment there in 1945. By the spring of 1938, Aalto had also actively established a number of acquaintances in the United States through correspondence, Richard Neutra among them.[23]

On his second trip to the United States in 1939, Aalto made friends with Frank Lloyd Wright, who became an important figure for Aalto (FIG. 5). Aalto, it is thought, even emulated some of his elder colleague's eccentric manners and impeccable style of dressing.[24] Their personal relationship has given rise to speculation and a number of legends. Their correspondence, however, confirms an intimate and mutually respectful friendship. After his visit to Taliesin in 1945, Aalto suggested to Wright that he planned to send his son Hamilkar, who was studying civil engineering in Helsinki, to apprentice with the American master.[25] The apprenticeship never took place, despite the fact that Wright responded positively: "Dear Alvar: all right. Send us your son. We will try to make as good a man as his father out of him."[26]

Yet another mutually significant friendship developed between Harry Weese and Aalto, who met at MIT shortly before the war. This personal relationship led to the establishment of the Baldwin Kingrey retail furniture store in Chicago during the summer of 1947, to which Aalto granted the Midwest franchise for Artek [the company founded by Aino and Alvar Aalto, Maire Gullichsen and Nils-Gustav Hahl in Finland in 1935 to produce and sell Aalto furniture] furniture that year.

The Baldwin Kingrey store, founded by Weese, his wife, Kitty Baldwin, and Jody Kingrey, focused on low-cost, space-saving modern furniture by Scandinavian and American designers such as Bruno Mathsson, Charles Eames, Eero Saarinen, George Nelson and Harry Weese, in addition to Alvar Aalto. The distribution of Aalto's furniture had been minimal in the United States, despite the prestigious show of Aalto's work at the Museum of Modern Art in spring 1938.[27]

The Museum of Modern Art exhibition and publication of the first book on Aalto's work, *Aalto: Architecture and Furniture*, strengthened his emotional ties with America. The architect and his first wife, Aino Marsio-Aalto, made their first trip to America in October 1938 after having won all the three prizes in the public design competition for the Finland Pavilion at the World's Fair in New York (FIGS. 6–7). Despite his rudimentary command of English, Aalto gave lectures at Yale University, the Museum of Modern Art, and New York University.

The Finland Pavilion at the 1939 World's Fair in New York was a great success professionally for Aalto. As Paul David Pearson describes, "The Finnish Pavilion attracted the interest of architects and critics alike, and for many architects it remains the one significant design that has yet to be eclipsed in its boldness and romantic modernism."[28] For Aalto personally, Frank Lloyd Wright's declaration after having visited the Finland Pavilion "Aalto is a genius" must have been especially encouraging.[29]

FIGURE 06 *The Aaltos' arrival in New York on the Gripsholm, 23 Oct. 1938. Photo: Aino Aalto.*

FIGURE 07 *Alvar Aalto in New York, 1939. Photo: Maire Gullichsen.*

The praise received by the Finland Pavilion seemed finally to open all doors for Aalto, presenting opportunities that must have appeared tempting. The lecture series Aalto conceived for Yale University and the University of California—Berkeley immediately after the opening of the New York World's Fair clearly reveals his desire for academic exposure and teaching in the United States. Aalto's outline for his seven lectures reflects the scope of his intellectual and professional interests that, as we shall see, were to develop further during his teaching and research activities at MIT as well as in his involvement with the task of reconstructing his native country after the Winter War.[30]

In addition to the wide publicity that Aalto received for the Finland Pavilion, MoMA called further attention to his work during the World's Fair, featuring it in an exhibition devoted to the five masters of modern architecture (in order of age): Frank Lloyd Wright, Ludwig Mies van der Rohe, Le Corbusier, Alvar Aalto, and Oscar Niemeyer.[31] The exhibition canonized Aalto's position in the pantheon of modern architecture.

The opportunity that American institutions provided Aalto for appearing in the role of a celebrated architect and lecturer must have been an important emotional consolation for him after he had lost the professorship of architecture at the Helsinki University of Technology to his older classicist colleague J. S. Siren in 1931. The fact that this professorship had been the chair held by his respected teacher Armas Lindgren, former partner of Eliel Saarinen, had undoubtedly increased Aalto's disappointment and sense of defeat. In the beginning of the 1930s, Aalto was still a controversial figure in the architectural circles of the Finnish capital. Onni Tarjanne, noted architect and professor, judged Aalto's qualifications for the professorial position with suspicion: "He has . . . mainly worked in the wake of the currently emerging fashionable architecture, functionalism, a style the development potential, duration, and permanent value of which cannot be foreseen."[32]

The fact that until the very end of his life Aalto preferred to use the title "professor" conveyed by his MIT appointment, regardless of the higher distinction of "academician" awarded to him in 1955 as member of the Academy of Finland, seems to echo his disappointment of 1931 and appreciation of the later academic association.

Redefining Rationalism

During his brief engagement with continental functionalist doctrine in the late 1920s and early 1930s, Aalto adopted a rationalist view of architecture. This would be reflected again in his teaching and research programs in America more than a decade later, regardless of the socialist tenor of its initial European formulation. By 1930, Aalto had appropriated a programmatic, ultra-rationalist attitude in the spirit of Hannes Meyer, to the point of questioning the relevance of a synthetic design aspiration altogether: "I do not believe that it is sensible to concentrate on synthesis in tackling an architectural assignment. . . . The Functionalist architect is an entirely different professional type from the old-style architect. In fact he is not an architect at all; he is a social administrator."[33] Aalto's extreme confidence in analytic rationalism was well illustrated by the title he used for two of his lectures at the turn of the decade, "Non-Synthetic Aspirations in Architecture," and by his initiative to publish a book in Germany with the very same title.[34]

The mid-1930s, however, brought a dramatic transition in Aalto, from that of an enthusiastic supporter of functionalism to a skeptic critical of rationalist principles, and more generally, the benefits of industrialization. This abrupt change is clearly reflected in his writings, perhaps even more so than in his designs. Aalto's conscious intellectual transitions were altogether more dramatic than the changes in his design work, which were perhaps guided more by intuition and emotion.

His subsequent conversion from rationalism was so complete that ten years later he would make a statement that exactly opposed his earlier condemnation of synthesis with equal assurance: "Architecture is a synthetic phenomenon covering practically all fields of human activity. An object in the architectural field may be functional from one point of view and unfunctional from another. . . . If there were a way to develop architecture step by step, beginning with the economic and technical aspect and later covering the other more complicated human functions, then the purely technical functionalism would be acceptable; but no such possibility exists. . . . Technical functionalism is correct only if enlarged to cover even the psychophysical field. That is the only way to humanize architecture."[35]

In the American research proposals that Aalto initiated in 1939 and 1940, he curiously returned to his earlier ideas of scientific rationality and to a research-based design approach. Presumably, the material and mental difficulties associated with the Winter War—the purely quantitatively overwhelming demands for reconstruction as well as the severe social problems brought about by the resettlement of people from the war zone—redirected Aalto back to his early rationalist ideals and confidence in the possibilities of research. In fact, at this time he seems to have been uneasily caught between the duality of analysis and synthesis. Consequently, Aalto's entire academic mission in the United States would be characterized by fervent research proposals that had the dual focus of a scientific method and a behavioral and psychological understanding of human reactions and architectural effects.

Proposals for Architectural Research

On his trip to California after the opening of the World's Fair, Aalto initiated, through William W. Wurster, a meeting on 1 June 1939 with a group of esteemed San Francisco Bay Region architects (FIG. 8). Aalto's objective was to discuss his idea of an international institute for architectural research.[36] Aalto emphasized the importance of producing studies of human reactions to different conditions, and of the need for social as well as scientific and physiological research. His idea was to establish an international institute that would feature laboratories in connection with industries and universities to study science, engineering, sociology, and other fields, centering on issues of architecture. The institute would coordinate research on architectural developments and problems in various countries. He also proposed to establish in Finland a small institute, a combined laboratory and school, for research on the small wooden house. Such a Finnish laboratory for wood research, he anticipated, would work with medical laboratories.[37]

The response of the American participants at the San Francisco meeting was polite, and a few concrete proposals were made concerning, for instance, potential sources of funding, but nobody seemed willing to commit himself to the cause. One of the participants,

Ernest Born, expressed a critical view of the Cranbrook Academy of Art, stating that it had begun as an institute of research comparable to that of Aalto's proposal, but it had turned too aesthetic and monastic.[38]

Regardless of the hesitant tone of the meeting, or, perhaps because of it, Aalto formulated a written proposal for the International Institute of Architectural Research twelve days later, after having returned to New York. In this paper, Aalto argued further for the importance of research: "Specialization, which characterizes our time, has forced us in various fields to separate research from practical production. . . . It is research in architectural

FIGURE 08 *Alvar Aalto in California, June 1939.*

synthesis itself that we need today—research in how to bind materials together, how to make a living totality from technical details—the HUMAN RESEARCH, how the human being reacts to this totality. . . . Because of this lack of research the greatest harm is . . . in the social sphere . . . the town, the village, the group of houses—HOUSING."[39] Aalto's expression "research in architectural synthesis" seems to resolve his philosophical dilemma.

Aalto then proceeded to argue in his proposal for the human basis of research: "Most of the problems which we call purely technical are solved. The next step in technical development is to become more closely merged with human needs." In his view, research in architecture cannot be carried out in a single laboratory, because architecture covers the entire field of human activity and human life: "To provide an institute for architectural research is a major world problem today requiring [an] international solution." Aalto proposed that research functions should be divided into various branches, because "some places in the world are more suitable for experimentation in some fields than others. . . . An experimental institute for artificial lighting, for instance, should be established in connection with a university, where not only architecture, but the medical sciences are especially studied." In Aalto's view, "there is no specialization in architecture. . . . Separate problems . . . belong to the same totality." Aalto ended his proposal with an assessment of contemporary architectural education: "There is today an urgent need for further education in the form of analytical and synthetic research to complete architectural teaching."[40]

In the same year, Aalto repeated his proposal for international cooperation in the field of architectural research during his lecture at the meeting of the American Federation of Art in Washington, D.C. He proposed that the institution of the World's Fair should be turned into "a permanent national educational institution in every country so that, taken together, they constituted a kind of universal school, shared by all countries."[41] Aalto returned to his pioneering ideas of research and university activities organized as an international collaboration in his ambitious research proposals at MIT and his related project for "An American Town in Finland."

The Human Side

After his return from New York to Finland, Aalto continued his idealistic projects in a proposal developed with his old friend Gregor Paulsson. Paulsson had visited Helsinki to participate in the preparation of the large Nordic Housing Exhibition initiated by Aalto.[42] Aalto's and Paulsson's proposal described an international "cultural-political periodical" designed "to bring to the knowledge of a large public in a matter-of-fact, responsible and popular way the symptoms of 'socio-biological responsibility' in the fields of culture, social life, industrial life and politics."[43] The publication project had already been discussed in the United States during Aalto's visit, as a letter from Aalto to William W. Wurster indicates. It was conceived as a six- to ten-page pamphlet to be published weekly. The contributors would be "leading, entirely independent, persons from the élite of the "democratic" countries, people with first hand knowledge of the problems the journal discusses."[44] The objective of the periodical, later titled *The Human Side*, Aalto and Paulsson stated ambitiously: "The ultimate purpose is thus a synthesis of culture, social life, industry and politics."[45]

Aalto and Paulsson might have dropped the idea because of the outbreak of war, but instead they stated in a new announcement: "In this time of war and conflict, the publication *The Human Side* is therefore considered even more important, if possible, than it would have been in a time of peace."[46] Regardless of their fairly vague plans, the editors had managed to assure a surprisingly authoritative and diversified collection of collaborators for the periodical, which certainly reflects Aalto's international reputation, and his extraordinary circle of friends deriving from the CIAM circles and his two trips to the United States.[47]

When the Soviet Union attacked Finland at the end of November 1939, the editors once more altered their plans and circulated another notice: "Since the war broke out in Finland, the character of the *The Human Side* has been revised and linked up as closely as possible with the war in Finland, but still within the ideological bounds of the original programme."[48] The further acceleration of the war, however, brought this idealistic enterprise to its final halt, as Aalto had to turn to more urgent problems.[49]

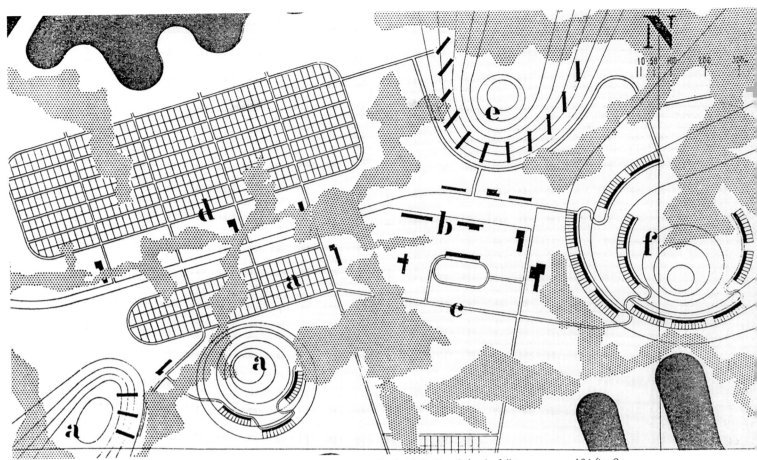

FIGURE 09 *"An American Town in Finland," a schematic plan for a model town in Finland, 1940. Detail; for the full image, see p.106 fig. 9.*

Aalto's Research Projects at MIT

In July 1940, John Burchard, director of the Albert Farwell Bemis Foundation, invited Aalto to teach and conduct research at MIT.[50] Burchard, in turn, had induced Walter R. MacCornack, dean of architecture, to appoint Aalto to the school's faculty.[51] Aalto's trip to the United States, however, was in actuality motivated by reconstruction plans in Finland. That the Finnish state authorities permitted Aalto and his family to travel to the United States during the Winter War reflects their confidence in his ability to raise economic help for Finland through his influential and wealthy American connections.

Based on his "Working Program for Architectural Research at MIT" of 3 September 1940, Aalto persuaded the Bemis Foundation and the School of Architecture to establish an architectural laboratory for examining the production of flexibly adaptable building units. The results of this academic research would be utilized in the construction of "An American Town in Finland," a project to be funded by For Finland, Incorporated, a civic fund-raising operation organized in the United States (FIG. 9).[52] As early as 17 October, however, Aalto was suddenly called back to Finland. Despite the extreme brevity of his stay in the United States, he managed to produce a schematic plan for the experimental town with his students, a rather programmatic and pedagogic illustration set within a schematized and idealized context.

In his lecture "The Reconstruction of Europe Is the Key Problem for the Architecture of Our Time," presented in Switzerland half a year after he had left his post at MIT, Aalto reported on his experiences with the "Architectural Experimental Institute of Massachusetts Institute of Technology."[53] He described his theoretical "chart method," created for the purposes of identifying variations in orientation, indicating ground characteristics in relation to the sun and to unfavorable external conditions. Any site could be described by these conditions. He also reported that he set up a "miniature factory" at the university to produce building components such as wall units, floor and roof elements, and windows at a miniature scale but complete with real technical characteristics and precision. The students were asked to design houses of a standard size using these elements in varying external and internal conditions.

Altogether, Aalto's report of his research and teaching experiment at MIT might have been exaggerated, considering that he had conducted the study for a period of only ten days. However, a letter from Dean MacCornack to the president of the Institute, which expressed regret over the fact that Aalto has been suddenly obliged to return to Finland, also highly praised the results of the study: "The work of the first group of students under Mr. Aalto's direction was completed with the exception of preparing a final report. . . . The work of this first group is exceptionally good and I feel that we were completely justified in introducing a study of housing for the very low income groups into the School of Architecture."[54] Dean MacCornack expected Aalto to return in March 1941.

By the time Aalto finally did return to Cambridge four years later in November 1945, his close friend William W. Wurster had been appointed the dean of the architecture school at MIT. But Aalto's fervent enthusiasm for research seems to have faded; he spent less and less time at MIT until 1948. A concrete reason for his diminishing involvement in research was MIT's decision to commission him in autumn 1946 to design the new seniors' dormitory, which came to be named Baker House.

Today it is evident that—regardless of Aalto's repeated ambitious proposals for research and education as elaborate systems of international cooperation, his attempt to tie academic activities at MIT with the construction of an entirely new experimental town in his own country, and his contribution to research as a professor—the architect's lasting impact on education as well as design thinking in America lies in the actual buildings that he managed to complete there, Baker House notable among them. "I cannot answer in words, I would rather answer with buildings," Aalto replied in 1953 to questions posed by the editor of *Arkkitehti*

(*Finnish Architectural Review*).[55] He was himself acknowledging the fact that the real synthesis of his thinking was to be found in his architectural designs rather than in his theoretical formulations.

Aalto's Views of American Architecture

Alvar Aalto used his contacts to have the "America Builds" exhibition, organized by the Museum of Modern Art and shown in Stockholm in 1944, to be shown also in Helsinki at the beginning of 1945, during the ceasefire with the Soviet Union. In his essay written in conjunction with the exhibition, Aalto provided an introduction to the history of American architecture. "[F]rom a doctrinaire perspective, American architecture seems to have a more superficial intellectual basis [than European architecture], but in reality its influence on practical life is stronger ... An excellent example is provided by Thomas Jefferson, the true father of American neoclassicism ... above all, however, he was the real originator of the democratic way of thinking and democratic forms of American everyday life."[56]

In another essay written for the same occasion, his somewhat surprising preface to the exhibition catalogue, Aalto praised American pragmatist attitudes, the democratic character of American architecture, the unconstrained and adaptive character of American colonial architecture, the spontaneous character of the ghost towns in the Sierra Nevada deriving from the time of the Gold Rush, and the indigenous Indian adobe structures of Arizona and Colorado. He also gave deserved praise to Henry Hobson Richardson as a strong influence over late-nineteenth and early-twentieth-century architecture in Europe and Finland, to Louis Sullivan, and, of course, to Frank Lloyd Wright. Of this final man Aalto wrote, "To be sure, his buildings are not rationalist architecture in the ordinary sense of the term, as they contain mystic elements and reflect a remarkable quest for decorative values, but even here he has often proved right even in the most recent years ... Frank Lloyd Wright seeks a form of society in which present-day antitheses can be juxtaposed and brought into harmony."[57]

At the end of his preface, Aalto praised the America of the New Deal: "Lately— particularly during the

Roosevelt administration—deliberate plans, even out-right planned economy has advanced in social planning. At the same time that the Russian five-year plan and England, France, and Germany paid attention to social aspects of city planning, the planned construction of great wilderness areas and the rebuilding of old communities was begun in America. The programmed construction of the Tennessee Valley, the planning of power plants, road networks, and residential centers attached to them as well as a multitude of social experiments are examples of this."[58]

Two years later, Aalto wrote an essay titled "Culture and Technology" for the Suomi-Finland-USA publication of 1947 in which he stated: "In any case, America is the land that anticipates the future of the world at large, warts and all. Apart from all the progress made, the industrial culture of America also contains its own "corrigenda."[59] Aalto's positive and active attitude toward the United States immediately after the war is also reflected in the fact that from 1945 to 1948 he was a member of the board of the Finland–America Association.[60]

The Finland–America Association (renamed The League of Finnish–American Societies in 1972) was founded on 1 July 1943. Its organizers felt that Finnish–American relations could be improved by establishing such an association to promote mutual understanding. Widely noted abroad, the creation of the association was regarded as a significant political phenomenon. The initial statute defining its purpose reads: "The aim of the Association is the advancement of relations between Finland and the United States." As an active member, Aalto spoke on American architecture and, at the beginning of 1945, helped in organizing the "America Builds" exhibition, which was seen by twenty thousand visitors, at the time a huge number for an exhibition on architecture.

Aalto's designs for the library of the U.S. consulate in Helsinki and for a partly subterranean twenty-car garage next to the ambassador's residence (1948), which was topped by a garden terrace with a roof punctured by sixteen pyramidal skylights, are further indications of his continued good relations with Americans (**FIGS. 10, 11**). He was also asked to design a new ambassadorial residence, but the project never advanced. In addition to the Finland Pavilion at the 1939 World's Fair in New York, and the Baker House senior dormitory for MIT (1946–49), Aalto completed two interiors in the United States—the Woodberry Poetry Room in the Lamont

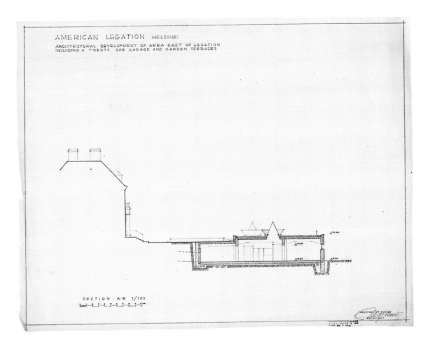

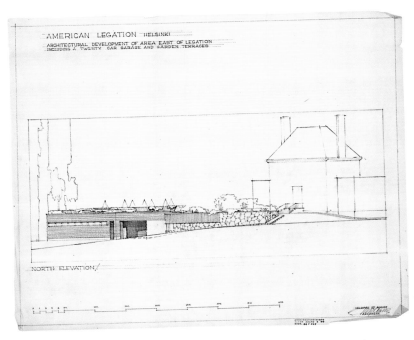

FIGURES 10–11 *Aalto, American Embassy, Helsinki, unexecuted garage with garden terrace, 1948. Section and northeast facade.*

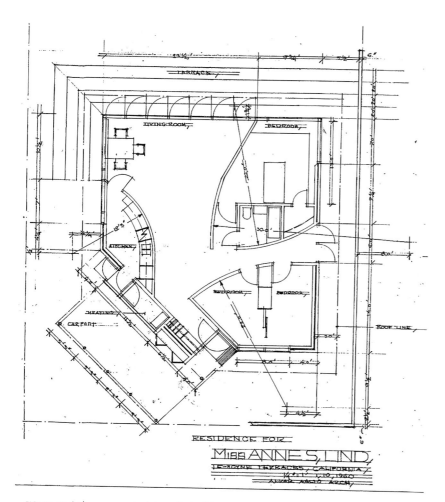

FIGURE 12 *Aalto, unexecuted Anne S. Lind house, Le Moyne Terraces, Calif., 1960. Plan.*

Library at Harvard University (1948) and the Edgar J. Kaufmann Conference Rooms at the Institute of International Education in New York (1963–64)—along with his third major project, Mount Angel Abbey Library in St. Benedict, Oregon (1963–70). In 1960, Anne S. Lind requested a design for a small house in California, and assistants in Aalto's office engaged in a playful design competition **(FIG. 12)**.

Aalto Turns Critical of American Culture

Immediately after the war, Aalto began to receive enticing commissions at home (albeit mostly through competitions), and in spite of the success of Baker House, he must have felt that, most authentically, his architecture derived from the Nordic soil and cultural

context. Regardless of his initial enthusiasm, by the late 1940s, Aalto began to develop a mental distance from the American reality.

In the years after the war, Aalto became increasingly disillusioned and disappointed with his former ideals. His philosophy of doubt made him skeptical of a theory-based approach to architecture, of the generative role of technology, and of rationalized design methods based on research and teamwork. In fact, from the mid-1960s onward, an ideological opposition developed between Aalto and his followers, on the one hand, and the young generation that had a confidence in the ideals that Aalto had supported early on in his career, on the other. He even became doubtful about democratic institutions as the clients of the architect. During the 1950s, he began to make increasingly sarcastic comments about America. He declared, "Even today it remains the fashion to copy, let us say, Hollywood, the most badly constructed city that I know," and "I recently read in *The New York Times* that a new kind of freedom had been invented, namely the freedom for the White House to withhold all important national security considerations from the public."[61]

He was equally critical of the course American architecture was taking. In a lecture in Vienna he stated, "Occasionally the problems of architecture are treated quite superficially, as in New York harbor, where tourists are asked on arrival: 'Are you modern or old-fashioned?'"[62] At another time he wrote, "Let us take some capital of entertainment—Hollywood, for instance. Of course all the houses are modern. [But] you can find very few houses that give human beings the spirit of the real physical life."

By the late 1950s, Aalto saw the future of architecture quite pessimistically and associated the negative formalist tendencies with America: "The horoscope for architecture today is so bad that my words are bound to be negative—that's no fun. The parallelepiped of glass squares and artificial metals—the inhuman dandy-purism of big cities—has produced a form of building from which there is no return. . . . Often [such housing areas] are like commercial fairs, and the public buildings exude a propagandistic formalism—industrial design and the awful imbalance of American cars."[63] In another instance he declared, "The freedom required by human nature has come into conflict with industrial mass production in America. While Americans

FIGURE 13 *Aalto, sketch for the Metropolitan Opera House, Lincoln Center, New York, 1956.*

FIGURE 14 Alvar Aalto, "Cape Cod, Hurricane," pencil sketch (1946).

today eat hygienically packaged and chilled food, and generally enjoy the benefits of systematic large-scale production, they also consult doctors more often than before."[64]

What exactly gave rise to Aalto's negativity toward American culture is unknown. His personal disappointments with his participation in the teams of international experts for the United Nations Headquarters (1947) and the Metropolitan Opera House in New York (1956) suggest at least two concrete explanations (FIG. 13).[65] The anti-Americanism of Aalto's later age is intriguing in relation to the fact that, since the early 1950s, America had served as a popular ideal of lifestyle in Finland —a country that has sometimes been jokingly labeled by foreign journalists as "the most American country outside of America." Perhaps

the emerging American values and informal style of life in his own country had become a source of irritation for the aging academician, who continued to be a supporter of classical European education, values, and manners.

During his years of active contact with the United States, Aalto must have been seriously considering the prospect of immigrating to that country, particularly given that the political situation of Finland might have turned intolerable for him, a potential consequence of the lost war against the Soviets. At the same time, Aalto's research-related activities in the United States during the war functioned, in part, as sincere attempts to raise economic, military, and political help for Finland. It is likely that Aalto wanted to maintain a foothold in America in case the war ended in a catastrophe for Finland. The success of many of his Bauhaus and CIAM friends in the New World as well as Eliel Saarinen's celebrated career as president of the Cranbrook Academy of Art served as encouraging precedents.[66] Since his youth, Aalto had envisioned America as the land of opportunity. Further, he found that those who had challenged his professional horizons were now open to him, given that his home country was entering the uncertain period of reconstruction and psychological recovery from the war.

Why did Aalto eventually decide to return to his homeland? Regardless of his cosmopolitan and internationalist character, deep in his personality Aalto remained emotionally tied to the Nordic landscape, culture, and values of life. Aalto viewed architecture, not as an abstract and contextually detached professional practice, but rather as a mediation between landscape, material culture, and people.

As Sigfried Giedion wrote of Aalto at the time he was already distancing himself from American ideals, "Finland is with Aalto wherever he goes. It provides him with that inner source of energy which always flows through his work. It is as Spain is to Picasso or Ireland to James Joyce. Part of the essence of present-day art is that its true representatives originate in a definite human environment and their work is not created in a vacuum."[67]

Alvar Aalto designed projects and built buildings in a dozen countries, but he chose to live and work in Finland all his life with the exception of his fairly short stays in the United States. His artistic sensibilities grew from the Finnish landscape and cultural soil to the degree that even his architectural works abroad are reflections of the characteristics of his Nordic homeland.

1 Reino Kero, *Suureen Länteen: Siirtolaisuus Suomesta Pohjois-Amerikkaan* [To the Great West: Immigration from Finland to North America] (Turku, Finland: Siirtolaisinstituutti, 1996).

2 Individuals born in Finland and their children are included in this number. Kero, *Suureen Länteen*, 131.

3 Kero, *Suureen Länteen*, 59–61.

4 On Nat Pinkerton, see Alvar Aalto, "A Fireside Story" (1921), in *Alvar Aalto in His Own Words, ed.* Göran Schildt (New York: Rizzoli, 1998), 12–13; on Huckleberry Finn, see Alvar Aalto, "Eldorado" (1921), in *Alvar Aalto in His Own Words*, Schildt, 13–15.

5 Alvar Aalto, "Menneitten aikojen motiivit," *Arkkitehti* 2 (1922); published in translation as "Motifs from Past Ages," in *Alvar Aalto in His Own Words*, Schildt, 32–5.

6 As an indication of the exceptional esteem held for Eliel Saarinen by members of his profession, the Finnish architectural journal *Arkitekten* greeted Saarinen, who had already settled in the United States, with an admiring and respectful fiftieth-birthday editorial article in 1923: *Arkitekten* 7 (1923): 97 [the editor-in-chief in 1923 was Carolus Lindberg].

7 "I was nine years old when first I saw the work of Eliel Saarinen. It was an early winter morning. The mail, brought by the train which had come from the south, lay on the family living room table. From among the newspapers and letters I selected a magazine which caught my eye, an attractive, red-covered periodical with a heraldic lion decorating the cover, *The Young Finland*. It contained . . . two

pages of colored pictures—architectural illustrations. Hardly any text at all accompanied these pictures, only the word 'Interior' in the lower left corner and the name 'Eliel Saarinen' in the lower right. . . . The impression made upon me by those architectural drawings was incredible. I became aware, so early, of the work of Eliel Saarinen. . . . My second view of Eliel Saarinen came when I, too, went to the United States and saw him against the broader horizon of the architecture of the Western world. During my periodic visits to the Massachusetts Institute of Technology I heard many discussions about design and Eliel Saarinen's contribution to contemporary architecture." Alvar Aalto, foreword to *Eliel Saarinen*, by Albert Christ-Janer (Chicago: Univ. of Chicago Press, 1948), ix–x. As a young architect Aalto was critical of the National Romantic architecture of which Saarinen was a representative. The relationship of the two compatriots became closer, however, when Saarinen visited his old homeland in 1936 and, a few years later, when Aalto was visiting and working in the United States. When Eliel Saarinen died in 1950, Aalto wrote an obituary that remained unpublished until recently. In it Aalto praised Saarinen's *oeuvre* and related Saarinen's work to a wider cultural philosophy: "In honouring his memory and the greatness of his work, we Finns feel such pride, joy, and gratitude that it cannot be readily expressed in a few words. Rather, our emotion is crystallized in the serene awareness that his creations and his vital contribution to the culture of his era will persist, as will his influence on future generations." Alvar Aalto, Eliel Saarinen obituary (1950, Alvar Aalto Archive); reprinted in *Alvar Aalto in His Own Words*, Schildt, 246.

8 Göran Schildt, *Alvar Aalto: The Decisive Years* (New York: Rizzoli, 1986), 166–67. The subject matter of Aalto's lecture is not known.

9 David Paul Pearson, *Alvar Aalto and the International Style* (New York: Whitney Library of Design, 1978), 188.

10 The acceptera group included Sven Markelius, Uno Åhrén, Erik Gunnar Asplund, Eskil Sundahl, Wolter Barclay Gahn, and Gregor Paulsson. The film club was founded on 7 March 1935, and its last showing took place in May 1936. The club closed due to deliberate measures by authorities that made its activity economically impossible. Schildt, *Decisive Years*, 114–16.

11 Schildt, *Decisive Years*, 87.

12 Alvar Aalto, "Hyvä asunto," *Soihtu*, 1932, published by Cay Sundström and Mauri Ryömä; excerpted as "A Good Home," in *Alvar Aalto in His Own Words*, Schildt, 76.

13 Alvar Aalto, "The Human Side as a Political Option for the Western World" (1939), in *Alvar Aalto in His Own Words*, Schildt, 115.

14 Aalto's Swedish leftist friends criticized him for accepting such an exclusive commission. Aalto's insistent description of the project as an experiment applicable in standard housing seems to be a rationalization against such accusations. Author's interview with Paul Bernoulli in Helsinki, 22 Aug. 1993.

15 Alvar Aalto, keynote speech at the centenary of Aalto's school, the Jyväskylä Lyceum, published as "What is Culture?" (1958), in *Alvar Aalto in His Own Words*, Schildt, 15–17.

16 This group of Finnish architects, working in the Reconstruction Bureau set up by the Finnish Association of Architects in 1942, was invited to visit Germany by Ernst Neufert. The delegation included Alvar Aalto, Aarne Ervi, Viljo Rewell, and Esko Suhonen. In an interview, Esko Suhonen recalled Aalto's bold public speeches in Germany during the visit of the Finnish delegation. Kirmo Mikkola, *Aalto* (Jyväskylä, Finland: Gummerus, 1985), 18.

17 Göran Schildt, "Anarchism as an Architectural Principle," in his *Alvar Aalto: The Early Years* (New York: Rizzoli, 1984), 242–59.

18 Alvar Aalto, RIBA Annual Discourse (1957) reprinted as "The Enemies of Good Architecture," in *Alvar Aalto in His Own Words*, Schildt, 204.

19 The Finnish Communist Party commissioned the House of Culture in Helsinki, one of Aalto's seminal works, in 1952. The sketches were finalized in 1955, and the building inaugurated in 1958.

20 Alvar Aalto, in interview for Finnish Television conducted by Göran Schildt, July 1972; transcription published *in Alvar Aalto in His Own Words*, Schildt, 269–75.

21 Alvar Aalto, "The Rational Cinema" (1928), in *Alvar Aalto in His Own Words*, Schildt, 71; Aalto, "An Independence Monument in Helsinki: The Olympic Stadium" (1927), in *Alvar Aalto in His Own Words*, Schildt, 66.

22 The following information on Aalto's American contacts derives mainly from Schildt, *Decisive Years*. 165–186.

23 Pearson, *Alvar Aalto*, 188. Aalto requested the address of Neutra, his acquaintance from CIAM meetings, from William W. Wurster.

24 Yrjö O. Alanen, psychoanalyst and emeritus professor of psychiatry, as well as Aalto's son-in-law, remarks on Wright's influence on his father-in-law's character: "When I first became acquainted with Alvar upon my engagement to Hanni in summer 1951 . . . he dressed in white shirts adorned with cuff links and fine sombre suits, or stylish informal leisurewear sporting silk cravats at the throat. It is claimed that he received the final sartorial touch from his new friend, Frank Lloyd Wright." Alanen, "Alvar Aalto—Fragments in Close-up," *ptah* 1 (2004): 46.

25 "Words cannot express how very much the visit to Talieson [sic] has meant to me—both in head and heart reactions. But I will say this . . . if it is acceptable to you, I shall immediately make arrangements to take my boy out of the Technical University in Helsinki, where he is taking the combined studies of Civil Engineering and Architecture and will send him to you by next summer or the following autumn. Will you, please, let me know if this will be acceptable to you." Letter from Alvar Aalto to Frank Lloyd Wright, 13 Dec. 1945, sent from MIT, in Cambridge, Mass. (Frank Lloyd Wright Foundation/Alvar Aalto Foundation) [A copy of the letter in the Frank Lloyd Wright Foundation is in the Alvar Aalto Foundation]

26 Letter from Frank Lloyd Wright to Alvar Aalto (at), 23 Jan. 1946 (Frank Lloyd Wright Foundation/Alvar Aalto Foundation).Another example of the intimate friendship between Wright and Aalto is the fact that in 1957, when Aalto was beginning to work on his art museum project in Baghdad, he sent a telegram to his American colleague inquiring about the percentage of the architect's fee that Wright had received for his work in Baghdad. In 1957 King Faisal invited several renowned architects to design important cultural and government buildings in Baghdad. Frank Lloyd Wright was commissioned to design a combined theatre and opera house, Aalto an art museum and central post office. (Göran Schildt, *Alvar Aalto: A Life's Work – Architecture, Design and Art* (Keuruu: Otava Publishing Company Ltd, 1994), 122) Telegram from Aalto to Wright, 2 July 1957 (Alvar Aalto Foundation archives). Again Wright responded, despite his advanced age (ninety): "Dear Alvar fee complete service including engineering and supervision ten percent of total cost of operation." Telegram from Wright to Aalto, 9 July 1957 (Archives of the Alvar Aalto Foundation).

27 John Brunetti, *Baldwin Kingrey: Midcentury Modern in Chicago, 1947–1957* (Chicago: Wright, 2004), 11, 13–14.

28 Pearson, *Alvar Aalto*, 184.

29 Göran Schildt, *Alvar Aalto: The Mature Years* (New York: Rizzoli, 1991), 244.

30 None of these lectures was ultimately delivered in California; the entire series was presented at Yale University in April and May 1939. Aalto's ambitious outline for the series contained seven lectures:

I. The problem of humanizing architecture;
II. Psychology—and problems of humanization—in town planning. The social value of humanizing the principles of town planning;
III. The problem of concentration of large groups of dwellings; the apartment dwelling; various concentrated types of dwelling. The protection of the individual and of the family unit in the midst of a large group;
IV. The problem of the small dwelling, its relation to town planning and mass production, its type and standard production;
V. The problem of standardized architectural forms. Humanizing standardization;
VI. Public buildings of collective function. The humane protection of the individual against the harmful influences of the great mass;
VII. The human dwelling—architecture—and its relation to the fine arts. The position of the fine arts in daily life and their architectural arrangement. (This lecture is based on Mr. Aalto's recently finished building [Villa Mairea], a family dwelling, where the family is especially interested in modern fine arts).

Appended to letter from Aalto to William W. Wurster, 29 March 1939 (William Wilson Wurster Archives, Environmental Design Archives, Univ. of California, Berkeley).

31 Peter MacKeith and Kerstin Smeds, *The Finland Pavilions: Finland at the Universal Expositions, 1900–1992* (Helsinki: Kustannus Oy City, 1992), 52.

32 Despite this remark, Onni Tarjanne concluded his evaluation with optimism: "Undoubtedly he is very talented and possesses noteworthy artistic qualifications which will probably in the future, if given the opportunity, even leave beautiful traces in our architecture." Quoted in Juhani Pallasmaa, "Alvar Aalto: Toward a Synthetic Functionalism," in *Alvar Aalto: Between Humanism and Materialism*, ed. Peter Reed (New York: Museum of Modern Art, 1998), 28. See also Raija-Liisa Heinonen, *Funktionalismin läpimurto Suomessa* [Breakthrough of functionalism in Finland](Helsinki: Museum of Finnish Architecture, 1986), 40.

33 Alvar Aalto, interview, *Nidaros* (Trondheim, Norway), 28 June 1930; quoted in Schildt, *Decisive Years*, 196.

34 Aalto held lectures at the Swedish Association of Engineers and Architects on November 18, 1929 and at the Finnish Association of Architects' annual meeting on February 16, 1932, but only the title of these two lectures remains, "Non-synthetic aspirations in architecture". In the summer of 1930 Aalto corresponded with Otto Völkers, the editor of Stein Holz Eisen about publishing a book with the same title "nicht synthetische bestrebungen in der architektur (the title excludes capital letters in accordance with the Bauhaus principle). The book was never published.

35 Alvar Aalto, "The Humanizing of Architecture" (1940), in *Alvar Aalto in His Own Words*, ed. Schildt, 102–7.

36 According to a memo containing thirty-four notes, the meeting was held in Wurster's office and the participants were Alvar Aalto, Ernest Born, Thomas Church, Gardner Dailey, Timothy Pflueger, and Wurster (William Wilson Wurster Archives).

37 Memo cited in preceding note, with references to Aalto's contribution. By collaboration with medical laboratories Aalto is presumably thinking of the psychological and physiological aspects of architecture, which he mentions frequently in his lectures and articles in the mid-1930s. In his lecture in Italy (1956), Aalto had called his Paimio Sanatorium (1929–33) "a medical instrument."

38 Memo cited in preceding notes.

39 Memo from Alvar Aalto to William W. Wurster, 13 June 1939 (William Wilson Wurster Archives).

40 Memo cited in preceding note.

41 Alvar Aalto, "Maailmannäyttelyt: New York World's Fair/The Golden Gate Exposition," *Arkkitehti* 8 (1939), published as "Comments on the 1930 World's Fair in New York," in *Alvar Aalto in His Own Words*, Schildt, 120-2.

42 The exhibition was opened on 7 Oct. 1939, but it was forced to close four days later because of the general order for mobilization (related to the Winter War). Schildt, *Decisive Years*, 182.

43 On 25 Oct. 1939, Aalto sent a letter to William W. Wurster containing the first program of the periodical. He also refers to discussions on this kind of an initiative during his trip to the United States (William Wilson Wurster Archives).

44 Göran Schildt, *Decisive Years,* 183.

45 Göran Schildt, *Decisive Years,* 182.

46 Quoted in Schildt, *Decisive Years,* 183.

47 The imposing list of would-be contributors included, among others, Alexis Carrel, Walter Gropius, László Moholy-Nagy, Lewis Mumford, Gunnar Myrdal, George Bernard Shaw, James Johnson Sweeney, and Frank Lloyd Wright. According to notes in the Alvar Aalto Archive, Eugene O'Neill, Ernest Hemingway, and Sinclair Lewis were also contacted. See Schildt, *Decisive Years,* 183–85. In a letter of Oct. 1939, Aalto invited Frank Lloyd Wright to contribute to the planned journal: "Mr. Gregor Paulsson from Uppsala and I have together with many Scandinavian friends founded a magazine of special nature. . . . It can probably help to solve the difficulties of all northern States [Nordic countries], this is the only part of the world, which is like your country and which is developing under the same kind of system as America. — I ask you, could you possibly become an author of this magazine, we think that you are just the man, whose help we need most. My sincere hope is that you will kindly accept." Alvar Aalto's letter to Frank Lloyd Wright, 24 Oct. 1939 (Frank Lloyd Wright Foundation/Alvar Aalto Foundation). [The letter in the files of the Alvar Aalto Foundation is a copy of the original in FLW Foundation.]

48 Quoted in Schildt, *Decisive Years,* 184.

49 A month after the outbreak of the war, Aalto again contacted Frank Lloyd Wright with a request for help: "As you know, the first real open fighting of the world-war has begun in Finland. It is the Russian terror-system which now shows its will to expand all over the world. . . . With this letter I send you some enclosures which show the real significance of the struggle and its technical possibilities as, I hope, that this will confirm to you the idea that the battle is 'our common'—in a way a religious battle. . . . The principle necessity is an increase of the aerial defence of Finland, i.e. international voluntary air-fighters with complete equipment. . . . Personally, I have a feeling that a special organization should be founded among technicians, architects, artists and literary people in your country, with this purpose as their solitary aim. . . . Dear Friend, it is perhaps a little unexpected that today my language is imbued with necessity of the fight, instead of constructive philosophy, but after all, our world is of no value if this fight against everybody, against intellectual creation, against constructive progress of development and against positive results already achieved does not turn out a victory [the logic of the sentence seems to be erroneously reversed]. If you can do anything, preferably in the shape of an organization as hinted at, please let me know from time to time how you progress." In the three-page attachment to the letter, Aalto gave a devastating criticism of the Soviet revolution: "The struggle,

originally of an ideal nature, adopted as a method a heritage from the Russia of the Tsars—the police-power. This permanent terror, which, by and by, has grown predominant, has made the realisation of a balanced life and organized economy impossible in that land of revolution even though its size is almost that of a continent and it thus should not be hindered by outside obstructions." Aalto to Wright, 8 Jan. 1940 (Frank Lloyd Wright Foundation / Alvar Aalto Foundation).

50 Pearson, *Alvar Aalto,* 194. The Bemis Foundation at MIT had already intensely focused on rationalizing the design and production of homes, especially the problems of prefabrication in wood. See Pekka Korvenmaa, "Crisis as Catalyst: Finnish Architecture, Alvar Aalto and the Second World War; A Case in Strategic Decision-Making," in the published proceedings of the Sixth International Alvar Aalto Symposium, *Architecture of the Essential* (Vammala: Alvar Aalto Symposium, 1995), 84.

51 "Alvar Aalto, distinguished Finnish architect who was chosen to direct reconstruction of his country following the Russian invasion, will join the faculty of the MIT School of Architecture for the new academic year, Dean MacCornack has announced. After spending some time in Finland starting the program of reconstruction, Mr. Aalto will return in the late fall to serve as research professor in architecture." *Pencil Points* 21, suppl. 22 (Sept. 1940).

52 A group of Americans founded the For Finland, Incorporated project. Korvenmaa, "Crisis as Catalyst," 83. See also Pekka Korvenmaa, "A Bridge of Wood: Aalto, American House Production, and Finland" in the present volume. The entire project came to an end due to concurrent political developments. Finland was forced to take sides between the two powers and chose Germany and its Axis allies. Later England and the Allied forces declared war on Finland and cooperation between the United States and Finland became impossible.

53 The lecture was originally published in *Arkkitehti* 5 (1941) and is reprinted in *Alvar Aalto in His Own Words,* Schildt, 149-57.

54 Letter from Walter R. MacCornack, dean, to Karl T. Compton, president of MIT, 23 Oct. 1940 (Massachusetts Institute of Technology Archives).

55 Alvar Aalto, "Julkisten rakennusten dekadenssi," *Arkkitehti* 9-10 (1953); translated as "The Decline of Public Architeture" in *Alvar Aalto in His Own Words,* Schildt, 210-1.

56 Alvar Aalto, "Amerikka Rakentaa" [America builds], *Arkkitehti* 1 (1945); translated as "The Intellectual Background of American Architecture," in *Alvar Aalto in His Own Words,* Schildt, 131–6.

57 Alvar Aalto, "Amerikkalaisen rakennustaiteen traditio ja sen nykyisyys", [The Tradition and Present of American Architecture], preface to *Amerikka rakentaa,* catalogue of the exhibition organized by the Association of Finnish Architects and the Finnish–American Society in the Ateneum Museum of Art, Jan. 6–21, 1945 (Helsinki: Suomalaisen kirjallisuuden seuran kirjapaino, 1945), 6–19. The same passage is translated in "The Intellectual Background," in *Alvar Aalto in His Own Words,* Schildt, 135.

58 Aalto, preface to *Amerikka Rakentaa,* 136.

59 Alvar Aalto, "Kulttuuri ja tekniikka/Culture and Technology," *Suomi-Finland-USA* publication, 1947; fully translated as "The Dichotomy of Culture and Technology," in *Alvar Aalto in His Own Words,* Schildt, 136–7.

60 The United States made attempts to keep Finland outside the wider theater of war, but after England declared war against Finland in Dec. 1941, Finnish relations with the United States worsened; the U.S. diplomatic presence was minimized and the ambassador was called back in Dec. 1942. In order to realize its aims, the Finland–America Association attempted to improve knowledge of Finland in the United States through dissemination of information and other means, and to familiarize Finnish citizens with the spiritual and economic life as well as the national and social order of the United States through lectures, artistic events, literature, and other related means. *Suomi–Amerikka Yhdistysten Liitto,* 1943–1993, fiftieth-anniversary publication of the League of Finnish–American Societies (Helsinki: 1993), v; and *Suomi–Amerikka Yhdistysten Liitto,* 1943–2003, sixtieth-anniversary publication of the League of Finnish–American Societies (Helsinki: 2003), 7.

61 Alvar Aalto, "Schöner Wohnen," lecture delivered at the Verband der deutschen Teppich- und Möbelstoff-Industrien, Munich, 15 Nov. 1957; published as "More Beautiful Housing," in *In His Own Words,"* Schildt, 177.

62 "The RIBA Annual Discourse", 1957, in *In His Own Words,* 202.

63 Alvar Aalto, "Artikkelin asemasta," *Arkkitehti* 1–2 (1958), translated as "In Lieu of an Article," in *Alvar Aalto in His Own Words,* Schildt, 264.

64 Aalto, "The Dichotomy of Culture and Technology" in *Alvar Aalto in His Own Words,* Schildt, 136.

65 Aalto was invited by his old friend Wallace K. Harrison to participate in the preliminary planning of Lincoln Center. Aalto worked in Harrison's office for ten days in Oct. 1956, proposing to build the entire center on a raised platform surrounded by closed walls, as "a fortification of silence." His ideas were not followed. Schildt, *Alvar Aalto: A Life's Work,* 103.

66 In addition to members of the multi-gifted Saarinen family, two Finnish women artists made successful careers at the Cranbrook Academy of Art: the textile artist Marianne Strengell and the ceramist Maija Grotell. Saarinen had also invited the Finnish sculptor Gunnar Finne as the sculptor-in-residence, but the fine, classicizing sculptor preferred to work in his homeland. George Booth and Saarinen even contacted Finland's "national painter" Akseli Gallén-Kallela during his extended stay in America (1923–26) and offered challenging and tempting commissions at Cranbrook. Juhani Pallasmaa, "The Finnish Vision at Cranbrook," *Form Function Finland* 2 (1984): 18–27.

67 Sigfried Giedion, *Space, Time and Architecture: The Growth of a New Tradition,* 2nd ed. (Cambridge, Mass.: Harvard Univ. Press, 1949), 455.

Aalto Goes to America

Eeva-Liisa Pelkonen

"Finland is with Aalto wherever he goes," Sigfried Giedion exclaimed in the article "Irrationality and Standard" in 1941.[1] Emphasis on Aalto's national origin has since become a dominant way to explain his architecture and persona. In this essay I will show that the concepts that we now use almost interchangeably to describe Aalto's architecture—national, international, regional, vernacular—were highly politically charged. In order to highlight their historicity I will focus on a particular period and place, around the year 1940, when Aalto's transnational contacts were focused on America. The discussion will cover some eight years around the Second World War, when the meanings of these concepts were particularly unstable. The cross-continental exchanges added to their fluidity.

First Contacts with the Museum of Modern Art: The Geopolitics of Fame

Aalto's first contacts with the Museum of Modern Art took place at the 1937 Exhibition Internationale des Arts et des Techniques Appliqués à a la Vie Moderne in Paris , where the Finnish Pavilion attracted the attention of museum affiliates. Among them was Henry-Russell Hitchcock, Jr., who in *Architectural Forum* singled out Aalto as "the greatest individual architect represented in the Exhibition."[2] The rise of nationalist sentiment in Europe turned out to be Aalto's good fortune: the exhibition was marked by the absence of works by most modernist architects, whom Hitchcock had championed in the "Modern Architecture: International Exhibition" of 1932—Le Corbusier's Pavillon des Temps Nouveau being the only exception.[3] When countries central to the development of the international modern movement—France, Germany, Russia, and Italy—turned to neoclassical monumentalism, the exhibition became a showcase of modernism from the smaller countries like Finland, Czechoslovakia, and Sweden, all of which gained Hitchcock's praise. Aalto's pavilion, designed in collaboration with his wife Aino, formed a particularly stark contrast to the scale of the surrounding buildings: the mostly one-storey, wood-clad building was located next to Palais de Chaillot at Trocadero at the end of the main axis along which most of the main pavilions were located. Its staggered massing that negotiated the wooden and sloped site formed an antithesis to the imposing order around it.

The fact that Aalto was already an internationally known architect at that time certainly helped him gain further attention. The Turun Sanomat Building had been featured in the 1932 "Modern Architecture: International Exhibition," organized by Hitchcock and Philip Johnson, and in the subsequent book entitled *International Style: Architecture since 1922*. Hitchcock, in fact, situated the Paris fair pavilion as still within the legacy of 1920s architectural modernism, albeit in its wooden version: It "offer[ed] possibilities of light construction in birch wood" without compromising those formal qualities of architecture the author identified as the constituent blocks for International Style architecture.[4] Hitchcock praised the "varied plan," "composition," and "spatial qualities" of the building choreographed around distinct spatial experiences:[5] the visitor entered through an intimate courtyard, then meandered through the mostly one-storey building, which had exhibitions organized around the perimeter and under light wells, before finishing the tour in a double-high sky-lit exhibition hall. The pavilion seemed to prove Hitchcock's and Johnson's assessment from 1932 that "if controlled by aesthetics, [wood] certainly lends itself to . . . the international style."[6]

After viewing the pavilion, John McAndrew, the curator of the department of architecture at the Museum of Modern Art, invited Aalto on the spot to have a solo exhibition at his museum, an honor the museum had granted to only one architect prior to that date: Le Corbusier in 1936. The subsequent exhibition catalogue, *Architecture and Furniture: Aalto*, was the first single-architect monograph published on Aalto's work and the first ever on a living architect published by MoMA. The exhibition opened on 15 March 1938, only a year after the Paris exhibition.

McAndrew's decision to invest in Aalto invites us to consider how Aalto fits into the curatorial and ideological agenda of MoMA. After all, Aalto was still a relatively unknown figure in America and was unlikely to draw huge crowds. The reasoning seems to have been two-fold. First, Aalto showed that European modern architecture was still alive despite the fact that many of its pioneers were forced to immigrate to the United States. Second, the representatives of MoMA must have also realized that, in order to stay alive, modernism had to provide an alternative to the monumental classicism present at the Paris exhibition. If that was the case, singling out Aalto for a retrospective at MoMA resulted, at least in part, from the rise of nationalist sentiments in Europe. Aalto's use of wood and quasi-vernacular motifs offered a path for modernism's future development.

Whatever the motives might have been, MoMA can be credited with cementing Aalto's reputation as a leading figure of the modern movement. The MoMA show, for example, occurred eleven years before Giedion's inclusion of Aalto as one of the modern masters in the second edition of *Space, Time and Architecture: The Birth of a Tradition*. In his foreword to the exhibition catalogue, McAndrew identified Aalto as one of "the younger men who have since then joined the established leaders",[7] and continued to state, following Hitchcock, that "among these none is more important than Aalto."[8] Yet, where Hitchcock emphasized continuity, McAndrew saw a larger paradigm shift within the modern movement.

In McAndrew's view, Aalto's and his generation's task was to reassess the legacy of modernism. Aalto's material and formal sensibility departed from the white, geometric purism of the 1920s, which had been represented at the museum's "Modern Architecture:

International Exhibition." McAndrew wrote: "Like the design of other men first active in the '30s, Aalto's work, without ceasing in any way to be modern, does not look like the modern work of the '20s. The younger men employ new materials and new methods of construction, of course, but these only partly explain the change. The buildings of men working naturally in an already established style are less assertive of that style's tenets than those earlier and more puristic buildings, which were establishing the style with a necessarily stringent discipline." McAndrew then continued to define the shifts and re-engagements of the new generation: "Certain materials and forms once renounced because of their association with non-modern work are now used again, in new ways or even in the old ones. To the heritage of pure geometric shapes, the younger men have added free organic curves; to the stylistic analogies with the painters Mondrian and Legér, they have added Arp."[9]

As all critics, McAndrew viewed his object from a particular vantage point, in this case, one informed by American art discourse of the late 1930s. He borrowed the idea that the modern movement was experiencing a shift from "geometric" to "organic" from Alfred H. Barr, Jr., the director of MoMA, who had in his exhibition catalogue *Cubism and Abstract Art* (1936) identified these qualities as the "two main traditions of abstract art" (FIG. 1). He called the first tradition "intellectual, structural, architectonic, geometrical, rectilinear and classical in its austerity and dependence upon logic and calculation," and the second one its polar opposite, "intuitional and emotional rather than intellectual; organic or biomorphic rather than geometrical in its forms; curvilinear rather than rectilinear, decorative rather than structural, and romantic rather than classical in its exaltation of the mystical, the spontaneous and the irrational."[10] In fact, it is possible that the Aalto retrospective might not have taken place if it were not for Barr's artistic and intellectual agenda.[11] This relatively unknown Finnish architect confirmed Barr's prediction that "the geometric tradition in abstract art . . . is in decline."[12]

Two years later, after having visited the Paris exhibition, McAndrew linked the formal shift from geometric to organic with the transition from internationalism to an emphasis on national character. As is usually the case, when transported into a new period and place,

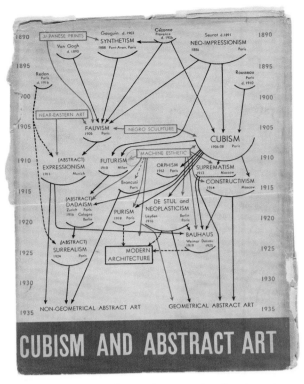

FIGURE 01 *A diagram showing the two strains of modern art, from Alfred H. Barr, Cubism and Abstract Art (New York: Museum of Modern Art, 1936).*

words and concepts change their meaning. In the late 1930s, American intellectuals started to associate internationalism with Marxism and other socialist ideologies. Hence, Aalto's presumably "national" style spoke for the need and ability to resist these forces. The shift from uniformity to "personal" expression rides the same political moment. Clement Greenberg's "Avant-Garde and Kitsch," written during the same years, countered kitsch, a product of totalitarianism, with the avant-garde, presumably an outcome of the individual artist's fight against authority. By using the conceptual pair "national" *and* "personal" to describe Aalto's architecture, McAndrew avoided any association with the "debased" totalitarian nationalism of Nazi Germany. The seamless link between the formal, psychological, and cultural taxonomies naturalized any ideological meanings.

The emergence of quasi-vernacular motifs in Aalto's work in the late 1930s can be explained to a great extent as his way of negotiating at times competing historical and ideological reference points: viewed from the United States, Aalto's vernacular represented a benign, non-aggressive, pacifist architecture in a

politically convulsed time. Tellingly, the sources of this "politically correct" version of national expression are ambiguous: the vaguely Japanese details of the Paris pavilion prove the case **(FIG. 2)**. The rustic sauna and fence added to Villa Mairea about the time of the MoMA exhibition allude more specifically to the Finnish vernacular building tradition. In both cases Aalto's use of the vernacular points to the innocence of the local culture prior to the birth of the nation-states. At the same time, MoMA had started to endorse America's own vernacular traditions, which would gain the most potent expression in California "Bay Region Style" architecture. The exhibition "Modern Architecture in California" had taken place at MoMA in fall 1935 as criticism started to mount of the "alleged reliance of the modernist on 'a German and French formula.'"[13] In this context, Aalto, like the Californians, showed the way toward a more benign national expression.

As the name "Architecture and Furniture: Aalto," indicates, MoMA's Aalto show was divided between two parts, which presented slightly different takes on Aalto's position within the modern movement. The architecture part of the exhibition sent somewhat mixed signals, as it showed how MoMA tried to negotiate the difficult terrain between what Johnson and Hitchcock had labeled "international style" modernism originating from Germany and France and the new national expression. With their white stucco walls and flat roofs the Turun Sanomat Building (1928–30), Paimio Sanatorium (1928–33), and Viipuri Library (1928–35) could easily be placed within the legacy of 1920s modernism. The extensive use of wood in Aalto's Own House (1936–37) and Finnish Pavilion at the Paris World's Fair (1936–37) made a case for a distance between 1920s and 1930s modernism. In order to highlight a paradigm shift toward national and personal expression during the 1930s, the catalogue identifies only their completion dates.

The furniture part of the exhibition presented a thesis of Aalto breaking new ground: Aalto's pieces of bent wood furniture were based on a single formal trope, curvilinearity, and a single material, wood. Mounting the chairs on the wall made the link to the "organic", which had been identified by Barr in his 1936 exhibition *Cubism and Abstract Art* as one of the "two main traditions of abstract art," **(FIG. 3)**.[14] A series of

FIGURE 02 *Aalto, Finland Pavilion, Paris World's Fair, 1938. View of exterior loggia.*

photo-collages with a reclining woman hovering over, yet not quite touching, the contours of the furniture suggested that, rather than based on functionalist dogma, Aalto's architecture was indeed based on a more grounded approach to human needs.

It is therefore no surprise that, more than the buildings, the furniture caught the fancy of the museum's large audience. In a letter to Aalto, McAndrew reported: "The exhibition of your architecture and furniture is a great success. Over 1000 people a week have come to the Museum to see it; we consider this an exceptionally good attendance. The visitors have been perhaps more interested in the furniture than the architecture, but that is to be expected, for there is no furniture as handsome or comfortable as yours to be

had in this country for anything like so low a price."[15] McAndrew's letter must have caused mixed feelings in Aalto's mind. He was surely pleased that the MoMA show functioned as an advertisement for his furniture but was probably frustrated about the lack of enthusiasm for his buildings. A review in *Art News* confirmed McAndrew's assessment; the husband and wife-team Aino and Alvar Aalto were presented as "the most original designers of furniture of the past decade" while the buildings on display were listed without comment.[16] Apart from ideological formulations, the Aalto exhibit was a success in terms of its popular appeal. Whereas the general public was turned off by modern abstraction, Aalto's furniture appealed to that public, not least because, as a consumer-good, it offered access to a new way of living.

The success of the exhibition meant a triumph for MoMA, which had already established itself as a kingmaker and arbiter of new trends and styles with the 1932 exhibition. McAndrew's letter to Aalto was jubilant at the Aalto exhibition's success: "We [have been] pleased to see the great number of architects who visited the show. [Frank Lloyd] Wright, [Walter] Gropius, [Marcel] Breuer, [Richard] Neutra, [Erik Gunnar] Asplund, [William] Lescaze and others have been here."[17] It is noteworthy that all but Wright and Asplund were European émigré architects working in America. McAndrew's positioning of Wright on the top of the list is telling of MoMA's changing attitude toward him; while underrepresented in the 1932 exhibition, his stature rose after the completion of Fallingwater in 1936, which paved the way for the emergence of a particularly American response to modern architecture. In fact, MoMA had dedicated an exhibition to the house in late 1937. Singling out Aalto as the man of the moment, MoMA also endorsed Wright's newly gained leadership, both of which led the way to defining an American modernism during the years throughout and after the Second World War.

When Elizabeth Mock recalled Aalto's role in shaping the future of modern American architecture in *Built in USA, 1932–1944* (1944), the political and ideological context had changed. Finland was just emerging from the so-called Continuation War with the Soviet Union, beaten but independent. In this context, the curvilinear form gained an additional reading: a sign of will to "freedom," which connected the Americans and the Finns. Mock's book implies that Aalto's architecture managed to fight against all tyranny, be it imposed by totalitarianism or the International Style: "Aalto had been notably successful in creating fresh and sympathetic forms, based as much on intuitive understanding of the way free people might like to live."[18] By 1944, what Mock labeled Aalto's "fresh and sympathetic forms" had already found their way into American architecture and design. What Mock termed a "free form" became the hallmark of a free (read: American) society by the mid-1940s.

In turn, even though Aalto was not able to travel to the opening of his MoMA exhibition, the American reception surely influenced the future development of his architecture. This effect was most apparent in the case of the Finland Pavilion for the New York World's Fair,

FIGURE 03 *Aalto-designed furniture in the exhibition "Architecture and Furniture: Aalto, Museum of Modern Art, 1938," as reproduced in the catalogue* Alvar Aalto: Architecture and Furniture *(New York: Museum of Modern Art, 1938)*

which won the first prize in an open national competition in late 1938. As if Aalto were somewhat cunningly reaffirming MoMA's prediction that architectural culture was facing a shift from the geometric toward the "organic," the project was dominated by a slightly tilted, curvilinear multi-media wall made of wooden battens (SEE FIG. 12 / p.146). What McAndrew labeled "personal and national qualities" and Simon Breines called a "vigorous expression of the work and culture of the Finnish people" were celebrated with photoenlargements of Finland and the Finns, which were curiously similar to those nationalistic photos seen at the German and Soviet Pavilions in Paris.[19]

In hindsight, it is possible to see the presence of populist, even nationalist ideologies in Aalto's New York pavilion. Its task was to communicate patriotic sentiments and create an image of a vigorous and unified nation on the eve of the Second World War. Judging by his pronouncements, Aalto was well aware that the monumental (read: classical) architecture seen at the Paris World's Fair went hand in hand with a debased form of nationalism. The title of an interview Aalto gave to *Helsingin Sanomat* in June 1939 demonstrates Aalto's characteristic sensitivity to his audience: "Large Exhibitions Suffer from So-called Exhibition Fatigue: Finland's Good Reputation in America Relies on Sensitive Use of Advertising."[20] As if to steer away from any explicit meaning, Aalto emphasized his desire to create "an impression on the visitor psychologically and instinctively," continuing, "a true image of a country cannot be conveyed with individual objects alone; it can be done convincingly only by the atmosphere such objects create together, that is, only by the overall effect perceived by the senses."[21] The creation of a politically innocent and materially elusive "atmosphere" was based on carefully considered representational strategies: the dismantling of objects and the boundaries between them, endless repetition of the undulating line in all scales, blurring the hierarchy between objects and their background, and the integration of different media—objects, photographs, film. These representational strategies shared with the vernacular what Roland Barthes called the "reality effect"; both were marked by the overabundance of details and images that, rather than forming a coherent narrative, simply claimed: "we are real."[22] The frantic overlapping of lines and textures added to their mystique (FIGS. 4A–B).

Travels to America and the Politics of Regionalism

The prize money from the New York World's Fair Pavilion competition and the subsequent commission to design and supervise its construction allowed Alvar and Aino Aalto finally to travel to America, which they did twice between 1938 and 1939. During the first trip, in fall 1938, Aalto was welcomed by New York's artistic and financial elite centered around MoMA[23] and championed by *Architectural Forum*. In the November 1938 issue, Aalto's Paimio Chair was used as an example of how from the "'wildest' theories often come the most vital ideas."[24] The fact that the magazine announced the Aaltos' second arrival during March 1939 in their events page speaks to Alvar's American fame. Several lectures were arranged in New York and nearby universities during both visits.

The lecture "The Home of a Rich Art Collector," given at Yale University in May 1939, demonstrates Aalto's ability to tailor himself to an American audience. Tellingly, he chose to present Villa Mairea, a house designed for one of Finland's most wealthy families, the Gullichsens, as if to demonstrate his importance

as a residential architect to a potential patronage. Furthermore, Aalto's call for "fighting the program" and his credo that only when one transcended a particular task could forms result in "what we today call true 'ARCHITECTURE'" came unusually close to Hitchcock's and Johnson's formalist position.[25]

The trip certainly broadened Aalto's outlook on American architecture culture and society. Soon after the Yale lecture the Aaltos left for California (via Chicago), first visiting Richard Neutra in Los Angeles before traveling north to attend the opening of the Golden Gate International Exhibition in San Francisco, which featured the Aaltos' furniture. William W. Wurster, who had visited the Aaltos in Finland two years earlier, acted as a host. The trip exposed Aalto to the distinct qualities of Californian modernism and earned him an intellectual companion in Wurster, a major representative of what would be called the "Bay Region Style" of architecture, which paid particular attention to topography, climate, and the use of local materials like wood.

Departing on his trip to California from New York, Aalto was surely informed of Wurster's growing reputation and apparently "felt right at home" when stepping into Wurster's Gregory Farmhouse in Scotts Valley (1928).[26] The compound consists of four iconic components: a three-story water tower, the L-shaped house proper, a mud-brick wall with a wide gate, and a courtyard. Wurster's deadpan description of the house implies that his architecture based on local vernacular occupied an ideologically unambiguous idea of the everyday life unfolding in the premises: "After passing through the front gate, you walk to the front door at the rear of the forecourt: it's on the right, at the inner corner of the L where two covered brick walkways intersect. The big door is in a long, blank, north-facing facade . . . . Open it and you enter the large white rectangular living and dining room with a fireplace on the right and a long refectory table on the left."[27] Wurster followed equally simple criteria when siting his buildings, for example, noting the value of a cool breeze reaching the veranda on a hot summer day.

When back in New York, Aalto wrote to Wurster about the need to establish a research institute to study the "technological," "social," and "regional" aspects of architecture.[28] These two former elements helped

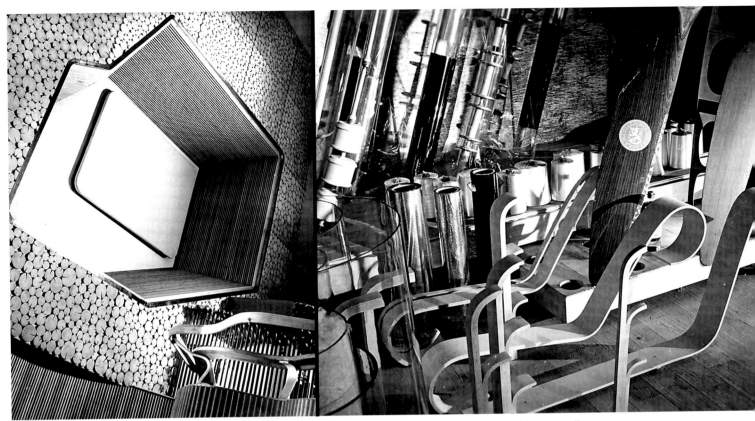

FIGURE 4A–B *Aalto, Finland Pavilion with photo-enlargements by Esko Mäkinen, New York World's Fair, 1939-40. Exhibition installation.*

the third, or "regional" aspect, to break loose from ideas about national or international culture based on an ethnicity bound to a particular place. Any ethnic group was able to inhabit a particular place as long as it adopted, at least in part, local social customs and technologies. It goes without saying that this idea of inhabitation was better suited to the United States, a country based on colonization and immigration. Nevertheless, Aalto was drawn to the formal outcome of this approach, a fact known to Wurster, who, unlike the representatives of MoMA, had actually seen three of Aalto's buildings during his 1937 visit to Finland, including Aalto's newly completed personal house in Helsinki. Similarities to Wurster's "regionalism" were apparent: Aalto's house employed wooden siding, the cozy backyard, continuity between indoors and outdoors, and split levels to accommodate changes in topography.

The trip to California had made Aalto aware of the fundamental difference between American and European culture and society; he returned home to Finland celebrating the state's "mixture of races and cultural

impulses."[29] The exposure to the advantages of such cultural plurality helped him also to acknowledge the nationalist subtext that fueled European architectural culture at the time. There followed in his thinking a desire to challenge the very foundation of European nationalism—that is, the idea of the insular, culturally and ethnically homogenous nation. "Everything good in Finnish culture is the result of the stimulating effect of having two competing languages," Aalto announced during a lecture in Gothenburg soon after the trip. He continued, "That Nordic collaboration has had an equally positive effect on Finnish culture. The unity is richer, giving an opportunity to see more clearly both from within and without."[30]

Regionalism was also connected to a political agenda. It was used in tandem with the word "organic," a key concept for both 1920s German and Scandinavian modernists and American regionalists. Lewis Mumford, a chief proponent of regionalism, used the word to explain social phenomena and relationships: for him, organic society was based on free individuals who shared the same values and mutual respect, as opposed to the "mechanical" totalitarian society based on order imposed from without.[31] Aalto used the term to celebrate a heterogeneous and dynamic society, exclaiming that the "unity and the ability to build an organism doesn't 'only result from similar phenomena. It is indeed necessary as well as meaningful for an organism to include various kinds of phenomena."[32] It should be noted that Aalto's endorsement of Scandinavian collaboration and diversity was not solely based on noble ideals: undoubtedly its aim was also to solicit Swedish solidarity on the eve of the Second World War.

The benign idea of coexistence and collaboration across national borders received a major blow when Russian forces attacked Finland on the 30 November 1939. Turning to his American friends for assistance, Aalto did not hesitate to use strong anti-Soviet rhetoric. A letter to Frank Lloyd Wright in early January 1940 explained his version of the affairs: "As you know, the first real open fighting of the world-war has begun in Finland. It is the Russian terror-system which now shows its will to expand all over the world. The Western social thinking—constitutive activity—has shown itself more of a success than the Russian collective system can stand. All of us who have worked for a real socially positive future, have now the same battle to fight, the battle that has begun here."[33] Aalto had written elsewhere that, as far as Finland was concerned, the war was "not a fight of a national character" unlike those fought in Western Europe.[34] In this political climate, Aalto was aware of the danger of over-emphasizing the Finnishness of Finnish architecture. He was equally aware of the need to avoid any association with "internationalism," which Americans would read as a sign of Soviet sympathies. Instead, Aalto referred to abstract universal values and human experiences in an attempt to overcome associations both with nationalism and internationalism. In this effort, Aalto was indebted to the universalism of Mumford's notion of organic society, which suggested that a healthy social development was founded on innate human qualities shared by people all over the world. It is clear that the letter to Wright was not without political motivation: Finland was desperate for military and humanitarian aid.

Working directly under the Ministry of Social Affairs, Aalto was able to convince his superiors that the country might profit from sending him to America as a sort of one-man propaganda unit engaged with soliciting American sympathy and aid for Finland. Aalto spent March to October 1940 in the United States, visiting his American friends, giving lectures, and writing articles. The article "Finland" for the June 1940 issue of *Architectural Forum* interpreted Finnish architecture and culture with his mission in mind (FIG. 5). In it Aalto avoided using words like "national," relying instead on regionalist elements like "climate, topography, [and] resources."[35] The attention drawn to the "absence of fortification" was meant to convey the idea of an innocent, politically neutral country.[36]

The Russian–German alliance and Russia's subsequent attack on Finland dismantled the Soviet sympathies common among American liberal intelligentsia. Mumford was among the first to initiate open discussion among the American Artists' Congress, which had strong ties to the American Communist Party.[37] Aalto, surely aware of the increasingly anti-Soviet position of the American intelligentsia, used the article "Finland" published the following June to convince his American audience that Finns had nothing to do with the presumably Communist-infested international modern movement. According to him, the best of Finnish modern architecture, in which Aalto probably was including his own, bore witness to this distance. It had shown independent development somewhat along the lines of American regionalism. He wrote, "As in other countries with a more or less provincial culture, modern architecture did not appear in Finland as a superficial style trend in imitation of the great European centers. Even though there is today in Finland, as in all countries, a good deal of superficial modernism, the country itself, its climate, resources, topography and ways of living afford a mass of material which forms a good base for the solution of problems of contemporary architecture."[38] In support of the regionalist agenda, Aalto described "the special forms of culture," "the use of wood," the "single house . . . without the heavy characteristics which fortifications buildings lend to architecture," and "decentralization" as the foundations of Finnish architecture.[39] Aalto's ideas for reconstruction after the destruction caused by the Winter War fostered the link between Finnish and American architecture. Basing his proposal on regionalist principles of decentralization and lessons learned from American mass-production, the goal was to rebuild in "complete harmony with nature" using "standard types of building."[40] The use of wood formed a further link between American and Finnish building traditions.

The Americanization of Finnish architecture went hand in hand with the desired Americanization of Finnish society. Gone was the idea about collective housing that Aalto had endorsed during the early 1930s; reconstruction was based on the American dream of everybody owning a house. His ideological move from collective "conveniences" to "private facilities" made this shift to the American ideal complete. Aalto explained, "Because there is such a great need for homes, they will be built and equipped in stages: first the roof and walls, then in the next step, heating and lighting, and later plumbing and other equipment. This will ensure the people immediate shelter, and, by the third step, a completely equipped house. Later stages would include better finishing materials and in the end there will be a complete modern home as a unit in the modern community."[41] Aalto's "modern community" was to be modeled after Mumford's ideal of a small New England town far from the ills of urban centers; a place where common good and individualism were presumably not mutually exclusive. Like Mumford, Aalto used the ambiguous word "community" to seek a way out of the deadlock of both American liberalism and Soviet collectivism. "Community" implied collectivity without collectivization. In fact, just before the war in 1939, Mumford had planned to write about the possibility of a "third way" in Aalto's magazine, *The Human Side*, under the title "Is Collectivization of the Social Organism the Only Alternative to Bourgeois Liberalism and to the Forms of Organization and Culture Inherited from It?" Aalto's magazine never came to fruition because of the Winter War.

Aalto's decision to endorse American planning ideas was at least in part motivated by his ambitious plan to get American money to fund part of the reconstruction in Finland. The results were meager—the Hoover Foundation managed to raise only $2 million—probably because Americans were never quite certain about Finland's political affinities, and rightly so;

FIGURE 05 *Title image from Aalto's article "Finland,"* Architectural Forum, *June 1940.*

Finland and Germany formed a military pact during the Continuation War (1941–44).[42] Aalto's long negotiations with the Rockefeller Foundation did result in financial backing for a research professorship at the Massachusetts Institute of Technology (MIT) after Aalto was able to convince the board that the project "An American Town in Finland" would yield reconstruction strategies for wider "universal" use. A little brochure titled *Post-war Reconstruction: Rehousing Research in Finland*, published through the Finnish Consulate in New York for American distribution in 1940, demonstrates Aalto's ability to negotiate a balance between general principles and the particular locale by focusing on the idea of flexible standardization: "Standardization here does not mean a formal one with all houses built alike. Standardization will be used mainly as a method of producing a flexible system by which the single house can be made adjustable for families of different sizes, various topographical locations, different exposures, views, etc."[43]

Aalto and his students at MIT began the work on "An American Town in Finland" in the beginning of October 1940. But the collaboration was interrupted after only ten days when Aalto was called to return to Finland due to the approaching Continuation War. Two sets of diagrams produced by Aalto, probably in September of that year, give clues about the emphasis of the studio. Both are organized by grid-like patterns, and each provides about twenty to thirty variations of a standard type according to differing site conditions. The first differentiates between positive and negative site factors **(FIG. 6)**. The second specifies the factors that would influence the planning and siting of the house: "size," "family requirements," and "natural conditions" **(FIG. 7)**.

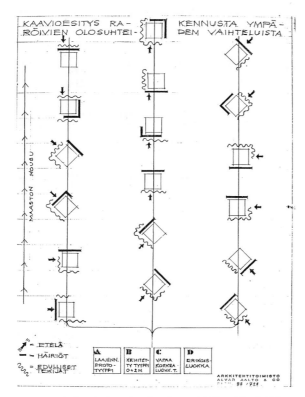

FIGURE 06 *Aalto, A chart showing the variability of the building environment surroundings, September 1941.*

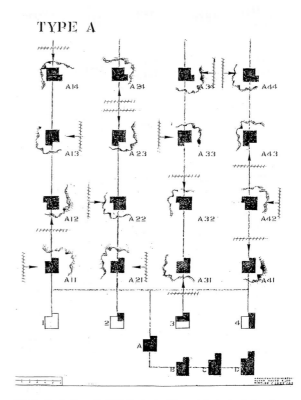

FIGURE 07 *Aalto with MIT Students, "Type A": A chart showing the effect of environment on the orientation of the house, September 1941.*

Lessons from America: Finland, Regional Identity, and International Conflict

Aalto's plans for reconstruction had a receptive audience in the three interest groups which dominated Finnish internal affairs during the late 1930s: the Social Democrats, who had long since given up the idea of revolution and were working toward a Scandinavian welfare state; the Agrarian Party, whose main loyalty was to people living in rural areas; and the small yet very powerful industrial elite in control of the country's dispersed forest industry. Aalto's program for reconstruction offered something for all groups: better housing for those in need; decentralization as a model for supporting the countryside; and a new market constructing single-family homes out of wood, which would please the Finnish forest industry.

Harry Gullichsen, the chief executive officer of Finland's largest forest producer, the A. Ahlström

Company, had perhaps most to gain; Aalto's reconstruction plans offered a new market for the AA-house system, which he had commissioned from Aalto in 1937. Reminiscent of American prefabricated single-family housing of the same era—in its simple rectangular floor plan with a pitched roof—the project bore Gullichsen's ideological stamp. His solution to the housing problem was simply to produce houses rather than to create utopias.[44] All in all, he believed that the country would be best run by professionals rather than by politicians, whom he viewed as being tangled up in ideological debates. Gullichsen's pragmatism convinced Aalto to endorse building single-family houses, which he had previously condemned for being "petit bourgeois" in 1932, at the height of his leftist sympathies.[45] Hundreds of them ended up being built in American-style company towns, where the factory acted as a developer, planner, builder, and bank. Photographs of housing areas built in Inkeroinen, Sunila, Valkeakoski and Varkaus (by Tampella) before the war bear witness to the bleakness that can result from uniformity (**FIG. 8**).

Aalto steered his prefabrication project in a new direction on his return from America in October 1940, with the intention of emphasizing variability based on programmatic and site concerns. He proposed two massing alternatives: A new V-shaped plan, in which the original core building and the bedroom wing would fan out, and a so-called growing house, where additional spaces could be added to a core unit consisting of a living room, a kitchen, and a bathroom (FIG. 9). Regionalist ideals of living in harmony with nature were most pronounced in his 1941 study for a prefabricated summer cottage. The building consisted of a bedroom wing, a living-room area, and a semi-open kitchen and dining area, which were loosely configured around landscape features (FIG. 10).

Aalto's efforts to introduce regionalist ideas within the AA-system diminished when the project was adapted to the booming reconstruction market after the Winter War. None of the new versions ever was built. The AA-House catalogue from 1941 makes only a meager and rather superficial concession to regionalist ideals: a drawing of a building is juxtaposed with an image of a forest landscape without any suggestion of how the integration of the two might happen (FIG. 11).[46] Variability was offered simply in terms of size and style, in thirty models ranging from the economic 51.2-square-meter basic to a luxurious 203-square-meter model. The catalogue reveals that the company used regionalism simply to give the old products a new marketing spin: house-building throughout the Finnish woods was presented as a foundation of individual and national wellbeing and security. Pictures of idyllic home scenes in rooms full of Aalto-designed furniture—a husband reading a magazine, mother working in the kitchen, kids playing—conveyed an image of a happy home in this period of distress.

The ideas about national/regional/vernacular architecture gained an added political dimension when the peace treaty of 1940 ordered Finland to cede a large part of Karelia to the Soviet Union. The loss of the region that had traditionally been considered the heartland of Finnish culture led to what could be called a second wave of Karelianism. The first wave had taken place at the turn of the century when scholars, artists, and architects made pilgrimages to the province to document buildings, folklore, and the way of life. The second wave led to countless exhibitions, magazine

OSA SUNILAN SULFAATTITEHTAAN OMAKOTIALUETTA ENSIMMÄISESSÄ RAKENNUSVAIHEESSA.

Koska 90 % rakennuskustannuksista on omakotiyhtiön hankkimaa lainaa, ja lähes puolet tästä määrästä valtion omakotilainarahastosta sekä näiden lainojen korko on hyvin kohtuullinen, tulee jos yhä ajattelemme edellämainittua 75.000: — maksavaa taloa lainojen osalta rakennuttajalle korkomaksuja ensimäisenä vuonna 3.180: — mk jonka jälkeen korkomaksut vuosi vuodelta alenevat.

Inkeroisten tehtaitten konttorissa huolto-osasto avustaa auliisti neuvoilla ja antaa yksityiskohtaiset ohjeet siitä, miten rakentajan on meneteltävä ryhtyessään kotiaan rakentamaan. Omakotiyhtiö huolehtii kaikista käytännöllisistä kysymyksistä, lainojen hankinnasta sekä muodollisista toimenpiteistä, joten omankodin rakentajan vain on allekirjoitettava omakotiyhtiön hänelle tarjoamat sopimukset ja asiakirjat sekä määrättävä, missä muodossa hän itse suorittaa oman osuutensa.

Tampereen Pellava- ja Rautateollisuus toivoo, että Inkeroisten Tehtaiden henkilökunnasta niin moni kuin mahdollista ryhtyisi oman kodin hankintaan yllä selos-

VIIHTYISÄ RUOKAILUNURKKAUS 1939 RAKENNETULTA OMAKOTIALUEELTA.

8

FIGURE 08 *Tampella house catalogue from 1941 showing housing areas completed in 1939.*

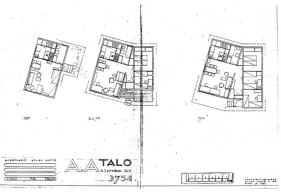

FIGURE 09 *Aalto, "A.A. Talo," designed for A. Ahlström Company in 1940. Three alternative house plans based on a single core unit.*

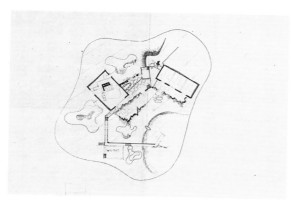

articles, and books, of which the best known is *Karelia: The Land of Memories*, by the pioneer of Finnish literary modernism, Olavi Paavolainen.[47] The book catalogued buildings, people, and landscapes from every town and village in the ceded territory.

During his early career, Aalto had been openly critical of National Romanticism and its values. He had talked about "birch-bark architecture" as lacking synchrony with new technological and economic realities. Although the construction of the Viipuri Library between 1928 and 1935 had taken him to the region, I have never encountered any proof that Aalto traveled, let alone sketched, buildings in the surrounding countryside. So when Aalto made his first written reference to Karelian vernacular architecture in the 1941 article "On Karelian Architecture," he did so without succumbing to nostalgia or national essentialism. Instead, he provocatively claimed that "it is difficult, even unnecessary to draw national borders when it comes to material culture."[48] The Karelian vernacular, according to Aalto, should therefore not be appreciated as Russian or Finnish, but rather for its ability to integrate architectural form, a way of life, and the physical site. By considering Karelian vernacular architecture "regional" rather than "national," Aalto denied the new rulers any right of authority to the culture. He used the organic analogy to emphasize Karelia's flexibility and thus its ability to resist totalitarianism. He described how each farmhouse evolved from a small "embryo" into a large unit based on wealth and need; new parts were simply added to the core unit. Alternating roof slopes bore witness to the flexible agglomeration of the building mass **(FIG. 12)**. Through this examination, the Karelian farmhouse is interpreted as a modular system. His goal was to extract universal principles from the local vernacular traditional rather than to emphasize its idiosyncrasies.

Aalto wrote the article after he had been forced to return to Europe, which was in war over national and racial hatred. The text suggests that Aalto was well aware of the negative connotations of the terms "vernacular" and "regional." In fact, Aalto never used the terms. By emphasizing universal principles, Aalto attempted to purify Karelian vernacular of any association with the *Heimatstil* vernacular preferred for buildings for Hitler Youth. Aalto's idea of a material culture that does not know national borders recalled

FIGURE 12 *An eastern Karelian farmhouse in 1894, published in Alvar Aalto's article "Karjalan rakennustaide," Uusi Suomi, 2 Nov 1941 Photo: Into Konrad.*

Sigfried Giedion's 1930 essay "Die Heutige Rolle der Malerei."[49] Giedion had claimed that the most promising new art came from small countries like Switzerland, which, "due to its location between German and French culture, is able to take a relatively free approach. Here the clear, neutral atmosphere is untouched by local considerations of a different kind."[50] With extreme nationalism on the rise all over Europe, Giedion had considered the ability to transcend national disputes and even national traits as a prerequisite for art's presumably pure, non-ideological essence to come forth. During this time, he started to prefer artists who were products of in-between regions with multiple cultural influences, considering hybrid culture the most fertile ground for artistic genius. For example, as an Alsatian, Jean Arp was neither French nor German, and even his use of two first names, Jean and Hans, indicated an ability to move between different linguistic groups and cultural identities. Giedion implied that Aalto's Finnish identity was equally fluid by referring to Finland as a *Randstaat*, or "borderstate," in his 1931 article "Architektur aus Finnland."[51]

Nothing better captures the metaphor of a fluid region than an aerial view of a Finnish lake landscape that Giedion juxtaposed with the plan of the Finnish Pavilion in New York and a picture of a Savoy Vase in the second edition of *Space, Time and Architecture: The Birth of a Tradition* in 1949 **(FIG. 13)**.[52] Aalto used the same image in several of the projects, articles, and lectures discussed earlier: for the exterior of the Paris pavilion, as part of the multi-media exhibition wall at the New York pavilion, in the article "Finland," and accompanying his lectures on reconstruction in 1941 **(FIG. 14)**. The article "Finland" captured the disguised political meaning of the image: the claim that Finland was an innocent region, both politically and culturally ambiguous, was supported by portraying the curvilinear form as an outcome of geological processes that took place well before the birth of the nation-states. The image gained an added political meaning after 1940, when a part of that soil or territory had been lost. The malleable forms of the lakes depicted in the image pointed ominously to the fact that Finnish politics could not ignore the landscape's current geopolitical

394. Finnish lakes and forests, Aulenko.

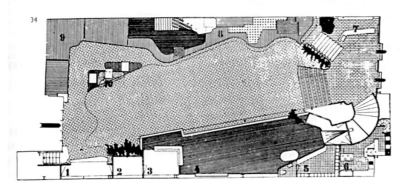

395. ALVAR AALTO. Finnish Pavilion, World's Fair, New York, 1939. *Ground plan.*

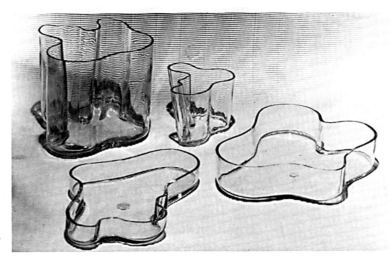

396. ALVAR AALTO. Glass vases.

635

FIGURE 13 *Illustration from the chapter "Alvar Aalto: Elemental and Contemporary," in Sigfried Giedion,* Space, Time and Architecture: The Growth of a New Tradition, *(2nd ed. Cambridge Mass.: Harvard Univ. Press, 1949)*

location. The country, its politics, and its boundaries were also susceptible to change due to overpowering external forces.

Giedion can be credited for trying to enforce a link between Aalto's architecture and these historical events. He starts his chapter on Aalto by pointing out that "Alvar Aalto's active life coincides with the most consistently agitated period of Finland's existence."[53] If Giedion considered Picasso's *Guernica* at the Paris World's Fair in 1937 as the artist's "first real historical painting," he saw in Aalto's organic lines the first sign of historical architecture by interpreting them as signs of a frenzied imagination and vitality that attempted to animate the inanimate, joyless outside world.[54]

American interpretations of biomorphic forms have emphasized psychological and formal taxonomies over historical interpretation. György Kepes's *Language of Vision* (1944) was most influential in this respect.[55] Kepes contended that the curvilinear forms of Jean Arp, for example, rose from the unconscious and were a sign of a free and uninhibited man. His emphasis on individual creativity was indicative of the wide disillusionment with the politically committed art of the 1930s, which gave birth to the abstract expressionism that swept the American art scene from the late 1930s onward.[56]

MoMA's exhibition "Modern Art in Your Life" in 1948 celebrated commercial applications of biomorphism and other modernist formal idioms as an indicator that modern art had become an integral part of American life (FIG. 15).[57] Probably in preparation for an exhibition that juxtaposed canonical European art and architecture from the 1920s with contemporary American designers working in a "modern vein," Edgar Kaufman, Jr., then the curator of industrial design, asked Aalto in March 1946:

> Could [you] help me by answering a question which has been much discussed here in the Museum in the past few days. That is, what do you think was the most important reason or reasons for you developing the curved forms that you have used in your furniture, particularly the pieces where the curves close back upon themselves. It seemed to be a very special expression, quite different from what other modern designers previously tried. I think that some main reasons, such as fitting the chair to the general postures of the human body, were always

> assumed by us, but perhaps there were other ideas in your mind while these pieces were designed about which we know nothing. The whole problem of the transition from geometrical shapes, which we much used in the early days of modern furniture, to the freer shapes. If you can help us to understand how this development occurred, we would be very grateful.[58]

Aalto never replied to Kaufman's question and, in fact, his furniture was absent from the exhibition. The "Abstract Organic Form" section paired Arp's wooden reliefs from the late 1920s with designs by Charles Eames and George Nelson. Aalto had by then become an absent mediator between 1920s European high modernism and post-war American architecture. If Aalto had tried to reply, he would have had to dwell on the links between forms and the culture that produced them. Yet, having been deeply influenced and involved in the events surrounding the Second World War, drawing simple causal relationships would have hardly done justice to the complex personal, political, and historical motivations and transcontinental exchanges behind his formal choices.

FIGURE 14 *Aalto, Paris World's Fair 1938, Finland Pavilion. Exterior photo collage.*

Abstract Organic Form

ARP· Two Heads. 1929 Painted wood relief, 47¼ x 39¼″

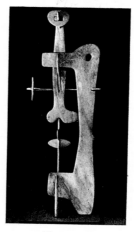

NOGUCHI· Kouros. 1945. Georgia pink marble, 9′ 9″ high

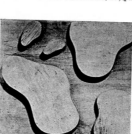

ARP Objects Arranged According to the Law of Chance *or* Navels. 1930. Varnished wood relief, 10¾ x 11⅛″

Assembled on the next four pages is a series of designs using shapes which, though abstract, suggest life. They are defined by an irregular, fluid contour that avoids the geometrically regular curve as consistently as the straight line. No part of this curve exactly resembles any other part. It is not produced by the repetition of a basic unit, but grows out of a growing, changing rhythm. The resultant form can therefore not be broken into parts and must be grasped as a unique whole. Similar organic

CALDER Spiny 1942. Stabile. Sheet aluminum, 26″ high. Collection Herbert Matter New York

Abstract Organic Form 26

FIGURE 15 *An illustration showing the correspondence between biomorphic forms in art and furniture, from the exhibition catalogue* Modern Art in Your Life *(New York: Museum of Modern Art, 1953).*

1 Sigfried Giedion, "Irrationalität und Standard," Zurich, ETH/Geschichte und Theorie der Architektur (Giedion Archive Document gta: 42-T-13-1941). The article formed the basis for the chapter on Aalto in Giedion, *Space, Time and Architecture: The Birth of a New Tradition,* 2nd ed. (Cambridge, Mass.: Harvard Univ. Press, 1949). The quotation appears on p. 567 of that book.

2 Henry-Russell Hitchcock Jr., "Paris Exhibition," *Architectural Forum,* Sept. 1937, 160.

3 The pavilion was a blue-and-white tent not to be confused with the Pavillon de l'Esprit Nouveau he had designed for the Paris Exposition des Arts Décoratifs et Industriels in 1925.

4 Hitchcock, "Paris Exhibition," 160.

5 Ibid, 160.

6 Henry-Russell Hitchcock, Jr., and Philip Johnson, *The International Style: Architecture since 1922* (New York: W. W. Norton, 1932), 83.

7 John McAndrew, ed. *Architecture and Furniture: Aalto* (New York: Museum of Modern Art, 1938), 1.

8 McAndrew, 1.

9 Ibid, 1.

10 Alfred Barr, *Cubism and Abstract Art* (New York: Museum of Modern Art, 1936), 19.

11 Indeed, Hitchcock's favorite (J. J. P. Oud) and Johnson's favorite architect (Ludwig Mies van der Rohe) might have been more likely candidates.

12 Barr, *Cubism and Abstract Art,* 200.

13 A. Conger Goodyear, *The Museum of Modern Art: The First Ten Years* (New York: MoMA, 1943), 113.

14 *Cubism and Abstract Art,* 19.

15 Letter from John McAndrew to Alvar Aalto, 16 April 1938 (Alvar Aalto Museum document)

16 A review of Aalto's exhibition at MoMA in *Art News,* 2 April 1938, 23.

17 Letter from John McAndrew to Alvar Aalto, 16 April 1938 (Alvar Aalto Museum document).

18 Elizabeth Mock, ed., *Built in USA, 1932–1944* (New York: Museum of Modern Art, 1944), 20.

19 McAndrew, op.cit,,3; Simon Breines, "Architecture," in *Architecture and Furniture: Aalto,* 9.

20 Alvar Aalto, "Suurnäyttelyiden Varjopuolena n.s. Näyttelyväsymys: Suomen Hyvä Maine Amerikassa Edellyttää Harkintaa Mainostuksessa," *Helsingin Sanomat,* 23 June 1939.

21 Alvar Aalto, "Maailmannäyttelyt: New York World's Fair, The Golden Gate Exhibition," *Arkkitehti* 8 (1939): 113; translation published as "Comments on the 1939 World's Fair in New York" in *Alvar Aalto in His Own Words,* ed. Göran Schildt (New York: Rizzoli, 1997), 120–122.

22 Roland Barthes, "The Reality Effect," in *French Literary Theory Today: A Reader,* ed. Tzetan Todorov (Cambridge: Cambridge Univ. Press, 1982), 131–35. For this reference, I am indebted to Romy Golan. See her article "A 'Discours aux Architectes'?," *Rivista de Architectura* 5 (June 2003): 153.

23 Göran Schildt has mapped out the contacts Aalto made during both trips in his book *Alvar Aalto: The Decisive Years* (New York: Rizzoli, 1986). Therefore, to avoid duplicating his work, I will concentrate on the reception of Aalto's artistic and intellectual positions, and on the artistic and intellectual ideals to which Aalto was exposed and with which he chose to engage during and after these trips.

24 Editorial in the Nov. 1938 issue of *Architectural Forum.*

25 Alvar Aalto, "A House for a Rich Art Collector," unpublished manuscript of a lecture delivered at Yale University, May 1939 (Alvar Aalto Foundation Archive, Helsinki), 5.

26 William Wurster, quoted in Daniel Gregory, "The Nature of Restraint: Wurster and His Circle," in *An Everyday Modernism: The Houses of William Wurster,* ed. Marc Treib (San Francisco: San Francisco Museum of Modern Art; Berkeley: Univ. of California Press, 1995), 107.

27 Wurster, quoted in Gregory, "The Nature of Restraint," 102.

28 Letter from Alvar Aalto to William W. Wurster, 13 June 1938 (Alvar Aalto Museum Archive, Helsinki).

29 Alvar Aalto, quoted in Göran Schildt, *Alvar Aalto: The Decisive Years* (New York: Rizzoli, 1986), 179.

30 Alvar Aalto, unpublished manuscript of a lecture delivered in Gothenburg, Sweden, 1939 (Alvar Aalto Museum document), 2–3.

31 To my knowledge, Aalto and Mumford met for the first time during Aalto's 1939 trip to the United States. It is, however, very likely that Aalto knew previously of his writings, since Mumford was a frequent contributor to German architecture magazines.

32 Alvar Aalto, unpublished manuscript of a lecture delivered in Gothenburg, Sweden, 1939 (Alvar Aalto Museum document), 2–3.

33 Letter from Alvar Aalto to Frank Lloyd Wright, 8 Jan. 1940 (Alvar Aalto Museum document).

34 An undated and unaddressed letter written in English by Aalto (Alvar Aalto Museum document).

35 Alvar Aalto, "Finland," *Architectural Forum,* June 1940, 399.

36 Aalto, "Finland," 399.

37 My discussion has been informed by Serge Guilbaut, *How New York Stole the Idea of Modern Art: Abstract Expressionism, Freedom, and the Cold War* (Chicago: Univ. of Chicago Press, 1983), esp. 38–39.

38 Aalto, "Finland," 399.

39 Ibid, 399.

40 Ibid, 399.

41 Ibid, 399.

42 For this and many other pieces of factual information, I have relied on Göran Schildt, *Alvar Aalto: The Mature Years* (New York: Rizzoli, 1991), 27.

43 Alvar Aalto, *Post-war Reconstruction: Rehousing Research in Finland* (n.p, 1940), 15.

44 Aalto was exposed to American prefabricated housing through, for example, *Architectural Forum,* to which he started subscribing in 1937.

45 Alvar Aalto, "Utwecklingslinje," *Granskaren* (July–August 1932), 88.

46 See *AA-Talo* brochure (Helsinki: A. Ahlström Company, 1941).

47 Olavi Paavolainen, ed., *Karjala Muistojen Maa* (Helsinki: Werner Söderström, 1940).

48 Alvar Aalto, "Karjalan rakennustaide", *Uusi Suomi,* 2 Nov. 1941, 12; published in translation as "Karelian Architecture." in *Alvar Aalto in His Own Words,* ed. Göran Schildt (New York: Rizzoli, 1997), 115–19.

49 Sigfried Giedion, "Die Heutige Rolle der Malerei," in *Produktion Paris 1930: Malerei und Plastik* (Zurich: Gallerie Wolfsburg, 1930).

50 Giedion, "Die Heutige Rolle der Malerei," 64.

51 Sigfried Giedion, "Architektur aus Finnland," *Bauwelt* 25 (1931), 34.

52 Sigfried Giedion, *Space, Time and Architecture: The Growth of a New Tradition* 2nd ed. (Cambridge, Mass.: Harvard Univ. Press, 1949), 467.

53 Giedion, *Space, Time and Architecture,* 458.

54 For further discussion on Giedion's reception of Aalto, see my essay "Alvar Aalto: The Geopolitics of Fame," *Perspecta* 37 (2005), 86–97.

55 Gyorgy Kepes, *The Language of Vision* (Chicago: Paul Theobold, 1944).

56 See Guilbaut, *How New York Stole the Idea of Modern Art,* for further discussion.

57 For further information about the exhibition, see Robert Goldwater, *Modern Art in Your Life* (New York: Museum of Modern Art, 1949).

58 Letter from Edgar Kaufmann, Jr., to Alvar Aalto, 29 March 1946 (Alvar Aalto Museum document).

A Bridge of Wood:
Aalto, American House Production, and Finland

Pekka Korvenmaa

On 25 October 1939, Alvar Aalto wrote to the California architect William W. Wurster regarding a plan for the journal, *The Human Side*: "It can probably help to solve the difficulties of all Northern states [Nordic countries], this only part of the world which is like your country and which is developing under the same kind of system as [the] American [one]."[1] Aalto had already anticipated the turmoil of war to come. A week later the Soviet Union attacked Finland and the Winter War began. Aalto's own professional activity and his already well-established ties to the United States were to be entwined for the coming years with the turns of the wars, first the Finnish Winter War (fall 1939 to spring 1940), and then World War II.

The relationship of Aalto with the United States has been described extensively by others as well as by me, in my essay "Aalto and Finnish Industry."[2] The present inquiry, however, focuses on the years around 1940 and attempts to illuminate one specific strain in the mutually rewarding ties between Aalto and the United States. It concerns the use of wood as a facilitator of communication between the two cultures of architectural design and industrial production. The scenes of action are mainly the Massachusetts Institute of Technology (MIT) and New York City. Aalto's cooperation with MIT received its physical manifestation in one of his noted projects, MIT's Baker House (1946–49). The events preceding this commission discussed here, however, were not productive for Aalto on the level of commissions for grand-scale buildings and were certainly much more frustrating in nature than the Baker House commission.[3] But before examining why Aalto perceived Finland as developing under the same system as the United States and how this enabled his strategies and operations to mesh with the American scene, I will embark on a brief excursion into the role of wood in Aalto's work.

Aalto and Wood: Novel Forms via New Technology

For Aalto, as for all Finnish architects of his generation, the knowledge of the properties of wood as a building material was a natural thing. The overwhelming majority of Finland's existing building stock was constructed of wood, either as solid logs or sawn to be used as frames and clapboarding; wood dominated construction until the years after WWII. Aalto, after having begun his career using this material, turned away from it in the mid-1920s and went on to explore the structural possibilities of other materials, first of brick and soon thereafter of reinforced concrete. However, his efforts to find new ways to utilize the most important raw material of his country in the service of design-based production were intensified by his simultaneous experiments in furniture design, starting in the late 1920s.[4]

Aalto's well-known chairs in bent and laminated wood, which dated from the early 1930s, have been duly hailed for their avant-garde design and formal qualities. Behind these achievements, however, lay his less visible research into the technical properties of solid and laminated woodwork which led first to Finnish patents and then to international ones (FIGS. 1–2). These patents as granted do not protect

FIGURE 01 *Aalto, experiment in comparing a naturally shaped piece of wood with one produced by gluing and pressing together wooden particles, early 1930s.*

FIGURE 02 *A demonstration of the lamination and bending construction of the legs used in the Aalto chairs and stools, early 1930s.*

design, but rather technical features. Of these seven patents, two from the 1930s concern the technology of wood in furniture design. The first patent, applied for in 1934 and received in 1938, covers the two versions of the so-called Paimio Chair, designed for the Paimio Tuberculosis Sanatorium in 1932; it demonstrates the flexible, spring-like properties of laminated wood (**FIG. 3**). The second patent covers "the way to bend solid wood by laminating the end part," which Aalto applied for in Great Britain in 1933 and in Finland in 1934, and was granted in 1940 (**FIG. 4**). A non-typical feature of these patents is that Aalto filed them under his own name as the architect-designer, and not under the name of the constructor-producer Otto Korhonen, whose plant, Oy Huonekalu-ja Rakennustyötehdas AB, and whose personal cooperation made it possible for Aalto's experiments to become items of furniture in serial production.[5]

Aalto began his most intensive work with solid and laminated domestic birchwood during the early 1930s, when the effects of the Great Depression reached Finland and architectural commissions were scarce. By sawing, glueing, bending, and pressing, he tested the properties of wood. These efforts he placed in the service of a modernist aesthetic in systematized production.[6] Samples from these tests were used as items with both the status of a design object demonstrating the basic ideas behind the furniture and as artifacts that virtually acquired the character of independent pieces of abstract sculpture (**SEE FIG. 2**). They complemented his furniture in exhibitions such as the one at Fortnum & Mason Department Store in London in 1933 as well as the one-man exhibition held at the Museum of Modern Art, which opened on 15 March 1938, "Architecture and Furniture: Aalto." This process of working with wood shows how Aalto integrated its technical and utility-related aspects with his design intentions. In the resulting whole, the implementation of an up-to-date knowledge of wood processing served an agenda that highlighted the aesthetic, psychological and physical well-being of the user.

In the mid-1930s, after winning the commission for the Sunila cellulose plant and the adjoining community, and having formed at the same time the extremely beneficial bond with Harry Gullichsen, the chief executive officer of A. Ahlström Corporation, the mightiest industrial actor in Finland, and with his wife, Maire

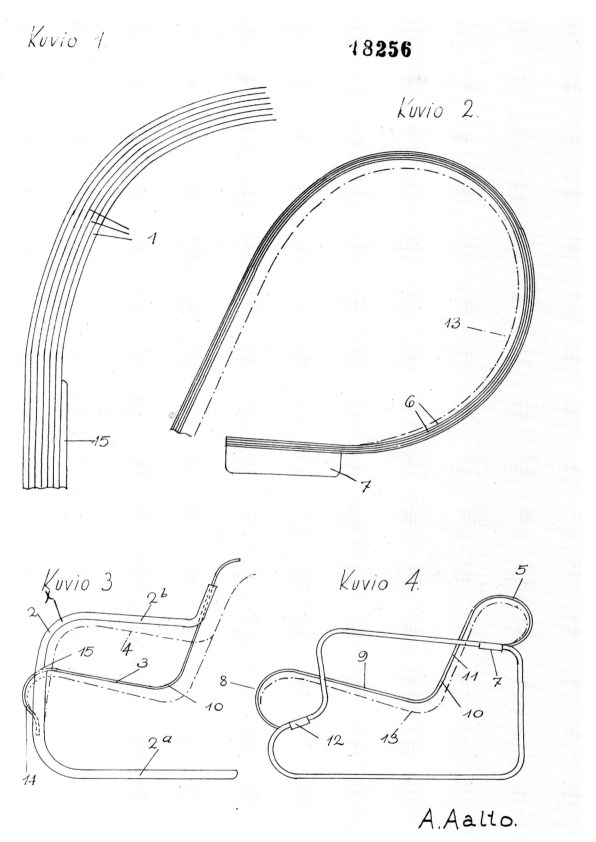

FIGURE 03 *Illustration from Aalto's patent application for the two so-called Paimio Chairs from the early 1930s. Application from 1934, patent approved in 1938 (Suomi Patentti nr. 18256).*

Gullichsen née Ahlström, Aalto's preoccupation with furniture design diminished. Major architectural commissions streamed into his office.[7] Still, Marie Gullichsen backed the founding of Artek Ltd. in 1935 to market and distribute Aalto's full range of furniture. This gave Aalto a rare position amid his generation of modernists: he had conceived an integrated model of furniture design, production, and distribution, which he kept at his service; this enabled a richness of experimentation in wooden furniture prior to his activity in industrialized wooden house production. As recent research makes evident, neither the design work nor the tactics of such integrated operations would have been possible without the collaborative input of his spouse and partner, the architect Aino Marsio Aalto.[8] Two factors came to be vital regarding Aalto's interaction with the United States. The first was his experimental, research-based approach to design from both its technical and human standpoints. The second was his ability to operate conjointly with the other stakeholders crucial for the realization of his design intentions.

To America: Aalto's Institute for Architectural Research

Like most of his modernist colleagues in Europe, Aalto had a curiosity about the American scene. This did not limit itself to architecture but encompassed societal aspects and especially the advancement of industrial production.[9] Yet Aalto's position differed in a remarkable way from the more typical patterns of volunteerism and enforced emigration that had characterized the general picture of European architects moving to the United States. Aalto's compatriot Eliel Saarinen, whom Aalto visited in 1938, had made his decision to emigrate in 1923 based on the pull of future American commissions following his success in the Chicago Tribune Building competition of 1922 and on the push generated by meager economic conditions in the newly independent republic of Finland. Le Corbusier's visit to the United States in 1935 was essentially an observation trip, and led to his insightful book *When the Cathedrals Were White* of the same year but not to deeper ties with the American architectural scene. Walter Gropius, Marcel Breuer, László Moholy-Nagy, and Ludwig Mies van der Rohe all emigrated for well-known reasons.

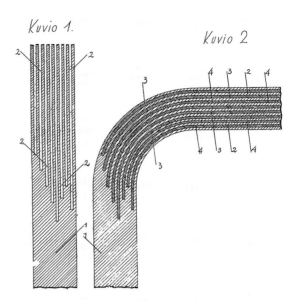

FIGURE 04 *Illustration for Aalto's patent application concerning "the way to bend solid wood by laminating the end part." Patent application 1933 in Great Britain, 1934 in Finland; approved 1940 (Suomi Patentti nr. 18666).*

But in the late 1930s Aalto was already well-established. At the time in his early forties, he was continuously advancing his career. Modernism was accepted in Finland even for public, official purposes and neither the domestic, economic, nor political climate gave cause to contemplate forced emigration.

Aalto was, therefore, free to establish ties in America and to learn from a context he had long waited to experience without the pressure of seeking a foothold for a permanent presence. But he was also determined to use his professional relationships and skills in the United States for the benefit of Finland. He had been pushed into that situation by the government of a Finland at war with the Soviet Union, because he had the connections and cultural prominence required for seeking help and understanding from the United States. Aalto, as a consequence, became an agent for his country. However tempting it might have been to remain in the United States and however apparently indeterminate his oscillation between the United States and Finland eventually became, he never took the decisive step but always remained a visitor, a friend, and loyal colleague—while keeping a distance.

During their second journey to the United States, for the opening of the World's Fair in New York on 1 May 1939, Alvar Aalto and Aino Aalto embarked on travel to the Midwest and then to the West Coast.[10] Before leaving, Aalto gave his well-known Yale lectures during April and May of that year. Of these seven lectures, the fourth and fifth would be seminal to his activity in the United States during the coming years. The fourth lecture concerned "the problem of the small dwelling, its relation to town planning and mass production, its type and standard production" and the fifth "the problem of standardized forms; humanizing standardization." He had drafted the themes in a letter to Wurster in the preceding March; he asked whether he also could deliver the lectures in California.[11] Whether this occurred is not known, but Aalto continued to develop the themes in a meeting at Wurster's office in San Francisco on 1 June. Aalto and Wurster, accompanied at the meeting by the architects Ernest Born, Thomas Church, Gardner Dailey, and Timothy Pflueger, drafted a thirty-four-point memorandum, which would serve as the basis for the founding of what Aalto called an Institute for Architectural Research. The draft, as described by Juhani Pallasmaa in the present volume, was both idealistic and brazenly pragmatic.

Later that June, and just before returning to Finland, Aalto wrote and mailed to Wurster a six-page program and mission statement further describing the planned Institute for Architectural Research. There he repeated his earlier pleas for human research and the importance of social factors; he emphasized that housing should function as the test bed for the coming research. But he also expanded the proposal to incorporate a laboratory comprising not only a single unit but several test locations around the world. These would function as branches of the institute tailored to specific climatic conditions. The first steps would be to "localize research in small wooden buildings . . . in California and Finland . . . because of the local materials and the local technical traditions." The research would then be implemented within industry, creating a circular flow of technical innovations coming from industry as well as architectural research that would, in turn, feed the industry with findings of human, social, and formal character.[12] Consequently, Aalto had formed a synthesis of research, laboratories, housing, industrial production, and wood as a material, which he would go on to develop further. This development would take place in 1940, during and after the Finnish Winter War, in an intellectual climate far removed from the relaxed days in California of the previous summer.

The 1940 Voyage: For Finland (and for Aalto)

When the Winter War ended on 13 March 1940, the magnitude of the reconstruction work needed in Finland became apparent. Hundreds of thousands fled toward the west from the part of eastern Finland that had been ceded to the Soviet Union. In addition, several towns had been bombed.[13] Soon after the ceasefire, both Aaltos left again for the United States. This time their task was to raise funds to help the ravaged country and to heighten the awareness that Finland belonged to the West and should not be forgotten. Aalto used architecture as his platform. This message, along with the urgency to provide shelter for the refugees, remained a core topic in his numerous talks and articles produced that spring. But the preparations for this activity had begun already during the Winter War, when Aalto became an officer operating under the Finnish War Office with the special tasks of propagating the Finnish cause in the West and especially in the United States, and of using his contacts there to the utmost to help his country. He had carefully orchestrated his operations in advance of this stay in the United States. During the visit, he acted as a de facto state agent and not as a private architect. Still, the lengthy visit produced two highly significant results: a tangible scheme to channel American funds for Finnish reconstruction and, for Aalto, the contacts with MIT that led to his appointment as a research professor in fall 1940.

In his letters to the United States, Aalto constantly stressed the fact that Finland had two fronts: a hostile eastern front and a Western front, the latter signifying a connection with the sphere of civilization to which Finland belonged. It was Aalto's duty to serve on that Western front as a propaganda officer. His operations in this sector started well before the Winter War ended, gained momentum through late May 1949 during his stay in the United States, and continued with lesser amplitude during the fall. Already in February 1940, Aalto had contacted Laurence S. Rockefeller and suggested that a still neutral country, the United States, could help another neutral country, Finland, with voluntary anti-aircraft devices and troops in order to protect civilians. The Winter War was the only war after the Spanish Civil War in which civil structures and citizens had become a main target for

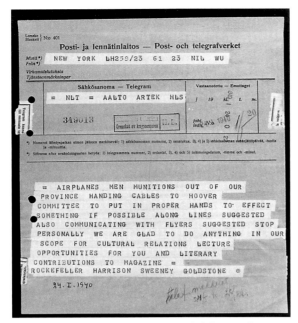

FIGURE 05 *Telegram from Laurence S. Rockefeller to Aalto, 24 Jan. 1940, answering his plea to provide airplanes and ammunition for the Finnish Winter War against the Soviet Union.*

destruction. Rockefeller replied to assess this kind of help as rather precarious in the turbulent situation of world politics (**FIG. 5**). That is when Aalto proposed that "perhaps the question of *reconstruction* suits America better, i.e. the renewal of what has been destroyed."[14] This mission of reconstruction, along with its architectural program combining social and human factors, consequently became the core agenda of Aalto's activity in the United States during 1940. First, he served as an undercover but state-monitored propagator of reconstruction, and second, he served increasingly as an individual operator that monitored the efforts of several actors toward a single goal: to channel funds and expertise from the United States to Finland. Both he finalized with the desired tangible result of an experimental town.[15]

Aalto's trip to the United States of spring 1940 was thoroughly prepared in unison with the Information Office of the Finnish Government.[16] Aalto supplied a detailed memorandum of the persons and institutions that should be approached, stressing the importance of contacting both cultural and architectural players, such as John Steinbeck, Lewis Mumford, and Frank Lloyd Wright, and the circles "of the younger highest financial levels such as the Rockefellers." Aalto explicitly stated that all this had been partly worked

out during his previous trip of 1939—and this was exactly why Aalto had risen to value among the Finnish officials: he was the only person in Finland with such connections previously formed on a personal and professional basis. Although the remodeling of the World's Fair pavilion for summer 1940 gave due cause for the trip, along with the presentation of the project in such a way that informed viewers about the new and disastrous conditions in Finland, Aalto's main purpose was to carry out the aforementioned activity.

Before embarking for the United States in March 1940, the Aaltos presented a detailed travel itinerary to the Finnish Information Office.[17] There they agreed that all official information exchanged between themselves and Finland should go through the Finnish Foreign Office and Embassy in a ciphered, coded form. The program in itself covered the period from March 16 to May 4, when Aalto proposed to travel back to Finland while Aino stayed a little longer.

The almost day-by-day program detailed meetings, lectures, and negotiations with possible supporters of the "Finnish cause." Regarding Finland's physical reconstruction, two items in the plan are of special interest. First, tentative negotiations were to occur with the Rockefeller Foundation on "the American builder's activity (ABA)" for "the protection of the homes and culture in Finland" and the "reconstruction of what is destroyed by the flying barbarians." Second, the ABA agenda was to be presented at several locations, including the central testing institute of the American wood industries in Madison, Wisconsin. As a rather unspecific agenda, it asked for help in the form of know-how from the American building industry and from its networks of expertise. It also requested direct financial aid from the wealthy circles exemplified by the Rockefeller Foundation.

Consequently, one of the leading modernist architects of the late 1930s had begun operating in the United States for the cause of his shattered country, with the full backing of the industrial and political power structure and even with formal ties to the operations of the Finnish Foreign Office. Had Aalto transformed from a rebellious, even leftist avant-garde architect and cultural critic of the late 1920s to a bedfellow of corporate capitalism and a servant of state politics? We have to remember that Aalto had during the late 1930s entered the inner circle of Finnish decision-makers in industrial policies, mainly via his connection to Harry and Maire Gullichsen.[18]

Harry Gullichsen was a member in an unofficial group of industrialists and policy-makers that had gathered to discuss the modernization of Finland through industry and with nonpartisan, liberal politics leaning toward Anglo-American models, thus uniting private, progressive industries and enlightened reform policies on the national level. This process of re-engineering also required the physical and visual modernization of the man-made environment, and for this, Aalto served as a key figure. Industrial leaders were determined to present publicly an example of an "official" power structure overwhelmingly concerned with the problems of their predominantly agrarian country. Thus, when the state appointed Harry Gullichsen as head of the reconstruction strategies at the end of the Winter War, it also gave Aalto a matching role with regard to city-planning and housing.

The Finnish government rapidly understood Aalto's value as related to the Western, and especially the American, scene. Consequently, it did not enroll him into normative front service—he was recruited instead to serve on the "Western front." And for Aalto this service was natural, as the whole existence of his country was endangered. The division of labor in this small circle of people was finalized when Maire Gullichsen became head of "Bureau A," operating under the State Information Office through the company Artek, which was led and mainly owned by her. This unit assumed the responsibility of campaigning for the Finnish cause in the West at large. It also formed the base for Aalto's activity. Maire Gullichsen would make operative her network of industrial tycoons, but the network also gained through her active role in the realm of modern art, architecture, and furniture design.[19]

From Research to Reconstruction: "An American Town in Finland"

I now return to the quotation by Aalto cited at the beginning of this essay, in which the architect underlines the parallels between American and Nordic/Finnish modes of operation—parallels that enabled Aalto to operate successfully as a mediator between the innovations of the United States and those of his home country. There already existed a strong tradition in Finland of looking at "America"; that is, to the United States for models not only of the democratic political system but also of scientific and especially technological advancement. This practice Finland naturally shared with the Old World at large, but in that country the United States also served as a role model of democracy, innovation, and modernity, which took on a specific importance first during Finland's nation-building era, from the late nineteenth century to independence in 1917, and then in an altered way thereafter.[20] As Finland strove toward national sovereignty and attempted to create a correspondingly indigenous cultural profile, features of late nineteenth-century American architecture—especially that of H. H. Richardson—served as one ingredient in the shaping of "Finnish" modernity during the first years of the twentieth century. Soon, these formal influences would be replaced with models tied to building techniques and serial production. The models, in turn, had ties to wood—prevalent in both geographic areas—as the common material basis for single-house production.

When Aalto began forming his contacts in the United States in the late 1930s, he followed a well-established pattern. Even though Germany still dominated as a center for emulation and innovation transfer in most areas of technological advancement as well as culture, the Anglo-American sphere was growing in significance. This significance was strengthened by the political situation in both Germany and the Soviet Union. For many in Finland, the American model of societal and technological modernity combined with a democratic system highlighting the role of the individual had become, during the 1930s, a beacon in a world of increasing dictatorship.

As previously mentioned, Aalto belonged to the informal group of top-level decision-makers who, in the late thirties, discussed the future as well as the political orientation of Finland. Harry Gullichsen, as a spokesman of industry, represented the liberal and internationally oriented, technocratic view of experts from the private sector. These experts were not bound by party-political ties and thus could operate freely within the domain of their enterprises and the societal context embedded in their industrial communities. In these areas, Aalto and Gullichsen, via the financial backing of the Ahlström Corporation, had already collaborated, constructing modernist housing such as the stepped multi-apartment block in Kauttua from 1938 and initiating the production in Varkaus of pre-sawn wooden one-family houses based on type-drawings by Aalto, beginning in 1937.[21] Technological advancement, as well as architectural and research-based analytical knowledge tied to social and psychological factors, was to lead the way to modernization, providing a model for Finland's slow and provincial-nationalistic public sector.

As a result, through the group of decision-makers to which Aalto belonged, we find the alignment of modern entrepreneurship and finance with a program of not only economic but also social advancement. All of this, it was thought, could be expressed via the construction of a modern infrastructure. In Finland and in the United States, a democratic political system with high esteem for individual incentive provided the framework. Such background factors facilitated Aalto's surprising swiftness in finding operational ground for his efforts by catalyzing the right circles, such as leading architects, universities, and the Rockefellers, for the cause of Finland—and soon enough for himself, as the architectural mastermind of the whole endeavor. It was with these assets that Aalto during his stay in America, from March to October 1940, set in motion a multifaceted network with the goal of reaching a tangible, built result intended to facilitate Finland's reconstruction, "An American Town in Finland." This initial success gave him a foothold on American turf.

A Home-Base for Research: The MIT Appointment and the "Experimental Town"

The gradually deepening contacts between Aalto and MIT around the effort of supporting reconstruction portended a complex but integrated process. In the end, MIT provided support for the accumulation of knowledge and for a consortium shaped around a building project, the "experimental town." Aalto conceived this project to channel funds and to function as an American–Finnish architectural interface.

John E. Burchard, the director of the Albert Farwell Bemis Foundation associated with the MIT School of Architecture, followed Aalto's stay in the United States, and after hearing about his proposed visit to see Gropius at Harvard University, he wrote to Aalto in early April 1940, asking him to give a couple of guest lectures at MIT. Burchard felt the students would be especially keen to hear him because, he wrote, "graduates who go to Europe regularly make pilgrimages to you."[22] Aalto replied with enthusiasm and delivered the lectures on 25–26 April. Besides speaking about Finnish and Nordic modern architecture and his own work, Aalto—in accordance with his special wishes—gave a talk on the reconstruction and rehousing problems of Finland. He pointed out the role that research would have in this massive task. Burchard, not surprisingly, also wished for Aalto to focus on the issues of reconstruction and research—the Bemis Foundation's mission emphasized precisely the same issues—to facilitate a larger mission of gathering information and conducting research on the problems of housing. The interests of the Bemis Foundation and those of Aalto, consequently, formed a perfect match. The university immediately produced an abstract of Aalto's lecture as a press release, and Aalto published articles on the same topic in the United States soon thereafter.[23]

Aalto's lecture on reconstruction would be seminal for his subsequent activity in the United States and Finland; in it, he laid out the main principles that guided his task in its entirety, stressing research, high quality, flexibility, and the positive chance to produce models that could also be applied elsewhere under similar circumstances. In this argument one can hear the echoes of the discussions at Wurster's office from the previous June, which had focused on the draft program for an Institute for Architectural Research. The Finnish situation, with the imminent need for rehousing, now provided a context motivating the actualization of those ideas. Thus Aalto, in his typically assured manner, envisioned in his talk that "it is proposed to build a laboratory community for reconstruction activities. This will be a special kind of model town, managed in a scientific way to carry out special human needs and to appraise the quality of construction of new homes and housing centers. Development of this laboratory town is expected to be of great value not only in guiding reconstruction in Finland, but for future colonization and reconstruction problems all over the world."[24] In early July, a tentative decision was made to offer Aalto a part-time teaching and research post at MIT with a three- or four-month period that he would spend full-time at the Bemis Foundation. Funds for Aalto's research were to be sought from the Rockefeller Foundation.[25]

After the formal decision had been made to appoint Aalto, MIT issued a press release on 24 July. In summarizing MIT's agenda for Aalto, Dean Walter R. MacCornack stressed the role of research to be carried out at the Bemis Foundation. He also stressed the feedback that would come from Finland via experimentation associated with reconstruction. Aalto would have the dual role of conducting research at MIT periodically and in between supervising reconstruction back home, testing research results in a hands-on setting and bringing the results back again to MIT for further elaboration.[26] In informing the editors of leading professional journals about Aalto's field of work, Burchard also stressed that "Aalto's appointment as a research professor is a true statement. It was neither his wish nor the Institute's that he be imported as a distinguished European who would be a critic of design."[27]

But what was this "research" that Burchard still acknowledged to be "vague" in its formulations—even while admitting that "there is no institute of architectural research at all"? He was also careful in clarifying that MIT would not be "basically interested in the Finnish problem."[28] This cautiousness can be ascribed to the fact that Aalto had already begun negotiations before his appointment with the Rockefeller Foundation. This resulted in an unofficial, oral decision that if MIT engaged Aalto, the Bemis Foundation would most probably receive a major donation from the Rockefellers for architectural research in low-cost housing. Officially, MIT and the Rockefeller Foundation operated independently, but, in fact, Aalto had tied them together to further his agenda as well as that of Finland.[29]

Burchard and Aalto together defined the working program for Aalto at MIT in early September.[30] The sectors of research were quite general and the practical reasons for the program's implementation—among them housing reconstruction—were not mentioned. The three "divisions" of research were: examining the flexibility of standardization; examining special sensitive reactions

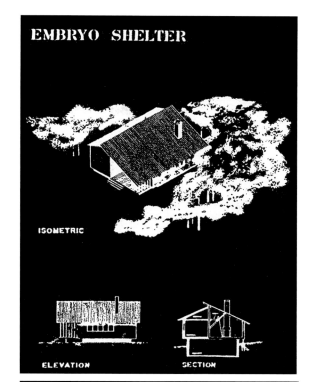

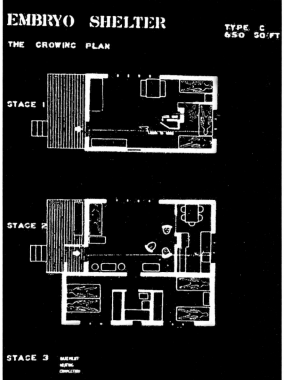

FIGURES 06–07 *Examples of work by Aalto and MIT students, 1940: a drawing of an "embryo shelter" that can be expanded, as illustrated in the second drawing.*

of the human being to architectural elements (especially light) in one room; and establishing the surface areas of the house (elevations). With this program, a schedule for the first year, and a group of enthusiastic, carefully selected students including I. M. Pei, Aalto and the Bemis Foundation set out to realize their joint scheme of research and education.[31] But they witnessed it come to an abrupt stop in mid-October of the same year. Aalto, his wife, and their two children—who had not left the United States in late spring as anticipated when they embarked in March—were warned by Finnish officials about the signs of an imminent war, the Second World War, and they took the only passenger ship available to Finland.[32]

Behind him, Aalto left a deep frustration, both within MIT's Bemis Foundation and among the MIT students. The ensuing correspondence from Burchard to Aalto, while considering the possibilities of continuing the work in anticipation of Aalto's return, mentions that it would now be conducted principally by Arnold Wasson-Tucker, who would ensure the continuation of the project. Even during Aalto's short time at MIT, the first sets of drawings for preliminary shelters had already been completed and gathered in a booklet (**FIGS. 6–7**). Also, negotiations with the American Red Cross and their Department of Disaster Relief had reached a positive stage—but were to suffer without Aalto "to lend them the force of his personality."[33] After Aalto's departure, Wasson-Tucker continued the work, reworking drawings for "expandable shelters," but also making it clear that without Aalto's presence the project would wither away.[34]

Nothing was heard of Aalto for many months, despite Burchard's inquiry to the Embassy of Finland in February 1941. In April, Aalto sent an explanatory letter, describing his efforts on behalf of Finland's reconstruction work and anticipating a return to MIT in the summer. He concluded a letter sent later in May: "I could say to you that the process here has been from point of view of architecture so complicated that I not before now had a real picture clear in my eyes."[35] The disruption in Aalto's work at MIT would last four years. But even though the project at MIT came to what everybody expected to be a temporary halt, work progressed along the opposite channel of action, the one aiming to build the "experimental town" in Finland.

Realizing the "Experimental Town": Post-War Housing

Aalto's work at MIT served as but one component of his larger vision for a collaboration between Finland and the United States, which included the realization of the "experimental town." As previously mentioned, he had formed a relationship with the Rockefeller Foundation and personally with Laurence S. Rockefeller well before his extended stay in the United States during March through October 1940. When Aalto suggested reconstruction aid as a possible intervention to help ravaged Finland, the foundation considered providing such aid a viable possibility. Rockefeller presented the matter to the president of the foundation in April and detailed discussions ensued. By early May, Aalto had already conceptualized the "experimental town," to be partially financed by U.S. funds. He cabled to Maire Gullichsen that the Rockefellers would send an observer to Finland.[36]

Parallel with this development, Aalto formed For Finland Inc. in April, a vehicle to collect and channel funds to Finland. It had among its objectives "to assist in and forward plans and means for the reconstruction and rehabilitation of Finland and its citizens." The ambassador of Finland, Hjalmar J. Procopé, served as the honorary chairman and members came from the circles of the wealthy and influential, with the honorary committee including Mrs. Eleanor Roosevelt.[37] Aalto, following his objective to propagate the Finnish cause, would empower his plans for the "experimental town" through this network. The scheme for the "laboratory town," already presented in one of Aalto's April 1940 lectures at MIT, was in a concrete way forwarded in a meeting in New York on 12 July of that year. In that meeting Aalto, together with Edgar Williams and two members from the For Finland Inc. New York Executive Committee, Dickson Hartwell and Henry W. Miller, conceived the scheme for the town in such a way that For Finland Inc. would function as the collector of funds, serving the committee of architects that were to supervise the project (**FIG. 8**).

After deliberating, For Finland Inc. decided by the end of July to inaugurate what they now called "An American Town in Finland." An American Architects' Committee, backed by the American Institute of

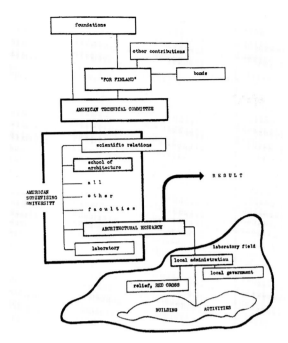

FIGURE 08 *Aalto, diagram explaining the structure to support the realization of "An American Town in Finland."*

Architects, would oversee the project. Three main decisions were reached: 1) an experimental town would be built in Finland with funds from the United States; 2) a research center in the United States would be installed to provide expertise for the project; 3) the project as a whole would be monitored by the committee of the architects. For Finland Inc. rapidly formalized the committee with Edgar Williams as chairman and members including renowned architects such as William Lescaze, George Howe, and Edward D. Stone, as well as, not surprisingly, Wurster and Burchard, who had released the news of Aalto's appointment at MIT through the Bemis Foundation the very same week.[38]

The development of the "American Town in Finland" can be followed from a couple of drafts into the detailed, budgeted version published as a booklet in New York in late summer 1940, titled "Post-War Reconstruction: Re-housing Research in Finland" **(FIG. 9)**.[39] The booklet included the schematic town plan prepared, as indicated earlier, with the anticipation of Aalto's affiliation with MIT. The plan was to serve as a concrete testing ground for the more generally conceived research at MIT's Bemis Foundation, which had the tentative promise of Rockefeller Foundation funding. In Aalto's late July meeting with the Rockefeller

Foundation, it was stipulated that "the Rockefeller Foundation would pay for the actual construction of a portion of this community."[40]

Even though funding from the Rockefeller Foundation was crucial to the further elaboration of the scheme, Aalto actively sought other U.S. funding too. He wrote numerous letters to top decision-makers and industrialists, and even to Franklin D. Roosevelt, enclosing the booklet for reference. In these letters, he attempted to strike a psychological chord in the receiver so that a feeling of sharing in a mutual project and its goals would ensue. He ended his letter to Herbert Hoover in California by saying, "My letter is probably too emotional to be . . . from one technician to another," and to Henry Ford he wrote, "I appeal to you as the man who has solved a great human technical problem by harmonising technical standards and the social human need and economy"—almost quoting himself from the booklet.[41]

That the Aalto family stayed in the United States longer than expected can be explained by the rapid advance of both a concrete financial method for helping Finnish reconstruction and Aalto's negotiations with MIT. The latter had been finalized in his appointment to the post of research professor at the university. But during the summer of 1940, the situation in Finland had worsened as the country tried to recuperate from the Winter War. The former population of the territories ceded to the Soviet Union had, in moving west, created the housing problem for which Aalto's "American Town in Finland" would serve as a model solution. Back home, Aalto's expertise would therefore have been of the utmost importance. Among Aalto's countrymen, then, a certain impatience grew with the Aaltos' lack of commitment to an imminent return.

In two letters from the summer of 1940, Maire Gullichsen made it clear that many thought the Aaltos would permanently choose the "Land of Plenty" instead of their ravaged Finland. Moreover, Nazi Germany had occupied Norway in the spring and the threat of a new war was imminent. Being aware of the scheme for the "experimental town," Gullichsen described the negotiations already completed in Finland with the aim of preparing the ground for the coming construction of the project. She also made it clear that Aalto's personal presence was crucial for furthering

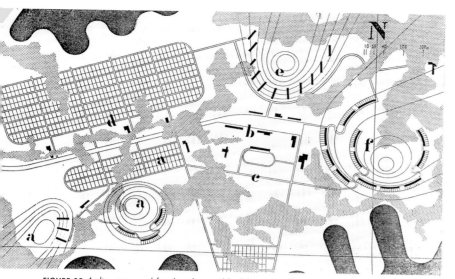

FIGURE 09 *Aalto, proposal for the plan and building types for "An American Town in Finland."*

any aspect of the project, both in the United States and in Finland. Aalto's personal identification with the scheme made it vulnerable and dependent on Aalto's location and involvement. Gullichsen ended one of her letters by strongly urging Aalto to return to Finland with the "American town as a flower in your buttonhole."[42]

At the beginning of his description of Finland's would-be reconstruction in his booklet "Post-War Reconstruction"—in fact his scheme for "An American Town in Finland"—Aalto set out for the first time principles he was to repeat in all of his writings during the coming years concerning rebuilding and housing. He emphasized key issues such as research, "scientifically conducted work," and the use of industrial and serial house production according to "flexible standardization." All of these were to be guided by the "human factor," that is, by the psychological, biological, and social variables that were to be considered in order to avoid the usual results of emergency reconstruction: barrack-like shoddy construction and monotony. After delineating this mission statement, Aalto emphasized the need for creating an actual test environment in order to get feedback for further explorations. The built results would "be turned over as dwellings for families and individuals to serve as a living center for refugees. In this way the laboratory field then begins to fulfill its task directly to humanity."[43] Finland is not mentioned, nor is MIT. This is unusual, given that in the next chapter, Aalto proposed the organization of the research and development and stressed the need

for an anonymous "American university or technical institute." But when Aalto considered the actual pragmatics of the scheme, Finland was shown as the perfect testing ground, due to the pertinence of its condition after the Winter War.

The idea was to finance the "experimental town" with combined U.S. and Finnish capital. The American funds—mainly from the Rockefeller Foundation—would add up to 60 percent of the estimated total cost of $560,800. The Finnish government and local authorities were to provide the remainder, including the "research field" (building site) along with the necessary infrastructure such as roads, plumbing, and electricity. The actual site was never determined, but without making it explicit, the plan was tied to the interests of the Gullichsens and their Ahlström Corporation, which had already initiated industrial, wooden one-family house production. During an interview, Aalto mentioned the Kokemäki River Valley district in western Finland as one option for a site.[44] In 1940, he was already envisioning a regional development plan for this area, vital to the industrial interests of Ahlström. The "experimental town" would fit well into the concept, land usage, and logistics of this larger scheme.

The proposed community comprised several types of houses. The wooden, one-family house would dominate alongside terraced apartment houses and row houses on both sloping and even ground. Aalto had already executed such types in the late 1930s, along with his designs in the industrial communities of Sunila and Kauttua. In addition, Aalto now envisioned taking advantage of prefabricated elements made of concrete. But it was the wooden house executed via prefabrication that lay at the core of the whole plan. The first stage of this prefabrication consisted of the "embryo human shelter," which was about the only result Aalto had time to take to the level of a set of drawings at MIT, and which was also titled the "expandable shelter" in the published dossier **(SEE FIGS. 6–7)**.[45] The bulk of the building program comprised "the one-family house: a product of pre-fabrication and industry." Aalto envisioned a flexible way to apply standardization, such that it would ensure a result "adjustable for families of different sizes, various topographical locations, different exposures, views, etc."[46]

The town would also include a community center, a school, and an athletic field. From the calculations and diagrams, it is hard to estimate the approximate number of people that were to inhabit the town. The budget, however, provides some idea: 168 single houses, 3 units of terraced apartment houses, and 3 units of row houses are mentioned. This does not match the schematic town-plan presented in which the first test-phase is indicated with letter "a." This more extensive town-plan also includes the construction completed after the experimental phase, and so utilizes its results. It indicates commercial buildings as well. Industrial or agricultural production is not mentioned or visually indicated, because "it is to be located in a place of flexible connections with various existing towns, industrial districts and agricultural centers."[47] In this way, the community could have functioned as a satellite of either two of the main production areas of interest for the Ahlström Corporation: the Kokemäenjoki River Valley in the west or the Varkaus sawmill and paper plant in eastern central Finland.

The Keystone: Wooden Prefabrication

Prefabrication constituted the core of Aalto's work in both the United States in 1940 and Finland during the early 1940s, in public and private spheres alike.[48] As mentioned earlier, Aalto had since 1937 produced type-drawings of wooden one-family houses for the Ahlström Corporation, to be used as company housing at several industrial sites in Finland. Their Varkaus sawmill, consequently, served as the housing's production site and first testing ground. With the lead of the Gullichsens, the company was determined to expand this production line, both for internal use and for external markets. By summer 1940, the activity was still at the stage of type-drawings to be realized through pre-sawn elements. But it had already been decided to take the next step toward the serial factory production of prefabricated elements, enabling a greater flexibility in the product palette.

While in the United States, Aalto had been dispatched by Finnish officials to examine the production methods and logistics of the local housing industry, already well-advanced in the mass-production of wooden one-family houses. Aalto thus visited several plants, such as those of the Gunnison Company, and collected data to serve his program of house production for the

Ahlström Corporation. In this way, his activity in the United States had a third thread in addition to his state-monitored role as a spokesman for the Finnish cause and his teaching and research work at MIT. This thread intertwined with the project for the "experimental town." In the service of the Finnish private sector, and of the Gullichsens with the Ahlström Corporation as a tool, Aalto had assumed the role of an industrial agent. He collected data for the installment of a new production line based on the already existing technological know-how of the Ahlström Corporation as well as on his own new set of type-drawings.[49] He further enriched this data collecting by the work carried out at MIT. Both formed the nucleus of the building program for the "experimental town."

It is not an exaggeration to assume that the provider of housing for the "experimental town" would have been the Ahlström Corporation. The company was the first to start in-factory house production in Finland at the beginning of 1941. In a way these houses, produced extensively during and after the war, became the physical manifestation of Aalto's transfer of American know-how to Finland (FIGS. 10–11). In the drawings and program Aalto produced for the Ahlström house factory he stressed, as he did in the booklet on reconstruction, the importance of "flexible" standardization. Although he admired the efficiency and logistics of American house production, he was highly critical of the resulting uniformity of the products. Thus the Ahlström collection of type-houses became one of high variation, making it possible to provide homes from 40 to more than 150 square meters in size, but all based on the 90-centimeter-wide wall panel—and even providing possibilities for later additions along the lines of the "expandable shelter."

The End, Intermission, and Return to MIT: What Was Achieved?

Although Aalto's research with his students at MIT's Bemis Foundation ceased in October 1940, his work on "An American Town in Finland" continued. Negotiations with the American Red Cross proceeded from Finland during that fall, but the requisite U.S.-based starting capital of $200 was still missing.[50] After his return, Aalto gave interviews to Finnish and Swedish newspapers explaining the scheme, fully confident that its actualization would begin in summer 1941.[51] Months passed, and the geopolitical position of Finland became increasingly precarious in war-torn Europe. The still neutral, isolationist United States had become ever more cautious about operating in a risk-zone like Finland. Pearl Harbor, along with Finland's pact with Germany in 1941 to oppose the Soviet Union, finally sealed the fate of the project.

But even though the American town never materialized on Finnish soil, Aalto gained from his experiences in the United States in other ways. As mentioned, he applied what he learned there in laying out the scheme for both the production and the actual architectural design of the Ahlström house factory. In 1942, he was appointed head of the Reconstruction Bureau of the Finnish Association of Architects, and in this capacity, he recommended a specific unit for standardization. In an extensive booklet published that year describing the principles of standardization in the service of reconstruction, "The Art of Building and Standards: Core Issues of Reconstruction," it is easy to identify many of the fundamental ideas behind Aalto's project for "An American Town in Finland". It would not be a single community, but a whole reconstruction plan operative during and after the war.[52]

Wurster and Aalto began to plan for Aalto's return to MIT immediately after the war in 1945. Wurster, now dean of the School of Architecture, was free to make decisions about Aalto's future work and salary.[53] In discussing the nature of Aalto's coming work, the two men took up the subject of continuing Aalto's research. But now that research would appear in the form of a series of lectures on his experiences during and immediately after the war in Finland—the country had ceased war with the Soviet Union in summer 1944. In these talks Aalto again picked up the role of standardization and its abuse in architecture: "By this [standardization] I do not mean the ordinary process of modern evil mania. What I aim at is the special architectural liberation from the grip of technical standardization."[54] Such a grip Aalto now viewed as ruling the American housing industry. Aalto resumed his work as a professor at MIT in fall 1945, but the momentum of 1940, as expressed in For Finland Inc.'s tightly knit plan for aid and cooperation, was gone. Politically, furthermore, the United States would have been unable to help Finland. The Soviet Union prevented the country from receiving the Marshall Aid the United States had intended to give.

It regarded Finland as belonging to its territory of dominance, as had been agreed by leaders of the United States, Great Britain, and the Soviet Union in Yalta in 1945. Although the Soviet Union had never occupied Finland, the political climate in the post-war years was extremely precarious.[55]

In his letters to Wurster of 1945, Aalto recalled the impressions he gained during his 1939 journey in the United States, when he visited the Wursters in California. Some of those experiences, such as his visits to wooden one-family houses, which followed the topography and the scattered nature of the local urbanism, suggested parallels to Finnish conditions, alluding to his own aspirations toward making architectural communication between these two cultures possible. Now Aalto had a real town to rebuild, Rovaniemi, the capital of Lapland, which the retreating German troops had burned down to ashes. Not only did he envision the new plan for Rovaniemi in 1947, but he later worked out a general plan for the future of the built environment of the whole of Lapland. Under these circumstances, his experiences in the United States and with the ambitious schemes for the Institute for Architectural Research and "An American Town in Finland" came into play—but more on the conceptual than the material level.

Lapland had to be developed under circumstances of the utmost scarcity, without any foreign investors or aid sources. At the same time, the country was paying severe war reparations to the Soviet Union. Consequently, the wooden houses came to be constructed on-site, without the anticipated promise of industrial house production. Nevertheless, what Aalto had learned in the United States about the union of research, housing, and prefabrication had already emanated into the private sector, through the rapid growth of industrial house production during and after the war, and into the public domain via the work of the Reconstruction Bureau of the Finnish Association of Architects. That Aalto continued to see this wooden bridge of innovation as vital and operative six years after his first visit to the West Coast became evident when he wrote to Wurster, conceptualizing the rebuilding of Rovaniemi: "The building program consists on the whole of wooden houses, about as your things in California except that Lapland has a cold, arctic climate."[56] Thus, Aalto had not forgotten his lessons from the United States.

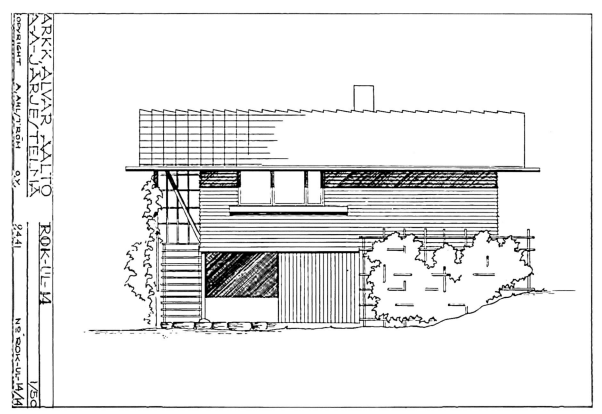

FIGURE 10 *Aalto, one of the type-house schemes of the AA-system for the house factory of the A. Ahlstrom Corporation, 1941.*

FIGURE 11 *Aalto, prefabricated AA-system homes for the A. Ahlstrom Corporation mill, Kauttua, western Finland, early 1940s.*

1 Letter from Alvar Aalto to William Wurster, 25 Oct. 1939 (William Wurster/Wurster Bernardi, and Emmons Collection, Environmental Design Archives, Univ. of California, Berkeley, hereafter EDA UCB).

2 Pekka Korvenmaa, "Aalto and Finnish Industry," in Alvar Aalto: Between Humanism and Materialism, ed. Peter Reed (New York: Museum of Modern Art, 1998), 70–92.

3 Aalto's American travels have been researched by Elina Standertskjöld; see her "The Dream of a New World: Alvar Aalto in America, 1938–40," in En Route! Finnish Architects' Studies Abroad, ed. Timo Tuomi (Helsinki: Museum of Finnish Architecture, 1999). Additionally, I have written elsewhere on topics related to the present chapter: see "Aalto and Finnish Industry"; "The Finnish Wooden House Transformed: American Prefabrication, War-Time Housing and Alvar Aalto," Construction History 6 (1990): 47–61; "From House Manufacture to Universal Systems: Industrial Prefabrication, the Utopias of Modernism and the Conditions of Wood Culture," in Timber Construction in Finland (Helsinki: Museum of Finnish Architecture, 1996), 162–75; and "Modern Architecture Serving Modern Production," in Sunila, 1926–54: Alvar Aalto Architect, vol. 7, ed. Pekka Korvenmaa (Helsinki: Alvar Aalto Foundation and Alvar Aalto Academy, 2004), 9–23. For extensive background about Finnish conditions and the wars, see the footnotes in "Aalto and Finnish Industry."

4 The most recent source on Aalto's furniture and nonarchitectural design is Pirkko Tuukkanen, ed., Alvar Aalto, Designer (Jyväskylä, Finland: Alvar Aalto Museum, 2002), especially the chapter by Kaarina Mikonranta, "Alvar Aalto: Master of Variation," 43–108. In order to contextualize Aalto's use of bent plywood and laminated wood in furniture, it is worth noticing the highly innovative design and production of such furniture very near Finland in Tallinn, Estonia, by the Luther Company, dating from late nineteenth century up to WWII. See Jüri Kermik, The Luther Factory: Plywood and Furniture, 1877–1940, (Tallinn: Museum of Estonian Architecture, 2004).

5 See Mikonranta, "Alvar Aalto." See also the archives of the Finnish National Board of Patents and Registers, Helsinki. Aalto held seven patents: five on furniture, one on a lamp, and one on a staircase solution. The patents discussed were date from the 1930s: for a metal-legged chair (Suomi Patentti nr. 16222; applied 1932 and granted 1934); for the construction used in the so-called Paimio Chair (Suomi Patentti nr. 18256; applied 1934, granted 1938); and for the way to bend solid wood by laminating the end part (the basis for most of Aalto's furniture) (Suomi Patentti nr. 18666; applied in 1933 in Britain and in 1934 in Finland; granted 1940). This information reached the author via an exhibition organized by the Board of Patents and Registers, Helsinki, in 2003. Marianna Heikinheimo published an article based on the exhibition: Heikinheimo, "Alvar Aalto's Patents," Ptah 2 (2004), 9–16. The documents were extensively laid out for the author by the kind help of Mrs. Kastehelmi Nikkanen, main archivist at the Board of Patents and Registers.

6 On Aalto's furniture in relation to Finnish modern furniture design in general, see Pekka Korvenmaa, "Opportunities and Ideals in Modern Furniture Design in Finland," in Finnish Modern Design, ed. Marianne Aav and Nina Stritzler-Levine (New Haven, Conn.: Yale Univ. Press, in association with the Bard Graduate Center for Studies in the Decorative Arts, 1998), 103–28.

7 These were mostly of industrial character and came largely through the Gullichsens and their circle of leading industrialists. This context is explained in Korvenmaa, "Aalto and Finnish Industry."

8 The crucial role that Aino Marsio Aalto played in the design of the range of furniture sold through Artek and her role as a designer of commissioned interiors realized by Artek and as the artistic leader of that enterprise has slowly emerged through research. See Ulla Kinnunen, ed., Aino Aalto (Jyväskylä, Finland: Alvar Aalto Foundation and Museum, 2004), esp. Renja Suominen-Kokkonen, "The Silent Central Figure: The Architect Aino Marsio-Aalto," 206–27.

9 See Standertskjöld, "Dream of a New World." Aalto, for example, owned the book Wie Baut Amerika?, by Richard Neutra. See also the three-volume work Alvar Aalto (New York: Rizzoli, 1984–1991), by Göran Schildt, especially the volume The Decisive Years (1986), 165–88.

10 Described in detail in Schildt, Decisive Years, 165–88.

11 Korvenmaa, "Aalto and Finnish Industry", 70–92.

12 The memorandum, dated 1 June 1939, was seminal to all of Aalto's coming activity in the United States for the next few years and was to radiate into his practice in Finland during and after the Second World War. The program and mission statement is dated 13 June of the same year in New York (WWA).

13 Again I refer to Korvenmaa, "Aalto and Finnish Industry," for a fuller picture of these events in relation to reconstruction.

14 Memorandum by Alvar Aalto, Jan. 1940 (Alvar Aalto Foundation Archive, Helsinki; hereafter referred to as AAA); letter from Aalto to Laurence S. Rockefeller, 8 Feb. 1940 (copy on file at AAA).

15 On the numerous talks and ensuing articles written by Aalto on reconstruction, published both in the United States and in Finland, see Korvenmaa, "Aalto and Finnish Industry."

16 Typed memorandum of four pages,undated, "The Ways to Distribute Propaganda and Its Different Forms" (AAA). Here Aalto stresses that all "elements that are vital to construct a modern life" should be included: literature, architecture, sociology, sciences, industry, and financial life.

17 "A General Outline: Work and Travel Program USA, 16.3.1940, Aino and Alvar Aalto" (AAA).

18 For a fuller account of this see Korvenmaa, "Aalto and Finnish Industry."

19 Memorandum on the planned activities and responsibilities of Bureau A (Toimisto A), written by Maire Gullichsen for the State Information Office, sine anno, but apparently prepared before Aalto left on his trip to the United States in March 1940 (AAA); description of the activities of Bureau A, produced by Maire Gullichsen for the State Information Office, 26 April 1940 (AAA). The domain of Bureau A was vast, including the Nordic sphere, Switzerland, Great Britain, and the United States. Persons involved included Morton Shand, Siegfried Giedion, and Hélène de Mandrot, among others. Norway and Sweden were active in realizing funds, but the well-begun Norwegian campaign stopped when Adolf Hitler invaded the country in fall 1940.

20 Here it is not possible to delve deeper into the architectural relationship between the United States and Finland. But it is worth mentioning in brief that, around 1900, to design "along the American style" was a conscious reference and symptom of modernity. Some years later, master-builders adopted the system of the American plank house; that is, the balloon frame.

21 For a further account, see Korvenmaa, "Aalto and Finnish Industry" and "Modern Architecture Serving Modern Production."

22 Letter from John E. Burchard to Alvar Aalto, 8 April 1940 (copy on file at MIT's Institute Archives and Special Collections, John Ely Burchard Collection; hereafter MITA, JEBC). On the Bemis Foundation in relation to the issues discussed here, see Korvenmaa, "Finnish Wooden House Transformed" and "Aalto and Finnish Industry."

23 Letter from Alvar Aalto to John E. Burchard, 17 April 1940 (MITA, JEBC); letter from John E. Burchard to Alvar Aalto, 18 April 1940 (MITA, JEBC); press release with notation: "Advance Matter: Caution, by the MIT News Service, to be released in morning papers," 26 April 1940 (MITA, JEBC).

24 Press release: "Advance Matter: Caution, by the MIT News Service, to be released in morning papers," 26 April 1940 (MITA, JEBC).

25 Memorandum from a meeting on Aalto's engagement held by John E. Burchard, Dean Walter R. MacCornack, and President Karl Taylor Compton, 3 July 1940 (copy on file at MITA, JEBA).

26 MIT News Service press release, 24 July 1940 (MITA, JEBC).

27 See, for example, a letter from John E. Burchard to Roger Sherman of the Architectural Record, 25 July 1940 (MITA, JEBC).

28 Letter from John E. Burchard to Roger Sherman of the Architectural Record, 25 July 1940 (MITA, JEBC). See also the letter from Burchard to D. J. Hartwell, 1 Aug. 1940 (MITA, JEBC).

29 All of this is explicitly stated in the "Memorandum of interview with Aalto and others at Rockefeller Center," 27 June 1940, written by John E. Burchard (MITA, JEBC). Although the foundation already had spent substantial sums in housing, mainly house production, the younger generation showed interest in Aalto's proposals: "Moreover, even hating housing as they do in a sense all of the sons seem convinced that they owe something to the housing problem" (1).

30 Proposal by John E. Burchard to Alvar Aalto, 16 July 1940; Aalto's scheme of 3 Sept. and Burchard's comments on it to Dean Walter R. MacCornack, 7 Sept.1940 (MITA, JEBC). The swiftness of the changing information was due to the fact that Aalto still remained in the United States.

31 Aalto's last minute letter (from New York, on 17 October) to Burchard, in which he apologizes for his disappearance and explains the reason for it (MITA, JEBC).

32 "Famous Finnish Couple—Alvar and Aino Aalto, Architects—Are Producing Unique Furniture in the United States," *Christian Science Monitor*, Women's Page, 12 Feb. 1941, edited by Vera Connolly.

33 Letters from John E. Burchard to Dean Walter R. MacCornack, 28 Oct. 1940, and to Edgar I. Williams, chairman of the committee behind the American Town in Finland, 9 Nov. 1940 (MITA, JEBC). Negotiations with the American Red Cross were begun by Aalto on 17 Sept. 1940. A letter and attached memorandum from a meeting between Aalto and Albert Evans, director of the disaster relief of the American Red Cross, show the enthusiasm Evans had for Aalto's ideas and the work conducted at the Bemis Foundation. See also the letter dated 26 Nov. 1940, when the promising start had already faltered due to Aalto's leave (MITA, JEBC).

34 Letter from Arnold Wasson-Tucker to Alvar Aalto, 8 Nov. 1940 (AAA). Although trying to sound positive, Tucker is rather anxious, wishing for Aalto's return. He also wrote that I. M. Pei would come to work at Aalto's office in Finland the next summer. After Pearl Harbor and the ensuing escalation of war this never happened.

35 Letter from John E. Burchard to Ambassador of Finland Hjalmar Procopé, 3 Feb. 1941 (MITA, JEBC); letter from Alvar Aalto to Burchard, 17 April 1940 (MITA, JEBC); letter from Aalto to Burchard, 15 May 1941 (AAA).

36 Letter from Laurence S. Rockefeller to Alvar Aalto in New York, 5 April 1940 (AAA); telegram from Aalto to Maire Gullichsen, 4 May 1940 (copy on file at AAA).

37 Certificate of incorporation For Finland Incorporated, 13 April 1940, New York, and other related documents (copies on file at AAA).

38 Memoranda from the "American Town in Finland" conference, held at 126 East Thirty-Eighth Street, New York, 12 July 1940 (copy on file at AAA); membership list of the American Architect's Committee, 31 July 1940 (copy on file at AAA). Members were: Leopold Arnaud, John Burchard, Gardner Dailey, William Emerson, Frederick Frost, Wallace Harrison, Claude Hooton, George Howe, William Lescaze, Walter MacCornack, Howard Meyers, Henry Miller (from For Finland Inc.), Andrew Reinhard, John Wellborn Root, Eliel Saarinen, Edward D. Stone, James Sweeney, Ralph Walker, and William Wurster, with Finnish ambassador Procopé as an honorary member.

39 This twenty-page booklet, Post-War Reconstruction: Re-Housing Research in Finland, is to be found at several locations such as the AAA and University of Pennsylvania Library, Philadelphia. The copy at the library indicates a private printing in New York, 1940, and is signed "compliments of Mrs. Aalto." The booklet was later reprinted in the Journal of the Royal Institute of British Architects (March 1941): 13–17. Typed drafts of budgets and working schemes, without date and signature (copies on files at AAA).

40 "Memorandum of interview with Aalto and others at Rockefeller Center," 27 June 1940, written by John E. Burchard (MITA, JEBC).

41 Letter from Alvar Aalto to Herbert Hoover, Palo Alto, 29 Aug. 1940; letter from Aalto to Henry Ford in Dearborn, Mich., 24 Sept. 1940 (copies on file at AAA).

42 Letter from Maire Gullichsen to Alvar Aalto, 1 Aug. 1940, and a draft for a letter to Aalto from late summer 1940 (copies on file at AAA).

43 *Post-War Reconstruction*, booklet, 10.

44 "America Builds a Town in Finland," interview with Alvar Aalto, newspaper and date unknown, but apparently from fall 1940, after Aalto's return to Finland, typed draft given to Aalto (AAA). For a fuller account of the regional plan and Ahöström, see Korvenmaa, "Aalto and Finnish Industry."

45 These drawings are referred to in letter from Arnold Wasson-Tucker to Alvar Aalto, 8 Nov. 1940 (AAA). Aalto published them in Finland in 1941, but they are not to be found in the drawing collection of the AAA. *Arkkitehti* (1941), 93–94.

46 *Arkkitehti* (1941), 93–94.

47 "Plan for the founding of an experimental town in Finland for research purposes of international scope," memo, no date or signature (AAA).

48 Again, for a fuller account see Korvenmaa, "Finnish Wooden House Transformed," "From House Manufacture to Universal Systems," and "Aalto and Finnish Industry."

49 In her letter of 1 Aug. 1940 to Aalto, Maire Gullichsen asks for more type-drawings and indicates that during the fall the new factory for prefabricated wooden houses will be ready (AAA).

50 Correspondence between American Red Cross and J. E. Burchard, 28 Nov. 1940 (MITA, JEBC); letter from Edgar Williams to members of the American Architects Committee, 4 Nov. 1940 (MITA, JEBC).

51 Interview drafts in both Finnish and Swedish for the Stockholm newspaper Aftonbladet (AAA).

52 *Rakennustaide ja standardi: Jälleenrakentamisen ydinkysymyksiä* [The art of building and standards: Core issues of reconstruction], booklet (Helsinki: Suomen Arkkitehtiliitto, 1942).

53 Correspondence between Alvar Aalto and William Wurster, 17 April–20 July 1945 (AAA).

54 Correspondence between Alvar Aalto and William Wurster, 17 April–20 July 1945 (AAA).

55 See Korvenmaa, "Aalto and Finnish Industry."

56 Letter from Alvar Aalto to William Wurster, 15 June 1945 (copy on file at AAA).

Aalto, Wurster, and the "New Humanism"

Gail Fenske

When construction neared completion on Alvar Aalto's Baker House in 1948, debate broke out within the Boston architectural community. Here, informed critics observed, stood evidence of an independent architectural thinker.[1] In a city in which architects equated the modern with the teachings of Walter Gropius's "Harvard Bauhaus," Aalto's Baker House demonstrated that an international modernist could indeed conceive a wholly different kind of modern building. In the strength of its serpentine shape, brick and wood materials, depth of color, and textural warmth, Aalto's design challenged the accepted image of the modern avant-garde: architecture's isolation within the surroundings through whiteness, austerity, and abstraction as an independent work of art.

In 1947, Aalto explained to a local reporter the distinguishing features of Baker House as a modern work of architecture (**FIG. 1**). He pointed to the structural advantages of its curving exterior and to the resulting distinctively shaped individual rooms with southern exposures that capture and reflect the play of light. The rooms' windows, he noted, provide diagonal vistas up and down the Charles River, affording a depth of perception and consequently, a "more interesting picture of movement on the water." He emphasized that he prioritized the "needs of human beings." These inspired him in making "a multitude of concessions to the people who will work and play in the building," among them his choice of materials for their "humanistic effect," such as wood, an "organic material," and "Boston common brick."[2]

The construction of Aalto's Baker House culminated the Finnish modernist's long association with MIT's School of Architecture and Planning. The association began in 1940, during Walter R. MacCornack's tenure as dean, when Aalto proposed that his "Institute for Architectural Research" be housed within MIT's Albert Farwell Bemis Foundation. Aalto's return to MIT in 1945, however, and his subsequent commission for Baker House in 1946 can be ascribed to the vision of

FIGURE 01 *Alvar Aalto in front of Baker House, MIT, ca. 1948.*

Wurster as a California Modernist

FIGURE 02 *William Wilson Wurster, portrait, ca. 1940.*

FIGURE 03 *Wurster, Schuckl Canning Company, Sunnyvale, Calif. Exterior showing roof terrace.*

the California architect William W. Wurster, then the school's recently appointed dean. From the outset, Wurster aimed to establish Aalto's distinctive, humanistic approach as a modernist within the curriculum at MIT and, more generally, within the architectural milieu of the United States.

At the time of his appointment at MIT in 1944, Wurster held an international reputation as a California-based architect and the founder of an indigenous style of modernism **(FIG. 2)**.[3] That year, the Museum of Modern Art featured his designs in its exhibition *Built in U.S.A. —1932–1944*, among them an office building for the Schuckl Canning Company in Sunnyvale, California (1942) **(FIG. 3)**. Composed with a disciplined structural module of wood posts and beams, the design featured stained wood sheathing, linear sunblinds, and horizontal bands of glass. The exhibition's curator, Elizabeth Bauer Mock, hailed the Schuckl Canning Company along with Wurster's houses as "a flexible native style" of modernism, the product of a well-established and "continuous but curiously unpublicized" tradition of wood construction in California.[4]

Mock also viewed Wurster's designs as architectural evidence of nativeness and authenticity; like the vernacular architecture of America's diverse regions, the designs invested California's distinctive climate, topography, and social life with a strong visual character. This Mock opposed to the "cold abstractions" of the 1920s European avant-garde, or the works of J. J. P. Oud, Walter Gropius, Ludwig Mies van der Rohe, and Le Corbusier, which had formed the core of the Museum of Modern Art's "Modern Architecture: International Exhibition" of 1932.[5] Mock's colleague and the museum's former curator of architecture, John McAndrew, may well have influenced her views, having called the International Style an "importation" in his *Guide to Modern Architecture: Northeast States* (1940), describing "many of our earlier modern buildings" as "architectural aliens."[6] Given the effects of the Depression years, McAndrew believed, American architects had placed greater value on the simplicities of vernacular buildings.[7] Wurster's California architecture, both McAndrew and Mock seemed to suggest, might serve as a suitable example in America for a regionally based yet fully advanced modernism.

Wurster had established his reputation as a California modernist primarily through his designs for houses. His Gregory Farmhouse of 1927–28, located in Scotts Valley, near Santa Cruz, California, had functioned as the masterpiece of his early career **(FIGS. 4–5)**. A clear visual statement of Wurster's fully developed architectural

FIGURE 04 *Wurster, Mrs. Warren (Sadie) Gregory Farmhouse, Scotts Valley, Calif. (1927–28). Exterior looking toward the courtyard.*

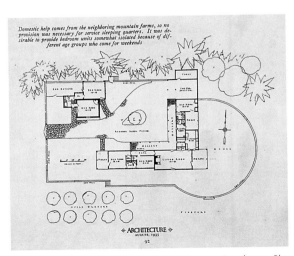

FIGURE 05 *Wurster, Mrs. Warren (Sadie) Gregory Farmhouse. Plan.*

principles, the farmhouse established the tenor for his future domestic designs.[8] Wurster's client for the farmhouse, Sadie Gregory, may well have inspired the architect's often-stated belief that his works should serve as "the frame for the client's living."[9] Gregory had pursued doctoral studies with Thorstein Veblen at the University of Chicago, so it is not surprising that she enlisted Wurster in her larger objective to avoid any trace of what Veblen called "conspicuous consumption." Perhaps inspired by Veblen's appreciation for the vernacular, Gregory believed the farmhouse's architectural character should be simple, camp-like, and should blend with the natural surroundings.[10]

As Alan Michelson has explained, Wurster trained as a Beaux-Arts architect at the University of California, Berkeley and while in the San Francisco Bay region had visited and studied the early modern domestic architecture of Ernest Coxhead, Willis Polk, and Bernard Maybeck—all of which visibly expressed in construction and materials the ideals of the Arts and Crafts movement. Inspired by their simplicity, authenticity, and reverence for the sense of rootedness in a particular place, Wurster traveled through the surrounding countryside, seeking out comparable examples of California's pre-industrial vernacular: gold mining towns, the ranches of the Central Valley, and the Spanish-influenced houses of old Monterey. During his student travels of 1922–23 in Europe, Wurster gravitated toward the vernacular buildings of Italy and southern Spain—products of a climate, topography, and culture resonating with that of California.[11] When designing the Gregory Farmhouse, Wurster brought these early experiences to bear on what had already become his objective to systematically update and to modernize the central California wood vernacular.

In responding to Sadie Gregory's vision of simplicity, Wurster incorporated within the farmhouse's sprawling composition terraces and courtyards, or outdoor "rooms," he placed windows high within interiors to extend the eye across space and out into the landscape, and he kept the massing of the house low to avoid obtruding on the natural surroundings. Ultimately, the farmhouse's design, built of what Wurster called "clean" wood carpentry, presented the viewer with a modern abstraction of California's pre-industrial wood vernacular through its composition of simple, geometricized forms. Wurster had mastered what he called the art of the architectural "understatement."[12]

During the 1930s, Wurster became more closely attuned to the polemics of the European avant-garde. In 1932, he reportedly showed a client, Frederic Benner, his copy of Modern Architecture, probably Henry-Russell Hitchcock, Jr.'s and Philip Johnson's Modern Architecture: International Exhibition (1932), and in 1935, his office's younger designers presented him with a copy of Le Corbuiser's and Pierre Jeanneret's Oeuvre complète (1934–1938).[13] Still, Wurster resisted abandoning his own place-inflected method of designing. In 1936, he stated, "Over and over again I would reiterate that Modern is a point of view—not a style."[14]

By the late-1930s, Wurster's designs had achieved international renown, appearing in journals such as Moderne Bauformen, Architectural Review (London), Casabella, and Architecture d'Aujourd'hui. Shortly thereafter, the journals highlighted the San Francisco Bay region as one of the most influential centers of domestic architecture in the United States.[15] In 1943, Architectural Forum called Wurster "the founder of a regional school of architecture," adding that the school "is easily the best the contemporary movement in this country has produced to date."[16]

During the early 1940s, Wurster's California version of the modern had attracted the attention of other East Coast critics besides the Museum of Modern Art's Elizabeth Bauer Mock and John McAndrew. The historian and cultural critic Lewis Mumford visited Berkeley in 1941 and taught at Stanford, in Palo Aalto, during 1942–44. Later, Mumford recounted that he and Wurster had visited the works of Bernard Maybeck and that from Wurster he gleaned "the autobiographic observations of one of the best of the Bay Region school." He had also discerned "the direct effect of Maybeck's poetic architectural imagination on [Wurster's] own work."[17] As a consequence, Mumford left the Bay region convinced that a separate but parallel tradition of modern architecture had established itself in California. In his widely read New Yorker essay of 1947, "The Skyline: Status Quo," Mumford would go on to champion what he christened the "Bay Region Style"—the architecture of Wurster along with that of his California predecessors and contemporaries—for its place-responsiveness as well as its fully developed modern character. In the California Bay Region's "humane form of modernism," Mumford further argued, could be found a "far more truly universal style than the so-called international style of the nineteen-thirties."[18]

When he became dean at MIT, Wurster already knew Aalto, but Mumford's point of view as a critic may well have influenced him in commissioning Aalto to design Baker House. Wurster would place the highest importance on establishing an institutional connection with the phenomenon that Aalto represented on the international scene—that is, on the Finnish modernist's comparably human-centered and environment-oriented convictions about design.

Wurster and Aalto

By Wurster's own account, the high point of his early years in practice, in fact, coincided with his meeting of Aalto in person on a visit to Finland with the landscape architect Thomas Church and his wife, Elizabeth Church, in 1937. According to Wurster, he and Aalto—whom he later called "one of the greatest architects in the world"—developed an instant rapport.[19] The encounter between the two men laid the groundwork for what became a lifelong friendship.

Wurster recalled that on his visit to Finland, he had failed to find Aalto at his office in Helsinki. Fortunately, he and the Churches stumbled on the architect's house and studio in Munkkiniemi, a neighbourhood on the outskirts of the city—"just what we had been dreaming of seeing" (FIG. 6).[20] There they met Aalto, who was apparently delighted to practice his English. Aalto made reference to a recently published plan of Wurster's McIntosh House (Los Altos, Calif., 1936) and Wurster, in turn, admired Aalto's bent plywood furniture. Aalto's house and studio, in fact, showed an affinity with Wurster's Gregory Farmhouse; for its design, Aalto had similarly drawn on indigenous wooden vernacular prototypes, in his case, those of Finland's East Karelia.[21] Aalto subsequently accompanied Wurster and the Churches to Helsinki. There they visited the Savoy (1937), a restaurant that Alvar Alto's wife, Aino Aalto, had designed for the city's paper industry executives, and afterward, they toured the city at night. Together in the following days, they traveled to the Sunila Pulp Mill near Kotka (1936–38) and to the Paimio Tuberculosis Sanitorium (1929–33).[22]

In fact, Wurster stated that his primary reason for journeying to Finland was to see Aalto's Paimio Sanatorium.[23] In designing the sanatorium, Aalto emphasized the patient's relationship to the health-inducing natural surroundings: he arranged the entire complex in a loose-knit fashion, echoing the topography, and oriented its solaria for direct access to open air and views of the adjacent fir trees and forest beyond. Such attention to the patient confirmed Wurster's own commitment to the centrality of the person in design. So did Aalto's focus on the patient as a reclining, "horizontal man," by contrast to the more typical "vertical man," and his prioritizing of

FIGURE 06 *Aalto, Aalto House, Munkkiniemi, Helsinki, 1936–37. Exterior from the garden.*

architectural details conducive to horizontal comfort, among them ceiling radiators focusing heat on the patient's feet and electric fixtures positioned to avoid harming the patient's eye.[24]

After leaving Finland, Wurster and the Churches traveled to Paris. There, they visited the 1937 World's Fair and Le Corbusier's newly completed Cité de Refuge (1937). The Cité's unhappy residents, Wurster later recounted, demonstrated an important contrasting lesson. Le Corbusier may have been a gifted sculptor, but the residents had covered the interior's floor-to-ceiling glass with newspapers in order to support their requirement for sleeping in eight-hour shifts through the day and night. Additionally, the air conditioning didn't function. Such a building had "nothing to do with the human being"; hence, it could not properly be considered architecture at all.[25] In short, Wurster had identified in Aalto a kindred spirit. Both had recently matured as independent-minded modernists producing designs fully in sympathy with the needs of the individual while also sensitively attuning those designs to the natural surroundings.

FIGURE 07 *New York City, view of Lower Manhattan from the across the East River, ca. 1930.*

FIGURE 08 *San Francisco, Market Street, 1939.*

Shared Sympathies

Aalto's having met Wurster in 1937, along with other American architects, may well have contributed to his growing fascination with the United States and more particularly with California. In the early 1920s, Aalto had lectured with Gustav Strengell on the architecture of New York City for the Association of Finnish Architects (**FIG. 7**). But soon enough, Aalto directed his interest toward the American West; he began writing popular essays on mythical American frontier outlaws and heroes, showing in the words of his biographer, Göran Schildt, a "weakness for cowboys."[26] As Juhani Pallasmaa has explained, by the early 1930s, Aalto along with other Finns openly admired America's technological inventiveness, emphasis on the freedom of the individual, optimistic spirit, and belief in progress. Aalto held in especially high regard the efforts of Franklin Delano Roosevelt and Roosevelt's "brain trust"—an "expert society" comprising professors, scientists, technicians, and businessmen—toward conceiving and implementing the country's program of recovery from the Depression, the New Deal.[27]

On the first of his two pre-war transatlantic journeys to the United States, in fall 1938, Aalto spent most of his time in New York. Shortly after he disembarked, he lectured at the Museum of Modern Art on "the humanization of architecture." Alfred Barr, Jr., the museum's head, and John McAndrew, its curator of architecture, had organized "Architecture and Furniture: Aalto" only eight months earlier.[28] Through other New York acquaintances such as the architect Harmon Goldstone, who worked for Wallace K. Harrison, and James J. Sweeney, who headed the museum's department of painting and sculpture, Aalto met members of the Rockefeller family: Mrs. John Rockefeller, the Museum's treasurer; Nelson Rockefeller, who became its president the following year; and Laurence Rockefeller, who with Goldstone had recently founded New Furniture, Inc., for importing and selling Aalto's furniture in New York.[29]

It was during the Aaltos' second trip to the United States in March through June 1939, however, that they chose to cross the continent to California, visiting Wurster in reply to the invitation he extended while in Finland. On the way, they stopped in Chicago to see László Moholy-Nagy, the founding director of the "New Bauhaus," and then in Los Angeles to visit

FIGURE 09 *Aalto panning for gold, Sutter's Creek, Calif., 1939.*

Richard Neutra (whose book *Wie Baut Amerika?* Aalto kept in his library) before journeying north to the San Francisco Bay region (**FIG. 8**).[30] After arriving in San Francisco, they toured Wurster's office, Aalto gave a lecture at the San Francisco Museum of Art, and with Wurster he attended the Golden Gate International Exposition, which featured Wurster's Yerba Buena Clubhouse and an exhibit of Alvar and Aino Aalto's furniture and decorative arts.[31] By car, Wurster showed the Aaltos his Gregory Farmhouse, Frank Lloyd Wright's Hanna House (Palo Aalto, 1936), and what Aalto later described as modern houses of "extraordinary refinement." The Aaltos instantly became enamored of California as a place, and more particularly, of its architecture, which Aalto described as adaptable to "the greatest variety of human needs, to terrain, and other conditions," and to the social life, which he characterized as the "happy disposition" existing among the mixture of peoples comprising native Californians.[32]

The Aaltos also spent a significant amount of time traveling on their own through the foothills of the Sierra Nevada, to the east of San Francisco. They marveled at the region's scenic wonders—sending Wurster a postcard of El Capitan from Yosemite Valley—and visited the "gold rush towns," where Aalto panned for gold at Sutter's Mill, playfully enacting the mythical history of the California frontier (**FIG. 9**). The simple wood-framed construction of these pioneer settlements, Aalto later suggested, exerted a favorable

FIGURE 10 *Placerville, Calif., ca. 1850.*

From an Old Daguerrotype

FIGURE 11 *Houses, Karelia, Finland, ca. 1895.*

influence over California's modern architecture: "On the slopes of the Californian side of the Sierra Nevada, one may still see the ghost towns of the Gold Rush, which have a spontaneous lightness and delicacy, and the temporary character that always accompanies this type of construction, providing an excellent illustration of the most recent trends in American architecture" (FIG. 10).[33] Aalto might have discovered in California towns such as Placerville, Coloma, and Sutter's Creek an affinity with Finnish Lapland's "gold rush town," Rovaniemi, or more importantly, he may well have appreciated the similarities between the towns' wood vernacular and Finland's indigenous Karelian vernacular (FIG. 11; SEE ALSO p. 89 FIG. 12).

Certainly, he recognized the parallels between Finland's geographical landscape and that of the Bay region—the watery topography of lakes and inlets, the heavily forested terrain, and the ever-present physicality of a seemingly pristine but wild nature.

Shortly after their meeting in California during 1939, Wurster wrote to the Aaltos that "our sympathies and joys are based on such a common root that words seem superfluous."[34] At their basis, Wurster's "sympathies" could be ascribed to important similarities in the backgrounds of him and Aalto. As Michelson has noted, both grew up in isolated but geographically distinctive locations, tangential to urban centers—Aalto in Jyväskylä, the "heart" of Finland, a region densely forested and filled with lakes, and Wurster in Stockton, to the north of California's San Joaquin Valley, the state's premier agricultural region. Both received exposure to Arts and Crafts principles during their architectural educations, Aalto at Helsinki's Polytechnic Institute and Wurster in the San Francisco Bay region at the University of California, Berkeley. In Berkeley, furthermore, Wurster mastered Charles Keeler's Arts and Crafts philosophy when reading *The Simple Home* (1904) and joined the intellectual community centered on the environmentally conscious Hillside Club. Yet, by the 1920s, both would resolve to transcend the cultural limitations imposed by their peripheral relationships with Europe and America's primary urban centers, chief among them Paris and New York.[35]

Given Aalto's appreciation for the architecture and landscapes of California, it is not surprising that on his visit to San Francisco in 1939 he should view the city as the ideal location for a key branch of his "Institute for Architectural Research," the international organization he had recently conceived for the study of modern housing and its relation to the new systems of factory production. Importantly, Aalto viewed San Francisco and Finland as the best places to work out the details of his favored housing prototype, the small wooden building.[36]

During the year coinciding with his visit to the California Bay region, Aalto watched construction on the most noted house of his career rise to completion, the Villa Mairea in Noormarkku, near the west coast of Finland (FIG. 12). Only a year earlier, Wurster had supervised the completion of his Dearborn Clark House on a

FIGURE 12 *Aalto, Villa Mairea, Noormarkku, Finland, 1933–39. Garden elevation looking across the courtyard.*

FIGURE 13 *Wurster, Clark House, Aptos, Calif., 1937. Ocean front. Photo: Roger Sturtevant.*

sandy beach in Aptos, California (**FIG. 13**). Aalto's Villa Mairea poetically engaged the natural surroundings while also representing those surroundings in complex, metaphorical ways. The villa's main living area, inspired by what Aalto called "forest dreaming," has been further described by Marc Treib as a "forest architecturally transformed."[37] Alternatively, Wurster's Clark House served as an open-air architectural device for appreciating the natural surroundings, in his words, "the frame for living and not life itself."[38] Wurster's design demonstrates by contrast to the Villa Mairea his emphasis on architecture's generic simplicity and severity, along with a strictness of indebtedness to California's humble vernacular roots.

However, a comparison between Aalto's Villa Mairea and Wurster's earlier Gregory Farmhouse—that is, between two houses built as comfortable weekend retreats on an equally generous scale—calls attention to Aalto's and Wurster's shared sympathies as designers (**SEE FIG. 4**). Both strongly evoked local craft traditions in wood, whether those of Monterey ranch houses or Karelian farmhouses. Both, moreover, demonstrated the potentials of thoroughly integrating a skilled composition of geometric forms with the natural surroundings, whether through the provocative use of native materials or through the incorporation of outdoor "rooms." And although the farmhouse's starkness and rusticity contrasts with the villa's sensuous quality in curved forms and luxurious materials, both feature emblematic references to local customs, Aalto's design with a sauna and Wurster's with a tankhouse that serves as a lookout tower flanked by a stockade-like entrance gate.

During the 1930s, Aalto had focused on achieving "the transfer from an orthodox internationalism to a deft modern vernacular," as Roger Connah has put it, whereas Wurster, already reputed for his indigenous modernism, had become increasingly attuned to the internationalism of the European avant-garde.[39] Yet, regardless of such distinctions in the trajectories of Aalto's and Wurster's development as modernists, their designs for the villa and the farmhouse exemplify their shared appreciation for the uniqueness of a particular landscape as well as the history and culture of their respective regions.

Mock and "Humanization," Mumford and the Regionalist Point of View

In the catalogue for the Museum of Modern Art's exhibition *Built in USA* of 1944, the curator Elizabeth Bauer Mock noted that, in Europe, Aalto had set the standard for the "humanization" of modern architecture and planning by "creating fresh and sympathetic forms," which emphasize the centrality of the person in design. "His humanizing influence," she further maintained, "could scarcely have found a more receptive public" than in the United States.[40] The recent interest shown by American architects in the nation's distinctive vernacular traditions—the "stone and wood barns of Pennsylvania, the white clapboard walls of New England, the rambling ranch houses of the West"—had reflected, in fact, not only a longing for a rootedness in the landscape, but also for a comparable attention to the person in architecture. In Mock's view, "the machine" would better serve as a tool for achieving the goals of humanization rather than being perpetuated as a false ideal.[41]

Such a recent impetus for humanization, Mock further argued, could be also ascribed to Frank Lloyd Wright's "renewed creative activity in the middle and later 'thirties.'" The California modernism represented initially by Maybeck and now by Wurster had found parallels in the career of Wright, who had continued to design houses strongly identified with their respective locations. Like Wright, Wurster had been "producing straightforward, essentially modern houses well before 1932"—the year of the museum's "International Style" exhibition—albeit based on "good sense and the California wood tradition rather than on specific theories of design."[42]

Mock's advocacy at the Museum of Modern Art of the indigenous, "humanized" modern architecture of Aalto, Wright, and Wurster, along with others, may well have been based on her appreciation for Lewis Mumford's history and criticism and, in particular, for his regionalist point of view. Mumford had developed that point of view by the mid-1920s in studies such as *Sticks and Stones* (1924) and *The Golden Day* (1926) and by 1923, he had codified it in practice through his founding with others of the Regional Planning Association of America. Indebted to the thought of Sir Patrick Geddes—the Scottish biologist, sociologist, and planning theorist—Mumford built his perspective on Geddes's philosophical tenet that all organisms, including human beings, thrive and mature to their benefit in communities interdependent with their natural surroundings. He identified with Geddes's conviction that all works of design should "embody the full utilization of local and regional conditions and must be the expression of local and regional personality." The latter held the utmost importance for Mumford: neither critics, historians, nor planners could fully understand societies or their works of architecture in isolation from a particular geographical setting.[43]

Throughout the 1930s, Mumford strengthened his emphasis as a historian and critic on what he considered the virtues of "regionalism" in both architecture and planning. In *Brown Decades* (1931) and later *The South in Architecture* (1941), he highlighted modern architecture's capacity for shaping the identity of a particular natural environment or geographical setting. He called Frank Lloyd Wright, for instance, "our greatest regional architect," because Wright had tried in many regions "to evolve a form that would identify [a house] with its landscape."[44] Such a regional sensibility, Mumford further argued in an essay for the *New Republic* in 1934, would continue to influence modern architecture: "Our regional cultures, which were blasted by a ruthless and over-rapid industrialization . . . may be putting forth stems from their buried but still vital roots."[45] Following a parallel line of thought, Mock organized the exhibition "Regional Building in America" for the Museum of Modern Art in 1941. Through its emphasis on "the influence of climate and locally available materials and techniques on the architecture of the past and present," Mock's exhibition provided a useful precedent for her "Built in USA" of three years later.[46]

During the same years, other architects, historians, and critics joined Mumford and Mock in their advocacy of regionalism. Louis Le Beaume, a St. Louis architect, wrote in 1936 that the Depression years had fostered the notion of architecture as a societal-based art, informed by the contemporary need for economy and simplification yet responsive to the desires of the human spirit.[47] In 1938, the historian Talbot Hamlin observed the recent emergence of "a certain regionalism of taste, a regionalism that is as much a difference of artistic ideals as it is of climate."[48] The new perspective in American criticism found parallels on the international scene; the English historian J. M. Richards, for instance, called attention in 1940 to the affinities between Aalto and Wright.[49]

By the late 1930s, as a consequence, there had emerged a clear argument on the part of critics for a less doctrinaire, more indigenous approach to modern architecture. During the 1940s, the argument continued to resound in Mock's exhibitions for the Museum of Modern Art as well as the writings of Mumford. In America, such a context of criticism would prove especially receptive to Aalto's work and ideas.

Housing Research and Humanization at MIT

By 1944, the regionalist point of view had established itself well enough in American architectural criticism to influence MIT's search for a new dean to lead its School of Architecture. That year, James R. Killian, the vice president of MIT, along with a search committee chaired by Frederick J. Adams, a professor of city planning, initiated the search.[50] According to Wurster's later account, his presence during 1943–44 as a student of city and regional planning at Harvard University, and at the same time also briefly at MIT, attracted the attention of Killian and the committee. Others noted, however, that the school had resolved to identify a dean at once convincingly "modern," "regional," and "American"—with the objective of creating a clear institutional alternative to Gropius's recently established "Bauhaus" at Harvard.[51]

By the early 1940s, Wurster's architectural reputation as the leading exponent of a California Bay region style of modernism had broadened to incorporate experiments with a range of types in social housing.[52] As Wurster explained in 1942, "the design of buildings emerged as a social art" during the Depression years.[53] After the outbreak of World War II, Wurster designed low-cost projects for California's war industries, among them Carquinez Heights (1941) and Chabot Terrace (1942) in Vallejo (FIG. 14).[54] Importantly, Wurster's marriage in 1940 to Catherine Bauer, the sister of Elizabeth Bauer Mock and the influential author of *Modern Housing* (1934) and *A Citizen's Guide to Public Housing* (1940), further deepened his commitment to the social bases of architecture as well as city planning.[55]

FIGURE 14 *Wurster, Chabot Terrace Experimental War Houses, Vallejo, Calif., 1941–42. Photo: Roger Sturtevant.*

The decision by MIT's Killian and the School of Architecture's search committee to appoint Wurster as dean in 1944 may well have been influenced by Lawrence Anderson, who at the time served as the school's head of architectural design. Mock's "Built in USA" had featured Anderson's MIT Alumni Swimming Pool of 1940, probably the first modern building built on any university campus.[56] Anderson had joined the MIT faculty in 1933, replacing Jacques Carlu. He had completed his master's degree in architecture at MIT three years earlier and then had studied at the École des Beaux-Arts in Paris after receiving the twenty-third Paris Prize from the American Society of Beaux-Arts Architects. Like Wurster and his San Francisco contemporaries, Anderson viewed Scandinavian architecture as an important inspiration and resource for modern design. During his travels in Europe during 1930–33, Anderson focused on "Nordic architecture"; then, in

1937, he made a special trip to Finland for the purpose of meeting Alvar and Aino Aalto and seeing their architecture, furniture, and designs in glass.[57] He designed MIT's Alumni Swimming Pool only two years later.

Wurster, according to his own account, aimed from the day of his arrival at MIT's School of Architecture to "humanize MIT." His stay at the school was relatively short, but in the view of Anderson, "his impact . . .[was] immense."[58] MIT's School of Architecture, according to the institution's contemporary report, had declined during the "war emergency" to a state of post-war chaos: enrollments had suffered, classes were small, and many of the faculty had departed.[59] The faculty who remained had split themselves between what Anderson called architecture's new "liberalist leanings" and the much older Beaux-Arts system, with its narrowness and so-called "philistine tendencies." The school needed "strong leadership," Anderson argued, especially given that Joseph Hudnut, the dean of Harvard's Graduate School of Design, had succeeded six years earlier in appointing the renowned modern architect and educator Walter Gropius to direct its department of architecture.[60] Shortly after his arrival in 1945, Wurster began recruiting new faculty for the MIT, later recounting his decision to write his very first letter to Alvar Aalto.[61]

Within a few months after Wurster contacted Aalto, he appointed the artist György Kepes, who came from László Moholy-Nagy's School of Design in Chicago; the historian Henry-Russell Hitchcock, Jr., who then chaired the department of art at Wesleyan University; and Kevin Lynch, a Taliesen-educated and Chicago-based city planner. All arrived in fall 1945. Wurster also secured a full-time appointment for Robert Woods Kennedy, who was already serving as an architect, critic, and instructor at the school. By the academic year 1946–47, Wurster had recruited Ralph Rapson, who had been exposed to Finnish modernism through Eliel Saarinen and the Cranbrook Academy of Art and who had recently worked as a collaborator with Moholy-Nagy. He also hired Vernon DeMars, known for his public housing funded by the Farm Security Administration in California, and Carl Koch, who had apprenticed in the office of Sven Markelius in Stockholm and the with Gropius and Meyer. Given that he had introduced Mumford to the architecture of the San Francisco Bay region in the early 1940s, it is not surprising that

Wurster brought the historian and critic to the school as a visiting lecturer in spring 1945 and spring 1947.[62]

According to his contemporaries at MIT, Wurster aspired to "create a more forward-looking curriculum without imposing a modernist dogma." At the same time, they also noted, he encouraged "robust and spirited differences of method and philosophy within the faculty."[63] By Wurster's own account, he aimed to strengthen the undergraduate and graduate programs in city planning, to create in effect a school of architecture and planning. He also aimed to make the school's programs more "scholarly" through the rigorous study of history, the social sciences, theoretical engineering, and the arts of drawing and design, as well as through connecting the school's curriculum more strongly with that of the institution at large.[64] Such sensibilities would have in their own right sharply distinguished MIT's new School of Architecture and Planning from Gropius's Bauhaus at Harvard. Still, Aalto, who visited regularly during the fall terms of 1946, 1947, and 1948, albeit for a total of five to six weeks during each visit, attracted notice as the most prominent and influential figure within the school. Rapson, De Mars, and others reportedly prized their years at MIT on account of Aalto having taught there.[65]

When Wurster wrote to Aalto in 1945, it would have been easy enough for him to recall that five years earlier Aalto had persuaded John Burchard and the Bemis Foundation to establish within MIT's School of Architecture his "Institute for Architectural Research"—in essence, one of the research laboratories for the international institution he had proposed in Wurster's San Francisco office the year before.[66] As Pekka Korvenmaa has noted, by 1940 Aalto had secured the promise of Rockefeller funds, and, equally important, his initiatives had the full support of the Finnish government. Finland had suffered severe devastation during the "Winter War" of 1939–40 and it faced the problems of reconstruction and of sheltering Karelian refugees.[67]

Aalto's research professorship began at MIT in fall 1940 and, within a few weeks, he and his students had prepared a schematic plan for an "experimental town," the starting point for the For Finland Inc. project, "An American Town in Finland." Equally important, Aalto published one of his most influential essays, "The Humanizing of Architecture," in MIT's *Technology Review*

that November. There he argued for his technique of "flexible standardization," that is, for subsuming the efficiencies of rationalized construction within what he considered architecture's larger goal: "to bring the material world in harmony with human life."[68] But earlier that October, Aalto was forced to abandon his work; he wrote to MIT President Karl Taylor Compton regarding the "present conflict in the world," later adding that "military duties" required his immediate return to Finland.[69] Aalto, as a consequence, would not return to MIT until Wurster invited him back, scheduling his arrival on the campus for November 1945.

When corresponding with Wurster in June 1945, Aalto supplied a detailed proposal for extending and augmenting his earlier program of housing research at MIT, albeit now placing still greater emphasis on the problems of postwar reconstruction. He asked that MIT "take the official initiative" in supporting his travel and study of reconstruction in the devastated cities of Belgium, Holland, France, and Italy.[70] This, along with his documentation of the recently destroyed Rovaniemi—Finnish Lapland's "gold rush town"—would allow him to focus at MIT on "new city plans up to types of houses and building practice." The future of Rovaniemi, Aalto told Wurster, would consist "on the whole of wooden houses," not unlike "your things in California."[71] As it turned out, Aalto's most meaningful contribution at MIT would eventually eclipse even such a socially engaged, broadly scaled research proposal. Within a year, he would conceptualize and construct Baker House, one of his most important designs, suggesting a new direction for his work and predicting the character of key projects produced in his later career, among them the Town Hall in Säynätsalo (1948–52).

The Baker House Commission: Aalto's Influence at MIT

Wurster announced to MIT's School of Architecture and Planning in November 1945 that Aalto would be arriving "fresh from the problems of reconstruction of the destroyed towns in Finland" and would lecture on both "city planning" and "the building of houses."[72] But Wurster had already envisioned what he considered a more timely and important project for Aalto at the school; that is, he had decided to commission the design of Baker House from Aalto. Wurster had conceived other projects for the school's faculty as well, among them a project for Robert Woods Kennedy of one hundred prefabricated, temporary houses for returning veterans—called "Westgate." **(FIG. 15)**.[73] But in identifying a comparable institute project for Aalto, Wurster recounted telling the MIT Corporation that "we had a genius in our midst" and that "the Corporation better get some advanced buildings done" as opposed to merely perpetuating its "old pattern."[74]

In July 1946, only eight months after he began his second visiting professorship at MIT, Aalto presented his ideas for the new "senior house" to the MIT Corporation. The site for the project faced the Charles River on the West Campus and bordered Memorial

Drive. Wurster described Aalto's presentation as a "performance" to Vernon De Mars, adding that he could "charm a bird out of a tree." The entire corporation was, in fact, charmed; according to Wurster, they "bowed their heads sagely and gave him the job."[75] The commission provided Aalto with the opportunity to demonstrate his "humanizing" philosophy of modern design through the construction of such an exemplary work; it also allowed him to build full-scale the "practical experiment" he believed so essential for testing new paradigms such as "flexible standardization."[76] Perhaps more important, Wurster and MIT supported and even encouraged Aalto in designing one of his boldest architectural works to date. In his Finland Pavilion for the New York World's Fair, viewers could only discover and appreciate its undulating wall after entering the building and arriving in the main space of the interior. But in Baker House, Aalto's serpentine lines completely infused the plan and massing of a prominent building sited in a prominent location, open to views from the city of Boston—an environment reputed for its colonial red-brick architecture but also recognized as one of America's preeminent intellectual and cultural centers.

For both Aalto and Wurster, Aalto's "senior house" served the equally important end of forging the desired link between their shared ambitions for a

FIGURE 15 *Aalto, Robert Woods Kennedy, and William Wurster at MIT, 1948.*

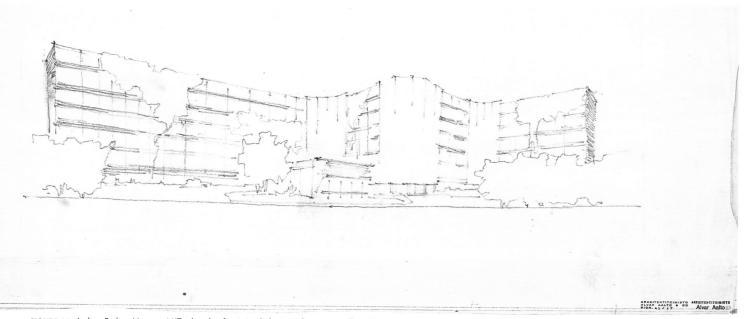

FIGURE 16 *Aalto, Baker House, MIT, sketch of original design showing trellis, 1947.*

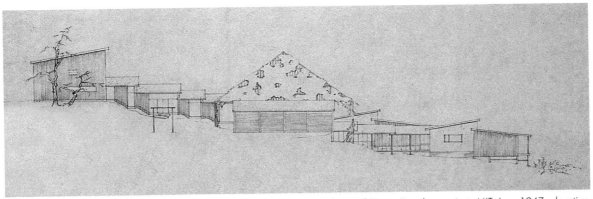

FIGURE 17 *Ming Li, "Dormitory for Girls: A Humanized Machine for the Mechanized Human" student project, MIT, June 1947, elevation.*

school-based program of architectural research and effective studio instruction. Wurster pointed out Aalto's design to incoming freshmen as a way of calling into question prevailing conceptions of the modern, asking "why is it curved?" (**FIG. 16**).[77] The design, not surprisingly, also influenced the students' studio projects, as illustrated by at least one project of 1947, a dormitory for girls by Ming Li, a young woman from China. Titled "A Humanized Machine for the Mechanized Human," Li's project comprised a stepped arrangement of angular forms terracing down a falling landscape (**FIG. 17**).[78] Constructed in wood with sloping roofs, it featured a prominent common space roofed with a vine-covered pyramidal trellis—echoing the trellis Aalto had featured in his earliest sketches for the "senior house." Although it is known that Aalto never organized or led a design studio of his own at MIT, he still stood out as an influential presence within the school. He gave sporadic lectures to the student body at large and served as an inspiring critic at numerous design reviews.[79]

Aalto's method of teaching was, in fact, informal and even "haphazard" according to Ralph Rapson, who occupied an office adjacent to Aalto's. He would arrive late in the day, talk with the students, and then he, they, and his colleagues—Rapson and DeMars among them—would proceed together to a bar or coffeehouse, where Aalto reportedly regaled his audience late into the night. Aalto's stories interwove Finnish folklore with his personal experiences; they followed a serpentine narrative, according to Rapson, but they always had a point.[80] In Aalto's teaching, as De Mars, Rapson, and others observed, his humanism consistently came through. Indeed, for DeMars, Aalto was "more interested in politics, the human condition, and the way the

world works than in how it *should* work."[81] Rapson, in a parallel vein, emphasized Aalto's "fantastically exquisite" drawings, which betrayed a deep sensitivity to materials and to the craft of building as well as his strong desire to design in concert with the natural surroundings.[82] Beyond his formal lectures and criticism, then, Aalto's stories, political views, and method of drawing, it appears, coupled with his larger, human-oriented philosophical perspective, made the most important impact on the design curriculum at MIT.

In addition to his selection of Aalto and the school's other faculty, Wurster's determination to establish at MIT a distinctive type of modernism evidenced itself in the school's studio projects. A 1946 project, for example, "A House for a Doctor with His Office Attached," sums up Wurster's design ethos. The project's clients, a Mr. and Mrs. Harding, espoused a liberal outlook in politics and taste. Mrs. Harding, in thinking about her house, had looked at hundreds of magazines and "all the publications of the Museum of Modern Art." After carefully considering a range of possibilities, she and Mr. Harding "decided against an international school house." Instead, they sought "a good plan" with a "warm feeling both inside and out."[83] The students' designs for the Harding house incorporated terraces and courtyards. Constructed out of wood, they featured pitched and overhanging roofs, suggesting the protection of their occupants while also signifying shelter. According to Rapson's later account, such designs represented for MIT's faculty and students alike the very antithesis of the contemporary projects produced in the studios at Harvard: cold and abstracted "international style cubes."[84]

Wurster later indicated that he had hoped to create an atmosphere of "controlled chaos" at MIT. This he opposed to a "master school where one person sets the dominant note, the dogma of the school."[85] Still, during Wurster's years at MIT there emerged within the school a shared philosophical perspective: architecture took its importance not merely from individual buildings designed as isolated works of art, but instead from their responsiveness to, in Anderson's words, "the landscape or cityscape . . . the local extremes of temperature, precipitation and winds . . . the appropriate materials and methods"—as well as to everyday human needs, whether physical or psychological.[86] Wurster further reflected on this view in 1956: "Architecture is not a goal; architecture is for life and pleasure and work and for people; the picture frame and not the picture."[87]

Wurster and his architectural contemporaries at MIT took pride in highlighting the distinctions between MIT's anti-dogmatic studio culture and Gropius's assertion of a singular modernist position within Harvard's Graduate School of Design.[88] Wurster, furthermore, abhorred the endless hours that Harvard students spent producing polished presentation drawings and models. Instead, he preferred and encouraged "roughness" at MIT.[89]

Consequently, by the late 1940s, MIT had become under the leadership of Wurster and Anderson—with Aalto as a celebrated visiting professor—the institutional proponent within the United States of a distinctive humanistic as well as modern philosophy of design. The school's faculty had been also influenced by Frank Lloyd Wright and Taliesen, by Eliel Saarinen and the Cranbrook Academy of Art, and by the New Bauhaus in Chicago. But it was the kind of modernism for which Aalto had become the most prominent representative—one indebted to Finland and substantiated in America by a clearly articulated ethos in recent American architectural criticism—that served as the school's most important educational resource.

For Aalto, the resonance of such an institutional culture with his own perspective may well have served to strengthen that perspective. By the mid-1930s, he had faced increasing suspicion and criticism in Finland from the local architectural community—a reaction to his having charted a new direction as a modernist. No longer classifiable as the expected orthodox rationalist, he had become, as Pallasmaa has put it, "a skeptic critical of rationalist principles" and, in the eyes of some,

a new type of "romantic."[90] But in America, Aalto had now identified a receptive audience for his work as well as for his humanizing philosophy of design.

Modern Architecture's "New Humanism"

That the modern architecture of Wurster and the California Bay region became in 1948 the focus of a vehement debate between Mumford and Henry-Russell Hitchcock, Jr., both now well-established as the nation's leading historian-critics, may well have caught even Wurster by surprise.[91] In response to Mumford's advocacy of the Bay Region Style in his 1947 *New Yorker* essay—which championed Wurster's designs as epitomizing a humanistic and place-inflected strain of modernism—the Museum of Modern Art's Philip Johnson and Alfred H. Barr, Jr., organized a symposium at the museum in February 1948: "What is Happening to Modern Architecture?"

Johnson and Barr suggested a lively debate between "the originators of the 'International Style'" and the recent proponents of the "new humanism of the 'Bay Region' school." But in the end the symposium did not serve as such an open and engaging forum. Instead, Barr focused on recapitulating Hitchcock's and Johnson's International Style visual principles of 1932—important among them "architecture as volume rather than mass"—which he thought continued to hold explanatory power. He then pointed out the disparity between the International Style and the Bay Region Style's "informal and ingratiating kind of wooden domestic building," which in his view was less rigorous because Wurster and his California contemporaries had emphasized the design of houses, or what he considered architecturally less significant "cottages."[92] Mumford's recent advocacy of the Bay region, Hitchcock further suggested, had constituted an ill-timed challenge to his and Johnson's still dominant mode of conceptualizing the modern: "We are not . . . ready for such a reaction."[93]

It is perhaps ironic that Hitchcock taught the history of architecture at MIT during the years surrounding the Museum of Modern Art debate, between 1947 and 1949.[94] Aalto never mentioned meeting Hitchcock at MIT, but the historian-critic had in all likelihood

FIGURE 18 *Ralph Rapson, Carl Koch, Vernon De Mars, Robert Woods Kennedy, and William Hoskins Brown, Eastgate Apartments, Cambridge, Mass., 1950–51.*

FIGURE 19 *Walter Gropius and the Architects' Collaborative, Harkness Commons Building, Harvard Graduate Center, 1948–50.*

conversed with Aalto in some capacity; Aalto's fall 1947 and fall 1948 appointments overlapped with Hitchcock's, and Hitchcock couldn't possibly have avoided the sight of Aalto's "senior house" rising on Memorial Drive. Robert Woods Kennedy, still also at MIT, published an essay clarifying his own viewpoint as an architect and critic while responding to the Museum of Modern Art debate. In it, he argued passionately for the virtues of a "live regional architecture" in New England.[95]

Aalto's "senior house," in fact, was approaching completion during the year of the debate; MIT officially dedicated the design on Alumni Day, 11 June 1949.[96] Aalto, however, had left for Finland the preceding November; Aino had suffered a recurrence of cancer. He anticipated returning to Cambridge in fall 1949 and again in fall 1950, but he did not in fact return until May 1963. Wurster recalled that by the early 1950s Aalto indeed had become extraordinarily busy with his practice, having won competitions for the Helsinki University of Technology and the National Pensions Institute; he had, furthermore, lost patience with the American contracting system.[97] But as Pallasmaa has noted, Aalto, a "Finnish architect," had also become disenchanted with the United States.[98] At MIT, he called attention to the school's recent "mechanistic way of thinking" and began to clash with Burchard, who he now considered too technocratic. He drew closer to Mumford, and after a visit to Talisen, he made note of Frank Lloyd Wright's observation that "my America no longer exists."[99]

A Wider Modernist Perspective

In 1950, a year after Baker House's dedication, construction began on Wurster's third "demonstration project" at MIT, Eastgate Apartments (**FIG. 18**).[100] Like Baker House, Eastgate was prominently sited on Memorial Drive. Eastgate's designers, "the younger stripe" of faculty at MIT (Ralph Rapson, Carl Koch, William Hoskins Brown, Robert Woods Kennedy, and Vernon DeMars)—with Rapson in a key role as delineator and designer—took Aalto's dormitory as their starting point.[101] After the project's completion, Wurster extolled its unique modern features, among them balconies for every apartment, a triple-floor skip-stop elevator system, and the "revolutionary idea of corridors only on every third floor."[102] Contemporaries considered its siting at 100 Memorial Drive in relation to Baker House, when viewed from across the Charles, as appearing like bookends framing the MIT campus. In this arrangement, the two designs provided a striking contrast with Coolidge, Shepley, Bulfinch & Abbott's 1920s neo-Georgian "Harvard River Houses" upstream. As a consequence, they proudly announced to the city of Boston MIT's commitment to a particular type of modernism.[103]

During the same year, construction neared completion on Walter Gropius's and the Architect's Collaborative's Graduate Center at Harvard (1949–50) (**FIG. 19**). Gropius threw a dinner party for Wurster. Although Gropius had criticized Aalto for not having used "the palest materials" in Baker House, thereby allowing "transparency in shadows," he acknowledged that Aalto's design had set an important example: it had convinced Harvard officials to sponsor an equally forward-looking faculty-designed campus building. Such a design, Gropius anticipated, would heighten public awareness of modern architecture.[104] MIT students might have mockingly chided the Graduate Center's Harkness Commons as an "international style cube." The design's ribbon windows, flat roofs, piloti, and light-colored limestone panels indeed showed less resonance with Gropius's earlier designs than with the work of Le Corbusier; such features echoed Hitchcock's and Johnson's International Style visual formula, now almost twenty years old.

In 1950, Wurster returned to California to become dean of the School of Architecture at the University of California, Berkeley, which he would soon with others restructure as the College of Environmental

FIGURE 20 *Eero Saarinen, MIT Chapel, Cambridge, Mass., 1953–55.*

of Design. He also reinvigorated his architectural practice, and called himself "a great believer in place" who required inspiration from "the land and customs" of California to produce convincing works of modern architecture.[105] MIT, faced with having to find a new dean, consulted with Wurster and chose Pietro Belluschi.[106]

Belluschi's architecture, like that of Wurster, had shaped the identity of a particular region, the Pacific Northwest.[107] Shortly after arriving at MIT, Belluschi, reputed for his church designs, witnessed the completion of Eero Saarinen's chapel for MIT. Wurster had awarded Saarinen, the son of the Finnish-American architect Eliel Saarinen, the commission for the chapel **(FIG. 20)**.[108] Saarinen's design, constructed in red brick, suggested for the viewer the same qualities of authenticity, strength, and warmth as Aalto's Baker House. The direction MIT had charted for its modern campus architecture, then, represented a clear contrast with that taken by other universities, not only Harvard, but notably the Illinois Institute of Technology. At IIT, Mies van der Rohe's steel and glass Chapel (1952) pointed to the future of spare modernist works favored by American corporations during

the prosperous and consumer-oriented 1950s. MIT's School of Architecture and Planning, however, would not lose sight of Wurster's and Aalto's "rough" and "humanist" vision of the modern.

Aalto's design for Baker House, consequently, had visually crystallized and decisively established a particular modernist position within the American culture of architecture. Along with the criticism of Mock, Mumford, McAndrew, and others, it demonstrated the significance of modern architecture's many humanistic and, indeed, person-oriented variables—those expressive of the individual, the community, local building methods, and, above all else, those which signified the character of a place. Such an ideological strain could not have diverged further from the formulaic and isolating model of the International Style. As a wider modernist perspective, emphasizing the embrace of the total environment, extending from the intimate scale of the decorative arts to the individual building and then beyond to large-scale regional planning, it continues to be appreciated—despite the broad appeal of the Miesian aesthetic during the 1950s—down to the present day.

1 Ann Richards, telephone interview with author, Sept. 1999. Richards, then a student of architecture at the Rhode Island School of Design, toured the Baker House with Aalto and others during spring 1948 as construction neared completion. An article in *Architectural Forum* echoed the local reception of Aalto's design, noting that "only an institution as self-assured as the Massachusetts Institute of Technology could afford to carry the experimental approach so far in a dormitory for 353 seniors," adding that "honest debate will be prolonged" and that "in heroism and character [Baker House] is big, draws a salute." "M.I.T. Senior Dormitory," *Architectural Forum,* Aug. 1949, 63. For the international reception of the Baker House, see Lisbeth Sachs, "Studentheim des Massachusetts Institute of Technology," *Werk* 37 (April 1950), 97–102; and "Senior Dormitory, Massachusetts Institute of Technology," *Architekten* 4 (1950), 53–64. Later, the American critic Paul Goldberger wrote that Baker House "resembled no other modern building in the United States" at the time of completion, and that after designing it, Aalto vaulted to prominence as "not only as his nation's preeminent architect but an acknowledged world master." Goldberger, "Alvar Aalto Is Dead at 78; Master Modern Architect," *New York Times,* 13 May 1976.

2 "Alvar Aalto, Noted Finnish Architect, Explains Why He Designed the Strange-Shaped M.I.T. Dormitory," *Boston Sunday Post,* 9 Nov. 1947. This article can be found at the MIT Institute Archives and Special Collections (hereafter MITA).

3 On Wurster, see Alan R. Michelson, "Towards a Regional Synthesis: The Suburban and Country Residences of William Wilson Wurster, 1922–64" (PhD diss., Stanford Univ., 1993); Marc Treib, "William Wilson Wurster: The Feeling of Function," in *An Everyday Modernism: The Houses of William Wurster,* ed. Treib (San Francisco: San Francisco Museum of Modern Art; Berkeley: Univ. of California Press, 1995), 12–83; R. Thomas Hille, *Inside the Large Small House: The Residential Design Legacy of William W. Wurster* (New York: Princeton Architectural Press, 1994); and Gail Fenske, "Lewis Mumford, Henry-Russell Hitchcock, and the Bay Region Style," in *The Education of the Architect: Historiography, Urbanism, and the Growth of Architectural Knowledge,* ed. Martha Pollak (Cambridge, Mass.: MIT Press, 1997), 40–47, 78–79.

4 Elizabeth Mock, "Built in USA—Since 1932," in Elizabeth Mock, ed, *Built in USA, 1932–1944* (New York: Museum of Modern Art, 1944), 14. Mock had toured the San Francisco Bay region in the early 1940s with her sister, Catherine Bauer, and her new brother-in-law, William W. Wurster. Michelson, "Towards a Regional Synthesis," 417 n. 26.

5 Michelson, "Towards a Regional Synthesis," 13.

6 John McAndrew, *Guide to Modern Architecture: Northeast States* (New York: Museum of Modern Art, 1940), 9. See also Michelson, "Towards a Regional Synthesis," 253–54.

7 McAndrew, *Guide to Modern Architecture,* 13–14, 16.

8 On the Gregory Farmhouse, see Daniel P. Gregory, "An Indigenous Thing: The Story of William Wurster and the Gregory Farmhouse," *Places 7* (Fall 1990), 78–93; Gregory, "The Nature of Restraint: Wurster and His Circle," in *Everyday Modernism,* ed. Treib, 98–113; and Treib, "William Wilson Wurster: The Feeling of Function," in *Everyday Modernism,* ed. Treib, 19–22.

9 See, for example, William W. Wurster, "The Human Equation in Architectural Practice," lecture delivered at the Collegiate Schools of Architecture meeting, 9 May 1950 (transcription on file in the William Wurster/Wurster, Bernardi, and Emmons Collection, Environmental Design Archives, Univ. of California, Berkeley, hereafter EDA UCB).

10 Gregory, "Indigenous Thing," 83, 87–88; and Gregory, "Nature of Restraint," 105.

11 Michelson, "Towards a Regional Synthesis," 78–79; Susan B. Riess, *William Wilson Wurster* (Berkeley: Univ. of California Regional History Project, 1964), 48–50, 54–56.

12 Riess, *William Wilson Wurster,* 82–83. Others have also used "understatement" to describe Wurster's work. See, for example, Gregory, "Indigenous Thing," 88.

13 Michelson, "Towards a Regional Synthesis," 240, 242.

14 William Wurster, quoted in "1936 Convention in Retrospect," *Architect and Engineer* 127 (Nov. 1936), 52 (italics original).

15 Michelson, "Towards a Regional Synthesis," 259–60.

16 "William Wilson Wurster," *Architectural Forum,* July 1943, 45. *Architectural Forum's* assessment of Wurster and his work was cited in an MIT press release by Maynard Norris, 8 Dec. 1949 (MITA).

17 Lewis Mumford, "The Architecture of the California Bay Region," in *Domestic Architecture of the Bay Region* (San Francisco: San Francisco Museum of Art, 1949), n.p. Mumford also knew Wurster's wife, Catherine Bauer. Their torrid love affair is well documented in Mumford's own writings and those of others. See, for instance, H. Peter Oberlander and Eva Newbrun, *Houser: The Life and Work of Catherine Bauer* (Vancouver: Univ. of British Columbia Press, 1999), 48–54, 75–88, 95–109.

18 Lewis Mumford, "The Skyline: Status Quo," *New Yorker,* 11 Oct. 1947, 110. Mumford argued that the universality of the Bay Region Style could be ascribed to its synthesis of "Oriental and Occidental traditions."

19 Riess, *William Wilson Wurster,* 91 (for quote), 92–96.

20 Riess, *William Wilson Wurster,* 92.

21 Michelson, "Towards a Regional Synthesis," 240.

22 Vernon DeMars notes that "Aalto suspended work and took Wurster to visit some of his major projects," including the pulp mill and the sanatorium. DeMars, "Humanism and the Mount Angel Library," *Cornell Architecture: The Preston H. Thomas Memorial Lecture Series: Alvar Aalto* (Ithaca, N.Y.: Cornell Univ. Department of Architecture, 1981), 7–9. Cornell Univ. Archives.

23 Susan B. Riess notes that Wurster went to Europe for the purpose of seeing three buildings: the Penguin Pool at Regent's Park Zoo in London, (Berthold Lubetkin and his firm, Tecton, 1933), Aalto's Paimio Sanitorium (1932), and Aalto's library in Viipuri (1934). This final work he decided to forego based on Aalto's recommendation and its distance from Helsinki. Riess, *William Wilson Wurster,* 96.

24 For Aalto's own description of the sanitorium, see Alvar Aalto, "The Humanizing of Architecture: Functionalism Must Take the Human Point of View to Achieve Its Full Effectiveness," *Technology Review,* Nov. 1948, 15–16.

25 Wurster, as quoted in Riess, *William Wilson Wurster,* 98–99.

26 On the view of America Aalto shared with some of his Finnish contemporaries in the late 1930s, see Göran Schildt, *Alvar Aalto: The Decisive Years* (New York: Rizzoli, 1986), 165–72, 170 (for quote).

27 See Juhani Pallasmaa, "Aalto's Image of America," in the present volume; and Schildt, *Decisive Years,* 166, 169–70.

28 Schildt, *Alvar Aalto: The Decisive Years,* 170–71, notes that Aalto arrived in New York on October 23, 1938, and that four days after that, lectured at Yale, then at the Museum of Modern Art. The museum published *Architecture and Furniture: Aalto* (New York: Museum of Modern Art, 1938) with the exhibition. John McAndrew wrote the foreword.

29 Schildt, *Decisive Years,* 170–72.

30 Neutra's book did not emphasize metropolises, as did accounts of America by other Europeans (e.g., Erich Mendelsohn, *Amerika: Bildersbuch eines Architekten,* 1926 and Le Corbusier, *Quand les cathédrals étaient blanches: Voyage aux pays des timides,* 1937), but rather southern California. Elina Standertskjold, "Alvar Aalto and the United States," in *Alvar Aalto: Toward a Human Modernism,* ed. Winfried Nerdinger (Munich: Prestel Verlag, 1999), 81.

31 Schildt, *Decisive Years,* 176–77.

32 Schildt, *Decisive Years*, 177, 179 (for quotes). Schildt references Aalto's catalogue introduction to the "America Builds" exhibition, shown in Stockholm and Helsinki in 1944 and 1945, and an interview published in the Helsinki newspaper *Nya Pressen* on 23 June 1939. After Aalto and his wife returned, they wrote to Wurster, "[We] have never lived more joyous days than those spent with you in San Francisco." Alvar Aalto and Aino Aalto to William Wurster, 12 June 1939. William W. Wurster/Wurster, Bernardi, and Emmons Collection, EDA UCB.

33 Alvar Aalto, "The Intellectual background of American Architecture" in *Alvar Aalto in His Own Words*, ed. Göran Schildt (New York: Rizzoli, 1997), 134. This publication information is different from what is provided in the Goldhagen ch. (Helsinki: Otava Publishing). The postcard, dated 5 June 1939, is housed in the William Wurster/Wurster, Bernardi, and Emmons Collection, EDA UCB.

34 William Wurster to Alvar Aalto and Aino Aalto, 6 July 1939 (William Wurster/Wurster, Bernardi, and Emmons Collection, 1922–1974, EDA UCB).

35 For a brief comparison of the backgrounds of Wurster and Aalto, see Michelson, "Towards a Regional Synthesis," 290–91.

36 "Meeting—Office of W. W. Wurster—Thursday, June 1, 1939," meeting minutes (William W. Wurster/Wurster, Bernardi, and Emmons Collection, 1922–24, EDA UCB). See also Alvar Aalto, memorandum on the International Institute of Architectural Research, New York, 13 June 1939 (William W. Wurster/Wurster, Bernardi, and Emmons Collection, EDA UCB). That February, Wurster had corresponded with John Burchard of MIT, director of the Albert Bemis Foundation, which Burchard described as "an endowed division of the Massachusetts of Technology, established to engage in the 'search for, and dissemination of, knowledge pertaining to adequate, economical, and abundant shelter.'" Letter from John E. Burchard to William Wilson Wurster, 25 Jan. 1939, and letter from Wurster to Burchard, 4 Feb. 1939 (William W. Wurster/Wurster, Bernardi, and Emmons Collection, 1922–24, EDA UCB).

37 Marc Treib, "Aalto's Nature," in *Alvar Aalto: Between Humanism and Materialism*, ed. Peter Reed (New York: Museum of Modern Art, 1998), 50 (quote by Aalto), 54 (quote by Treib). See also Richard Weston, "Between Nature and Culture: Reflections on the Villa Mairea," in *Alvar Aalto*, ed. Nerdinger, 70.

38 William Wurster, quoted in Richard C. Peters and Caitlin King Lemperes, "An Architectural Life," in *An Everyday Modernism*, 91.

39 Roger Connah, *Finland: Modern Architectures in History* (London: Reaktion, 2005), 70.

40 Mock, "Built in USA –Since 1932," 20.

41 Mock, "Built in USA –Since 1932," 13–14.

42 Mock, "Built in USA. –Since 1932," 14.

43 Patrick Geddes, *Cities in Evolution* (1915), as quoted in "Mumford on Geddes," *Architectural Review* 107 (Aug. 1950), 87. For Geddes's influence on Mumford, see Fenske, "Lewis Mumford, Henry-Russell Hitchcock, and the Bay Region Style," 57, 60–61; and Robert Wojtowicz, *Lewis Mumford and American Modernism: Eutopian Theories for Architecture and Urban Planning* (New York: Cambridge Univ. Press, 1998), 11–15.

44 Lewis Mumford, *The Brown Decades: A Study of the Arts in America, 1865–1895* (1931; New York: Dover, 1971), 49–82; and Lewis Mumford, *The South in Architecture* (1941; New York: Da Capo, 1967), 102, 107, 127 (for quote); Fenske, "Lewis Mumford, Henry-Russell Hitchcock, and the Bay Region Style," 64, 68–69.

45 Lewis Mumford, "Orozco in New England," *New Republic*, 10 Oct. 1934, 231; quoted in Michelson, "Towards a Regional Synthesis," 416 n. 17.

46 Mock's *Built in USA, 1932–1944* lists the architectural exhibitions and publications of the Museum of Modern Art (126). The "Regional Building in America" exhibition traveled to at least fifteen museums in addition to MoMA.

47 Louis Le Beaume had served as a vice president of the American Institute of Architects. Louis Le Beaume, "Appraising the Controversy," *Architect and Engineer* 126 (July 1936), 55. See also Michelson, "Towards a Regional Synthesis," 248–49.

48 Talbot Hamlin, "Architectural League Exhibition," *Pencil Points* 19 (June 1938), 353–54.

49 For Richards, Aalto demonstrated how "modern architecture might, without compromising its principles, achieve the depth and richness and sense of human values also associated with the peculiar genius of Frank Lloyd Wright." J. M. Richards, *An Introduction to Modern Architecture* (London: Cassell, 1940), 93. See also Connah, *Finland*, 107–8.

50 On MIT's search, see Oberlander and Newbrun, *Houser*, 216–17. Wurster had received a Wheelwright fellowship from Harvard University and had completed all of the work necessary to earn a doctorate in regional planning with the exception of a thesis. See also Riess, *William Wilson Wurster*, 104, 108–9.

51 Lawrence Anderson, "William Wilson Wurster," unpublished essay, 19 Dec. 1992, n. p. (MITA), notes that Wurster represented the tendency within modernism that emphasized "diverse regional conditions." Jane King Hession, Rip Rapson, and Bruce N. Wright state that Wurster told Rapson that "he wanted to build a truly 'American school' of architecture." Hession, Rapson, and Wright, *Ralph Rapson: Sixty Years of Modern Design* (Afton, Minn.: Afton Historical Society Press, 1999), 61.

52 These included small, prefabricated houses, such as the Unit Steel House (1937), designed for the Soule Steel Company, and large, community-scale public housing projects such as the United States Housing Authority's Valencia Gardens in San Francisco (1939–42), the latter of which Mock featured in her exhibition "Built in USA." Greg Hise, "Building Design as a Social Art: The Public Architecture of William Wurster, 1935–1950," in *Everyday Modernism*, ed. Treib, 141. Mock, "Built in USA—Since 1932," in *Built in USA*, praised Valencia Gardens for avoiding an "institutional effect" (24).

53 William W. Wurster, notes from a 1942 office tour; quoted in Hise, "Building Design as a Social Art," 145.

54 Carquinez Heights and Chabot Terrace were two among a number of commissions that Wurster received for war workers' housing in the vicinity of San Francisco, financed by the Lanham Act, which Congress passed in 1940. Hise, "Building Design as a Social Art," 144–52.

55 Catherine Bauer, *Modern Housing* (Boston: Houghton-Mifflin, 1934); and Bauer, *A Citizen's Guide to Public Housing* (Poughkeepsie, N.Y.: Vassar College,1940). It was said that Wurster's relationship with Bauer "politicized" him. Gwendolyn Wright, "A Partnership: Catherine Bauer and William Wurster," in *Everyday Modernism*, ed. Treib, 189. H. Peter Oberlander and Eva Newbrun note that Bauer "gave him hell about his political leanings. . . . She made a liberal out of him." Oberlander and Newbrun, *Houser*, 197.

56 Stanford Anderson, lecture on MIT's School of Architecture during the 1930s and 1940s, for the seminar "Boston and American architecture," MIT, spring 1983. Lawrence B. Anderson, "Architectural Education at MIT: The 1930s and after," in *Architectural Education in Boston: Centennial Publication of the Boston Architectural Center, 1889–1909*, ed. Margaret Henderson Floyd (Boston: Boston Architectural Center, 1989), 87, 89; and Mock, ed., *Built in USA*, 82. For Anderson's description of his own design, see "Interview with Lawrence Anderson Conducted by Robert Brown, January 30, 1992," (Archives of American Art, Smithsonian Institution, Washington, D.C., hereafter AAA), 45.

57 "Interview with Lawrence Anderson Conducted by Robert Brown, January 30, 1992" (AAA), 43. On the view of Scandinavia shared by Wurster and his San Francisco contemporaries, see also Michelson, "Towards a Regional Synthesis," 425 n. 83.

58 Lawrence Anderson, "William Wilson Wurster," unpublished essay, 19 Dec. 1942, n.p. (MITA).

59 Walter R. MacCornack, "Architecture," in "President's Report Issue, 1941–42," special issue, *Massachusetts Institute of Technology Bulletin*, vol. 77, no. 1 (October1942), 111.

60 Lawrence Anderson, "William Wilson Wurster," unpublished essay, 19 Dec. 1942, n.p. (MITA); "Talk Given on Wurster's Retirement from University of California's College of Environmental Design, Berkeley, June 4, 1963," in Riess, *William Wilson Wurster,* 312; and "Interview with Lawrence Anderson conducted by Robert Brown, 30 Jan. 1992" (AAA), 49.

61 Riess, *William Wilson Wurster,* 94. Wurster subsequently telegraphed Aalto. Letter, Alvar Aalto to William W. Wurster, 15 June 1945 (MITA), references Wurster's "instructive and hearty cable of June 5."

62 William W. Wurster, "School of Architecture and Planning," in "President's Report Issue, 1944–45," special issue, *Massachusetts Institute of Technology Bulletin,* vol. 81, no. 1 (Oct. 1945): 138–40; Wurster, "School of Architecture and Planning," in "President's Report Issue, 1945–46," special issue, *Massachusetts Institute of Technology Bulletin,* vol. 82, no. 1 (October 1946), 146–48; and Lawrence B. Anderson, "Architecture," in "President's Report Issue, 1946–47," special issue, *Massachusetts Institute of Technology Bulletin,* vol. 83, no. 1 (October 1947), 142.

63 Hession, Rapson, and Wright, *Ralph Rapson,* 64. See also Michelson, "Towards a Regional Synthesis," which notes that Wurster cultivated "widely varying viewpoints" at MIT (320).

64 William W. Wurster, "The Architectural Life," *Architectural Record* 109 (Jan. 1941): 91–92 (for quote). See also interview with Lawrence Anderson conducted by Robert Brown, 30 Jan. 1992 (AAA), 60; and William W. Wurster, lecture delivered to the San Francisco Planning and Housing Association, San Francisco, 12 July 1948, William W. Wurster/Wurster, Bernardi, and Emmons Collection, EDA UCB.

65 According to Hession, Rapson, and Wright, in *Ralph Rapson,* "Rapson's exposure to Aalto left a strong impression" (69). Vernon De Mars recounts sharing an office with Aalto in "Humanism and the Mount Angel Library": he "learned some bad habits, but also some fundamental wisdom from Aalto" (7–9).

66 In the minutes taken of a meeting in 1939, Wurster noted that the Bemis Foundation was "looking for outlets for its money." "Meeting—Office of W. W. Wurster—Thursday, June 1, 1939" (William W. Wurster/Wurster, Bernardi, and Emmons Collection, EDA UCB).

67 In a press release written by MIT's John J. Rowlands, 24 July 1940, Aalto is described as "the distinguished Finnish architect who was chosen to direct reconstruction of his country after the Russian invasion." (MITA) MacCornack reported to Rowlands on "plans for expanding research in architecture" with the assistance of the Bemis Foundation: "One of [the program's] most important objectives will be the study of low-cost housing, a matter of national significance."

68 Aalto, "Humanizing of Architecture," 14–16, 36.

69 Letter from Alvar Aalto to Dr. Karl Taylor Compton, 17 Oct. 1940 (MITA). Göran Schildt, *Alvar Aalto: The Mature Years* (New York: Rizzoli, 1991), 40, 96. Indeed a new war, the "Continuation War" against the Soviets, would break out in June 1941.

70 Letter from Alvar Aalto to William W. Wurster, 14 July 1945 (MITA). MIT was not forthcoming with the initiative Aalto proposed; it was never mentioned again.

71 Letter from Alvar Aalto to William W. Wurster, 15 June 1945 (MITA).

72 Letter from William W. Wurster to John J. Rowlands, director, News Service, MIT, 14 Nov. 1945 (MITA).

73 Wurster described Westgate as a pioneering effort in prefabricated housing in which MIT was the first. William W. Wurster, "To the Freshmen," transcript of lecture 16 Sept. 1949 (William Wurster/Wurster, Bernardi, and Emmons Collection, 1922–1974 EDA UCB). See also Wurster, "School of Architecture and Planning," in "President's Report Issue, 1944–45," 139–40.

74 William W. Wurster, quoted in Riess, *William Wilson Wurster,* 116.

75 William W. Wurster, quoted in DeMars, "Humanism and the Mount Angel Library," 9, and in Riess, *William Wilson Wurster,* 116.

76 Schildt, *Mature Years,* 120–21, 123 (for quotes).

77 William W. Wurster, "To the Freshmen," transcript of lecture, 16 Sept. 1949 (William Wurster/ Wurster, Bernardi, and Emmons Collection, 1922– 1974 EDA UCB).

78 Ming Li's project is housed in MITA.

79 Schildt, *Mature Years,* 119–21.

80 Ralph Rapson, telephone interview with author, Sept. 1999; and Hession, Rapson, and Wright, *Ralph Rapson,* 68–69. Rapson also recalled Aalto's "lamentations about the current design scene." Hession, Rapson, and Wright, *Ralph Rapson,* 69.

81 Hession, Rapson, and Wright, *Ralph Rapson,* 69; De Mars, "Humanism and the Mount Angel Library," 8 (for quote).

82 Hession, Rapson, and Wright, *Ralph Rapson,* 69.

83 The 1946 project statement (grade 3 and grade 4), along with examples of student design solutions, is housed in MITA.

84 Ralph Rapson, telephone interview with author, Sept. 1999. "International style cubes" was probably a reference to Le Corbusier's Villa Savoye, in Poissy, France (1929–31). Mock, in "Built in USA—Since 1932", similarly refers to "'cardboard boxes on stilts,'" and to the "'hollow box' formula" (13, 14).

85 Wurster, as quoted in Peters and Lemperes, "Architectural Life," 92.

86 Lawrence Anderson, "William Wilson Wurster," 19 Dec. 1992, n.p. (MITA).

87 William W. Wurster, "Competition for U.S. Chancery Building, London," *Architectural Record* 119 (April 1956): 222; quoted in Richard C. Peters, "William Wurster: An Architect of Houses," in *Bay Area Houses,* ed. Sally Woodbridge, 2nd ed. (Salt Lake City: Peregrine Smith, 1988), 121.

88 Peters and Lemperes, "Architectural Life," 90; and Lawrence Anderson, "William Wilson Wurster," 19 Dec. 1992, unpublished essay, n.p. (MITA).

89 Ralph Rapson, telephone interview with author, Sept. 1999. Rapson had told Wurster that, to the contrary, he was "disgusted" with the MIT students' presentations and that he thought those at Harvard were more "polished."

90 Connah, *Finland,* 68–69, 81–85.

91 For a description and analysis of the debate, see Fenske, "Lewis Mumford, Henry-Russell Hitchcock, and the Bay Region Style," 37–47, 78 n. 5; and for its postwar implications, see Stanford Anderson, "The 'New Empiricism–Bay Region Axis': Kay Fisker and Postwar Debates on Functionalism, Regionalism, and Monumentality," *Journal of Architectural Education* 50 (Feb. 1997): 203–13.

92 "What is Happening to Modern Architecture? A Symposium at the Museum of Modern Art," *Museum of Modern Art Bulletin* 15 (Spring 1948): 4. The organizers noted that the second group, the Bay Region school, also included its counterpart, the English-invented (actually Swedish) "New Empiricism."

93 "What is Happening to Modern Architecture?," 5–10.

94 In "What is Happening to Modern Architecture?" Hitchcock identified himself as a "lecturer on architecture, Massachusetts Institute of Technology" (3). Under "Fine Arts" in "Catalog Issue, 1947," *Massachusetts Institute of Technology Bulletin, vol. 82, no. 4* (1947), 12; Hitchcock's name is listed as a "Lecturer" in "Architectural History" along with John McAndrew's. Both Hitchcock and McAndrew continued to be listed as lecturers in the 1948 catalogue. Hitchcock's name alone appears in the 1949 catalogue. But in 1950, according to Lawrence Anderson, "Professor Henry-Russell Hitchcock resigned. His work in Architectural History has been taken over by Professor John McAndrew." Anderson, "Architecture," in "President's Report Issue," special issue, *Massachusetts Institute of Technology Bulletin,* vol. 86, no. 1 (Oct. 1950), 193.

95 Robert W. Kennedy, "The Small House in New England," *Magazine of Art,* April 1948, 123–28. Kennedy's essay echoed points that he made earlier in "Toward an Old Architecture," *Pencil Points* 25 (Aug. 1944): 78–83. Peter Blake and Philip Johnson responded to Kennedy with "Architectural Freedom and Order: An Answer to Robert W. Kennedy," *Magazine of Art,* Oct. 1948, 228–31. Blake and Johnson treated Kennedy's argument for a modern architecture inflected by the region's vernacular as another argument for the "cottage style."

96 Wurster spoke at the dedication. The program for the dedication and reception is housed in MITA. The senior dormitory was named "Baker House" in honor of Everett Moore Baker, MIT's dean of students, in 1950. That year, Baker had been killed in a plane crash in Egypt. Stanley Abercrombie, "Happy Anniversary, Baker House," *Architecture Plus,* July 1973, 61.

97 Riess, *William Wilson Wurster,* 117. Paul David Pearson, in *Alvar Aalto and the International Style* (New York: Whitney Library of Design, 1978), notes that "the time-consuming trips to teach a few months, or sometimes only a few weeks at a time, must have created many obstacles to his burgeoning practice in Finland" (207). Göran Schildt notes that after Aino's death, Aalto distanced himself from the United States with "an aversion that resembled fear" and that Aalto could only return to MIT and Boston in 1963, when he "felt strong enough to face the painful past." Schildt, *Alvar Aalto: His Life* (Jyväskylä, Finland: Alvar Aalto Museum, 2007), 692, 699.

98 See Juhani Pallasmaa, "Aalto's Image of America," in the present volume.

99 On Aalto's growing disenchantment with America, see Schildt, *Mature Years,* 103 (for quote), 106–7. Wright also told Aalto that "democracy has yielded; various fascisms and such have given us a worldwide mobocracy. America has become much more imperialistic than in our days" (103). For Mumford's criticism during the late 1940s, see Fenske, "Lewis Mumford, Henry-Russell Hitchcock, and the Bay Region Style," 72–74.

100 Margaret Henderson Floyd, "Ralph Rapson: Modernism Implemented at MIT," in *Architectural Education and Boston,* ed. Floyd (Boston: Boston Architectural Center, 1989), 94.

101 Ralph Rapson, telephone interview with author, Sept. 1999; and Suzanne B. Riess, *Vernon Armand DeMars: A Life in Architecture; Indian Dancing, Migrant Housing, Telesis, Design for Urban Living, Theater, Teaching* (Berkeley, Calif.: Univ. of California Regional Oral History Office, 1992), 276–80. Rapson indicated that he was responsible for 90 percent of the design, whereas DeMars maintained that Rapson contributed only 50 percent. Still, Rapson produced most of the drawings and even DeMars acknowledged that "the guy holding the paintbrush, or the pencil, has a lot of influence." Riess, *Vernon Armand DeMars,* 280.

102 Wurster, "To the Freshmen," transcript of lecture 16 Sept. 1949 (MITA), 3–4; and Riess, *Vernon Armand DeMars,* 276–77. Hession, Rapson, and Wright, in *Ralph Rapson,* provide a full account of the project, the idea for which originated in a studio project at MIT (70–76). The project was widely known as the earliest example of a triple-floor skip-stop elevator system in the United States. Le Corbusier developed a similar concept for his Unité d'habitation in Marseilles (1947–52) during the same years, albeit with elevators that stopped at every other floor.

103 Ralph Rapson, telephone interview with author, Sept. 1999.

104 According to Wurster, Gropius treated him at the dinner as an "honored guest." Gropius's assessment of Baker House is explained by Lawrence Anderson in "Interview with Lawrence Anderson Conducted by Robert Brown, January 30, 1992" (AAA), 58.

105 DeMars, "Humanism and Mount Angel Library, 3; and Lawrence Anderson, "William W. Wurster," unpublished essay 19 Dec. 1992 n.p. (MITA). Anderson noted that "Wurster made no secret of his intention to return to the Bay Area when suitable inducements came up."

106 Meredith Clausen, *Pietro Belluschi: Modern American Architect* (Cambridge, Mass.: MIT Press, 1994), 193. On MIT's School of Architecture and Planning during the years immediately following Wurster's departure, see Anderson, "The New Empiricism–Bay Region Axis," 211–13.

107 Clausen, *Pietro Belluschi,* 200–201. Clausen also reports that Wurster encouraged Belluschi to come to MIT, telling him that the school needed his perspective as a West Coast architect, adding that "the whole international, tight point of view of the MoMA needs healthy questioning" (193).

108 Clausen, *Pietro Belluschi,* 205.

Aalto's Work in America

These essays, which focus on Aalto's architecture in America, examine his three major works, all of which are well known: the Finland Pavilion for the New York World's Fair (1939–40), Baker House at MIT (1946–49), and, finally, Mount Angel Abbey Library (1964–70) at the Benedictine abbey near Portland, Oregon. They also examine two less well known but important interiors: the Woodberry Poetry Room at Harvard University's Lamont Library (1947–49) and the Edgar J. Kaufmann Conference Rooms at the Institute of International Education in New York (1961–64).

It was with the completion of the Finland Pavilion for the New York World's Fair that Aalto secured renown on American shores. He returned in 1940, when the fair reopened; later that year, he began his appointment as a research professor at MIT. But it was not until 1946 that he designed his second major American work, Baker House at MIT, which followed his reappointment as a visiting professor at the university in 1945. This commission marked a turning point in his career. As construction began on the dormitory in 1947, Aalto designed the Woodberry Poetry Room at Harvard. During the same years, major commissions began pouring into his studio at Tiilimäki, following a dearth of commissions during World War II. From 1950 onward, his encounters with America were few. He returned to New York and Cambridge in 1963, to see the Kaufmann Conference Rooms while under construction and to visit the completed Baker House. In 1967, he would return again to inspect the site of Mount Angel Abbey Library, the third and final of his major American works, well after he had begun its design in 1964. After 1967, Aalto never visited America again. He would never see Mount Angel Abbey Library after it was completed—despite its importance in the trajectory of his thought and work.

The earliest of Aalto's American works is the subject of Sarah Menin's "Embracing Independence: The Finland Pavilion, New York, 1939." In analyzing Aalto's design, Menin emphasizes its symbolic agenda in the international context of the World's Fair, particularly as expressed by its great "wooden wave." She links this agenda, on one hand, with the representation of a Finnish identity but, on the other, with Aalto's deep attachment to the forest and to the richness of meaning it holds for him as well as for his countrymen.

The design and construction of Baker House is examined in three essays that follow. In his "Baker House: The Individual and Mass Housing, a Delicate Balance," Michael Trencher analyzes the significance of MIT as an institutional setting, the postwar ethos of which corresponded with Aalto's belief in the centrality of the person in design and which stimulated Aalto's exploration of spatial ideas in support of the delicate relationship between the individual and the collectivity, ideas that were indebted to but diverged from modernist paradigms of mass housing. Lawrence W. Speck's "Baker House and the Modern Notion of Functionalism" examines Aalto's process of designing Baker House and its strong indebtedness to Aalto's distinctive, humanistic version of "organic" functionalism. Finally, Ákos Moravánszky explores Aalto's approach to brick as a building material in "Baker House and

Brick: Aalto's Construction of a Building Material." He contrasts existing notions of the "scientific" standardization of brick construction with Aalto's organic notion of the brick as a "living cell" embedded in the mortar that offers it freedom, or "the soul of elasticity," in the shaping of architectural form.

Two subsequent essays assess the "afterlife" of Baker House as a design. In "Illuminating Aalto: The Renovation of Baker House," David N. Fixler explores the relationship of Baker House to Aalto's later works as well as to Aalto's original intentions for its design—among them the great planted trellis—as weighed against the realities of the built work, to which he gave meticulous study during the process of restoration. In "The Significance of Baker House," Paul Bentel argues for the persisting forcefulness of experience engendered by Baker House for those who have encountered it over time—its "gravity as a physical and spacial object" outperforms it interpretations in contemporary and later historical writing.

Two short essays on Aalto's interiors, Kari Jormakka's "Poetry in Motion: Aalto's Woodberry Poetry Room at Harvard" and Matthew A. Postal's "Aalto and the Edgar J. Kaufmann Conference Rooms," examine the circumstances surrounding the commission of each project—in both cases involving a distinguished supporter of the arts, Harry Harkness Flagler and Edgar J. Kaufmann, Jr., respectively. Each author notes the issues involved during the construction of the interiors without Aalto's direct supervision, while also calling attention to Aalto's hand in the rooms' spatial uniqueness: in the Woodberry Poetry Room, to "shifting centers," asymmetries, and "echelons," and in the Kaufmann Rooms, to coves with "tree-like constructions," a wave-like ceiling, and spaces of varying geometries.

In the concluding essay, "Mount Angel Abbey Library and the Path from Viipuri," Michael Spens describes the library as a "master work" of Aalto's late career and a "distillation" revealing his mature philosophy of design—reinforcing key themes in the earlier essays. Spens investigates Aalto's final work in America in a total way, from its origins as a commission through the process of its design. In the process, he links Aalto's three schemes for the library to his earlier libraries and so illustrates the Mount Angel design as a perfection of the library type. Spens's analysis calls attention to the materiality of the completed design, and the details of furniture, fittings, and lighting. He also highlights the significance of the completed work within the Benedictine community. Importantly, Spens additionally documents and assesses the life of the building in architectural criticism, aiming, in his words, to "restore the balance"—that is, to assign Mount Angel Abbey Library its deserved place in the history of modern architecture. In doing so, he alludes to the broader reception of Aalto's works in America.   **G.F.**

Embracing Independence:
The Finland Pavilion, New York, 1939

Sarah Menin

Unfortunately I lack the means to explain to you solely in words what we have tried to say with the Finnish pavilion and the exhibition. Exhibitions are in and of themselves a kind of "accounting," but they should derive their impact from their substance, not from words.

Alvar Aalto, "World's Fair: The New York World's Fair and the Golden Gate Exposition" (1939)

In the Finland Pavilion at the New York World's Fair, Alvar Aalto and his wife, Aino Marsio Aalto, made a creative account of Finland and matured their attitude about the role of architecture in human experience. What is more, the pavilion gave Alvar the opportunity to establish himself in the New World.

The competition to design Finland's pavilion for the New York World's Fair was launched during the completion of Aalto's Finland Pavilion at the Paris World's Fair, in 1937. Karl Fleig, writing with Aalto's authority, suggests that "friction between government officials and the architect prompted Aalto to commit a small breach of ethics; he submitted not just one but two projects, beside that, Aino Aalto secretly submitted a third project without her husband's knowledge."[1] Having been reluctant to have further involvement with the Pavilion Committee, Aalto began his competition designs only three days before the competition deadline. Aalto's two entries came first and second, and Aino's third. These three designs from the Aalto atelier have quite similar themes, and the resultant pavilion seems to be an assemblage of elements of them all (FIGS. 1–3). Ultimately the couple worked on the design together, and Aino was fully acknowledged in subsequent literature as co-author of the eventual

Finland Pavilion.[2] Malcolm Quantrill comments that Aino's entry was "by far the most conventionally functionalist"—an interesting comment on the division of skills between the couple, with Aino rooting Aalto's often fantastical conceptions.[3]

Finland could not afford to construct a free-standing building from scratch, so the competition brief called for the design of an interior for one of a series of restrictive, rectangular, box-like enclosures within a large building rented to nations by the New York Exposition Committee. The windowless white stucco and gypsum box measured 31 by 14.5 meters, with a height of 16 meters. The Aalto's conceived a forested interior of four half-levels representing Finland's produce, her industry, the people, and the nature of the country beneath a representation of the all-enveloping aurora borealis.

Readings of Aalto's Finland Pavilion to date have tended to find a representation of "Finnishness." For instance, Juhani Pallasmaa famously read it as "a kind of symphony in wood," but according to Richard Weston, "whatever nuances one chooses to see in the design, the message of Aalto's 'Modernist forest' was clear for all to see: Finland is a modern, creative country with deep roots in the landscape and culture of the forest." The most detailed explication of the pavilion is by Kerstin Smeds and Peter MacKeith in The *Finland Pavilions: Finland at the Universal Expositions, 1900–1992.* The thoroughness of their description of the pavilion relieves this essay of the task of describing the schematic wrangles of the design and building process, and the exact exhibition layout, enabling the focus to remain on the consideration of its symbolic agenda for Finland, for the Aalto's themselves, and for the visitor.[4]

FIGURE 01 *Aalto, winning competition entry for the Finland Pavilion, New York World's Fair, 1939. Sketch of undulating wall.*

FIGURE 02 *Aalto, second-place competition entry for the Finland Pavilion, 1939. Sketch of pavilion interior.*

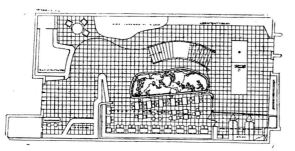

FIGURE 03 *Aino Aalto, third-place competition entry for the Finland Pavilion, 1939. Sketch plan.*

Following a description of the pavilion, this essay will discern three significances in the design: a political-cultural clarion and a personal agenda, which together lead to the third significance, the formal composition. I will also suggest that there is a continuum among these significations—between the impending world war (and Finland's geopolitical vulnerability) and the symbolism of a forested haven, both for Aalto personally and the Finns more generally, but also for others. In the course of this argument, I trace the etymology of "wood" to its Latin root in the etymon *materia*, which is closely related to the word *mater*, meaning mother and maternal love.[5] In so doing, I seek to understand the "unity" that Aalto sought to create in New York, in which he consciously brought the physical and the metaphysical together, inextricably linking the material and the psychological.[6] In this effort, I follow the lead of Aalto himself, who repeatedly linked the making of architecture to the metaphysical when he suggested that the root of "disharmony" in architecture arises at "the break with the individual's genuine psychological needs."[7]

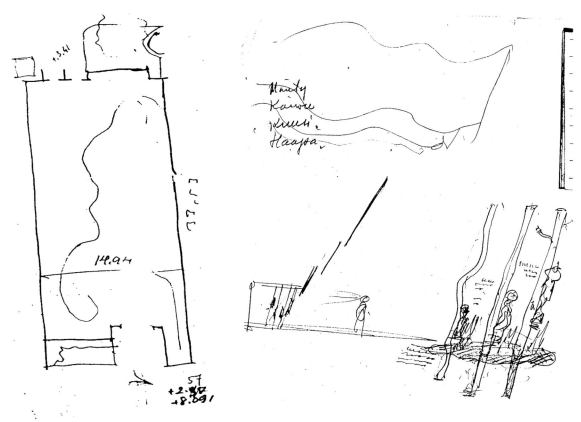

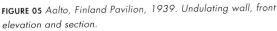

FIGURE 04 *Aalto, Finland Pavilion, New York World's Fair, 1939. Sketch plan of the pavilion.*

FIGURE 05 *Aalto, Finland Pavilion, 1939. Undulating wall, front elevation and section.*

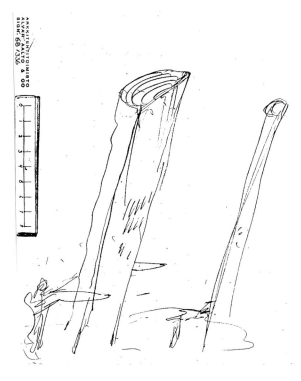

FIGURE 06 *Aalto, Finland Pavilion, 1939. Inhabiting the forest: sketch exploring the undulating wall as a spliced tree trunk.*

The Finland Pavilion: "A kind of symphony in wood"

The parti of Aalto's New York design was to undermine the rectangularity of the "box" **(FIG. 4)**. The waving wooden ceiling from the Viipuri Library had reappeared as the "raised hall with a serpentine wall front" in sketches for Villa Mairea earlier in 1938.[8] It made another appearance (only three weeks later) in the last minute sketches for the New York pavilion competition. In answer to the brief, Aalto's introverted, top-lit solution cut an undulating line through the "box," and projected it upward, to create an imposing, serpentine wall that was adorned with enormous photographic images. The wall was inclined toward the visitor, both to aid the viewing from a low level, and to create a sense of envelopment. Archive sketches show Aalto's conceptual thinking; he drew the wall as if it were cut through the wood, as if to inhabit it **(FIGS. 5–6)**. These concept sketches seem to show that he thought of this as a forested wall as much as a representation of the northern lights—and the inclined angle of the wall further suggests its enveloping gesture.

FIGURE 07 *Aalto, Finland Pavilion, 1939. Wood battens adorn the restaurant window.*

FIGURE 08 *Aalto, Finland Pavilion, 1939. "Globe" locating latitudes of Helsinki and New York over entrance to Pavilion.*

FIGURE 09 *Aalto, Finland Pavilion, 1939. Interior perspective sketch showing view out from beneath the "wall."*

FIGURE 10 *Aalto, Finland Pavilion, 1939. Ground floor plan. Ground floor plan key: 1) Information counter and office; 2) Administration office; 3) Travel bureau; 4) Exhibition area for the 1940 Helsinki Olympics; 5) Employee space; 6) Kitchen; 7) Bazaar and souvenir sales; 8) Exhibition area of industrial products; 9) Exhibition area of furnished rooms; 10) Exhibition area, standing glass cabinets*

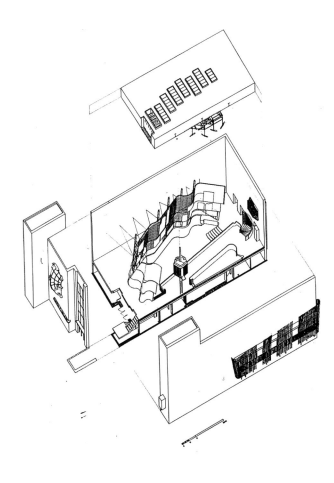

FIGURE 11 *Aalto, Finland Pavilion, 1939. Axonometric of the pavilion. Drawing by Peter McKeith.*

From the outside the pavilion appeared like a white modernist box. When the final logistical arrangements were made, rather than a "box" in the middle of a conjoined series, the Finns were allocated one at the end, opposite the host pavilion of America. This location gave the pavilion an unplanned side wall, on which was a long window. The architects adorned this with tightly but seemingly randomly placed light wood slats (FIG. 7), which gave a sole clue about the nature of the interior space. On turning the corner to the entrance (a "given" opening that suggested art-deco proportioning), the visitor was confronted by a sculpture of a "skeleton globe" identifying a line between the latitudes of Helsinki and New York (FIG. 8).[9] From the entrance level the visitor was drawn into the forested interior (FIG. 9), missing the offices which were discretely hidden to the right of the entrance (FIG. 10). The visitors found themselves beneath and within the forest. At one moment the visitor would be enticed, protectively, under the huge cantilevered wall to the left, aware of a forest clearing beyond. Opposite the wall ran the balcony of the first-floor restaurant that extended in a straight but diagonally inflected path, as if it were seeking, yet failing to resist, the power of the main force of direction of the snaking undulation. To the left of the entrance, still under and within the forest wall, visitors were invited into "typical" furnished rooms. In front of these

FIGURE 12 *Aalto, Finland Pavilion, 1939. Every aspect of growing, felling, moving, and processing timber was depicted on the "forest wall."*

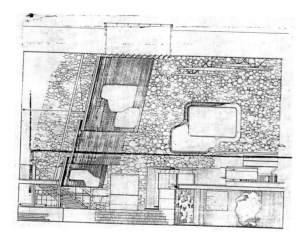

FIGURE 13 *Aalto, Finland Pavilion, 1939. Design drawings demonstrate how the use of the space was conceived from the outset. The restaurant balcony allows a view across to the upper tiers of the "forest wall."*

were three free-standing glass cases, in which ceramics and glass designs were displayed. Only in moving out from beneath the "wall" would the visitor be struck by how Aalto had cut the cantilevered three-tiered timber wall through the single pavilion volume, thereby totally fragmenting the cubic volume of the "box." The architectonic reality of this inclined wall required Aalto to use every structural contrivance to lean the forested interior on steel "I-hangers" between the roof of the "box" and the floor, and suspended back on wires to the side walls. The pavilion was contrived as a great undulating "as if," designed to affect the experience of being within a forest realm, with timber in all its states, from unrefined to crafted and molded, and with plants growing, "as if" up the trunks of trees. The visitor would be drawn by the axis between the wall and the restaurant, which linked the off-set entrance and exits, through the space, and up, at the far end, to other levels (FIG. 11).

The "inside elevation" (or "facade inside") was to be, as the architects put it, "a great decorative wall (composed of three screens in a waving form). They explained that "These screens are built on a fundamental iron structure in the same waving form. . . . To be completed with wooden construction and covered with plywood . . . to be brought from Finland."[10/11] This hanging, undulating wall was thus made of a composite birch plywood-clad structure which was adorned with long timber battens running vertically, at small intervals, down each tier of the undulating wall—each coded by species: pine, birch, fir, and alder. Gaps in the battening were shaped around the subjects of the enormous photographic images that depicted different aspects of Finnish life, including her nature, people, and industry—but mostly related to the forest (FIG. 12). Akin to Akseli Gallen-Kallela's frescoes in the Finland Pavilion at the Paris World's Fair of 1900, the almost life-size images assisted in creating the desired portrait of Finnish culture. However, while in 1900 the objective was a quasi-romantic portrait of Finland's mythology, in 1939 it had become a representation of contemporary reality. The top tier of the wall was taller than the others, adding to its imposing nature. Nestling beneath it all was a display of artifacts, from skis to propellers of pressed wood, cheeses to Savoy vases, axes to clothing, and ceramics to boxing gloves.[12] There were, of course, also industrial rolls of paper representing Finland's massive pulp industry. Throughout the pavilion were posted facts about Finland, boasting, for the most part, about her economy.[13]

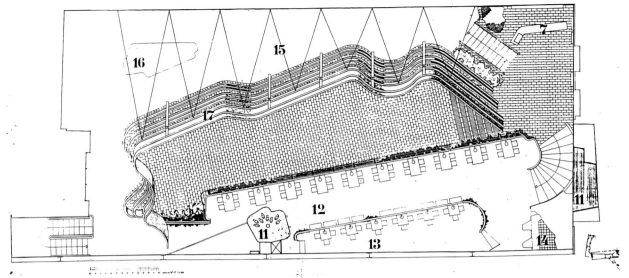

FIGURE 14 *Aalto, Finland Pavilion, 1939. Mezzanine floor plan. Key: 11) Cinema screens and the projection booth; 12) Restaurant, main level; 13: Restaurant, upper level; 14) Buffet and pantry; 15) Exhibition area of Finnish economy and culture; 16) Model of ideal planned Finnish community; 17) Curving wooden exhibition wall*

FIGURE 15 *Aalto, Finland Pavilion, 1939. Steps leading to upper exhibition area behind "forest wall."*

The restaurant was on two levels. Suspended above it was an undulating, timber-clad projection box, which cast films of Finland into a curved inset screen-box, set on the exit wall that was otherwise covered with sawn ends of logs (SEE FIG. 22). Over the restaurant whirred wooden propellers, used as fans—an image of the state of the art of the aviation industry in Finland (FIG. 17). From the elevated level of the restaurant the visitor could look directly across at the undulating wall of huge images (FIG. 18).

Opposite the undulating wall was another long, low-level display area boasting Aalto's own Paimio chairs among other artifacts, in this case nestling beneath

the raised restaurant level (FIG. 13). At the far end of the pavilion a rise of six steps led to a curving half level, where a booth offered souvenirs for sale. From here the visitor could either move up to the restaurant and buffet on the right, or left to a large exhibition about the Finnish economy and Aalto's concept for an "ideal planned Finnish community" behind the cantilevered wall (FIGS. 14–15). Aalto's two competition designs had placed the restaurant and a cinema behind the wall. In moving them to a position opposite the undulating element, he adopted aspects of Aino's third-place scheme, and opened up a more powerful, vertical forest clearing. The hand-hugging handrails throughout epitomized his approach to the whole scheme—one of accommodating the visitor physically and psychologically—while contriving to offer an image of Finland (FIG. 16).

Cultural Clarion and Political Act

The Finland Pavilion opened on 4 May 1939, the eve of the Winter War, when the Russian Bear threatened to sit on its diminutive neighbor, which had been a grand duchy of Russia until it seized independence at the moment of the revolution. At this time the creativity and fame of Finland's two greatest cultural ambassadors (Aalto and Sibelius) were called on to draw the world's attention to the plight of their far-off land, which found itself between a rock and a hard place.[14] At the opening ceremony there was a live broadcast of Sibelius

FIGURE 16 *Aalto, Finland Pavilion, 1939. Finnish made propellers used as fans, and undulating projection booth, all hung from the ceiling.*

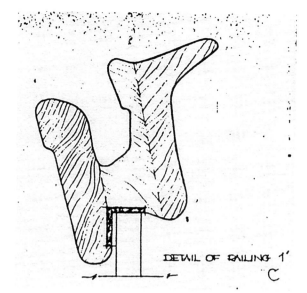

FIGURE 17 *Aalto, Finland Pavilion, 1939. Detail of hand-hugging handrail of main staircase.*

conducting a performance of his searing *Andante Festivo* live from Helsinki.[15] This political moment was critical; Finland needed to project a favorable image to the world, one of a neutral, free democratic industrialized state about to host the 1940 Olympics.

Aalto's expression of Finland and Finnish identity was thus crucial—politically, economically, and creatively. Aalto said that it was his and Aino's determination to offer what they called a "spontaneous unity" in their scheme, which comprised sections that, from the lowest level up, covered the cultural-historical foundations of Finland, the Finnish economy today, and the cultural life of the nation.[16] Smeds suggests that this bore features of an "almost Marxist" stratified structure.[17] Yet the Aaltos seemed to view this as a simple, holistic

world view, in which man, the land, his work, and his home were interrelated to an indistinguishable degree. And this is something that Aalto's subsequent (unrealized) project for a journal called *The Human Side* sought to continue.[18]

The fact that a wooden wave was chosen by the competition judges to represent Finland evinces the crux of many matters regarding (expedient) conceptions of "Finnishness"—something that was a critical political necessity for the nation's existence at that time. Indeed, the title of Aalto's winning competition entry, "Land, People, Work, Products," continued as the dominant motif throughout. The creation of an "image" for the nation was crucial in attracting attention to the floundering fledgling nation. It is difficult now to conceive of there being no "image" of Finland, so deep is the effect of Finnish image-making now. Yet in 1939 Aalto's capacity to fantasize may have been pivotal in creating the image of Finland that the world then held, and which drew attention to the impending Red doom. It is interesting here to note a comment from his biographer, Göran Schildt: he observed Aalto's "tendency to confuse his own wishes with reality"—something that has a fundamental impact on the composition of the pavilion interior.[19] The fantasy in New York was yoked to reality, and the undulation yoked enough to Euclid's hand to hold off the critics, yet emotive enough to stir the hearts of Americans.

FIGURE 18 *Aalto, Finland Pavilion, 1939. Restaurant level, showing projection booth, screen, and skylights.*

Looking Forward: Finland as a Modern Industrial State

Aalto's desire to describe the specificity of Finland in 1939, to celebrate the "original," authentic forest culture, was counter to what he called the "absurd birch-bark culture of 1905 which believed that everything clumsy and bleak was especially Finnish."[20] While shunning the stylistic cocktail parties of his National Romantic forebears, in his architectural detailing Aalto actually came closer to the back-wood techniques of wrapping bark and saplings than had the Finnish National Romantic architects such as Eliel Saarinen and company at their Hvitträsk home, as elsewhere. Indeed, in both Paris and New York Aalto used what Weston calls "a promiscuous array of columns," rope-lashed bundles of saplings, and

fluted trunks **(FIG. 19)**.[21] But, of course, Aalto's use of the same material and even the same technique would be far from "absurd."

In Aalto's Finland Pavilion in Paris in 1937, Finland announced itself to the world, not only as "a producer of wood," but as a social state—something that Smeds suggests Aalto achieved through "comprehensive planning."[22] Aalto wanted total control, believing, "An exposition ought to be what it has been since its origin: a bazaar where all kinds of heterogeneous objects are displayed indiscriminately whether they be fish or fabrics or cheeses. For this reason I've looked for the greatest possible concentration, a place stuffed with juxtaposed, superimposed merchandise, industrial products and groceries separated from each other by only a few centimeters. It was no easy task to bring

FIGURE 19 *Aalto, Finland Pavilion, 1939. Columns, poles, and slats bound with twine.*

together these elements and create a harmonious whole."[23] A whole that, with reference initially to Paris and then to New York, Aalto described as an "organic exhibition" **(FIG. 20)**.[24] This deep motivation for disparate elements to come together to form "a totality that can be grasped instinctively," is crucial to an understanding of the pavilion.[25] The indivisible whole would, he seemed sure, offer a "momentary impression" that must be backed up by "a profound and penetrating analysis of the times and their spirit"—an aesthetic vision based on social foundations. Aalto believed that, generally speaking, expositions had the capacity to be "motors for humanity's development."[26]

In Paris the Finnish Fair Committee (and Finnish industry) had challenged Aalto's reading of the priority for an overall cultural picture, instead favoring the production of an export promotion. The crux of the matter was the manner in which artifacts were chosen and displayed in the pavilion. Rather than a trade fair, Aalto wanted a "coherent cultural demonstration, with material and spiritual aspects consistently dovetailed to make up a single . . . total image . . . which is not just a futile aesthetic doctrine." Because of this debacle in Paris, Aalto stated from the start of the New York project that there should be "no interference" by the authorities. The desire for coherence is interesting since the architects' method of achieving this is in no way simple—often appearing, as Aalto also suggested, "like a country store."[27]

The Pavilion was to be a *Gesamtkunstwerk*; a total work of art in which all individual elements were composed into a unified whole. Although Finnish industry had felt side-lined by his aesthetic intent—his big idea of a "symphony"—they eventually appreciated Aalto's willingness to accommodate their wish to demonstrate the capacity of Finnish industry within this idea.[28] Central to his idea were the rich resources of the forest that were key to Finland's industrial progress. Aalto also wanted to relate practical, economic, or political realities in a way that was aesthetically and indeed humanely pleasing.

The key to all this was wood—that "scientific" element, as he put it, that was to be "the general theme that holds it together."[29] As in Paris, the forest and its resources were the central structure of the piece—a main theme and what Smeds describes as a "macroeconomic core."[30] Indeed, that the machinery of industry was featured in the enormous exhibition photographs (itself a modern feat) was crucial to Aalto, who saw himself as a "modern," progressive Finn.

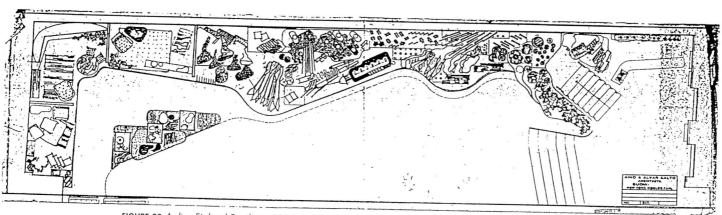

FIGURE 20 *Aalto, Finland Pavilion, 1939. Exhibition layout plan.*

FIGURE 21 *Aalto, Finland Pavilion, 1939. Nets were hung dramatically, lending a mystical air to the exhibition.*

In fact, Aalto had come to be close to progressive industrialists. Chief among these was the Gullichsen family, who ran the A. Ahlström Corporation and had already commissioned Aalto to design housing complexes associated with its forest enterprises in Sunila and Kauttua, in addition to the Villa Mairea, completed just before the New York pavilion opening. The "progress" they sought had a particular focus, rooting a modern standard of living in the natural environment.[31] Aalto had already expressed his idea that "contact with nature and enjoyment of its constant variation is a way of life that cannot be reconciled with overly formalistic ideas."[32] In the pavilion, modern living comprises the co-mingling of industry, products, and people in a socioeconomic realm that is inseparable from the natural environment. This is congruent with Aalto's repeated claim that progressive modernity should be conceptually rooted in the "nuances" of nature, the symbolism of nature (that is, "freedom"), and its materiality (that is, wood).[33] His model and inspiration for this is the forest, as his writings and designs testify.[34]

In Sunila and Kauttua (and not least in Villa Mairea) Aalto had begun to look more closely at the vernacular tradition of building in Finland. Highlighting the "affinity with nature" in this tradition, Aalto challenged the notion that the grouping of such vernacular settlements exhibited "disordered incoherence."[35] He was determined to offer something of this "other" ordering system to counter what he saw as modernity's monotonies—and in this wish he was not far from Hugo Häring's *Leistungsform* (or content-derived form).

In the pavilion many vernacular artifacts from forest life—fishing nets hanging as ghostly swathes (**FIG. 21**), bearskins, and even the infamous ryijy rag-rugs (that Aalto personally hated)—were placed in a dynamic, almost sculptural way alongside the contemporary painting of Tyko Konstantin Sallinen, the Aaltos' own furniture and glass designs, and the fourteen-foot-tall Maiden of Finland sculpture by Wäinö Aaltonen, which referred to Finnish mythology in modern guise.

Fighting for Independence and Identity—Again

The title of the New York World's Fair was "The World of Tomorrow," to which Aalto added the motto for the Finland Pavilion, "Finland—the country of freedom and democratic spirit" (**FIG. 22**).[36] This addition was crucial. Before the New York World's Fair, Finland had only been known as an eastern Baltic state, rubbing shoulders with Stalin's Russia, and home to Sibelius. After 1939 Finland became known as a small Western democratic industrialized nation in Scandinavia, home of Sibelius and Aalto.[37] Aalto's contrivance had worked—his propaganda campaign had been successful.

Writing with hindsight, Frederick Gutheim, author of the first book on Aalto, suggests that, "beyond [the pavilion's] assertive irrationality and visual excitement, its denial of the rule of geometry and affirmation of the organic, nature became a symbol of political freedom."[38] However, Gutheim's critique fails to recognize the complex and profound way in which Aalto sought to allow gestures of the organic to cling to Euclid's hand.[39] Indeed, the pavilion undoubtedly represented the relationship between the natural context (the forest) and political freedom. Though the Aaltos, like many Finns, knew there were dangers of the forest, at the same time they carefully represented the nation's mastery over this powerful realm of Tapio—the god of the forest in Finnish mythology. Both the dangers and the fecundity of forest-survival came to the nation's aid when, within a few months of the pavilion opening, inexperienced Russian troops crossed the border into Finnish Karelia, grossly outnumbering Aalto's white-clad, ski-mounted compatriots, who in thirty degrees of frost held back the Red Army against all the odds. Aalto was not among their numbers.

The Conceptual Landscape: Personal Reformation

In 1938 the exhibition "Alvar Aalto: Architecture and Furniture," held in New York at the Museum of Modern Art, lauded the Finn for the first time.[40] The museum's new building was inaugurated in 1939, concurrent with the World's Fair, and Aalto was again honored by that institution, as one of the five world "masters" of architecture (alongside Frank Lloyd Wright, Le Corbusier, Ludwig Mies van der Rohe, and Oscar Niemeyer), all of whom were asked to exhibit their work. He chose to display the eclectic new Villa Mairea.[41] Thus Aalto had the greatest opportunity of his career so far, and indeed experienced the beginning of his truly international reputation.

The contrast between this international success and the personal low that began at the outbreak of the Winter War is marked. Aalto suffered an initial episode of what Schildt describes as terrified "psychosis" on the outbreak of war. Once he had regained some mental composure, Aalto sought "more or less to flee" Finland.[42] In March 1940, family in tow, he successfully engineered an official transfer back to the land of the free, where he had so recently been lauded.[43] Ironically the peace treaty between Finland and Russia was signed when they were less than half way to America.[44]

The World's Fair was due to re-open in spring 1940, which offered an opportunity, according to the new Finnish Chief Fair Commissioner, "to remind the world that the democratic Republic of Finland exists, and that it is bravely fighting for the principles of Western liberty and justice."[45] The Americans, not yet in the war, loved this sentiment, paying through donations for the reorganization of the exhibition.[46] Aalto was now "on site," ready to redesign aspects of the interior to reflect the immediate need for reconstruction (with the sections on sport and tourism being replaced by images of bombed buildings). When the pavilion re-opened on 16 May 1940, its use as an instrument of propaganda became even more crucial. Under the new theme of reconstruction, it acted as a magnet for political and financial assistance. Aalto's personal needs (to flee the war) and Finland's political needs (for an ambassador) were, temporarily (and conveniently), congruent.[47] While reorganizing the pavilion, Aalto undertook a varied lecture program—visiting the Massachusetts

FIGURE 22 *Aalto, Finland Pavilion, 1939. Opening of the pavilion, at which Sibelius's* Andante Festivo *was broadcast from Finland.*

Institute of Technology, Yale University, Princeton University, the Cranbrook Academy of Art, and the Pratt Institute, among others—in which he spoke, often fantastically, of reconstructing Finland. At this time he wrote the important essay "The Humanizing of Architecture," in which he argues for architecture to challenge the limited analyses of modernism, and to allow sufficient latitude for individual creativity and the human psyche.[48] Aalto began work as a visiting professor at MIT on 8 October 1940, but had to leave from New York on 20 October after he was ordered by Finnish officials, ignominiously, to return to Finland. From the land of the free (the "peaceful, bright, vital America," as Schildt puts it) Aalto was forced to ground the theories of reconstruction in "Finnish reality."[49]

The identification of these personal problems in no way belittles either Aalto or his work; on the contrary, it helps to identify a key to the empathy he practiced in his buildings, and to that which concerned him repeatedly in his writing—the psychological world.

For Aalto the political, the artistic, and the personal were intertwined, and nowhere more so than in the New York pavilion. Although politics in itself did not interest him, he was keenly aware when it impinged on people's lives (and the future of his homeland). However, in his design for New York,

Aalto was acting at the cusp of both the political and the artistic, and there the image of the culture of a nation was forged. He wrote: "[T]he concept of culture should not be misunderstood or misused. It is not an isolated phenomenon, separable from life. . . .Even the smallest daily chore can be humanized and invested with harmony." To Aalto those daily human experiences were crucial, and without them, "man is forgotten. . . . And architecture—the real kind—only exists where the little man is at the center. His tragedy and his comedy—both." While in the United States he was in the process of seeking to make architecture that maintained the links with individual psychological needs, stimulated, perhaps, by a certain degree of psychological vulnerability of his own at the time.[50]

In the specific context of the New York pavilion design, although not wanting to "brag," Aalto admits to seeking "to make an impression on the visitor psychologically and instinctively."[51] "Bragging" is an interesting term. Why should it be taken as "bragging" to identify his deep agenda of "humanizing architecture"? It seems that the Aaltos were not, as some commentators suggest, interested solely in "upholding the primacy of specifically Finnish conceptions, forms and materials."[52] Rather their agenda was much broader, and concomitantly their appeal is much broader, and indeed much deeper.

Mediating Reality

In this context of understanding the more "general" appeal of the pavilion, and its non-nationalist agenda, it is profitable to ask why the architectural critic Reyner Banham could write in the late 1950s, "No other architect in the world, let alone Finland, could have produced at that moment anything quite so spectacular, so appropriate, and so completely original as that great disquieting, irregularly planked wall of wood sagging wavily out over the visitors to the pavilion."[53] Here Aalto's originality is undoubted, yet in isolating the sense of the wall being "disquieting," Banham is almost alone in offering a critical awareness of the effect of the pavilion at the level of what Aalto described as one's "mental and emotional being."[54] Since Aalto was keen to expose this fecund realm of architecture, it is appropriate to examine the

creative root of this interest in "the unknown depths of our own being," as he put it, and of note is his capacity to put himself at the heart of this by using the word "our."[55] Yet, there is an underlying challenge in Banham's critique of the pavilion, to the tectonic aspects of Aalto's composition that are rooted in the forest. Banham's derogatory description of a carefully detailed wood wall as the "sagging" of "planks" identifies his own distrust of Aalto's material aesthetic, far as it seemed from the machine age so favored by that particular critic—a value he shared in common with his modernist forebear the herald Giedion. In this sense Banham's words do more to conjure the pavilion's "disquieting" character than they do to offer an accurate description of the pavilion's tectonic reality.

Aalto was particularly interested in the individual experience of the exhibition. In his exploration of the nature of contemporary expositions, he pinpoints their potential to inform the public about "valuable experimental activity," and even to stimulate what "begins with primitive inquisitiveness and ends in that drive to creative work which exists in every individual." He also expresses the need for the material of the expositions to be unmediated, to be "without go-betweens." In this text, Aalto relates the activity of conceiving the pavilion, and its subsequent role as a stimulant to the creativity in others (directly and without explanation)—indeed, "in every individual."[56] In this way, Aalto conceived his work as catalyst for creative experience, modeling a "conceptual landscape" that can be experienced—inhabited even—in a completely intuitive way, while being carefully constructed to appeal to the visitor who desires (or requires) a factual exposition of Finland.[57] It was to be an "experience" not easily forgotten. The visitors would take something away with them (something enveloping, or even something "disquieting') and would feel very close to it, in part because the architecture may have stimulated a deeper sense of themselves—their inner reality.[58] Thus, at the intuitive level, the pavilion becomes an experience of mediation: a space in which one may access a personal (inner) reality at the same time as outwardly experiencing representations of Finland.

Consequently, the pavilion can be argued to be a "transitional object" through which an inner life of the individual and an outer reality could be simultaneously related: "those damned realities which make up our work," as Aalto put it to Sigfried Giedion.[59] In other words, there is a mediation between the "inner" reality of an individual's experience of their own being-in-the-world (which might explain the "disquieting" sense that Banham perceived) and the outer "reality," which in this case is the experience of Finland and the forest that Aalto constructed. Here is an example of Aalto's penchant for connecting the practical with the personal—something that he had honed during his many episodes of personal collapse, in which (he intimates) he learned the importance of "humanism" (or the psycho-social elements) in the built environment. This capacity to trigger the inner world of the self and thus let aspects of the self bleed into the experience of the outer place adds to the fecundity of the architectural experience. Of the techniques the Aaltos' implemented in their New York pavilion, not least was their use of the imagery of the forest, and all it represents, not just to Finns but to humanity generally.[60]

Primary Comfort

In his ideas about expositions, Aalto also challenged the American Pavilion in particular, reading it as lacking "architectural seriousness" and being "of a transitory nature." Aalto suggested that, on the contrary, his experience of "America" rather mirrored his own agenda, which "willingly leaves out everything superfluous to the structure's task or to primary comfort."[61] "Primary comfort"—that physical experience that speaks of mother and the primary position of envelopment—is crucial to the psychosomatic experience of architecture. Colin St. John Wilson has since translated it into most valuable architectural language in his essay "The Natural Imagination," and later, at the First International Alvar Aalto Symposium, applied it specifically to Aalto's work.[62] It refers to the pre-verbal language of space and spatial relationships, "the sole metaphor you had for dealing with every emotion, frustration or fantasy, fear or joy and which owes its emotional charge to its reconciliation of contradictory material. And it is one of the most marked characteristics of Aalto's work that it so dangerously engages with contradictory elements which it yet manages to control."[63] In such ideas architectural place is understood as having the potential to provide a place of mediation, a transitional object, or "in-between" realm

which can translate Melanie Klein's psychoanalytical "primary positions" of separation and merger into the more architectural positions of "exposure" and "envelopment"; phenomena that seem to have been active in visitors' experience of the tilted (even overbearing) wooden wall in New York.[64]

The Meaning of the Forest

In the 1930s substantial parts of the culture of which Aalto spoke were still, in one way or another, related to the forest. As well as offering the physical resources for survival, the forest also offered metaphysical sustenance; symbolically the forest represented both the reality of Finland and something more universal. A document in the Alvar Aalto Foundation Archive suggests that Aalto sought to create a "warm and homey tone"—a haven offering "primary comfort"—that would also do the job of "characterizing and symbolizing the Finnish mental make-up in a concentrated fashion."[65] Since there may not be such a thing as the "Finnish mental make-up," may it not, in part, be a projection of Aalto's own mental make-up? Although there was an obvious scientific basis for Aalto's choice of wood, there were also deeply personal reasons for this decision. It is of particular import that this document uses the expression a "warm and homey tone," since the pavilion is at the same time disquieting. Yet the nature of human experience of the forest is at one moment enveloping and the next disquieting. The pavilion replicates the difficult reality in which conflicting opposites demand to be reconciled in ways that are not simplistic, and which thus follows the movement of the psyche. The pavilion allows the joining of the dissimilar, inviting them to relate, and it therefore represents one of the deepest motivations for Aalto: "the simultaneous solution of conflicting problems."[66]

During his childhood, the forest had been a haven for Aalto, who had traipsed through it endlessly with his father, a forest surveyor. When his mother died (Alvar was just eight) the forest may have provided a further, metaphorical haven. Undoubtedly, the forest remained an emotive creative stimulant for him. Such a metaphoric return to the forest is often described in literature about the "meaning" of the forest to Finns.[67] Aalto's desire to use forest material to make a "primary embrace" is apparent; and the relation of material to 'mater' and 'mother' is important (SEE FIG. 5). Indeed, discussing his use of the term "material," he wrote, " Of course I primarily mean substance, and yet the word material means more to me, for it translates purely material activity into related mental process. . . . Matter is a link. . . . It has the effect of making a unity. . . . The links in material leave open every opportunity for harmonious synthesis . . . Wood is the natural material closest to man, both biologically and as the setting of primitive civilizations." Interestingly, he also wrote, "I do use wood, but not for sentimental reasons." Rather, he suggests, "as a timeless material with an ancient tradition wood is readily available, and not merely for constructive purposes but also for psychological and biological ones" (FIG. 23).[68] Although written in 1970, toward the end of his life, this statement epitomizes both his manner of integrating the material and psychological and, importantly, his method of using nature (or in this case more specifically wood) as a tool of mediation—an agenda quite different to that of his modernist colleagues.

FIGURE 23 *Aalto, Finland Pavilion, 1939. Aalto in the pavilion during construction.*

Attitudes toward the Forest

The Finnish philosopher Juhani Pietarinen has defined four attitudes toward the forest among Finns—utilism, humanism, mysticism, and primitivism—and each can be seen to some degree in the Aaltos' Finland Pavilion in New York.[69] Utilism sees the forest merely as an objective resource, both a means of increasing the standard of living and a tool for the welfare of mankind—just as the huge images on Aalto's undulating wall demonstrate.[70] The humanist attitude to the forest is purely human-centered, striving for forests to be used in the service of the Socratic intellectual ideals of beauty and of ethics, and seeking to facilitate mental balance. In their realization that the forest represents both the resource of hope and the threat of danger, the Aaltos demonstrated a mingling of humanism and utilism; it is no accident that the great height of the leaning wall in New York was (and is) felt, by some, to be overpowering, even "dangerous." In the mystical attitude, man searches for unity with nature through sensory or spiritual experience. Nature is experienced as a sacred totality, as something beyond reason. That the so-called scientific basis of the pavilion was wood is epitomized in and on the emphatically intuitive gesture of the undulation. Pietarinen notes that such

mystical attitudes are common at times of cultural crisis, when there is a desire to be other than where one is (that is, to be united with something beyond the crisis context). This attitude tallies both with Finland's time of national crisis and Aalto's own need of a refuge from the war. Throughout Finnish history the lakes and the forest have heaved with grief for a people suppressed politically yet free in the natural environment to fight for life. It is perhaps in this way that the forested interior of the pavilion was "disquieting." Finally, Pietarinen suggests that primitivism denies all human privileges in nature, and secures the rights of all species, overriding the ideals of civilization. The New York pavilion clearly declares the Finns' active exploitation of natural resources, confirming Aalto's distaste for primitivism (SEE FIG. 12).

In finding the project "a productive, harmonious symbiosis between man's intellectual and material culture, and nature," Weston saw "a vision of what Finland could aspire to more than what it already was." Weston went on to make a crucial point: "For Aalto, ever a Modernist, the world was about becoming not being."[71] Herein Weston draws attention to Aalto's preoccupation with drawing the "underlying pattern" for the pavilion from both the ever-changing relationship with the forest and the experiential process that the pavilion would offer. Indeed, a drawing sets out how the photographic images would depict the journey from subsistence forest settlement to export of timber products, visually rooting the Finnish economy and therefore prosperity in the forest (FIG. 24). Aalto had come to a belief that modern life everywhere was improved if more connections back to nature were offered, one way or another—be they in dwellings opening directly from nature, or in the re-planning of new towns. These were ideas that appeal far beyond the image of Finland, to the borders of the human psyche "and beyond."[72] Nevertheless, in including archetypal Finnish figures carved in wood,[73] Aalto located this meta-agenda in the specifics of Finland—located, but not fixed—and borrowed something of the specific life in Finland that appeals more universally.

Formal Revolution

However "disquieting" it may have been, the pavilion was never "fatiguing." Aalto spoke out strongly against such "toxins" that most often cause physical and psychological fatigue in exhibitions. He believed that monotony is often "tied to the formal language" used by the designers. Thus demonstrating how close he felt the psychical and the physical to be, Aalto also reveals how he considers a formal language to be created for the specific circumstance and context. Challenging decorative and architectural irrelevancies in other pavilions, Aalto sought to make the architecture and the artifacts isomorphic—thus avoiding those physical and psychical toxins that make up exhibition fatigue by way of experiential stimulation.[74]

The Principle of Unity?

In Ancient Greek society there was a conception that "the healthy soul is 'symphonic,' i.e., harmonious."[75] Aalto's explanatory words characterize the pavilion variously as "a harmonious whole," and a "symphony."[76] Rooting beneath the concept of symphony to the Greek etymon *sum*, which is an assimilated form of *sun* (with), we can better understand Aalto's reference, relating it through the Greek *sumphonos* (sounding together) to *sumphusis* (growing together), which is more suitable in architectural terms. Importantly, both the notion of harmony and symphony that Aalto used repeatedly are based on a notion of "mutual adjustment" of parts in the forging of a balance of consonance and dissonance.[77] The key to this is *harmos*—the etymon of harmonia (meaning joint)— which brings the philosophical notion back to the

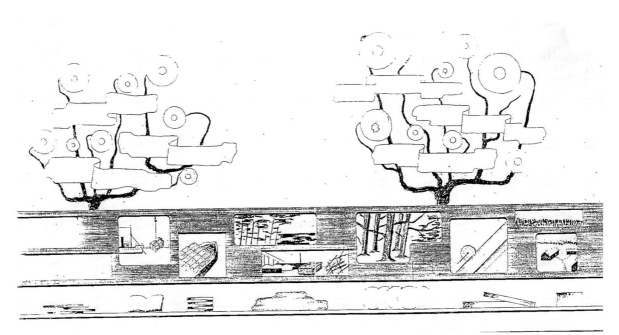

FIGURE 24 *Aalto, Finland Pavilion, 1939. The conception sketch of the "forest wall" panels demonstrates the path from forest settlement to manufacture to export.*

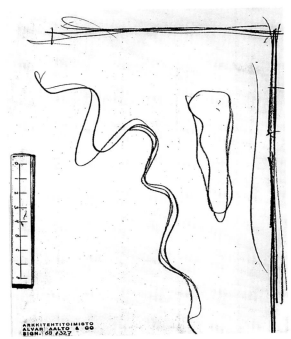

FIGURE 25 *Aalto, Finland Pavilion, 1939. Concept sketch of the box and the undulation.*

The Bar and the Wave

The manner in which Aalto's first sketches for the pavilion destroyed the "box" is quite different from other challenges to Euclid by the architectures of Wright, Gerrit Rietveld, and Mies van der Rohe. Aalto's was the agenda of "the organic line," as he had put it in a letter to Gropius in 1930.[83] In sketches for the Paris pavilion, Aalto explores an undulating gesture tied to a fractured "box." In the Lapua Forest Pavilion of 1938 (designed during the construction of the New York pavilion) there is no such argument, since the whole pavilion, carried out by Aalto's assistant, Jarl Jaatinen, has become an unmitigated undulation, unchallenged and unyoked to Euclid's grasp—and consequently loses its power. Nevertheless, in the New York pavilion Aalto is still dependent on the "box"—which Weston points out "proved to be his best friend"—as a retaining and restraining idiom, against which his serpentine wall can lash but remains contained and anchored **(SEE FIG. 25)**.[84] It must be noted too that the undulation comes to signify Aalto's humanist agenda, gesturing to the "little man," as he puts it,[85] alongside the more shallow readings of "Finnishness" for a country that comprises over sixty thousand undulating lakes. Shallower still is the notion that the "wave" is self-referential, since aalto means "wave" in Finnish—something that Aalto, with his irreverent sense of humor, was happy to play with.[86] However, if we read only such totemic meanings in his compositions we miss his deeper, more challenging agenda.

From the philosophical notion of *symphysis* comes Aalto's actual technique, by which the form was developed architecturally. His yearning for a "synthesis" is revealed in the first sketches of the New York "box" and the undulation. Wilson finds this "argument" is central to Aalto's compositional technique, and "can be epitomized by drawing two forms—an ideograph of two lines—one straight, the other serpentine . . . a complementarity between the rigorous plane of analysis and the turbulent wave-like surge of fantasy."[87] Between the "bar" and its distinct formal partner (that is, the wave), "an axis of difference" is established.[88] Aalto described this as "the simultaneous reconciliation of opposites."[89] These oppositions bring the dynamic and auxiliary functions of life together in many buildings, but this phenomenon is best epitomized in the plan of the House of Culture. To Aalto's friend Sigfried Giedion, in the New York pavilion the wave was a "rude and almost

physical, joining the dissimilar and the disparate. This concept became central to Aalto's compositional technique in and beyond New York. Indeed, it seems to have become a means of ideal thinking toward which Aalto increasingly strove, and to which end he soon developed the notion that "architecture is thus a kind of super-technical creation, and the harmonization of many disparate forms of activity is central to it."[78] In New York, as elsewhere, there were no disparate elements to unite, so it was necessary from the start to construct the dichotomy and then work to harmonize it.

However, it must be noted that not everyone experienced the New York pavilion as a modernist integrated presentation,[79] let alone as a "symphony" of elements. As if declaring the king was naked, the correspondent for the *Architectural Review* found that too much was "crammed" in, creating a "general confusion," reminiscent more of a cacophony than a symphony.[80] Indeed, it might be said that Aalto's process is one of creating tension in form and of then letting forms "dialogue" until these are resolved "into harmony," a precarious symbolic resolution of the tension, the argument, or the relationship—use what metaphor you will.[81] This method seems to have been critical for Aalto as a process of bringing his art to a place that reflected life—"the ethical line," as Sibelius put it.[82]

barbaric" dynamic, a reading which demonstrates Giedion's closed, modernist mindset that sought a more aphoristic minimalism than Aalto's intuitive approach would offer.[90] Indeed, it is a mindset that infected Banham's second-hand disquiet, which is far from Smeds's contemporary understanding of the pavilion as a description of the forest, which I have already discussed.

Modeling Interiority: 'A Building with a Facade Inside'

As early as 1926 Aalto had referred to "that curving, living, unpredictable line," suggesting a link between an organic unpredictability and what some experience as precarious, even, as Banham says, "disquieting," or as Quantrill puts it, "threatening."[91] Having used the term "organic exhibition," Aalto cast the die for the formal outworking of the physical exposition; it would be generated by the idea of a "process" of experiencing the exhibition. As suggested, this came at a time when he had begun to be more interested in the observation that deeper into the forest (and the further east in Finland), less Euclidean and more "organically living and flexible forms" of settlements were apparent.[92] Pallasmaa broadens this notion: "Finns tend to organize space topologically on the basis of an amorphous 'forest geometry' as opposed to the 'geometry of town' that guides European thinking."[93] The "forest geometry" infuses the conception of the New York pavilion, but not for the first time in Aalto's work. From Viipuri to Noormarkku, Aalto had conceived wooden waves as features in his designs. In New York, however, he inaugurated the wooden wave as a multivalent force. No longer just a feature, it becomes the main sculptural tool for "carving" space out of the very nature of wood; from its tectonic malleability and its symbolic embrace comes the mechanism for symphysis.

In the 1900 pavilion, Finland had sought a window open to Europe, as historians put it,[94] drawing the cultural agendas from the center toward the northern periphery of the continent. In 1939 Aalto was happy to be offered a windowless edifice in which the Finland Pavilion could reside, allowing the big idea to generate its own, unique forest geometry—that "non-architectural free-form design" that provided

the scientific basis for the whole idea.[95] Why was there a need for the creative idea to be scientifically based? Why could it not simply be justified in creative, metaphorical terms? Whatever its raison d'etre, in this way the pavilion could hold itself together—form and content—indivisibly in the minds of the architects, and deeply rooted in wood; in matter, material, mater, and "primary comfort."[96] It is at this level that Aalto challenges modernism's limited rationalism. Indeed, to Aalto functionalism must solve "problems in the humanitarian and psychological fields."[97] In the pavilion he addresses this architectural imperative head on with a "disquieting" undulating wall.

Conclusion

In the eyes of his dogma-driven, International Style colleagues, Aalto's modernism was personal. In liking the man Aalto, they were forced to address a pavilion that identified the process of making architectural modernism phenomenal, and in a way that Le Corbusier was to do at Ronchamp in 1955.

Aalto's New York pavilion was not widely reported on in Finland. Only later did the Finns recognize Aalto's architectural gestures as signifiers of themselves, their experience, and their place in the world. At this late point, they adopted the undulating metaphors (be they in the Savoy Vase or the New York pavilion's wooden wall) as their own. As a creative gesture, the pavilion was of course a creative admixture rather than a scientific representation of the reality of Finland. The modern "image" of Finland that Aalto wished to construct was an amalgamation of his authentic personal experience of Finland and his fantasy of his progressive modern homeland. Take for example the "model of the ideal planned Finnish community" (SEE p.106 / FIG. 9)—the like of which Aalto spent time planning at MIT and then in Helsinki, but which came to nothing. Smeds suggests that Aalto's image of Finland "was not entirely concurrent with the nationalist Finns' general views—their self-perception."[98] This possibility does not devalue the pavilion itself, but helps us see it for what it was—a complex architectural gesture with broad appeal that spoke to many strata of the human condition, not least—but not only—the human experience in Finland's northern climes. It seems that although the pavilion appeared to be waving, desperately, to the free world, Finland as a whole was largely oblivious to its gesture, despite the fact that it was part of Aalto's role in the nation's propaganda office. Thus, the fact that, moments before retreating in personal terror of the war, Aalto threw down a gauntlet to modernists in Finland's pavilion offers a significant correlation of creativity and personal vulnerability. Although a multi-leveled representation of Finland in the late 1930s, the pavilion's uniqueness lies in the creation of an architectural space that probes the realities of Finland at the time, and that is rooted in requisitioning aspects of the forest culture—both past and present, collective and personal, and, I suggest, both conscious and unconscious. In the pavilion, with its remarkable architectural form, Aalto was seeking to yoke Finnish culture both backward to the heart of the forest and forward to the heart of the twentieth century—to engage both its progress and its grief.

1 Karl Fleig, ed., *Alvar Aalto Complete Works: 1922–1962*, trans. William B Gleckman (Zurich: Architektur Artemis, 1990), 1:124.

2 Alvar Aalto, "Suomen Osasto New Yorkin Maailmannäyttelyssä," *Arkkitehti* 8 (1939), 117–28. In this article, the credit for the built scheme is given as "Arkkitehdit Aino ja Alvar Aalto," Architects Aino and Alvar Aalto (119). Aino Aalto had received independent notice of her third-prize honor in the American press. See Earlene White, "Modern Women," *Gadsden County Times* (Florida), 16 Dec. 1938; this press clipping is available at the Alvar Aalto Foundation Archive, Helsinki, hereafter referred to as AAA.

3 Malcolm Quantrill, *Alvar Aalto: A Critical Study* (London: Secker and Warburg, 1983), 93.

4 Juhani Pallasmaa, ed., *The Language of Wood* (Helsinki: Finnish Museum of Architecture, 1987) 22; Richard Weston, *Alvar Aalto* (London: Phaidon, 1995), 113; Kerstin Smeds and Peter MacKeith, *The Finland Pavilions: Finland at the Universal Expositions, 1900–1992* (Helsinki: Kustannus Oy City, 1992).

5 J. Macfarlane, *Latin–English Dictionary* (London: Eyre and Spottiswoode, 1933) 266.

6 Aalto employs the term "unity" in an interview, "Helhet och Kvalitet," *Hufvudstadsbladet* 24 (March 1937) trans. Kerstin Smeds. Cited in Smeds and MacKeith, 53–4, footnote 47.

7 Aalto, "The Reconstruction of Europe Is the Key Problem for the Architecture of Our Times" (1941), in *Alvar Aalto in His Own Words,* ed. Göran Schildt (New York: Rizzoli, 1998), 149-157.

8 Quotation from Göran Schildt's description of the sketch design of one element of Villa Mairea. Schildt, *Alvar Aalto: The Decisive Years* (New York: Rizzoli, 1986), 165.

9 The globe is referred to in this way in the "Definitive Specification for Interior Work Except Construction Made by New York World's Fair Corporation" (Alvar Aalto Office, 1938 held in AAA).

10 "Definitive Specification" (AAA).

11 The report "Definitive Specification for Interior Work Except Construction Made by New York World's Fair Corporation" (AAA) describes the complex composite structure of the Pavilion interior: "There are two kinds of steel construction. The north side of the mezzanine is to be constructed on a pillar system. The south side above the exhibition area is to hang from the ceiling" (AAA).

12 Aalto had the vast cheeses carved from solid wood. He refers to this fact in Alvar Aalto, "The Relationship between Architecture, Painting and Sculpture (1970)," in *Alvar Aalto in His Own Words,* Schildt, 268.

13 A report outlines the thrust of the exhibition, with section titles such as "Finland, the Country of 68,000 Lakes," "Finland, the Country of Freedom and Democratic Spirit," "Finland, a Country of Forestry," "Finland, a Country of Independent Farmers Who Have Never Been in Serfdom," "Finland, a Country of Farms with Broad Base of Subsistence," "A Country of Rapid Progress . . . the Agriculture Raw Production Has Become Redoubled During 20 Years Time of Finland's Independence," "A Country of Cooperation," "A Country Exporting Animal Products," and "A Country of Low Cost of Living." From a typescript report on copy paper, with obliterated title (Alvar Aalto Office, 1938, AAA).

14 Finland was a pawn between Germany and the USSR at this time. A secret agreement signed on 23 Aug. 1939 between Adolf Hitler and Joseph Stalin gave Finland to the Soviets and Poland to the Nazis. Russia invaded Finland on 30 Nov. 1939. See Eino Jutikkala and Kauko Pirinen, *A History of Finland* (Helsinki: Weilin and Göös, 1984), 247–49. The meeting between Aalto and Sibelius was the one and only meeting of the creative energies of Finland's two most famous creative sons. See Sarah Menin, "The Profound Logos: Creative Parallels in the Lives and Work of Aalto and Sibelius," *Journal of Architecture* 8 (Spring 2003): 131–48; and Menin, "Aalto, Sibelius and Fragments from Forest Culture," in *Sibelius Forum*, Proceedings of the Third International Sibelius Symposium, eds. Matti Huttunen, Kari Kilpeläinen and Veijo Murtomäki (Helsinki: Sibelius Academy, 2003), 347–55.

15 Sibelius's musical utterance was incidental musicologically (indeed, he may not have suggested the piece himself), but crucial politically.

16 'Suomen New Yorkin näyttelyn rakenne ja yleissuunnitelma', undated, Finnish Fair Corporation Archive, 'New York 1939–40 file', trans. Kerstin Smeds.

17 Kerstin Smeds, 'The Image of Finland at the world exhibitions 1900–1992' in Smeds and MacKeith, *Finland Pavilions,* 61.

18 See details of Aalto's proposed contents for the journal in the form of ideas for articles and a list of possible topics, AAA; see also Schildt, *Decisive Years.* 184-5.

19 Göran Schildt, *Alvar Aalto: The Mature Years* (New York: Rizzoli, 1991), 47.

20 Alvar Aalto, untitled and undated article (AAA).

21 Weston, *Alvar Aalto,* 109.

22 Smeds, in Smeds and MacKeith, *Finland Pavilions,* 48.

23 Aalto, quoted in Fleig, *Alvar Aalto,* trans. Clare and Grahame Thompson (Zurich: Arcchitektur Artemis, 1974), 74.

24 Alvar Aalto, "Pariisin maailmannäyttelyn 1937: Suomen paviljongin piirustuskilpailun ohjelma," Manuscript, 1937 (AAA); and Aalto, "A Suomi Pariisin maailmannäyttelyssä," *arkkitehti* 7 (1937), 138.

25 Aalto, "World's Fair: The New York World's Fair and the Golden Gate Exposition" (1939), in *Sketches: Alvar Aalto,* ed. Göran Schildt (Cambridge, Mass.: MIT Press, 1978), 64.

26 Aalto, "Inledningsanförande vid Svenska Arkitektföreningens mote den 18 the October 1937," *Form* 9 (1937): 116; translated and cited by Smeds, in Smeds and MacKeith, *Finland Pavilions,* 177.

27 Aalto, "Helhet och Kvalitet", trans. Smeds; See also Aalto's own words in *Alvar Aalto Complete Works: 1922–1962,* 1:124. Trans. William B Gleckman; Aalto, quoted in Smeds and MacKeith, *Finland Pavilions,* 136.

28 Aalto's use of the term "symphony" is cited in Fleig, *Alvar Aalto Complete Works: 1922–1962,* 1:130.

29 Alvar Aalto, in the working document produced for the Finnish Fair Corporation; "Suomen New York näyttelyn rakenne ja yleissuunnitelma," undated (Finnish Fair Corporation Archive, "New York 1939–1940" file).

30 Kerstin Smeds in Smeds and MacKeith, *Finland Pavilions,* 57.

31 See Sarah Menin, "The Meandering Line from Sunila to Marseille," *Ptah* (Journal of the Alvar Aalto Academy), no. 1 (2003): 42–51.

32 Alvar Aalto, "Rationalism and Man" (1935 speech to the Swedish Craft Society), in *Sketches,* ed. Schildt, 93.

33 Defining Erik Gunnar Asplund's greatest contribution to architecture, Aalto wrote of his determination to design for "man, with all the innumerable nuances of his emotional life and nature." Alvar Aalto, "E. G. Asplund in Memoriam" (1940), in *Alvar Aalto in His Own Words,* ed. Schildt, 242–43. See also Aalto, "Finland as a Model for World Development" (1949), in *Alvar Aalto in His Own Words,* ed. Schildt, 171; and Aalto, "Karelian Architecture" (1941), in *Alvar Aalto in His Own Words,* ed. Schildt, 115–9. Although he claimed not to have a feeling for folklore, he admitted feeling that "the traditions that bind us lie more in the climate, in the material conditions, in the nature of the tragedies and comedies that have touched us." Conversation between Aalto and Schildt (1967), in *Alvar Aalto in His Own Words,* ed. Schildt, 171.

34 See Sarah Menin, "Fragments from the Forest: Aalto's Requisitioning of Forest Place and Matter," *Journal of Architecture* 6 (Autumn 2001): 279–305.

35 Aalto, "Karelian Architecture," 119. This subject is also addressed in Menin, "Fragments from the Forest."

36 This motto was taken up by the Finnish Fair Corporation.

37 Juhani Paasivirta, "Suomen kuva Yhdysvalloissa 1800-luvun lopulta 1960-luvulle," *Ääriviivoja* (Helsinki: Wsoy, 1962): 73, 77; cited and trans. Kerstin Smeds, in Smeds, 71.

38 Frederick Gutheim, *Alvar Aalto* (New York: Braziller, 1960), 11.

39 See the discussion of the Church of the Three Crosses in "Chapter 6: Spiritual Space as a Holding Environment" in Sarah Menin and Flora Samuel, *Nature and Space: Aalto and Le Corbusier* (London: Routledge, 2003).

40 The exhibition of Aalto's work was subsequently shown at the George Walter Vincent Smith Art Gallery in Springfield, Mass., in Dec. 1938. Press clipping (AAA).

41 Maire Gullichsen and Harri Gullichsen saw the villa complete for the first time at the exhibition, in the form of photographs, which had been flown over to the United States, arriving before their boat.

42 The context of war was not insignificant for Aalto personally. On being called up, his younger brother, Einar, killed himself, and Alvar fled to a Stockholm hotel in an extremely vulnerable mental state. Death in the air triggered both men, and Aalto's subsequent strategy that would enable him to flee danger and sojourn in the States met, eventually, with both personal and official disapproval. Maire Gullichsen wrote to him, "We cannot help feeling a little disappointment about the new postponement of your journey and do not understand the reason. . . .Now the home front is the most important one." (Letter from Gullichsen to Aalto, 26 Aug. 1940, in Schildt, *Mature Years,* 19.) Schildt quotes a telegram of 8 Oct. 1940 from the Finnish authorities that read: "Res.2nd Lieutenant Aalto ordered to return to his post." Aalto himself avoided active service by engineering a role for himself in propaganda work. Schildt also cites a conversation with Yrjö Alanen, Aalto's son-in-law, in which he explores the meaning of these for Aalto. Schildt, *Mature Years,* 14, 16.

43 A letter dated 19 Jan. 1940 (AAA) is addressed to "My dear friend," and may have been sent to Aalto's many contacts in the United States, rather than being written with only one person in mind. It reads: "Yesterday I had a conference with the Minister of Cultural Affairs. . . . It was decided that a special department should be founded for the cultural work abroad and for mutual contact. . . . This department will start work at once and one effect is sure to be that, for instance, our cultural intercourse with your country will be increased and intensified." Although this explanation suggests that Aalto's work would encompass general cultural activity, the letter goes on to describe the organization of a specifically architectural show. The letter further details an exhibition that Aalto would take around to different universities. In fact, he did lecture at a number of schools, but did not take with him an exhibition of Finnish cultural life.

44 There was an unholy (but strategically vital) alliance of Finland with Nazi Germany in the Continuation War against the Soviets in summer 1941. Intitially an attempt by Finland to regain the lost Eastern territories, it was later viewed as a belligerent attempt by Finland's great General Carl Gustaf Emil Mannerheim to make further in-roads in order to create a greater Finland.

45 Alvar Aalto cites this in *Finland Builds* (New York: Finnish Fair Committee, 1939), 78.

46 This support was mostly financed by the Volunteer Guide Corps of students from the New York School of Visual Arts.

47 Aino Aalto's brief diary entry notes how, as soon as they arrived in New York on 19 March, they met their close friends, and many celebrities flocked to meet them. They stayed in the guest wing of Fallingwater (the house Frank Lloyd Wright designed for Edgar and Liliane S. Kaufmann) for two weeks in August, and visited Eliel and Louise (Loja) Saarinen in Cranbrook for a weekend. The Finland Pavilion moved, with the exhibition as a whole, to Cleveland in autumn 1940. See Schildt, *Mature Years,* 31–33.

48 Alvar Aalto, "The Humanizing of Architecture," in *Alvar Aalto in His Own Words,* ed. Schildt, 102-7.

49 Schildt, *Mature Years,* 42.

50 Alvar Aalto, "What is Culture?," speech for the Hundred-Year Jubilee of the Jyväskyla Lycée" (1958), in *Alvar Aalto in His Own Words,* ed. Schildt, 16; Aalto, "In Lieu of an Article" (1958), in *Alvar Aalto in His Own Words,* ed. Schildt, 264; Aalto, "The Reconstruction of Europe Is the Key Problem for the Architecture of Our Time" (1941), in *Alvar Aalto in His Own Words,* ed. Schildt, 155.

52 Alvar Aalto, interview, *Hufvudstadsbladet,* 23 June 1939; interviewer unknown.

52 Peter MacKeith, "Architecture and Image in the Finland Pavilions," in *Finland Pavilions,* ed. Smeds and MacKeith, 150.

53 Reyner Banham, "The One and the Few: The Rise of Modern Architecture in Finland," *Architectural Review,* April 1957, 247. This article was written at the time of Aalto's visit to London to receive the Royal Institute of British Architects Gold Medal.

54 Aalto used this expression in a talk "My Frank Lloyd Wright" in 1940. Unpublished manuscript, registrar's file, exhibition 114, Museum of Modern Art, New York. Quoted in Peter Reed, "Alvar Aalto and the New Humanism of the Postwar Era," in *Alvar Aalto: Between Humanism and Materialism,* ed. Reed (New York: Museum of Modern Art, 1988), 97.

55 Aalto, "My Frank Lloyd Wright" (1940). Aalto addressed psychological needs, even hinting at his own experiences: see, e.g., Aalto, "Rationalism and Man," 49.

56 Aalto, "World's Fair," 65.

57 The phrase "conceptual landscape" appears in the conclusion of MacKeith, "Architecture and Image in the Finland Pavilions," in Smeds and MacKeith, The Finland Pavilions,150.

58 Reyner Banham uses the term 'disquieting' in Reyner Banham, "The One and the Few: The Rise of Modern Architecture in Finland," Architectural Review, 723 (April 1957), 247. This was written at the time of Aalto's visit to London to receive the RIBA Gold Medal.

59 Letter from Alvar Aalto to Sigfried Giedion, autumn 1930; quoted in Schildt, *Decisive Years,* 66.

60 Aalto, "World's Fair," 65.

61 Aalto, "World's Fair," 65.

62 See Colin St. John Wilson, "The Natural Imagination" and "Alvar Aalto and the State of Modernism" (originally a talk that received a standing ovation at the First International Alvar Aalto Symposium, 1979), in Wilson, *Architectural Reflections* (Manchester, UK: Manchester Univ. Press, 2000), 2–19 and 82–99. See also Sarah Menin and Stephen Kite, *An Architecture of Invitation: Colin St. John Wilson* (London: Ashgate, 2005).

63 Colin St. John Wilson, "Alvar Aalto and the State of Modernism," 90.

64 Melanie Klein *The Psychoanalysis of Children* (London: Hogarth and Institute of Psycho-analysis, 1973). See also Wilson, "Natural Imagination"; and the work of Adrian Stokes, an English aesthete and art theorist whose work stimulated Wilson to make the connection with Klein's thinking. Stokes, *The Quattro Cento and Stones of Rimini* (University Park, Pa.: Pennsylvania State Univ. Press, 2002).

65 Alvar Aalto, undated document (AAA).

66 Alvar Aalto, "Art and Technology" (3 Oct. 1955 lecture on the occasion of his installation into the Finnish Academy), in *Sketches,* ed. Schildt, 127.

67 See, e.g., *Information* (Metsähallitus, Finland: Vantaa and Lusto, 1995), n.p. "Lusto" is an old Finnish word for a tree's growth rings, from which a new forest museum of that name takes its form. Lusto Forestry Museum is in Savo, in eastern Finland.

68 Aalto, "The Relationship between architecture, painting and sculpture," 1960, in *Alvar Aalto in His Own Words,* ed. Schildt, 267–68.

69 Pietarinen discusses these four attitudes, for example, in "Ihminen ja Metsä: Neljä perusasennetta" (Man and the Forest: Four Basic Attitudes), *Silva Fennica* 21, no. 4 (1987): 323–31; and "Principle Attitudes towards Nature," in *Sport for All,* ed. Pekka Oja and Risto Telama (Amsterdam: Elsevier, 1991), 581–88.

70 After the Second World War, shortages led to the substitution of wood for more modern materials in the making of shoes, cloth, and even bicycle tires, marking a positive return to the subsistence wood-culture.

71 Weston, *Alvar Aalto,* 113.

72 Aalto, "Rationalism and Man," 93.

73 Kerstin Smeds argues that in this inclusion Aalto "expressed the Finnish mentality in the form of wood." Smeds, 'The image of Finland at the World Exhibitions 1900–1992' in *Finland Pavilions,* ed. Smeds and MacKeith, 58.

74 Aalto, "World's Fair," 65.

75 Leo Spitzer, *Classical and Christian Ideas of World Harmony* (Baltimore: Johns Hopkins Univ. Press, 1963), 17.

76 See Karl Fleig, *Alvar Aalto,* 3rd ed. (Zurich: Architektur Artemis, 1992), 74; and Fleig, *Alvar Aalto Complete Works: 1922–1962,* 1:130.

77 See Heraclitus, *The Cosmic Fragments* (Cambridge: Cambridge Univ. Press, 1962), frag. 51. See also Edward Hussey, *The Presocratics* (London: Duckworth, 1972), 44–47.

78 Aalto, "The Reconstruction of Europe," 154.

79 Weston, *Alvar Aalto,* 113.

80 "Finnish Pavilion, New York Fair," *Architectural Review,* Aug. 1939, 64.

81 For quotes, see Aalto, "Art and Technology," 125. Aalto and Karl Fleig both employ "synthesis" in reference to the New York Pavilion. See Fleig, *Alvar Aalto Complete Works: 1922–1962,* 1:124. Indeed, Aalto increasingly used the word in later essays and interviews. See, e.g., a conversation with Göran Schildt in 1967, in which Aalto suggested that "what is needed is synthesis." Published as "Conversation," in *Sketches,* ed. Schildt, 170.

82 Jean Sibelius, statement from 20 May 1918, quoted in Karl Ekman, *Jean Sibelius: His Life and Personality* (New York: Knopf, 1938), 154–55.

83 Letter from Alvar Aalto to Walter Gropius, autumn 1930; quoted in Schildt, *Decisive Years,* 66.

84 Weston, *Alvar Aalto,* 112.

85 Aalto, 'What is Culture' 1958, in Schildt, *Alvar Aalto in his own words,* 16.

86 Take, for instance, the iconographical status of the Savoy vase, which, in typical irreverent fashion, Aalto originally named *An Eskimo Woman's Leather Breeches.* In equally irreverent manner, Roger Connah has demonstrated how such an artifact has become iconographic due to Finland's need for a patriotic identity. Connah, *Waving Not Drowning* (London: Finnish Institute, 1994–96).

87 Colin St. John Wilson, "Alvar Aalto and the State of Modernism" (1979), in Wilson, *Architectural Reflections* (Manchester, UK: Manchester Univ. Press, 2000).

88 Douglas Graf, "Strange Siblings—Being and No-Thinness: An Inadvertent Homage to Ray and Charles Eames," *Datutop* 14 (Tampere, Finland: Tampere University of Technology, 1991), 14. See also Gareth Griffiths, "The Polemical Aalto," *Datutop* 19 (Tampere, Finland: Tampere University of Technology, 1997).

89 Aalto, "Art and Technology," trans. by author. See also Schildt, *Alvar Aalto in His Own Words,* 174.

90 Sigfried Giedion used these words in *Space, Time and Architecture* (Cambridge, Mass.: Harvard Univ. Press, 1949), 468.

91 Alvar Aalto, "The Hilltop Town" (1926), in *Alvar Aalto in His Own Words,* ed. Schildt, 49; Quantrill, *Alvar Aalto,* 96.

92 Aalto, "Architecture of Karelia," 82. See also Menin, "Fragments from the Forest."

93 Juhani Pallasmaa, "Tradition and Modernity: Feasibility of Regional Architecture in the Post-modern Society" (1988), *Arkkitehti* 3 (1993): 17–30.

94 This is a general expression widely used about Finland at the time.

95 Aalto, quoted in Smeds, 58.

96 The project outline was probably a collaboration between Alvar and Aino. See E. and A. Aalto, "Suomen New Yorkin näyttelyn rakenne ja yleissuunnitelma," undated document (Finnish Fair Corporation Archive, "New York 1939–40" file). It is significant that, when he fled to New York in 1940 and began to compose the book *Finland Builds* (which accompanied the re-opening of the pavilion), Aalto was also preoccupied with reconstructing Finland. His subsequent concept of the "the growing house," somewhat rooted in his (partly erroneous) understanding of the adaptability of Karelian houses, was explored in his propaganda article "The Architecture of Karelia" (originally published in *Uusi Suomi,* 2 Nov. 1941).

97 Aalto, "The Humanizing of Architecture," 102.

98 Smeds, in *Finland Pavilions,* ed. Smeds and MacKeith, 72.

Baker House 1949

FIGURE 01 *Aalto. Baker House, Massachusetts Institute of Technology, Cambridge, Mass.. Aerial view in context of West campus. The ceremonial domed entrance to the MIT Main Group is at the upper right.*

FIGURE 02 *South elevation looking east along Memorial Drive.*

FIGURE 03 *North elevation with entry pavilion and cantilevered stair.*

FIGURE 04 *East elevation; top of north stair at upper right.*

FIGURE 05 *View from north with west end of north stair.*

FIGURE 06 *Main entry at night.*

FIGURE 07 *Main entry at night.*

FIGURE 08 *Dining Commons, upper level, looking southwest.*

FIGURE 09 *Dining Commons, upper level, with trellised columns.*

FIGURE10 *Dining Commons from lower level at night.*

FIGURE 11 *First floor fireplace lounge*

FIGURE 12 *Double room with Artek and custom furniture*

FIGURE 13 *"Wedge" single room with custom furniture.*

Baker House: The Individual and Mass Housing, a Delicate Balance

Michael Trencher

The attitude among the leadership at the Massachusetts Institute of Technology concerning the place of the individual in the postwar years was surprisingly sympathetic to Alvar Aalto's ideas. Having grown dramatically as a result of war-time research and development, the institute set about re-evaluating its educational mission, attempting to focus on its role in the new postwar environment and the place of the individual's education within that role. As members of MIT's Committee on Educational Survey enthusiastically stated in the foreword to their "Lewis Report" of 1949 (initiated in 1947):

> Democracy as we have known it for more than two hundred years is the fruit of leadership that rises from the initiative and individuality of the people. . . . Since the war, there has appeared a new national consciousness of the responsibility for providing education to all of our young men and women commensurate with their ability. But in broadening the educational base, let us not stifle individuality by seeking uniformity; let us not fail to discern the gifted mind, to foster special talents, and to provide an environment in which these may flourish.

> We believe that the mission of the Institute should be to encourage initiative, to promote the spirit of free and objective inquiry, to recognize and provide opportunities for unusual interests and aptitudes; in short, to develop men as individuals who will contribute creatively to our society in this day when strong forces oppose all deviations from set patterns.[1]

There is in this statement and the report itself a sense that the dawn of the atomic age had made it imperative that scientific and technical education be framed within a broader humanistic cultural context, for the very survival of civilization. While promoting a democratically nurtured respect for individual differences within an acknowledged and shared moral universe, the educational context would assure that the individual would accept personal moral responsibility for his actions. This existential position would require special vigilance and awareness for those professionals operating in the scientific and technical realms.[2]

Just prior to the Lewis report as the war drew to a close in June 1945, Aalto had written a letter to his friend William W. Wurster, who, subsequent to their initial meeting in Finland in 1937, had become dean of MIT's School of Architecture.[3] Regarding his upcoming lectureship at MIT, Aalto mentioned two critical issues that he felt it imperative to address:

> 1. Architectural Standardization. By this I do not mean the ordinary process of modern evil mania. What I aim at is a special architectural liberation from the grip of technical standardization. During the last years I have been busy with these problems, leading the work at the Standardization Centre of the Institute of Finnish Architects, where "an elastic standardization" has been worked out, which is meant to release the post-war architecture from the necessity of following certain types in building. . . .

> 2. In conjunction with the above I would rather pose the delicate relationship between Collectivity and Individualism both as regards city planning and ordinary building structure.[4]

In keeping with these priorities, when Aalto received the commission in 1946 for the "senior house," the first postwar residential building for MIT students, the institution expressed the paramount need for a humanistic structure that celebrated, enriched, and nurtured the individual within a modern social context that was dominated by science and technology. This was understood if not explicitly stated in the mind of the architect and the leaders of the educational community.

Mass Housing: The Framework for a Continuing Dialogue

One of Aalto's major preoccupations as an architect was redefining the place of the individual in a modern society faced with industrialization, urbanization, and the political ideologies of extreme left and right. Given that housing was one of the most important items on the modernist's architectural and planning agenda, architects' philosophical differences were played out as an extended dialogue in their mutual, lifelong definition of the mass-housing typology. In this context, Aalto expressed a philosophical opposition to Le Corbusian paradigms of Platonic idealism based on perfected cellular elements. He was also opposed to accepting the Communist models of communal living with their rigid suppression of individuality through architecture. For these reasons, he set out in MIT's Baker House to redefine the modern mass-housing model.

Aalto respected the genius of the great Swiss-French pioneer Le Corbusier, but as a second-generation Scandinavian modernist, he frequently took issue with Le Corbusier's perfectionist, rationalist, and formalist visions. Le Corbusier's predilection toward synthesizing French neoclassical traditions with contemporary forces of industrial mechanization set up a contrast with Aalto's lifelong pursuit of a more naturalistic, organic, and humane architecture.

The Le Corbusian View

Le Corbusier's Platonic idealism framed his world view and dominated his vision of architecture. His devotion to pure form (the sphere, cone, cube, pyramid), his search for clarity and the universal, and his commitment to Euclidean geometry as the fundamental ordering system placed him squarely in the French tradition of Cartesian thinkers for whom reason dominated emotion.[5] Underlying these beliefs was the classical emphasis on number, mathematics, proportion, and the golden

section. Thus, the classical ideal of harmony could be attained through the regulation of physical reality by appropriate mathematical laws. Imperfect and rude nature could be transformed by the enlightened architect into a model of a utopian world governed by reason.

The integration of these Platonic ideas into the modern world could be accomplished through the utilization of modern science, technology, and industry. Further, industrial logic and functionalist design would produce a world that through "mechanical selection" would be filled with pure types, elements of clear rational design that would reflect the universality of Platonic form. As Stanislaus von Moos has written in regard to Le Corbusier's seminal treatise on modern architecture, *Vers une architecture*:

> While the text insists on rational methods of design, it also emphasizes that functionalism is not enough. This is even more clearly suggested by the illustrations: they were selected according to criteria of pure form. Ultimately, the point of view that emerges is Neo-platonic and idealist. . . . In accordance with its own rules, technology seemed to have found its way to the primary forms; cubes, cones, spheres, cylinders, and pyramids, and that was proof enough that it was in agreement not only with the "lesson of Rome" but also with the beauty of the elementary forms referred to by Plato in Philebos. A pseudo-Darwinian law of mechanical selection seemed to have brought about the premises of a new harmony in the sphere of man-made forms.[6]

Le Corbusier's Cartesian frame of mind and celebration of mechanization put him at odds with all that was naturalistic, imperfect, and complex.

Although prior to his important trip to Germany in 1910, Le Corbusier had in fact enthusiastically supported the medieval tradition and the ideas of Camillo Sitte in city planning, by 1925 he had completely reversed himself and come to idolize the straight line as a rational work of man while condemning the irregular as something bestial in origin.[7] On this subject he wrote disdainfully in 1925 in *Urbanisme*, carrying out his argument at length and with great vehemence: "Man walks in a straight line because he has a goal; he knows where he's going. He decides to go somewhere and walks right up to it. A donkey ambles absentmindedly along, zigzagging to avoid large stones, skirt steep inclines, and stay in the shade. He exerts himself as little as possible. Man's feelings are governed by his reason; he subordinates his feelings and instincts to his goal. His intelligence gives order to his animal nature."[8] Thus, in planning, Le Corbusier seemed to scorn the pragmatic, experiential, and sensorial except as a basis for establishing absolute rules, clear and rigid ordering systems that govern decision-making regardless of time or context or levels of complexity. He preferred mechanistic systems to organic ones, which are fundamentally complex and contextual. Warming to his condemnation of the natural and medieval, Le Corbusier continued: "The donkey doesn't think about anything at all, except avoiding effort. The donkey marked out all our European cities, including Paris, unfortunately. . . .The religion of the donkey path has just been set up. The movement started in Germany, the result of a wrong-headed book by Camillo Sitte on town planning, glorifying the curve and demonstrating its peerless beauties. . . .The curving street is the way for donkeys, the straight street is the way for men."[9] It was just this kind of thinking that led Le Corbusier to his grand residential schemes, such as "A Contemporary City" of 1922–25, in which vast geometric patterns obliterated all in their way, whether in the center of Paris or the rural countryside, where millions of men of the new spirit would live in great prismatic towers accessed by broad straight bands of endlessly flowing traffic intersecting at precise right angles.

Aalto's Contrasting Position

Although Aalto shared a respect and love of the classical tradition, as well as its underlying notions of harmony, his personal and cultural values drove him in a completely opposite direction to that pursued by Le Corbusier. Aalto's rural upbringing in the woods of central Finland filled him with a deep love of the natural world, a respect for its organic vitality, and the human need to engage it. This reinforced a deep-seated individualism and a social egalitarianism typical of Scandinavian societies.[10] Further, elitism, authoritarianism, and centralization were understood to be antagonistic to human dignity. Thus, excessive formalism was seen as a destructive constraint and the pursuit of perfection as a threat to human nature.

Aalto's early works in the decade of the 1920s were marked by a carefully constructed mannerism that reflected the designs of Scandinavia's most renowned architect of the period, Eric Gunnar Asplund. In the young Aalto's first major building, the Jyväskylä Workers Club of 1924, early Renaissance motifs were used to create subtle asymmetries. These elements broke down the implied aristocratic order into a more irregular composition, suggesting something more suited to the informal lives of the users. Historical type created a desired dignity but was ameliorated by discrete imperfections.

That this was not just a whimsical stylistic detailing but instead based on serious philosophical issues, Aalto clearly stated in one of his early essays, "From Doorstep to Living Room." After discussing the need for northern homes to have gracious transitions between inside and outside and using the English entry hall and the Pompeian atrium as models, Aalto displayed a sketch of a proposed residential design for his brother (Casa Väinö Aalto) with a formal atrium at the center. A perspective showed the small but elegant court surmounted by a clothesline, from which was suspended a pair of shorts and other laundry! Aalto wrote: "The hall has the only decorative floor in the house, made of limestone. Thus the architectural character of the room is a little severe. . . . It is a ceremonial room, but its stiffness is toned down by the glimpse the visitor has of the upper storey of the house, with its bedrooms, children's rooms and a line with drying articles of clothing on it, hanging there as a somewhat careless piece of evidence of the chores of everyday life; the commonplace as a crucial architectural element, a piece of Neapolitan street in a Finnish home interior!"[11] In an almost heretical statement for an architect, certainly one that would offend the idealist values of any Platonist or true classicist, Aalto further stated, "But if you want my blessing for your home, it should have one further characteristic: *you must give yourself away in some little detail.* Your home should purposely show up some weakness of yours. . . . If it is not there, the link with real life is broken. . . . Perhaps the reader should not immediately start cultivating the clothesline between the columns in his hall. It is enough to be aware that 'the open visor' is and will remain the true mark of the modern gentleman, and his home reflects this attitude."[12] Thus, in opposition to the purist atmosphere of Le Corbusier's villas, in which the Swiss architect characteristically placed the aggressive figure of the boxer fighting for the new spirit—a new classical modernism—Aalto envisioned instead an

FIGURE 01 *Le Corbusier and Pierre Jeanneret, Swiss Pavilion at Cité Universitaire, Paris, 1929–33. View of housing block.*

environment in complete sympathy with and accepting of the reality of human life with its aspirations and its imperfections.

Likewise, in contrast to Le Corbusier's Cartesian town plans, which obliterated the three-dimensional diversity of nature with the imposition of prismatic forms and rigidly geometric patterns, Aalto held up the Italian hill town as his paradigm for urban development. He saw in such a town the ideal integration of nature and human habitation. In a 1924 essay, written after returning from his first trip to Italy, he stated: "Rome was built on seven hills. But not only Rome, for many of the gems of urban planning can thank the hills on which their pavements are laid for their beauty. Whoever has once been bewitched by the magic of small Italian towns . . . will be left with a strange bacillus forever circulating in his veins, and the disease caused by it is incurable."[13] For the young Aalto, whose name in Finnish means "wave," the recognition of this

"bacillus" constituted a profound discovery of self and the beginning of a lifelong exploration of the organic in form and symbol. As he continued in the same essay, "For me 'the rising town' has become a religion, a disease, a madness, call it what you will: the city of hills, that curving, living, unpredictable line which runs in dimensions unknown to mathematicians, is for me the incarnation of everything that forms a contrast in the modern world between brutal mechanicalness and religious beauty in life. It is an everyday yet wonderful form of art, and one that the modern age denies; indeed, the predominant mentality today goes to great lengths to avoid it."[14] Thus the very things Aalto celebrates—the curving unpredictable line, the organic town integrated into a dominating natural setting—are what Le Corbusier condemns.

Aalto, consequently, aligned himself with Camillo Sitte and his paradigm of the medieval city with its contextual, humanly scaled environment filled with well-defined public spaces.[15] For Aalto, the wandering path formed by a living being engaging the three-dimensional landscape is not the mark of an indolent donkey, but the graceful sensual line of life. In Le Corbusier's rationalist cities, the individual aided by mechanical transport rushes directly to his goal, oblivious and condescending of anything that may deflect him from reaching it. For Aalto, the experience of the path, with its sensorial stimulation, is as life itself—the way is as important as the end.

Le Corbusier's Swiss Pavilion, Soviet Utopianism, and the Russian Avant-Garde

During the years 1930–32, Le Corbusier designed and built the Swiss Pavilion, a dormitory for Swiss students at the Cité Universitaire, in Paris (FIGS. 1–2). Le Corbusier's dormitory would serve as the typological frame of reference for Aalto's Baker House and the starting point of Aalto's critique of the modern mass-housing paradigm. At this time, Le Corbusier had established communications with the Russian avant-garde architects in Moscow who, like other Soviet cadres, were actively involved in defining a new housing model for the utopian world of the new revolutionary society. Their progressive ideas focused on the creation of communal settlements that could provide shelter and amenities for individuals and families in a society facing the economic and material crises following years of war, revolution, and civil war and their accompanying destruction, dislocation, and deprivation. The youth of the country were particularly hard hit by these circumstances, leading to the spontaneous development of youth groups in need of shelter.

In his *Pioneers of Soviet Architecture*, Selim Khan-Magomedov clarifies the conditions that gave rise to the collective dormitory:

> "The creation of communes among the young was also greatly stimulated by the fact that large numbers of them were directed to workers' colleges and institutes of higher education, or employed in the construction of new cities.... Lonely students or building workers, a long way from home and their childhood peer groups and communities, as yet without new families of their own, naturally chose company

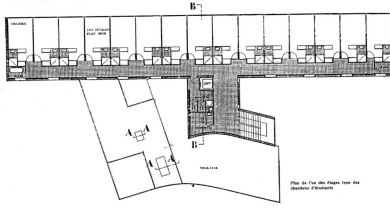

FIGURE 02 *Le Corbusier and Pierre Jeanneret, Swiss Pavilion. Plan.*

over solitude and preferred to live communally.... It must be stressed, however, that youth communes came into being before any communal houses specifically intended for a fully collectivized way of life were designed and built."[16]

Consequently, the Soviet model of mass housing for institutions of higher education was deeply connected to a particular set of individual needs; as Khan-Magomedev puts it, "These houses met a genuine social requirement."[17]

In response to such needs, Ivan Nikolaev designed an experimental communal student hostel in Moscow (1928–30) for two thousand students, with a massive eight-story bedroom wing set against the lower block of communal facilities (FIGS. 3–4). The latter included a sports hall, dining hall, study spaces, laundry, and sun terrace. The bedroom wing contained double units so small that all activities other than sleeping were assigned to the communal center. Thus, the juxtaposition of the massive dormitory wall and the lower, more plastically defined community facility served as a bold advertisement in the older urban context for the new social conditions of the revolutionary era. The individual could find his identity and fulfillment only within the totality of the community.

Moise Ginsburg's Narkomfin Apartment collective of 1928–30 restates such formal and social themes, but in a richer manner, leaning heavily on previous housing studies done under Ginsburg's direction at Stroikim (the Russian Republic's Committee for Construction) (FIGS. 5–7). In this major work, of which Le Corbusier was

FIGURE 03 *Ivan Nikolaev, student hostel, Moscow, 1928–30. Exterior showing dormitory block.*

within Soviet society at large and its political and architectural leadership in particular.

As noted in the theoretical essays of the radical and revolutionary Nikolai Kuzman, as well as in his communal housing proposal of 1928–29, the new collective spirit was supreme—the bourgeois traditional family was to be eliminated entirely in the new, communist utopia. Kahn-Magomedov describes Kuzmin's architecture: "Kuzmin completely discarded family flats. Instead, he divided the residents into age groups and designed separate accommodations for each of these. The rooms provided in special blocks were reserved for sleeping, and the remainder of free time had to be spent by everyone in a cultural centre. The family as such did not exist. Children were brought up collectively, in separate age groups. Meals were taken communally. Life was strictly regulated, and the programmes prescribed for each age group were reckoned out to the minute."[20] Thus Kuzmin's radical social engineering destroyed the heterogeneous family unit with its intimate social fabric by segregating age groups and communalizing activities, and thereby established the most extreme paradigm for a new social order.

well aware, and in which are integrated his famous five points of modern architecture,[18] Ginsburg responds to the diverse needs of individuals and families within the housing collective by providing a wide range of units, varying circulation systems, and options for contrasting lifestyles (for example, variations in where and how food was to be prepared). The rich variety of residential spaces in the large rectilinear block are juxtaposed to the condensed social spaces of the smaller cube, which contained a canteen, gymnasium, library, day nursery, and roof garden.[19] The dramatic contrast between Nikolaev's and Ginsburg's treatment of the individual and the degree to which individual needs were to be accommodated within the collective reflects the deep divisions between the more radical and liberal factions

With Nikolaev's and Ginsburg's bold new Soviet models recently finished or under construction by 1930, the similarities between them and Le Corbusier's Swiss Pavilion should not come as a complete surprise. As noted by von Moos, Le Corbusier's housing block, similar to Nikolaev's model—a large, rigid residential block juxtaposed to a lower, more irregular group facility—is based on the repetition of a standard unit, which supplies the ideal conditions to support the intellectual work

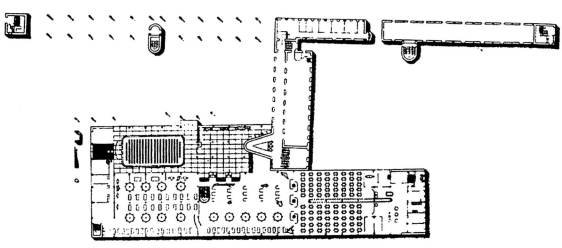

FIGURE 04 *Nikolaev, student hostel. Plan.*

FIGURE 05 *Moise Ginsburg, Narkomfin Apartment collective, Moscow, 1928–30. Perspective.*

of the ideal student. This perfect room seems based on Le Corbusier's favorite unit: the medieval monk's cell, with its geometric clarity and associated rectitude (**SEE FIG. 2**). Except for the top floor with its special units, the ideal room is provided for each student, so that each may have equal access to the best environment. Each is lifted above the ground with a southern view and accessed from a north facing, single-loaded corridor. There is here an assumption on the part of Le Corbusier that reason can ascertain what is best, what is absolutely true, and that architecture can give access to that truth through standardization and repetition. This belief represents a complete transfer of purist ideas of type, mechanical selection, and the primacy of standard to the world of architecture.

As with Nikolaev's scheme, the Swiss Pavilion's group facility is nonetheless highly differentiated. Unlike the rigid, mechanical block of lightweight steel-framed units lifted on pilotis above the ground plane, Le Corbusier's communal hall is treated as a part of nature and the landscape and is full of sensual elements and materials (concrete and rubble walls), non-Euclidean forms, and indeterminate exterior-like space. Whereas the individual cells celebrate the rationalistic, mechanical, and industrial, the lower element celebrates the poetic, painterly, and imaginative—the creativity of the subconscious—in an organic extension of the purist manipulation of sensual form, which is in turn akin to the cubist explorations of the image of a guitar.

Le Corbusier wrote in 1930 after a visit to Moscow: "In Moscow I had the chance of visiting a communal house. The structure was solid and well-executed and the management impeccable, but the interior arrangement and architectural concept were entirely cold. . . . The subtle artistic intention that should have animated the building was totally lacking, and I was moved by the sadness of the thought . . . that several hundred individuals have thus been deprived of the joys of architecture."[21] It seems clear that for Le Corbusier, the individual intellect could best concentrate under Euclidean conditions, safely removed from the distractions of nature, while the group of several hundred individuals could best interact while sharing the subtle artistry and sensual joys of a communal architecture that engaged the landscape. Certainly Le Corbusier found a weakness in the revolutionary Soviet rendering of the new social order; art and form were to be celebrated even if the individual was not.

FIGURE 06-07 *Ginsburg, Narkomfin Apartment collective. Exterior view.*

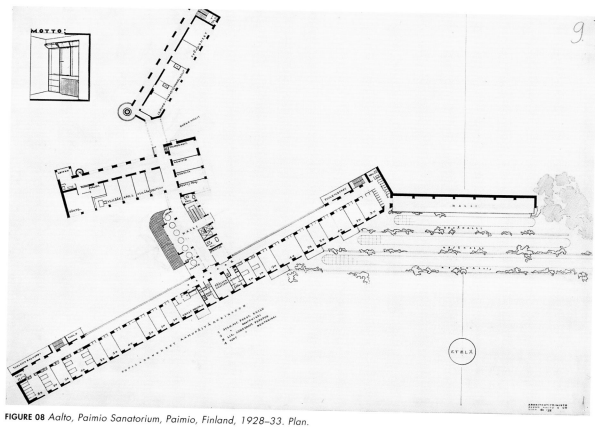

FIGURE 08 *Aalto, Paimio Sanatorium, Paimio, Finland, 1928–33. Plan.*

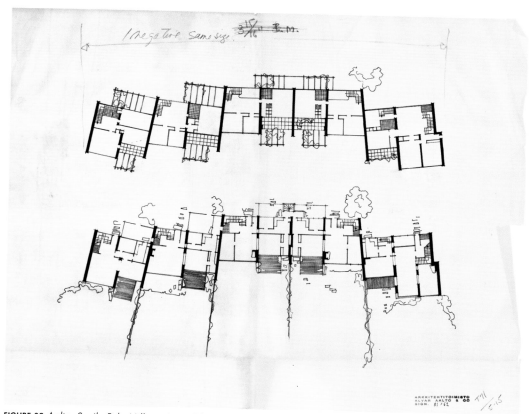

FIGURE 09 *Aalto, Sunila Pulp Mill, engineers' housing, 1936–37. Plan.*

Aalto in the 1930s:
The Prelude to Baker House

Although not commissioned to design a model community residence until MIT presented him with the opportunity of a "senior house" in 1946, Aalto's work during the 1930s amply prepared him for the task. In his first and perhaps most famous completely modern building, Paimio Sanitorium (1928–33), Aalto seems to have accepted aspects of the Russian housing model, yet he also significantly altered them to assure an appropriately scaled human environment that would accommodate diverse individual needs (FIG. 8). He organized the building masses into distinct blocks—service, communal, and patient accommodations all linked by a thin slab of circulation—not unlike Le Corbusier's organizational methods in La Cité du Refuge (1932–33). But here, on an open site, each block has its appropriate massing and exposure. Aalto initially proposed that all the patient rooms be organized into one massive plane facing in the most appropriate orientation, southeast, so that each patient could gain the salutary benefits of sunshine and fresh air without overheating or glare. The single-loaded corridor opened to the northwest, allowing more air and light to penetrate the thin, inhabited wall plane. A careful look at the competition entry plans shows that there were to be a variety of room sizes allowing for diverse social conditions, although this was not ultimately carried out.

At the end of each open corridor, the patients on each floor had access to a sun terrace; these were stacked vertically into another thin plane facing due south, like a great heat and sun absorber. Surmounting both the patients' and terrace wings was a long sheltered roof deck high enough above the surrounding pine forest to gain maximum sunlight and air on a daily and seasonal basis. Thus, although recognizing that the cure for tuberculosis required exercise, fresh air, and sunshine, Aalto still managed to incorporate the needs of the individuals within the changing population of the hospital by proposing diverse bedroom units and a range of opportunities for self-curing, from sitting by the open window of one's room, to gathering in the smaller terrace or going to the main roof deck, to finally exiting the building and walking throughout the grounds on a defined exercise pathway. In this way, Aalto supported the uniqueness of each individual by providing for a broad range of interactions, by articulating throughout

the design a complete scale of social hierarchies. These aspects helped de-institutionalize the institution and transform it into a more hospitable hospital.

Developing an approach he would follow throughout his career, Aalto extended these ideas of individualization, social hierarchy, and differentiation into the housing facilities for the institution's supporting staff. Each housing type was afforded its own design, massing, and siting: a large single residence for the director in a remote corner of the site, a series of attached L-shaped villas (reminiscent of Le Corbusier's Immeubles Villas) adjacent to the entry drive, and a dormitory-like, compact, and ingeniously efficient series of staff residential cellular units in close proximity to the hospital. Even in these final units, variation and choice was the rule. The lower floor was broken into a series of group living rooms, each with its own separate external entry, kitchen, toilet, and storage. To the rear, a series of bedrooms opened to the living rooms in such a way that one, two, or three sleeping spaces could be linked to the four communal living rooms, thus allowing the individual residents to gain some degree of self-directed social flexibility, a type of dynamic and organic self-clustering. The second floor was not a repetition of the first; overlaid on the clustered units below were a series of small single-occupant cells opening directly onto a generous exterior corridor walkway that doubled as a communal terrace accessed in turn by an enclosed stair with a separate entry.

Fortunately, Aalto had other opportunities in the 1930s to explore the humanization of housing. As at Paimio, in these other projects integration with nature was paramount in providing richness, diversity, and health for the occupants. At the site of the Sunila Pulp Mill, for instance, Aalto provided an entire village of diverse units scaled to the appropriate social and economic needs of the employees. All were integrated into the rocky, forested, and sloping landscape to afford intimate settings for all inhabitants. Aalto considered each housing condition an opportunity for exploration and experimentation, using the corporate owners as patrons for the support of socially viable housing types.

One experiment in particular seems to have been the basis for some of Baker House's units: the engineers' attached houses at the Sunila Pulp Mill, of 1936–37 (FIG. 9). These form a radiant pattern closed to the north, but opening widely to the south. Externally,

FIGURE 10 *Aalto, Baker House, 1946–49. View of south elevation.*

FIGURE 11 *Aalto, relief (detail), wooden slats, 1931–33.*

the units were meant to be covered with plantings, increasing their integration into the natural environment. Internally, although based on the planning of the Paimio's doctors' villas, the standard repetition of a single unit is purposely avoided; in fact, the series of units are graded from smallest to largest in an organic and dynamic growth pattern with subtle changes in room distribution and size leading to the culmination in the chief engineer's house to the east. Here, as well as in the smallest units—the famous terraced row houses on the northern edge of the site, where each of

the three floors of flats are designed differently—Aalto purposely avoided using identically repeated standardized elements, a significant and purposeful rejection of Le Corbusier's purist and Platonic concepts of type. Instead, a standard was to lead to variation based on a carefully differentiated functional analysis; as with cellular growth in nature, organic processes would lead to distinctive species and subtypes.

Although it is perhaps beyond the scope of this essay to discuss Aalto's many experiments in prefabricated and serial housing during the latter half of the 1930s, it should be mentioned that he spent a great deal of time developing systematic approaches to the problem of industrialized housing, in particular of housing systems based on modular cellular spaces that could be combined in different ways to respond to different sites, economic conditions, family sizes, and so on.[22] His enthusiasm for flexibility in systems as is found in natural, organic systems, as opposed to the mechanistic rigidity of industrial minimalism, grew throughout the 1930s and the ensuing war years. For Aalto, the creation of humane habitats could be attained by the utilization of responsive systems more supportive of diverse human needs, both physiological and psychological, if the resources were available and the added effort extended. The accepted biological paradigm of natural selection was not to be eradicated by Le Corbusian notions of "mechanical selection," or mechanistic repetitions of perfected types.

Aalto and the Design of MIT's "Senior House"

Aalto's concerns for the place of the individual in modern society and for the humanization of mass housing found a receptive environment at MIT. Certain conditions of the Baker House's site and program, however, required that he search for an appropriate balancing of contending forces (SEE p. 163, FIG. 1). The senior house's rectilinear site, oriented east-west, was tightly bounded on either end by existing structures. An access path from the monumental neoclassical main campus thrust into the site at an acute angle. Most importantly, the site's shallow depth and long east-west dimension meant that Aalto's decision to provide each room with a southern orientation would result in a taller-than-desired structure.

FIGURE 12 *Aalto, Baker House, 1946–49. North elevation.*

During the design process, the natural economic pressures to include more and more rooms (to cover the costs of the building and meet student needs) resulted in the rejection of Aalto's early schemes of layered and overlapping wings. Aalto had analyzed several alternative schemes utilizing the same formal motifs employed earlier by Le Corbusier, Nikolaev, and Ginsburg: the centralized communal facility set in juxtaposition to the wall of cells. Yet if the site could not grow, the height could not change, and the rooms could not receive a northern exposure, then the only logical possibility was to increase the linear dimension on the site by abandoning the site geometry—that is, by including an undulating curve that increased the southern perimeter without blocking views (**FIG. 10**). Moreover, such a shifting perimeter would give a range of diverse views from individual rooms, views that would render the riverscape in perspective, as Aalto noted, affording a more dynamic vista. Thus, even though MIT's Lewis Report had emphasized the needs of the individual, the project's programmatic demands led logically to a dynamic distortion and individualization of the Russian housing paradigm.

In developing this modulation, Aalto combined several ideas: 1) the formal devices explored in his undulating reliefs of the 1930s and 1940s; 2) the linear cellular organization from Paimio Sanatorium; and 3) the radiant variations from Sunila's engineers' housing. The reliefs themselves are constructivist studies in tension and compression-bending that result from the distortion of linear malleable wooden slats (furniture segments) anchored on pegs (points of force application) to a rigid geometric base (site) (**FIG. 11**). The wave patterns three-dimensionalize the Aalto form,[23] thus actualizing a signature, a statement of identity that simultaneously draws into the modern morphological debate the historical "bacillus" of Bergamo, the Italian hill town, and the modernists' rejected medieval city of Camillo Sitte. As it modulates from a straight to a curving line, the dynamic configuration of the residential wall amply articulates the energy of the new era and its play of competing interactive forces, yet it does so through a poetic, sensual, lyrical composition. This is a far cry from the static, sterile rationalism and mechanistic affect of Le Corbusier's Swiss Pavilion residential wing, an homage to the straight line. Most significantly, the shifting form also encourages the development of diverse room configurations on each floor, so that, as Stanley Abercrombie has noted, twenty-two different configurations could be developed from simple common types— a living example of Aalto's flexible standardization as opposed to Le Corbusier's typological duplication and Nikolaev's minimalistic redundancy.[24]

FIGURE 13 *Aalto, Baker House. View of stair.*

As important as the variation in room layout is the rich and diverse nature of public space on each floor. Going beyond the linear devices of the Paimio block, Aalto ingeniously incorporated a continuous hung stair on the back of the shifting dorm wall—the stair itself acting as a unifying communal element **(FIG. 12)**. The spreading wings of risers are asymmetrically focused on the point of penetration of the diagonal campus axis, while they simultaneously intersect each floor differently, creating special conditions on each level. The entry portal conditions vary by location and type, and, most significantly, as the stair wings rise past each floor, the inner hallway wall is removed and the adjacent corridor space increased by the dimension of the stair **(FIG. 13)**. Thus, the western lounge is repeated on each floor, but the central lounge modulates from level to level, absorbing to the east and west excess circulation spaces that then can double as gathering spaces.

Each open corridor is unique in its spatial topography, broken down into small, differentiated sub-zones and providing distinct spaces for spontaneous social gathering outside the adjacent rooms **(FIG. 14)**. The idea of a complete range of well-scaled, naturally-lit social spaces that originated in Paimio is realized here. The undulating circulation system replicates the organically generated fabric of pedestrian spaces characteristic of an Italian hill town **(FIG. 15)**. It rejects the modernists' images of linear streets dedicated to high-speed traffic, as in Le Corbusier's city plans or his contemporaneous broad interior streets of the Unité d'habitation at Marseilles.

The topography of the interior's pedestrian streets is modulated by the purposeful interaction of three zones of structure, each aligned with a particular section of the site-generated composition **(SEE FIG. 14)**. The central section is organized around the skewed entry axis and the northwestern quadrant around the orthogonal site geometry, while the western main wing shifts in response to the site's compaction. To make the form even more complex, the shell of the northeastern wall takes up the formal shift of the western wing and thus dislocates (by approximately 6 degrees) the orthogonal orientation of the skewed entry axis. These complex dislocations dramatically enhance the quality of movement through space, especially since so much of the visual environment is experienced in a non-orthogonal manner when traversing each floor, through rotation, diagonal penetration, and non-parallelism. Thus each floor is not only unique in configuration but defined by non-Euclidean, indeterminate space, much more akin to the complex spatial configurations of our own contemporary era than the static linearity of traditional axial planning **(FIG. 16)**. In addition, the extensive fenestration of the rear walls combines with the semi-permeability of the many-doored corridor wall to enhance the transparency of the space and transform the internal corridor into a sheltered yet exterior volume flooded by natural light. Instead of living in an enclosure isolated from ground and sky, the students inhabit a porous wall plane permeated by outdoor space, an organic reef-like structure of extensive spatial interconnectedness and variability.

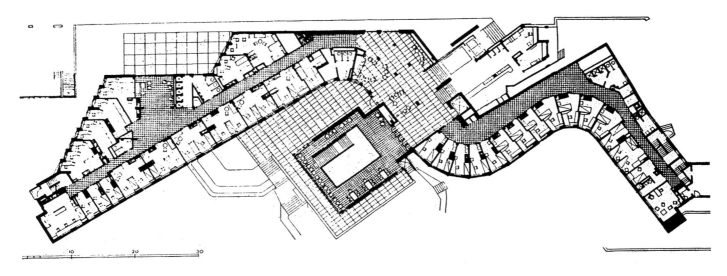

FIGURE 14 *Aalto, Baker House. Plan.*

FIGURE 15 *Bergamo, Italy. View of street in upper town.*

FIGURE 16 *Aalto, Baker House. Interior, showing corridor.*

Against this backdrop of highly differentiated and individualized space is set the low volume of the central dining hall and lounge (FIG. 17). Recalling the salient architectural idea of Viipuri Library's main reading room—a stair rising through a court-like space crowned by a plane perforated by circular skylights—the rectilinear volume brings the entire community together in a geometry strongly reminiscent of the communal spaces of classical antiquity. Although completely modern in detail and materialization, the spatial characteristics are traditional, as if Aalto wished to underline the need for communal cohesion through historical reference as a natural balance to the equal contemporary necessity for energetic individualism—his own working out of the "delicate relationship between Collectivity and

FIGURE 17 *Aalto, Baker House. Exterior, view showing the common space (dining hall and lounge) juxtaposed with the student dormitory units.*

Individualism." The physical and social setting is the complete reversal of Le Corbusier's statement at the Swiss Pavilion, where the individual is controlled in the cell through traditional references and liberated in the group setting by modern aesthetics.

When one enters on the main axis, the importance of the group space is heightened by the experience of its being hidden behind the mass of the dormitory and then its subsequent sudden appearance as a raised skylit viewing platform, thus creating a dramatic terminus to the entry procession. Its diminutive size and non-monumental character allow a celebration of the collective without asserting its dominance, a reversal of the normal institutional condition.

Conclusion

Consequently, within the monumental and institutional Beaux-Arts, neoclassical context of MIT's main building complex, Baker House reconstructs the balance between group and individual in a humanistic manner by validating history, tradition, and collectivity, but within an environment that is distinctly modern, individualistic, and democratic, just as the Lewis Report had suggested. The delicate balance within the building is a mirror of the social and political dynamic of the modern era: the dilemma of how to avoid, on the one hand, the pitfalls of anarchical individualism and fragmentation, and, on the other hand, the potentially crushing weight of institutional control and centralization. For Aalto, the solution was obviously reached by recognizing, respecting, and celebrating the uniqueness of all the individuals and supporting their free actions while simultaneously honoring those essential cultural binding elements that enhance and enable individual activity. In a telegram to John Burchard at MIT in December 1958, Aalto wrote:

> In ordinary discussion in recent decades traditional imitation has been pointed out as (the) main enemy of contemporary art. I think, however, the enemy number one today is modern formalism, not traditional[ism], where inhuman elements are dominating. True architecture, the real thing, is only where man stands in centre.[25]

1 "Report of the Committee on Educational Survey to the Faculty of the Massachusetts Institute of Technology" (the "Lewis Report"), Dec. 1949 (MIT Institute Archives and Special Collections, hereafter MITA), 5.

2 For an interesting reference in the Lewis Report, see p. 42, first paragraph: "In our increasingly complex society, science and technology can no longer be segregated from their human and social consequences."

3 As described by Göran Schildt, Aalto and Wurster had become friends during Wurster's visit to Finland in 1937. Their relationship became more deeply developed in 1939 during Aalto's tour of the United States and visit to San Francisco, where Aalto promoted his idea of establishing an Institute for Architectural Research in the United States and discussed his ideas of flexible standardization. Their close professional and personal friendship later led to Aalto's work at MIT, following Wurster's arrival in Cambridge. Schildt, Alvar Aalto: The Decisive Years (New York: Rizzoli, 1986), 167, 177–78.

4 Letter from Alvar Aalto to William W. Wurster, June 1945 (MITA).

5 Stanislaus von Moos, Le Corbusier: Elements of a Synthesis (Cambridge, Mass.: MIT Press, 1979), 48–51.

6 Von Moos, Le Corbusier, 48–49 (for quote).

7 Le Corbusier's initial thoughts on urban issues are represented in his unpublished "La construction des villes," which is based on Sitte's seminal work City Planning According to Artistic Principles (1889). See William Curtis's comments in his Le Corbusier: Ideas and Forms (New York: Rizzoli, 1986), 30. For a more complete review and discussion of Sitte and Le Corbusier, see H. Allen Brooks, Le Corbusier's Formative Years (Chicago: Univ. of Chicago Press, 1997), 200–207. Brooks quotes Le Corbusier from 1910: "The lesson of the donkey should be retained!" Le Corbusier further asserts that planners must learn from donkeys how to design streets that respect and enhance the landscape; he ridicules the grid system for failing to respect the gradations of nature (202).

8 Le Corbusier, quoted in Maurice Besset, Le Corbusier: To Live with the Light (New York: Rizzoli, 1987), 151.

9 Le Corbusier, quoted in Besset, Le Corbusier, 151.

10 For an extensive discussion of many of Aalto's fundamental beliefs and their generation from his early life, family, and culture, see Göran Schildt, Alvar Aalto: The Early Years (New York: Rizzoli, 1984), especially sec. 6, "Cultural Themes in Aalto's Work," 148–259.

11 Alvar Aalto, "From Doorstep to Living Room" (1926), in Schildt, Early Years, 218.

12 Aalto, "From Doorstep to Living Room," 218.

13 Alvar Aalto, "The Hilltop Town" (1924), in Göran Schildt, Alvar Aalto in His Own Words (New York, Rizzoli, 1998), 49.

14 Aalto, "The Hilltop Town," 49.

15 Some of the essential linkages between Sitte's and Aalto's thinking can be traced to Gustaf Strengell, the Finnish architect and critic whose book Staden som konstverk (The City as a Work of Art) of 1922 was well known to Aalto. Aalto and Strengell maintained a personal and professional friendship until the latter's death in 1937. For a more detailed discussion, see Schildt, Early Years, 244–45.

16 Selim O. Kahn-Magomedov, Pioneers of Soviet Architecture: The Search for New Solutions in the 1920s and 1930s (London: Thames & Hudson, 1987), 390.

17 Kahn-Magomedov, Pioneers of Soviet Architecture, 390.

18 For discussions concerning Le Corbusier's interactions and communications with the Russian avant-garde during this period, see von Moos, Le Corbusier, 152; Curtis, Le Corbusier, 88–89; Kenneth Frampton, Modern Architecture: A Critical History (New York: Oxford Univ. Press, 1980), 179; and William Blumfield, Gold in Azure: One Thousand Years of Russian Architecture (Boston: Godine, 1983), 352.

19 See Frampton, Modern Architecture, 174–75.

20 Frampton, Modern Architecture, 389.

21 Le Corbusier, as quoted by Stanislaus von Moos, in his Le Corbusier, 152–53.

22 See, for example, the wooden houses for the Savonmaki district in Varkaus of 1937, a forerunner of the AA-system. See also Göran Schildt, Alvar Aalto: A Life's Work; Architecture, Design and Art (Helsinki: Otava, 1994), chap. 8, "Housing," 228–30. Aalto's various projects for mill workers at Sunila, Varkaus, Inkeroinen, Kauttua, and other locations serve as particularly clear illustrations of his systematic method.

23 See my earlier discussion of what Aalto called "that curving, living, unpredictable line" on p.180.

24 Stanley Abercrombie, "Happy Anniversary, Baker House," Architecture Plus, July 1973, 58–65.

25 Telegram from Alvar Aalto to John Burchard, Dec. 1958 (MITA).

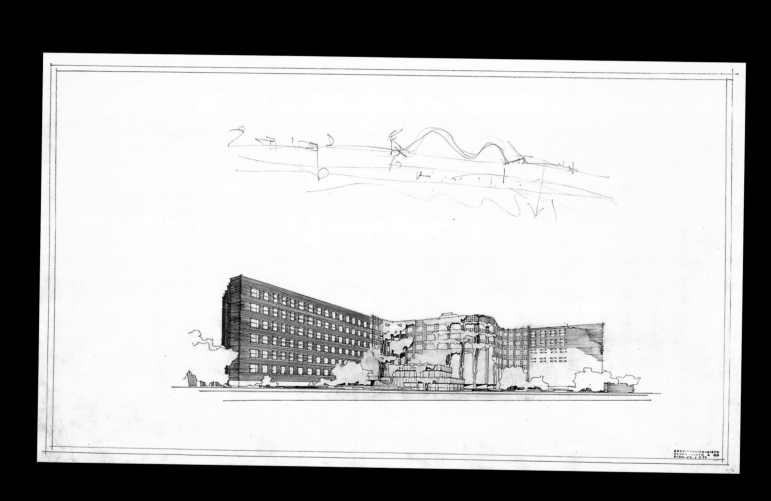

Baker House and the Modern Notion of Functionalism

Lawrence W. Speck

During the first half of the twentieth century one of the most prominent notions fueling the discussion of the emerging modern architecture was the concept of functionalism. Alvar Aalto wrote in his article "The Humanizing of Architecture," published in MIT's *Technology Review* in 1940, "In contrast with that architecture whose main concern is the formalistic style a building shall wear, stands the architecture we know as functionalism. The development of the functional idea and its expression in structures are probably the most invigorating occurrences in architectural activity in our time."[1] This essay will investigate Aalto's attitudes toward functionalism and will examine, in particular, his application of these in the design of Baker House at MIT, his most important building project in the United States.

Aalto received the commission for Baker House in 1946, after having served as a visiting professor at MIT in 1940. The site for the dormitory, which MIT originally called "senior house," stretched long and thin on the north bank of the Charles River, just west of the primary academic core of the MIT campus. On completion in summer 1949, it housed 353 students, providing important relief for the housing shortage created by the surge of young men returning to school after World War II. Baker House was not a glamorous project. As a building type, dormitories are intrinsically "workhorse" buildings. The budget was modest. The schedule for design was tight and inflexible. Through his extraordinary investigation of the real and authentic issues of function inherent in the program and site he was given, Aalto created a very responsive and original building, unprecedented in his own work and emblematic of a fresh new direction for modern architecture.

Aalto and Functionalism

It is important to differentiate Aalto's approach to functionalism from what is often called (perhaps inappropriately) modern functionalism in the work of Le Corbusier, Walter Gropius, Ludwig Mies van der Rohe, and others in the 1920s. Sigfried Giedion describes that "emphasis on function" as a road that Europe had to take to "free itself from the devalued language of the ruling taste" in a period when "architectural expression had become so debased that it could no longer follow any direct path." In that instance, he notes, "the curative process could only succeed if one pruned away everything so that there remained only the healthy base bearing the insignia of the period—a steel and concrete skeleton."[2] The results were sometimes buildings seen as technical machines.

This reductionist approach is a far cry from the bold but natural expressiveness advocated by Aalto and evident in his work. A more inclusive humanist and organic approach to functionalism in aesthetic realms had deep roots, even by the early twentieth century, in both Europe and America. It is richly embedded in the work of Johan Wolfgang von Goethe, Georg Wilhelm Friedrich Hegel, Thomas Carlyle, and Samuel Taylor Coleridge, as well as Walt Whitman, Ralph Waldo Emerson, Henry David Thoreau, and Horatio Greenough. Architects such as Louis Sullivan, Hugo Häring, and, later, Aalto advanced these traditions in their very specific applications to building.

Aalto observed, "Architecture is a synthetic phenomenon covering practically all fields of human activity. An object in the architectural field may be functional

193

from one point of view and unfunctional from another. During the past decade, modern architecture has been functional chiefly from the technical point of view. . . . But, since architecture covers the entire field of human life, real functional architecture must be functional mainly from the human point of view. . . . The present phase of modern architecture is doubtless a new one, with the special aim of solving problems in the humanitarian and psychological fields. . . . To make architecture more human means better architecture, and it means a functionalism much larger than a merely technical one."[3]

So how does the architect achieve this "functionalism much larger than a merely technical one?" For Aalto, the first step was accepting a great freedom of form. He wrote in 1938, "In order to meet its responsibility of helping toward a solution of the extensive humanistic, sociological, and psychological problems, architecture must be allowed as much inner and formal flexibility as possible. Every external, formal pressure—whether it be a deep-rooted tradition of style, or a superficial homogeneity born out of a misunderstanding of modern architecture—hinders architecture from playing a really active part in human development and thus lessens its importance and intensity."[4] Logically, if one is to be able to create a definite explainable relationship between form and the causes that shape it, Aalto suggests, one must rely on an understanding of the particular formal pressures internal to the situation and reject external formal pressures.

A second step toward achieving a "functionalism much larger than a merely technical one" involved, in Aalto's mind, a serious process of analysis and research. The myriad of factors constituting the architectural problem needed to be studied, analyzed, researched, and understood as part of what elucidates the internal forces that would shape the form of the building. In the 1940 *Technology Review* article, he wrote, "Architectural methods sometimes resemble scientific ones, and the process of research, such as science employs, can be adopted also in architecture."[5] In Aalto's case, this process was exhaustive and exhausting. He noted in 1947, just as he was in the midst of designing Baker House, "Whenever I have to solve an architectural problem, I am inevitably held up by the thought of its realization—it is a sort of 'three o'clock in the morning-feeling,' probably due to the difficulties caused by the weight of the different elements at the moment when the design is being carried out. The social, human, technical, and economic demands which are found alongside psychological factors and which concern each individual and each group, their rhythm and the effect they have on each other, are so numerous that they form a maze."[6]

At this point in the design process, Aalto was able to see the limitations of analytical methods. As he noted, "Architectural research can be more and more methodical, but the substance of it can never be solely analytical. Always there will be more of instinct and art in architectural research."[7] After a thorough process of analysis and investigation, then, Aalto spoke of "giving free rein" to instinct as a means of linking the "numerous, often contradictory elements" and bringing them "into harmony with each other." So the third step in achieving a "functionalism much larger than a merely technical one" (after accepting a freedom of form and conducting research and analysis) involved using intuition to bring together and to synthesize the various, often divergent forces inherent in the particular architectural problem.

From Aalto's previously referenced writings in the decade before Baker House, it is clear where he stood both in terms of his advocacy of a very broad, inclusive functionalism and in terms of his methodological notions about what steps might be taken in order to bring his design goals to fruition. The commission to design Baker House, as a consequence, became an opportunity to build an extraordinary physical manifestation of its author's long-considered aspirations.

The Baker House Commission

From 1939 to 1946, Aalto had not produced a single major work. Just as he reached his forties and might have been expected to begin the most productive years of his career, World War II disrupted virtually all building in Finland. The Finns suffered greatly during the war, being defeated first by the Nazis and later by the Allies. They emerged from the peace settlement poor and demoralized by the loss of critical territories to Russia. Though Aalto could think and write about architecture in this critical seven-year period, he could not build. Aalto, then, secured the Baker House commission at a critical juncture of his career, after he had firmly established his position on a functional yet humanistic approach to design. Given the dormitory as a function-centered building type, the site with its clearly preferred sun and view orientation, and a client strongly inclined to research and analysis, this commission provided a great opportunity for Aalto. He would produce a landmark work.

What were the key functional issues in the case of Baker House—the "social, human, technical and economic demands" from which Aalto worked?[8] Reinforcing his stated interest in "the humanitarian and psychological fields," Aalto rooted his design firmly in the social demands of the students. Everett Moore Baker, dean of students during the design process, and the person for whom the building was later named, believed strongly that the physical conformation of a building could affect the socialization and social well-being of students. Indeed, some of the seminal research on spatial determinism—the extent of environmental influence on friendship patterns and other socialization factors—was being conducted in student housing on the MIT campus in the late 1940s. Research for the groundbreaking book *Social Pressures in Informal Groups*, by Leon Festinger, Stanley Schacter, and Kurt Back, and published in 1950, was based on observations made in the Westgate and Westgate West temporary housing projects located where Briggs Field is today, virtually adjacent to the Baker House site.[9]

Though in the 1960s the case for spatial determinism would get overstated and exaggerated in terms of its potency,[10] *Social Pressures in Informal Groups* was modest both in its ambitions and its claims. It observed, simply, that both physical distance and functional distance (taking into account common daily patterns of activity) had an effect on patterns of acquaintance and friendship formation. The students and their families had arrived at Westgate and Westgate West from all parts of the world. They had no role in determining which unit they occupied. The study simply confirmed that students made personal acquaintances with those among whom they were most easily put into contact. The study is impressive in that it observed the influence spatial configurations have on these patterns of contact.

Certainly one of the social demands thoroughly considered in the design of Baker House was how student rooms would be organized—whether students would

share a room or live in singles, and how the rooms might be clustered together. These concerns had been at the core of the Festinger, Schacter, and Back research. For the new dormitory, the decision was made to create a range of individual student accommodations with about 60 percent of the students in single rooms, about 25 percent in double rooms, and about 15 percent in triples. The range of accommodations would allow students to choose from among more social or more private options according to personal preference, the stage of their college career, or simply their desire for change or experimentation.

Private rooms were also intended to be clustered in sub-groups of fifteen to twenty students who could share bathroom facilities and a small, informal lounge. For the entire dormitory of three hundred students, there would be some large central social spaces—a dining room, living room, library, music room, and more—for interaction with the broader, house-wide community. Movement through the dormitory—from the entry to the front desk and mailboxes, past large social spaces, up stairways, along corridors, past sub-group lounges, and to one's private room—was considered critical in the social function of the building. As the research Festinger, Schacter, and Back were conducting indicates, these paths and arrangements of spaces were critical factors in friendship formation and in the ease with which students adjusted to campus life. These "social demands," as Aalto referred to them, were critical in the conceptualization of the building.

Aalto was also interested in addressing what he termed "human demands"—maximizing the comfort, amenity, and well-being of the building's inhabitants. At the conceptual level of the building, two factors were critical to this task. The project site had access to extraordinary views to the south, with the Charles River Basin in the foreground and the city of Boston beyond. Aalto wanted to give every resident of the building access to that view from their private room.

While in the United States, Aalto had read *The Adventures of Huckleberry Finn* by Mark Twain, and was taken by an observation by Twain that one should not address a great river by looking across it, but by looking up the river and down the river. The Charles River is certainly not as vast as the Mississippi, but it still seemed desirable to Aalto to orient as many of the student rooms as possible at oblique angles upstream toward the end of the basin or downstream toward the peninsula of downtown Boston, rather than across the river only to see the opposite bank.

A second "human demand" critical to Aalto was privacy in the student rooms. It was important that the "senior house's" occupants be able to keep their windows open without worrying about neighbors looking in across a courtyard or even across the inner corner of a building with 90-degree angles. Aalto's concern with "the individual and the group" led him not only to be attentive to opportunities for interaction but also to understand the importance of protecting privacy and the ability to have time to oneself without constantly feeling the presence of others.

"Technical demands" were also seminal in the formulation of the building's conceptual design. Aalto considered it critical to capture the south sun's illumination and warmth in as many of the student rooms as possible. From the very earliest stages of design, built-in student desks under a south facing window became his standard module. The long Cambridge winter, which consumed much of the school year, demanded such optimization of both light and heat gain from the low winter sun.

In terms of construction, the building was conceived as a structural frame—a reinforced concrete skeleton—from the very beginning. This allowed flexibility for window shapes and sizes. The skeleton with small, irregular bays also made good sense in terms of both constructability and schedule. But about midway through the design process, Aalto began to render the south facade as a solid masonry wall with punched openings. The exterior expression of the frame disappeared. Boston was, of course, a "brick city" in the late 1940s. MIT's other dormitories and buildings near the site were also built of brick. In the end, Aalto created a load-bearing brick wall outside the frame, revealing the concrete columns, beams, and slabs (painted white) inside, but expressing a robust masonry character on the outside. The brick selected was a very coarse "clinker" brick laid with deeply recessed mortar joints. Exploded in the kiln while being fired, the clinkers created a richly textured wall and a very clear and explicit expression of brick technology. Rather than perfect, machined objects, the bricks indicate the still somewhat crude process behind their making.

"Economic demands" were critical as well. Since the project was planned to pay for itself, receipts from student rentals had to cover amortization of the construction loan. If rents were too high, students would seek housing elsewhere and MIT would price itself out of the market, so construction costs had to be tightly controlled. The six-story height of the building was set, in part, by the desire to stay beneath "high-rise" construction levels, which would have created greater costs in code compliance, construction process, and types of elevators. Minimizing the number of expensive elevators required in a building with many daily student trips was also a cost factor to be considered.

These and the myriad of other "social, human, technical and economic demands" of this tightly constrained project would certainly have been enough to give Aalto the "three o'clock in the morning feeling" he described in 1947. How did he negotiate this "maze of problems" and come to such a satisfying solution?

The Design Process

From the design process, a series of four drawings remain, which illustrate a wide variety of approaches to the conceptual form of Baker House. The twelve schemes that they show constitute a sequence and demonstrate a progression of thought about the project. The series of drawings is almost compulsively analytical (not something one might generally expect of Aalto). It very clearly illustrates Aalto's stated belief that "architectural methods sometimes resemble scientific ones," and that "architectural research can be more and more methodical."[11]

Each scheme in the series is documented by a plan, an axonometric drawing, and a score sheet on the right listing positive and negative traits of the scheme. The first drawing illustrates three schemes that are all composed of clean, rational, orthogonal boxes six stories high, lined up like soldiers (FIG. 1). (The second scheme is remarkably similar to the concept used by José Luis Sert thirty years later in the design of New House for MIT, just up the river from Baker House.) The only positive feature that Aalto noted for these schemes is that they could accommodate a very high density of student rooms, well over the three hundred deemed to be necessary for economical operation. On the negative side, all of them fail in terms of their

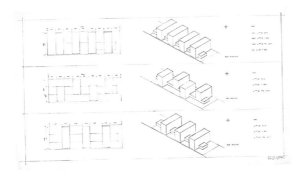

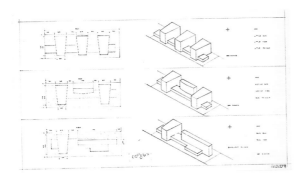

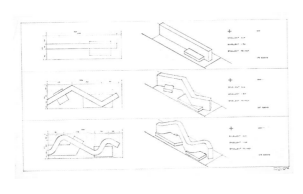

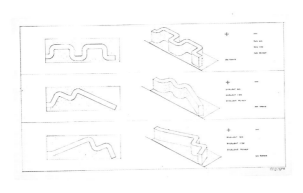

FIGURES 01–04 *Aalto, Baker House, Massachusetts Institute of Technology, Cambridge, Mass.. Early site plan diagrams, sheets one to four, 1946.*

provision for the human and technical demands for sun, view, and privacy.

The second drawing illustrates three schemes with the side walls of the boxes canted out (**FIG. 2**). When the density and spacing of the first score sheet is roughly maintained in the top scheme, rankings for sun, view, and privacy remain low. But when the ranks of soldier-like buildings of the earlier schemes are broken a bit by segments of a single-loaded linear building facing south in the bottom two schemes, rankings rise to medium sun and view and fair privacy in one case, and to fair sun and view and excellent privacy in the second case. (There is a little doodle of another unranked scheme made up of polygonal pods in what is almost certainly Aalto's own hand at the very bottom of this sheet.)

The third drawing takes the south-facing, single-loaded linear approach to massing a step further (**FIG. 3**). The top scheme is just one simple bar building with all student rooms facing south. It is deemed to provide excellent sun, view, and privacy, but enables only 179 rooms—far short of the 300 required. By bending the bar and better utilizing the depth of the site, more rooms are achieved while maintaining excellent sun, view, and privacy—207 rooms in the middle scheme and 225 rooms in the bottom scheme.

The fourth drawing explores the curved form introduced in the last scheme of the third drawing more extensively (**FIG. 4**). The top version increases the number of rooms to closer to 300, the amount required. But in so doing, it reduces sun, view, and privacy ratings from excellent to just fair. The second and third schemes, which are almost mirror images of each other, recapture the excellent sun, view, and privacy, but lose capacity in doing so. The last scheme illustrated is, of course, the general diagram for the building which was built.

The challenge of Aalto's diagram as it progressed to building design was how to fit the full 300 rooms into the lengthened, but still not quite sufficient, southern perimeter. The documentation moves at this point from a diagram to specific architectural drawings. A very clever scheme was developed fairly thoroughly (**FIG. 5**). It increased the number of rooms on the west end of the scheme by curving the building one more time and on the east end by adding a flat, re-entrant volume which is almost an extension of the adjacent row houses and is very different from the long curved volume. Much of what is wonderful about the eventual

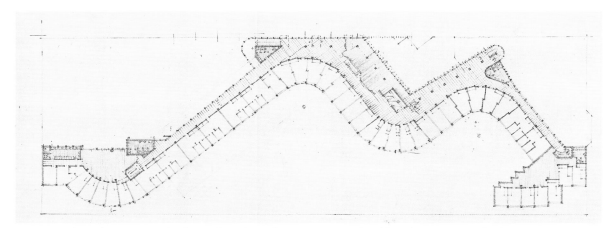

FIGURE 05 *Aalto, Baker House. Study of upper-floor plan with curve on west end and flat volume on east end, 1946.*

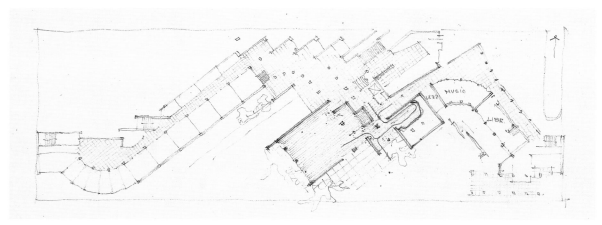

FIGURE 06 *Aalto, Baker House. Study of ground-floor plan with curve on west end and flat volume on east end, 1946.*

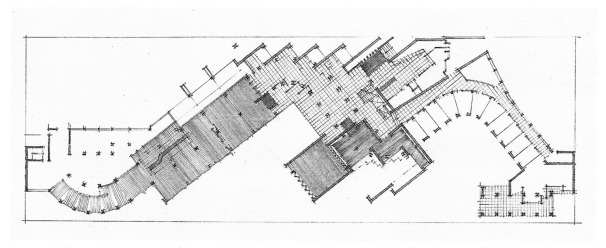

FIGURE 07 *Aalto, Baker House. Study of ground-floor plan with curve on west end and flat volume on east end, 1946.*

Baker House is already evident in this early version—the cascading stair on the north face, the winding corridor that opens into informal lounge spaces, and the great variety of rooms and views.

Several ground-floor treatments were developed for this scheme; they show a shifting of public spaces back and forth to find optimal locations (FIGS. 6–7). The entry sequence on the campus side is already similar to the eventual plan, with carefully orchestrated movement from the steps of the entry, through the open lounge, and to the garden, the river, and the view on one side and the dining pavilion on the other. This more detailed schematic design demonstrated that the original diagram, noted with only 212 beds, could be stretched to accommodate about 280 students, close to the 300 needed.

Aalto gained a few more spaces on the ground floor by pulling the library out of the main volume of the building and tucking it back on the north side in a series of polygonal pods (FIG. 8). The end of the west wing is thickened, adding a few west rather than south facing rooms to gain more capacity. Aalto's sketches are littered with numbers tallying rooms gained or lost by various design decisions. The dining pavilion is explored as a fan-shaped volume reiterating the curves of the larger building.

The front and rear elevations begin to get more attention at this phase of the design as well. Aalto seems to be just as committed to functionalist form-making in elevation as he was in the massing, conformation, and plan of the building. He is seeking to make outward appearances resemble inner purposes and is examining all parts of the building to create forms by awakening the essential form enclosed within. The great stair on the north facade is an extraordinary example of functionalist form-making (FIG. 9). It is easy to read through the building form to its purpose and reason for being. The act of students entering and distributing themselves as they rise up the stairs to their rooms is palpable in both general shape and in detail. The contrasting building material sets this lighter "hung" element apart from the heavier mass of the building, which expresses a change in the technological building function as well.

The sketches show that on the south face of the building, Aalto grappled with the appropriate expression of the great wall of student rooms. As previously noted, in early drawings the building is rendered as a frame, which would have been appropriate in terms of its

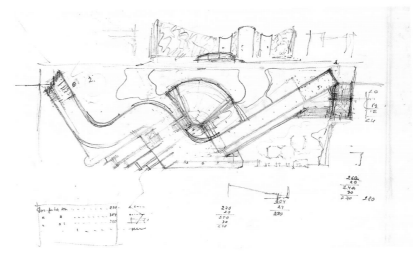

FIGURE 08 *Aalto, Baker House. Study of ground floor with polygonal library and fan-shaped dining pavilion, 1946.*

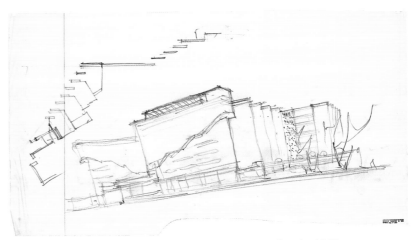

FIGURE 09 *Aalto, Baker House. Sketch of great stair on north facade, 1946.*

technical character (FIG. 10). But, if one believed, as Aalto did, that "real functional architecture must be functional mainly from the human point of view," and if one was seeking, as Aalto had stated, a "functionalism much larger than a merely technical one," then the expression simply of a frame might have seemed a bit hollow. As the design developed (and in the final building), Aalto emphasized the wall as an assembly of windows, each standing for an individual student (FIG. 11). The single rooms received one window, the doubles two, the triples three.

Windows vary in size, proportion, groupings, and rhythms, as do the rooms behind them. The smallest singles have only a double-hung window. The larger singles (generally occupied by seniors) have a double-hung window with a sidelight. The three windows

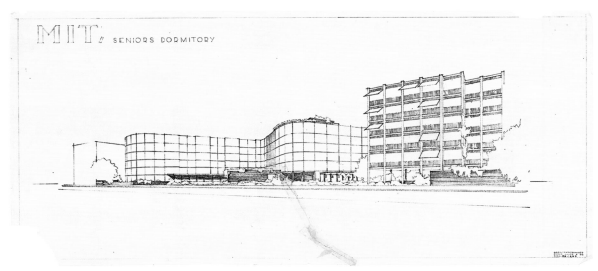

FIGURE 10 *Aalto, Baker House. Perspective from southeast of scheme with curve on west end and flat volume on east end, 1946.*

for the triples at the east end of the curve are grouped together to make them clearly different from the windows of three single rooms. On the north facade, the ability to "read" functions through the windows is striking. Lounge windows are dramatically large, creating a vertical bank that completely interrupts the masonry wall. Bathroom windows, by contrast, are thin, horizontal slits.

The dining pavilion received a radically different treatment in shape, fenestration, and materials, as its function is radically different from the repetitive student rooms. Its broad expanses of glass and limestone cladding make it public and open, in contrast to the more contained and private parts of the building with punched windows and a cladding of domestic New England red brick. Its interior has a much brighter quality of light and is filled with bustling, dynamic shapes and surfaces (**FIG. 12**).

Aalto's commitment to functionalism pervades every element of the design. The form "entry hall" is the function "entry hall" made visible (**FIG. 13**). The space draws you up and pulls you into the building. The form fireplace explains the function fireplace with its generous hearth for gathering and its firebox faced in casually laid stone (**FIG. 14**). The form hand rail speaks for the function handrail with steel bars creating strength and support while wood caps receive the human touch—the cap shaped, in fact, to perfectly catch the heel and the grip of the hand (**FIG. 15**).

But it is perhaps an episode that took place during late summer 1947 that most clearly demonstrates Aalto's commitment to form as generated by functional parameters. By mid-July 1947 the design was nearly complete.

Working drawings were well on their way, and a final model had been produced. At that very late point in the process, MIT decided that more rooms were needed to make the project work economically.[12] On 15 July, a very frustrated William Wurster, dean of the School of Architecture and Planning and a member of the small client team directing the project, wrote to Aalto informing him that fifty or so new rooms had to be added and the library eliminated.[13] On 17 July, Robert Dean, along with Perry, Shaw & Hepburn, the Associated Architects, sent sketches to Aalto showing how fifty-three additional students could be accommodated by compromising and remodeling the original design. Wurster wrote Aalto again on the same date lamenting, "I think it is OK to decide to add these rooms, but for God's sake let us not confuse things by saying it is *just as good*."[14] He too was ready for compromise.

But not so for Aalto. To the architect, the problem had changed and, therefore, the solution should change as well. On 13 August he wrote to Robert Dean, "I consider it necessary that we redesign the whole dormitory starting from President Compton's economical program, but of course it is up to us to give this problem an architecturally pure solution in harmony with its real significance."[15] He enclosed a totally new scheme that had the ability to accommodate up to four hundred students with very little increase in the cubic volume of the building. The same day he also sent a copy of the new plan to Wurster along with a letter which stated, "The enclosures show that

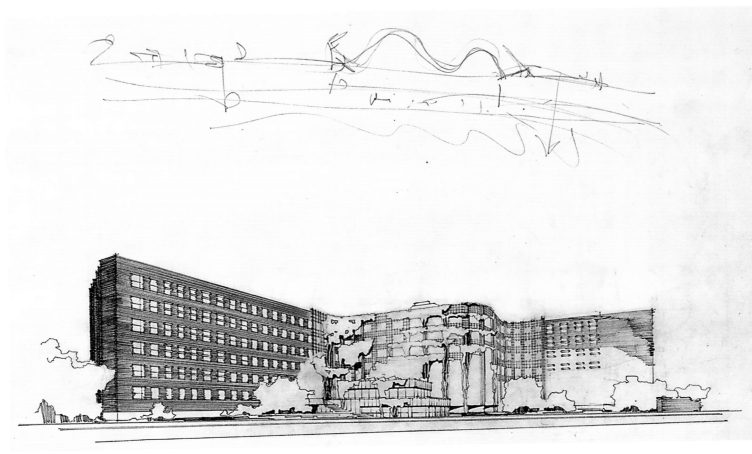

FIGURE 11 *Aalto, Baker House. Perspective from south with brick and window pattern rendered, 1947.*

there are possibilities of a simpler economy; if we are poor we should not make a mixed work and dream of architecture that is not logically perfect. I prefer a clean shirt" (FIG. 16).[16] Aalto wrote to Wurster again on 19 August and reiterated his belief that, given the altered parameters, "a plainer shape of the building would better harmonize with the stiffening economics."[17] The new design represented a radical change indeed. It consisted of three angled wings, the westernmost one similar to the west end of the original design (the footprint of old building was ghosted-in on the plan). The great curve was completely gone. The cascading stair on the north side was gone. The dining pavilion had been subsumed into the larger structure.

It is quite amazing to think of an architect who had produced such creative and original forms being able to just give them up. But it indicates something very important about Aalto. For him, design was about fit—about response to the "social, human, technical, and economic demands" of the "architectural problem"—about functionalism. If the demands changed, they

must be matched by a changed solution. He preferred a "clean shirt."

Wurster, it seems, was not so meticulous with his laundry. He was in California when Aalto's drawings and letter of 13 August arrived in Cambridge. He talked to Aalto by telephone in early September and, while he understood from that conversation that Aalto had agreed to add more beds, he did not understand that Aalto's changes in the design would be so fundamental.[18] When he finally saw the new drawings, he immediately wrote back to Aalto on 8 September: "I understand your reaction so well, but I still cling to the brilliance of the first concept. . . . Of course, you are the architect and, in the final analysis, must be the boss and make the decisions, but with all my heart I make the plea that we proceed on the former plan with some necessary revisions."[19] In the end, Wurster won the day. Aalto added about fifty student spaces on the northwest end of the building and working drawings continued, as did construction at a breakneck pace until the building was completed in the summer of 1949.[20]

FIGURE 12 *Aalto, Baker House. Sketch of interior of dining hall, 1948.*

Baker House and Functionalism

In the context of mid-century architectural dialogue, Baker House was clearly viewed as a "functionalist" building. Steen Eiler Rasmussen, in his book *Experiencing Architecture* from 1959, called Baker House, "One of the important monuments of twentieth century architecture."[21] He admired the fact that "the entire design is based on the functions of the building, on the life of the students for whom it was built." He continued, "For these young people Aalto has created a building which entirely avoids the stereotyped rooms and ant-hill atmosphere of old-fashioned dormitories, and the students love it. He has sought to give each one a chance to exist as an individual as well as to lead a corporate life. In Baker House the students can gather in large groups in the lounges on the main floor or in smaller groups in the common rooms on their own floors. Or they can retire to the privacy of their own

rooms, which, like all parts of the building, are so very human because their design was based on the life that was to be lived in them. . . . The building should be experienced in function."[22]

Sigfried Giedion agreed with Rasmussen, even repeating one of his key phrases in later editions of *Space, Time and Architecture*. He notes of Baker House's organic functionalist approach, "The sober program of a dormitory is given a new interpretation. All means are employed in an attempt to avoid the ant-hill atmosphere often emanated by such buildings."[23] Jürgen Joedicke, in his 1969 book *Architecture since 1945* observed the immediate influence of Baker House on the work of other leading architects. He points to it as one of the first buildings where "individual functional elements are boldly emphasized as deliberate architectural features."[24] He isolated Baker House as an influential work in the development of emerging

FIGURE 13 *Aalto, Baker House. Interior sketch of entry hall, 1948.*

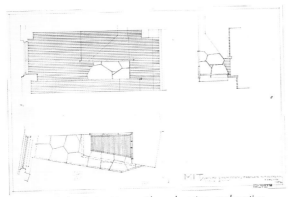

FIGURE 14 *Aalto, Baker House. Plan, elevation, and section drawings of fireplace, 4 Dec. 1948.*

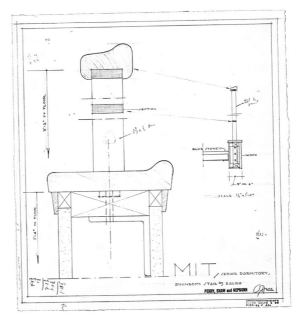

FIGURE 15 *Aalto, Baker House. Section drawing of dining hall stair rail, 1948.*

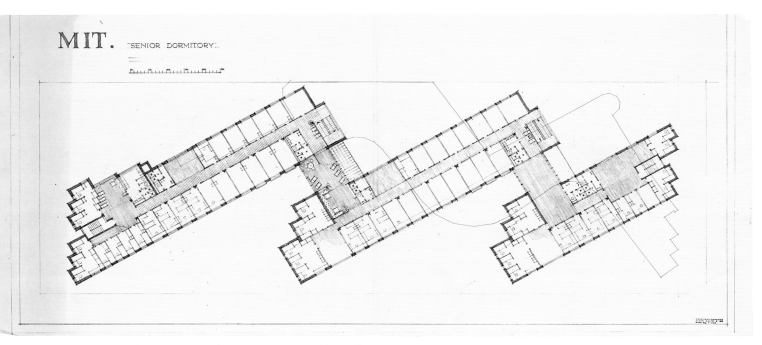

FIGURE 16 *Aalto, Baker House. Revised plan that accompanied letter of 13 Aug. 1947 to Wurster.*

architects in the 1960s like James Stirling and Peter and Alison Smithson.

Whatever happened to functionalism? In the current renewed respect for modern architecture, the term "functionalism" seems to have unfortunately been excised from discussion. While there has been a rejuvenated appreciation for the formal character of modernism there has been less interest in the ideas which created those forms to begin with.

Baker House demonstrates the potency of a design philosophy that seeks to express the authentic life of the building in architectural form. Aalto's humanism as well as his organic approach to form-making broke new ground for modernism. The freshness and vigor that he managed to infuse into so many of his mature buildings grew out of his belief that design was a process of constantly drawing inspiration from "social, human, technical and economic demands" to create an architectural form that was particular and responsive to them.

But in the 1950s and 1960s, modernism became a style with amazing rapidity. Its proper language, as codified in texts like Hitchcock's and Johnson's *The International*

Style, began to replace the breadth of vocabulary prevalent in earlier decades.[25] Aalto, in his mature career, saw the tendency and decried it. In correspondence with Dean John Ely Burchard of MIT in December 1958, he railed, "The enemy number one today is modern formalism, not traditionalism."[26] Is there a danger of the same being true today?

There is a genuineness, a sincerity, a particularity to Baker House which sets it apart from any sort of stylemaking. There is an inventiveness, a problem-solving, and a creativity that grounds it far more than buildings based on aesthetic pretensions. Though its forms are fascinating—even voluptuous—they are not trendy or self-absorbed. They are authentic, real, and unique to the particular situation. Notably, Aalto did not produce a succession of buildings with sinuous curving walls or with great cascading stairways. Unlike so many leading designers today, he really could invent new forms, materials, and configurations in response to the "social, human, technical and economic demands" of each particular "architectural problem" he approached. His works, like Baker House, continue to set a daunting and inspiring standard.

1 Alvar Aalto, "The Humanizing of Architecture," *Technology Review,* Nov. 1940, 14.

2 Sigfried Giedion, *Space, Time and Architecture: The Growth of a New Tradition,* 5th ed. (Cambridge, Mass.: Harvard Univ. Press, 1967), 618.

3 Aalto, "Humanizing of Architecture," 14.

4 Alvar Aalto, "The Influence of Construction and Materials on Modern Architecture" (1938), reprinted in *Synopsis: Painting, Architecture, Sculpture* (Basel: Birkhäuser Verlag, 1970), 12. (Originally published from a lecture held at the Nordic Building Conference in Oslo, 1938; published in 'ARK', 1938, 129–131 (in Finnish).)

5 Aalto, "Humanizing of Architecture," 15.

6 Alvar Aalto, "Abstract Art and Architecture" (1947); reprinted in *Synopsis,* 17. Originally an answer to an inquiry in 'Domus' Magazine; published in 'Domus', 1947, 223–225; 3–20; 'Werk', February 1959, 43–44.

7 Aalto, "Humanizing of Architecture," 15.

8 Aalto, "Abstract Art and Architecture," 17.

9 Leon Festinger, Stanley Schacter, and Kurt Back, *Social Pressures in Informal Groups* (Stanford, Calif.: Stanford Univ. Press, 1950).

10 For a survey of the literature of this period on spatial determinism, see William Michelson, *Man and His Urban Environment* (Reading, Mass.: Addison-Wesley, 1970), 168–90.

11 Aalto, "Humanizing of Architecture," 15.

12 The loosely defined group that acted as client for the project included President Karl Taylor Compton, executive assistant to the President James R. Killian (who himself later became MIT president in 1948); Dean of Students Everett Moore Baker (for whom the building was named); Dean of Architecture and Planning William W. Wurster; and Chair of the MIT Building Committee E. L. Moreland. The decision to add rooms was made in a meeting at 10:45 AM on 15 July 1947, in President Compton's office with Compton, Baker, Wurster, and Moreland in attendance. (Killian was away on vacation.) William W. Wurster to Alvar Aalto, July 15, 1947 (personal correspondence, MIT Institute Archives and Special Collections, AC 400, MIT School of Architecture and Planning. Office of the Dean. Records, 1934–1992. Box 1. Folder: Aalto-Dormitory).

13 Letter from William W. Wurster to Alvar Aalto, 15 July 1947 (personal correspondence, MIT Institute Archives and Special Collections, AC 400, MIT School of Architecture and Planning. Office of the Dean. Records, 1934–1992. Box 1. Folder: Aalto-Dormitory).

14 Letter from William W. Wurster to Alvar Aalto, 17 July 1947 (personal correspondence, MIT Institute Archives and Special Collections, AC 400. MIT. School of Architecture and Planning. Office of the Dean. Records, 1934–1992. Box 1. Folder: Aalto-Dormitory.

15 Letter from Alvar Aalto to Robert Dean, 13 Aug. 1947 (personal correspondence, MIT Institute Archives and Special Collections, AC 400. MIT. School of Architecture and Planning. Office of the Dean. Records, 1934–1992. Box 1. Folder: Aalto-Dormitory).

16 Letter from Alvar Aalto to William W. Wurster, 13 Aug. 1947 (personal correspondence, MIT Institute Archives and Special Collections, AC 400. MIT School of Architecture and Planning. Office of the Dean. Records, 1934–1992. Box 1. Folder: Aalto-Dormitory).

17 Letter from Alvar Aalto to William W. Wurster, 19 Aug. 1947 (personal correspondence, MIT Institute Archives and Special Collections, AC 400. MIT School of Architecture and Planning. Office of the Dean. Records, 1934–1992. Box 1. Folder: Aalto-Dormitory).

18 The telephone conversation is referred to in a letter: William W. Wurster to Alvar Aalto, 4 Sept. 1947 (personal correspondence, MIT Institute Archives and Special Collections, AC 400. MIT School of Architecture and Planning. Office of the Dean. Records, 1934–1992. Box 1. Folder: Aalto-Dormitory).

19 Letter from William W. Wurster to Alvar Aalto, 8 Sept. 1947 (personal correspondence, MIT Institute Archives and Special Collections, AC 400. MIT School of Architecture and Planning. Office of the Dean. Records, 1934–1992. Box 1. Folder: Aalto-Dormitory).

20 In a note to the author from 24 June 2003, David Fixler observed: "I have been led to believe that in the end it was Aino Marsio Aalto [Aalto's first wife] that persuaded Alvar to be pragmatic and try to come up with a solution to this dilemma while saving the essential original scheme, and that she may in fact have been responsible for the idea of the echeloning setbacks along the northwest face that finally enabled the scheme to work."

21 Steen Eiler Rasmussen, *Experiencing Architecture* (Cambridge, Mass.: MIT Press, 1959), 153. Rasmussen was a Danish architect and town planner, professor at the Royal Danish Academy of Fine Arts, occasional visiting professor at MIT, and a prolific writer of books and essays, including *London: The Unique City* (1937), *Towns and Buildings* (1951), and *Experiencing Architecture* (1959). This final work has remained in print for over four decades.

22 Rasmussen, *Experiencing Architecture,* 155, 157–58.

23 Giedion, *Space, Time and Architecture,* 636.

24 Jürgen Joedicke, *Architecture since 1945: Sources and Directions* (New York: Praeger, 1969), 115.

25 Henry-Russell Hitchcock, Jr., and Philip Johnson, *The International Style: Architecture since* 1922 (New York: W. W. Norton, 1932).

26 Telegram from Alvar Aalto to John Ely Burchard, 4 Dec. 1958 (M.I.T. Archives and Special Collections, AC 400, Box 1, folder: Aalto, 1945–50).

Baker House and Brick: Aalto's Construction of a Building Material

Ákos Moravánszky

Sigfried Giedion, in Space, Time and Architecture, gave his chapter devoted to Aalto the title "Alvar Aalto: Irrationality and Standardization." The focus of the chapter is Baker House, a student dormitory of the Massachusetts Institute of Technology (1946–49). Giedion's text was first included in the second, enlarged edition (eighth printing) of his book in 1949, the year of the building's inauguration (SEE P.163, FIG. 1).

The inclusion of a new chapter in Space, Time and Architecture was not simply an extension of the book; it shows, rather, that the history of architectural modernism took a new turn. Giedion claimed that "the combination of standardization with irrationality" is intended to fulfill the moral imperative of the avant-garde, "to reestablish a union between life and architecture."[1] The undulating wall became a leitmotiv, not only in Aalto's oeuvre, tying Finnish lakes, glass vases, exhibition spaces, and the MIT dormitory together, but also in the context of Space, Time and Architecture, where it continued what Giedion describes as a "tradition" that started with the facade of Francesco Borromini's church of San Carlo alle Quattro Fontane and the crescents of Bath. The importance of the constellation of Frank Lloyd Wright, Ludwig Mies van der Rohe, and Le Corbusier, dominant in the first edition, faded. The new hero Aalto received more pages and illustrations in the volume than any other architect, as Giedion himself pointed out in a letter.[2] However, one wonders if Giedion willfully misread Aalto, who had no interest in irrationality. In fact, Aalto writes in an article in 1940: "It is not the rationalization itself which was wrong in the first and now past period of Modern architecture. The

wrongness lies in the fact that the rationalization has not gone deep enough."[3]

Giedion is not very specific on the issue of Aalto's irrationality in his analysis of Baker House. He describes the facade as a kind of mask that gives the individual lives a collective expression: "The sober program of a dormitory is given a new interpretation. All means are employed in the attempt to avoid the ant-hill atmosphere often emanated by such buildings."[4] Later, in his description of the bentwood furniture, Giedion notes that Aalto's rococo-ish wood macaroni reminded a physician of "certain organisms within the large intestine."[5] For Giedion, "irrationalism" seems to be a fitting term for everything that is not based on an orthogonal raster.

The remarks quoted here and Giedion's interest for what he calls Aalto's "human side" paved the way for a connection between the late-baroque mobilization of space by Borromini and Aalto's contribution to modern irrationalism. The reception of Borromini has always been guided by a psychologizing mode, stressing the role of the constant headaches, depressions, and the ultimately suicidal disposition of the architect in his capricious irregularity of form. In an analysis reminiscent of the psychograms of Borromini by his critics in the eighteenth century, Giedion wrote, "Aalto is restless, effervescent, incalculable. Aino [Aalto's first wife] was thorough, persevering, and contained. Sometimes it is a good thing when a volcano is encircled by a quietly flowing stream."[6]

In "On Alvar Aalto's Work," an article published in the Swiss architectural magazine Werk in 1948, Giedion made this connection between the two architects explicit: "Aalto takes on what was announced by Le Corbusier with the curved wall of the Swiss Pavilion of the Cité Universitaire in Paris . . . or with his plans for Algiers. This continues the tradition of undulating walls, which have determined the shaping of space in a masterly way since their inventor, Francesco Borromini, and later in English city planning."[7] It is Aalto's "human side," his temperament, that appears to Giedion as a key to a synthesis similar to the one achieved in the work of Borromini: the ecstatic individualism of the artist is harnessed by reason (standardization, scientific and technological development, and, of course, the encircling by the "quietly flowing stream"). The innovations of the creative personality and the rules that he has to obey propel historical development to a new, higher stage.

Rationalism, Standardization, and Brick

Giedion's somewhat short-sighted perception of irrationalism, however, should not deter attention from Aalto's own interpretation of the rationality of standardization. The use of brick as a facade material is a good example. In the 1920s, when Aalto started his career as an architect, the red brick facades of Scandinavian National Romanticism belonged to the past. His Aira Building in Jyväskylä, Finland (1924–26), a block of flats for officials of the national railways, is a three-story brick structure, coated with a thin layer of plaster and whitewashed. But the texture of the brick, still visible in this case, disappeared in his subsequent "functionalist" work with the exception of industrial buildings, such as the cellulose mills in Oulu (1930–31) and Sunila (1936–39). As Simo Paavilainen notes, it is the ensemble of terraced houses built for the engineers of the Sunila factory (1937–38) that shows again a facade rendering similar to that of the Aira Building, with ivy climbing up the facades to the cornice. Obviously, Aalto is about to leave the purity of functionalism behind.[8] Baker House is the key example of Aalto's work establishing a dialectic relationship between the organicist line of functionalism and the revival of sensitivity to material effect characteristic of National Romanticism.

393. ALVAR AALTO. Finnish Pavilion, World's Fair, New York, 1939. *Undulating wall in the interior.*

634

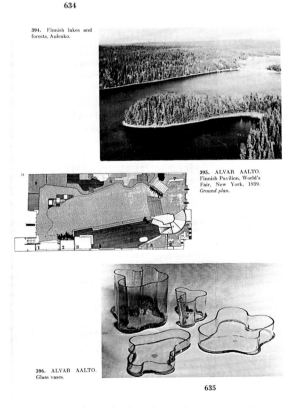

394. Finnish lakes and forests, Aulenko.

395. ALVAR AALTO. Finnish Pavilion, World's Fair, New York, 1939. *Ground plan.*

396. ALVAR AALTO. Glass vases.

635

FIGURE 01A–B *Aalto, Finland Pavilion at the 1939 World's Fair in New York as shown and compared in Sigfried Giedion,* Space, Time and Architecture *(1967).*

The relation between building mass and facade is an important aspect of this dialectic. Not only Baker House but also interiors, such as that of the Finland Pavilion at the New York World's Fair of 1939 or of the Opera House in Essen, Germany (competition design 1958–59), show Aalto's strategy of using undulating surfaces, in New York piercing one with "windows" of photographs (FIGS. 1A–B, 2). The horizontal layers of the undulating wall in the New York pavilion are cantilevered, evoking a feeling of dangerous instability.[9] The illumination of its surface creates the impression of polar light: an atmospheric phenomenon, the natural sublime. The solidity of the facade of Baker House, similarly, was to have been dissolved by ivy on an aluminum trellis attached to the brick.[10] This idea was not realized, but still, the facade lacks the smooth, seamless quality of the early Aalto buildings. Its purity is contaminated by the use of deformed, burnt, discolored bricks.

Aalto's assistant Olav Hammarström reported that Aalto located near Boston a brick manufacturer on the brink of bankruptcy that produced "the lousiest bricks in the world."[11] Aalto noted: "The bricks were made of clay from the topsoil, exposed to the sun. They were fired in manually stacked pyramids, using nothing but oak for fuel. When the walls were erected, all bricks were approved without sorting, with the result that the colour shifts from black to canary yellow, though the predominant shade is bright red."[12] In his 1955 lecture "Art and Technology," Aalto emphasized the local quality of brick: "An ordinary brick is for all appearances a primitive product, but if it is made correctly, properly processed from the country's own raw materials, if it is used in the right way and given its proper place in the whole, then it constitutes the basic element in mankind's most valuable and visible monuments and is also the basic element in the environment that creates social well-being."[13] This means that the brick must occupy its proper place as a basic element, not only in a given structure, but also in the matrix of needs, the society, and its culture. Processing the bricks means giving amorphous clay a clear geometric body and durability, creating an individual element that has to play its well-defined role within a structure.

Paradigm changes within the modern movement are reflected in the statements and theories surrounding the use of brick. The construction of the identity of

FIGURE 02 *Aalto, Opera House, Essen, Germany, 1959 (competition), 1981–88 (execution). Interior of the auditorum.*

brick as a building material is a process fluctuating between the poles of sentimental and technological responses to questions of a given period. Brick signifies earth and fire, the touch of its maker's hand—even if the actual brick in question is a modern industrial product. At the same time, brick is the result of early standardization, the document and prerequisite of mass production as a factory-made product—even if the coordination of its size with the grid of the measuring system never quite succeeded.

The brick, besides being a source of fascination for generations of architects, also presented them with problems, both as a stereometric volume and as a material object. Names for bricks tie them to certain places, and to sorts of clay and fuel; color, surface, and the size of the brick varied accordingly, an enormous obstacle on the way toward standardization. Efforts to establish a norm even in one country reflected the political interests of the moment: in Austria in the nineteenth century, for example, the question was discussed

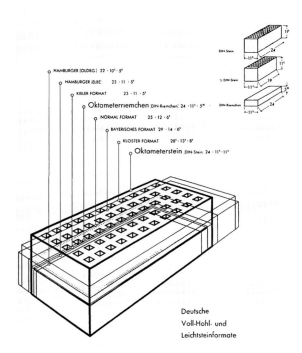

FIGURE 03 *German brick formats from Ernst Neufert, Oktameter-System (1941).*

whether the Austrian brick-building tradition was more closely tied to Lombardy or to southern Germany.

Architecture in ancient times meant the correct combination of nature's materials, as Aalto emphasized in a 1938 talk delivered at the Nordic Building Forum in Oslo: "This primitive art arouses in us a curious kind of admiration, since here one can recognize most clearly the first modest victories of the human intellect over nature."[14] The brick is a first product of this intellect, "an expression of human intellectuality based on 'materia.' . . . I think of the word 'materia' in a broader sense in which the purely material activity is closely connected with an intellectual process"—he explained later.[15]

Aalto's Oslo talk, "The Influence of Construction and Material on Modern Architecture," demonstrated his concern about the issue of "true standardization," which was very different from what Ernst Neufert, the author of the famous Bauentwurfslehre, termed "the conclusive logic of the brick."[16] However, while having a great deal of admiration for the brick, both Aalto and Neufert (who knew each other personally) wanted to reform it, albeit for different reasons.

Neufert recognized that the size of the brick that had been in use in Germany since 1869 was only seemingly logical. Its basic dimension, its length of twenty-five centimeters, appears to conform with the metric system, but if we consider the mortar joint, this conformity is a mere illusion, and there is no way to coordinate the size of building parts and rooms with that of the brick. Neufert focused his efforts on developing a system that he called octametric; the length of a brick within this system was reduced to twenty-four centimeters, and as a result, one meter equaled four bricks with mortar joints. He claimed that the octametric system finally creates the missing link between house, room, furniture, and body (**FIGS. 3–4**).

Neufert (like many other architects using anthropometry to build a theory of proportions) modified the standard size of the human body to fit it into his system. He called this "eine Generalbereinigung auf der ganzen Linie" (a general clean-up on all fronts).[17] In the first, 1936 edition of the Bauentwurfslehre, the shoulder height of a "well-built man" was 1.46 meters; in 1944, it was already 1.5 meters, while the full height remained the same, 1.75 meters. This means that Neufert had to shrink the size of the head and neck by 4 centimeters—a remarkable decision for a time when anthropometry was a discipline with ominous consequences in Germany.

It would be a mistake to view Neufert's position (and that of modernism in general) as diametrically opposed to Aalto's notion of standardization. Neufert's concern was to present his octametric system as the result of a timeless rationality of building technology vis-à-vis the formalism of "international style," thereby creating a common platform for traditionalists and technocrats. In this context, brick signifies the timeless material of a militant globalization which facilitates the saving of materials crucial for war. At the same time, for the traditionalists the meaning of brick as a durable material associated with certain "material landscapes" (Materiallandschaften) played an eminent role.[18]

Between 1929 and 1932, when Aalto designed standardized fixtures and furniture for the Paimio Sanatorium and the Turun Sanomat Building, his idea of standardization was still in full agreement with the Congrès Internationaux d'Architects Modernes (CIAM) position regarding mass production. The large number of his prototype drawings shown at the "Minimum Apartment" Exhibition in Helsinki in November 1930 reflected the CIAM conviction that technological standards are responses to standard biological needs.[19] The minimal apartment is based on standardization, industrialization, and Taylorization. Brick and advances in the speed of bricklaying were a main argument for the benefits of Frederick Taylor's scientific management, who used scientific analysis and organization methods to raise the efficiency of the work process. In 1911, Taylor advanced his proposal with reference to the bricklaying system by Frank B. Gilbreth.[20] Gilbreth's system served as proof that it is possible to triple the work output of a bricklayer merely through optimal organization.

In his 1932 speech at the Nordic Building Forum in Helsinki, Aalto argued for scientific standardization.[21] However, in the years immediately following he grew increasingly critical of technological rationalization in general. Returning from the United States, Aalto gave a lecture in Zurich and six other Swiss cities in 1941 on the reconstruction of Europe after the war ("Der Wiederaufbau Europas stellt die zentralen Probleme der Baukunst unserer Zeit zur Diskussion").[22] In it he criticized the practice in the United States of basing standardization in architecture on car-manufacturing models, despite the fundamental difference in the way the objects relate to their environment and to nature. He stressed that standardization in architecture should be based on biological models: "If the character of the landscape is such—should we really build this way?"— he asked rhetorically, not only showing images of the Finnish landscape and standardized houses, but also pictures of "life starting anew": a woman baking bread in the oven of a destroyed home, and the re-use of bricks taken from the rubble. He continued, "And so life goes on. Despite its primitive character, it slowly and touchingly takes on ever richer forms (**FIG. 5A–F**)."[23]

In this lecture, he spoke of blossoms as examples of the standardization in nature: "We find that every blossom on a spring-flowering fruit tree differs from all the others. . . . And yet this immense variety of function and form, this total dissimilarity, has arisen within an extremely strict system of standardization."[24] He criticized the fact that standardization in technology did not allow for the same variety of forms, and that architecture itself was seen as a form of technology: "A building is not in the least a technological problem; it is an architechnological problem. Therefore, technical planning methods cannot be applied to it. Even the standardization applied to it must thus be architechnological."[25] He declared that "centralizing standardization" was leading

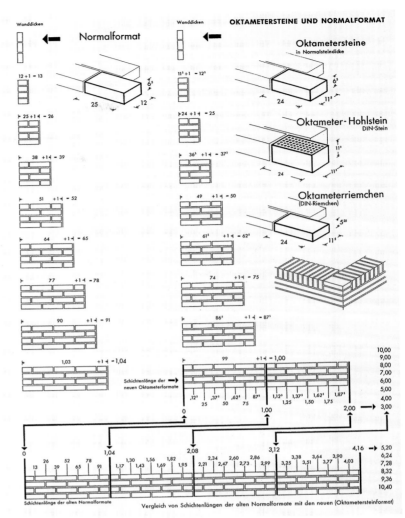

FIGURE 04 *A comparison of the "normal format" with the octameter brick format, from Ernst Neufert,* Oktameter-System *(1941).*

to the emergence of "a new type of slum—the psychological slum"; therefore, decentralizing standardization was needed.

The standardization necessary both for the reconstruction of the country and the use of damaged bricks were parts of the same context: the morality of these practical and at the same time symbolic actions was evident. Of course, the construction of Baker House was not part of this specific context, but still, we should not forget that for Aalto Finland's reconstruction and what he termed his "laboratory experiments" at MIT were closely connected. He used this phrase to refer to his search for methods to replace rigid technical standardization by flexible solutions—for instance, by developing a system of specially designed furniture for the wide range of room shapes in Baker House.

FIGURE 05A–F *Six illustrations to Alvar Aalto's lecture on the reconstruction of Europe (1941).*

Baker House and Architechnological Standardization

Baker House was an experiment with brick as the basic element of architechnological standardization. In an iconological sense, however, the emphasis was on the archaic rather than on the technological. Observing the transformations of the facade wall in Aalto's oeuvre, we can follow how brick became an instrument for giving the wall depth. The wall becomes stratified, with overlapping layers, folded and curved, and with strong color and textural effects. When Aalto noticed that bricks were sticking too far out from the facade of Baker House, he instructed the workers to remove them with a chisel and let the rough surface show.

"In primitive times the supporting skeleton was almost the only problem, and it was also the basic element of architecture," Aalto noted in his 1938 Oslo lecture, meaning that "the whole of architecture" consisted of walls, lintels, and posts, all playing a structural role. The details were "only slight protuberances on the skeleton, and often practically inseparable from it." But by his day, Aalto noted, the situation had changed: "The basic element of architecture at that time—the skeleton—is, for example, reduced to a light metal grid, and the production of this grid is only a small part of the whole building process." The skeleton, therefore, has lost its primacy: "The skeleton of a modern building is often in its volume, but above all in its importance, certainly always a smaller part of the whole building than formerly. However, while the importance of the skeleton has decreased, other problems and new basic elements are taking its place in the architectural process."[26]

The incompatibility of the rectangular geometry of the brick with the undulating façade of Baker House as a whole is obvious, particularly for an architect convinced of the benefits of standardization. This is a morphological incompatibility, not the merely numerical (geometrical) one that Neufert had to solve. Still, it is again the disregarded non-element of architecture, the mortar joint, that is crucial to solving the problem. In Neufert's case, the size of the brick had to be modified because the joint had been previously and wrongly disregarded. For Aalto, the joint had now to carry the curve, but at a price; the intelligence of the single brick, its precise fitting into a well-defined role, is not obvious at all. "The shape of the brick wall will retain its cubism, until a brick is found which allows free expression of form. It must be possible to find such a form which can stand as a brick wall and yet create at the same time a round or negative, convex, concave or square wall," Aalto said in his 1955 lecture "Between Humanism and Materialism," delivered in Vienna.[27] This argument was based on the analogy between the form of the building and of the brick, but also on buildings such as Erich Mendelsohn's Einsteinturm in Potsdam, which demonstrated that even fluid forms can be much more easily and efficiently realized using regular-shape brick than concrete, which would require an enormously complicated wooden formwork.

Aalto was familiar with many earlier attempts to produce a range of special brick shapes to achieve variations of form. He himself later used special wedge-shaped bricks that allowed the sharper curves of his House of Culture in Helsinki (FIG. 6). But such practices were not without question for architects who believed in "truth to materials." Cutting the brick was seen already by the authors of nineteenth-century brick manuals such as J. Lacroux's La brique ordinaire (Paris 1878) as going against the rule, the "nature" of the brick. Frank Lloyd Wright, beyond any doubt an authority for Aalto, criticized the use of special bricks to build the Monadnock Building in Chicago (Burnham and Root, 1891; Holabird and Roche, 1893). He wrote, "The flowing contours, or profile, unnatural to brick work was got by forcing the material—hundreds of special molds for special bricks being made—to work out the curves and slopes (FIG. 7)."[28]

FIGURE 06 *Aalto, House of Culture (Kulttuuritalo), Helsinki, 1955–58. Side view from street.*

The Brick as Cell

The resistance to the production of special bricks as well as Neufert's attempts to subordinate all aspects of architecture and life to an all-embracing metric grid are similar in giving the brick a well-defined singular geometry. But Aalto had a different view: "We are far from having the right materials for architectural form to hand which we need. Not only the brick should have a universal form which can be used for anything; all other forms of standardization are the same. When we have reached the stage of being able to achieve different ends with a standard unit which has a soul of elasticity incorporated in the object, then we shall have paved the way between Charybdis and Scylla, between individualism and collectivism."[30] "The soul of elasticity" that Aalto spoke about is not an immanent quality of the modern brick, but rather of the mortar joint, itself the product of the bricklayer on the site. In his Oslo talk in 1938, "The Influence of Construction and Material on Modern Architecture," he spoke of brick as a living cell: "In nature standardization appears . . . only in the smallest units, the cells. This results in millions of elastic combinations in which there is no trace of formalism. Furthermore, this gives rise to the enormous wealth of organic growing shapes and their eternal change. Architectonic standardization must follow the same path."[31]

FIGURE 07 *Burnham and Root, Monadnock Building (first phase), Chicago, 1891. Raking street view.*

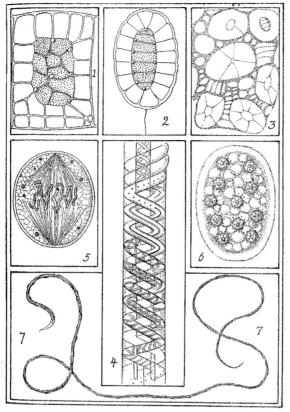

Abb. 2. Protoplasma. (Erklärung nebenstehend.)

FIGURE 08 *Protoplasm. Illustration from Raoul H. Francé,
Die Pflanze als Erfinder (1920).*

The visual model of a living cell with no trace of pre-established form was the amoeba, a primary cell of living matter, discussed by a large number of popular science publications that transported the vitalist philosophy of hugely popular authors such as Ernst Haeckel, Raoul H. Francé, Wilhelm Ostwald and others into the twentieth century, where they influenced the biocentric and biomechanic ideas in the works of László Moholy-Nagy and others. Moholy-Nagy and György Kepes were familiar with these theories, partly through the work of Francé **(FIG. 8)**. Moholy-Nagy, in his Bauhaus book *Von Material zu Architektur,* quoted Francé as the founder of the research discipline that he was using, biotechnology (Biotechnik).[32] Moholy-Nagy further discussed Bewegungsformen (forms of movement) and the artificial epidermis of technological objects. He presented his friend Aalto with a copy of this book when visiting him in 1931. Aalto found the book "magnificent, lucid and beautiful."[33] The principles of biotechnology seem to have influenced his thinking **(FIG. 9)**.

It was the philosopher Hermann Friedmann who, living in Finland between 1906 and 1934, developed a philosophical theory of form that abandoned the pseudo-scientific and ultimately irrational mythology of vitalism. Friedmann analyzed the influence of perception on thinking, and understood haptic and optic as two distinct modes of perception that lead us to the cognition of very different aspects of reality. The goal of Friedmann's most important book, *Die Welt der Formen* (The world of forms), was the "systematic enhancement of the haptic concept of the world up to a level where it becomes more rich, closer to the symbolic and optic."[34] Friedmann criticized the consequences of explaining space by merely optical terms, since the epistemological basis of its measuring reveals haptic origins (e.g., "inch," "foot," etc.). Describing illnesses where the patient can no longer recognize objects visually, he emphasized the role of haptic memories in consciousness, and therefore the importance of tactility for human development. The most difficult task of his inquiry, Friedmann realized, is the precise localization of the terms of our language in one of the realms of haptic and optic in order to determine and analyze their transferability into the other.

The dualism of haptic and optic perception is a very important aspect in the architectural concept of Baker House. Aalto's choice of the "lousiest bricks in the world" is a metaphoric representation of a problem rather than its solution.[35] He referred to the archaic forms of brick architecture, the massive walls built of amorphous lumps of dried clay.

Aalto spoke of the material experiments in architecture as a play rich in historical resonance. He was convinced that the architect can play and experiment with the values of a society, rather than simply "express" them. "When my old friend Yrjö Hirn, Professor of Aesthetics and the History of Literature, says that one of the fundamental elements of art is play, I agree with him wholeheartedly," he said in an interview.[36]

Johan Huizinga's book *Homo Ludens*, first published in 1938, was very popular during the post-war years.[37] The thesis of Huizinga's book is that in the industrial age the playing man, homo ludens, will free society from the pressures of the productivism of homo faber, which resulted in war.

FIGURE 09 *László Moholy-Nagy, The constructive scheme of the kinetic constructive system, 1922, from* Von Material zu Architektur *(1929).*

For Aalto, architectural sketches, oil paintings, and material experiments—such as the various brick panels in the patio of his small house on Muuratsalo Island—had to play the role described by Huizinga and Hirn (FIG. 10). They were not demonstrations of an ideal language, as were the still-life paintings of Le Corbusier or the collages of Mies van der Rohe. "It gives the architect a shock to suddenly find yellow parasites thriving on his stones and small though these things may be, they are a stimulant," wrote Aalto, stressing the importance of the contamination of Le Corbusier's "pure creation of the spirit."[38] In his buildings there is no trace of purism, not even the white panels appear "pure." Their surfaces show solid materials and flows: "In my work I have seen no other relationship between the three art forms than the material one. Whether I draw sketches, do them in watercolors or in oil is, for me, an experimenting with different materials. . . . The material, this intellectual challenge it offers, the 'materia' in fact, is the substance which unites all three arts."[39]

The playful experimentation with various media and materials was expected to result in the transformation of material. Aalto, in his Vienna lecture "Between Humanism and Materialism," quoted Frank Lloyd Wright on this issue: "I was once in Milwaukee together with my old friend Frank Lloyd Wright who gave a lecture which he opened as follows: 'Ladies and gentlemen do you know what a brick is?—It is a small, worthless, ordinary thing which costs 11 cents but has a peculiar quality. Give me this brick and it immediately becomes worth its weight in gold.' It was the first time I had heard an audience told so bluntly and expressively what architecture is. Architecture is the turning of a worthless stone into a nugget of gold."[40] The bricks of Baker House, the "lousiest bricks in the world," are ingredients in this alchemical process, transforming the ordinary and valueless into something precious. These bricks show a greater similarity to pieces of natural stone than to the bricks of Neufert. They can be associated with standardization only if we project the use of the grid back into Stone Age, finding its origins (as did Gottfried Semper) in techniques of weaving. From this point of view, brick is a mediator between archaic patterns and modern design based on grids. Art playfully fulfills a necessity, and also the desire for order.

Aalto's interest in deformations shows that the modern cannot exist without its other, the archaic, the geological, the biological, and the primitive. For Neufert, however, the starting point is the concrete, physical space that is endless but can be divided into the cells of cities, houses, apartments, and rooms, down to the smallest unit, the brick. For Aalto, it all starts with the basic cell, the brick, with its "soul of elasticity." The multiplication of this unit results in rich variations of apartments, schools, or dormitories.

In 1947, Aalto wrote, "In one sense architecture and its details is biology and the circumstances of its origins are probably just as complicated." He continued, comparing architecture to a salmon, driven by "basic feelings and instincts." He then remarked, "Construction—in this case intelligence, reason or whatever name you choose to call it—is at one with creation—the part it plays in creation being sometimes more, sometimes less important. Indefinable depths of sentiment are involved here. No doubt we have reached an advanced stage of development, if we consider the results achieved by modern art. Someone who has not the constructive intelligence indispensable to a creative artist is nevertheless enabled to receive positive impressions thanks to this crystallized form, simply with the aid of that undefinable thing

FIGURE 10 Aalto, Experimental house on Muuratsalo Island, 1952–53. Courtyard facade.

called sentiment."[41] Brick no longer functions as an organizer of all processes on the building site as it did earlier, when its manufacturing, transport, and handling determined all aspects, from the rhythm of building to the composition of the building team. Now brick is a monument, a sign of its own history, a reminder of the fact that the architect works in a culture that also determines his or her concept of rationality.

Aalto's use of materials was, as we have seen, firmly based on his understanding of natural sciences (biology in particular), technology, and art. Like many of his contemporaries, he was convinced that the researchers and engineers who spend their student years in Baker House would develop an understanding for their disciplines on the same theoretical basis of a shared cultural field of forces that motivated Aalto. Playing with brick on the building site or experimenting with chemical substances in a laboratory is a common source of creativity in culture. The "contamination" of the place of experimentation, generally seen as a danger, since it affects the results by compromising the ideal condition of purity, in the architectural realm represents the hope of overcoming a period of one-sided "pure technology that has recently invaded architecture."[42]

1 Sigfried Giedion, *Space, Time and Architecture: The Growth of a New Tradition*, 5th ed. (Cambridge, Mass.: Harvard Univ. Press, 1967), 618.

2 Letter to Aalto, 12 October 1949, quoted in Teppo Jokinen and Bruno Maurer, "Alvar Aalto und die Schweiz: 'Der Magus des Nordens' und seine Zauberlehrlinge," in *"Der Magus des Nordens": Alvar Aalto und die Schweiz*, ed. Jokinen and Maurer (Zurich: gta Verlag, 1998), 74.

3 Alvar Aalto, "The Humanizing of Architecture: Functionalism Must Take the Human Point of View to Achieve Its Full Effectiveness," *Technology Review*, Nov. 1940, 14–16, reprinted in Alvar Aalto, *Synopsis: Painting, Architecture, Sculpture* (Basel: Birkhäuser Verlag, 1980), 15.

4 Giedion, *Space, Time and Architecture*, 636.

5 Giedion, *Space, Time and Architecture*, 662.

6 Giedion, *Space, Time and Architecture*, 667.

7 Sigfried Giedion, "Über Alvar Aaltos Werk," in *Werk 9*, no. 35 (Sept. 1948): 274.

8 Simo Paavilainen, "Alvar Aalto: Modernist in Brick," in *Alvar Aalto: The Brick*, ed. Hanni Sippo (Helsinki: Alvar Aalto Foundation, 2001), 43–74.

9 See Sarah Menin, "Embracing Independence," in the present volume.

10 Göran Schildt, *Alvar Aalto: The Mature Years* (New York: Rizzoli, 1991), 126.

11 Schildt, *Mature Years*, 159.

12 Schildt, *Mature Years*, 159.

13 Alvar Aalto, "Art and Technology" (1955), in *Alvar Aalto/Sketches*, ed. Göran Schildt (Cambridge, Mass.: MIT Press, 1978), 127.

14 Alvar Aalto, "The Influence of Construction and Material on Modern Architecture" (1938), reprinted in *Synopsis*, 12.

15 Alvar Aalto, "The Relationship between Architecture, Painting, and Sculpture," from a discussion with Aalto in February 1969, published in Synopsis, 25. See also Menin, "Embracing Independence."

16 The *Bauentwurfslehre* is a handbook of design standards, first published in 1935. Its later, revised editions are still in use.

17 Ernst Neufert, *Oktameter-System* (1941?), quoted in Gerd Kuhn, "Die Spur der Steine: Über die Normierung des Ziegelsteins, das Oktametersystem und den 'Maszstab Mensch,'" in Ernst Neufert: *Normierte Baukultur*, ed. Walter Prigge (Frankfurt: Campus, 1999), 344.

18 Ákos Moravánszky, "Materiallandschaften," *Kritische Berichte* 28, no. 2 (2000): 20–28.

19 Göran Schildt, *Alvar Aalto: The Decisive Years* (New York: Rizzoli, 1986), 68–70.

20 Frederick Winslow Taylor, *The Principles of Scientific Management* (New York: Harper & Brothers, 1942), 77–84.

21 Schildt, *Decisive Years*, 86; to the question of standardization see also Alvar Aalto, "The Geography of the Housing Question," lecture given at the annual meeting of the Swedish Craft Society, 9 May 1935, in Sketches, ed. Schildt, 44–46.

22 Jokinen and Maurer, "Alvar Aalto und die Schweiz," 177–187.

23 Alvar Aalto, "The Reconstruction of Europe Is the Key Problem for the Architecture of Our Time," in *Alvar Aalto in His Own Words*, ed. Göran Schildt (New York: Rizzoli, 1998), 149–157.

24 Aalto, "Reconstruction of Europe," 154.

25 Aalto, "Reconstruction of Europe," 154.

26 Aalto, "Influence of Construction," 12.

27 Alvar Aalto, "Between Humanism and Materialism", lecture at the Central Union of Architects in Vienna (Summer 1955), publ. in *Der Bau 7–8/1955*, 174–176, reprinted in *Synopsis*, 21.

28 Frank Lloyd Wright, The Future of Architecture (New York: Horizon, 1953), 151.

29 Fritz Schumacher, *Das Wesen des neuzeitlichen Backsteinbaues* (Munich: Callwey, 1920).

30 Aalto, "Betweeen Humanism and Materialism," 21.

31 Aalto, "Influence of Construction," 13.

32 László Moholy-Nagy's *Von Material zu Architektur* was published in a revised English edition as *The New Vision: From Material to Architecture* (New York: Brewer, Warren & Putnam, 1930).

33 Schildt, *Decisive Years*, 77.

34 Hermann Friedmann, *Die Welt der Formen: System eines morphologischen Idealismus*, 2nd ed. (Munich: C. H. Beck, 1930), 45.

35 Schildt, *Mature Years*, 159.

36 Alvar Aalto in an interview with Göran Schildt, July 1972, included in *Alvar Aalto Volume III: Projects and Final Buildings*, ed. Elissa Aalto and Karl Fleig (Zurich: Verlag für Architektur Artemis, 1978), 232.

37 Johan Huizinga, *Homo Ludens: A Study of the Play-Element in Culture* (London: Routledge & Kegan Paul, 1949).

38 Aalto, "Between Humanism and Materialism," 21.

39 Aalto, "Relationship between Architecture, Painting, and Sculpture," 25.

40 Aalto, "Between Humanism and Materialism," 20–21.

41 Alvar Aalto, "Abstract Art and Architecture," in Synopsis, 18.

42 Aalto, "Reconstruction of Europe," 154.

Illuminating Aalto:
The Renovation of Baker House

David N. Fixler

The 1998–2003 renovation of Baker House at the Massachusetts Institute of Technology provided a unique opportunity to refresh our evaluation of Alvar Aalto and one of the pivotal works of his career, created at a time that was both the temporal mid-point and a critical juncture in the evolution of his architectural sensibility. At the same time, the renovation process also provided a platform for undertaking a critical examination of how the evaluation and renovation of a work of this importance might inform the ever-growing debate on establishing appropriate methodologies for the preservation of significant works of the recent past. The object in pursuing these inquiries was to use the resultant dialogue to inform an architectural intervention designed to sustain and enhance the building's essential qualities without appearing either mimetic or insensitive to the delicate nuances of Aalto's design.

In 1946, Aalto received his first significant building commission since before the Second World War, to design a new residence hall for upperclassmen at MIT. This commission, which followed closely after Aalto's return to his "professorial duties" at MIT at the close of the war,[1] gave Aalto the opportunity to explore and realize some of his own ideas about the form and nature of social housing. The design of Baker House, as the seniors dormitory came to be known, was to become a pivotal point in Aalto's career, both in the evolution of his architectural sensibilities and in his ongoing relationship with America and American culture.

Aalto's Architectural Elements and the Design of Baker House

By 1940, the completion of the Villa Mairea and the onset of war signaled the close of the first epoch of Aalto's career. Had he stopped practicing architecture at this point, he would perhaps be perceived as a very different architect today. Although Aalto had established the position from which he developed the distinctive elements that would come to define his design language as early as 1927 in the Turun Sanomat Building, only the sinuous wall of the 1939 New York World's Fair pavilion gave a strong hint as to how these formal strategies might eventually come to dominate his work. While most of the signature ingredients of Aalto's architecture had already appeared by this time—the wave form, banks of circular skylights, plan deformation, and the integration of natural motifs through the use of trellises and plantings—these became the elements of what was to become a more comprehensive synthesis that increasingly dominated his work, in both plan and three dimensions, in the later stages of his career.

The identification of these design elements and the ways in which they are used to create an "authentic" signature in Aalto's work was a key ingredient in the establishment of a working methodology as the renovation design team began the daunting course of charting interventions into Baker House. Authenticity is a topic of constant and heated debate within the preservation community, and it is a concept that is evolving in particular with relation to the evaluation of the heritage of the modern movement. In establishing design guidelines for the renovation the design team, led by Perry Dean Rogers & Partners, Architects, sought to define and then respond to an operable concept of authenticity as it may be applied to Aalto's work. This concept may briefly be defined as a sensibility toward materials—both traditional and contemporary—as they have been selected and employed in Aalto's configuration of form and space, balanced with the distinct quality of his understanding of the need to shape the elements of architecture in response to the centrality of the human experience.

As completed, Baker House can serve as a fulcrum that enlarges and focuses the elements of Aalto's unique sensibility. The direction he took in this project evolved and gained definition in those that followed soon afterward—projects that defined the onset of Aalto's mature career. In particular, these are the Town Hall at Säynätsalo (1949–50), and the National Pensions Institute (1952) and the Kulttuuritalo (House of Culture, 1952–55), both in Helsinki. Through the mining and interpretation of Aalto's design intent, it is possible to better understand how this gestalt produced not only the work under study but also how it catalyzed the great works of his mid-career. Further, this analysis enables the elucidation of the unique character of the building, an essential component in focusing the direction of the renovation project.

Baker House was the first manifestation of a major post–World War II initiative by MIT, championed by Dean of Students Everett Moore Baker (for whom the building is named), to increase the role of residential life in the educational experience of the undergraduate student. The choice of Aalto to design the building came through the advocacy of William W. Wurster, a close friend of Aalto's from the 1930s who became dean of the MIT School of Architecture and Planning during the Second World War and recognized Aalto's growing reputation as both a champion for progressive social housing and an iconoclast within the modern movement. The commission was Aalto's second in the United States, the first being the Finland Pavilion at the 1939 New York World's Fair. The monumental wave form in the interior of that building quickly assumed almost mythic status in Aalto's oeuvre and, in the minds of many, prefigured the distinctive, undulating slab of Baker House.[2]

The Baker House parti is one of Aalto's most brilliant conceptions. A single-loaded six-storey slab of dormitory rooms is bent and shaped to fit on a constricted site facing the Charles River in such a way that more than 90 percent of the student rooms enjoy river views. Piercing the slab on a diagonal is a sequence of low pavilions and lounge spaces, which define the communal axis of the building (FIG. 1). The dormitory slab is constructed of reinforced concrete and is clad in an unbroken envelope of rough, water-struck New England brick, a nod to the domestic Georgian vernacular of this region and Aalto's first use of brick as an exposed exterior material outside of its use on industrial structures like the Sunila Pulp Mill. This is a material that he subsequently came to champion and with which he came to be closely identified in the canonic works of his mid-career.[3] In contrast, the pavilions are presented in stone, natural wood, glass, and steel detailed in a manner that imparts a collective, monumental identity to these spaces. The dining commons, a two-story terraced pavilion clad in limestone, with wood-framed ribbon windows and a bank of Aalto's signature circular skylights, embodies the communal essence of the building. Aalto referred to the commons as the jewel of the composition, nestled in the embrace of the undulating brick slab, facing the river, and marking the end of the processional path that leads back to the dome of Building 7, the representational entry to the MIT campus (SEE p. 163 FIG. 1).[4]

Background: Process

Aalto's prominence rests on his skill as a designer, not as a theoretician, although there is nonetheless a significant polemical aspect to his work, a point emphasized by Göran Schildt in his editions of Aalto's collected writings, and by others in the considerable scholarship that has emerged on Aalto surrounding the centenary of his birth in 1998.[5] With Aalto, as with many architects of the modern movement, it is necessary to understand the meaning and architectural consequences of his generative idea in order to begin to develop a strategy for intervention in renovating his buildings. As our understanding of modernism continues to evolve, and particularly as it continues to inform contemporary architectural practice, it should follow that preservation, as it embraces the buildings of this era, should acknowledge and respond to this condition. As John Allan has stated, interventions in modern buildings should respect the "spiritual authenticity"

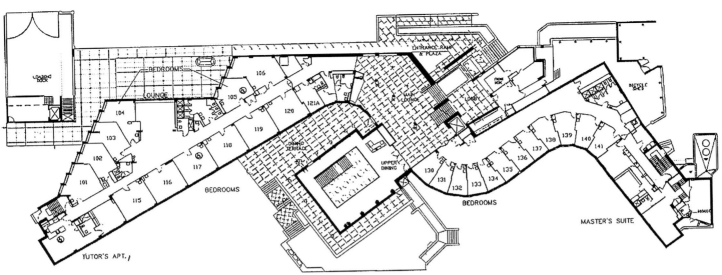

FIGURE 01 *Aalto, Baker House, Massachusetts Institute of Technology, Cambridge, Mass. Renovated (1999) Plan first floor.*

of the modern movement, and continue to elucidate a *representation* of the social, technical, and aesthetic principles of modernism, and a "commitment to change."[6] The challenge, therefore, in establishing a preservation methodology for Baker House was to formulate a sympathetic approach that expanded on Aalto's unique spatial consciousness and architectural vocabulary without interfering with those features of the work that establish the authenticity of the original artifact. In Aalto's work, ideas are embodied in the essence of both the large gesture and the detail, and it is for this reason that it is important to understand the essential design elements of Baker House as significant markers in the context of his work from this period (ca. 1946–1955).

Understanding the fundamental importance of this idea to the success of the project, MIT presented the design team with a mandate to research and set in detailed perspective the design history of Baker House, and then to use this knowledge to infuse the structure with the programmatic, physical, and technological improvements necessary to produce a functional, twenty-first-century residence hall. The initial study produced a position paper that included a historical narrative situating Baker House as a pivotal work in Aalto's career, and a preservation philosophy that uses this history to provide appropriate measures to sustain, enhance, and update the unique design and culture of Baker House. The analysis of the existing conditions and program needs generated key design initiatives, which became starting points in crafting a formal

strategy for approaching the design of the project. Several of these initiatives will be explored as case studies of particular design aspects of the project that serve as examples of how this philosophy was applied to the realization of the building program.

From the outset, it was understood that this work was to be a renovation, and that changes would have to be made in some areas to the original design. This decision was not taken lightly; it was determined that the nature of the building, its use, and the degree of intervention that would be required for certain aspects of the upgrade mandated changes that would go beyond those normally found in a restoration project. However, it was also felt that the flexible and robust quality of the structure would lend itself to a series of interventions that could illustrate the power of the original idea of the building through engaging these necessary changes in a meaningful design dialogue stretching across a half-century. Because this was a project with a high profile among many diverse and articulate constituencies, it was necessary first to formulate a working methodology sufficiently transparent to the parties following the process that all could understand the reasons for the decisions made. The initial step was to document the degree to which Aalto's original intent for the design of Baker House had been realized, in order to use this material to inform both restoration decisions and the renovation design process. Archival research done locally and at the numerous Aalto archives in Finland produced enough information to reconstruct, with a reasonable degree of accuracy, the sequence of the Baker House design process. These findings were greatly enhanced by the availability of Veli Paatela and Olav Hammarström, Finnish architects who successively managed the project for Aalto in Cambridge from 1946 to 1949, and who provide insights into many of the issues left unresolved at the completion of the research.[7]

This material was synthesized, along with program information, a building-conditions survey, and construction cost and phasing projections, into a feasibility study, which became the foundation on which the subsequent design was based. An important component of the design process was the evaluation—by both the design team and a peer-review committee of scholars, architects, and preservation professionals—of why key original design features had been either changed or deleted during the critical design and construction phases between 1947 and 1949. Once these determinations were made, there ensued a delicate process of evaluating whether the needs and aspirations of the present project mandated consideration of these features' reconstruction. The original alterations fall into three categories: budget-driven deletions of architectural features to save money, changes made for technical reasons (if, for example, the contractor was unable to build certain systems as detailed, or the material technology for a particular construction was insufficiently developed for MIT to sanction its use), and interpretations of some of Aalto's designs made in his absence (on site in the course of construction).

There was much debate as to where the lines should be drawn when considering whether to propose the rebuilding of any unexecuted elements. Orthodox preservation practice states that the original built form of the structure—regardless of its final design—should provide a normative touchstone from which to reconstruct or restore any work of architecture. The exceptions to this rule typically are buildings that have had significant additions or alterations made over time that have enhanced the quality of the primary structure, or those that have had changes made that cannot be reversed without causing irreparable harm to the original building. According to these guidelines, the approach to Baker House would be straightforward. Unsympathetic changes of the 1960s and 1970s would be reversed, building systems would be

installed or replaced for contemporary use, and alterations would be unobtrusively made to bring the building into compliance with modern codes and standards of accessibility.

This outline does, in fact, describe much of the project's scope, including the restoration of the central lounges on the upper floors via the removal of the 1962 bedroom additions, as well as the replacement of the 1976 aluminum windows with teak wood units matching the original design profiles. (Teak will acquire a patina similar in color to the original painted wood, with far greater longevity.) However, many believed that, given the building's pedagogical role and its importance as the first realized work of Aalto at mid-career, this project represented a rare opportunity to explore the possibility of using hitherto unrealized aspects of the architect's design to enhance the renovation. Within the areas to be restored (as opposed to areas that were changed through insertion or addition), the interpretation and development of Aalto's ideas were considered only as they met our criteria as interventions consistent with original intent. The work in question is all well documented and was clearly part of the design at the time of the completion of working drawings and the start of construction. It is important to note that any of the changes proposed for inclusion in the restored work were also justified on the grounds that they would improve the safety or functionality of the building, as well as providing the expected aesthetic enhancements.

Design Intent: Case Studies

One of the design characteristics that most concerned Aalto was the plain appearance of the brick facade on the river side of the building. Although clearly enamored of the rough brick as a facade material, Aalto nonetheless sought, as he did in many of his projects, to use plantings to "soften" the architecture with a material that could provide variety, color, texture, and a direct bond to the natural world of its site. Numerous drawings and a model from 1947 reveal Aalto's intent to overlay a system of aluminum trellises onto the curved portions of the south facade.[8] These were to be part of a larger trellis network that was originally proposed to cover a portion of the dining pavilion and the unexecuted first-floor library (also present in this model), and

FIGURE 02 *Aalto, Baker House. Building model from south with proposed trellises, 1947.*

then to extend up the building and spread out over the roof. In Aalto's correspondence to his site representatives through 1948, he repeatedly states the importance of these elements (particularly the trellises along the curved facade) in creating fine scale and architectural interest on this part of the building (**FIG. 2**).[9]

Trellis-like elements in Aalto's oeuvre date back to the Viipuri Library and continually reappear as a design trope throughout his career, although the prominence of the Baker House trellises goes beyond their usage in his earlier work. In Aalto's Finnish buildings these elements, usually executed in rough-hewn wood, evoke the rusticity and filtered light of the northern forest. At Baker House they are transformed—via the use of modern American technology, a concurrent fascination of Aalto[10]—into a visually brilliant, machine-made frame designed to be softened over time by nature, in the form of vines.

Although not ultimately present in the 1947 model, studies exist for a developed roofscape including a pergola and even (in one study) a thin concrete shell pavilion, similar in character to the rooftop terrace

at the Paimio Sanatorium from 1932. Its importance to Aalto had to do both with the health and recreational possibilities of a terrace for the students, as well as with giving the building a strong horizontal "cap" when seen from afar. This advocacy of the use of the roof to promote physical well-being, also ties Aalto directly back to Le Corbusier, who cites the use of a developed flat roof as one of his key five points of modern architecture.[11] The feature of an active roofscape appears less frequently in Aalto's later work, as both the nature of the programs and his experiments with more elaborate skylights and pitched or curved roof forms inhibit the possibility of inhabited roofs.

Analysis showed that construction of the south trellises would be difficult to justify as a purely formal intervention and that they would be expensive and difficult to maintain—all reasons for their deletion in 1949, which could not be overcome fifty years later. Thus they were not considered for incorporation into the work. However, the culture of Baker House has always supported an active roofscape, so here the opportunity

FIGURE 03 *Aalto, Baker House. Rooftop pergola, addition 1999.*

was seized to celebrate the role of the roof with the construction of a pergola linking the elevator lobby and the main stair penthouses. The actual design of the pergola is inspired by Aalto's domestic precedents (at his own house in Munkiniemi, the Villa Mairea, and the terraces of the Kauttua and Sunila Pulp Mill housing, all from the 1930s), but it is also clearly a contemporary intervention—no direct connection is made between the new fabric and any of Aalto's previously existing work. The pergola strengthens the center of the composition and frames the view back along the processional axis to the dome of MIT's Building 7, the representational campus entry. It also marks the place of activity on the roof and provides an architectural backdrop for the life of the terrace (**FIG. 3**).

The second example of a difficult design choice considered by the renovation team generated the greatest debate of any issue surrounding the renovation process. The north stair wall at Baker House, a cascading constructivist element that plays masterfully off the serpentine dormitory block and the old industrial landscape of East Cambridge, which it originally faced, was a subject of intense study by Aalto and his

assistants. The exterior cladding system was originally proposed to be metal. Studies exist for an aluminum curtain-wall system, although Aalto eventually rejected aluminum on the grounds that the contrast between the large areas of bright metal and the dark, water-struck brick would be too harsh. (It was never considered that the aluminum be painted.) Anecdotal evidence abounds that "black copper" (a copper alloy similar to that subsequently used by Aalto on several projects in Finland) was also proposed for the wall cladding.[12] This would have produced a rich mix of texture and color similar to that found in designs Aalto prepared shortly following Baker House—for the Säynätsalo Town Hall, the National Pensions Institute, and the House of Culture—designs that strengthen the notion of Baker House as a pivotal work in Aalto's emerging postwar aesthetic (**FIG. 4**).

Ultimately, Aalto settled on a system of vertically striated, unglazed terracotta tile secured with grout on metal lath over composition board on a light-gauge steel frame to clad the stairway. (Examples of such tile can be seen as part of the material collage on the courtyard wall of Aalto's Experimental House at Muuratsälo.) The record shows that in the course of construction, the contractor stated that they could not guarantee completion of the building on time with the tile cladding and that MIT therefore agreed to accept the change to a three-coat stucco system (which also involved a substantial reduction in cost). This decision was met with scathing objection from William Wurster, who saw himself as the guardian of Aalto's vision and claimed, in a letter to MIT President James Killian, that stucco was a cheap, shoddy material that would severely compromise the integrity of Aalto's design.[13] Exploration of this issue in interviews with Aalto site assistant Olav Hammarström revealed that the contractor was wary of the technical design of the tile cladding, and that the contractor had in fact told MIT that they would not guarantee the integrity of this system.[14] Taken in this light, MIT really did not have a choice in this decision, as the project team would have been unwilling to risk the failure of a substantial part of the exterior wall.

A preservation dilemma thus arose at this juncture. The present stucco system, although not particularly attractive and in need of repair, had held up remarkably well for over fifty years. Standard preservation

FIGURE 04 *Aalto, Baker House. Building model from north with metal stair cladding, 1947.*

FIGURE 05 *Aalto, Baker House. Computer rendering of north facade with tile cladding, 1998.*

practice would dictate the conservation of the stucco, as the authentic fabric—or, should the material failure turn out to be greater than suspected, its removal and replacement with new stucco. There was, however, significant sympathy among many of the project participants and experts familiar with the issue to the idea that the present initiative represented a unique opportunity to restore a component of Aalto's unrealized design intent, while simultaneously enhancing the appearance and integrity of the exterior envelope. In

this manner one could postulate a strategy that sought to extend the life of the building for centuries, whereby an analogy could be drawn between the north wall of Baker House and portions of late medieval and early Renaissance structures that awaited completion with temporary materials, pending either the availability of funds or the development of the building technology necessary to complete the work.

To gain a clear picture of the issue, the design team conducted detailed studies of the projected appearance of the tile wall (FIG. 5). Through this effort it became apparent (even to preservationists philosophically opposed to the change) that implementing the tile cladding would significantly enrich the quality of the north stair as an architectural element, as well as the building as a whole. The primary reading of the brick facades is rough and horizontal, punctuated by the projecting accents of the clinker bricks, which cast long shadows in the raking light that falls along the undulating north elevation. This same light, in early morning and late afternoon, would create a subtle vertical counterpoint in the raised striations of the tile, thus energizing the rich material contrast. The effect of this material ensemble

FIGURE 06 *Aalto, Baker House. Dining Commons from lower level with wood ceiling, 1999.*

would also be significantly heightened with the restoration of units to match the original wood windows, which would provide a light, harmonic contrast to the dark earth tones of the brick and tile.

After lengthy debate, a consensus was achieved that the value of the stucco to the collective memory of the MIT community tipped the scales in favor of the conservationist argument; the authentic material was ruled to be the stucco, due to the physical fact of its existence and by virtue of tradition, rather than the tile by virtue of intent. This decision was facilitated by concerns over budget and by the durability of the existing finish. Taken in the larger context of Aalto's oeuvre, it is significant to note that when tile was finally utilized for the exterior of later works, such as the Seinäjoki Town Hall, it was the heavy, vertical tubular tiles—developed by Aalto with Arabia Finland, a leading manufacturer of ceramics, and designed to be set in three inches of grout to absorb and withstand the thermal swings inherent in a northern climate—that

proved to be the sound choice.[15] The difficulty surrounding the choice regarding the Baker House tile system as designed was heightened by lingering concerns on the part of the present design team about the feasibility of creating a technically sound tile panel system without a radical reconsideration of the original detailing. Such a change would in all likelihood modify the appearance of the finished product and would significantly compromise the concept of the tile as the authentic original system. However, the exploration of this issue has shown that, given a material at the point of failure (for example, if the stucco had proven to be in as bad condition as it looked) and an option to retrieve a more robust alternative clearly preferred by the original architect, a strong philosophical argument can be made to make the change.

The final illustration of the difficult decisions encountered by the renovation team falls into both the categories of second-guessing in Aalto's absence and conformance to current building and accessibility codes mandating changes to the original design. Before 1998, the balustrade of the balcony in the dining pavilion was a solid wall approximately twenty inches high, capped by an open steel railing with a carved wooden top-rail. Drawings dated as late as February 1949 show a solid balustrade with a more richly articulated wood rail serving as a wall cap. Given Aalto's treatment of similar balcony motifs in subsequent Finnish works such as the Rautatalo office building in Helsinki, it seems likely that the solid balustrade was Aalto's final design intent. This assumption is confirmed by Hammarström, who claims that Aalto intended the higher walls of the balustrade within the light well to act as reflectors for the "moon garden" skylights to the dining room below and to create a more private space for the café and lounge users upstairs on the balcony level. (This final point was also echoed by the building's users in the course of defining the program for the renovation).[16]

Because the original design had to be changed to meet current life-safety standards, large-scale models were built and mock-ups constructed in situ to explore the range of alternatives that could be considered for the railings and balustrade that would satisfy contemporary requirements of height and opening size. It quickly became apparent that a conforming balustrade fabricated of any of the conventional infill materials such as thin steel rods, mesh, or glass would fail to retain the character of Aalto's design. Moreover, the more elaborate handrail of 1949 was too heavy an element to be comfortable in the space (which may explain its ultimate rejection). However, it was determined that the higher balustrade did in fact enhance and reinforce qualities of the original room and that this change could be accomplished by conserving and reassembling the existing rail and wood-cap system with shorter metal struts on the taller wall. The resulting design bears similarity in proportion and articulation to balcony designs for the library of the National Pensions Institute and the Academic Bookshop in Helsinki, both skylit, multi-level spaces with a separate top rail hovering lightly over a solid balustrade. Baker House's stair railings, which were originally articulated with a steel rod running centered between each of the support posts, have been brought to code through the addition of two parallel intermediate rods in each section. The banister continues to provide a light, sweeping counterpoint to the solid wall of the balcony rail and

the delicate vertical vanes of the wood fascia edging the lower level. Thus it was possible simultaneously to preserve much of the railing fabric, to prove the merit of Aalto's aesthetic intent, and to retain the iconic character of this space (**FIGS. 6–7; SEE ALSO p.173 FIG. 10**).

Design Interventions

Álvaro Siza noted in 1999 that while Baker House is unmistakably an Aalto building, it is simultaneously an unmistakably American building.[17] By this he means that Baker House has an austere, rough-and-ready quality that clearly places it at the edge of the unique tradition of delicate material juxtaposition and refinement found in many of Aalto's works, even of this period, in Finland. However, in its raw materiality it is both an honest expression of the essential material durability needed in an undergraduate-student residence and a poignant commentary, not unlike that so powerfully expressed several years later in Le Corbusier's monastery at Sainte Marie de La Tourrette, of the austere realities of building (even in the United States) in the immediate postwar era. Aalto also recognized that the culture of building in America was such that details should not be made too fine or idiosyncratic lest the intent of the gesture become lost in its execution,

FIGURE 07 *Aalto, Baker House. Dining Commons from kitchen, 1999.*

FIGURE 08 *Aalto, Baker House. Dining Commons with trellised columns and wood ceiling, 1999.*

FIGURE 09 *Aalto, Baker House. Student room with wood soffits, 1999.*

and he thus cautioned his assistants to avoid creating anything that would require explanations beyond those that would be easily understood by the contractors.[18] The renovation project team was often confronted with this issue in evaluating whether or not to implement certain design interventions, or in deciding the materials and finishes in which they should be executed, even where the details were those specifically mandated by Aalto. The result—a work with an aura that is in subtle ways both more finished and perhaps Finnish than the original—attempts to be simultaneously a reflection of its original author's intent, an appropriate response to contemporary expectations for and demands on the building, and a commentary on the impossibility of creating a "true" restoration.

The greatest challenge facing the design team in upgrading Baker House was the sympathetic integration of contemporary systems and technology into a reinforced

concrete structure with masonry interior partitions and nine-foot floor-to-floor heights. It is in these interventions that the architect must take the greatest care in devising both system configurations and a language of expression that are sympathetic without being mimetic. In 1949 Baker House had no air conditioning, no sprinklers, minimal telecommunications wiring, and sparse lighting. Thus it became an overriding necessity to devise a method for the provision of these amenities in a harmonious, architecturally integrated fashion.

In the principal public spaces, the new systems are entirely accommodated by the extension of architectural elements originally designed by Aalto for these areas. New mechanical systems were integrated into the first-floor (fireplace) lounge by selectively extending the original system of wood slat soffits out and back to locations where the systems within could be run vertically to the lower level. At the upper level of the dining room, it was necessary to provide supplemental heat and air conditioning through discreet fan coil units above the ceiling of this space. New lighting and fire protection systems also had to be added. Simultaneously, the students requested a greater degree of acoustic control and isolation in the dining hall. Research uncovered original drawings executed during the construction phase for an accessible, open wood-slat acoustical ceiling that, if implemented, could conceal all of the necessary systems and eliminate the need for access panels in an already visually crowded plane. In this case then, original intent and present necessity dovetailed to create a practical and aesthetically pleasing solution to a difficult problem. It should also be noted that these wood ceiling details, integrated with Aalto's trademark circular skylights, were later developed by his office and executed in the library for the Benedictine Mount Angel Abbey, in Oregon, in the 1960s (**FIG. 8; SEE ALSO p.172 FIG. 9**).

On the residential floors, it was decided that the corridors and their adjacent lounges, the principal public spaces, should retain as much of their original appearance as possible and that it made greater architectural sense to run the miles of piping and wiring required to service the student rooms within soffits inside the rooms, which would run parallel to the corridor. Given the tremendous cost and impact of this system on the building (affecting every student room), a series of mock-ups were built and refined to arrive at the optimal mix of aesthetics, economy, and ease of service accessibility. As eventually executed, the natural-finish millwork units cover the concrete beams already present over the doors and windows, and allow access to the piping and wire trays run adjacent to the beams. In doing so they provide a subtle contemporary update (much desired by the students) to the rooms, lend additional warmth to the spaces, and complement the original Aalto furniture, which was custom designed for the rooms. These pieces, dubbed "elephants, giraffes, and armadillos" by the students, were restored between 1995 and 2000 as an independent project (**FIG. 9**; **SEE p.175 FIG. 13**).

Throughout the lower level, the opportunity was taken to build out underutilized, unfinished spaces as new program areas. A glazed wall system was developed whose material, wood-to-glass proportions, and plan form were carefully studied to complement the existing space and language of the building, while also employing the generous proportions and precise detail with

which Aalto infused windows throughout his career. Along the east side, the upper level of all of the perpendicular dividing partitions was glazed in order to reveal and reinforce the perception of the full sweep of the serpentine dormitory slab. At the ceiling, the reorganization of the mechanical systems allowed for the development of a new soffit system, which provides services to the new spaces along the east corridor, as well as increased height and consequently greater daylight, as the original ceiling was lower than the high windows in these rooms (**FIG. 10**).

A conscious decision was made throughout the building to finish all interior woodwork, old and new, in the same manner, rather than attempt to introduce an artificial patina in the materials used in the restoration. (Exceptions were made only in areas of original woodwork that needed spot repairs.) This approach, utilizing the same clear-finish varnish formula used in 1949, produced a subtle contrast between the old and the new work that will fade, but never entirely disappear, over time.

FIGURE 10 *Aalto, Baker House. New lower-level recreation and study area, 1999.*

Aino Marsio Aalto, Alvar's first wife and professional partner, was a close collaborator in creating the refinements of furnishings, plantings, and fabric designs developed to grace their unique spaces. Aino's final illness and untimely death took Aalto away from Baker House for almost the entire final year of construction, and there is considerable evidence that, with the exception of the moon-garden lights in the dining room, the Aaltos had little if any part in the design of the building's lighting. In 1949 Baker House's lighting primarily consisted of naked, indirect "A" lamps and a series of square, recessed fixtures with Fresnel lenses in the public spaces—standard commercial lighting of the period. The naked lamps had long since been replaced with newer, fluorescent fixtures, but both the quality and quantity of light has always been a serious issue within the building (FIG. 11; SEE p.174 FIG. 11).

From the early phases of the renovation project, a program of custom lighting was proposed to permanently enhance the lighting in Baker House. Here again, a conscious effort was made to interpret the ambiance achieved in Aalto's work of this period in Europe in a manner appropriate to the somewhat more austere environment of Baker House. Working with the custom design departments of the Louis Poulsen Company in Denmark (whose primary designs were developed between the 1920s and the 1950s by Poul Henningson, Aalto's early mentor in lighting design) and Edison Price Lighting in New York, the architects and lighting designer developed five new fixture types, with variations, based on similar designs created by the Aaltos between the late 1930s and the early 1950s. The reactions to these modifications have been perhaps the most divided of the renovation. While no one doubts the efficacy and added quality of the modifications to the lighting, some—notably Lawrence Speck—have commented that the "off the shelf" quality of the original fixtures particularly contributed to the "American" feel of the spaces, and that the interventions yield an increased preciosity that, while not out of character with Aalto's European work, is arguably a misleading reflection of Baker House as originally executed (FIG. 12).[19]

Conclusion

There can be little argument that living buildings must accommodate change to maintain relevance and even to survive. Aalto himself said it plainly: "It is not what a building looks like on opening day—but what it is like 30 years later that counts."[20] This assertion speaks not only to the value of spatial and material accommodation but also to the importance of time and patina in imparting character to architecture. As a principle, it acknowledges the modernist notion of transitoriness while simultaneously accepting the possibility of material change to foster durability as a means of resisting obsolescence. As I have noted, with Aalto there are few universals; form and materials are instead carefully calibrated to human experience and to the vicissitudes of construction, to the "the methodical accommodation to circumstance," so carefully analyzed by Stanford Anderson.[21] This design approach—which is perhaps a more personal interpretation of Louis Sullivan's "form follows function"—in fact posits an opposition to the relentless inevitability of the big idea that characterizes much of orthodox modern architecture, and also mandates the critical evaluation of present "circumstance" to properly assess appropriate change.[22] At the point where the intervention begins to take shape, some subjectivity becomes inevitable, and if a decision is made to accept the authority of Aalto as the hypothetical final

FIGURE 11 Aalto, Baker House. Main lounge with extended soffits and new lighting, 1999.

FIGURE 12 *Aalto, Baker House. Lobby at night with relocated desk and new lighting, 1999.*

arbiter of what best suits his own buildings, we may then logically conclude that when the sustainability of these buildings mandates physical change, Aalto, where it can be proven that he has thought through these changes, should remain the best source for guidance.

This point is not made easily; it is a subjective, qualitative judgment that will often challenge the established autonomy of later interventions by subsequent architects. It is however a critical point, one on which the delicate balance of quality, honesty, and authenticity all come to bear. Throughout the design process the renovation team repeatedly confronted guidelines three and nine of the "Standards for Rehabilitation" in *The Secretary of the Interior's Standards for the Treatment of Historic Properties*, which stipulate that conjectural reconstruction should be avoided and that new work should be of its time and clearly distinguishable from existing fabric.[23] Bearing this in mind, it is instructive to remember the milieu in which these standards were crafted. Historic preservation crystallized as a

profession shortly after the cresting of the modern movement in America, and its crafters were primarily architects and historians who believed both in the appropriateness of modernism to contemporary design and in the fundamental gulf that existed between the work of the modern movement and what became labeled "traditional" architecture. These guidelines (particularly guideline nine) are thus in essence a modernist response to the problem of adding to or updating a traditional structure for which the adaptation of the language of the original fabric would in some real sense deny history and not be an honest reflection of the time, construction methodology, and (in all likelihood) function of the intervention.

Although, as David De Long and others have demonstrated, significant and irreversible changes have occurred in architectural theory and practice between the high-modern postwar period and the late modernism of today (as it should be perceived by the preservationist),[24] we still remain essentially a culture defined by many of the aesthetic and functional aspects of modernism, but with critical philosophical differences. "Modernism" in practice today is a more complex, heterogeneous, self-conscious, and even historical idea—one lacking a clear social or political agenda and with perhaps a thoroughly postmodern sensibility of its own inevitable obsolescence. Nonetheless, from the point of view of design language and aspiration, there are still many connections that can be made between the postwar design milieu that produced both Baker House and the preservation movement, and contemporary design culture. It can also perhaps be argued that stylistically Aalto's work has a unique but relatively timeless quality that settles comfortably into any decade of our era from mid-twentieth century on. Taken together, and with a conscious decision to read more of Aalto into the work, these circumstances fostered the evolution of what came to be understood as an optimal design methodology for the interventions at Baker House—to utilize Aalto's own ideas where change was necessary and where he had clearly planned it (minimizing the possibility of the conjectural) and otherwise to remain sympathetic and evolutionary. It was simultaneously agreed that to attempt a consciously different, contemporary approach would be seen at best as an attempt to upstage a subtle design and at worst as an insensitive, and quickly dated, intrusion.[25] The project team made these decisions fully cognizant of the inevitability of controversy—a predicament best summed up in the words of Antero Markelin: "It doesn't matter what you do—it will be wrong."[26]

These are the pitfalls of the close engagement of this approach. There is no doubt that significant architecture is, in most cases, the result of an ongoing, open collaboration between a talented architect, an enlightened client, and a skilled and sympathetic builder. The design philosophy employed for the renovation recognizes that the complexity, timing, and resultant stresses involved in any large construction effort are such that often ultimate decisions, even when made with the full consent of all of the principals involved, may be cause for critical reflection. It also accepts the

inevitability of the physical evolution of the structure, and it gambles that the resultant perceptual shift will be toward understanding the completed project as a contemporary work that elucidates both the original fabric and the greater idea of Aalto's project at mid-century.

This approach also inevitably rekindles the nineteenth-century debate on the nature and validity of restoration, championed by Eugène-Emmanuel Violet-le-Duc, but condemned by John Ruskin as a lie.[27] Ruskin's verdict is perhaps a harsh indictment of something generally done with the best of intentions, but it is nonetheless a succinct and lucid description of the inevitable truth that any intervention into an existing structure will irrevocably alter its original character. Any solution therefore must involve compromise and the recognition that preservation is both an ideal and a pragmatic art. Where the building's pedagogical mission and its projected long-term use have been clearly defined and restated, these in turn will inform the logic for the preservation of the structure. It should emerge, as did the examples cited in this essay, from a process that includes an open dialogue between the design team and the various constituencies with stewardship over the historic property.

In the final analysis, preservation, especially as it is applied to the work of the modern movement, must acknowledge and to some degree interpret the idea of a building as well as its fabric as an historic artifact. This is especially critical in the work of an architect of Aalto's stature. Therefore, in the course of the renovation, Aalto's original ideas have been utilized, openly but selectively, to reinforce and elucidate the highly idiosyncratic design of Baker House; to reemphasize its critical role as a pivotal work that propelled Aalto toward the great works of his mature career; and to balance, comment on, and complement the new work necessary to prepare it for the century ahead.

1 Aalto was initially brought to MIT by John E. Burchard in fall 1940, through funding from the Albert Farwell Bemis Foundation.

2 Sarah Menin, "Embracing Independence," in the present volume.

3 Aalto used whitewashed brick on several structures in Finland in the 1930s, including the Villa Mairea and his own house in Munkiniemi, but to my knowledge his only use of unfinished brick prior to the construction of Baker House—with the exception of purely industrial structures such as the Sunila Pulp Mill—was one exposed interior wall of Roman brick in the dining room of the Villa Mairea. Beginning with the Säynätsalo Town Hall, Aalto designed a succession of works, including the House of Culture, the National Pensions Institute, the Technical University at Otaniemi, and the Pedagogical Institute of Jyväskylä, where brick is the signature exterior material. These works were instrumental in the promulgation of Aalto as an architect championing the use of natural materials and a non-Cartesian "organic" sensibility in moving away from the functionalist aesthetic. It is interesting to note that on his return to Finland after the experience of Baker House, he made a challenge to the Finnish masonry industry to work with him in promoting and evolving techniques of brick construction in Finland.

4 Veli Paatela, interview with the author, 25 June 1996 at the Alvar Aalto Foundation

5 Göran Schildt, ed., *Alvar Aalto: Collected Writings* (New York: Rizzoli, 1996), 7–9, from the foreward, "Theoretician and Practitioner."

6 John Allen, "A Challenge of Values," in *Back from Utopia: The Challenge of the Modern Movement*, ed. Hubert-Jan Henket and Hilde Heynen (Rotterdam, Netherlands: 010 Publishers, 2002), 21.

7 Veli Paatela, interview with author, 25 June 1996, Alvar Aalto Foundation in Helsinki; Olav Hammarström, interview with author, 8 Aug. 1996 at the Hammarström house in Welfellet, Massachusetts.

8 The Drawings referenced are primarily sketches on file at the Alvar Aalto Foundation in Helsinki, but also include one sketch indicating the presence of trellises in a preliminary working drawing that is part of the set of original construction documents housed in the archive of Perry Dean Rogers & Partners in Boston, Massachusetts. The 1947 model no longer exists, but the photos are on file at the MIT Museum Archive in Cambridge, Massachusetts.

4 Letters from Alvar Aalto to Olav Hammarström, July 7, August 16, and September 15, 1948,(Archives of the Alvar Aalto Foundation, translations into Englaish 1996). In each successive letter, Aalto becomes more adamant about the necessity of the trellises, finally stating in the last letter that "the hovel will be too bare without it."

10 Veli Paatela, interview with author, 25 June 1996; Olav Hammarström, interview with author, 8 Aug. 1996.

11 Le Corbusier and Pierre Jeanneret, "Fünf Punkte zu einer neuen Architektur," in *Bau und Wohnung: Die Bauten der Weissenhofsiedlung*, by Deutscher Werkbund (Stuttgart, Germany: F. Wedekind, 1927), 27–28.

12 I first heard of the reference to black copper as the original choice for the cladding through the MIT Professor Will Watson, headmaster of Baker House during the course of the renovation. Veli Paatela also made reference to copper having been explored as a possible cladding material, but the recollection was vague and had to be taken as such. No references to the prospective use of this material have been found in the correspondence relating to Baker House, either at MIT or the Alvar Aalto Foundation.

13 Letter from William W. Wurster to MIT President James Killian, Nov. 22, 1948 (MIT Institute Archives and Special Collections).

14 Olav Hammarström, interview with author, 8 Aug. 1996.

15 Aalto did not use tile on the exterior of earlier projects except for a small area of flat blue tile surrounding the exterior fireplace at Villa Mairea.

16 Olav Hammarström, interview with author, 8 Aug. 1996.

17 Álvaro Siza, remarks made at the "Interpreting Aalto, Baker House and MIT" symposium, held at MIT, Oct. 1-2, Sept. 1999. Alvaro Siza delivered the annual Pietro Belluschi Memorial Lecture as part of the symposium, but the remarks quoted were made to a smaller group in conversation following his talk.

18 Veli Paatela, interview with author, June 25, 1996, (Alvar Aalto Foundation).

19 Lawrence Speck, "Back to School," *Architecture*, Jan. 2000, 42.

20 Alvar Aalto, address to Royal Institute of British Architects, London, 1956, quoted in Colin St. John Wilson, "The Other Tradition," London, Academy Editions, 1995, 123, Introductory quote.

21 Stanford Anderson, "Aalto and 'Methodical Accommodation to Circumstance,'" in *Alvar Aalto in Seven Buildings/Alvar Aalto in sieben Bauwerken*, ed. Timo Tuomi and others (Helsinki: Museum of Finnish Architecture, 1998), 142–49. The title comes from a statement made by Aalto about the Karelian farmhouse in Aalto, "Karjalan Rakennustaide", Usi Suomi (2 Nov. 1941).

22 Louis Sullivan, "The Tall Building Artistically Considered," *Lippincott's 57*, March 1896. The actual phrase used by Sullivan is "Form ever follows function."

23 United States Department of the Interior, *The Secretary of the Interior's Standards for the Treatment of Historic Properties*, 1995, "Standards for Rehabilitation," guidelines 3 and 9, www.cr.nps.gov/local-law/arch_stnds_8_2.htm.

24 David De Long, keynote address, "Preserving the Recent Past 2" conference, Philadelphia, 11 Oct. 2000. These remarks were also made in a similar address given by Professor De Long at the First Annual James Marston Fitch Symposium, Columbia University, New York, 12 Feb. 2000.

25 Guideline 9 of the "Standards for Rehabilitation" in the U.S. Department of the Interior's *The Secretary of the Interior's Standards for the Treatment of Historic Properties* mandates that interventions be sympathetic to the original design but clearly of their own time. While the interventions at Baker House generally harmonize with and update the original design, the work as executed sometimes errs on the side of blurring distinction rather than toward overt contrast. It was felt that this kind of discipline was necessary to ensure that Aalto's vision was not encumbered with subjective contemporary interventions. The pitfalls of the impetus to update mid-century modernism are exhibited in the renovations to Harkness Commons at the Harvard Graduate Center, originally designed by Walter Gropius and the Architects Collaborative. This building, an exact contemporary of Baker House, was given a makeover in 2004 that "modernized"—and largely obliterated—the austere and delicate material palette of the original, rendering it largely indistinguishable from the banal but sumptuous facilities found in corporate conference centers and office parks around the country.

26 Antero Markelin, in conversation with the author at Baker House, April 1998.

27 John Ruskin, *The Seven Lamps of Architecture* (New York: Noonday, 1961), 184–85.

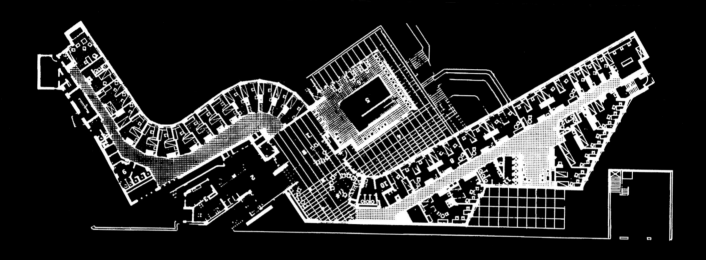

The Significance of Baker House

Paul Bentel

Baker House sends a message that beauty matters, quality matters, excellence matters in all human endeavors.

Rosalind Williams, former Dean of Students and Undergraduate Education, Massachusetts Institute of Technology

Since its first appearance in Sigfried Giedion's *Space, Time and Architecture* in 1949 until the present, Baker House has held a position in the architectural canon as a work representative of the design sensibilities of Alvar Aalto and that strain of the modern movement he has come to personify. The building is regularly mentioned and poignantly illustrated in historical literature ranging in subject matter from modern architecture to the architecture of American colleges and universities **(SEE p.163 FIG. 1)**.[1] Seeing the dormitory is a priority for architecture students on their pilgrimage to the great buildings of North America.[2] As the epigraph to this essay demonstrates, there is a reliable public consensus about its value as well. Baker House is routinely presented as an architectural monument whose aesthetic qualities make it an important historical figure.

This is remarkable given the building's idiosyncratic form and the specificity of its program. Certainly, Baker House is a noteworthy building with special material, formal, and spatial qualities. Yet the fact that there is such broad agreement about its significance is a matter that deserves some attention. How is it that the historical persona of this building transcended its particularities to garner high and unanimous esteem?

The relationship between the historical significance of a building and its intrinsic architectural qualities is not a simple one. To the architectural historian, physically remarkable buildings such as Baker House are self-evident focal points for investigation since their uniqueness suggests a noteworthy commitment by a patron and an architect. Writers with a strong point of view about historical change may use such buildings to illustrate their understanding of prevailing or emerging sensibilities. Once present in the historical discourse, these buildings acquire authority as evidence of the historical narrative they have been called on to substantiate. Subsequent historical interpreters may choose to accept, redefine, dismiss, or ignore the building and the historical narrative with which it has been associated. Some buildings may rise to the level of a canonic work and are commonly cited. Once ensconced in this discourse a canonic building operates as an intellectual touchstone whose status inspires conflicting claims about why it is important but whose authority as a significant building is undiminished over time.

Baker House is a case in point. Despite disagreements among pundits about the lessons that Baker House offers the student of history, the building has retained its role as a monument for over fifty years. Its emergence as a canonic work demonstrates how difficult it is to disentangle the historian's celebration of its aesthetic qualities from his or her interest in the building as proof of a historical thesis. For example, Sigfried Giedion—its earliest and staunchest proponent—argued that the building's curvilinear facade links it to Le Corbusier's Swiss Pavilion (1930–32) and to what he described as

FIGURE 01 *Alvar Aalto. Baker House, Massachusetts Institute of Technology, Cambridge, Mass.. Aerial view in context of West campus. The ceremonial domed entrance to the MIT Main Group is at the upper right.*

82. FRANCESCO BORROMINI. Undulating wall of San Carlo alle Quattro Fontane, 1662–67. *This late baroque invention, the undulating wall, reappears in English town planning toward the end of the eighteenth century.*

FIGURE 02 *Francesco Borromini, San Carlo alle Quattro Fontane, Rome, 1662–67. This facade image appeared in* Space, Time and Architecture *accompanied by this caption: "This late baroque invention, the undulating wall, reappears in English town planning toward the end of the eighteenth century."*

an evolving tendency among modern masters like Le Corbusier and Aalto to "free architecture from the threat of rigidity."[3] We might regard this as an apt reading of the building's form and a sensitive interpretation of Aalto's ambitions as an architect. It is also clear that the building's value to Giedion as historical evidence was immeasurable, because it supported his prior claim that the "undulating wall" was one of the recurring "constituent facts" in architecture, "producing a new tradition."[4] For Giedion, Baker House revealed a link between the plasticity of the baroque, the formal invention of eighteenth-century English town planning, and the sculptural shapes of modern architecture. He reinforced the point by including an aerial view of Baker House that suggestively recalls illustrations of Francesco Borromini's San Carlo alle Quattro Fontane (Rome, 1662–67), Lansdowne Crescent (Bath, 1794), and Le Corbusier's "Scheme for skyscrapers in Algiers" (1931) that appear in an earlier chapter of Space, Time and Architecture (FIG. 1–4). According to Giedion, Baker

83. Lansdowne Crescent, Bath, 1794. *Its serpentine windings follow the contours of the site.*

FIGURE 03 *Image of Lansdowne Crescent, Bath, England, as it appeared in* Space, Time and Architecture

85. LE CORBUSIER. Scheme for skyscrapers in Algiers, 1931. *Late baroque space conceptions came very near to contemporary solutions like this one.*

FIGURE 04 *Image of "Scheme for skyscrapers in Algiers, 1931," by Le Corbusier, as it appeared in* Space, Time and Architecture

House showed that the human aspiration for formal invention in buildings was inexorable and destined to resurface no matter how vigorously it was challenged by the popular taste for ornament.[5] From the moment Giedion first advanced this claim, the historical figure of Baker House would grow, nurtured by the ideologue's continuous endorsements of its significance and the rising influence of his writing on a generation of architects and architectural historians. Propelled into the historical discourse by Giedion, Baker House has remained one of the central and defining examples of modern architecture.

There is now an opportunity to consider not only this building as a work by Alvar Aalto but also the ways in which we define—and then subsequently work with—the significance of canonic buildings. I will give examples from elsewhere in Giedion's work as well as the ensuing discourse on the building's significance in which interpreters reinvent its historical meaning. I will examine Baker House's rise within the history of the modern movement, its resurfacing in the postmodern critique, and its past and current role as an international emblem of its institutional patron, MIT. I will conclude with a brief reflection on the effect that its status as a canonic work has on us individually, as spectators of the building itself. But first let us consider the circumstances that compel us to rely on such declarations of significance.

The Epistemology of Significance

As the case of Baker House shows, collective or institutional determinations of significance have an impact on the maintenance and, by extension, the appeal of a structure. Baker House also demonstrates how fickle the custodians of historic resources can be. The success of MIT's recent meticulous renewal of Baker House should not cause us to forget the deleterious effects of prior inattention. Alternatively, determinations of significance may provoke overzealous reactions, embalming the building as a monument. Such has been the fate of other canonic works whose historical importance challenges their contemporary use-value. Le Corbusier's Carpenter Center for the Visual Arts comes to mind as an example of a building whose cultural value as an art piece with clear provenance

has, at times, preempted its role as an art center so that its guardians have enshrined it as a testament to its historical legacy.[6]

The process of signification and the subsequent public actions that flow out of it put us at risk of losing historic buildings physically, for reasons of neglect, or emotionally, because of their estrangement from our private lives. In view of the latter, establishing the significance of Baker House is urgent since among the qualities most highly prized by its historical chroniclers are those that present themselves gradually through an individual's direct experience of the building. Aalto interpreters attribute this to the unpredictability of the architect's resolutions of programmatic and structural issues and to his unusual juxtapositions of uses and materials, as well as to peculiarities in the siting of his buildings. The singularities that result yield unanticipated consequences for the user, making it necessary to experience the building for oneself and, presumably, impossible to comprehend through secondhand accounts.[7]

The idea that Baker House is critically unintelligible to those who do not know it through personal encounter is part of its historical lore. Sigfried Giedion was among the first to encourage this point of view. Not having seen the building firsthand, he presented the words of a surrogate, the "English Observer," to evoke its special qualities in editions of *Space, Time and Architecture* before 1967.[8] In remarking on Aalto's accomplishment, Giedion went so far as to characterize the effect as an emancipation of the "individual," stimulating his or her sensibilities with its spatial, material, and programmatic variations. Aalto, Giedion maintained, "imbues things with an almost organic flexibility."[9] More recently, Stanford Anderson described the variety and unpredictability of Aalto's work as a result of the architect's eschewal of patterned responses to the design problems he encountered. For this reason, Anderson notes, "The programmatic thinking of critics seeking formal or even stylistic consistency over a body of work . . . reveals a mindset that cannot incorporate a method like Aalto's that generates diversity not only within his oeuvre but even in aspects of the same building."[10] By all accounts, Aalto's work is intimate and episodic. It places demands on viewers' powers of observation and rewards them for the time they spend in close contact. Efforts to circumscribe the individual's experience—whether by historical narration or physical barriers—can impede this revelatory process.

Yet conventional determinations of a building's historical significance based on a prevailing canon by their nature fall back on a modality of knowledge that is both arbitrary and authoritative. For example, historic preservation, an increasingly familiar discipline which marshals legal and economic support for historic buildings on the basis of their cultural value, depends on a strong and enduring "statement" of historical significance as a point of departure. Within this and other fields of cultural-heritage management an "epistemology of significance" predominates, characterized by standards of cultural value that do not change over time.[11] Institutional patrons of historic buildings such as MIT are also encouraged by definitive and enduring assessments of historical significance, because they offer hope of a result whose good outcome will not be overturned simply by changes in fashion or taste.

While authoritative proclamations of significance may legitimize an official act of preservation or undergird an institution's will to restore a significant historic building, they also tend to exclude unprecedented points of view, especially those that depart from the mainstream. This dichotomy has drawn much recent critical attention and fomented a backlash from cultural conservators and historic preservationists against assessments of historical significance which invoke a fixed canon that excludes diverse points of view about the cultural value and meaning of the buildings themselves.[12]

Baker House presents us with an intriguing test case since its power as a building capable of fomenting diverse and private reactions lies at the heart of its historical persona. Commentators claim historical significance for this building on the basis of, on the one hand, its impact on a professional discourse and, on the other, the emotive power of its form. Is it possible that Baker House possesses intrinsic architectural qualities so potent they preclude an expression of its value as mere historical evidence? Or are the claims for its significance that tout its evocative power self-serving punditry intended to bolster some historical narrative? To probe these questions, let us consider Sigfried Giedion's use of Baker House in *Space, Time and Architecture* more closely.

Baker House, Giedion, and the Modern Movement

From the moment Giedion first included Baker House in *Space, Time and Architecture* in 1949, he heralded its historical significance and proclaimed its architect a dominant figure who carried forward "new means of expression and their elements—standardization, new methods of construction and, above all, a new space conception." Giedion presented Aalto as a successor to Frank Lloyd Wright, Walter Gropius, Le Corbusier, and proponents of De Stijl, among others.[13]

Beyond this, Giedion saw in Baker House a relationship to the core strategies that he associated with the modern movement: a new "space conception" liberated from the confinements of structure-bearing walls, a rejection of period styles and historical references, a relating of form to program, and the incorporation of contemporary building technologies. Recalling the ambitions of early modernists to achieve an "existenzminimum" in their housing units, Giedion also reported that the dormitory's "bedrooms and workrooms . . . were as small as possible without destroying the vitality of the atmosphere." In black and white, Baker House presented itself as an "unadorned" building that demonstrated the volumetric possibilities presented by the rigid concrete frame. To emphasize its stylistic independence, in the 1959 edition of *Space, Time and Architecture* Giedion added a comparison to the Harvard dormitories "built in the style of English country houses of the eighteenth century." In contrast to these, Aalto's work demonstrated a modern aesthetic brought to life by the creative vision of the architect.[14]

At the same time, Giedion perceived evidence in Baker House of a shift within the modern movement. In its "organic" formal vocabulary, the dormitory avoided the regularity and repetition of the earlier work of European modernists, such as Gropius, without departing ideologically from the movement Giedion espoused.[15] Its design was novel with respect to both the stylistic eclecticism of the École des Beaux-Arts and the rigid and sanitized work of the *Neue Sachlichkeit*. It possessed a vigorous free-form plan, "flexibly" organized to accommodate different needs; sculptural features such as the curvilinear facade; and, finally, the contrasts of rough and smooth surfaces by which these formal features were enhanced.[16] It is in this capacity that Baker House became definitively intertwined with the historical evolution of the modern movement as Giedion narrated it, cementing Aalto's role as the "integrator" of its early and later phases.[17]

The aesthetic possibilities presented by Baker House appear to have had a powerful impact on Giedion, causing him to change the words he used to describe its historical significance. In the 1949 edition of *Space, Time and Architecture*, in which his first reviews of the dormitory appeared, he titled the chapter on Aalto "Elemental and Contemporary" to evoke the sculptural simplicity of the architect's work. Giedion subsequently renamed the chapter "Irrationality and Standardization," as a public acknowledgment that the unpredictable forms that characterized Aalto's work constituted a legitimate formal strategy for the new architecture. This change in the chapter title coincided with Giedion's inclusion of his own firsthand observations of the building, suggesting that his reclassification of Aalto's work was provoked by his experience of Baker House in person.

The spirit of change that Baker House signaled to Giedion was not merely to be construed in its formal or material character. The historian's growing conviction of the significance of Aalto's work, demonstrated by his increasing coverage of it in *Space, Time and Architecture*, followed his ruminations on the more essential shortcomings of modern architecture as a vehicle of contemporary culture. Giedion revealed this line of thinking as early as 1943, when he prepared a short manifesto with José Luis Sert and Fernand Léger titled "Nine Points on Monumentality."[18] In it the three declared a desire to move the modern movement beyond its commitment merely to satisfying humankind's physical requirements for shelter toward service to its social and symbolic life as well. This assertion led Giedion to contemplate the ways in which architectural form might stimulate a transcendent collective social memory.[19]

In his search for architectonic forms that were "abstract" and yet still stirred the human imagination, Giedion found something in Baker House that answered the challenge, namely Aalto's derivation of a modern formal vocabulary linked to human experience. Of Baker House, he wrote, "As Joan Miró is rooted

in the Catalan landscape, as the cubists transmitted experiences—tables, glasses, bottles, newspapers—of a Parisian café into a new conception of space, so Aalto found a direct incentive in the curved contours of the Finnish lakes, shaped with astonishing smoothness by nature itself and set in high relief by forest masses pressing on all sides down to the water's edge."[20] In its plasticity and formal inventiveness as well as its recall of landscapes and the material richness found in nature, Baker House served Giedion in a way that the rigid and functional work of the *Neue Sachlichkeit* never could. It both enlarged the movement formally and enabled him to weave a historical narrative describing Aalto's work—and by extension, the work of his modernist colleagues, such as Le Corbusier in his later years—as fully rounded, satisfying the human instinct for lyricism and metaphor.

But did Giedion's assessment of Baker House and the significance he accorded it accurately reflect qualities that he apprehended in the building, or was he inspired to celebrate these qualities of the building because they revealed a way forward to a new design thesis for the modern movement? A direct answer to this question is not available to us. However, the tension between the demands of historical narration and the discrete revelations of the building itself becomes apparent when we compare Giedion's written descriptions of Baker House before and after 1967, the date of issue of the fifth edition of *Space, Time and Architecture*. As I have noted, prior to 1967, Giedion used the reported impressions of an unnamed "English Observer" as a substitute for his own words, since he had not seen the building firsthand. That borrowed text makes note of many of the features that relate the building to its locale and revel in its material richness. For example, it references the relationship between the curvilinear wall of Baker House and the Boston brick bowfront. The English Observer is also prescient in her observation of a lyrical connection between the curving facade and the waterfront beyond, establishing what has surely become one of the most often repeated explanations for this form. Following this narrative, Giedion explained why he dwelled on the local influences on Aalto's design: "Aalto's attempt to free architecture from the threat of rigidity, points, like every constituent work, forward and backward, and is rooted at the same time in its own soil."[21]

After 1967, Giedion removed the text of the English Observer. He replaced it with his own words describing Baker House's relationship to other significant buildings by Gropius, Le Corbusier, and Sert.[22] Instead of discussing the curvilinear shape in its relationship to local architectural forms, he focused on its connection to the "undulating wall," on the basis of which the historical lineage from Borromini to Le Corbusier could be traced. Why the change? Why omit the reference to those intrinsic characteristics of the building that so influenced a firsthand encounter with the building and replace them with comparisons that situate the building in abstract relationships across time and space? Perhaps, by 1967, Giedion had seen Baker House and found it less stimulating than anticipated. More likely, he focused his descriptive faculties on the historical legacy of the building rather than its local associations or material qualities because the narrative of canonic significance best fulfilled the rhetorical expectations of his readership.

Baker House after the Modern Movement

Aalto's role as a modern master was canonized inalterably by Giedion's embrace of his work (which grew, as Stanford Anderson has pointed out, to 9% of the total volume of illustrated works in the final editions of *Space, Time and Architecture*).[23] Nevertheless, Giedion's assessments of both Aalto and Baker House would be challenged. Nikolaus Pevsner criticized Aalto's design methods as being irrational and aberrant when viewed against the historical trajectory of what he termed "modern design," this judgment notwithstanding his recognition of Baker House as evidence of the movement's international reach.[24] Frank Lloyd Wright, with whom Aalto is occasionally associated in historical accounts of the modern movement as having enriched its formal vocabulary, was also a critic of the building. Wright's reaction to an interviewer's suggestion in 1952 that Baker House had influenced his design of the Solomon R. Guggenheim Museum (1943–59) stated his position clearly when he wrote, "Incidentally, Aalto's work on MIT affects me as inspirational as a clumsy grub. No chrysalis is that Dormitory of his."[25]

Despite the exception taken by Pevsner to Aalto's design sensibility on ideological grounds or Wright's put-down of Baker House, historical surveys of Western architecture written before 1980 that regarded the modern movement as historically inevitable included Aalto as a de facto modern master and as a link between its early and later phases. For example, in his collection of essays on American architecture titled *The Impact of European Modernism in the Mid-Twentieth Century* (1972), William Jordy connected Aalto with Marcel Breuer, Le Corbusier, and Wright on the basis of their use of wood and brick to create texture in walls. He also pointed to Aalto's and Breuer's common study of folk craftsmanship.[26] In his contribution to the Pelican History of Art series, *Architecture: Nineteenth and Twentieth Centuries* (1977 edition), Henry-Russell Hitchcock presented no illustrations of Baker House. But he stressed Aalto's leadership role within the modern movement particularly in the formal and material richness he brought to the modern idiom. Hitchcock linked Aalto with Louis Kahn and the "Neo-Brutalism" of Paul Rudolph.[27]

By the 1980s, however, both the inevitability of the modern movement and the role Aalto played in restoring continuity between its rational and organic phases were subject to critical revision. In *Modern Architecture: A Critical History*, Kenneth Frampton described Aalto's work as a synthesis of Nordic "Romanticism" and a prevailing "Doric sensibility" in Scandinavia that resulted in a merging of idiosyncratic tendencies and the normative "rules" of classicism. By explaining Aalto's work in relationship to his personal history rather than as the consequence of a historical imperative, Frampton's *Modern Architecture* gave a hint of things to come in the historiography of Aalto, who would be increasingly celebrated for his idiosyncratic design sensibilities. In Frampton's view, Baker House was "a somewhat unresolved design" that looked forward to the rustic Säynätsalo Town Hall rather than back to the Bauhaus or Borromini.[28]

Histories of American architecture during the same period are less consistent in their coverage and assessment of Baker House. This is understandable since the theme of the modern movement (and the related International Style) did not figure centrally in studies that dealt with national or regional architecture.

Among those that acknowledged Aalto's historical status as a modern master, *The Architecture of America: A Social and Cultural History* (1961), by John Burchard and Albert Bush-Brown, was the most vigorous in its praise. It states: "By 1960, acclaimed from Zurich to Tokyo as one of Aalto's greatest buildings, Baker House remains a landmark in American university architecture."[29] No doubt the authors' MIT affiliation played some role in their strong affirmation of its significance. Marcus Whiffen's and Frederick Koeper's *American Architecture, 1860–1976* (1983) describes Baker House as "forward looking, forecasting the experiments of the sixties." This book, it must also be pointed out, was published by MIT Press. In his *American Architecture* (1985), David Handlin accorded Baker House high praise, attributing to it an influential role in the transformation of the work of Louis Kahn from light tubular steel structures to his monumental and classically inspired work in concrete and masonry.[30] In contrast, Robert Stern's *Pride of Place: Building the American Dream* (1986) and Dell Upton's *Architecture in the United States* (1998) make no mention of either the architect or the building, a circumstance that stands to reason since both books embrace American exceptionalism, emphasizing the historical influence of national and popular culture (in the case of Stern) and regional or local circumstances (in the case of Upton) on architectural production.

The range of treatment of Aalto and Baker House that we see in the writing of Frampton, Stern, Upton, and others can also be explained by the waning influence of the modern movement and its supporting historical ideology. As a consequence of the declining authority of this canon, it became possible for survey histories such as those by Stern and Upton to exclude Aalto or Baker House. When Aalto does appear it is for his iconoclasm as a modernist rather than his role as a modern master. We see such a representation in the regroupings of prominent architects by Reyner Banham and Vincent Scully, both of whom put Aalto in with the New Brutalists. While Banham's *Theory and Design in the First Machine Age* (1960) failed to include Aalto as a modernist alongside Walter Gropius, Le Corbusier, and Ludwig Mies van der Rohe, his polemic, *The New Brutalism: Ethic or Aesthetic?* (1966), portrayed Aalto's work as having influenced that of architects such as Peter and Alison Smithson, Paul Rudolph, Denys Lasdun, Louis Kahn, and James Stirling.[31] In his textbook, *American Architecture and Urbanism* (1969), Scully presents Aalto within the context of a younger generation of American architects such as Rudolph, Kahn as well as John Johansen and Moshe Safdie. Scully goes on to describe Baker House as having reinforced a nascent movement toward strong and rough shapes carried out in inexpensive but permanent masonry and brick which would

397. ALVAR AALTO. Dormitory (Baker House), Massachusetts Institute of Technology, 1947–49. *Air view.*

FIGURE 05 *Image of Baker House as it appeared in* Space, Time and Architecture.

become the material and formal well-spring of a contemporary vernacular architecture.[32]

Writers who championed postmodernism saw Baker House as a manifestation of Aalto's modernist apostasy, a claim that coincided with the rise of the historical thesis proclaiming the epistemological failure of modernism. Notable among them was Robert Venturi, an architect whose polemical work, *Complexity and Contradiction in Architecture* (1966), attacked the reductive simplicity of the modern movement and presented Aalto as its ideological opponent.[33] Baker House, Venturi wrote, was "exceptional" because its curvilinear river front contrasted with the rectangularity of the back of the building. In celebrating this discontinuity between front and back, Aalto disclosed the "complexity and contradiction" inherent in the relationships of program and structure, which modernists—eager to express the universality of industrial technology—would otherwise attempt to conceal.[34] As with the Philadelphia Savings Fund Society Building (George Howe and William Lescaze, 1932), a building Venturi praised in his text, the dormitory had two different sides in recognition of "its specific urban setting" and its role as "a fragment of a greater exterior spatial whole." To illustrate the point, Venturi compared the plan of the dormitory to that of a "double axis" Parisian hotel, the Hôtel de Matignon, whose "ingenious double axis . . . accommodated outside spaces differently at the front and back," and the Florentine Palazzo Strozzi, whose plain side elevation similarly contrasted with its heavily rusticated street front and referenced two different urban conditions (**FIG. 5**).

How different is Venturi's interpretation of the historical significance of Baker House from that of Giedion, who compared the dormitory to Borromini's San Carlo alle Quattro Fontane and English crescents of the eighteenth century? Where Giedion perceived formal coherence forged by the powerful gesture of the curving line, Venturi saw the opposite; namely, the building as a matrix of formal gestures, each responsive to its local condition. As an example of a modernist sensibility, the building evoked a comprehensible unity forged by artistic vision and the rational deployment of program and structure. As an example of a postmodern ethos, the same building demonstrated the architect's acceptance of disunity and discontinuity, a trait Venturi advocated in *Complexity and Contradiction in Architecture*.

Sixteen years after Venturi's book, Dimitri Porphyrios published *Sources of Modern Eclecticism: Studies on Alvar Aalto*, in which he claimed not merely that Aalto's work diverged from the rationalism of the modern movement but that it represented an ideological shift away from the "homotopia" of European rationalism. In its place, Aalto substituted a "heterotopia" that "was to destroy the continuity of syntax and to shatter predictable modes of the homogeneous grid."[35] Porphyrios's characterization of Aalto's work as eclectic created a new historical role for the architect in the 1980s and removed him from the pantheon of modern masters whose singular vision Giedion had heralded years earlier. Remarkably, Aalto's stature as a historical figure rose meteorically in this period despite the growing intellectual disaffection for the modern movement with which he had been so intimately connected.

Spiro Kostof's architectural survey, *A History of Architecture* (1985), is the most important re-affirmation of the significance of Baker House within the historical narrative of postmodernism. The dormitory is described in the text and appears in a stunning aerial photograph, which depicts it against the backdrop of the rectilinear buildings of the MIT main campus, a view that highlights its sculptural form (this view is reproduced in the Baker House Photo Essay fig. 1). Baker House assumes the role of a visual icon alongside other significant modern buildings (it is located between Oscar Niemeyer's Church of St. Francis Assisi [1942–43] and Le Corbusier's Notre-Dame-du-Haut at Ronchamp [1950–55]) and within the sweeping context of architectural history spanning back to 400,000 BCE. In his written description of the building, Kostof noted the architect's "lyrical" sensibilities, his formal inventiveness, and the "undulating" wall, repeating language that had appeared forty years earlier in *Space, Time and Architecture*. The "coarse brick" and random spacing of the clinkers of Baker House, to which Kostof drew parallels with the rough concrete of Le Corbusier's Unité d'Habitation in Marseilles, was a "deliberate affront to the International Style sensibilities." The building also provided Kostof the opportunity to explain Aalto's role in turning an international generation of architects away from the "doctrinaire rationalism of the Germans" and back to the lineage of "traditional" architecture, thus helping

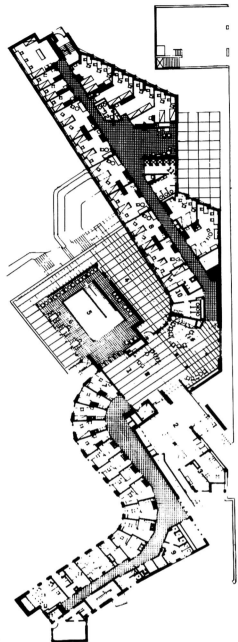

205. Aalto. Baker House Dormitory, M.I.T., Cambridge. Plan

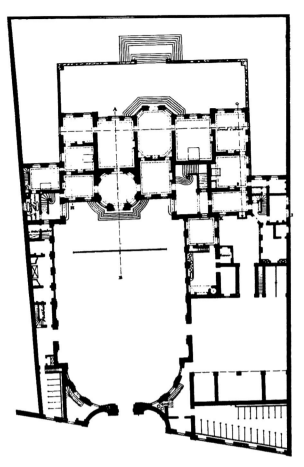

206. Courtonne. Hôtel de Matignon, Rue de Varenne, Paris. Plan

207. Maiano. Strozzi Palace, Florence. Perspective

FIGURE 06 *Comparative figure from Robert Venturi,* Complexity and Contradiction in Architecture *(New York: Museum of Modern Art, 1966), showing the plan of Baker House; the plan of a Parisian hotel that Venturi reprinted from Nikolaus Pevsner,* An Outline of European Architecture *(London: Penguin Books, 1943); and the side elevation of the Palazzo Strozzi, Florence.*

to conclude the revolutionary experiment that had commenced with the *Neue Sachlichkeit* and pointing the way toward new aesthetic possibilities for those who sought to reconnect with the architecture of the past.[36]

With the endorsement of Kostof and after almost six decades of constant historical attention since the 1949 edition of *Space, Time and Architecture*, Baker House's significance can hardly be contested.[37] In fact, the circumstance is reversed: due to the unquestioned significance of Baker House, an author's ability to demonstrate the veracity of his or her historical thesis can be demonstrated by the success he or she has in showing it to be pre-ordained in Aalto's work generally and Baker House in particular. This condition is borne out even in the face of the supposed decentralization of the historical discourse through the medium of the World Wide Web: as of the writing of this essay, the Wikipedia entry for "modern architecture" listed Aalto as one of two "mid-century masters," alongside Eero Saarinen, and Baker House as one of five "significant buildings" cited for Alvar Aalto.[38] From the point of view of the historiography of the building and Aalto, contemporary studies of the dormitory need not dwell on the legitimacy of its canonic significance. Now ensconced in the historical canon, Baker House is part of the lingua franca that both facilitates and shapes our discussions about architectural production in our own day.

Baker House and MIT

When it was completed, Baker House was as distinct in its immediate physical context as it was in its historical relationship to the work of Aalto's modernist forebears. Since its construction, the curvilinear form of the riverfront dormitory has provided a powerful sign of MIT's presence in the Boston metropolitan area and among other academic institutions with a prominent position on the Charles River, such as Harvard and Boston University. It is reasonable to suggest that the significance of Baker House to its institutional patron has gone well beyond its utility as a dormitory.

At the time that it was constructed, Baker House was one of the first dormitories built by the institute for "on-campus" housing. It fulfilled the administration's desire to create a distinct academic community within the city. Aalto's prior relationship to the school—first, through his affiliation with the Albert Farwell Bemis Foundation and then as a faculty member in the architecture department at MIT—is not to be discounted as an influence on his selection.[39] Nevertheless, his status as an internationally recognized modernist carrying out his first permanent building in the United States suggested a progressive outcome. Apparently content with the results of the process, MIT administrators praised the architect for a "stimulating and unconventional design" at the inauguration of the building.[40]

In order to appreciate the forward-mindedness Aalto demonstrated in his design of Baker House, the dormitory must be considered in the context of both American campus planning and the modern movement. MIT was not the first major American university or college to engage a prominent architect associated with the modern movement. Before the war, with the aid of the Rockefeller Foundation and the spiritual leadership of supporters of modernism such as Lewis Mumford, a series of competitions featuring modern designs were held throughout the Northeast.[41] Frank Lloyd Wright's work at Florida Southern College in Lakeland (started in 1938) had provided an internationally recognized architect the opportunity to build a whole campus. Also in 1938, the most famous example of academic modernism was initiated by Ludwig Mies van der Rohe on behalf of Illinois Institute of Technology in Chicago. But even with these as precursors, Aalto's project was distinctive due to its stunning proximity to MIT's existing neoclassical buildings, which were so different in design from Baker House. As Paul Turner has pointed out, Baker House was among the first of several buildings, including the Alumni Pool (Lawrence Anderson, 1939), that would be carried out by the Institute according to a novel design methodology ostensibly based on the modernist goals of functionality and flexibility but also preoccupied with the clarity of these buildings as objects set against the other buildings on the campus. This agenda marked a departure from the "traditional" American campus planning, which had sought permanence, stability, and visual continuity in the designs of buildings for institutions of higher education.[42]

It would be incorrect to suggest that the distinctiveness of Baker House rests completely on its visual difference from the William Welles Bosworth campus or, as Giedion pointed out, the "Georgian" dormitory format adopted by Harvard and present in numerous exemplars just up the river. Baker House was also remarkable as a building within the modern idiom, as I have already noted, by virtue of its rough brick walls and formal complexity, features that were inconsistent with standardization and the machine-made. As an academic building, Baker House gave expression to the relationship between the student and the institution. Commentators from within the MIT community noted this quality in the plan layout, in which a variety of room sizes and shapes were present, each with their own relationship to public spaces. These aspects were evidence of a sophisticated response to the "communal" program of the dormitory and further signified the progressive cant of the school following World War II.

The significance of Baker House to MIT remains in its symbolic role as a progressive, modern, communal building with a distinctive presence in the public domain. The institute recognizes, as well, the importance that the building has acquired by virtue of the repeated commentary by Giedion and others. This understanding is reflected in the words of MIT's own promotional literature describing Baker House as "one of the pivotal modern buildings in North America."[43] By its current, well-thought-out, and highly visible stewardship of Baker House, the institute has acquired more than just the reputation of a public guardian of important architectural heritage. Its image as a first-rate technical university is burnished by its patronage of and commitment to good, modern design. The words of Rosalind Williams, dean of students at MIT at the time of the renovation of Baker House, suggest the self-awareness with which the rehabilitation of the building was carried out in 1998. "Baker House," she wrote in the promotional literature that accompanied the re-opening of the building after its refurbishing, "is part of the postwar vision that MIT should become a place where communal life is important and is leveraged for educational benefit. As President [James R.] Killian was fond of saying, our campus should give our students 'a sense of the first rate.'"[44]

Though dichotomous, these two forms of signification—the one celebrating Baker House's association with Aalto, the other describing its intrinsic qualities as a building of excellence—overlap and amplify one another. It is undoubtedly reassuring to those who believe in Aalto's importance among his contemporaries that this building should still provoke positive responses from audiences who witness it today. MIT's commitment to "excellence" in cultural and scientific pursuits, as expressed in Rosalind Williams' pronouncement in the epigraph to this essay, is reinforced by this tasteful and important monument. But these circumstantial and fortuitous relationships between our evaluations of architectural quality and historical significance hide a fundamental conflict between the criteria of cultural value on which we base them. Indeed, there is danger in the use of one kind of signification to substantiate the claims we make to the other. Allusions to Baker House's historical significance threaten to undermine the credibility of our admiration of its gravity as a physical and spatial object, because they raise the possibility that we are celebrating its physical attributes in order to substantiate historical claims. The zealousness with which Aalto's proponents seek a place in history for him and his building undoubtedly provokes a positive response in popular taste which privileges the Aalto aesthetic. To what extent, we might ask, is the current approbation of the building a result of an authentic and individual response to its architectural qualities, the residual effect of a prior evaluation of historical significance, or a mixture of both?

The current re-estimation of Baker House as a monument testifying to the values of MIT has gained greater depth in recent years with the commencement of an MIT building program that includes new dormitories. In this regard, Baker House provides an example of the utility of the progressive designs with which the school is associated. The former dean of the School of Architecture and Planning, William Mitchell, used the example of Baker House to foment support for the new building project by Steven Holl, who was designing a residence hall while the Baker House renovation was ongoing. In this context, Mitchell's comments about Baker House are revealing: "Baker House shows the value of investing in thoughtful, well-designed buildings that are fundamentally good in basic human terms and that have a robustness that allows them to adapt over time. It sets a very high standard for the new student residences MIT will be constructing over the next few years."[45]

Baker House Itself

In the current critical climate, it is difficult to sustain the belief that our opinions about the architectural qualities of a building are not influenced by prior evaluations of historical significance. Professional evaluators of Baker House—historians, critics, architects, representatives of MIT—are limited in what they can say about a building like Baker House by the larger historical project they have underway. We have seen that Giedion's favorable comments on Baker House coincided with his efforts to redirect the modern movement toward greater formal diversity. His interpretation of the building as a "constituent work," locked in its place in time and destined to play out its role as evidence of a historical continuum reaching back to classical antiquity, cannot be divorced from his celebration of the curvilinear wall. His interpretation of the building form as "free" is linked inalterably to his portrayal of Aalto as an aesthetic liberator whose independence and creativity were bulwarks against the "threat of rigidity" borne by standardization. Vincent Scully's use of Baker House to demonstrate a point of origin within the modern movement for the historical events leading to the work of Louis Kahn or the New Brutalists is an example of how opportunistic the treatment of canonic works can be. MIT's relatively sudden rekindling of enthusiasm for the dormitory, its deserving qualities notwithstanding, coincides with the institutional recognition of the way in which progressive design, in the past and today, can reflect well on the school. In each case those making claims for the significance of Baker House can be shown to have interests which those claims also service. Were we to rely on these competing claims as the basis for determining historical significance we would inherit their limited and biased view.

One would be hard-pressed to show that this kind of appropriation of meaning for the purposes of constructing a historical narrative leads to untruthfulness. It is, nevertheless, troubling that historical narration diminishes the artifact by yielding to it a meaning that only partially reflects its intrinsic value as architecture. We have seen this in the way that Baker House lost its historical identity as a building with regional associations in Giedion's text when the author committed himself to codifying its role as the marker of continuity between the first and second generations of the modern movement. We also see it in Robert Venturi's claim that Baker House was a fragment that was rooted in an urban context, an interpretation that disregards the building's powerful formal integrity. Estimations of value based on extrinsic, historical, or associational significance seem invariably to cause this kind of loss of depth in our interpretation of buildings.

Yet Baker House is instructive in this regard as well. The dormitory continues to foment a desire for close observation and rewards viewers for the time they spend with it by disclosing additional qualities of space, form, and surface. Students, alumni, visitors to the building from outside the MIT community, architects and non-architects, all comment positively on its siting and shape. The persistence with which we find critics and historians returning to Baker House as an example of this or that particularity of history is itself reassuring, since it suggests that the building retains its ability to stimulate the individuals who witness it even though their attentions may be focused elsewhere. Despite the role of the building as a historical touchstone, our strong reactions to Baker House's sculptural forms, its robust material features, and its idiosyncratic plan suggest that it is possible for the building to outperform its historical persona.

Could we suppose that the significance of Baker House lies in its ability to attract our attention, compel us to engage it as a physical object, and, subsequently, to write our histories around it? By its presence and entrancing physicality, Baker House challenges the intellectual abstractions with which we support the thesis of its historical significance. In a moment when we seem to be able to muster so little conviction in the capacity of things to inspire a collective sense of their unmediated value, recognition of this quality is no faint praise.

1 Survey histories on modern architecture, American architecture, and academic buildings in which Baker House is mentioned are identified in the sections that follow. Among regional and local histories in which the dormitory is described or illustrated, consider G. E. Kidder Smith, *The Architecture of the United States*, vol. 1, *New England and the Mid-Atlantic States* (Garden City, N.Y.: Doubleday, 1981), 264–65 (with illustration); and Boston Society of Architects, *Architecture Boston* (Barre, Mass.: Barre, 1976), 170–71 (with illustration). Books on architectural compositions specifically addressed to architecture students that use Baker House as a subject of analysis include Francis Ching, *Architecture, Form, Space, and Order* (New York: Van Nostrand, 1979), 223 (with plan); and Roger Clark and Michael Pause, *Precedents in Architecture* (1985; New York: Van Nostrand, 1996), 197 (with plan). Figure 1 in the Baker House Photo Essay in the present volume appears both in Spiro Kostof, *A History of Architecture* (New York: Oxford University Press, 1985), and in Demetri Porphyrios, *Sources of Modern Eclecticism: Studies on Alvar Aalto* (London: Academy Editions, 1982).

2 This has been true since the building was first constructed. In his short account of the travels of architecture students from Texas A&M University in 1949, Max Levy describes "field trips" throughout the Midwest and Northeast. Their first stop in the Boston area was at MIT, where, after meeting William W. Wurster, dean of architecture, the group was invited to spend the night in the Baker House dormitory even before the building was completed. "The building, which famously looks up and down the Charles River rather than at it, offered the students the unexpected opportunity of actually living in modernism for a few days." Max Levy, *Chasing the Modernist Rainbow* (College Station, Tex.: Texas Architect Press, 2000), 29–30.

3 Sigfried Giedion, *Space, Time and Architecture*, 5th ed. (Cambridge, Mass.: Harvard Univ. Press, 1967), 637. All subsequent references are to the 1967 edition unless otherwise noted.

4 Giedion, *Space, Time and Architecture*, 18. "Constituent facts are those tendencies which, when they are suppressed, inevitably reappear. Their recurrence makes us aware that these are elements which, all together, are producing a new tradition. Constituent facts in architecture, for example, are the undulation of the wall, the juxtaposition of nature and the human dwelling, the open ground plan."

5 Giedion, *Space, Time and Architecture*, 18.

6 Having been a student in the Visual and Environmental Studies Program at Harvard College in the late 1970s, I can attest to the difficulties which we, as students, had in gaining access to the Carpenter Center for the Visual Arts for use as a studio environment.

7 For descriptions of Aalto's work that make reference to the unfolding experience of the visitor to an Aalto building, see Kostof, *History of Architecture*, 732; Kenneth Frampton, *Modern Architecture: A Critical History* (New York: Oxford Univ. Press, 1980), 200; and William Curtis, "Modernism, Nature, Tradition: Aalto's Mythical Landscapes," in *Alvar Aalto in Seven Buildings/Alvar Aalto in sieben Bauwerken*, ed. Tino Tuomi and others (Helsinki: Museum of Finnish Architecture, 1998), 132.

8 The "English Observer" may have been Mary Jaqueline Tyrwhitt (1905–1983), the distinguished, South African–born, British town planner and town-planning educator. Tyrwhitt met Giedion around 1947 through her association with the Congrès Internationaux d'Architecture Moderne and would become his translator and editor. She also traveled and provided images to Giedion for his publications. The collection of her images dating from between 1950 and 1957 intended for Giedion's use in *Space, Time and Architecture* as well as *Architecture You and Me: The Diary of a Development* (Cambridge, Mass: Harvard Univ. Press, 1958) is part of the Tyrwhitt collection at the Royal Institute of British Architects (RIBA) archive. Tyrwhitt held a teaching position at the New School of Social Research in New York City starting in 1948, so she was in a position to travel to see Baker House, which was finished in 1949. It is known that Tyrwhitt was in New England in 1949, carrying out research on soil conservation at the farm of Walter Hadala in Adams, Mass. See "Tyrwhitt, Jaqueline, 1905–1983" (British Architectural Library at the RIBA archive, Acc. M98 and M150). For the collection of images intended for use in the Giedion publications, see RIBA Archive Record Control Number P005203, P005151. For a synopsis of Tyrwhitt's life and work see Catharine Huws Nagashima, "M. J. Tyrwhitt: Annotated Curriculum Vitae," *Ekistics* 314/315 (Sept.–Oct. and Nov.–Dec. 1985): 403–7.

9 Sigfried Giedion, *Space, Time and Architecture*, 2nd ed. (Cambridge, Mass.: Harvard Univ. Press, 1952), 472

10 Stanford Anderson, "Aalto and 'Methodical Accommodation to Circumstance,'" in *Alvar Aalto in Seven Buildings*, ed. Timo Tuomi (Helsinki, Museum of Finnish Architecture, 1998) 143.

11 Joseph Tainter and G. John Lucas, "Epistemology of the Significance Concept," *American Antiquity*, 48/4 (Oct. 1983): 707–19.

12 See, for example, Daniel Bluestone, "Preservation and Renewal in Post–World War II Chicago," *Journal of Architectural Education*, 47/4 (May 1994): 210.

13 Giedion, *Space, Time and Architecture*, 618–19.

14 Giedion, *Space, Time and Architecture*, 3rd ed. (Cambridge, Mass.: Harvard Univ. Press, 1959), 636–40.

15 See for example, Giedion, *Space, Time and Architecture*, liv. See also Alan Colquhoun, "Rationalism: A Philosophical Concept in Architecture," (1987) reprinted in Alan Colquhoun, *Modernity and the Classical Tradition: Architectural Essays 1980–1987* (Cambridge, Mass.: MIT Press, 1989), 84; and Kostof, *History of Architecture*, 732.

16 Giedion, *Space, Time and Architecture*, 640.

17 In the fifth edition of *Space, Time and Architecture*, Giedion described Aalto as an integrator of the "rational geometric" and "organic" sides of the modern movement. Aalto's work resolved an epochal confrontation of opposites visible in the early work of Le Corbusier but not fully resolved until the 1960s in the work of Aalto and late Le Corbusier. Giedion, *Space, Time and Architecture*, liv–lv.

18 Written in 1943 and published in Giedion, *Architecture You and Me: The Diary of a Development* (Cambridge, Mass: Harvard University Press, 1958), 48-52.

19 Kenneth Frampton has described the task as forging a connection between "the abstract forms of modern art and the traditional representative forms of collective memory." Frampton, "Giedion in America: Reflections in a Mirror," *Architectural Design* 51, no. 6/7 (1981): 50.

20 Giedion, *Space, Time and Architecture*, 640.

21 Giedion, *Space, Time and Architecture* (2nd ed), 472.

22 Giedion, *Space, Time and Architecture*, 637.

23 As Stanford Anderson has pointed out, illustrations of Aalto's work grew to 9 percent of the total volume of illustrated works in the final editions of *Space, Time and Architecture*. These forty-nine pages eclipsed the page totals of sections on any other architect with the exception of Le Corbusier. Giedion, *Space, Time and Architecture*, 618–67.

24 On Pevsner's critique of Aalto's work, see Kostof, *History of Architecture*, 732. His reference to Baker House as an example of the "internationalism" of the "style of the twentieth century" first appears in the seventh edition of Nikolaus Pevsner, *An Outline of European Architecture* (London: Penguin, 1963), 421.

25 Letter from Frank Lloyd Wright to Joseph Samona [Giuseppe Samonà], 20 March 1952; reprinted in Bruce Brooks Pfeiffer, *Letters to Architects: Frank Lloyd Wright* (Fresno, Calif.: California State Univ. Press, 1984), 191.

26 William Jordy, *The Impact of European Modernism in the Mid-twentieth Century* (New York: Oxford Univ. Press, 1972), 188, 372.

27 Henry-Russell Hitchcock, *Architecture: Nineteenth and Twentieth Centuries* (New York: Penguin, 1977), 579–80.

28 Frampton, *Modern Architecture,* 200.

29 John Burchard and Albert Bush-Brown, *The Architecture of America: A Social and Cultural History* (Cambridge, Mass.: MIT Press, 1961), 483.

30 Marcus Whiffen and Frederick Koeper, *American Architecture: 1860–1976* (Cambridge, Mass.: MIT Press, 1983), 343; David Handlin, *American Architecture* (New York: Thames & Hudson, 1985), 255.

31 Reyner Banham, *Theory and Design in the First Machine Age* (London: Architectural Press, 1960); Banham, *The New Brutalism: Ethic or Aesthetic?* (New York: Reinhold, 1966): 14, 47, 75. Two years after the publication of *Theory and Design,* Banham affirmed Aalto's historical role as a "Master" of the modern movement and "the quiet man of the Big Four" alongside Ludwig Mies van der Rohe, Le Corbusier and Walter Gropius. See Banham, *Guide to Modern Architecture* (London: Architectural Press, 1962): 126.

32 Vincent Scully, *American Architecture and Urbanism* (New York: Praeger, 1969), 209–10.

33 Robert Venturi, *Complexity and Contradiction in Architecture* (New York: Museum of Modern Art, 1966), 18.

34 Venturi, *Complexity and Contradiction,* 86.

35 Demetri Porphyrios, *Sources of Modern Eclecticism* (London, Academy Editions), 2, 93.

36 Kostof, *History of Architecture,* 730. The image of Baker House used by Kostof is the same as that which appears in Porphyrios's *Sources of Modern Eclecticism.*

37 A bibliographic search in the Avery Library Architecture Catalogue at Columbia University for titles in which Aalto's name appears revealed over eighty different book citations, twenty-one of which were published between 1995 and 2005.

38 See *Wikipedia,* s.v. "Modern architecture," http://en.wikipedia.org/wiki/Modern_architecture (18 July 2011).

39 During his first academic visit to MIT, Aalto received support from the Rockefeller Foundation to carry out studies of postwar relief housing. He was also a personal friend of William W. Wurster, dean of architecture, at the time the Baker House commission presented itself.

40 Quoted in "Baker House at Fifty: Renewing the Commitment," a pamphlet printed by MIT on the occasion of the reopening of the building after its renovation in 1998, n.p.

41 On the history of the pre–World War II competitions for modern academic campus buildings, see James Kornwolf, ed., *Modernism in America, 1937–1943* (Williamsburg, Va.: Muscarelle Museum of Art, 1985); and Paul Bentel, "The Re-examination of Modern Architecture: A Review of Modernism in America, 1937–43," *Places* 3/1 (Winter 1986): 43–53.

42 Paul Turner, *Campus: An American Planning Tradition* (Cambridge, Mass.: MIT Press, 1984), 260–61.

43 "Baker House at Fifty," n.p.

44 "Baker House at Fifty," n.p.

45 "Baker House at Fifty," n.p.

Poetry in Motion:
Aalto's Woodberry Poetry Room at Harvard

Kari Jormakka

While completing the work on Baker House at the Massachusetts Institute of Technology's campus in Cambridge in fall 1947, Alvar Aalto received a commission from Harvard University to design a poetry reading room for the undergraduate Lamont Library (**FIG. 1**).[1] A gift of Harry Harkness Flagler, the Woodberry Poetry Room had been established in May 1931 in honor of George Edward Woodberry, a poet and professor at Columbia University who graduated from Harvard in 1877.[2] Woodberry and Flagler wanted a space where one could hear the voice of modern poets, either live or animated by the motion of a turntable: from the beginning, the concept included not only recitals but also a phonograph archive. In 1933, the first recording made for the Poetry Room featured T. S. Eliot reading "Gerontion" and "The Hollow Men." Bearing the label Harvard Vocarium, the collection today includes tens of thousands of recordings by Robert Frost, William Carlos Williams, Ezra Pound, e. e. cummings, Vladimir Nabokov, Jorge Luis Borges, Dylan Thomas, Italo Calvino, Allen Ginsberg, John Ashbery, Sylvia Plath, Yevgeny Yevtushenko, Robert Pinsky, and others.[3]

Originally, the Poetry Room was situated on the third floor of Widener Library, but in 1948, with a second grant from Flagler, it was moved to better quarters in the new Lamont Library, overlooking the President's Garden. Responding to the spatial ambiguities in the library's design, Aalto created an intimate and unpretentious space with a number of custom-made elements, including a display case, bookshelves, and wall panels of elm and birch, as well as elements from earlier designs, including Artek's bentwood chairs and desks with bronze foot cups; elm partition screens, first installed in the Savoy Restaurant (1937) in Helsinki; and kultakello (golden bell) lighting fixtures out of brass, previously used in the library of Villa Mairea (1939) in Noormarkku, Finland (**FIG. 2**).[4]

For the listening stations that were central to the concept of the poetry archive, Aalto designed four polygonal wooden cabinets to hold record turntables and earphones, with the lids opening and closing over the records in a counterweighted vertical movement. In early plans, the audio units were hexagonal,

FIGURE 01 *Aalto, Woodberry Poetry Room, Lamont Library, Harvard University, Cambridge, Mass., 1948. Photo: 1979.*

FIGURE 02 *Aalto, Woodberry Poetry Room, Lamont Library. Photo: 1979.*

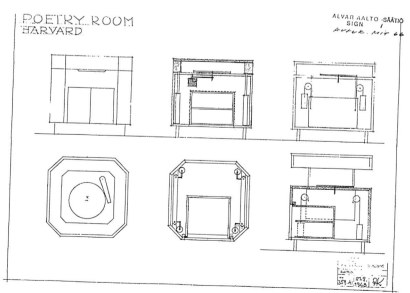

FIGURE 03 *Aalto, Woodberry Poetry Room, Lamont Library. Fabrication drawing for the phonograph consoles, Sept. 27, 1948.*

in order to fit in a minimal space when not in use. Later, however, it was determined that eight students should be able to use the units at the same time, and the cabinets assumed an octagonal shape, which in its symmetry and proportions recalls Nordic classicism **(FIGS. 3–4)**. There were also four smaller, rectangular listening posts with sliding tops for accessing the electronics within.

As Artek was unable to export the furnishings from Finland, all the products were delivered by Svenska Artek (Swedish Artek) in Hedemora, and marked on their lower surface "Aalto Design Made in Sweden." The curator of the Poetry Room, John L. Sweeney, pointed out that the dark-green upholstery fabric for the sofa and lounge chairs was "designed, woven, and

FIGURE 04 *Aalto, Woodberry Poetry Room, Lamont Library. Phonograph console, 1948.*

dyed in Sweden under the direction of the late Aino Aalto," Aalto's first wife.[5] He also described the octagonal phonograph listening stations as "an interesting example . . . of American–Swedish cooperation," as the cabinets of Swedish elm housed sophisticated American electronic equipment.[6] In addition to the furnishings of the Poetry Room, Artek also shipped a hundred or so Aalto chairs and tables for Lamont Library's main reading room.[7]

Harvard records indicate that the work on the Poetry Room was sufficiently far along to make possible a preliminary cost estimate on 3 December 1947.[8] In October 1948, receiving the news of the illness of his wife, Aino, Aalto returned to Finland. Completed—like Baker House—in Aalto's absence, the Woodberry Poetry Room was opened either in January or February of 1949.[9]

Lamont Library

When Aalto received the commission, the design of Lamont Library was in its final stages: the architects of the building, Coolidge, Shepley, Bulfinch & Abbott, completed their working drawings in March 1948.[10] Since major changes to the structure were precluded, Aalto's sketches for the Poetry Room never go beyond the boundaries of the room and do not deal with issues of construction beyond the cabinetry and millwork details for his installations.

Situated at the corner of Quincy Street and Massachusetts Avenue, Lamont Library was the first modern structure in Harvard Yard, and it represents a definitive break with precedent both for the university and for its designers. Coolidge, Shepley, Bulfinch & Abbott and earlier iterations of the firm had been responsible for defining the present ambience of Harvard more than any other architects.[11] Looking toward Harvard from the Boston side of the Charles River, one sees an almost solid wall of their designs in neo-Georgian brick, including seven dormitories (or River Houses) from the 1920s and 1930s, as well as the Indoor Athletic Building (1931) and, in the distance, the spire of the Memorial Church (1933) in the College Yard.[12] Closer to Lamont Library, the firm also built the Fogg Museum (1927). Historians have praised "the neo-Georgian genius of Charles Coolidge," in particular the freedom in the manipulation of historic motifs that characterizes his office's best work.[13]

In the thirties, paradoxically, the senior partner Henry Richardson Shepley became an early patron of modern architecture in the Boston area. When Walter Gropius first came to Harvard in 1937, it was Shepley who brought him together with the Storrow family to obtain the plot of land for the émigré to build his house in Lincoln, Massachusetts. At around this time, Coolidge, Shepley, Bulfinch & Abbott started to add contemporary accents to work based on the New England building tradition. An example is the Hemenway Gymnasium in the North Yard on the Harvard campus (1937–39), next to H. H. Richardson's Austin Hall. The gymnasium design is characterized by simple massing, regular fenestration, and the lack of ornamentation, save for a simplified Georgian lantern.[14] However, the use of waterstruck brick, typical of New England, gives the building a quasi-ornamental, tactile concreteness quite unlike much of modern architecture and anticipates similar brickwork in Aalto's Baker House (1947–49). Incidentally, Perry, Shaw & Hepburn, the Boston office that collaborated with Aalto on MIT's Baker House, was to build the last neo-Georgian building on the Harvard campus, Houghton Library, in 1941; six years later, Lamont opened Harvard's gates to modernism.[15]

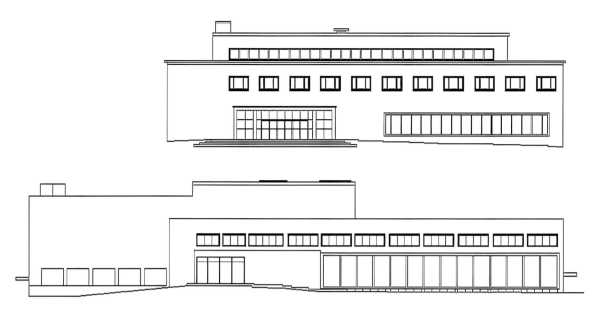

FIGURE 05 *Coolidge, Shepley, Bulfinch & Abbott. Lamont Library, 1948. Main elevation (top). Aalto, Viipuri Library, 1935. Main elevation, (bottom).*

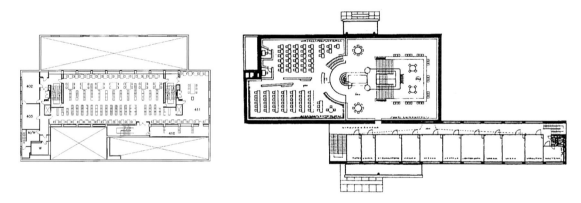

FIGURE 06 *Coolidge, Shepley, Bulfinch & Abbott, Lamont Library, 1948. Plan (left). Aalto, Viipuri Library, 1935. Plan (right).*

As David N. Fixler has observed, the design of Lamont Library is "an understated though demonstrably contemporary response to its brick Georgian context that also takes considerable cues in massing and detail from Aalto's own 1932 library for Viipuri, Finland (now Vyborg, Russia), the first great library of the modern movement."[16] Completed in 1935, the Viipuri Library features several technological and aesthetic innovations, including an ingenious air-circulation system, an idiosyncratic acoustic ceiling in the auditorium, and skylights that fill the library proper with shadowless light. However, these are not the features that one finds in Lamont Library. Rather, the similarities are to be sought in elevation, plan and section.

In both cases, the main entrance is situated asymmetrically to the left-hand side and pulled out to make a horizontal volume (FIG. 5). It is balanced on the other side of the facade by a continuous band of full-height windows. On the floor above, these modernist devices are juxtaposed with a series of punched windows.[17] Moreover, both plans can be seen as three-bar schemes.[18] In Viipuri, the tripartite organization is shown by the exterior inflections that correspond to the surrounding streets, while in the interior, two bars merge to make the main library space.[19] At Harvard's Lamont Library, the tripartite arrangement can be seen in the interior, while the exterior suggests a composition with two volumes (FIG. 6).[20] Finally, both buildings use complex sections to organize the program. In Lamont Library, the open book stacks are placed in the central zone, surrounded by double-height spaces. In Viipuri, the sectional complexities relate primarily to circulation.

Viipuri Library

Aalto's library design may be best analyzed in terms of Paul Frankl's architectural theory which claims that "spatial form is crystallized around center points and center lines (vertical, horizontal, diagonal) which, in a schematic but concentrated way, indicate the prevailing movement."[21] To illustrate his point, Frankl contrasts the "series" design scheme with that of the "group" in terms of how they relate to movement. An example of the former is a Gothic cathedral, the linearity of which draws the visitor to a distant goal, to the choir and beyond. The opposite, the group, is exemplified by Renaissance centralized churches that aspire to a perfect, serene symmetry. Arguing that such symmetry is impenetrable since any opening would create an imbalance, Frankl complained. "We are supposed, as if by magic, to arrive with one bound at this central point and to experience there the unique quiet, the secluded, serene independence that seems to be realized in such geometrical formations."[22] Frankl is obviously right— but only if one remains on one plane.

While Viipuri's spatial organization is asymmetrical as opposed to centralized, Aalto does establish a center point which resonates with another symmetrical Renaissance typology, that of the palazzo with a central cortile. In Viipuri, the "cortile" is formed by the sunken reading room surrounded by book stacks and the librarian's desk at a higher level.[23] In its symmetrical centrality, the lending office rehearses some themes of Erik Gunnar Asplund's Stockholm Public Library (1920–28).[24] However, instead of Asplund's monumental staircase, which drives a wedge into the rotunda, thus challenging its formal purity, Aalto engages in a complex gambit of centering through changes in level and orientation. From the Viipuri Library's generously dimensioned and brightly lit foyer one walks up a wide staircase that leads to a windowless, dark, and low vestibule. Here, one has a choice: either one takes a left and, passing the control desk, enters the reading room on the same level, or one turns right and goes up a few steps to emerge, miraculously, in the middle of the palazzo

configuration of the reference and reading room at mid-level, with book stacks on the higher level. Here, the spatial "group" of Frankl is no longer impenetrable but, by virtue of the section, as dynamic as the "series."

Not only in the entry sequence but time and again in the building, a center (or a central axis) is set up only to be broken in the next step. Richard Weston explains, "Aalto drove an axis through the two blocks: at one end the main entrance was located in a projecting vestibule, while at the other was a smaller projection for the separate entrance to the children's library." He goes on to point out that "the main reading room at ground level is reached around a half-cylinder, which forms an apse-like balcony for the library above and lies on the cross axis along which the stairs, stacks and desks are disposed. The presence of these two axes, and the symmetry of the library space, are surprising in what initially appears to be a 'free' volumetric organization."[25] What we should not forget, however, is that the "axis" from the main entrance to the vestibule of the children's library, as discovered by Weston in the plan, can never be experienced in the real building, as the two entries are not connected physically or visually (FIG. 7). Similar exercises with virtual axes and suggested symmetries can be found in Lamont Library as well, both in Coolidge, Shepley, Bulfinch & Abbott's plan for the building and Aalto's design for the Poetry Room.

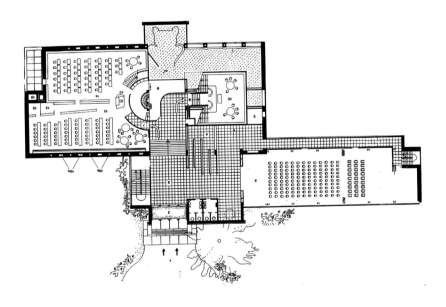

FIGURE 07 *Aalto, Viipuri Library, 1935. Plan.*

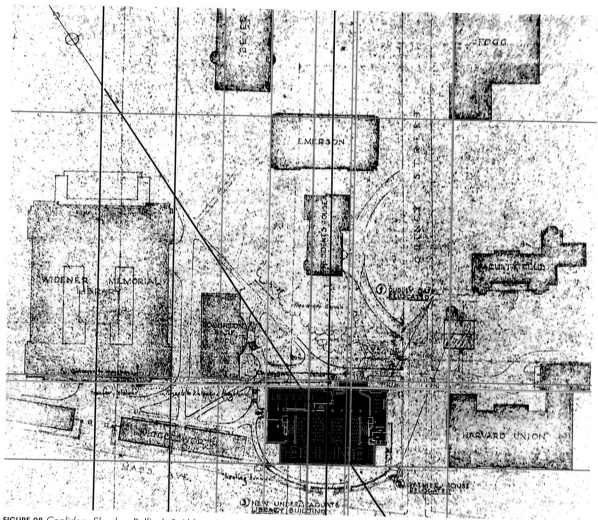

FIGURE 08 *Coolidge, Shepley, Bulfinch & Abbott, Lamont Library, 1948. Site plan with part of Harvard Yard. Author's overlay of axes.*

Shifting Centers

In addition to referencing Aalto's Viipuri design, Lamont Library reacts to its site, both to the edges of surrounding buildings and to their central axes. The southern facade facing Massachusetts Avenue continues the edge determined by Barker Center, while the setback that defines the volume of the reading room has the same dimension as Wigglesworth Hall, the neighboring building to the west. The northern facade is positioned on the same line as the back facade of Widener Library, and the southern end of Houghton Library sets the depth of Lamont's portico. Coolidge, Shepley, Bulfinch & Abbott positioned the western wall of its building so that Houghton is equidistant from Lamont and Widener.

While Harvard's yards are arranged as traditional quadrangles, this typology breaks down in the President's Garden. From the axial order of the yard, as marked by Widener and the Memorial Church, a diagonal path leads to Lamont through a transitional space with Houghton as the center. Finally, Loeb House (formerly President's House) appears as a figural solid in the center of the garden, almost aligning with the central axis of Lamont. The entrance to the library, however, lies still further to the east **(FIG. 8)**.

Once inside the building, the game of shifting centers continues, but the axial displacements follow in the opposite direction, to the west. The first central axis is defined by the symmetrical entry; once one reaches the lobby, a new center, slightly to the west of the first one, presents itself as the corridor that allows one to view the entire volume of the library. This apparent central axis (that incidentally aligns with the eastern edge of the President's House) is mirrored on the western side of the building. This symmetry means that the real center of the building is at the central axis of the stacks area, to which the visitor is drawn in order to reach the main stair. However, even this central axis is unstable: while the back of the building respects this center, the front volume is stretched slightly to the west in order to establish Houghton's position as equidistant from Widener and Lamont Libraries. The stair supports the central axes moving to the right by defining yet another central axis at the landing on the fourth level (**FIG. 9**).

This constant re-centering does not extend to Coolidge, Shepley, Bulfinch & Abbott's version of the Poetry Room, though. In the original design, the room had occupied the entire corner in an L-configuration, echoing the plan of the entry level beneath.[26] The grid that governs the rest of the library was continued to the corner, with bookshelves dividing the space into equal niches around a central axis marked originally by a window with neo-Georgian detailing. The original entrance picked up the axis of the right-hand corridor of the stacks area, also aligning with a window. In this design, the listening rooms were placed in the area defined by the central stair in order to maintain clear edges (**FIG. 10**).

With his intervention, Aalto breaks this static organization and continues the original plan's play with axes, centers, and symmetries (**FIG. 11**). He reconfirms the axis, as indicated by the special window, by positioning the librarian's desk and an entry to the next space, the Farnsworth Reading Room, on the line that is situated exactly in the middle of the room.[27] Perpendicular to this axis, he defines another axis of symmetry by extending the space to the area originally occupied by the listening rooms. Instead of being closed inside solitary cubicles, the students would now listen to the poetry recitals in a collective setting with mobile phonographs. The space left over is occupied by the curator's office. While in Coolidge, Shepley, Bulfinch & Abbott's original, unbuilt design the axis was terminated by a bay window on the western facade of Lamont Library, Aalto's perpendicular axis gestures toward a bay window on the southern facade of the President's House.

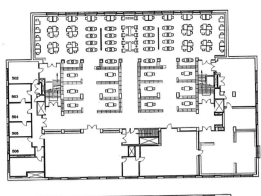
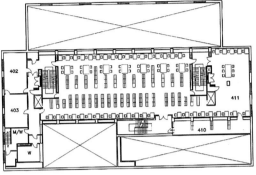
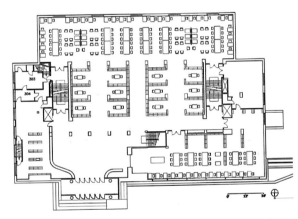

FIGURE 09 *Coolidge, Shepley, Bulfinch & Abbott, Lamont Library. Plans of levels 3, 4, and 5.*

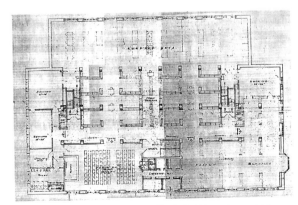

FIGURE 10 *Coolidge, Shepley, Bulfinch & Abbott, Lamont Library. Plan including a poetry reading room.*

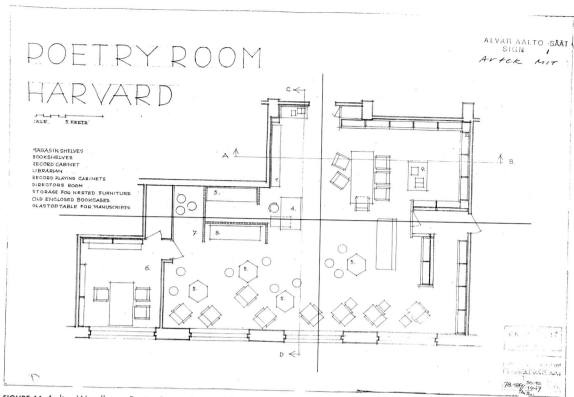

FIGURE 11 *Aalto, Woodberry Poetry Room, Lamont Library. Plan, 30 Oct. 1947. Author's overlay of symmetry axes.*

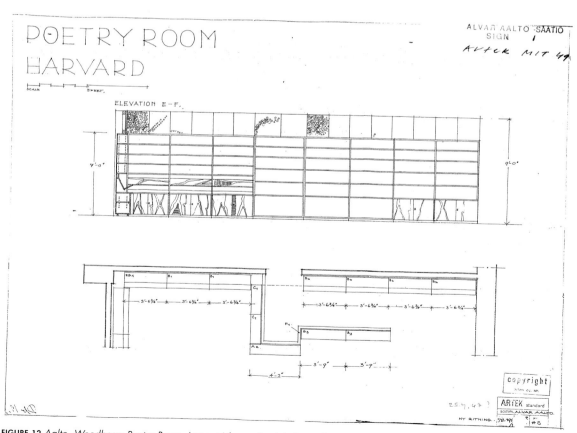

FIGURE 12 *Aalto, Woodberry Poetry Room, Lamont Library. Bookshelves, plan and elevation, 28 April 1948.*

The resulting organization corresponds to two central axes but the space is experienced as irregular. Moreover, Aalto positions the shelves in an echelon, a device he had applied at a large scale in two unrealized projects, one for an art museum in Tallinn, Estonia (1937), the other for a mining museum at the Johnson Institute in Avesta, Sweden (1944).[28] In these designs, the galleries are separated by parallel walls staggered in a way that maintains the orthogonal grid of the plan while tracing a diagonal trajectory through the space.

In the back of the room, the bookshelf meanders, creating a comfortable corner with the display table as a center. The table can also be seen as a suggestion of a further step in the echelon that opens up to the light from the windows. In the original design, in order to enhance the perspective effect of this organization, Aalto gives the shelves in the front different dimensions from the standard ones. Thus, the piece in the front has a width of 4 feet and 2 inches, while the next row has two shelves of the width of 3 feet and 9 inches, and the furthermost row has four shelves of the width of 3 feet and 6 3/4 inches.[29] The echelon has the additional advantage of hiding a door to the Farnsworth Room, creating an effect of surprise and beckoning the visitor to explore the adjoining space (FIG. 12).

The echelon is repeated in different scales and orientations all over the plan in order to reduce the formality of the room. For example, Aalto destabilizes the symmetry of the entrance by pushing the wall on one side to the exterior corridor and on the other side pulling it in. The regularity of the window wall is counteracted by the furniture arranged in a diagonal in a kind of landscape, with ceiling lamps suggesting Aalto's hallmark "forest space."[30] The apparently random placing of lighting fixtures contributes to the relaxed atmosphere and invites the patrons to rearrange the chairs, side tables, and phonograph consoles as they wish.[31] In its club ambience, with easy chairs and work desks, the room resembles the library at Villa Mairea.[32]

A Decayed House

The Poetry Room survived virtually unchanged for more than half a century, although at some time an extra shelf was added to the display of periodicals at the entrance, many of the desk chairs were replaced by generic ones, one of the unusual spherical lamps

FIGURE 13 Aalto, Woodberry Poetry Room, Lamont Library. After renovation in September 2006.

FIGURE 14 Aalto, Woodberry Poetry Room, Lamont Library, as refurnished in May 2007.

was lost, and one of the small audio units destroyed. In summer 2006, Harvard University had the room renovated. In the interest of meeting university norms and saving energy, the original lighting was replaced by brighter fixtures, which completely changed the domestic character of the space. This modification is particularly unfortunate for an Aalto design, since he always insisted that in a library, the primary consideration is light.[33] "A library can be well constructed and can be functional in a technical way even without the solving of this problem," he would argue, "but it is not humanly and architecturally complete unless it deals satisfactorily with the main human function in the building, that of reading a book."[34]

Only one spherical light fixture survived the renovation. All of the rectangular audio consoles are now gone, their place taken by a low bookshelf on the window wall. Out of four octagonal consoles, two remain, but they have been fitted with new countertops surfaced in plastic laminate and supported by original Aalto bentwood legs taken from desks previously in the main reading room.[35] At first, the couch and the eight armchairs were replaced by four anonymous lounge chairs in black leather, arranged around a coffee table (**FIG. 13**). Later, these were replaced with a set

of a couch and two armchairs, which better approximate the original furniture in both design and material (**FIG. 14**). In 2006, a listening station, an armchair, a stool, a floor lamp, and three other light fixtures were donated to the Busch-Reininger Museum at Harvard, while other pieces have been auctioned.

Most damaging of the changes is the rearrangement of the shelving. In the name of security and control, the echelon has been crippled: only a stump of the elegant design remains, shape without form, gesture without motion (**COMPARE FIGS. 1 AND 14**).[36] Today, instead of the witty repartee with which the Woodberry Poetry Room responded to Lamont Library's discourse on moving centers, there is silence.

1   Keyes D. Metcalf, director of the Harvard University Library from 1937 to 1955, conceived the idea of a library designed specifically for undergraduates and contacted Henry Shepley regarding this plan as early as 1938. At the end of World War II, through the donation of Thomas W. Lamont, Harvard class of 1892, the planning started.

2   Harry Harkness Flagler (1870–1952) was the only son of Henry Flagler, who together with John D. Rockefeller and three other partners founded Standard Oil in 1870. In 1894, Harry married Annie Louise Lamont, a daughter of the millionaire Charles A. Lamont.

3   For a complete list, see "Woodberry Poetry Room (Harvard College Library) poetry readings: Guide," last updated 23 March 2010, http://oasis.harvard.edu:10080/oasis/deliver/~hou00305.

4   *Kultakello*, designed in 1939, is still for sale as A330S in Artek's catalogue. It is a streamlined version of the original Savoy lamp, A330. The furniture company, Artek, was founded in 1935 by Aino and Alvar Aalto, Maire Gullichsen, and Nils-Gustav Hahl to promote and sell designs by the office.

5   From a letter dated 8 April 1949 from John L. Sweeney to Marshall W. S. Swan, quoted in Stanley Abercrombie, "Aalto's 1949 Poetry Room at Harvard," *Journal of the Society of Architectural Historians*, 38:2 (May 1979): 122. Aino Aalto died on 13 Jan. 1949. John L. [Lincoln] or "Jack" Sweeney was a scholar, art collector, poet, and the brother of the art critic and museum director James Johnson Sweeney, who was perhaps Aalto's closest personal friend in the United States. See Göran Schildt, *Alvar Aalto: The Decisive Years* (New York: Rizzoli, 1986), 171. For these reasons, one wonders if Jack Sweeney was the person at Harvard who brought up the name of Aalto as a possible architect for the Poetry Room.

6   The emphasis on Sweden is explained by the fact that Marshall W. S. Swan was the curator of the American Swedish Historical Museum in Philadelphia. See Abercrombie, "Aalto's 1949 Poetry Room at Harvard," 122.

7   Göran Schildt, *Alvar Aalto: The Complete Catalogue of Architecture, Design and Art* (New York: Rizzoli, 1994), 251, 253.

8   The earliest drawings for the project in the Alvar Aalto Archives in Helsinki are dated 15 Oct. 1947. The last drawings for the cabinets were signed 5 Feb. 1949. Most drawings were signed by Hans Slangus and Maija Heikinheimo, two assistants in Aalto's office.

In the following year, Aalto prepared drawings for acoustic panels above the bookshelves (4 March 1950) but they were never executed. New drawer unit designs are dated 10 Aug. 1959.

9   Most sources in Harvard's Houghton Library give the date as January, but Abercrombie argues that notices of the shipments of furniture and lighting fixtures indicate that the room could not have been completely furnished as planned until February, which is also what the drawings suggest. Records at Houghton mention various figures for the cost of outfitting the room, but the total seems to have been slightly less than $20,000, with Aalto's fee specified as $2,000. Moreover, Harvard archives contain a copy of a letter, dated 7 April 1949, in which Aalto requests that the rest of his fee be paid to Olav Hammarström, a young designer who had been brought to Boston in 1946 to assist Aalto on the design of Baker House. As this remaining sum amounts to $1,000, half of the total fee, it is fair to assume that Hammarström had a significant role in the later stages of the design. However, Abercrombie argues that in the earlier stages Aalto was personally in charge, and quotes a note dated 4 June 1948 from Sweeney to "Dear Alvar," asking

Aalto to consider eliminating a planned vitrine, if that "could be carried out without impairing" the design. Abercrombie points out that in the archives there are copies of several letters to Aalto, and a reference to a conference with him about the design as late as 19 Oct. 1948. It is difficult to determine Aino Aalto's role in the design of the Poetry Room, but the Aalto Archives include a complete list of furnishings, signed by her. Abercrombie, "Aalto's 1949 Poetry Room at Harvard," 121n2.

10   The first set of drawings is dated July 1946; in the plans of 17 July 1947, the design is close to the built version.

11   At this time, the partners were Charles Allerton Coolidge, Henry Richardson Shepley, Francis Vaughan Bulfinch, and Lewis B. Abbott, but the office can trace its roots to Henry Hobson Richardson. When Richardson died in 1886, a group of associates continued the practice under the name of Shepley, Rutan & Coolidge. From 1915 to 1924, the Boston office was called Coolidge & Shattuck; between 1924 and 1952, Coolidge, Shepley, Bulfinch & Abbott; after 1952, Shepley, Bulfinch, Richardson & Abbott. See J. D. Forbes, "Shepley, Bulfinch, Richardson & Abbott, Architects: An Introduction," *Journal of the Society of Architectural Historians*, 17: 3 (Autumn 1958): 19–31.

12   The River Houses by Coolidge, Shepley, Bulfinch & Abbott include Lowell House, topped by a copy of the Independence Hall tower; Eliot House, crowned by an approximation of an Asher Benjamin cupola; Dunster House, with a Georgian version of Tom Tower at Oxford; and Adams House, which incorporates older dormitories. The serpentine organization of Dunster House could be seen as setting a precedent for Aalto's Baker House.

13 Bainbridge Bunting, *Harvard: An Architectural History*, completed and ed. by Margaret Henderson Floyd (Cambridge, Mass.: Belknap Press of Harvard Univ. Press, 1985), 219.

14 In 1938, Coolidge, Shepley, Bulfinch & Abbott designed the B&B Chemical Lab on Memorial Drive, the first fully developed modern industrial building in Cambridge. Jean-Paul Carlhian of the Shepley firm designed Harvard's Allston Burr Hall in 1951, which featured Aalto-like "fan-shaped forms" in the lecture halls. (The building won the Harleston Parker Award in 1953 but was demolished in 1982 to make way for James Stirling's Arthur M. Sackler Museum.)

15 Despite its neo-Georgian exterior, Houghton Library used the latest climate control technology to protect the rare book collection. After Lamont, major European modernists were able to make their mark on Harvard: Walter Gropius and the Architects Collaborative with the Graduate Center in the North Yard (1948–52), Le Corbusier with the Carpenter Center for the Visual Arts (1961), José Luis Sert with Peabody Terrace (1963–65) and other buildings.

16 David N. Fixler, "Cambridge Modern, 1930–1970: One Architect's View" in Daphne Abeel, ed., *Cambridge in the Twentieth Century* (Cambridge, Mass.: Cambridge Historical Society, 2007), 58–79. In terms of facade material—red brick and limestone—Lamont connects to the campus tradition, and the projecting entrance with its columns in antis can be seen as a simplified, modernist variation of the monumental portico of Widener Library. In the plans from July 1946, the design was more traditional, with accentuated cornices, a portico with four columns, and a single Georgian window on the western facade. Otherwise, the fenestration is made of ribbon windows.

17 The northern facade of Lamont Library has a more vertical emphasis, reminiscent of Aalto's competition scheme for Viipuri (1927).

18 In Aalto's design, all the bars are of equal width, while in Coolidge, Shepley, Bulfinch & Abbott's library, the central bar is slightly wider than the flanking ones.

19 The long bar picks up on the approximate position and width of the Koulukatu street while the double-width volume of the library corresponds to the Suokatu street on the opposite side.

20 In Lamont, the first bar contains the entry and the café, the second the open stacks, and the third the study area.

21 Paul Frankl, *Principles of Architectural History: The Four Phases of Architectural Style, 1420–1900* (1914; Cambridge, Mass.: MIT Press, 1982), 157.

22 Frankl, *Principles of Architectural History*, 28.

23 The main stacks are in the basement.

24 Asplund's library was the major inspiration for Aalto's entry to the Viipuri Library competition (1927).

25 Richard Weston, *Alvar Aalto* (London: Phaidon, 1995), 64.

26 See the drawing dated 4 Nov. 1946, in the Aalto Archives.

27 Positioning the librarian at a point from which the entire space can be surveilled is a constant theme running through almost all of Aalto's library plans.

28 The foyer of the Viipuri Library includes a rudimentary version of the same principle, and later variations can be found in Aalto's designs for art museums in Aalborg, Denmark (1958), Baghdad (1958), and Shiraz, Iran (1969).

29 These dimensions are specified, for example, in a plan dated 28 April 1948 (Aalto Archive signum 78/198) In several earlier drawings, metric equivalents of the measurements are also given: 4 ft. 2 in. (127 cm), 3 ft. 9 in. (114.5 cm), and 3 ft. 6 3/4 in. (109 cm). Curiously, there are discrepancies here: while 4 ft. 2 in. does equal 127 cm, 3 ft. 9 in. is actually 114.3 cm and 3 ft. 6 3/4 in. is 108.3 cm. There is some reason to believe that the design was first determined in inches and only then translated into approximate metric dimensions for the Artek factory: the front bookshelf is 50 inches wide, the middle ones 45 inches and the back shelves 42¾ inches wide—which means that the width of the second shelf is 90 percent of the first, while the third one is 95 percent of the second, thereby creating the perspectival illusion of foreshortening. Moreover, the side shelves are 2 ft. 6 in. or 30 in. wide.

30 The concept of "forest space" does not appear in Aalto's own writings. As elaborated by Göran Schildt in his biography of Aalto and by Juhani Pallasmaa in many essays, "forest space" refers to a grid of vertical elements arranged in a rhythmical, irregular pattern. In the lobby, staircase, and living-room area of the Villa Mairea, for example, Aalto fuses structural columns and nonstructural ornamental poles into a continuity of vertical rhythms that resonates with the forest outside the building, merging interior spaces with the outdoors. See, e.g., Juhani Pallasmaa. "Image and Meaning," in *Alvar Aalto: Villa Mairea, 1938–39*, ed. Pallasmaa (Helsinki: Alvar Aalto Foundation/ Mairea Foundation, 1998), 70–125.

31 In his plans, Aalto shows several alternative arrangements for different events and activities.

32 Originally, in 1939, the library or study at Villa Mairea was separated from the living room by moveable bookcases and cabinets for storing works of art. In 1941, in order to provide a private workspace, the space was enlarged by one-third in the direction of the living room and the walls were fixed to the floor and extended to the ceiling. The resulting organization anticipates the Woodberry Poetry Room in that, in the new Mairea library, the entry lies on the central axis, and one first arrives in an asymmetrical space that takes a more regular shape as one proceeds toward the windows. The alteration plans of 13 Nov. 1941, are signed by Aino. See Renja Suominen-Kokkonen, "The Interior Design," in *Alvar Aalto*, ed. Pallasmaa, 112, 128–30.

33 Alvar Aalto, "Viipuri Library," *Alvar Aalto: Projects and Final Buildings,* ed. Elissa Aalto and Karl Fleig (Zurich: Les Editions d'Architecture Artemis, 1978), 1:48.

34 Alvar Aalto, "The Humanizing of Architecture," *Alvar Aalto in His Own Words*, ed. Göran Schildt (New York: Rizzoli, 1998), 104–5.

35 In order to save at least some of the octagonal consoles, the architects wrapped two of them with "aprons" so that they would provide table space for students' laptops. The legs on the aprons were designed as simple black cylinders to differentiate them from the original Aalto pieces. Nonetheless, Harvard decided to use bentwood legs from deaccessioned Artek desks.

36 Harvard feared that the likes of D. H. Lawrence and Gavin Ewart would lure unsuspecting freshmen into sordid trysts in this small, secluded alcove.

Alvar Aalto and the Edgar J. Kaufmann Conference Rooms

Matthew A. Postal

Visitors to the Edgar J. Kaufmann Conference Rooms enter an early 1960s office building and take the elevator to the top floor. Passing through the low-ceilinged vestibule, they come to a spacious reception hall, hung with brass lighting fixtures and furnished with chairs of birch and black leather. This luminous interior has a soft golden hue, in part due to the sunlight that filters through a grid of louvers, but also due to the generous use of lightly finished woods—ash and birch—silhouetted against angled walls of white plaster (FIG. 1). On the far side of the room is a wood sculpture. Constructed from long, flat pieces of laminated birch, this striking assemblage resembles a snapshot of a thickly forested landscape. Equally dramatic is the ceiling, gently rising in stages to a height of twenty-two feet.

Located in the headquarters of the Institute of International Education at 809 First Avenue (also known as United Nations Plaza), near Forty-Sixth Street, the conference rooms are Alvar Aalto's only extant commission in New York City. Adjoining the reception hall are smaller meeting rooms and an outdoor terrace, overlooking the headquarters of the United Nations, and across the East River, Queens. It was there, for the 1939 New York World's Fair (held at what is now Flushing Meadows Corona Park), that Aalto supervised the assembly of the Finland Pavilion inside the Hall of Nations. This structure was intended to be temporary and was demolished at the close of the fair in late 1940. Twenty-five years separate these interiors, a period when Aalto tried, but was unable, to build in New York, a city that many Europeans associated with the promise of the post-World War II era. Undamaged by war, it became home to the United Nations and many leading

architects pursued work there during this period, from Ludwig Mies van der Rohe and Marcel Breuer to Gio Ponti and Pier Luigi Nervi. Aalto's relationship with New York was long and complex, consummated only by the installation of the Kaufmann rooms, a project that raises issues about the challenge of exporting architectural designs, as well as Aalto's patronage in the United States.

Aalto and Edgar J. Kaufmann, Jr.

Aalto first traveled to the United States in October 1938. During the six-week trip he and his first wife, Aino Marsio Aalto, met Edgar J. Kaufmann, Jr., future patron of the conference rooms. Kaufmann was working as an unsalaried assistant to the curator John McAndrew in the Department of Architecture and Industrial Art at the Museum of Modern Art, where Aalto's work had been the subject of an exhibition during March and April 1938. Trained as an architect at Harvard University, McAndrew had reservations about the direction contemporary architecture was taking. Though he organized "The Bauhaus: 1918–38" (in collaboration with Walter and Ise Gropius and Herbert Bayer) in December 1938, McAndrew tended to favor lesser-known parallel developments, particularly aspects of the modern movement that were shaped by local traditions and materials found in nature. Aalto exemplified these ideals and the full breadth of his production was presented, with photographs, models, studies, and about fifty pieces of furniture. Kaufmann remembered: "McAndrew started the whole thing. He was filled with admiration for Alvar Aalto's Finnish

FIGURE 01 *Aalto, Edgar J. Kaufmann Conference Rooms, Institute for International Education, New York, 1963–64. View facing south, 2000.*

Pavilion at the Paris world's fair, 1937. Next year he organized an exhibition of Aalto's work. . . . His enthusiasm was catching, for Aalto's designs represented a breath of fresh air."[1] Born in 1910, Kaufmann was the only child of Liliane and Edgar Jonas Kaufmann. His family owned Kaufmann's Department Store, the most prominent retailer in Pittsburgh. Following high school, he pursued a somewhat unconventional education; rather than attending a prestigious American college or university, he studied at the Österreichisches Museum für Angewandte Kunst in Vienna during 1928–29, painting and typography in Florence with Victor Hammer from 1930 to 1933, and design at Taliesin in Wisconsin with Frank Lloyd Wright.[2] His stay at Taliesin was relatively brief, probably lasting only five months during late 1934 and 1935, but it became a defining period in Kaufmann's life. Not only was he introduced to Wright's aesthetic philosophy, but a visit from his father in

October 1934 led to the commission of Fallingwater (1934–37), the architect's most famous work. This association benefited Kaufmann immensely; setting in motion a sequence of events that would introduce him to McAndrew, who was among the earliest visitors to the house, and ultimately, to Aalto.

In conjunction with the New York fair, Aalto visited the United States twice, in March 1939 to supervise construction of the Finland Pavilion and in 1940 to "hold propaganda lectures and gather funds to aid Finland at war."[3] During the latter trip, which lasted seven months, he visited Kaufmann at Fallingwater twice, first during spring 1940, and later, for three weeks in August of that year.[4] The length of the second visit strongly suggests that a friendship had developed between the two men. Aalto returned for a brief time in late 1945 or early 1946 and in subsequent letters addressed Kaufmann as "Cher Edgar."[5]

Despite personal and professional contacts in New York, Aalto chose Cambridge, Massachusetts, as his base in the United States. He traveled to New York often, to speak about his work and promote sales of his furniture, but was unable to secure a commission of any lasting consequence. In 1947 he was asked to design a new facade for the Finnish Evangelical Lutheran Church in the Sunset Park section of Brooklyn. Veli Paatela, who worked in Aalto's office from 1946 to 1949, was responsible for the project. A front of plaster, brick, and limestone was proposed, but due to funding problems it was never executed. In addition, Aalto may have contributed to the design of a two-level restaurant in Finland House, sponsored by the Finnish Consulate, at 41 East Fiftieth Street in Manhattan.[6]

Kaufmann returned to Pittsburgh in 1939 to work in his family's department store but remained in steady contact with associates at MoMA. He accompanied "A New House by Frank Lloyd Wright" – the Fallingwater exhibition – as it toured, and contributed to McAndrew's *Guide to Modern Architecture, Northeast States* (1940). Following service in the U.S. Air Force Intelligence Office, he moved permanently to New York in 1946 and was appointed director of the Department of Industrial Design at the museum.

The most important exhibitions organized by Kaufmann were devoted to mass-produced consumer goods, particularly household products, including "One Hundred Useful Objects of Fine Design" (1948) and the "Good Design" series, staged during the early 1950s with the Merchandise Mart of Chicago. Related projects were devoted to the design of interiors, including "Modern Rooms of the Last Fifty Years." This 1947 exhibition, and the 1953 booklet that summarized its content, identified the characteristics that gave modern interiors a unique appeal.[7] Though several pieces of furniture by Aalto were illustrated in the booklet, Wright received the highest praise. Kaufmann called him the "dean of architectural design" and included more examples of his work than of any other architect.[8]

Despite significant achievements as a curator, Kaufmann's tenure at MoMA was overshadowed by Philip Johnson. The museum's architecture and industrial design departments merged by 1949, with Johnson as director and Kaufmann as research associate and consultant. This development allowed

Johnson's agenda to dominate and a feud developed between the two men.[9] Whereas Kaufmann could not forgive his colleague's fascist leanings during the late 1930s, Johnson did not share Kaufmann's strong interest in organic design and Wright's work. The impact of their curatorial activities is still contested, but there is no doubt that the glass-and-steel aesthetic favored by Johnson had a greater impact on architecture in midtown Manhattan, particularly in the blocks between Kaufmann's East Fifty-Second Street apartment and his office at the museum.

Kaufmann resigned from MoMA in 1955—his departure coinciding with his father's death in April 1955. He had threatened to leave many times and having done so was free to pursue independent scholarship, as well as philanthropic activities. Over the next decade, he used his wealth and the assets of the Edgar J. Kaufmann Charitable Foundation to promote excellence in design. Established by his father following the sale of the department store in 1949, the foundation primarily supported causes in the Pittsburgh area. After 1955, however, a greater emphasis was placed on international issues and the arts.[10] Gifts were made to the Chicago Art Institute, the Metropolitan Museum of Art, and Columbia University. Kaufmann also began to prepare Fallingwater for its eventual donation to the Western Pennsylvania Conservancy in 1963. He furnished the interiors with objects he exhibited at MoMA, including a Savoy Vase by Aalto, and asked Wright to design a gatehouse for the grounds. It was the first time Kaufmann had commissioned a work of architecture and it was only because of a disagreement over Wright's fee that the project was never executed.[11]

The Commission

Kaufmann's contact with the Institute of International Education began around 1958 when he wrote the introduction to *Fulbright Designers*, the catalogue for an exhibition organized by the Museum of Contemporary Crafts (now the Museum of Arts and Design) in New York. Founded in 1919 to promote peace through international scholarly exchange, since 1946 the institute had administered the Fulbright Program for the U.S. Department of State, providing travel grants to foreign and American students.[12] Kaufmann expanded his involvement during 1959 when he established the Kaufmann International Design Award. Administered by the institute, it recognized general rather than specific contributions to the field, including the work of Charles Eames and Ray Eames, Walter Gropius, the Olivetti Corporation, and a trio of critics—Lewis Mumford, Charles Alexander, and Ada Louise Huxtable.

In 1960, the institute launched a campaign to raise $4.5 million to construct a headquarters that would function as a "center for international exchange."[13] For about a decade the organization had been located in a late-nineteenth-century mansion at the corner of Fifth Avenue and Sixty-Seventh Street. For its new location, a large site across from the public entrance to the United Nations was acquired and Harrison, Abramovitz & Harris, who worked on many buildings in the immediate area, including the United Nations, were hired as architects.

To help raise funds for construction, a lavish prospectus was published, illustrating possible interior configurations. Various spaces were loosely rendered in a conventional modern style—rectangular rooms with low ceilings and walls of glass or marble. On the top floor, a covered terrace was planned. Kaufmann recalled: "The plans were approved for a small and aggressively routine building which failed to represent the character or the scope of the Institute's ideals. I was asked to make a contribution to the building funds through the charity established by the residual estate of my father. I'd been working with the Institute . . . and suggested it might be appropriate to invite a foreign designer to create a top-level conference suite."[14] Aalto was the logical candidate to design these rooms. Not only was he "a foreign designer," but he enjoyed an international reputation and had developed a personal relationship with the building's architect, Wallace K. Harrison, in collaborating on a series of preliminary sketches for the Metropolitan Opera House at Lincoln Center during a ten-day visit to New York in 1956.[15] Kaufmann and Aalto had several face-to-face meetings to discuss the Institute of International Education commission, starting at Fallingwater in June 1961.[16] They also met in Venice during September of that year, and by late November 1961 Aalto's participation had been approved by Kenneth Holland, president of the Institute.

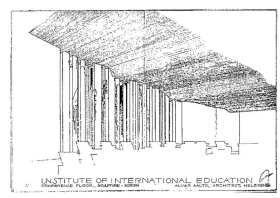

FIGURE 02 *Aalto, Edgar J. Kaufmann Conference Rooms. Early rendering of "sculpture screen."*

For Kaufmann, the commission served a dual purpose. It would be, in name, a memorial to his father, but it would also provide a permanent symbol of his contributions to mid-twentieth-century architecture and design. This second goal had been especially evident in his evolving relationship with Wright. Not only had he been his student and publicist, but during his later years, he depicted himself as a patron and collaborator, promoting the view, that he, rather than his father, had been responsible for the creation of Fallingwater.[17]

Aalto, in effect, became a surrogate for Wright, who had died in 1959. Their intersecting careers and sympathetic design philosophies must have been immediately clear to Kaufmann. During early 1938, when Kaufmann was working for McAndrew, Wright and Aalto were featured in consecutive exhibitions at MoMA. When Kaufmann visited the Finland Pavilion at the New York World's Fair the following year, he was accompanied by Wright, who reportedly declared Aalto a "genius." Aalto reciprocated the compliment, writing a tribute to his American colleague for MoMA's 1940–41 exhibition, "Frank Lloyd Wright, American Architect." This unpublished essay, titled "My Frank Lloyd Wright," praised the human character of the architect's work, highlighting their mutual objections to functionalism and the idea of a modern style without borders.[18]

Wright had also designed an intimate private office for Edgar J. Kaufmann, Sr. Completed in 1938, it would be the architect's only realized project in Pittsburgh. The room features a geometric relief made of cypress panels set over a large conference table, as well as several Wright-designed chairs. Dismantled at the time of the

FIGURE 03 *Aalto, Edgar J. Kaufmann Conference Rooms. Early model of south wall and ceiling.*

elder Kaufmann's death, it was reinstalled in the First National Bank Building in Pittsburgh and served as the office of the Kaufmann Foundation until 1963.[19] Literally and figuratively, the wood-paneled office provided a starting point for Aalto's design. Kaufmann recalled: "When I phoned Aalto he was at first not clear what was wanted, but when he said, would it be like the office Frank Lloyd Wright created for your father inside the existing shell of his business building? When I answered yes, but rather larger, he agreed to think it over. He could build an entire environment, limited only by the dimensions and exposure of the IIE Building."[20] Aalto's initial design confirmed the importance of this early conversation. He later described the proposed character of the reception hall as "based on the idea of having rich wooden surfaces, including the floor, ceilings and walls. Our intention was for every room to have the character of high quality like a stringed instrument."[21]

For Aalto, the commission held two attractions: the opportunity to work with an old friend, Kaufmann, and its location in Manhattan, opposite the recently completed United Nations complex. Because of Finland's position during the Second World War, Aalto was disqualified from participating in the design of the complex. Members of the Board of Design included Harrison, who served as director of planning, as well as Le Corbusier, representing France, and Oscar Niemeyer, representing Brazil. More meaningful to Aalto, perhaps, was the involvement of several Scandinavian colleagues. The Conference Building, located beside the East River, included the chambers of the Economic and Social Council, designed by Sven Markelius of Sweden; the Trustee Council, by Finn Juhl of Denmark; and the Security Council, by Arnstein Arneberg of Norway. Aalto's biographer Göran Schildt maintained that Aalto was hurt by his exclusion and viewed the Kaufmann project as a "chance for revenge."[22]

Design and Construction

Aalto began work on the conference rooms at the end of 1961. His office was crowded with international projects and he accepted the commission with the proviso that all work would be done in Finland. Kaufmann and the institute agreed to this arrangement, believing it would reduce the cost to a level more acceptable than

FIGURE 04 *Aalto, Edgar J. Kaufmann Conference Rooms. Assembling the wood sculpture. Alvar Aalto studio participants not identified.*

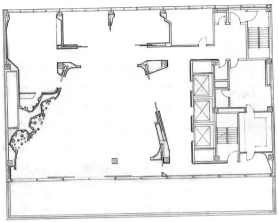

FIGURE 05A *Aalto, Edgar J. Kaufmann Conference Rooms. Plan, 1962.*

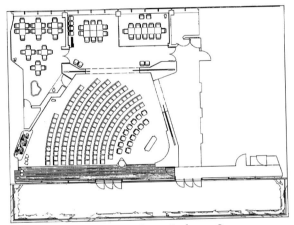

FIGURE 05B *Aalto, Edgar J. Kaufmann Conference Rooms. Plan, 1964.*

that of building the Finland Pavilion at the New York World's Fair. Moreover, the plainly designed structures that housed these interiors—the Hall of Nations at the fair, and now, the proposed institute headquarters—were designed in the office of the same architect, Wallace K. Harrison. A happy coincidence, the commission presented Aalto with challenges similar to those faced in 1939. It would be, in some ways, a nostalgic exercise for the architect, incorporating some of the ideas explored earlier in his career without direct re-creation.

A preliminary design was completed in mid-1962. Hans Christian Slangus, who had been associated with Aalto since 1945, oversaw the project. Sketches were delivered in March 1962, followed by a model in early October (**FIGS. 2–3**). All of the rooms were to be of irregular shape, including the vestibule, meeting rooms, and reception hall. The most memorable feature was

the reception hall's south wall, consisting of a series of wood-paneled coves, enlivened by groups of tree-like constructions. Despite an enthusiastic response from Kaufmann, two months later, in December 1962, Aalto modified his design. Though the overall plan was retained, it now had considerably less wood and fewer free-standing sculptural elements. These changes came as a shock to Kaufmann, who immediately telegrammed Aalto: "Cannot accept the latest revision. Regret. Believe Architecture More Important."[23]

A letter dated the same day addressed the issue more thoroughly. Kaufmann criticized the revisions on aesthetic and practical grounds, maintaining the increased use of plaster "will look cold, will give harsh acoustics to the smaller rooms, and will show dirt quickly."[24] Aalto's team defended the changes. A letter co-signed by Slangus and H. Mattson, Aalto's secretary, responded: "We wish to apologize for the confusion caused by our letter to you and Mr. [Michael] Harris. . . . We feel the difficulties arising from the fireproofing, possible damage in transit, and fitting on the site nearly rule out fabricating the wood in Finland."[25] Slangus did suggest that American-made panels could, if Kaufmann insisted, be substituted, but Aalto himself dismissed the idea, stating: "In my original sketch is a little bit too much wood, the whole thing getting too monotonous, without counter-point and cadence enough. . . . [It will be] simpler in construction but not less good in architecture."[26] Kaufmann eventually accepted the explanation and in May 1963 thanked Aalto, writing: "Were my father here to see your plans, I'm sure he would be immensely happy, and in terms of honoring his memory I feel an extra gratitude to you too."[27] Still, Kaufmann harbored mixed feelings about the modifications. In summer 1964, at about the time when the installation was set to begin, he cautioned Aalto: "If we can only be average, why bother you? Time and money will be wasted if we get only routine details. Please protect our hopes!"[28]

Aalto's representative in New York was twenty-eight-year-old Erik T. Vartiainen. A recent graduate of the University of California, Berkeley, he joined the Helsinki office midway in the project, in August 1963, replacing another American, Theodore William Booth.[29] Unlike Booth, he was born in Finland and was fluent in both Finnish and English. Vartiainen assisted Slangus with the preliminary assembly of the wood sculpture in Aalto's studio, and was sent, accompanied by a cabinetmaker from Artek, to New York in July 1964 (**FIG. 4**). There he worked closely with Harrison's partner Michael M. Harris and the main contractor, John Lowery.[30] Because the elevators of the Institute for International Education were small, larger elements, particularly the sculpture, were assembled on the second floor and raised by crane. The installation lasted approximately two-and-a-half months and, according to Harris, went "more smoothly than many."[31]

The Kaufmann rooms occupy most of the Institute's twelfth floor, almost 4,500 square feet (**FIG. 5A–B**). The vestibule, which widens near the entrance to the reception hall, has a low ceiling and the walls are faced with dark cobalt tiles. Manufactured in Finland, these curved porcelain tiles are set vertically in concrete around steel reinforcing rods. Aalto had used these elements before, in the public corridors of the National Pensions Institute (1948, 1952–57) in Helsinki, and in the lobby of the auditorium at the Helsinki University of Technology (1953–66). He compared their character to "the finest coffee cups." Vartianien remembers that this aspect of the installation was difficult, and poorly aligned pieces frequently needed to be hammered out.[32]

Visible from the elevators is the reception hall, a roughly triangular space that can be configured for lectures, luncheons, meetings, and public events. This multi-purpose room has the highest ceiling of all of the conference rooms, reaching approximately twenty-two feet near the windows. To achieve this height, Aalto persuaded Harrison's office to make "structural and mechanical" changes. A "cube" of machinery was shifted to the rear of the roof, allowing him to raise the ceiling and take full advantage of the room's unobstructed eastern exposure. The wave-like ceiling steps downward in four stages. While in form it recalls the auditorium of the Viipuri Library (1927–35) and particularly the profile of the ceiling that links various rooms in the Maison Louis Carré (1956–59) in France, due to local fire code restrictions Aalto was required to substitute plaster for thin strips of bent wood lath. This came as a disappointment to Kaufmann, as well as to Vartiainen, who in 2002 still regretted the change, commenting that the bare surface "begs for it [the wood embellishment]."[33]

Wood, however, was used generously elsewhere. Ash veneer covers most of the walls, extending from the floor to about a foot above the doors. Manufactured in the United States, these panels were finished with lacquer that Aalto sent from Finland. Attached to the panels are vertical battens. These elements project slightly from the walls, and above the paneling onto the plaster. Assembled on site, each "spaghetti" batten is composed of sixty-one slender birch rods. These poles, placed at regular intervals, create a subtle visual rhythm.

In the southeast corner is the element that most recalls Aalto's original plan (**FIG. 6**). Tucked into a shallow cove near the windows, the sculpture group is the room's most distinctive feature. In contrast to the wall battens, which are compressed and hexagonal, these flat, bent wood elements are multi-layered and highly organic. Similar, though more ambitious, wood constructions were incorporated into Finlandia Hall (1961–75) in Helsinki and the Opera House (1959, 1981–88) in Essen, Germany. These features play an important role in Aalto's late work. In 1965, Aalto said: "We have to soften up the architecture sometimes with sculpture. . . . You have to give a reception hall for an Institute like this an air of certain festivity—something enormously different. . . . I take the wood fresh from the forest, bend it and dry it after. . . . You see . . . we have done the proper thing: the joints show."[34]

To the east, a grid of plate glass, framed by aluminum moldings, separates the reception hall from the terrace. Square ash louvers, set in alternating directions, diffuse the sunlight, as did originally opaque wool draperies of Knoll design. Seating is typically arranged in semicircular rows, curving away from the windows and toward the entrance. All furnishings were designed in Aalto's office, including the armless leather chairs, lectern, and bar. Aalto was particularly proud of the lighting fixtures. Commenting on the small vertical rods that function as filters, he said: "You cannot see the bulb through. This took me half a year to work out. The material is gold on copper; the yellow is very healthy for the human eye."[35] Tiered cylindrical lighting fixtures hang from long cords throughout the reception hall. They give off a soft gold glow and are similar to those used in the council chamber of the City Hall in Seinäjoki, Finland (1961–65).

For Kaufmann, Aalto had assembled a room of somewhat familiar and recognizable signature motifs. While some elements do appear in other commissions, it is in the broader gestures—the use of wood,

FIGURE 06 *Aalto. Edgar J. Kaufmann Conference Rooms. View east along south wall.*

the curving walls assembled inside a rectangular shell, and the diagonal orientation of the plan—that a single work from Aalto's career was given prominence. Almost twenty-five years had passed since his participation in the New York World's Fair. Now in his mid-sixties, he was an international figure and the recent recipient of the American Institute of Architects Gold Medal. One can imagine the aging architect strolling out onto the terrace that adjoins the reception hall. Facing east, he could gaze past the United Nations toward Queens, recalling both the fair and the site of his earliest triumph in the United States.

Epilogue

Aalto returned to New York with his second wife Elissa Aalto in late November 1964 to receive an honorary doctorate at Columbia University, where Kaufmann was adjunct professor from 1964 to 1983, and to attend the dedication of the Edgar J. Kaufmann Conference Rooms.[36] Ada Louise Huxtable praised the project and its patron in the New York Times, calling it a "tribute to one of this country's devoted and most discriminating patrons of architecture—Edgar J. Kaufmann, Jr."[37]

Despite an enthusiastic reception, the rooms did not become well known. This can partially be explained by their location. Aside from the terrace, which is only partly visible from the street, no sign (aside from the building directory) indicates the presence of the Kaufmann rooms. Furthermore, the institute's annual reports oddly failed to acknowledge Aalto's participation at all, focusing only on how construction was financed and what events took place there.

Historians have generally given the Kaufmann rooms a lukewarm appraisal. Schildt dismissed the project as "perhaps not fully successful" and most books devoted to Aalto omit it entirely. When MoMA curator Peter Reed mounted an ambitious retrospective of Aalto's work in 1998—fifty years after his first exhibition at the museum—hardly any mention was made of his only surviving project in New York.[38]

In retrospect, whatever shortcomings the final design has, it should be remembered that the rooms were planned from a great distance, with limited face-to-face contact between parties. It did not turn out to be an ideal arrangement—Aalto's team was unfamiliar with the local building code and misunderstandings resulted. Aalto visited only twice, briefly during construction in October 1963 and to approve the final installation in August 1964.[39] By this time, the rooms were nearly complete and the brown carpet, designed by Elissa Aalto, was being laid.

It is difficult to gauge how Aalto and Kaufmann felt about their collaboration. The tone of their letters and telegrams suggest a somewhat strained relationship. When Aalto asked Kaufmann if he was happy with the sculpture, he politely responded, "I'm happy if you are happy with it." Kaufmann, in fact, never lost this reticence. In 1984, he summed up the results with remarkable objectivity: "This is not a major work of architecture, of course, but it carries, I believe, the spirit of a splendidly individual artist."[40]

The institute sold the building in 1998. Though an agreement with the new owner permitted occasional use of the conference rooms, following minor "improvements" rumors circulated that the interior was being shopped around for possible sale, with the idea that major features could be disassembled and installed elsewhere—as the Kaufmann office in Pittsburgh had been. At this time, the rooms became a public issue. Interest from the New York City Landmarks Preservation Commission toward possible designation as an interior landmark heightened attention, but no action was taken. Reacquired by the Institute in 2001, a careful restoration, supervised by a private group, the New York Landmarks Conservancy, was completed during 2002.[41]

Aalto's prestige, perhaps, was the most significant factor that saved the Edgar J. Kaufmann Conference Rooms. Though relatively few New Yorkers have visited these interiors, through the media and preservation community they have become more widely known and some city residents simply refer to them as the "Aalto rooms."

1 Research for this essay began in 2001 and was sponsored by the New Your City Landmarks Preservation Commission. Kaufmann's only account of the conference rooms' creation was published in 1984. For his remark about McAndrew, see Edgar J. Kaufmann, Jr., "Aalto on First Avenue," *Interior Design* (September 1984), 270.

2 Terence Riley and Edward Eigen, "Between the Museum and the Marketplace: Selling Good Design," in *The Museum of Modern Art at Mid-Century: At Home and Abroad,* ed. John Elderfield, Studies in Modern Art 4 (New York: Museum of Modern Art, 1994), 153.

3 Elina Standertskjöld, "Alvar Aalto and the United States," in *Alvar Aalto: Toward a Human Modernism,* ed. Winfried Nerdinger (Munich: Prestel Verlag, 1999), 86.

4 Standertskjöld, "Alvar Aalto and the United States," 86.

5 Letter from Alvar Aalto to Edgar J. Kaufmann, Jr., 26 June 1961. All correspondence referred to in the text and endnotes (except where otherwise noted) is in the collection of the Avery Architectural and Fine Arts Library at Columbia University. These letters, as well as materials to Fallingwater, were donated by Edgar J. Kaufmann, Jr. I would like to thank Janet arks and Louis DiGennaro, both of the department of Drawings at the library, for their help.

6 Other than mention by Schildt, there is little known about these New York projects. See Göran Schildt, *Alvar Aalto: The Complete Catalogue of Architecture, Design and Art* (New York, Rizzoli, 1994) 40, 253. The church facade was ultimately rebuilt by the architects Katz, Waisman (Väisänen) & Co.

7 Edgar J. Kaufmann, Jr., *Modern Rooms of the Last Fifty Years* (New York: Museum of Modern Art, 1953).

8 See Riley and Eigen, "Between the Museum and the Marketplace," 150–79. It is also likely that Kaufmann worked on exhibitions devoted to Wright and Louis Sullivan, as well as the Olivetti Company. For a list of exhibitions mounted by the museum, see Russell Lynes, *Good Old Modern: An Intimate Portrait of the Museum of Modern Art* (New York: Athenaeum, 1973), 446–69. The Paimio Chair, designed by Aalto in 1931–32, was donated to the museum by Kaufmann before 1955.

9 This stormy relationship is described by Russell Lynes, 322 , as well as in Peter Blake, *No Place Like Utopia* (New York: Knopf, 1993), 130; and Franze Schulze, *Philip Johnson: Life and Work* (New York: Knopf, 1994), 181–82.

10 E-mail from Franklin Toker to author, 6 Dec. 2002.

11 Franklin Toker, *Fallingwater Rising* (New York: Knopf, 2003), 376.

12 See the website of the Institute of International Education, http://www.iie.org. As of 2006, the institute's website refers to the rooms as both the "Alvar Aalto Conference Facility" and the "Kaufmann Conference Center."

13 "Vanderbilt's Fifth Ave. Mansion to Be Razed," *New York Times,* 12 June 1961; "Education Group Plans New Home," *New York Times,* 10 Jan. 1962. Also see *Institute of International Education Annual Report 1960* (New York, 1960), second from last page. In these articles, Harrison, Abramovitz & Harris, the contracted architects, were not identified as the architects.

14 Kaufmann, *Modern Rooms of the Last Fifty Years,* 272.

15 Though Aalto was not invited to work on the project, according to his biographer, Göran Schildt, the fruits of his collaboration with Harrison are discernible in Aalto's 1959 proposal for the Essen Opera House, completed in 1988. See Schildt, *Alvar Aalto: The Mature Years* (New York: Rizzoli, 1991), 240–41.

16 Letter from Edgar J. Kaufmann, Jr. to Aalto, 26 June 1961.

17 This is Franklin Toker's central thesis in *Fallingwater Rising.*

18 Wright's declaration is frequently cited. See Kristian Gullichsen, preface to *Alvar Aalto: Between Humanism and Materialism,* ed. Peter Reed (New York: Museum of Modern Art, 1998). For Aalto's unpublished essay on Wright, see Reed, "Alvar Aalto and the New Humanism of the Postwar Era," 97, endnote 12 on 114.

19 Toker, *Fallingwater Rising,* 337–38. Kaufmann donated his father's office to the Victoria and Albert Museum in London in 1973. It has been on public display since 1993.

20 Kaufmann Jr., "Aalto on First Avenue," *Interior Design,* September 1984, 272.

21 Letter from Alvar Aalto to Edgar J. Kaufmann, Jr., 22 Jan. 1963.

22 Schildt, *Mature Years,* 244. "New U.N. Building Will Open Feb. 27," *New York Times,* 13 Feb. 1952.

23 Telegram from Edgar J. Kaufmann, Jr. to Alvar Aalto, 28 Feb. 1963.

24 Letter from Edgar J. Kaufmann, Jr. to Alvar Aalto, 28 Feb. 1963.

25 Letter from H. Mattson and Hans Christian Slangus to Edgar J. Kaufmann, Jr., 22 Feb. 1963.

26 Letter from Alvar Aalto to Edgar J. Kaufmann, Jr., 27 Feb. 1963.

27 Letter from Edgar J. Kaufmann, Jr. to Alvar Aalto, 16 May 1963.

28 Schildt, *Mature Years,* 246.

29 Booth worked with Aalto from September 1962 to August 1963. In a September 2002 telephone interview with the author, Booth said that he left because of "language problems." Nonetheless, he called the time spent an architectural education, "better than Harvard." Booth described Kaufmann as "really pissed" about the changes to the design. He also recalled that there had been tension with Harrison's office.

30 Vartiainen recalled, "I was fortunate to have my aunt, who was an opera figure in Finland and who knew Aalto rather well, as well as William Wurster, my dean. . . . Both influence[d] my opportunity to get to the Aalto office after which it was up to me to perform and earn my stay." Aalto was clearly pleased with Vartiainen's work. He was associated with Aalto until December 1966 and served as the project manager of the Mount Angel Abbey Library, completed 1970. Vartiainen, telephone interview with author, 16 Sept. 2002; and Vartiainen, e-mail exchange with author, 24 Sept. 2002.

31 Michael Harris, quoted by Ada Louise Huxtable, "Aalto in New York," *Interior Design*, Feb. 1965, 180. This is the most complete article on the rooms. In addition to the text, it includes a plan, section, and a detailed description (p. 184) of the various materials used.

32 For reference to coffee cups, see Huxtable, "Aalto in New York," 184; Vartianien, telephone interview with author, 16 Sept. 2002.

33 Vartianien, telephone interview with author, 16 Sept. 2002.

34 Alvar Aalto, quoted in Huxtable, "Aalto in New York," 182.

35 Alvar Aalto, quoted in Huxtable, "Aalto in New York," 184.

36 Elissa (Mäkiniemi) Aalto is likely to have played a marginal role in the design of the Kaufmann rooms. Although she did attend the dedication, she did not travel to New York during the installation. Elissa did design the original wool carpet which had a "random brown" pattern. Her contribution is mentioned in "A Room of His Own," *Time,* 11 Dec. 1964. Vartianien said she had her "own projects" and was not involved in the Kaufmann commission. He also reported that Aalto insisted she receive credit.

37 Huxtable, "Aalto in New York," 180. Huxtable also wrote "Architecture: Alvar Aalto, Finnish Master, Represented Here," *New York Times,* 30 Nov. 1964. See also Harriet Morrison, "Furniture Is a Sideline," *Herald Tribune,* 30 Nov. 1964; "Home Is Dedicated by Education Group," *New York Times,* 1 Dec. 1964; "A Room of His Own," *Time,* 11 Dec. 1964; "Interviewing Aalto," *Progressive Architecture,* Jan. 1965, 48–50; and "Softener," *Architectural Review,* Oct. 1965, 60. C. Ray Smith, former editor of *Interiors and Progressive Architecture* and a friend of Kaufmann, characterized Aalto's use of a diagonal plan in the conference rooms "as then seemingly arbitrary but now enduringly vital." See Smith, *Supermannerism: New Attitudes in Post-modern Architecture* (New York: Dutton, 1977), 103.

38 Schildt, *Mature Years,* 243. The project is also omitted in the timeline devoted to Aalto's work on the webpage for the MoMA exhibition, "Alvar Aalto: Between Humanism and Materialism," on the museum's website. See http://www.moma.org/exhibitions/1998/aalto (accessed 10 April 2011).

39 Telegram from Alvar Aalto to Edgar J. Kaufmann, Jr., concerning October visit, June 1963.

40 Kaufmann, "Aalto on First Avenue," 272.

41 As of early 2008, the Landmarks Preservation Commission had not designated the Kaufmann rooms a landmark. See Erika Kinetz, "Can a Landmark Be By Invitation Only?" *New York Times,* 15 Sept. 2002.

Mount Angel Abbey Library and the Path from Viipuri

Michael Spens

Architecture and its details are in some way part of biology. Perhaps it and they are for instance like some big salmon or trout. They are not born fully grown; they are not even born in the sea of water where they normally live. They are born hundreds of miles away from their home grounds, where the rivers narrow to tiny streams in clear rivulets between the fells, in the first drops of water from the melting ice…. So too do we need time for everything that develops and crystallizes in our mind.

Alvar Aalto, "The Trout and the Stream" (1948)

Time and space have especially characterized the condition that gave birth to Alvar Aalto's final and consummate library building, built for the Benedictine Mount Angel Abbey, commenced in 1964 and completed in 1970. The monastery's perception of excellence traces back to ancient times, to precepts established by its founder, St. Benedict, in AD 529. The architect's evolution of library design stretched back to the beginning of his career. And the architect in his atelier in Munkkiniemi (literally "monk's promontory"), shoreward on the outskirts of Helsinki, was distant by some five thousand miles from the abbey near Portland, Oregon, when they decided to get in touch.

If, in the early 1960s, Alvar Aalto had been asked to nominate one ideal building type and his preferred location for a site, he would almost certainly have said, "a library, and preferably on a landscape promontory." He might also hope for it to be part of an established community, either in Finland or Italy. He was already famous for his libraries, and on the table in the Helsinki atelier at Tiilimäki in 1963 and 1964 already lay designs for two spectacular new library

buildings within Finland, the Seinäjoki and Rovaniemi civic libraries. It was a common feature that each lay on more or less flat and open plots. At Rovaniemi one is distantly aware of the undulating landscape of Lapland, and later Aalto was to reflect its outline in the low-slung curved profile of the three auditoria of the adjacent theatre center. Aalto sought always to harmonize his buildings with whatever topography prevailed. In the abstract mural relief he had designed for the Nordic Bank in Helsinki (1962) this was evident (**FIG. 1**). In dark and light gray marble he juxtaposed "built forms" within a generalized model of Kotka and Sunila as an idealized Finnish landscape: these tectonic forms seem always either to lie close to water or else to hang like snow on the steeper contours. But the two contemporaneous town libraries occupied only flat, prairie-like expanses. Suddenly now in America, a longstanding religious community was offering a superb, deeply contoured site.

At any event, it was an extraordinary piece of good fortune when in 1964 Father Barnabas Reasoner (Barnabas the Reasoner, as he was known) of the Benedictine monastery of Mount Angel, close to Portland, Oregon, wrote to Aalto. The architect responded: "I am very interested in your suggestion as libraries are my favorite subject."[1] Certainly the Benedictine Mount Angel Abbey was not new: this particular community had established itself in 1882. Monks from the seven-hundred-year-old Engelberg Benedictine monastery in Switzerland sought a New World sanctuary, following a period of religious oppression in their homeland. Now, for Aalto, the opportunity to design the new library seemed the manifestation of a long-held dream.

FIGURE 01 *Aalto, mural relief in dark and white marble showing an imagined Finnish landscape, Nordic Bank (later Union Bank), Helsinki, 1962.*

FIGURE 02 *Abbey of Monte Cassino, Italy, viewed from the Rapido Valley. Photograph 1981.*

The Benedictine tradition had, of course, originated in Italy much earlier, in 529, at Monte Cassino, between Naples and Rome (FIG. 2). St. Benedict had established precise terms for the rule of the order: "A company of monks, secure and protected by religion, who read, toiled the soil, and exercised the arts in the midst of a great society that was coming apart through barbarism, was laying the seed of the future civilization and recomposition of the people."[2] The Benedictines built the new abbey firmly atop Monte Cassino itself. Siting was all important, as it was with the placement of the Oregon community. Soon after receiving the commission, Aalto received the fullest possible information about the site, with visual documentation. From Aalto's base close to Helsinki, however, the Oregon site tantalizingly became almost an abstract ideal. Only four years later, when construction was to start, did Aalto discover the full beauty of the place. Coming to America in 1967, he stood on the site for the first time, in quiet contemplation. There were virtually no changes to be made by then to what had been designed in prior years.

Despite the exigencies of distance (still a major factor in the mid-1960s), and regardless of his age and the pressure of major projects such as Finlandia Hall and other work, Aalto conceived, designed, and completed an undoubted masterwork at this late stage of his career. Abroad, Aalto was engaged with the Riola Church in Italy (1966), projects in Iceland (1965–68) and Lucerne, Switzerland (1965–68), and the Essen Opera House, Germany (1963–64). Indeed, only the longstanding friendship and commitment of key Americans known to him from his time at the Massachusetts Institute of Technology, William W. Wurster and Vernon De Mars, ensured that the whole venture could be achieved.

To those who have followed Aalto's oeuvre across the years, it seems that the Mount Angel Abbey Library still remains obscure, and its impact curiously muted in the minds of subsequent and contemporary architectural historians. What should obviously have been appraised as a climactic fulfillment of a life's work was somehow marginalized in later years. It is generally now recognized, however, that one of Alvar Aalto's key contributions to the historical discourse on architecture has been the codification of distinctive typologies throughout his work. Four years or so after Aalto's death, Demetri Porphyrios, in a seminal article in *Oppositions*, was the first commentator to recognize Aalto's particular significance in the revision of modernism.[3] The architect, he noted, recognized the possibility of form as a linguistic device, and hence established a recognizable set of typologies within his own work as it progressed and diversified.

Aalto's particular role within the modern movement as appraised by earlier critics is now recognized to have been somewhat misconceived. The Paimio Sanatorium (1928–1933) is a key case in point. Aalto's masterly manipulation of the codices of functionalism, these writers contended, had brought him early fame and success as a modernist pioneer. Yet recent assessments of the Viipuri Library project offer a rather more interesting insight into Aalto's actual position as a modernist, both then and later. This project, on the boards simultaneously with the sanatorium, suggests that Aalto pursued a seemingly divergent methodology, one initiated in deference to a historically recognizable typology, one founded within a generalized classical Italian cultural context. Sigfried Giedion and others assumed of Viipuri that when the initial and then the amended modernist versions appeared, Aalto had developed an unquestioning and irrevocable affiliation with the "International Style."[4] In fact, as the typological development of all of Aalto's libraries reveals, he was by this time both looking forward to a more "natural" and humanist (that is, less mechanistic) modernism as well as looking legitimately to the past. There he sought verification of the symbolic essence of libraries in their meaning and "propriety" with regard to the specific communities they served. Nor was this approach only applicable to his libraries. Porphyrios has shown that in most building types, whether they be the libraries, city halls, concert halls, office buildings, or even villas, Aalto scrupulously

revisited precedent, not to replicate, but to advance his typologies. This methodology constituted Aalto's modernism; it led him forward throughout his career as an innovator in every aspect of design.

Historical Amnesia and the Negligence of Critique

Aalto's "prototype" library at Viipuri (1935), after an initial burst of acclaim by critics in the 1930s, had by the 1950s slowly passed into distant memory (**FIGS. 3–4**). This neglect was surely the result of major historical turmoil. The library became inaccessible when Soviet Russia gained Eastern Karelia and the city of Viipuri following the Winter War. The Viipuri Library was, in fact, virtually impossible to visit from the west, and the Baltic port, now Russian Vyborg, fell within a highly sensitive Soviet defense zone. By the late 1940s, Sigfried Giedion, a major advocate for Aalto, was to proclaim that the library had been "almost razed to the ground" in the war. In actuality it had stood solidly, despite serious damage (and re-opened as the town library on 12 March 1961).[5]

The state of Oregon may be sandwiched between Washington and California, with its own share of high and low desert, but it still has an active seaboard and community around Portland, near the Pacific Ocean. By contrast to Viipuri, it has never been overrun by hostile forces in time of war, and has never been a victim of enforced partition, as had been the fate of Finnish Karelia. And yet a curiously similar critical destiny has seemed to dog the Mount Angel Abbey Library.

Actually, like Viipuri Library, the abbey library, on dedication, was crowned with major and repeated accolades. *Architectural Record* described "the complete individuality of the solution based on the uniqueness of the building's requirements and of the site."[6] Ada Louise Huxtable celebrated "a small and perfect work" in the *New York Times*.[7] A decade later, Huxtable reiterated this praise, describing Aalto's various U.S. works as being chiefly institutional rather than commercial projects. She also recalled, "These buildings frequently puzzled their admirers because they were so far out of the mainstream; critics struggled with their covert disappointment when so few of the expected hallmarks appeared."[8] Only later, with the advent of architectural postmodernism as a revisionary critique, was Aalto (somewhat ironically) more fully appreciated in the United States. Even so, as early as 1965, Robert Venturi was outspoken in his recognition of Aalto's complexity, insightfully countering those who sought disingenuously to label his work as "picturesque." In proposing *Complexity and Contradiction in Architecture* as a manifesto against simplification or picturesqueness, Venturi perceptively saw "Aalto's complexity [as] part of the program and structure of the whole rather than a device."[9] Within two years, construction on the Mount Angel Abbey Library would begin, amply fulfilling this assessment.

Just as Viipuri was "off limits" along the Aalto pilgrimage circuit until the 1990s, Mount Angel was similarly a victim of remoteness.[10] Even Giedion was no longer able to enthuse followers. This may not have been all that disadvantageous, since by 1961 the validity of Giedion's (as much as Bruno Zevi's) romantic-classical standpoint had already been thrown into doubt by Vincent Scully, Jr.'s "romantic-naturalism," described in his own prescient re-appraisal of Aalto.[11] But within five years of Aalto's death in 1976, the abbey library had been seemingly relegated to critical obscurity: like Viipuri, it had become a forgotten masterpiece—or at least almost. But whereas Viipuri has in the past decade been enthusiastically restored to its position as a seminal Aalto work, thus firmly rehabilitated in the canon of modernism, Mount Angel Abbey Library curiously languishes in a remarkable fog from which it has barely emerged.[12]

This is not to argue that Aalto's work in the United States failed to serve as a precedent for later modern architects. In the postwar period MIT's Baker House (1947), a highly influential work, was a proud and recognizable formal precedent, notably for Richard Meier's early Olivetti offices project in Tarrytown, New York (1971–73), and for his Cornell University student-housing project (1974). But by Aalto's centenary date in 1998, it was clear that the Mount Angel library had slipped out of the frame both for contemporary architects and for historians. In three prestigious European and American publications on Aalto, there is no recognition of the library, other than the necessary listing within the catalogues of works.[13] In the postwar period, Aalto said of Viipuri that "it had lost its architecture."[14] But the paradox of the Mount Angel work,

the summit of the glorious trajectory of Aalto libraries, must be that in actuality it has lost its public.

One of the primary purposes of this study is to avowedly restore this balance. Mount Angel Abbey Library, it can be argued, today stands as a superb distillation of Aalto's mature philosophy of design. Aalto first sprang to prominence in 1927, winning the Viipuri Library competition with his first modern but deliberately classicizing scheme. It was over a year later that he designed the Paimio Sanatorium and the Turun Sanomat newspaper offices and works (completed 1930). The actual trajectory of Aalto's architectural development that is most relevant for this essay is documented in the schematic transformation of the three projects for the Viipuri Library, which Aalto spent over five years developing. In a memorable statement he described the germ of an idea, a utopian vision from which all of his subsequent library projects were conceived: "When I designed Viipuri City Library (and I had plenty of time—a whole five years) I spent long periods getting my range as it were, through naïve drawings. I drew all kinds of fantastic mountain landscapes, with slopes lit by many suns in different positions, which gradually gave birth to the main idea of the library building. The architectural framework of the library comprises various reading and lending areas stepped at different levels, while the administrative and supervisory center is at the peak" **(SEE p.27 FIG. 7)**.[15] Not only was this fundamental principle of organization initially presented by Aalto through Viipuri, but subject to accruing variations, it was characteristic of all Aalto's library designs, in various mutations, across some dozen schemes over forty years, until the final climacteric at Mount Angel.

Aalto's Mount Angel Abbey Library, the final movement of his library "symphony," clearly bears the closest reference of all his libraries to his initial sketch, that is, to the opening movement. Yet, as historians came to recognize the Paimio Sanatorium as pivotal in establishing the "fundamental Functionalist style of his first mature period," Viipuri Library was simultaneously relegated by the same token to a less formative position.[16] Viipuri, as the design progressed from 1928 to 1930, revealed a dramatic amendment of the functional premise, leading to a more organic and naturalistic expression of the humanist philosophy to which the architect was already firmly committed. And if at

Viipuri this tendency was still constrained within the orthogonal, rectilinear schema, Aalto's subsequent expansion of the "book pit" concept (initially derived from Erik Gunnar Asplund's Stockholm City Library) broke out dramatically with the sequence of libraries for Seinäjoki (1960–1965), Rovaniemi (1961–1966), Kokkola (1966), and, finally, Mount Angel Abbey. In this final work, the fan-shape, coupled with stepped contouring, achieved a topographical perfectibility not otherwise available. The Mount Angel Abbey Library must indeed be recognized as Aalto's ultimate library masterpiece, and the conclusion of that evolving typology which Aalto mastered as no architect has before or since. Consequently, America contains this quiet, dedicated masterwork, and the discrete religious brotherhood which gave it life continues to cherish the building, idiosyncratic yet also uniquely "Aalto," to a degree perhaps only fully recognizable when experienced on the site itself.

FIGURE 03 *Aalto, Viipuri Library, Vyborg (Viipuri), Russia, 1927–35. Main elevation.*

Initial Development: The Concept for the Commission

The Benedictines had reached Oregon from Switzerland almost as refugees, in search of new freedoms. In the early 1880s, the relatively small number of monks had settled within a community that was largely rural, composed primarily of Swiss and German migrants. From the beginning, they appreciated the advantages of the landscape butte there, almost three hundred feet long, so evidently right for the siting of a typical Benedictine community. Initially, they established what would become Mount Angel Abbey as a timber-built priory and church at the base of the site. Ten years later a disastrous fire reduced the emergent complex to a charred ruin. But the monks persevered under adversity, this time building anew on the plateau along the top of the butte. There the order established its central facility, a library, expanding its holdings rapidly to reach some twenty thousand volumes by 1926. Then, in that year, a second fire broke out. Again, the central buildings were rebuilt, this time with deeper foundations and a more solid construction. The library's destruction, however, had been so devastating that for some thirty years the books were to remain dispersed within the monastery, inappropriately housed and fragmented as a collection.

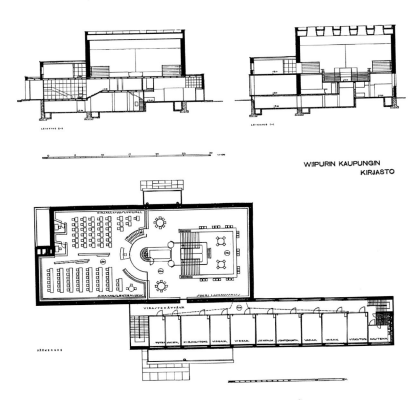

FIGURE 04 A–B *Aalto, Viipuri Library. Sections and Plan of upper floor.*

FIGURE 05 *Antonello da Messina*, St. Jerome in His Study, *oil on lime (ca. 1475), (45.7 x 36.2cm). National Gallery, London.*

Within the original Benedictine code, the Cassino Rule of 529 prescribed that all monks, in specified hours, had to read, collectively or individually. In the fifteenth century, Antonello da Messina expressed the ideal of the religious bibliophile in the iconic painting St. *Jerome in His Study* (**FIG. 5**).[17] More recently, Umberto Eco's novel, *The Name of the Rose*, focused somewhat obsessively on the vicissitudes of medieval Benedictine tribulation and survival.[18] In that book, the abbot recites, confronting the cryptic mass of the library, "Monasterium sine libris, est sicut civitas sine opibus, castrum sine numeris" (A monastery without books is like a city state without wealth, a camp without troops). The abbot elaborates on the importance of preserving the treasure of wisdom. Given the desire to access such knowledge, he describes the function of the *scriptorium*, where monks

reproduce illuminated texts for further dissemination. Knowledge, for Eco, is power, embodied in the story by the librarian, a forbidding and all-knowing figure in the abbey, who allows few monks access to more than the small fraction of the library's holdings deemed essential for their work.[19]

The circumstances of life were not quite as bad at Mount Angel Abbey, but following the fire and the loss of the library, access to texts had become complicated. So Father Barnabas Reasoner was at last chosen by the monastery to solve the problem, in 1953. By 1962, after much campaigning within the order, he was authorized "to make the hilltop a regional cultural center and recapture some of the monastery's older aspirations" by securing "the best available architect."[20] In continuance with the Benedictine pursuit of excellence, the new building was to become a focal point of Mount Angel Abbey second only to the church.

By this time, an enlightened and deliberately expansionist acquisitions policy managed by Father Barnabas had necessarily raised the total number of bound volumes again, to some fifty thousand with a planned expansion to two hundred thousand, so rendering the new building absolutely vital. Father Barnabas was not unaware of the respective talents of international architects, even out in Oregon. His interest in architecture grew out of his interest in history, and his breadth of modern knowledge had convinced him that the building had to be a contemporary facility, "a building worthy of our monastic tradition and of the natural beauty of the setting of Mount Angel." At this time a church policy was emerging that would be ratified in the Second Vatican Council, encouraging the faithful to "live in very close union with the men of their time."[21]

Contemporaneity would be reflected in the library's architecture. The abbey considered both I. M. Pei and Louis Kahn before settling on Aalto. Father Barnabas had learned of the prewar achievement of the Viipuri Library as a model through a librarians' professional journal, thus recognizing in the architect a sympathy for literature, a technical and poetic understanding of the quality of light, and an awareness that the library as building type had a special communal role. Still, Aalto had yet to be contacted, and persuaded.

First Realization of the Idea and the Means of Fulfillment

Father Barnabas wrote in his letter of 1964 to Aalto: "We need you. We have this magnificent monastic site and we don't want to spoil it. We want you to improve our site, and give us a building that will fulfill our needs in a beautiful and intelligent way." It was some time before Aalto replied. Was it a Finnish postal strike? But Aalto replied eventually, and very positively: "Libraries are my favorite subject."[22] Only later that year did Barnabas meet Aalto, faithfully tracking him to a hotel in Zurich.[23] Then a fatigued Aalto finally committed himself to travel to Oregon to visit the site. That too was an act of faith, since only one-third of the necessary finances had yet been raised.

Various positive developments were now to occur. Aalto received the Thomas Jefferson medal in architecture in 1967 (following his acceptance of the American Institute of Architects Gold Medal in 1963). Coming to the United States to receive the honor, Aalto visited Mount Angel Abbey for the first time. More significant, also at this time, Vernon DeMars of the University of California, Berkeley, who was connected with Aalto since their communal days at MIT, linked up with Erik Vartiainen, Aalto's former student who had already been appointed in Helsinki as the design associate on the library, and the architect John Wells.[24] The design team was now in place. Stefan Medwadowski (familiar as a structural engineer to DeMars and Wells) was also appointed to the team. Medwadowski's work turned out to be critical to the library's structural schema, which had been developed initially by Vartiainen with Aalto at Tiilimäki.

The Benedictine achievement in Oregon was not the development of an American-designed library in the manner of Aalto, but instead categorically a full-fledged, definitively Alvar Aalto building. This was a fortuitous consequence of the network of Americans who were enthusiastic about Aalto; they fostered a closely integrated liaison with Helsinki. William W. Wurster, dean at MIT in 1946, had been instrumental in bringing Aalto to the United States as a visiting professor and later in enabling him to carry out the MIT Baker House design.[25] Wurster in turn had brought Vernon DeMars to MIT and put him in contact with Aalto in 1947. Wurster intended that DeMars alternate with Aalto in the role of visiting professor, but their engagements ultimately overlapped.

It is not recorded that Wurster saw the Viipuri Library when he had gotten to know Aalto during his visit to Europe of 1937, but in 1938, close to the time that Wurster was showing Aalto his own new work in the Santa Cruz Mountains, DeMars by coincidence traveled to Viipuri. Viipuri can be said to have been the crucible for Mount Angel Abbey Library, but the godfather for the Oregon project was surely Wurster, because he united the principal parties. The financial backing of Howard and Jean Vollum was secured as a direct result of the initial commitment of Aalto.[26] Now Father Barnabas, by going to Zurich, had consolidated the full engagement of Aalto. The project was now ready to begin construction, managed by the associate architects of DeMars and Wells, with Vartiainen acting as the permanent arm of the Aalto office.

Initial Proposals and their Genesis

The initial scheme for Mount Angel Abbey Library had been completed by Aalto as early as 9 May 1964 (FIGS. 6–7). The Aalto office's library schemes in the preceding decade had ensured that it maintained and developed its expertise in the library field. The library designs for Jyväskylä University (1951–1955) and for Helsinki University of Technology at Otaniemi (from 1964) represented a transition of Aalto's evolving library-design concept. The genesis of the fan-shaped orchestration of book stacks (a development of the initial Viipuri book "pit" concept) appeared first at the civic library at Seinäjoki, where the library and auditorium were transformed between 1960 and 1963 into an asymmetrical, fan-shaped lending and stack room emerging out of the rectilinear plan conformation. However, the specific Aalto book "pit" and the juxtaposed, rectilinear block at the Mount Angel library trace a modernist genealogy direct from Viipuri. In the competition project submitted by Aalto for the Wolfsburg Cultural Center in Germany (1958) the auditoria are grouped in a fanned cluster, and the library, with three groupings of twenty-five conical, recessed roof lights, is organized with a "pit" in a manner still similar to Viipuri (FIG. 8; SEE p.40 FIG. 4). However, the emergence of the very first "fanned" plan form can be dated earlier still, to the competition entry for the Kuopio Theatre (1952). In the

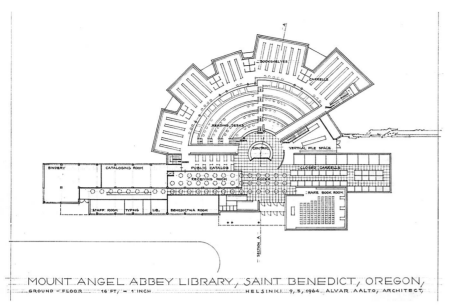

MOUNT ANGEL ABBEY LIBRARY, SAINT BENEDICT, OREGON,
GROUND FLOOR 16 FT/ = 1 INCH   HELSINKI 9,5,1964 ALVAR AALTO, ARCHITECT,

FIGURE 06 *Aalto, Mount Angel Abbey Library (1964–70), St. Benedict, Ore. Plan, 9 May 1964.*

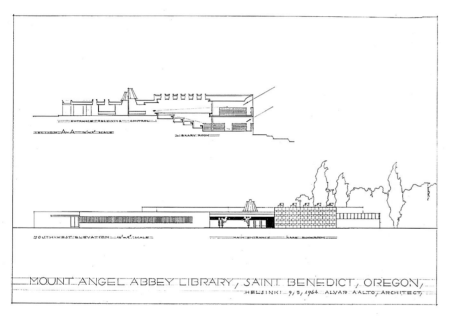

MOUNT ANGEL ABBEY LIBRARY, SAINT BENEDICT, OREGON,
HELSINKI 9,5,1964 ALVAR AALTO, ARCHITECT,

FIGURE 07 *Aalto, Mount Angel Abbey Library. Section and elevation, 9 May 1964.*

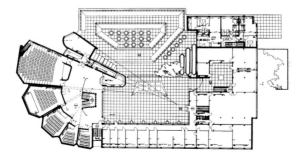

FIGURE 08 *Aalto, Wolfsburg Cultural Center, Wolfsburg, Germany, 1958–62. Plan.*

Wolfsburg church-center kindergarten, a similar horizontal block adjoins a fan-shaped array of classrooms of varying sizes—representing a smaller-scale variant of the same formal combination.

What most strikes a follower of Aalto's library-design sequence about the May 1964 Mount Angel library scheme is perhaps the tectonic resolution of the whole. This comes from fulfilling both the specific requirements of the Mount Angel site and the library brief. Together, they represent the ultimate development of a long-evolved typology of Aalto library designs. The five-tiered stepped section of the abbey library very dramatically echoes the conceptual "mountain" drawing that predicated the Viipuri Library, yet the Mount Angel design even more dramatically fulfils this earliest proposal. Its arrangement of a rectilinear administrative auditorium and servicing block is a sequential development from the built design for the Viipuri Library, but the dramatic outward opening of the library area itself is a perfection of the combined book "pit" and fan. Aalto created five divisions containing bookshelves, accompanied by four sets of grouped carrels in the interstices, with reading desks in the pit below, superbly lit by the skylights. All these areas are supervised from a single central control point, at the radial apex of the plan.

Of particular significance in this early scheme for the Mount Angel Abbey Library is the formal and symbolic status allocated to the rectangular rare book room. This compartment stands to the east of the entrance and is elevated in prominence over the long administrative block. Against the extremely long southward entrance elevation that Aalto originally proposed, there also rose, most emblematically, a high roof lantern, situated immediately over the library control desk.

Mount Angel's lantern was intended by Aalto to convey a symbolic centrality at night. The whole face that the library presents to the abbey lawn is enigmatic **(SEE FIG. 7)**. To Aalto, this entire building comprised the Benedictine "aedificium," both promising yet withholding knowledge inside the community, glowing mysteriously at night (from the abbey lawn), with little inkling conveyed of the dedicated activities pursued inside. The ancient Benedictine instruction, that Cassinese edict to read, was here interpreted by Aalto to signify the library in abbey life, its role second only to that of the abbey church. Here again, Aalto had realized (perhaps, after Viipuri, with some relief) the manifest absence of any notable "campanile." At Viipuri the library took on an enforced horizontality, being adjacent to the city's rhetorically vertical cathedral. Aalto could choose his own site there, and personally selected the area over which the spire of the nineteenth-century cathedral loomed.[27] The Mount Angel Abbey Library, conversely, having a pronounced horizontal disposition across the lawn, might duly compensate for a presumed lack of significant form evident at Mount Angel, at least as of yet.

The Final Design

Aalto and Vartiainen sent the initial scheme for the Mount Angel Abbey Library to Father Barnabas and the Benedictine community shortly after its completion in May 1964. A number of changes were then requested by the abbey, reflecting a need for reduced cost, but without any lack of commitment whatsoever (FIGS. 9-10). The book-shelving bays, hitherto numbering five, of varying depth and width with pronounced interstitial re-entrants, were reduced to four, of closer configuration and with the intervening spaces minimized. More reductively, the five layered "steps" containing the reading desks were effectively reduced to three levels, containing the control desk, reading area, and mezzanine, with the upper and lower level bookshelves in stacks. The reading area was still naturally lit through the overhead strip of roof lighting, taking over from the original unbroken array of cone lights and the parabolic lantern light over the control desk. Overall, the library became more closely organized along the lines of a large reference library. The study carrels, accordingly, were established all along the periphery, increasing individual privacy for study as required.

Following the visit in 1964 of Father Barnabas to Aalto, whom he found suffering from fatigue and failing health, Aalto and the design team realized that given the revised basis of the design and the gift of a donor, adequate funds now existed to go ahead. This acted as a stimulus to Aalto and the office in Helsinki, and motivated Aalto's 1967 trip to Mount Angel. It is recorded by the monks that when the architect reached the monastery, he "stood silently on the site for a long time." Finally he said: "It's like an acropolis, more beautiful than I imagined."[28] Then, in a pragmatic yet ritual respect for the natural site, Aalto instructed that a small stand of evergreen trees, awaiting felling, be

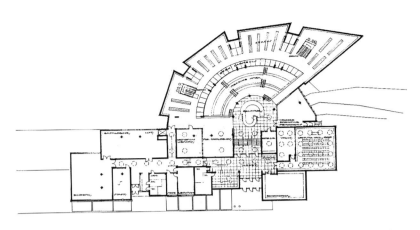

MOUNT ANGEL ABBEY LIBRARY, SAINT BENEDICT, OREGON,
MAIN FLOOR PLAN ³⁄₁₆" = 1'-0"   HELSINKI 10,2,1966   ALVAR AALTO ARCHITECT

FIGURE 09 *Aalto, Mount Angel Abbey Library. Plan. 10 Feb, 1966.*

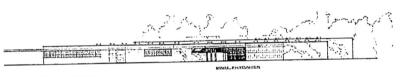

SOUTHWEST · ELEVATION

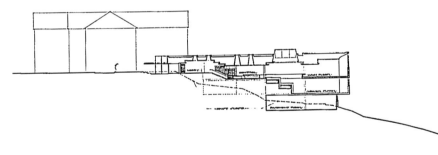

MOUNT ANGEL ABBEY LIBRARY, SAINT BENEDICT, OREGON
SECTION A—A ³⁄₁₆" = 1'-0"   HELSINKI 10,2,1966   ALVAR AALTO ARCHITEC

FIGURE 10 *Aalto, Mount Angel Abbey Library. Elevation and section, 10 Feb. 1966.*

saved by moving the entire design some ten feet along the butte. Also on this visit Aalto was asked why the library did not include larger glass areas overlooking these superb northward views. He simply replied, "I have designed a place for study, not a lounge."[29] Criticized by others on the grounds that the library bore a close resemblance to preceding libraries he had designed for Finland, he said that he did not mind using good ideas more than once.

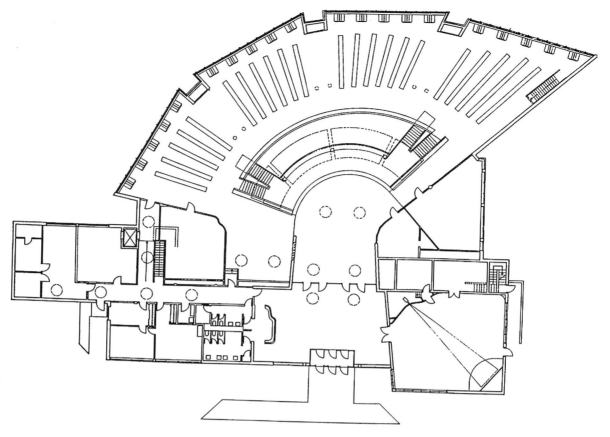

FIGURE 11 *Aalto, Mount Angel Abbey Library. Plan as built.*

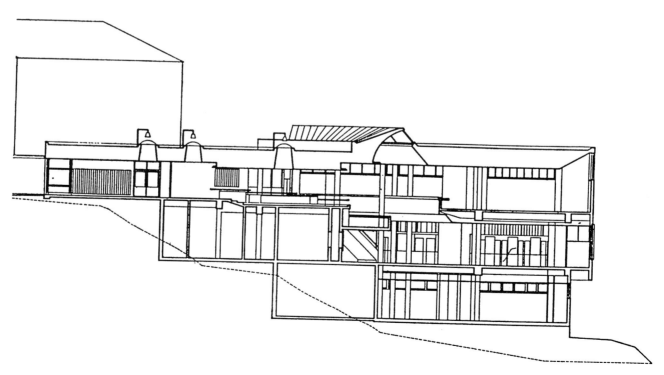

FIGURE 12 *Aalto, Mount Angel Abbey Library. Section as built.*

FIGURE 13 *Aalto, Mount Angel Abbey Library 1964–70. Main elevation showing entrance from the abbey's lawn.*

The Mount Angel Abbey Library, Built (1967–1970)

In its final form, the Mount Angel Abbey Library reveals a considerably more efficient disposition of the key library elements of book stacks and reading space than suggested by the initial and revised schemes **(FIGS. 11-12; SEE ALSO FIGS. 6–7 AND 9-10)**. The rings of reading desks proposed in the first scheme, positioned to be under close supervision of the librarian, appear to have been resettled as individual carrels, open on the upper level. The lower level, by contrast, is for the most part enclosed; the length of book-shelving is virtually identical to that of the upper level. And where an apparently "dead" area of filing space and a side exit to the right of the librarian's desk had previously existed, is now found the periodicals room, revealing a superb lateral view over the landscape through a continuous window.

Small open views are now offered through windows inserted between the segments of the "fans." Over the librarians' control desk at the entrance level (where the lantern had been), two cone skylights trace a provenance back to the Viipuri Library.

FIGURE 14 *Aalto, Reading Room, Mount Angel Abbey Library.*

Similarly, the Aalto office achieved major economies with respect to the clients' brief for efficiency in the library's various operational and organizational facilities. It shortened the length of the building facing the abbey lawn by further rationalizing the rooms allocated to such operations as bookbinding and cataloging. It made few changes in the entry lobby space, although it reduced the phalanx of fifty or so light cones by over half. The important, top-lit rare book room and auditorium, to the right (east) of the long lawn-facing elevation, remained in place, but more visibly in its role as the library's sole auditorium, with the speakers' desk and projection screen now shifted to the diagonal axis, and with discreet clerestory windows providing daylighting. The simple entrance canopy is now lighter as a superstructure, and the original three columns are replaced by four, which are brought forward of the building line. These steel-exposed columns are enclosed in Aalto's typical timber cladding strips (**FIG. 13**).

There is greater literal transparency in the built design too, with large windows revealing more of the interior, previously blocked by the location of the mysterious traditionally "Benedictine" ante-space adjacent to the entrance (**SEE FIG. 13**). Perhaps the presence close by of a full stand of evergreen trees, together with those spared by Aalto, provides a greater natural screening for the library entry than was initially taken into account in Helsinki. But the emphatic horizontality, combined with the more elevated block of the small auditorium, conspicuously announces the library diagonally from across the abbey lawn, without any loss of Aalto's original intention. Clearly his revision still maintains the presence of the "aedificium," and the low-profiled sense of mystery of a Benedictine library still persists.

Structurally, the library's schema of radially disposed columns, the inner ring being singular, and the second ring being paired (three radial dispositions in all), allowed the columns to securely support the radiating beams (**FIG. 14, SEE FIG. 11**).

FIGURE 15 *Aalto, Mount Angel Abbey Library 1964–70. Aerial view of site from the south with completed library.*

FIGURE 16 Aalto, Mount Angel Abbey Library, 1964–70. View from below the butte.

According to a local story, some of the Benedictine monks asserted it was regrettable that the dramatic northward-fanning profile of the library was not immediately perceptible from the butte itself (FIGS. 15–16). But it was always Aalto's intention to maintain the library's dramatic, almost medieval visual presence from below and afar, as with the abbey of Monte Cassino, where the building visually dominates the Rapido valley for miles below (SEE FIG. 2). Still, Aalto's building was far from a faithful homage to this older structure; Mount Angel Abbey Library was built of brick rather than travertine, and while the Cassinese library ran almost the full length of the abbey, Mount Angel's library constitutes no more than perhaps one-eighth of the loose assemblage of buildings overlooking the valley below the butte. But it is nonetheless the sole signifier there of the dedicated community. And so, in spring mists or russet-leaved fall, it establishes that presence unequivocally, an architectural evocation of St. Benedict's rule to the monastic community at large: to read.

Belated Critical Acclaim

Colin Rowe visited Mount Angel Abbey for the first time in May 1995, less than five years before he died, and during the year in which he received the Gold Medal of the Royal Institute of British Architects. When he wrote of the visit, he announced that he had become a convert to this particular Aalto library (SEE FIGS. 15–16). "It's on a butte which you approach through a forest with stations of the cross, all suggestively Italiano: and if, following this, the monastic buildings are nothing to write home about, the extreme reticence of the library suddenly becomes a consummation of the site. Screened or veiled by dark existing trees you can scarcely see it; but all the same its very modest and scarcely disclosed vertical surface collaborates with the horizontal surface of the butte to emphasise, without any exaggeration, the very powerful view over the valley."[30] Indeed, the view is only ultimately to be revealed from inside, by the entry to the book "pit." Stepping past the control desk, one emerges from below the lowering canopy to experience the full splendor of the book stacks and the reading galleries, concentrically disposed within the coordinating geometry of the outward-opening fan and looking out to the landscape beyond (SEE FIGS. 13–14).

The upper level, supported by the three pairs was thereby cantilevered over the well, while the single columns supported and braced the semicircular skylight overhead. The threesome columnar plan allows the eastward fan enclave to shift the radial inclination further toward its closure at the east wall. The thrust of this divergence is visually returned in the plan, not only to the librarians' desk, but beyond this and back again as the incline at a slight angle in the auditorium's lobby wall. This impetus is gently apparent from the actual entry point to the library, a specific moment in the Aalto formal dynamic.

In this way the asymmetrical axis of the composition is enforced and enhanced in the final design in a manner not achieved in the May 1964 and later proposals (SEE FIGS. 6, 9). The orthogonal axis leading from the entry and down through the actual reading desks in the original version of the design has been elegantly dispensed with as a result of Aalto's discreet but subtle adjustment of the plan.

Calascibetta. FZ

FIGURE 17 *Aalto, Sketch of Calascibetta, Sicily, 1952.*

In the design as finally built, and thus as pleasingly observed by Rowe (in something of an eleventh-hour conversion by one not known, prior to his visit to Mount Angel, as an Aalto aficionado), the impact of the library remains dramatic for the observer. In the initial scheme of May 1964, the most evident feature in the elaboration of the longstanding ideal Aalto held for this library type is the five-stepped section (SEE FIG. 7). Indeed Mount Angel stands as the consummation of that long-held vision first expressed by Aalto in his "The Trout and the Stream" (1947). This is shown by comparing the "mountain" sketch to the May 1964 Mount Angel Abbey Library section: one identifies the "tiering" process again in the accompanying sketch of the same period (SEE p.27 FIG. 7). In Aalto's work, invariably the building becomes the landscape, and the landscape spreads within and without the building. Routes within the building's circulation system reveal a topological awareness of place, somehow acting as paths through the forest, its rides, clearings, and openings. But its ambience remains always the same, familiar "forest" welcoming rather

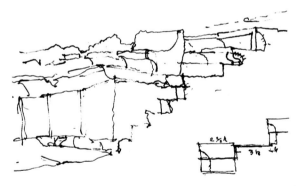

FIGURE 18 *Aalto, Sketch of the Theater of Dionysus, Athens, 1953.*

than alienating, offering landmarks, promontories, and private retreat.[31]

Throughout Aalto's oeuvre one can reference ultimate design choices back to a number of key surviving topographical or conceptual sketches. Whether the *Sketch of Calascibetta, Sicily* (1952) or the *Sketch of the Theatre of Dionysus, Athens* (1953) or even *Trees, Delphi* (1953), such drawings remind us that Aalto wove his buildings into the landscape (**FIGS. 17–18**). The early *Cyclopean Wall at Delphi* (1929) encapsulates this poetic vision of a landscape site. Frequently, in Finland or Germany, for example, there was little range of contour on which Aalto could redeploy these memories in a literal sense. So more often than not, he emphasized this aspect of his creative process through his language of detail, recognizable in his cultural buildings ("amphitheaters," for example) as an extended, internal typology. Such messages, consequently, are decoded and realized even for the uninitiated.

At Mount Angel Abbey, although still sight unseen by Aalto until 1967, all such memories were in play. The sectional progression from the summit monastery lawn to the valley below would unfold naturally in Aalto's mind. In the office at Tiilimäki (on the "monk's promontory," i.e., Munkkiniemi), newly under further expansion, the two civic libraries then under development at Seinäjoki and Rovaniemi were thus joined—around the same privately constructed office "amphitheater"—by Mount Angel, now the ultimate version of a long-treasured ideal. So this library, a new "aedificium" for a most ancient monastic order, was in 1964 cautiously begun: as if by the same ancient token of miracles, it would obliquely disappear through a change of client priorities. But, like some kind of mythopoetic fantasy, in Aalto's mind it persisted. As Stanford Anderson has convincingly argued: "What we may see in the work of Le Corbusier, Aalto, Kahn and others is not history, but exercises in memory, and invention in relation to memory."[32]

It is also worth mentioning in this context that by co-incidence, Le Corbusier had in 1961 just completed his Dominican monastery of Sainte Marie de La Tourette. This work followed the major realignment of modernism established by Le Corbusier's Notre-Dame-du-Haut at Ronchamp. The rhetoric consolidating this shift was as strident as that accompanying his first modernism.

To Aalto, such critiques, such eulogies to Le Corbusier as that of Colin Rowe's "Dominican Monastery of La Tourette" (1961), possibly constituted a challenge.[33]

A World of Books

Mount Angel's internal fittings, furniture, and lighting all conspire to establish what Aalto had always intended, "a world of books" (**SEE FIG. 14**).[34] A separate, studious world was to be fostered, one where movement exists, but is also invariably connected with the activity or provision of reading. This had long been Aalto's world too, for he was a pronounced bibliophile ever since childhood. Aware of the weight of words, Aalto was never verbose. Of his own skills, he would only say: "Of course I have written poems. A few, but naturally good ones. But they are written in sand. And poems written in the sand are not suitable for publishers and journals. Their publisher is the wind, a splendid publisher."[35] Still, Aalto appreciated the words of others; he valued books.

Lighting, as Aalto first explored it at Viipuri, was fundamental to this environment. At Mount Angel he attached great importance to the combination of natural and reflected light—especially through the total elimination of glare. Aalto's radial plan and stepped section for the abbey library, like those of the Seinäjoki and Rovaniemi libraries, facilitated such an objective (**SEE FIGS. 11–12**). The Viipuri library had also shown the effectiveness of the free section, and the value of the book "pit." But this system he could perfect in detail internally only by abandoning the rectangular box, and so he eventually substituted the radial fan-shaped assemblage, as at Mount Angel.

The benefits of such a plan assemblage are accentuated by the employment of timber furniture and fittings wherever possible. In the auditorium, Aalto recalls the Viipuri Library fleetingly by the fan-shaped screen of timber slats, which has a curving boundary that hovers over the seating area itself (**FIGS. 19–20**). He also equipped the stage with a sweeping timber canopy behind the speaker. Likewise the librarians' control desk is formed as a unitary element of curved timber (**FIG. 21**). Surfaces likely to be touched Aalto typically designed in timber; the individual carrels, for example, provide an essential harmony and privacy through the universal use of Aalto furniture within timber-detailed enclosures. It is

FIGURE 19 *Aalto, Mount Angel Library. Auditorium.*

FIGURE 20 *Aalto, Mount Angel Abbey Library. Auditorium, detail.*

appropriate here to recall the fifteenth-century ideal of the religious bibliophile as expressed in *St. Jerome in His Study* as well as Aalto's observation about the library itself: "I have designed a place for study, not a lounge" (SEE FIG. 5). Similarly, the monks have stated in the abbey's own catalogue, "Our library is a space which makes one want to sit and read."[36] The carrels are places of privacy designed specifically for this purpose, carefully defined as small study compartments with their own timber doors (FIGS. 22–23). Opposite to this area, all ends of the communal book stacks are finished with vertical timber slats, a device that Aalto adapted even for screening the fire extinguishers, to the tolerant chagrin of fire-prevention officers. In this world of books, it is left to the books themselves to provide the incidental color.

Finally, brass is used in Aalto's door hardware, including the entry-door handles that effectively and discreetly provide Aalto's signature. Of Aalto's design, the Benedictines have said: "We are fortunate to be

FIGURE 21 *Aalto, Mount Angel Abbey Library. Librarians' control desk.*

FIGURE 22 *Aalto, Mount Angel Abbey Library. Study compartments, lower level.*

FIGURE 23 *Aalto, Mount Angel Abbey Library. View of single carrel, lower level.*

heirs to a very long and great transition of Benedictine libraries. From this we gain certain convictions about what a library should be. First of all, we believe that a library must be a place of peace and a place that gives visual delight."[37] Aalto may well have provided a library that exceeded their expectations.

Conclusion: The Ultimate Accolade

The recognition of Mount Angel Abbey Library as an outstanding American masterpiece by the hand of Alvar Aalto is now more than overdue. Given the recent global celebrations of Aalto's centenary, one must now ask to what extent this building was, here or in his homeland, justifiably considered in the reappraisal of his contribution to posterity. Invariably, comparisons of Aalto with Le Corbusier have proliferated in the critical arena, especially in the years following Aalto's death in 1976. For example, Alan Colquhoun wrote: "Architecture as the symbol of, and vehicle for, the collective life was a recurrent theme in Le Corbusier, as it was in Aalto."[38] The critical mood of the late 1970s revealed a confusion in discourse about the ensuing direction of modernism. In his memorable critique of the time, Colquhoun went on to argue that what was lacking in Aalto's work was the equation of

functionalism and rationalism. So what appealed to Aalto in nature was "its emergent and phenomenal forms, rather than the rational order to which it may be reduced." But times change.

In the past twenty years there has been a shift in the biological concept of life as a relentless Darwinian mechanism. The concept of the organism as such has faded from a central, commanding role, to be replaced by a focus on the activity of the cellular and molecular process. It is not necessary to be a neo-Darwinian to entertain the idea that organisms are indeterminate in their activity fields, their respective internal and external boundaries, their inside, their outside. Likewise, recent biological thinking concerning animal-built structures tends now to assume such structures as being part of the animal itself.[39] The physiologist today examines such an organism in terms of its operation, its energy and activity flows—and indeed, the information both within the organism and between the organism and the immediate environment. Consequently, what Richard Dawkins has called "the extended phenotype," does recognize the architectural "container" of an organism, which mediates between its external surroundings and internal characteristics.[40]

If one were to assess the Mount Angel Abbey Library in relation to such recent biological thought, it could

FIGURE 24 *Alvar Aalto, untitled oil painting (1963).*

be argued that the design's chief virtue lies in its superb functioning, both internally and externally, with regard to ancient Benedictine traditions. What is most interesting today and most positive about Aalto's libraries, and in particular Mount Angel, is precisely that interaction with the surroundings, that topological construct, and the extent to which it too can evolve and be manipulated to ensure adaptively the continuity of such perfect library conditions. Aalto, it seems, was not interested in establishing "archetypes," per se; rather his work seems to correspond more closely to establishing through architecture the concept of the "extended phenotype" as it is known today.

Aalto, of course, never concerned himself with the universality to which the early moderns aspired; instead he drew significant aspects of his work from the problem at hand, deriving them from the site as well as the context of the institutional or individual brief for the building concerned. In other words, he rejected mechanistic, a priori constructs. An analysis such as that of Colquhoun a generation ago would note how at the Viipuri Library, for example, the separate blocks signify a De Stijl–related compositional methodology, whereby overlapping volumes seem to be disconnected organizational types rather than irreducible spaces. There was then, by the same token, seen to be a "clumsiness in the entry system, which comes from trying to create an axis across the stratified volumes." This, in turn, "leads to the projecting porch and large window terminating the block—both of whose relationships to the main masses seem unresolved."[41] But such a methodology was deliberate on Aalto's part.

The architect did employ repetition in a manner that recalls the Russian Constructivists, as did his great friend László Moholy-Nagy. He was, as early as 1935, however, also searching for a more fruitful analogy between mechanical reproduction and biological or, equally important, geological processes.

In this respect, Aalto was already seeking a path outward, to create each building as a socially connected microcosm—as we understand it in contemporary terms—whose energy fields clearly must exist beyond their immediate premise. This was Aalto's "naturism," and it would be made still more manifest in subsequent designs. In reaching back for typological roots, Aalto, as I have suggested, seems to have anticipated the changes in biological thought which have emerged to shape the science of today.

What, then, are the implications of the Mount Angel Abbey Library within the varied typologies of Aalto's life work? On the one hand, the library stands as wholly Benedictine in its contemporary realization of an ancient tradition, thus positioned on the abbey lawn, unassuming internally for all its primary significance to the community. On the other, it presents externally a prominent profile on the landscape butte. Yet Mount Angel also represents a more generalized consummation of Aalto's evolving typology for the library. This began at the Viipuri Library, and given that Aalto returned repeatedly to the plan, Viipuri by definition has to be generic. Mount Angel also closely relates, as the monks realized, to both the Seinäjoki and Rovaniemi civic libraries. Indeed, Aalto had, by the end of his life, fulfilled a library architecture that repeated primary characteristics shared in common between projects, while also permitting each project to incorporate characteristics peculiar to an individual historical context, client, or site contour and the routes of movement related to the site.

Aalto undoubtedly sought through his architecture a practical affinity with nature. Initially, the building of the abbey library was designed to harness natural light where appropriate and to sustain heat as a first priority, as well as to adapt within rather than to ignore existing site contours in the formation of the eventual topology. Through his many drawings cited here, as well as others showing natural phenomena such as typhoons or foliage, he sought to identify and celebrate the nature of such happenings. Aalto's

buildings recognize the flows, pools, and eddies of circulation around them, human and material; his paintings metaphorically express such conjunctions (FIG. 24). These spaces are transmuted into the internal containers for human movement, separation, and congregation, and these qualities are channeled and duly accommodated within tactile surfaces and perceivable orientations. Thus the concept of phenology, as it is known today, has already been instinctively realized by Aalto in his work, where a particular site in his mind was always deemed to extend its sphere far beyond the immediate "footprint" of the building plan. At Mount Angel Abbey Library, as in Aalto's paintings, the materials so diligently utilized by Aalto were selected during a creative, harmonizing, all-embracing process. In this way, in the abbey stands one of Aalto's ultimate masterworks. Even though the library has been neglected by historians and critics, and ignored by centennial commentators, the Benedictine monks themselves were not at all displeased to simply be left in peace to continue their mission. Posterity, however, must surely do justice to this American masterwork by recognizing its historic importance now.

As Aalto once said, "It is neither the sentimental critics nor the need to learn refinement in proportions that draws me to Italy. Every culture, like every religion or ideology has an original, pure simplicity about it. The fundamental problem of architecture is not that of attaining formal perfection, but the task of creating an attractive environment with simple means in harmony with our biological needs. For me, Italy represents a certain primitivism, characterized to an astonishing degree by attractive forms on a human scale."[42] It could be said, then, that Mount Angel Library fulfilled at the deepest level Aalto's Italy-inspired humanistic ideal.

This too, Colin Rowe seemed to understand: "You gotta go look. I never expected to be impressed. I never liked Aalto at MIT, but all this leaves me extremely émotionné."[43]

1 Donald Canty, *Lasting Aalto Masterwork: The Library at Mount Angel Abbey* (St. Benedict, Ore.: Mount Angel Abbey, 1992), 22. Canty's book is the abbey's official guide.

2 The rule formulated by St. Benedict when the first Cassinese monastery was founded is well described in Tommaso Leccisotti, *Monte Cassino*, English ed. (Montecassino, Italy: Pubblicazioni Cassinesi, 1987). The rule became the fundamental code governing the growth and development of the Benedictine movement. "Reading" was to become a defining characteristic, with the provision, where possible, of a fully stocked library in every monastery.

3 Demetri Porphyrios, "The Retrieval of Memory: Alvar Aalto's Typological Conception of Design," *Oppositions* 22 (1980): 54.

4 Sigfried Giedion, *Space, Time and Architecture*, 3rd ed. (Cambridge, Mass.: Harvard Univ. Press, 1954), 565–608 (a chapter on Aalto is new to this edition).

5 Giedion states, "It [the library] was damaged in the first Russo-Finnish war and almost razed to the ground in the following conflict." Reyner Banham repeats that the library was "destroyed in the Russo-Finnish War." Karl Fleig states that it was "totally destroyed in the Russo-Finnish War and stands today in ruins." Charles Jencks simply claims that the library was "totally destroyed, 1943." The damage is qualified by Sergei Kravchenko, who explains how the library was in some part open to the elements in the immediate postwar period and traces the efforts to bring the library back into full use in the period following the changes in Soviet leadership in 1955. With international collaboration, efforts to restore the library continue to the present. See Giedion, *Space, Time and Architecture*, 578; Banham, *Guide to Modern Architecture* (London: Architectural Press, 1962), 126; Fleig, *Alvar Aalto* (Zürich: Artemis, 1963), 44; Jencks, *Architecture Today* (New York: Abrams, 1982), 302; and Kravchenko, quoted in Michael Spens, *Viipuri Library: Alvar Aalto* (London: Academy Editions, 1994), 72–81.

6 Unattrib., "Aalto's Second American Building: An Abbey Library for Oregon," *Architectural Record* 149 (May 1971): 112.

7 Ada Louise Huxtable, "Finnish Master Fashions Library for Abbey in Oregon," *New York Times*, 30 May 1970.

8 Ada Louise Huxtable, "Alvar Aalto's Humane Environments," *New York Times*, 17 June 1979.

9 Robert Venturi, *Complexity and Contradiction in Architecture* (New York: Museum of Modern Art Papers on Architecture, no. 1, 1966), 26–27.

10 Spens, *Viipuri Library*, 18 n. 1.

11 Vincent Scully, Jr., *Modern Architecture* (New York: Braziller, 1961), 37–44.

12 *Acanthus*, 1 Helsinki: Museum of Finnish Architecture, 1990), with articles on Viipuri Library by Simo Paavilainen, K. Nivari, Sergei Kravchenko, and others. See also Eija Rauske, "Viipuri City Library," in *Alvar Aalto in Seven Buildings/Alvar Aalto in sieben Bauwerken*, eds. Tino Tuomi, Kristina Paatero, Eija Rauske (Helsinki: Museum of Finnish Architecture, 1998), 28–33; and Spens, *Viipuri Library*.

13 See Peter Reed, ed., *Alvar Aalto: Between Humanism and Materialism* (New York: Museum of Modern Art, 1998), including a comment in Kenneth Frampton's chapter in that volume: "The Legacy of Alvar Aalto: Evolution and Influence." "Aalto's checkered reception in North America could hardly have been more paradoxical" (133). See also Elina Standertskjöld, "Alvar Aalto and the United States," in *Alvar Aalto: Toward a Human Modernism*, ed. Winfried Nerdinger (Munich: Prestel Verlag, 1999), 77–90; and Richard Weston, *Alvar Aalto* (London: Phaidon, 1995), which is thematically selective. The index of works in these volumes nonetheless lists the library along with Aalto's other American works: Baker House, MIT (1947–48); Woodberry Poetry Room, Lamont Library, Harvard University (1949); and Edgar J. Kaufmann Conference Rooms, Institute of International Education, New York (1963–65).

14 Frederick Gutheim, *Alvar Aalto* (New York: Braziller, 1960), 26.

15 From Alvar Aalto, "The Trout and the Stream" (1948), in *Alvar Aalto in His Own Words*, ed. Göran Schildt (New York: Rizzoli, 1998), 107–9.

16 Kenneth Frampton, *Modern Architecture: A Critical History* (London: Oxford Univ. Press, 1980), 196–98.

17 The artist was one of number of a large number of Renaissance painters who selected St. Jerome (ca. 340–420) in his idealized "carrel" as a subject to represent individual learning through books.

18 Umberto Eco, *The Name of the Rose* (London: Martin Secker & Warburg, 1983).

19 Eco, *The Name of the Rose*, 38.

20 Canty, *Lasting Aalto Masterwork*, 20, 21.

21 Canty, *Lasting Aalto Masterwork*, 20–21.

22 Correspondence quoted in Canty, *Lasting Aalto Masterwork*, 22. Aalto's attitude to mail correspondence was famously relaxed, as testified to by Vernon DeMars: "Incoming mail would pile up on Aalto's desk. He would flip through it, looking for Finnish stamps (the sign of a letter from his wife): the rest he would merely ignore." DeMars, "Humanism and Mount Angel Library," unpublished paper, presented at the Alvar Aalto Symposium, Cornell University, 21 Feb. 21, 1981, 8. See *Cornell Architecture: The Preston H. Thomas Memorial Lecture Series: Alvar Aalto* (Ithaca, New York: Cornell Univ. Department of Architecture, 1981)

Cornell University Archives. The British critic P. Morton Shand had a similarly frustrating experience while seeking a reply to correspondence. Aalto's secretary Mrs Sargit Avellan wrote to him to explain the delay: "A fishing tour some time ago resulted with a broken bone in Professor Aalto's foot, that putting him out of circulation for a few weeks. There are no telephone facilities." Letter from Aalto's secretary Mrs Sargit Avellan to Shand, 23 July 1948. Archive of P. Morton Shand (Curator Michael Spens) University of Dundee.

23 The monk flew across the United States and the Atlantic Ocean to Switzerland from Portland to meet Aalto, at the Hotel Eden au Lac in Zurich, where Aalto confirmed he would be staying. Father Barnabas "at the appointed hour approached Aalto in the lobby of the luxury hotel and introduced himself as 'Father Barnabas from Mt. Angel.'" What seemed improbable when first proposed now came to fruition. Göran Schildt, *Alvar Aalto: His Life* (Jyväskylä: Alvar Aalto Museum, 2007), 700–701.

24 Erik Vartiainen worked for the Aalto office for all of Aug. 1962, and then from 15 Aug. 1963 to 31 Dec. 1966. DeMars, "Humanism and Mount Angel Library," 7–12. On DeMars's time at MIT with Aalto, see p. 8.

25 On the San Francisco architect William W. Wurster, see Gail Fenske, "Aalto, Wurster, and the 'New Humanism'" in the present volume.

26 Howard Vollum and Jean Vollum, known as "friends of the abbey," contributed $1 million in support of the library's construction. See Canty, *Lasting Aalto Masterwork*, 28.

27 See letter from Alvar Aalto to P. Morton Shand, 17 July 1948 (archive of P. Morton Shand, University of Dundee). As above; see note 22. "Together with the town architect of Viipuri I finally found an area close to the Cathedral. After this my new library project and its location were approved of. Then suddenly hell was raised from clerical circles (too close to the Cathedral!). . . . The fight lasted three years. The City Council was correct and kept calm, accepting my new project." Viipuri Cathedral, despite surviving the war, was demolished on the grounds of safety shortly afterward. This removed a key contextual factor that Aalto had intentionally sought to engage in his final, built design.

28 Canty, *Lasting Aalto Masterwork*, 26, 28.

29 Canty, *Lasting Aalto Masterwork*, 29.

30 Letter from Colin Rowe to the author, 29 May 1995. In fact, a former student of Aalto, James Tice, Professor of Architecture at the University of Oregon, had traveled with Rowe to visit Mount Angel earlier that month. In subsequent discussion with me, and later on the occasion of his Royal Institute of British Architects Gold Medal address in 1995, Rowe was emphatic in his praise for Aalto generally.

31 The subject of Aalto and topology is more fully explored by Michael Spens in "Alvar Aalto, New York Before and After," *Architectural Design,* Vol 68, Issue 11/12 (Nov. 1998): vi–ix, esp. viii, which refers to the unbuilt Kokkola library (design, 1966–71).

32 Stanford Anderson, "Memory in Architecture," *Daidalos* 58 (Dec. 1995): 22–37. There is important consideration here of "memory," particularly the conclusions on "typology/formal precedents," 31–34.

33 Colin Rowe, "Dominican Monastery of La Tourette," "*Architectural Review* 129, no. 772 June 1961; reprinted as "La Tourette" in Rowe, *The Mathematics of the Ideal Villa and Other Essays* (Cambridge, Mass.: MIT Press, 1976),., 185-203.

34 The quote is not verifiable as Aalto's, but was referenced in the Aalto office in 1996 by Elissa Aalto to the author.

35 Alvar Aalto, "In Lieu of an Article," an interview with Sigfried Giedion (faked by Aalto with the collusion of the editor Nils Erik Wickberg), *Arkkitehti* 1–2 (1958); reprinted, with comment, in *Aalto in His Own Words*, ed. Schildt, 262–63.

36 Canty, *Lasting Aalto Masterwork,* 28.

37 Ibid, 28.

38 Alan Colquhoun, "Alvar Aalto: Type versus Function," *L'Architecture d'aujourd'hui* (1976); reprinted in Colquhoun, *Essays in Architectural Criticism* (Cambridge: MIT Press, 1981), 75–81.

39 Richard Dawkins, *The Extended Phenotype* (Oxford: W. H. Freeman, 1982). Dawkins had defined "extended phenotype" as "the extension of the action of the genes beyond the outermost boundaries of the organism itself." This is a major theme repeated throughout Dawkins.

40 J. Scott Turner, *The Extended Organism: The Physiology of Animal-Built Structures* (Cambridge, Mass.: Harvard Univ. Press, 2000). Here Dawkins' theory is developed with special reference to built structures in nature (and summarized on pp. 211–12).

41 Colquhoun, *Essays in Architectural Criticism,* 75.

42 Alvar Aalto, Interview from *Casabella Continuità,* no. 200 (Feb/March 1954), translated/reprinted as "Journey to Italy" in *Alvar Aalto in his Own Words,* ed. Schildt, 38–39, 39 (for quote).

43 Letter from Colin Rowe to the author, 29 May 1995. Rowe added: "I became a convert: and I don't mean to the order of St. Benedict, but to this particular Aalto library."

Documents: Aalto on America

TECHNOLOGY REVIEW 43

November 1940

The Humanizing of Architecture

Functionalism Must Take the Human Point of View to Achieve Its Full Effectiveness

In contrast with that architecture whose main concern is the formalistic style which a building shall wear, stands the architecture which we know as functionalism. The development of the functional idea and its expression in structures are probably the most invigorating occurrences in architectural activity in our time, and yet function in architecture — and so also functionalism — are not so very easy to interpret precisely. "Function" is the characteristic use, or work, or action or a thing. "Function" is also a thing or quantity that depends upon, and varies with, another. "Functionalism" the dictionaries boldly define as "conscious adaptation of form to use" — it is both less and more than that, for truly it must recognize and reckon with both or the meanings of "function."

Architecture is a synthetic phenomenon covering practically all fields of human activity. An object in the architectural field may be functional from one point of view and unfunctional from another. During the past decade, Modern architecture has been functional chiefly from the technical point of view, with its emphasis mainly on the economic side of the building activity. Such emphasis is desirable, of course, for production of good shelters for the human being has been a very expensive process as compared with the fulfillment of some other human needs. Indeed, if architecture is to have a larger human value, the first step is to organize its economic side. But, since architecture covers the entire field of human life, real functional architecture must be functional mainly from the human point of view. If we look deeper into the processes of human life, we shall discover that technic is only an aid, not a definite and independent phenomenon therein. Technical functionalism cannot create definite architecture.

If there were a way to develop architecture step by step, beginning with the economic and technical aspect and later covering the other more complicated human functions, then the purely technical functionalism would be acceptable; but no such possibility exists. Architecture not only covers all fields of human activity; it must even be developed in all these fields at the same time. If not, we shall have only one-sided, superficial results.

The term "rationalism" appears in connection with Modern architecture about as often as does "functionalism." Modern architecture has been rationalized mainly from the technical point of view, in the same way as the technical functions have been emphasized. Although the purely rational period of Modern architecture has created constructions where

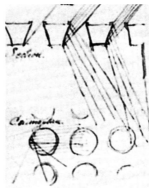

Diffused sunlight enters the combined hall and reading room of the Viipuri Library through conical skylights calculated to catch the sun's rays at even their highest angle and scatter light uniformly on the reader's book, as the designer's croquis indicate.

rationalized technique has been exaggerated and the human functions have not been emphasized enough, this is not a reason to fight rationalization in architecture. It is not the rationalization itself which was wrong in the first and now past period of Modern architecture. The wrongness lies in the fact that the rationalization has not gone deep enough. Instead of fighting rational mentality, the newest phase of Modern architecture tries to project rational methods from the technical field out to human and psychological fields.

It might be well to have an example: One of the typical activities in Modern architecture has been the construction of chairs and the adoption of new materials and new methods for them. The tubular steel chair is surely rational from technical and constructive points of view: It is light, suitable for mass production, and so on. But steel and chromium surfaces are not satisfactory from the human point of view. Steel is too good a conductor of heat. The chromium surface gives too bright reflections of light, and even acoustically is not suitable for a room. The rational methods of creating this furniture style have been on the right track, but the result will be good only if rationalization is exercised in the selection of materials which are most suitable for human use.

The present phase of Modern architecture is doubtless a new one, with the special aim of solving problems in the humanitarian and psychological fields. This new period, however, is not in contradiction to the first period of technical rationalization. Rather, it is to be understood as an enlargement of rational methods to encompass related fields.

During the past decades architecture has often been compared with science, and there have been efforts to make its methods more scientific, even efforts to make it a pure science. But architecture is not a science. It is still the same great synthetic process of combining thousands of definite human functions, and remains architecture. Its purpose is still to bring the material world into harmony with human life. To make architecture more human means better architecture, and it means a functionalism much larger than the merely technical one. This goal can be accomplished only by architectural methods — by the creation and combination of different technical things in such a way that they will provide for the human being the most harmonious life.

Architectural methods sometimes resemble scientific ones, and a process of research, such as science employs, can be adopted also in architecture. Architectural research can be more and more methodical, but the substance of it can never be solely analytical. Always there will be more of instinct and art in architectural research.

Scientists very often use exaggerated forms in analyses in order to obtain clearer, more visible results — bacteria are stained, and so on. The same methods can be adopted in architecture, also. I have had personal experience with hospital buildings where I was able to discover that especial physical and psychological reactions by patients provided good pointers for ordinary housing. If we proceed from technical functionalism, we shall discover that a great many things in our present architecture are unfunctional from the point of view of psychology or a combination of psychology and physiology. To examine how human beings react to forms and construction, it is useful to use for experimentation especially sensitive persons, such as patients in a sanatorium.

Experiments of this kind were performed in connection with the Paimio Tuberculosis Sanatorium building in Finland and were carried on mainly in two special fields: (1) the relation between the single human being and his living room;

(2) the protection of the single human being against large groups of people and the pressure from collectivity. Study of the relation between the individual and his quarters involved the use of experimental rooms and covered the questions of room form, colors, natural and artificial light, heating system, noise, and so on. This first experiment dealt with a person in the weakest possible condition, a bed patient. One of the special results discovered was the necessity for changing the colors in the room. In many other ways, the experiment showed, the room must be different from the ordinary room. This difference can be explained thus: the ordinary room is a room for a vertical person; a patient's room is a room for a horizontal human being, and colors, lighting, heating, and so on must be designed with that in mind.

Practically, this fact means that the ceiling should be darker, with an especially selected color suitable to be the only view of the reclining patient for weeks and weeks. The artificial light cannot come from an ordinary ceiling fixture, but the principal center of light should be beyond the angle of vision of the patient. For the heating system in the experimental room, ceiling radiators were used but in a way which threw the heat mainly at the foot of the bed so that the head of the patient was outside the direct heat rays. The location of the windows and doors likewise took into account the patient's position. To avoid noise, one wall in the room was sound absorbing, and wash basins (each patient in the two-patient rooms had his own) were especially designed so that the flow of water from the faucet hit the porcelain basin always at a very small angle and worked noiselessly.

These are only a few illustrations from an experimental room at the sanatorium, and they are here mentioned merely as examples of architectural methods, which always are a combination of technical, physical, and psychological phenomena, never any one of them alone. Technical functionalism is correct only if enlarged to cover even the psychophysical field. That is the only way to humanize architecture.

A picture of a typical patients' room at the sanatorium accompanies this article. Two other examples — from the Viipuri Municipal Library — show similar problems. The flexible wooden furniture is a result of experiments also made at the Paimio Sanatorium. At the time of those experiments the first tubular chromium furniture was just being constructed in Europe. Tubular and chromium surfaces are good solutions technically, but psychophysically these materials are not good for the human being. The sanatorium needed furniture which should be light, flexible, easy to clean, and so on. After extensive experimentation in wood, the flexible system was discovered and a method and material combined to produce furniture which was better for the human touch and more suitable as the general material for the long and painful life in a sanatorium.

The first picture of the Viipuri Municipal Library shows only one part, but the most important part, of this building. The main problem connected with a library is that of the human eye. A library can be well constructed and can be

Lecture hall in the Viipuri Municipal Library.

functional in a technical way even without the solving of this problem, but it is not humanly and architecturally complete unless it deals satisfactorily with the main human function in the building, that of reading a book. The eye is only a tiny part of the human body, but it is the most sensitive and perhaps the most important part. To provide a natural or an artificial light which destroys the human eye or which is unsuitable for its use, means reactionary architecture even if the building should otherwise be of high constructive value.

Daylight through ordinary windows, even if they are very large, covers only a part of a big room. Even if the room is lighted sufficiently, the light will be uneven and will vary on different points of the floor. That is why skylights have mainly been used in libraries, museums, and so on. But skylight, which covers the entire floor area, gives an exaggerated light, if extensive additional arrangements are not made. In the library building in the accompanying illustrations, the problem was solved with the aid of numerous round skylights so constructed that the light could be termed indirect daylight. The round skylights are technically rational because of the monopiece glass system employed. (Every skylight consists of a conical concrete basement six feet in diameter, and a thick jointless round piece of glass on top of it without any frame construction.) This system is humanly rational because it provides a kind of light suitable for reading, blended and softened by being reflected from the conical surfaces of the skylights. In Finland the largest angle of sunlight is almost 52 degrees. The concrete cones are so constructed that the sunlight always remains indirect. The surfaces of the cones spread the light in millions or directions. Theoretically, for instance, the light reaches an open book from all these different directions and thus avoids a reflection to the human eye from the white pages of the book. (Bright reflection from book pages is one of the most fatiguing phenomena in reading.) In the same way this lighting system eliminates shadow phenomena regardless of the position of the reader. The problem of reading a book is more than a problem of the eye; a good reading light permits the use of many positions of the human body and every suitable relation between book and eye. Reading a book involves both culturally and physically a strange kind of concentration; the duty of architecture is to eliminate all disturbing elements.

It is possible in a scientific way to ascertain what kinds and what quantities of light are ideally the most suitable for the human eye, but in constructing a room the solution must be made with the aid of all the different elements which architecture embraces. Here the skylight system is a combined product of the ceiling construction (a room almost sixty feet wide needs a ceiling construction with beams high enough for the erection of the deep cones) and special technical limits in horizontal glass construction. An architectural solution must always have a human motive based on analysis, but that motive has to be materialized in construction which probably is a result of extraneous circumstances. The examples mentioned here are very tiny problems. But they are very close to the human being and hence become more important than problems of much larger scope.

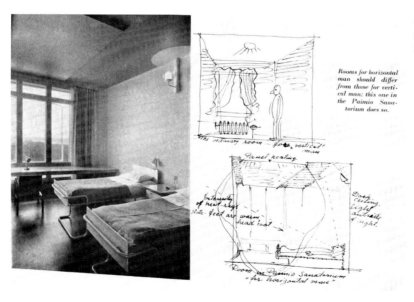

Rooms for horizontal man should differ from those for vertical man; this one in the Paimio Sanatorium does so.

ARKKITEHTI

No. 1, 1945

The Intellectual Background of American Architecture

The most conspicuous quality of American architecture is its democratic spirit. By this I do not mean its direct links with political democracy, a republican form of government, etc., but that architecture itself tends to pay more heed to the general public than in most other countries.

Politically, America is a daughter of the Enlightenment, and her architecture also dates from that period, at least insofar as post-Revolutionary architecture is concerned. The democracy of American architecture is not easy to explain to the Finnish public. I am here taking as my point of reference the Hegelian philosophy of [J. V.] Snellman— that is, an opponent to the Enlightenment world of ideas. Snellman once published a manly and elegant critique of his opponents that provides the best bridge I know to understanding the Enlightenment and the great Western cultural paradigm it represents. Snellman indirectly hints that he considers the Enlightenment philosophers somehow superficial, somehow as dilettantes in philosophy, but notes that they were, and indeed still are, a major influence in defining life and the world in their own era. This is how Snellman puts it: "Before God, there is in this superficiality more warmth and more seriousness about 'the thing in itself' than in all contemporary German philosophy." By this he naturally means that the influence of Enlightenment philosophy went deeper and its outlook on life was more practical than the doctrinaire continental way of thinking.

In exactly the same way, from a doctrinaire perspective, American architecture seems to have a more superficial intellectual basis but in reality its influence on practical life is stronger.

An excellent example is provided by Thomas Jefferson, the true father of American neoclassicism. The more doctrinaire schools would hardly consider him a philosopher at all: they would probably relegate him to the category of dilettantes. The practical results he achieved, however, decisively influenced American life. He was one of the authors of the Declaration of Independence and the third President of the young republic; above all, however, he was the real originator of the democratic way of thinking and democratic forms of American everyday life. Jefferson himself thought of architecture as one of his main occupations, and laid the foundation for an American architecture.

While neoclassicism in Europe turned to rigid forms serving as a stage set for the continental empires, in America it took a completely different turn. Paradoxically, we might say that there the rigid Palladian tradition gave rise to architectural democracy.

The post-neoclassical period turned America into a land of small, elegant, white wooden houses. There architecture belonged, in the best sense, to everyman, and adapted to a wide variety of social conditions. The vernacular character of this architecture was increased by a striking flexibility, permitting buildings to be used for a whole range of purposes. This colonial architecture was not based on symmetrical building volumes, but adopted instead a practice of asymmetry, even permitting buildings to grow as necessary, adapting flexibly to their terrain. It is precisely this freedom that expresses the democratic spirit of American architecture.

Owing to these qualities, the American architectural tradition has had far greater vitality than its European counterpart. The American tradition has been more flexible and better adapted to the practical demands of everyday life; it has followed transformations in society far more readily right up to the present day. The strength of this tradition has been such that we may say without exaggeration that American neoclassicism formed a bridge that directly led up to the most recent developments in architecture and thus, as it were, sired present-day, socially oriented architecture.

This extensive architectural flexibility and freedom partly explains the boom periods that have occurred time and again in American architecture, so powerful that they have significantly influenced even architectural thinking in the Old World.

An example of this is the gradual advance of rationalist architecture seen in the United States since the middle of the last century, forming a continuous chain with no end in sight. Richardson, Sullivan and Frank Lloyd Wright hold an undisputed place among the great names in world architecture, and as the forceful heralds of present-day trends.

It has been said that the United States, as it were, ran through all of architectural history within the space of one century (the seventeenth), from lean-to shelter to log cabin, then on to primitive stone buildings and to modernity. The comparison, of course, is misleading. Though true enough in a formal sense, on closer examination we find that life on the American continent was simply a direct extension of the ways of life the same people and nations had previously worked out for themselves in Europe. Obviously, swift colonization left its mark on American architecture, adding certain properties without isolating it from international developments. The influence of the colonial era can still be felt; it brought a distinctive freshness to architecture, and the resulting special characteristics have long been very useful to the Old World, too.

The colonial era is responsible for a fatal error made by many Europeans in judging American culture. Europeans tend to forget that the Americans have established a strong architectural tradition that shows no other break with European cultural developments than that arising naturally from geography. America already possessed a noteworthy architectural heritage at the time when the United States came into being, and it was during that very period that it acquired independent features, with a new self-confidence giving rise to brilliant forms. Further light is cast on the architectural tradition by the fact that Thomas Jefferson—author of the Declaration of Independence, third President of the United States and founding father of the new nation's democratic form of government and general democratic attitudes—was also a notable architect, a promoter of neoclassicism in America.

The American "colonial style" is, of course, well-known in Europe, but the extraordinary vitality of the style is not. At the same time as European neoclassicism, the official court style of Berlin and St Petersburg, among others—led to rigid, purely representational architecture, the neoclassical movement in the New World, inspired by newly-won independence, evolved in a completely different direction. There it gave rise to an architectural freedom giving the human imagination free rein, while generating forms that expressly served the whole nation and could be adapted to a wide variety of everyday needs. Paradoxically, we might say that the American application of the Palladian tradition thus gave rise to architectural democracy.

This remarkable freedom of form can be seen equally in the buildings, the plans of garden towns, and the interiors, even in technical furnishing details. The evolution of the American colonial style and Georgian architecture culminated in a conception of flexibility that is still undeniably influential today. This flexible approach gave rise to remarkably refined housing design, enabled the adaptation of buildings to the needs of many different kinds of people, terrain, and natural conditions, and permitted the growth of buildings in stages. It was thus responsible for present-day American residential architecture, which consists primarily of small, light, elegant timber structures, adapted to a free town plan reminiscent of a rural setting. The fact that the United States contain several different geographical areas with contrasting climate conditions has contributed to this flexibility.

The high quality of old American architecture, its democratic human value, and above all its flexibility have contributed to maintaining, longer than in Europe, the predominance of tradition in this modern, supposedly "unscrupulous" pioneer country. The tradition is so strong that it provides fruitful, direct points of contact even with the most recent construction, i.e., that following the architectural revolution of the twenties.

The colonial era did not end with the architectural style to which it gave its name. It subsisted in some form or other almost up to the present day. Migration from the east to the formerly uninhabited wilds of the west kept American architecture on the move, in a condition that lent it a certain mobility and lightness that cannot be found elsewhere on a comparable scale. On the slopes of the Californian side of the Sierra Nevada, one may still see the ghost towns of the Gold Rush, which have a spontaneous lightness and delicacy and the temporary character that always accompanies this type of construction, providing an excellent illustration of the most recent trends in American architecture.

Among the traditions that have influenced American architecture, we should also include the primitive buildings of Native Americans. The straightforward adobe structures of the Indian villages of Arizona and Colorado have had an influence on even the most recent New World architecture, and a small but significant role has also been played by the archeological excavations and studies being carried out further south, in Mexico and the Yucatan.

In contemporary architecture, America has given as good as it has taken, and since the middle of the last century American architects have been creating intensely independent forms revealing a certain rationalism. One of the earliest pioneers of the modern trend was indubitably Henry Hobson Richardson, who had a strong influence on European designers; for example, many turn-of-the-century Finnish architects (including Sonck, Saarinen, and Lindgren) owe a significant debt to Richardson. A southerner educated in France (at the École des Beaux-Arts), Richardson developed certain fundamental features of contemporary architecture quite extensively. Among his major works, Glessner House, Ames House, and the Marshall Field department store in Chicago particularly deserve to be mentioned. His work is characterized by the use of natural materials, plain, masculine exteriors, and a functionalist approach to big-city problems.

Another pioneer who must be mentioned is Louis Sullivan. He followed Richardson in introducing constructive features into architecture. Like his predecessor, Sullivan also exercised a considerable influence on European architects. For many years Sullivan was the grand old man of American architecture, and many outstanding architects rose from the ranks of his assistants. The confidence inspired by Sullivan is shown by the fact that he was entrusted with the task of judging the architectural competition for the Chicago Tribune building on his own. The rival entries of Raymond Hood and Eliel Saarinen made this competition particularly significant with respect to skyscraper design. Among Sullivan's works, the present exhibition features the Pirie Scott department store in Chicago, a graphic illustration of its designer's pioneering achievement.

Curiously enough, the emphasis in American architecture—whether we speak of spontaneously generated new forms, new plan solutions, or remarkable personalities—is not on the East Coast but in the Midwest, the source of so much of the mature creative work that typifies America. The leading contemporary American architect, Frank Lloyd Wright, also hails from the Midwest, from the forests of Wisconsin. His home in Taliesin has long been the site of a private academy with an influence that extends well beyond architecture to other spheres of American cultural life. An eccentric personality, Wright towers as one of the undisputed leaders of contemporary architecture.

Assessments of American architecture during the past few decades often suffer from two mistaken assumptions: first, that the architectural revolution that took place in Europe after the Great War, leading to the breakthrough of rationalism, functionalism and a basic social way of thinking, took place on an equally dramatic scale in America; and second, that the impulse came entirely from Europe. This is simply not true. America's contribution to the emergence of modern architecture is fully comparable with that of Europe. Here again, the name of Frank Lloyd Wright alone is enough to prove my point. He was one of the first architects, if not the first, to make use of free forms in the modern sense, as made possible by concrete. The many private houses designed by him in the Midwest, primarily in Chicago and its surroundings, also combine comfort with gentle psychological insight. To be sure, his buildings are not rationalist architecture in the ordinary sense of the term, as they contain mystic elements and reflect a remarkable quest for decorative values, but even here he has often proved right even in the most recent years.

Frank Lloyd Wright seeks a form of society in which present-day antitheses can be juxtaposed and brought into harmony. His buildings do not spring up, rootless, from the mere material architectural assignment; they have a social background that can always be detected, though often in a remarkably veiled form. With the experience of a long career and, more importantly, as a creative architect, Wright represents a link with the art nouveau style of the turn of the century—not an entirely alien feature to the European architecture of the last few decades, either. Like Richardson and Sullivan before him, but with even greater success, Wright uses those elements of the American colonial and post-colonial architectural tradition that are still valid in the modern world. His ground plans are particularly interesting in this respect. The true foundation of his art, however—as, indeed, the foundation of all coherent, balanced creative work—lies in the way he has resolved hundreds of different kinds of contradictions. In Wright's work, Chinese philosophy, the systematic housing standards of Japan, and the mysticism of the natives of Yucatan merge with modern social rationalism.

Naturally enough, contemporary American architecture was also influenced by the transition in Europe in the twenties. A special characteristic should be stressed here. Intellectual life in America is in some ways free of complexes: artificial national aspirations have not prevented the Americans from accepting foreign influences. Indeed, the reverse is true: the structure of American cities is in part based on freely imported ideas. The Americans understand that such imports enrich the nation in a spiritual sense without fearing that they might undermine the equilibrium of their lives or damage the characteristic features of American-ness. In many respects, America is now assuming a role reminiscent of that of France in the period when European life was governed by French culture. In those days, it was said that every civilized person had two homelands, his own and France. Architects, at least, might well say the same with reference to America.

Thus, a large number of notable European architects are now working in America. For us Finns, the emigration of Eliel Saarinen in the early '20s demonstrated the magnetic attraction of American culture. Saarinen's career in America as an architect and director of Cranbrook Academy has been a natural continuation of his work in Finland, without any intervening artificial metamorphosis. It is a prime example of internationalism and of how abilities developed in one country can serve to enrich another country, and universal culture.

Many pioneering architects in the Old World, including many of those involved in implementing the great transition, are now active in America, foremost among them Walter Gropius, director of the Bauhaus in the days of the Weimar Republic, who has also almost directly continued his earlier work in the capacity of director of the Harvard School of Architecture.

One of the reasons for the ease with which European designers have found their niche in America is that European architecture has for many years, though often inadvertently, been subjected to the influence of pioneering American architecture. But young American architects have also been involved in the recent transition. First and foremost among them is Raymond Hood, the skyscraper architect, with many others in his wake.

Many Europeans think that American society, in all its individualism, is not the result of planned development in the same way as Europe is. This is another misconception. It is true that American cities appear to have grown spontaneously, with big-city contrasts taking on sometimes abnormal forms, but the same hazards and the same social ills are by no means less well-known in Europe, although there may be differences of scale. In this respect, the growth of American communities is linked with the British colonial empire, the centers of which appear to have grown in an unplanned way compared with continental cities; and yet, curiously enough, they have also given rise to outstanding town plans. The doctrinaire neoclassical town planning of the Old World finds a freer counterpart in America, where it arose as a result of self-discipline and individual (often amateurish) architectural instinct and interest. The innumerable residential garden towns from the early and later colonial era stand as living proof of this.

In recent years—and especially under the Roosevelt administration—a more planned approach, even outright economic planning, has come to the fore. At a time that has seen the promulgation of the Russian Five-Year-Plan and the rise of social town planning in Britain, France, Germany and the smaller western states, America has begun the planned construction of large empty spaces and the renovation of old communities. Systematic development of the Tennessee Valley, with the planned construction of power stations, road networks, and related communities stands as an example of this trend; various social experiments have also been initiated.

In the past few years, the war has wrought many changes in America. The shift of emphasis to the arms industry generated an industrial boom in conditions that differed radically from previous periods. This meant the mass construction of communities, various ways to build quickly, and new methods of social planning that are in many instances the result of planning processes so far-reaching that they will continue to exercise an influence on architecture after the war. We may surmise that the war culminated a process that has led away from individualism and towards a focus on the overall social fabric in America, but this trend is likely to be balanced by the American tradition, preventing the obligation to plan and the collectivizing influence of social superstructures from getting out of hand.

Select Bibliography

There are a number of bibliographies on Alvar Aalto and his works, which provide an overview of the scholarship on Aalto. Among these are William C. Miller's Alvar Aalto: An Annotated Bibliography (London: Garland Publishing, 1984) and more recently the bibliographies in the publications accompanying the Aalto centennial of 1998, such as Peter Reed's Alvar Aalto: Between Humanism and Materialism (New York: Museum of Modern Art, 1998). This bibliography, in keeping with the theme of the book, emphasizes Aalto's relationship to American architectural thought and practice.

Aalto, Alvar. "Finland" *Architectural Forum* 72 (1940) 399–412.

Aalto, Alvar. "The Humanizing of Architecture: Functionalism Must Take the Human Point of View to Achieve Its Full Effectiveness" *Technology Review* (1940) 14–16, 36; republished as "The Humanizing of Architecture" in Göran Schildt, ed. *Alvar Aalto in His Own Words* (New York: Rizzoli, 1998) 102–07.

Aalto, Alvar. "The Intellectual Background of American Architecture" *Arkkitehti* 1 (1945); republished as "The 'America Builds' Exhibition in Helsinki, 1945" in Göran Schildt, ed. *Alvar Aalto in His Own Words* (New York: Rizzoli, 1998) 131–36.

Aalto, Alvar. *Post-War Reconstruction: Rehousing Research in Finland* (New York: n.p., 1940).

Anderson, Stanford. "The 'New Empiricism - Bay Region Axis': Kay Fisker and Postwar Debates on Functionalism, Regionalism, and Monumentality" *Journal of Architectural Education* 50 (1997) 197–207.

Burchard, John E. "Finland and Architect Aalto" *Architectural Record* 125 (1959) 127–36.

Canty, Donald. *Lasting Aalto Masterwork: The Library of Mount Angel Abbey* (St. Benedict, Oregon: Mount Angel Abbey, 1992).

Colquhoun, Alan. "Alvar Aalto: Type versus Function" in Alan Colquhoun, ed. *Essays in Architectural Criticism: Modern Architecture and Historical Change* (Cambridge, Mass.: The MIT Press, 1981) 75–81.

Connah, Roger. *Aalto MANIA: Readings Against Aalto?* (Helsinki: Building Information, 2000).

Connah, Roger. *Finland: Modern Architectures in History* (London: Reaktion Books, 2005).

Fleig, Karl, ed. *Alvar Aalto: 1922–1962* [The complete works in 3 volumes], Trans. William B. Gleckman, Henry A. Frey and H. R. Von der Mühll (Zurich: Les Editions d'Architecture Artémis, 1970).

Fenske, Gail. "Lewis Mumford, Henry-Russell Hitchcock, and the Bay Region Style" in Martha Pollak, ed. *The Education of the Architect: Historiography, Urbanism, and the Growth of Architectural Knowledge* (Cambridge, Mass.: MIT Press, 1997) 37–85.

Floyd, Margaret Henderson, ed. *Architectural Education in Boston: Centennial Publication of the Boston Architectural Center, 1889–1989* (Boston: Boston Architectural Center, 1989).

Giedeon, Sigfried. *Space, Time and Architecture: The Growth of a New Tradition* 5th ed. (Cambridge, Mass.: Harvard University Press, 1967).

Goldstone, Harmon Hendricks. "Alvar Aalto" *Magazine of Art* 32 (1939) 208–21.

Gutheim, Frederick. *Alvar Aalto* (New York: Braziller, 1960).

Hession, Jane King, Rip Rapson and Bruce N. Wright. *Ralph Rapson: Sixty Years of Modern Design* (Afton, Minn.: Afton Historical Press, 1999).

Hoseli, Bernhard, ed. *Alvar Aalto: Synopsis. Painting, Architecture, Sculpture. Malerei, Architektur, Skulptur. Peinture, architecture, sculpture* (Basel: Birkhauser Verlag, 1970).

Huxtable, Ada Louise. "Aalto in New York" *Interior Design* (1965) 180.

Huxtable, Ada Louise. "Finnish Master Fashions Library for Abbey in Oregon" *New York Times* (30 May 1970).

Johnson, Stewart. *Alvar Aalto: Furniture and Glass* (New York: Museum of Modern Art, 1984).

Jormakka, Kari, Jacqueline Gargus, and Douglas Graf. "The Use and Abuse of Paper: Essays on Aalto" *Datutop* 20 (Tampere: Tampere University of Technology, 1999).

Kaufmann, Edgar J., Jr. "Aalto on First Avenue" *Interior Design* (1984) 270.

Kinnunen, Ulla, ed. *Aino Aalto* (Helsinki: Alvar Aalto Foundation, 2004).

Korvenmaa, Pekka, ed. *Alvar Aalto, Architect: Sunila, 1936–54* (Helsinki: Alvar Aalto Foundation/Alvar Aalto Academy, 2003).

Korvenmaa, Pekka. "The Finnish Wooden House Transformed: American Prefabrication, War-Time Housing and Alvar Aalto" *Construction History* 6 (1990) 47–61.

Lahti, Louna. *Alvar Aalto - ex intimo: Alvar Aalto Through the Eyes of Family, Friends, and Colleagues* Trans. Roger Connah and Tomi Snellman (Helsinki: Building Information, 2001).

MacKeith, Peter, and Kerstin Smeds. *The Finland Pavilions: Finland at the Universal Expositions, 1900–1992* (Helsinki: Kustannus Oy City, 1992).

McAndrew, John, ed. *Architecture and Furniture: Aalto* (New York: Museum of Modern Art, 1938).

Menin, Sarah and Flora Samuel. *Nature and Space: Aalto and Le Corbusier* (London and New York: Routledge, 2003).

Michelson, Alan R. "Towards a Regional Synthesis: The Suburban and Country Residences of William Wilson Wurster, 1922–64" PhD diss., Stanford University Press, 1993.

Mock, Elizabeth, ed. *Built in USA, 1932–1944* (New York: Museum of Modern Art, 1944).

Mumford, Lewis. "The Skyline: Status Quo" *The New Yorker* (11 October 1947) 104–10.

Nerdinger, Winfried, ed. *Alvar Aalto: Toward a Human Modernism* (New York: Prestel, 1999).

Pallasmaa, Juhani. *Alvar Aalto, Architect: The Aalto House, 1935–36* (Helsinki: Alvar Aalto Foundation/Alvar Aalto Academy, 2004).

Pallasmaa, Juhani and Tomoko Sato, eds. *Alvar Aalto through the Eyes of Shigeru Ban* (London: Blackdog, 2007).

Pallasmaa, Juhani, ed. *Alvar Aalto: Furniture* (Helsinki and Cambridge: Museum of Finnish Architecture and MIT Press, 1985).

Pearson, David Paul. *Alvar Aalto and the International Style* (New York: Whitney Library of Design, 1978).

Pelkonen, Eeva-Liisa. *Alvar Aalto: Architecture, Modernity, Geopolitics* (New Haven: Yale University Press, 2009).

Pelkonen, Eeva-Liisa. "Alvar Aalto: The Geopolitics of Fame" *Perspecta* 37 (2005) 86–97.

Poodry, Deborah, and Victoria Ozonoff. "Coffins, Pies, and Couches: Aalto at MIT" *Spazio e societa* 5 (1982) 104–23.

Quantrill, Malcolm. *Alvar Aalto: A Critical Study* (New York: Schocken Books, 1989).

Ray, Nicholas. *Alvar Aalto* (New Haven: Yale University Press, 2005).

Reasoner, Barnabas. "Alvar Aalto at Mount Angel Library" *Society of Architectural Historians Journal* 31 (1972) 224.

Reed, Peter, ed. *Alvar Aalto: Between Humanism and Materialism* (New York: Museum of Modern Art, 1998).

Schildt, Göran. *Alvar Aalto: The Early Years* Trans. Timothy Binham (New York: Rizzoli, 1984).

Schildt, Göran. *Alvar Aalto: The Decisive Years* Trans. Timothy Binham (New York: Rizzoli, 1986).

Schildt, Göran. *Alvar Aalto: The Mature Years* Trans. Timothy Binham (New York: Rizzoli, 1991).

Schildt, Göran. *Alvar Aalto: His Life* Trans. Timothy Binham, Nicholas Mayow (Jyväskylä: Alvar Aalto Museum, 2007).

Schildt, Göran, ed. *Alvar Aalto in His Own Words* Trans. Timothy Binham, (New York: Rizzoli, 1998).

Schildt, Göran. *Alvar Aalto: The Complete Catalogue of Architecture, Design and Art* Trans. Timothy Binham (New York: Rizzoli, 1994).

Schildt, Göran. *Sketches* (Cambridge, Mass.: MIT Press, 1978).

Sippo, Hanni, ed. *The Brick* (Helsinki: Alvar Aalto Foundation, 2001).

Spens, Michael. *Viipuri Library 1927–1935* (London: Academy Editions, 1994).

Treib, Marc, ed. *An Everyday Modernism: The Houses of William Wurster* (San Francisco and Berkeley: San Francisco Museum of Modern Art and University of California Press, 1995).

Trencher, Michael. *The Alvar Aalto Guide* (New York: Princeton Architectural Press, 1996).

Tuomi, Timo, et al., eds. *Alvar Aalto in Seven Buildings* (Helsinki: Museum of Finnish Architecture, 1998).

Venturi, Robert. *Complexity and Contradiction in Architecture* (New York: Museum of Modern Art, 1966).

Wilson, Colin St. John. *The Other Tradition of Modern Architecture* (London: Academy Editions, 1995).

Weston, Richard. *Alvar Aalto* (London: Phaidon Press, 1995).

Wojtowicz, Robert. *Lewis Mumford and American Modernism: Eutopian Theories for Architecture and Urban Planning* (New York: Cambridge University Press, 1998).

Zevi, Bruno. *Towards an Organic Architecture* (London: Faber and Faber, 1949).

Figure Credits

Architectural Forum: Pelkonen 5 (June 1940)

Arkkitehti (Finnish Architectural Review): Korvenmaa 6-7 [unlocated originals (1941), 94; Menin 1-3 (1939), 116-7].

Belousek, Gustav, Legat of Carla Bindner: Kuhlmann 9.

Berkeley, University of California, College of Environmental Design Archives: Fenske 2, 4, 15 [WBE Collections (1976-2); photographs Roger Sturtevant].

Bern, Switzerland, Zentrum Paul Klee, on loan from a private collection: Goldhagen 1.

Boston, MA, Boston Public Library, Fine Arts Department: Fenske 3, 14 [*Architectural Forum* 79 (July 1943)], 5 [*Architecture* 72 (August 1935)],

Boston, MA, Perry Dean Rogers & Partners, Architects: Fixler 1.

Boston, MA, Shepley, Bulfinch & Abbot, Architects: Jormakka 6 (right), 8 (author's overlay), 9, 10.

Cambridge, MA: Harvard University Archives, call # HUV 211 (8-6): Fenske 19.

Cambridge, MA: Massachusetts Institute of Technology
Bentel 5.
Institute Archives: Bentel 1.
MIT Museum: Baker House Photo-Essay 1, Bentel 1, Fenske 17; Fixler 2, 4
Rotch Visual Collection: Fenske 1 [photograph Curtis Green], 20 [G. E. Kidder-Smith Collection]
Technology Review: Goldhagen 3

Coy, Owen Cochran, Pictorial History of California (Berkeley: University of California, 1925): Fenske, 10.

ESTO Archive
Photographer Ezra Stoller: Fenske, 18; all images in the Photographic Essay of Baker House [photos 1949] except Figure 1; Trencher 12.
Photographer Jeff Goldberg: Fixler 3, 6-8, 10-12.

Francé, Raoul H., Die Pflänze als Erfinder (Stuttgart: Kosmos, 1920): Moravanszky 8.

Giedion, Sigfried, *Space, Time and Architecture* (2nd ed., Cambridge, MA: Harvard University Press, 1949): Pelkonen, 13; Moravanszky 1a-b; Bentel 2. 3 [© 2011 Aerofilms Ltd], 4 [© 2011 Artist Rights Society (ARS), New York/ADAGP, Paris/F.L.C.], 5 [MIT Archive].

Helsinki, Museum of Finnish Architecture: Korvenmaa 1, 2, 9 [photograph; location and source of original is unknown], 10 [photograph; original Alvar Aalto Museum], 11 [Foto Ross]; Fenske 6, 11 [photograph Into Konrad Inha], 12; Menin 11, 19, 22.

Helsinki, National Board of Antiquities: Pelkonen 12.

Helsinki, National Board of Patents and Registers: Korvenmaa 3, 4.

Jyväskylä, Finland, Alvar Aalto Museum Collections, © The Alvar Aalto Foundation, Finland: Goldhagen 2, 4-15; Kuhlmann 7, 8, 10, 12, 13, 16, 17; Pallasmaa 1, 4-14; Pelkonen 2, 4, 6-11, 14; Korvenmaa 5; Fenske 9, 16; Menin 4-10, 12-17, 18 [photograph H. Iffland], 20, 21, 23 [photograph E. Mäkinen], 24, 25; Trencher 8, 9, 15; Speck 1-16; Moravanszky 2; Jormakka 3, 6 (left), 7, 11 (author's overlay), 12; Postal 3, 4 [photographers Eva Ingervo and Pertti Ingervo], 5a-b; Spens 1, 3, 4, 6-12, 17, 18, 24.

Johnson, Chris: Fixler 9.

Johnson, Tim (computer rendering): Fixler 5.

Jokkinen, Teppo, and Bruno Maurer, eds., *"Der Magus des Nordens": Alvar Aalto und die Schweiz* (Zurich: gta Verlag, 1998): Moravanszky, 5a-f.

Jormakka, Kari: Jormakka 13, 14.

Kahn-Magomedov, Selim O., *Pioneers of Soviet Architecture: The Search for New Solutions in the 1920s and 1930s* (London: Thames & Hudson, Ltd., 1987): Trencher, 5.

Kopp, Anatole, *Town and Revolution: Soviet Architecture and City Plannning, 1917–35* (New York: George Braziller, 1970): Trencher 3, 4.

Kuhlmann, Dörte: Kuhlmann 1-6, 11, 14, 15.

Le Corbusier, *Oeuvre complète* © 2011 Artists Rights Society (ARS), New York/ADAGP, Paris / F. L. C.: Trencher 2.

Leccisotti, Tommaso, *Monte Cassino* (Badia di Montecassino: Pubblicazioni Cassinesi, 1967): Spens 2

London, National Gallery Picture Collection: Spens 5.

Moholy-Nagy, Laszlo, *Von Material zu Architektur* (Mainz, Berlin: Florian Kupferberg, 1968): Moravanszky 9.

Moravanszky, Ákos. Moravanszky 6, 7, 10.

New York, Columbia University, Avery Library: Postal 2.

New York, Museum of Modern Art: Pelkonen 1, 3, 15a-b. [1 and 15: Digital Image © The Museum of Modern Art/Licensed by SCALA/Art Resource, NY].

New York, Museum of the City of New York, Gottschok-Schleisner Collection: Fenske 7.

New York, New York City Landmarks Preservation Commission (photographer Carl Forster): Postal 1.

New York, Robert Mann Gallery [©Wijnanda Deroo]: Postal 6.

Oakland, CA, Oakland Museum of California: Fenske 13 [Bequest of Roger Sturtevant]

Pallasmaa, Juhani: Pallasmaa 2, 3.

Post-War Reconstruction. Rehousing Research in Finland (New York: private printing, 1940): Korvenmaa 8.

Prigge, Walter, ed., *Ernst Neufert: Normierte Baukultur* (Frankfurt, New York: Campus, 1999): Moravanszky 3, 4.

Quiroga, Grace (drawing): Jormakka 5.

Robinson, Cervin, photographer (1979): Jormakka 1, 2, 4.

Rosskam, Edwin, *San Francisco: West Coast Metropolis* (New York: Longman, Green, 1939): Fenske 8.

Strode Eckert Photographic, Richard H. Strode © 1991: Spens 13-16, 19-23.

Trencher, Michael: Trencher 1, 6, 7, 10, 11, 13, 14, 16.

Venturi, Robert, *Complexity and Contradiction in Architecture* (New York: Museum of Modern Art, 1966): Bentel 6, reprinted by permission, ©1966 The Museum of Modern Art, New York [left, MIT Archive; top right, from Nikolaus Pevsner, *An Outline of European Architecture* (London: Pelican Books, 1943) ©Nikolaus Pevsner, 1943; bottom right, au concessione dei Ministero per i Beni e le Attività Culturali, Rome].

Index

optic perception, 214; lighting and furnishings, *174–75*, 196, 227, 230, *231*; models, *223, 225*; plans and schematics, *189, 192, 197, 198, 200, 201, 203, 204, 221, 244*; relief of (wooden slats in design), *176, 186, 187*; room types, 38; site, 126, *163*, 186, 193, 195–96, 220, 236; sketches, *126, 199, 202, 203*; stair wall, *10, 165*, 188, *188*, 224–26; trellises, *126*, 209, 219, 222–23, 233n9; undulating curve, 187, *197, 198, 199*, 208–9; wood-slat acoustical ceiling, 228

— *renovation*: building and accessibility codes, 226, *226–27, 227*; design elements identified, 219–20; methodological concerns in, 220–22; original intent of AA considered, 222–26; reflections on, 230–32; scope, 222; success, 238; systems and technology interventions, *228*, 228–29; underutilized, unfinished areas developed, 223–24, *224, 229*, 229–30

— *views*: aerial, *163, 236, 236, 242*; computer rendering, *225*; entry, *168–69, 231*; exterior, *10, 164–67, 186, 187, 190*; exterior, rooftop pergola, 223–24, *224*; interior, common areas, *vi, 170–73, 189, 218*, 226–30; interior, dormitory rooms, *174–75, 228*

Baldwin Kingrey furniture store (Chicago), 63

Ban, Shigeru, 2

Banham, Reyner, 153, 154, 158, 242, 249n31, 296n5

Barr, Alfred H., Jr., 78, 79, *79*, 119, 128

Barthes, Roland, 43, 82

Bauer, Catherine, 123–24, 133n55

Bauhaus: AA's exposure to, 20, 61, 73; building at Dessau, 15; exhibition on, 263; Harvard and Gropius's design ethos of, 113, 123, 125, 306. *See also* New Bauhaus

Bay Region Style: advocacy for, *79*, 116, 128, 132n18; debate about International Style vs., 128, 130, 134n92, 134n94; site appropriate to, 82. *See also* Wurster, William Wilson

Beaume, Louis de, 123, 133n47

Belluschi, Pietro, 131

Bemis, Albert Farwell, 5, 9n14

Bemis Foundation: AA's association with, 67, 103, 245; funding for, 103, 105, 111n29; mission of, 5, 102; prefabrication studies of, 75n50;

reconstruction projects and, 125, 134nn66–67. *See also* Massachusetts Institute of Technology

Benedictine Mount Angel Abbey (Oregon): AA's visit to, 276, 281, 283; history of, 275–76, *276*, 279–80, 290; reading in, 280, *280*, 282, 296n2. *See also* Mount Angel Abbey Library

Benner, Frederic, 116

Bentel, Paul: essay by, 235–49; references to, 4, 8, 139

Binder, Joseph, 43, *44*

biotechnology, 214

Blake, Peter, 135n95

Booth, Theodore William, 269, 273n29

Born, Ernest, 65, 99

Borromini, Francesco, 207–8, *236, 236*, 241, 243

Boston: colonial red-brick tradition of, 7, 126, 196, 220. *See also* Harvard University; Massachusetts Institute of Technology

Bosworth, William Welles, 245–46

Bourdieu, Pierre, 39, 41

Breines, Simon, 81

Breton, André, 16

Breuer, Marcel, 81, 98, 241

brick: AA's use of, in general, 7, 47, 208, 220; as cell or standard unit, 46, 51n22, 213–14, 216–17; as material object and as stereometric volume, 209–10, *210, 211*; mortar joints of, 196, 210, 212, 213; playful experimentation with, 216–17; re-use of damaged, 211, *212*; whitewashed, 233n3; *specific projects*: Baker House, 47, 48, *48*, 196, 209, 216–17; Cranbrook School, *48*; Harvard's Austin Hall (gymnasium), 253; House of Culture, 213, 233n3; National Pensions Institute, 233n3; Sunila Pulp Mill, 208, 220; Villa Mairea, 233n3

Brooks, H. Allen, 191n7

Brown, William Haskins, *129*, 130

building site: AA's changing views about, 46–47; attention to context of, 26, 32, 38; in Bay Region Style, 82; chart method for describing, 67–68; variability of, charted, *86*. *See also* construction materials; *and specific projects*

Bulfinch, Francis Vaughan, 130, 253. *See also* Coolidge, Shepley, Bulfinch & Abbott

Burchard, John E.: AA's clash with, 130; AA's correspondence with, 54, 190, 204; AA's MIT

appointment and, 5, 67, 233n1; AA's research and, 103–4; on Baker House, 242; experimental town scheme and, 105; institute proposal and, 133n36; position of, 102

Burnham and Root (firm): Monadnock Building, 213, *213*

Bush-Brown, Albert, 242

C

Calder, Alexander, 62

California: AA's critique of Hollywood, 54, 62, 70; AA's lecture in, 64; AA's visit to and view of, 6, *65*, 82, 83, 99, 108, *119*, 119–20, 122, 305; Finnish housing compared to Placerville in, 120, *120*; Lind house in, 70, *70*; war industries and housing in, 123–24, 133nn52–54. *See also* Bay Region Style; San Francisco Bay region; Wurster, William Wilson

Cambridge (Mass.). *See* Harvard University; Massachusetts Institute of Technology

ceilings: color of, 24; wavy, 31–32, 270, 301, *301*; wood-slat acoustical, 228. *See also* sound and acoustics

Chicago: AA's furniture sales in, 63; AA's visit to, 82, 119; architecture of, 305; Illinois Institute of Technology in, 131, 245; New Bauhaus in, 119, 128, 214

Chirico, Giorgio de, 16

Choisy, Auguste, 15

Church, Thomas, 99, *117*

cinema, 21, 61, 62, 73n10

Cité Internationale Universitaire de Paris. *See* Swiss Pavilion

Clausen, Meredith, 135n107

Colquhoun, Alan, 293, 294

Compton, Karl Taylor, 125, 205n12

Congrès Internationaux d'Architects Modernes (CIAM): AA as member of, 24, 26; AA's friends in, 61, 73; orthodoxies of, 14, 53, 54, 55; standardization ideas of, 210–11

Connah, Roger, 122, 161n86

construction materials: of AA vs. other modernist architects, 78; authenticity and renovation of, 219–20; contamination of, 216, 217; mixing of various, 13, 47; natural elements in, 41, 46, 51n9; sensory effects of diverse, 32; sound-absorbing, 24, 27; *specific*: aluminum, 222–23, *224*; black

to, 290, 295; site of, 275; tile used in, 226

Sert, José Luis, 196, 240, 241

Shand, P. Morton, 62, 110n19, 296n22

Shepley, Henry Richardson, 130, 253, 256. *See also* Coolidge, Shepley, Bulfinch & Abbott

Sibelius, Jean, 147–48, 151, 157, 159n14, 159n15

Sicily (AA's sketch), *289*, 290

signs and signifiers: brick, 209, 217; empty, 43; epistemology of significance and, 238–39; floating, 37, 40

sinks, noiseless, 3, 24, *24*

Siren, J. S., 64

Sitte, Camillo, 178, 179, 180, 187, 191n7, 191n15

Siza, Àlvaro, 2, 9n7, 227, 233n17

sketches. *See* drawings and sketches

Slangus, Hans Christian, 269

Slott, Robert W., 62

Smeds, Kerstin, 141, 148, 149, 150, 158, 161n73

Smith, C. Ray, 273n37

Smithson, Alison, 204, 242

Smithson, Peter, 204, 242

Snellman, J. V., 303

social fields concept, 39, 41

sound and acoustics: AA's ideas for Lincoln Center, 75n65; materials to absorb, 24, 27, 301; noiseless sinks, 3, 24, *24*; wavy ceiling for, 32; wood-slat acoustical ceiling for, 228. *See also* Woodberry Poetry Room

Soviet-Finnish Winter War (1939–40): AA's efforts to gain support for Finland, 84, 98, 99–101, *100*, 102, 104, 111n33; AA's response to outbreak, 152, 160n42; civilian targets in, 99–100; Finland Pavilion in context of, 147–48, 159n14; mobilization for, 5, 66, 74n42; peace treaty of, 87, 105, 152; Soviet invasion in, 84, 95, 159n14; travel to U.S. during, 67; Viipuri Library and, 277, 296n5. *See also* Continuation War (1941–44); Karelia region; reconstruction projects

Soviet Union: AA's view of, 75n49, 84; communal housing in, 181–83; German pact with, 159n14; postwar Finland controlled by, 108; as social utopia, 61. *See also* Continuation War (1941–44); Karelia region; Soviet-Finnish Winter War (1939–40); World War II

spatial determinism concept, 195–96

Speck, Lawrence W.: essay by, 193–205; references to, 3–4, *7*, 137, 230

Spens, Michael: essay by, 275–97; references to, 3, 8, 139

standardization: AA's view of, 99, 177; architechnological type of, 211–14, 240, 248n19; avoided in mass housing, 185–86; brick, rationalism, and, 208–11; flexibility applied to, 13, 33, 85, 87, 106, 125, 187; irrationality combined with, 207; nature as model for, 46, 211, 213–14, *214. See also* brick; prefabrication

Steinbeck, John, 100

Stern, Robert, 242

Stirling, James, 204, 242

Stone, Edward D., 105

Strengell, Gustaf, 43, 60, 119, 191n15

Sullivan, Louis, 68, 193, 230, 233n22, 304, 305

Sunila and Kauttua projects: brick used in, 208, 220; commission for, 96; community envisioned for, 106; engineers' housing design, *184*, 185–86, 187, 208; landscape of, 275; vernacular tradition and, 151; visitors to, 117

surrealism vs. rationalism, 16

Sweden: acceptera group in, 61, 73n10; "America Builds" exhibition in, 68, 133nn32–33

Swedish Association of Engineers and Architects, 74n34

Sweeney, James Johnson, 260n5

Sweeney, John L. ("Jack"), 252–53, 260n5

Swiss Pavilion (Le Corbusier and Jeanneret): Baker House in context of, *7*, 187, 190, 235–36; curved masonry wall of, 41, 208; description of, 181, 182–83; plan for, *181*; view of, *180*

T

TAC (The Architects Collaborative, Harvard), 8, 130, *130*, 233n25

Tarjanne, Onni, 64, 74n32

Taut, Bruno, 33

Taylor, Frederick, 211

technology: AA's view of, 54; climate control for rare books, 261n15; human and social consequences recognized, 177, 191n2; novel forms in wood due to, 95–96, *96*, *97*, 98, *98. See also* architechnological standardization; furnishings

Technology Review, 22, 125, 193–94

Tennessee Valley Authority, 69, 307

Tice, James, 296–97n30

Treib, Marc, 122

Trencher, Michael: essay by, 177–91; references to, 5, *7*, 137

Turner, Paul, 245

Turun Sanomat Building, 77, 79, 210, 219, 278

Twain, Mark, 195

Tyrwhitt, Mary Jaqueline, 248n8

U

undulating curves and walls: as constituent fact, 236; development in AA's work, 219; in dialectic of sensitivity to material and organicist line of functionalism, 209; geometry of brick vs., 212–13; other architects' use of, 236, *236*, *237*; signification and metaphors of, 157–59; tradition of, 207–8. *See also* Baker House; ceilings; Finland Pavilions (New York and Paris)

United Nations Headquarters, 72, 267. *See also* Institute of International Education

United States: AA's disillusionment with, 62, 70, 130; AA's visits to, 1, 63, *63*, 82, 98–99, 137, 160n47; anti-Soviet attitudes in, 84–85; Finnish relations in WWII and, 69, 75n52, 75n60; as model for Finland, 101–2; prefabrication plants in, 107; as social utopia, 61; standardization ideas in, 211. *See also* Aalto's engagement with America; American architecture; World War II; *and specific places and universities*

University of California—Berkeley, 64, 116, 120, 130–31

Upton, Dell, 242

utopianism, 181–83, 278

V

Valéry, Paul, 54

Vartiainen, Erik T., 269–70, 273n30, 281, 283

Veblen, Thorstein, 115

Venturi, Robert: on AA, 38, 39, 51n3, 53, 278; on Baker House, 243, 247; on Neue Vahr, 46

vernacularism: Karelian, 87–89, *89*; modern living and natural environment linked in, 151; nationalism of 1930s and, 78–79; simplicity